DATE DUE

NO 12 '96		
MY 10 '97		
AP 5 '01		
JE 13 '05		

DEMCO 38-296

Pay Any Price

PAY ANY PRICE

Lyndon Johnson and the Wars for Vietnam

LLOYD C. GARDNER

Ivan R. Dee   Chicago   1995

PAY ANY PRICE. Copyright © 1995 by Lloyd C. Gardner. All rights
reserved, including the right to reproduce this book or portions
thereof in any form. For information, address: Ivan R. Dee, Inc.,
1332 North Halsted Street, Chicago 60622. Manufactured in the United
States of America and printed on acid-free paper.

Photographs by Yoichi R. Okamoto, courtesy of the
Lyndon B. Johnson Library Collection

Map by Victor Thompson

Library of Congress Cataloging-in-Publication Data:
Gardner, Lloyd C., 1934–
Pay any price : Lyndon Johnson and the wars for Vietnam / Lloyd C. Gardner.
p.   cm.
Includes bibliographical references and index.
ISBN 1-56663-087-8 (alk. paper)
1. Vietnamese Conflict, 1961–1975—United States.   2. United States—Politics and
government—1963–1969.   3. Johnson, Lyndon B. (Lyndon Baines), 1908–1973.   I Title.
DS558.G37   1995
959.704'3373—dc20   95-13208

This Book Is Dedicated to My Parents and My Sister

Contents

Acknowledgments

MUCH OF THE BASIC RESEARCH for this book was done in the manuscript collections and other holdings of the Lyndon Baines Johnson Library in Austin, Texas. The papers housed there provide an immense resource for students of the diplomacy of the Vietnam War, of course, as well as for other topics related to the history of recent American politics. I am grateful, first, to Professor Robert Divine of the University of Texas for his review of an earlier book on Vietnam, and for steering me toward a full-scale study of President Johnson's fateful struggle to control the legacy of the war. The Johnson Library is directed by Harry Middleton, whose friendly and tireless staff excels in providing an academic research environment and support services beyond anything I have previously experienced. Middleton's unstinting determination to make the materials at the library accessible to scholars provides a high standard for other presidential libraries to emulate. Archivists Claudia Anderson and Linda Hanson are faithful guides in the research room. Regina Greenwell kept me up to date on the status of newly declassified documents, while Mary Knill did the same for computer disks. I am especially grateful to Ted Gittinger for help not only on this book but with a conference held at the library in the fall of 1993 on the early decisions of the Johnson administration. Finally, a special word of thanks to David Humphrey, now moved from the LBJ Library to the State Department's historical office, for his ability to pinpoint the location of any document in the library's foreign policy files, and for many, many conversations over the years about how the Johnson administration made foreign policy and about other topics, and for his friendship to a fellow Johnson scholar.

I am indebted to Gerry McCauley for his encouragement and his vast knowledge about baseball and anything to do with Pittsburgh. Mark White of St. Andrews University, Scotland, spent many hours with the documents to help me prepare to write. Ivan Dee must be the best editor and publisher that any author could hope to have interested in his work. Somehow he still manages to survive all my quirks and obsession for rewriting up until books actually appear in stores. As always, Nancy was there when I needed her. To all these people, thanks again.

L. C. G.

Dutch Neck, New Jersey
March 1995

Preface

AFTER WORLD WAR II the American "reformist" impulse underwent a profound transformation. In the 1930s the collapse of the world economy had severely challenged the legitimacy of ruling elites, even in nontotalitarian countries. Roosevelt's New Deal, as first conceived, tried to contain those challenges by expanding the limits on reform and isolating the U.S. economy from the shock waves and tremors sweeping across Europe and Asia. It aimed to protect American domestic institutions, in so far as possible, by shielding them from outside interference. It was experimental—and not a little frightening. As America mobilized for war, the New Deal became "unfinished business." Roosevelt talked about "Dr. Win-the-War" replacing "Dr. New Deal," a phraseology that suggested concern about the perils awaiting policymakers in the postwar era.

The New Deal liberated American leaders from constricting assumptions about the ability of capitalist institutions to absorb experiments without essential damage. Postwar reformers concentrated on completing the New Deal's "unfinished business" without encouraging rash adventurism in government intervention and regulation. That did not mean returning to a weak federal government—not at all, in fact quite the reverse. Saving the American "system" in the prewar decade demanded internal change; protecting it after the war depended upon expanding the state's capacity to "contain" the supposed military threat of the Soviet Union, but even more to provide a credible integration of military and political policies. The greatest symbol of American power might be the Pentagon, and the biggest cost item (surely the showiest) might be the long-range bomber, but these were instrumentalities, created to serve the same function as the British navy in the Pax Britannica. "We can see," future Secretary of State Dean Acheson had explained of America's situation at the start of World War II, "that British naval power no longer can establish security of life and investment in distant parts of the world, and a localization of conflict nearer at home." During the Korean War, when he presided over foreign policy debates, Acheson continued this exegesis. The sole purpose for which America waged war, he said, was "to create and to maintain the environment in which the American experiment in liberty could flourish and exist."[1]

That experiment depended upon a hospitable climate abroad for the expansion of American ideas, especially the equation between free markets and free men, while maintaining a balance at home between the rights of the individual and the needs of society. Acheson's ability to raise cold war questions to the level of abstract issues of good versus evil sometimes obscured his more important message. He saw the primary achievement of the Pax Britannica (and therefore the primary responsibility of a successor Pax Americana) in the amazing increase in the general production of wealth. This permitted the amelioration of social ills and the redress of injustices without limiting individual freedom—or, put in the immediate postwar context, the achievement of social peace without a super New Deal.

Criticisms of Harry Truman as a proponent of a global "New Deal," and later of Lyndon Johnson in the Vietnam War as a champion of "Welfare Imperialism," were not without merit; but they misread both men's purposes and objectives—as set forth in Dean Acheson's panoramic rendering of two centuries of English-speaking rule. Lyndon Johnson understood the stakes. Throughout his career LBJ remained a solid New Dealer, if one defines that credo as a belief in government's positive role as a promoter of economic development. Roosevelt's programs had meant everything to Johnson's Texas hill country and had launched LBJ's political career as a proponent of federal leadership in public power projects. He was still doing that for Texas in the Truman and Eisenhower years, though by that time the primary beneficiaries of federal support were of a different class. Dirt farmers and giant construction firms had little in common with each other, but LBJ's vision encompassed them both.

Validation of his beliefs played a crucial role in Johnson's personal life and in his politics. On the most personal level, in the aftermath of the Kennedy assassination he vowed he would not be the president who lost Vietnam. That was what Kennedy would have done, Johnson thought, and even if it was not, LBJ feared he would be judged against that standard. Both Kennedy and Johnson were wary of being trapped in the murky politics of South Vietnam. They constantly sought reassurance, political as well as military, that the path they were being asked to follow led somewhere besides deeper into the unknown. Johnson initially displayed no great eagerness to plunge into Southeast Asia; certainly he did not encourage the Joint Chiefs with promises to conduct a war. Indeed, he paid relatively little attention to the situation in Vietnam until the 1964 presidential campaign. Then, opposed by the right-wing Republican Barry Goldwater, Johnson inflated the events of the PT-boat "attacks" on American warships in the

Gulf of Tonkin in order to display Kennedy-style mettle in "crisis manage-ment." By the time he and his key advisers grasped that Vietnam was not like Cuba in 1962, the forces they had helped to set in motion had reached high speed.

Explaining American involvement in Vietnam is not that simple, of course. To argue that Lyndon Johnson felt aggrieved, as had Harry Truman at Franklin Roosevelt's death, that fate had played a cruel trick on him, leaves us to conjecture about matters of psychology. It requires a much greater effort to go beyond how LBJ felt about his burdens, and to break free from the grip of assassination-centered history. But only by such an effort can we engage the abiding questions of causation that historians must attempt to resolve.

Johnson's personality inclined him to exaggerate the slights of an East-ern elite into a campaign to destroy his presidency. Either way he went, he believed, his critics were sure to put Vietnam on his shoulders. If he aban-doned the Saigon regime, it would be said he had deserted the watchtowers on the walls of the Free World. If he pursued the enemy and struck at his base of operations, it would be said he had stupidly enlarged the war to sat-isfy a vainglorious quest, dragging everything down with him as the war consumed American spiritual and material resources.

But that explanation still leaves us a good distance away from under-standing LBJ and the escalation of American involvement. In an earlier book, *Approaching Vietnam* (1988), I discussed the origins of American involvement in Southeast Asia. A key factor, it emerged, was the need to reintegrate postwar Japan into the American-led world economy. Simply put, Japan needed economic outlets if it was to become a prosperous mem-ber of the Free World community and thus a reliable ally in an increasingly volatile area of the world. Around that issue swirled complicated problems: allaying European fears of Japanese economic competition, and providing incentive to newly independent countries to overcome their colonial-era suspicions and view the West as their mentor in the difficult transition years to full nationhood. In the 1950s Vietnam was seen as crucial to the success of this American policy, particularly after the ambiguous results of the Korean War. American leaders had no wish to settle for a permanently divided Vietnam as in Korea. They finally accepted the results of the 1954 Geneva Conference only because they offered a way of speeding France's exit from the scene so as to give American nation-building a chance to work. Washington never intended to allow Communist leader Ho Chi Minh to reunite Vietnam under his leadership by military means—or by elections.

In the 1960s the original causes of American involvement in Vietnam were transformed into more abstract questions. Japan was prosperous. Europe had fully recovered. The perspective of American policymakers shifted from the tasks of creation to those of sustaining the Pax Americana. Shortly before Kennedy's death, American policy in Vietnam had been complicated by complicity in the overthrow of Premier Ngo Dinh Diem. Fighting the war became a two-sided affair—holding back the rebellious National Liberation Front while coercing Diem's successors into accepting American guidance in developing a viable political system to meet the legitimate demands of the population.

Johnson thus needed a two-sided policy. He found it in the link between his New Deal experiences and what he had been told about the potential for a Mekong River development project. He proposed the Mekong Valley project because it supplied an answer to the fundamental question: What were we doing in Vietnam? From the beginning of the Kennedy administration to the end of American involvement in the war during Richard Nixon's presidency, the United States maintained that its only goal was to guarantee South Vietnam the right to self-determination against a Russian-sponsored (or latterly, Chinese) attempt to spread the Communist revolution across Asia. Probably more aware than his advisers that simply opposing Communist aggression in a far-off place—where the sides were far from clearly drawn—provided a less than compelling reason for being in Vietnam, Johnson drew on his New Deal experiences. He also understood that the United States had compromised its moral claims to be in South Vietnam by participating, however passively, in the plot to overthrow its premier, Ngo Dinh Diem. The only way to reconnect cold war assumptions and Vietnam was therefore to go beyond the "containment" of communism by offering North Vietnam a share in the Great Society. Even if Ho Chi Minh did not respond to the offer, LBJ had addressed the issue of American self-image, crucial to his success with the Great Society legislative program, as well as to support for his foreign policy. He sometimes rationalized his military decisions by referring to the power of the conservative bloc in Congress. To ward off the threat to his Great Society programs, he would argue, he had to keep conservatives happy with promises to bring back that coonskin to display on Capitol Hill. And he fantasized away public doubts, including his own, with the promise of a Mekong Valley project to surpass even the New Deal's Tennessee Valley Authority.

Complaints that such grandiose thinking hurt the military effort were heard even then, and even from those intimately engaged in formulating policy. And because, with the exception of the Eisenhower years, cold war Washington was under "liberal" control, foreign policy failures were soon being blamed on misguided attempts to export the Great Society to Southeast Asia. General Maxwell Taylor, who served as ambassador to South Vietnam and participated in decision-making at the highest levels all the way to the end of the Johnson administration, voiced such criticism in his memoirs:

If we made a mistake in this period [1964–1965], it was in trying too much in the civil field before an adequate level of security was reached. . . . We should have learned from our frontier forebears that there is little use planting corn outside the stockade if there are still Indians around in the woods outside.[2]

Integral to understanding the war's development, on the other hand, was the American environment at home. If LBJ had to win in Vietnam to satisfy conservatives, he also had to stand for something to keep liberals aboard. Policymakers in the 1960s had to deal with a whole series of challenges to the givens of the previous decade. Unlike the 1950s, protest movements linked the war with neglect of the poor, repression of blacks, and profits for the military-industrial complex. Johnson and his advisers were plainly perplexed by the accusations. From the time of the Truman Doctrine in 1947, a basic premise of national politics had been that America could not have liberty and prosperity at home without overcoming the Communist threat abroad. Vietnam undermined that credo.

We are still too close to the events to suggest what the final fallout from America's lost crusade will be. Some now argue that Vietnam was simply the last colonial war of the twentieth century. Others talk about lost innocence and the growth of a more realistic sense of America's place, morally and politically, in the world. Still others see the war marking the end of American hegemony in the world, as well as the last gasp of the New Deal system that governed American politics from Roosevelt to the end of the Johnson years, to be followed by an era of unparalleled cynicism. I have written the story largely from Lyndon Johnson's perspective, nonetheless attempting to see the unfolding tragedy not as one of personalities but of ideas and contexts.

Lyndon Johnson traveled a long way from the hill country of Texas to the White House. He gained a view of the "American Century" along the way that was not identical to that of Eastern liberals; but it shared with them a profound conviction about the power of the federal government to promote economic development as an antidote to regional and class struggles—even as far away as Vietnam. His first actual experience with Vietnam, in 1961, reconfirmed the validity of this conviction as a solution to international problems. So we must begin with Lyndon Johnson arriving in Washington.

Those three main strands of action—defeating aggression, building a nation, and searching for peace—were tightly braided together in all that we, the other allies, and the Vietnamese tried to accomplish.

—Lyndon B. Johnson, *The Vantage Point*

How is it with our general?

Even so, as with a man by his own aims empoison'd,
And with his charity slain.

—*Coriolanus*, Act 5, Scene 4

Pay Any Price

Part One

COMMITMENTS

Decoding
Lyndon Johnson

LYNDON JOHNSON CAME TO WASHINGTON in 1931, at the depth of the Great Depression. His father, Sam Ealy Johnson, a sometime politician who eked out a precarious living for his family farming the parched Texas hill country, had managed to secure a position for his high-school-teacher son as secretary to a newly elected member of the House of Representatives, Richard Kleberg. A conservative Democrat whose family owned the fabulous King Ranch, Kleberg looked upon elected office as the sort of sinecure owed to a man of his background. The young man who accompanied him to the nation's capital started from a very different place.

In deliberations presided over by Sam Ealy, the elder Johnson and his populist-oriented cronies often talked well into the night about who was to blame for the farmer's plight in bad times. Lyndon was a good listener, and he never forgot the verdict Sam Ealy's front-porch jury handed down at the end of those evenings: the bankers were the guilty ones. "If we ever have a revolution," LBJ confided to a biographer even after he left the presidency, "and throw out our system for Communism or fascism, they'll be the prime reason for it and the first victims. I believed it as a child, and I believe it still." All the intervening years, he told Doris Kearns, he had had to keep those views under wraps and maintain that America was a classless society.[1]

Lyndon Johnson frequently rearranged elements in his personality to meet new challenges over the course of a political career that lasted nearly four decades. But no matter how much his constituency and its demands changed, or how high his personal fortunes rose above those of former neighbors living around Johnson City, Texas, he always retained something of the old-time populist religion and its deep suspicion of the men who sat in leather chairs behind mahogany desks presiding over the nation's affairs from large offices on Wall Street. His lifelong attitude toward Eastern "intellectuals" grew from the same mind-set. Deeply imprinted on Johnson's psyche was an image of regional imperialism, economic and cultural, that determined the fate of his kind. "My daddy always told me," he confided to Doris Kearns, "that if I brushed up against the grindstone of life, I'd come away with more polish than I could ever get at Harvard or Yale. I wanted to believe him, but somehow I never could." And, Kearns added, "Johnson sincerely believed that he would have been the greatest President in his country's history had it not been for the intellectuals and the men of words."[2]

This intensely personal, intensely persistent theme bears more weight and explains more than abstract geopolitics or balance-of-power theories in coming to terms with LBJ's vision of America's role in the world. Sometimes reappearing in strange guise, it is nearly always present. Johnson cut a poor figure as a geopolitician. And when the Eastern establishment finally abandoned the war in Vietnam at the end of Johnson's political career, he was half-expecting it to happen. He found that development perfectly consonant with the elite's historical refusal to share the American dream with those whose resources had produced the wealth it took for granted.

Vietnam ultimately became for Johnson the Texas of yesterday, a feat of stupefying imagination. At the crucial moment of decision in Southeast Asia he recalled his beginnings in the Depression and the glory years of the New Deal, when for the first time the South and the West were offered a roughly equal role in the nation's economic development. If the North Vietnamese ceased their aggression, Johnson promised in a speech at Johns Hopkins University in April 1965, linking the heritage of the New Deal to American objectives in Vietnam, they would find the United States eager to help them overcome "the bondage of material misery." "The vast Mekong River can provide food and water and power on a scale to dwarf even our own TVA."

"In the countryside where I was born," the speech continued, now in the form of an emotional reminiscence about what the New Deal had accomplished with the Tennessee Valley Authority,

> and where I live, I have seen the night illuminated, and the kitchen warmed, and the home heated, where once the cheerless night and the ceaseless cold held sway. And all this happened because electricity came to our area along the humming wires of the REA.[3]

It had taken the New Deal and World War II to break the bonds of internal imperialism. And the critics who now rose to confront him he saw as the heirs of those frowning Yankees who had once sought to deny the South and West an equal role in the nation's economic development. This was an elaborate construction, no doubt—a protective shield Johnson used to ward off a full awareness of the costs of American intervention for the people of Vietnam—and for his own dream of the Great Society.

What the New Deal had accomplished, and even more what his generation had discovered about the federal government as a force for economic change, became the promise and obligation that held Johnson fast to his fateful course. To understand Johnson on the Mekong River in 1965 at the point of no return in Vietnam, we must seek his beginnings on the Colorado River.

WHEN YOUNG LYNDON first arrived in Washington, Louisiana senator Huey Long was at the summit of his power. Democrats and Republicans alike were scared to death of the "Kingfish," whose finger-waving threats to end poverty by taxing the rich sounded a tocsin across the land. Demagogic rhetoric abounded in those years, inside and outside Congress. But Huey Long was special. He ruled his home state as a personal fiefdom, yet for the first time Louisiana children had free schoolbooks, and the back country was being given a chance to enter the modern world. Fascinated by Long, Johnson would "perch" in the Senate gallery for hours listening to the Kingfish's raspy speeches for people "who needed some speeches made for them." Years later in the White House, Johnson was still fascinated: "I heard 'em all," he told historian Eric Goldman. "Don't forget," he added to his press secretary, "that Long never niggered it."[4]

Richard Kleberg's office was not the place, however, for a young secretary who sought to impress his boss, and to establish himself with the congressman's constituents, to be talking about Huey Long—except to condemn or make fun. "He was just a young fellow feeling his way around," recalled Representative Maury Maverick's widow, "and smart and catching on." "We considered him and felt that he was heading toward being a real, honest-to-God liberal."[5] But Johnson was careful not to get too involved with Maverick's liberal crowd, and to stay within shouting distance of the Kleberg people.

"I think Johnson probably lived in both worlds," recalled James Rowe, a White House assistant to Franklin D. Roosevelt who came to know LBJ during the early New Deal and remained a close political friend ever after.[6] In the heady atmosphere after FDR's election, the "Harvards" descended on Washington in droves, posing a challenge to tradition altogether different from the Kingfish and his ilk. Johnson never warmed up to them the way he had to Huey Long, but no one in Washington outdid Lyndon's enthusiasm for FDR himself.

Roosevelt listened to Maury Maverick and Sam Rayburn extol Johnson's virtues, then appointed him to head the Texas office of the National

Youth Administration—a grand vote of confidence for a twenty-seven-year-old. The NYA was the New Deal agency charged with helping young people stay in school. Johnson welcomed the challenge. "Those were the great days," he said later. He worked terribly hard, not only to find sponsors and sources of revenue beyond government appropriations, but to see that blacks received at least some of the NYA benefits. It was especially important to change the lives of youth, he believed, because that was the best chance to break the poverty cycle.[7]

Johnson's success as head of the Texas NYA only swelled his desire to return to Washington as an elected member of Congress. The sudden death of James B. Buchanan created an opening for Johnson to run in a special election for the Tenth Congressional District seat in April 1937. He conducted his campaign like an oath of fealty to Roosevelt and the New Deal—at a time when Texas Democrats and other Southern politicians were beginning to pull back from all-out support for FDR's reform program.

Robert Caro has written that Johnson's political career was launched by powerful men like Alvin Wirtz, a state senator with connections, particularly to the Austin publisher Charles Marsh; and, perhaps crucially, George Rufus Brown, who, with his brother Herman, headed Brown & Root, a Texas construction firm also based in Austin. What the Browns had in mind was to secure federal funds to complete a dam on the Colorado River. According to Caro, Wirtz chose a pro-Roosevelt strategy for Johnson because voters in the Tenth District would not elect anyone else. Backing Johnson made sense in any event because he was someone who had Roosevelt's ear.[8]

FDR took to Representative Johnson immediately. Roosevelt once made the interesting comment that Johnson "was the kind of uninhibited young pro he'd like to be"—and might have been, "if he hadn't gone to Harvard." In the next generation, predicted the president, "the balance of power would shift south and west, and this boy could well be the first Southern President."[9] Over the next four years Johnson's private lobbying efforts in the White House helped to produce $14 million in funds for various Texas dams, and millions more for other purposes, and to turn Brown & Root from a small road-building company into a multimillion-dollar business.[10]

Tommy Corcoran, a Roosevelt intimate put in charge of tending to Johnson's needs, would say, with good reason, "Lyndon Johnson's whole world was built on that dam."[11] But George and Herman Brown did not want anyone to think that they or their friend Lyndon Johnson were "public power" advocates. "He wasn't trying to revolutionize public power all over the United States," George Brown said of Johnson, "he never had that idea in his mind." He simply wanted to improve the Tenth District, and the only way was "to have something like the TVA. . . ."[12] While he was happy to accept the funds Washington provided his company, Herman Brown sometimes raved and ranted about New Deal spending, causing Johnson to snap back, "What are you worried about? It's not coming out of *your* pocket. Any money that's spent down here on New Deal projects, the East is paying for." Johnson saw Roosevelt as the first president to give the South a break.[13]

However well the Browns knew Johnson, or thought they knew him, his votes in Congress generally reflected a populist agenda, favoring welfare measures and public power projects. Still, Johnson was highly patriotic, and properly cautious as a Texan had to be about civil rights and too much government regulation.[14] As he moved from his position as Kleberg's secretary to director of the National Youth Administration in Texas, to congressman and then senator, Johnson's political base changed. The anonymous Texas hill country people were increasingly replaced by well-known individuals like Alvin Wirtz and Charles Marsh, and behind-the-scenes movers like George and Herman Brown.

Who really knew what drove Johnson's political career? Lady Bird Johnson recalled that her husband took time off to see the 1940 film of John Steinbeck's *Grapes of Wrath* "and sat in his seat crying quietly for about two hours at the helpless misery of the Okies. I do not think he has ever forgotten it."[15] Like other New Dealers, Johnson was enthusiastic (and probably a bit amazed) at the discovery that government really did have immense powers to change the life of the downtrodden.

Johnson might not have been trying to "revolutionize public power," but he certainly sounded those themes in speeches to Texas citizens, urging them to form rural cooperatives to buy power from the Lower Colorado River Authority. If the people did not act, he wrote to an Austin newspaper, "The power companies will be the chief beneficiaries of this huge government investment, supposedly made in the interest of the people of Texas."[16]

In a 1939 radio address Johnson envisioned the whole region sharing in the ultimate success of the LCRA and electric cooperatives. It was high time, he said, that the physical resources of the South, and the profits therefrom, stayed in the South.

> Our private utilities in Texas are owned in New York. We have sold our Texas gas and oil to other corporations owned in New York. We have sold our cattle to be processed with New York capital. We have sold our cotton to be processed with New York and London capital. We have sold our cheap labor to be processed in New York and Massachusetts. What resource haven't we sold to be processed somewhere else?

"When we have begun the conservation of our natural resources," Johnson concluded, only "then we can enter into our proportional share of

industrial activity." By such means would the South rise, at last, to its proper place in the nation, no longer subordinate to the North and East, and a
contributor as well to "the raising of the standards in other sections of the
country."[17]

At the University of Texas in Austin, historian Walter Prescott Webb,
who occasionally advised Johnson in the 1950s, had written a book about
the crisis of democracy in a frontierless society. In it Webb provided a
bridge to connect the views of the Browns and Johnson toward Roosevelt's
New Deal. In the years since the Civil War, he wrote, the North had established a feudal system that put the South and West in thrall, well-to-do and
poor alike. Anyone could look out his window at the university and see what
that feudalism meant.

> If I could paint a picture representing the general scene, it would be in
> the form of a great field stretching from Virginia and Florida westward
> to the Pacific and from Texas and California northward to Canada, an L-
> shaped region comprising nearly four-fifths of the country. Here mil-
> lions of people would be playing a game with pennies, nickels, dimes and
> dollars, rolling them northward and eastward where they are being
> stacked almost to the moon.[18]

Roosevelt's peaceful revolution had, for the first time since the Civil
War, challenged the rules of the game. But could FDR sustain a middle
course between fascism and socialism? That depended on whether he could
find a quick way out of the economic crisis before powerful forces swept the
New Deal into the still-deepening "chasm between the increasing poor and
the decreasing number of increasingly rich corporations."[19]

If he were to prevent this final catastrophe, Roosevelt needed support
from an alliance between the South and the West. A hopeful sign was the
budding cooperation of political leaders from those sections on the public
utilities question. But ultimately it would come down to the feudal lords
themselves.

> They can now decentralize industry through electric power; they can co-
> operate more with the government, state and national, if they will; they
> can more generously pour out their largesses to education in those sec-
> tions from whence their wealth comes. America is too rich for them to
> own, too independent for them to rule, too wise, we hope, for them to
> fool indefinitely.[20]

Roosevelt, meanwhile, had heard others voice similar concerns about
the fate of democratic government in a world dominated by totalitarian
powers. In early 1938, after worrisome months of economic decline questioned the viability of the New Deal, the president declared that government intervention was a way to bring the whole economy back to health.

From the nation's earliest days, he noted, "we have had a tradition of substantial government help to our system of private enterprise."

> It is following tradition as well as necessity, if Government strives to put idle money and idle men to work, to increase our public wealth and to build up the health and strength of the people—to help our system of private enterprise to function.[21]

Johnson thought it was exactly the right kind of message to give the nation. He had little difficulty, moreover, distinguishing Roosevelt's aims from those he believed the Harvards kept locked up with their Phi Beta Kappa keys, and who, he also fervently believed, had little real empathy for politicians from places like Texas, or for their constituents, or, it seemed increasingly obvious, for the success of capitalism.

The Harvards pinned their hopes on socialist-style planning, solving overproduction by allotments, putting people to work raking leaves. Their credo was redistribution of wealth and lowered expectations—for others. They had theirs, the rest could scramble. Not consciously exploitative like the bankers, well-meaning New Deal intellectuals (as opposed to Roosevelt himself) nonetheless blocked the true fulfillment of the American dream. That dream, Johnson believed, depended on programs like the NYA to educate the poor, and positive government efforts to stimulate wealth creation in the private sectors of the nation's economy—and in previously neglected regions.

Sometimes, of course, it was difficult to know whether the impact of a federal program advanced "socialism" or "private enterprise." Roosevelt's "Second" New Deal emphasized government spending in place of the redistributionist bias of the National Industrial Recovery Act and the Agricultural Adjustment Act. Where it would have taken the country had World War II not intervened, neither Johnson nor anyone else knew. As imperfect as LBJ's understanding of the situation might be, as imperfect as the New Deal itself was, the Texan's suspicion of a fundamental division among liberals on government's proper role never left him—not when he planned the Great Society, and not when he reacted to criticism of the Vietnam War, which, he believed, originated at least in part in arguments over who ought to be helped and how.

Partly, of course, his suspicions arose out of a belief that New Deal intellectuals would never accept him or his kind under any circumstances. They looked down their noses at anyone from west of the Mississippi. "You New Dealers, you are a bunch of intellectual snobs," he told James Rowe. He "worked" on these feelings, recalled Rowe, so that by the time he came to the presidency he had a well-developed sense of injured pride, which he displayed as readily as he would his gall bladder scar to embarrassed hospital visitors.[22]

What people in the South and West wanted, Johnson would say, was to "live American lives."[23] That opportunity came with World War II. Johnson had failed in a first attempt to win election to the Senate in 1941 and was feeling stymied in the House of Representatives. With a commission he entered the navy after Pearl Harbor but returned when Roosevelt recalled all members of Congress to legislative duties. From that vantage point, Johnson watched the war transform his section of the country and the fortunes of his most powerful backers.

The dam builders of the Colorado, Brown & Root, became shipbuilders for the navy. They built 355 vessels during the war, and, as George Brown recalled in 1969, reached toward higher plateaus.

> After the war we had these engineers whom we'd accumulated building ships and designing all the inside of the ships. We put them to work on chemical plants and industrial plants of all kinds, power plants, and became a very large integrated engineering-construction concern— which we are now. We're one of the biggest involved in the construction-engineering business in the United States and overseas.[24]

They formed a triumvirate, said George Brown—Alvin Wirtz, Lyndon Johnson, and himself. And Lyndon, according to Brown, swore that "we will not let any of our friends or enemies come between us as long as we are alive." What bound them together, he added, was a set of common feelings about the "burning questions of free-enterprise and socialist form of government," and the belief that Johnson thought as they did about the need to "have good government to keep from having a socialist form of government."[25]

How this was to be accomplished involved, for Brown & Root at least, something like the subsidies the East received in the nineteenth century to build railroads across the continent. A major military contractor in the cold war, Brown & Root spread worldwide, from Thailand to Haiti to Australia to the Persian Gulf, and South Vietnam, as builders of military infrastructure. Abroad, the powers that conservatives feared to give the government at home were exercised by foreign aid administrators and other "viceroys," thus enabling Washington to create a favorable climate for such investments on a scale far greater than anything dreamed of during the Pax Britannica.

Was it possible not to succeed under these conditions? With an annual $1.77 billion volume, Brown & Root eventually became, by 1969—the year Johnson's political career ended—the nation's largest construction company.[26] As Brown & Root went, so did the economy of the Southwest. Thus the war did for the region what funding the national debt did for the new American Republic. If the original New Deal spirit across the South and West was Jeffersonian, it emerged after the war in Hamiltonian garb. Johnson biographer Robert Dallek notes the changed outlook: "Where before 1941 southern state governments saw white supremacy and social stability as their primary goals, after that, encouraged by a Roosevelt administration which saw the war partly as a chance to transform the southern economy, business and industrial development became their central purpose." [27]

Johnson's personal fortunes were transformed as well. He refused an offer of oil lands from Texas supporters who said they wanted to make him "independent" of private pressures, fearing it would damage his political career. But with the help of George Brown and other friends, he and Lady Bird acquired a radio station in Austin for $17,500 in 1943 that became the basis for a variety of holdings that would one day be estimated at $14 million. [28]

The cold war promised more and more wealth for Texas, stimulated by military spending, and Johnson operated from the center of the scramble. As a member of the House Armed Services subcommittees concerned with industrial mobilization, he fought for large defense budgets and special support for the development of the synthetics industry. "In an age of synthetics," Johnson promised, "Texas—as the fountainhead of natural gas and oil—may easily become the kingpin state in a new industrial age." [29]

Newly prosperous Texas Democrats saw little for themselves, on the other hand, in the domestic side of Harry Truman's Fair Deal. The antigovernment, anti–labor union trend that began in the later Roosevelt years accelerated after the war in keeping with the entrepreneurial spirit that dominated the state. A symbolic turning point was the 1946 gubernatorial primary, in which the New Dealer Homer Rainey, ousted from his position as president of the University of Texas by anti–New Deal regents for not firing liberal economists, lost to the conservative Beauford Jester. [30]

While Brown & Root successfully lobbied the Texas state legislature for stronger antiunion laws that would make it one of the most antiunion states in the nation, they were also funneling money into Lyndon Johnson's 1948 campaign for the United States Senate "like Texas had never seen." [31] In his primary fight with Coke Stevenson, Johnson tried to paint his conservative opponent as the candidate of "labor bosses" who had come to Texas with their black bags full of money to defeat Lyndon Johnson. Replying in kind, Stevenson portrayed Johnson as an ardent New Dealer whose recent conversion to conservative views was purely opportunistic. [32]

It was the most famous campaign in modern Texas history, salvaged in the end for Johnson by a battery of lawyers, led by an old friend from the New Deal years, Abe Fortas. When the losing Stevenson forces sought an injunction based on claims of fraudulent returns, Fortas managed to persuade Supreme Court Justice Hugo Black not to grant it. Significantly, Black did not rule on the merits of the case, only that it had been erroneously introduced in federal instead of state courts. Certified the victor by just eighty votes, Johnson emerged from this dubious battle with the tag "Landslide Lyndon."[33]

Nevertheless, he now represented Texas, not just the Tenth District. Populist resentment had given way to Texas "nationalism," which easily accommodated attacks on "foreign owned" private power companies, and to defense of the Texas oil and gas industry against "big government." Where Walter Prescott Webb had feared that in the end the West would succumb to the same semicolonial fate as the South, a later historian, Donald Worster, now wrote that it had been transformed by the war from an empire in intention to one in being, from a source of strength for others to a master's role. "Indeed, since the war it has become a principal seat of the world-ordering American Empire."[34]

Oklahoma senator Mike Monroney made perhaps the most relevant comment on what was happening in Johnson's "country" in the 1950s and 1960s:

> The sharecroppers of the "Grapes of Wrath" days have become ranchers. Their sons, who would have had no opportunity, have gone to vocational trade schools and have become industrial workers. They live in suburbia today. They try to keep up with suburbia standards, with air conditioning bought on the installment plan, or with automobiles that are of higher standard than the beaten-up jalopies that their families once had. Their daughters have to be as well-dressed in the junior high school as the banker's daughter.[35]

Johnson was not unaware that some shared little if any in the region's new prosperity. But old acquaintances wondered what had happened to Lyndon. His new friends were the powerhouses in the Senate, Oklahoma's Robert Kerr, an oil man himself, and Georgia's Richard Russell. Eisenhower's election in 1952 was declared a triumph for "modern" Republicanism. But where were the modern Democrats? If the New Deal had succeeded in meeting the crisis of the Great Depression, the coming showdowns over civil rights required a solid party structure. Johnson was already beginning to see a new alliance between the South and West, with Texas, and himself, as natural leaders. Long ago protesting populists had failed to achieve such an alliance in the years before Woodrow Wilson's time, and the New Deal had only suggested such a possibility.[36]

If it materialized, the alliance would have to be based upon reasonable trade-offs to prevent the Republicans from regionalizing their opponents on questions like tidelands oil, public power projects, and, most crucially, civil rights. Johnson busied himself developing friendly relations not only with Kerr and Russell but with certain Midwestern and Western liberals, such as Minnesota's Hubert Humphrey and Idaho's Frank Church.

Convinced the only way he could reach the White House was through the vice-presidency, Johnson wangled an arrangement with Richard Russell, who believed he had a chance for the 1952 Democratic nomination. According to their pact, LBJ would support Russell for the presidency in exchange for the Georgian's efforts on his behalf—whoever was nominated—for second place on the ticket. But when Adlai Stevenson won the nomination and the dubious honor of opposing Eisenhower, he shunted Johnson aside in favor of Alabama's John Sparkman. A Stevenson-Johnson ticket would have made little difference. Eisenhower won simply by saying that he would go to Korea. He did not even have to promise to end the war; that was assumed by an electorate willing to trust the man who defeated the Nazis in World War II.

Neither would it have made any sense for Johnson to take a definite stand that year on the issue that agitated Texans perhaps more than Korea. The Truman administration had moved to assert national ownership of tidelands oil, thus setting up a perfect opportunity for Texans to use old populist arguments to protect the oil companies against federal taxes. Conservative Democrats like Price Daniel jumped ship. In 1952 Daniel ran for Texas's other Senate seat vowing to oppose the federal threat to usurp states' rights over natural resources. Eisenhower declared against the scheme, and Republicans saturated the state with clever ads funded by oil money, showing Stevenson sneering at a classroom of children: "Tideland funds for those kids? Aw, let them pick cotton." LBJ tried hard to straddle the issue, campaigning only briefly for Stevenson while making it clear he differed on federal ownership of tidelands mineral rights.[37]

In 1953 he became Senate minority leader, and when the 1954 elections produced a Democratic victory, Johnson stepped into the majority leader's office. If not the most effective majority leader ever, he certainly had a good claim to the title. In 1956 he again sought the vice-presidential nomination, and again Stevenson rebuffed his bid. This time, however, the senator felt doubly aggrieved because he had sent word to the likely nominee that his status in the party entitled him to be consulted before the final choice was made. Stevenson turned his back on tradition that year, throwing the convention open to allow the delegates to select the vice-presidential nominee, no doubt hoping that the contrast with the "rigged" renomination of the still controversial Richard Nixon by the Republicans would detract from Eisenhower's popularity.[38]

Once again Johnson was probably lucky not to have his colors attached to a losing cause. Afterward he received a timely warning from James Rowe not to allow his failed bids for the vice-presidency to embitter him. Rowe was fast developing a belief in Lyndon Johnson as perhaps the only politician capable of holding the Democratic party together in the civil rights crisis that had already begun to force its way to the top of the national agenda. Johnson was never of a mind to follow Southerners down the path of

narrow sectionalism, because he still believed in the potential of a South-
ern/Western alliance, and because he still believed himself capable of reaching the top of the ladder.

Eastern intellectuals simply did not understand that no Democrat
could win election as a "labor" party candidate. American politics did not
fall out that way. But that seemed to him where Adlai Stevenson's
"egghead" supporters wanted to steer the party. Throughout the Eisenhower years Johnson worked hard to build the Southern/Western alliance
in the Senate while quietly exploiting differences in the Republican party.
He liked pushing the notion, for example, that he was more "loyal" to
Eisenhower than the right wing of the president's own party.[39]

More than any foreign policy issue, more than any other domestic
issue, civil rights focused attention on Congress. The stage had been set by
the Supreme Court's 1954 decision in *Brown v. Board of Education* declaring
school segregation unconstitutional. The decision had set in train a nationwide civil rights movement whose momentum threatened to push politicians into confronting, at long last, the most fundamental questions about
American society. Eisenhower was unhappy with *Brown v. Board of Education*, but he made clear his determination to enforce the law of the land. As
Johnson was well aware, Republicans still hoped to divide, or "section off,"
the Democrats by pushing a pro–civil rights stance. All that would change
in the next decade, but in the 1950s Republicans sought the black vote in
the North and were delighted by the consternation that civil rights caused
the Democratic party in the South.

At the 1956 Democratic Convention, James Rowe, who read these
portents with growing apprehension, witnessed Averell Harriman's strange
plea for Johnson's support against Stevenson. "Now, Lyndon," Rowe quoted the New Yorker, "you don't have to worry about me on this civil rights
business. All I have to do to keep my people happy is to make a few speeches. I will make the speech, but I'm not going to do anything about it." After
Harriman left, Johnson stared over at Rowe. "You liberals," he snorted,
"you're great!"[40]

However much he might have relished another example of Eastern liberal hypocrisy, Johnson knew the real tests were about to begin. His personal voting record until then was solidly states' rights, but he fully realized
that the race issue could not be resolved that way, nor put off much longer.
When a strong civil rights bill sponsored by the Eisenhower administration
passed the House of Representatives in June 1957, the Southern bloc in the
Senate set out to weaken it with amendments calling for jury trials in contempt cases. A Southern jury was hardly likely to hand down guilty verdicts
in such cases. Here was a real challenge to the ingenuity of Johnson's leadership, as well as a test of his physical stamina after recovery from a serious
heart attack in 1955.

Like Eisenhower, he was less than happy that the civil rights question had been posed as a social issue instead of a political question. Convinced that racial turmoil would impede the South's economic progress, Johnson favored efforts to secure black voting rights as less disruptive than federal intervention to enforce desegregation in schools and at soda fountains. This was not a view shared by most Southern politicians. Working closely with Richard Russell, Johnson brokered a "deal" committing certain Southern senators to vote for a hydroelectric project at Hell's Canyon, Idaho, in exchange for Western votes in favor of his amendments to the House version of the civil rights bill. Johnson pulled out all the stops, one senator recalled.[41] He cajoled liberals with warnings that nothing stronger could get past a Southern filibuster, and prodded Southerners with a threat that if they blocked his version of the bill they could expect something much worse. Neither liberals nor conservatives were happy with the final Civil Rights Act of 1957, but Johnson received credit, however grudging, for passage of the first such legislation since Reconstruction. So while some liberals now talked about blocking Johnson's path to the White House, he had demonstrated, at least to his own satisfaction, that a Southern/Western alliance could hold together on key issues. And it was especially gratifying to see that alliance take shape around a favorite topic: federal aid to power projects.

Only weeks after he signed the Civil Rights Bill, President Eisenhower nationalized the Arkansas National Guard to enforce a court-ordered desegregation plan for Little Rock. Here was exactly the sort of thing that worried both the president and the majority leader. But then came Sputnik, the satellite that Moscow successfully placed in orbit, beeping its message back to earth that the Russians had beaten the United States at its own technological game. Perhaps only the first round in outer space had gone to the Soviets, but even that was hard to take, especially coming as it did in the midst of the turmoil over Little Rock and with the American economy struggling along in a recession.

Soviet Premier Nikita Khrushchev's boasts about communism's superior performance now had a focal point, with perhaps more to come before America's space program got off the ground. Exactly how Sputnik would influence political events on earth was not clear, but anything that added such enormous prestige to the Communist system worried policy planners. Russia's success in putting a satellite in orbit on October 4, 1957, offered Democrats an opportunity, on the other hand, to regroup for the battle against whomever the Republicans might name to succeed Eisenhower. Johnson's press secretary, George Reedy, grasped Sputnik's political significance at once. Properly handled, he wrote the senator, it "would blast the Republicans out of the water, unify the Democratic Party and elect you President."

Reedy went on:

> The integration issue is not going to go away. The troops are still in Lit-
> tle Rock and it will be difficult to get them out. . . . It is a dynamic issue
> which is not going to be solved by reason. The only possibility is to find
> another issue which is even more potent. Otherwise the Democratic
> future is bleak.[42]

It really didn't matter, added Reedy, whether or not Sputnik had immediate military significance, because the race for control of the universe had
begun. Eisenhower promised that the United States would put up a "better"
satellite soon, wisecracked the aide, "maybe even equipped with chrome
trim and automatic windshield wipers." But that did not begin to answer the
nation's legitimate questions about the future. Sputnik might not be much of
a gadget, argued Reedy, but neither was the Wright brothers' first airplane.[43]

The first step was to hold a congressional inquiry, headed by a senator
with a statesmanlike reputation in the preparedness area, "who is not
involved too heavily in the emotional issues surrounding segregation." No
one fit the bill better than Lyndon Johnson himself, Reedy advised. "This
may be one of those moments in history when good politics and statesman-
ship are as close to each other as a hand in a glove."[44]

Johnson had already acted. He had anticipated Reedy's memo with his
own order for Senate hearings, which he would chair, to probe the supposed failings of the nation's space program. The initial challenge confronting the majority leader was how to strike the right balance between a
reassuring Roosevelt-style fireside chat and a Paul Revere gallop across the
land shouting, "The Russians are coming!" Johnson presided with a presidential pose throughout, but he made each session seem like an emergency
summons to rally a sleeping nation. "He held the hearings in the morning,
he held them in the afternoon, and he held them at night," recalled an aide.
"I remember on one occasion," added another aide, Solis Horwitz, "[Air
Force] Secretary [Donald] Quarles appearing at a night hearing in tails," on
the way back from a White House dinner.[45]

Eisenhower liked none of it—not his dinner guests being hustled over
to Capitol Hill, and certainly not the senator and the Democrats conjuring
up a "missile gap" crisis. He was particularly annoyed when Johnson started
delivering "state of the union" speeches to his colleagues, perhaps because
he thought the Senate majority leader was the strongest candidate the
opposition party had to offer.[46]

On the opening day of the Senate preparedness hearings, Johnson
asserted that the nation faced an even greater challenge than it had on
December 8, 1941. "In my opinion, we do not have as much time as we had
after Pearl Harbor." Knowing "the facts" should not, however, lead to

national hysteria: "I believe the facts will inspire Americans to the greatest effort in American history."[47]

To present the "facts," Johnson introduced his first witness, Dr. Edward Teller. Before Teller could begin his testimony, Johnson had to bang his gavel repeatedly to get the photographers crowded around the star witness to step aside and stop blocking the senators' view. Besides J. Robert Oppenheimer, Teller was the most famous of all the scientists who had worked on the atomic bomb. He was also the most political of the atom scientists, highly prized by conservatives for his alarmist views of Soviet capabilities and intentions.[48]

Dr. Teller did not disappoint the subcommittee. Within a decade or so, he began, whoever dominated outer space could even control the weather, causing floods and drought at his command. "What kind of a world will it be," he asked, looking gravely around the room for his answer, "where they have this new kind of control and we do not?"[49] He knew the final answer: Russia could control the plant and animal life of the seas! Vermont's Ralph Flanders quipped that it all reminded him of H. G. Wells and the purple algae. Without a pause, Teller readily agreed, and added, "I am an enthusiastic reader of H. G. Wells, and, in fact, it is practically the only science fiction I read."[50]

Purple algae aside, Teller's somber descriptions of the Russian threat left a darkening cloud over the witness table. And when Deputy Secretary of Defense Donald Quarles showed up to testify in evening dress, he provided the perfect foil for Johnson to skewer Eisenhower. "There is a great feeling in the committee and in the country," intoned the chairman, "that there has been nobody in a real hurry about this whole situation and there have been a lot of public officials who have been making statements which are calculated to laugh the whole thing off." At another point in the hearings, Johnson interrupted testimony to tell everyone in the room that the president had suffered "another form of heart attack," even though the bulletin he read referred to a less serious cerebral episode.[51]

These allusions to supposed administration incapacities, public and personal, were not followed up, however, by exactly what the senator wanted to get on the record from Pentagon spokesmen. Admiral Arleigh Burke, chief of naval operations, for example, refused to credit cold war gains the Russians had made, or might make, to military factors. Both nations had the capacity to destroy one another, he said, and that would not change because of Sputnik or what came after. Where the Russians succeeded, he argued, it would be through economic and psychological means. Johnson would not leave it at that.

> Senator Johnson. What, in your opinion, could do more for Soviet psychological penetration than Soviet successes in missiles and satellites? The Soviet boasts about missiles had its effect on Suez, did it not?

Admiral Burke. I don't think so, sir. I don't think it did. It might have, because, you never can tell.[52]

Burke and other military brass slowed LBJ's missile-gap ride to the White House, but Johnson closed the hearings with an appropriately balanced Rooseveltian flourish:

I don't think this is any time to panic or to be hysterical, but it is certainly time, when the Russians get something in the air that we cannot get 4 feet off the ground, for us to take a notch in our belts, . . . and roll up our sleeves and go back to working a little bit like our dads did.[53]

Much of that work, of course, would be contracted for and accomplished in Johnson's home territory. James Rowe and another Johnson fan, *Washington Post* owner Phil Graham, were anxious that Johnson use the missile hearings to project the picture of the complete modern liberal, one who devoted heavy attention to world as well as domestic affairs. Rowe wrote at the conclusion of the hearings to remind the would-be president that undoubtedly he would now be asked to write several articles on missiles and defense policy. That being so, it would be wise to line up some ghost-writers, such as Sidney Hyman, whose articles often appeared in think magazines like the *New York Times Sunday Magazine*, *The Reporter*, and *Harper's*.[54]

Johnson always preferred oratory to expository writing. He had begun his teaching career as a debate coach. In a statement to the Democratic congressional conference on January 7, 1958, the majority leader summed up the themes he thought the party needed to emphasize. Teller's sci-fi predictions were offered up to his colleagues as the authoritative "testimony of the scientists," upon which Johnson would now draw out the fullest picture yet of America at Soviet mercies:

Control of space means control of the world, far more certainly, far more totally than any control that has ever or could ever be achieved by weapons, or by troops of occupation.

From space, the masters of infinity would have the power to control the earth's weather, to cause drought and flood, to change the tides and raise the levels of the sea, to divert the gulf stream and change temperate climates to frigid.[55]

If "men of selfish purpose" were dedicated to those goals, Johnson continued, it was also true that "men wholly dedicated to freedom" could thwart their evil design. They could create a world at last liberated from tyranny and from the fear of war. "There is something more important than any ultimate weapon. That is the ultimate position—the position of total control over earth that lies somewhere out in space." Much had to be done to regain supremacy in space. In the next breath, however, Johnson ticked

off what had to be done in nonmilitary ways to get the country moving—
and that turned out to be a traditional liberal agenda dealing with unemployment, farm problems, education, housing, and small business.

The speech to his fellow Democrats ended with a plea that the goals
of the "human race" were too great to be divided as spoils, too great for
wasted efforts in a blind race between competitive nations. Real hope for
the future rested not in weapons superiority to the farthest reaches of the
universe. "The conference table is more important now than ever it has
been, and we should welcome to its chairs men of all nations."[56]

Johnson cosponsored the bill that created the National Aeronautics
and Space Administration (NASA), but as biographer Robert Dallek notes,
he was already turning to other issues. Jim Rowe told him that, "speaking
solely from a selfish point of view," he had gained all there was to gain from
space and missiles: "You have received a tremendous press, increased your
national stature and got away scot-free without a scratch. . . . The obvious
new issue . . . is unemployment."[57]

Yet Johnson always believed that the challenge of Sputnik was crucial
to the "revolution of the '60s," in ways that had hardly anything to do with
the direct Russian military challenge. It reopened minds to the power of the
federal government to accomplish things undreamt of not only in outer
space but at home, and in other parts of the world to halt the spread of communism. People began to understand, and to ask, said Johnson, if you can
send a man to the moon, why can't you do something for grandma with
Medicare? Where John Kennedy felt the adventure of space, writes historian Walter McDougall, Johnson viewed the space program as demonstrating the role government could play, and should play—an assignment
handed down "by some Promethean party boss in the form of command
technology and federal management."

> To Eisenhower, the essence of courage was to resist the temptation to
> use dangerous tools; to Johnson, the essence of courage was to take them
> up in a good cause. Whether in decaying cities, outer space, or Third
> World jungles, American technology would overwhelm the enemies of
> dignity.[58]

What the Depression had done to spur government to action with the
New Deal, Sputnik now did to launch the New Frontier and the Great
Society. Like Johnson, Walter Prescott Webb, whose Western sensibilities
had paralleled LBJ's original notions, got hooked on the space program. As
late as 1951 the famous Texas historian had believed that civilization was
still suffering "a great pain in the heart" at the closing of the frontier, "and
we are always trying to get it back again." But after Sputnik he wrote to
Johnson with delight that he had apparently settled too soon on the closing
of the frontier. How fitting it was then, that the area "last to be occupied by

the Anglo-American civilization," as Webb now described the once down-trodden Southwest, should become the launching pad for the thrust into outer space.[59] George Reedy reintroduced Webb to Johnson because he believed his boss needed more contact with the intellectual world, and Webb was a perfect match. The historian was soon drinking J&B scotch after hours in the majority leader's office, and writing speeches for him on the subject of Southern and Southwestern economic development.[60]

The 1958 midterm elections looked like a domestic turning point to Johnson. The results strengthened the Democratic party's majorities in Congress, and LBJ began to think about a bid for the presidency, all the while denying any such intention. If he could get elected, Johnson told a group of New Yorkers, he would be "more liberal than Eleanor Roosevelt." But he had to get elected first. And that was the tricky part. The country was still comfortable as it was, whatever might be stirring under the surface. Liberals in the Senate were scaring people. "Have a revolution, all right," he told a well-known liberal visitor to his office, "but don't say anything about it until you are entrenched in office. That's the way Roosevelt did it."[61]

He was certainly Dean Acheson's choice for 1960. "He is a giant among pygmies," Acheson wrote former president Harry S Truman. With John Kennedy as his running mate, he was the best chance to defeat Adlai Stevenson's likely bid for a third nomination. What was needed, Truman's secretary of state told the Senate majority leader, was a dramatic revival of U.S. and NATO military power and huge increases in development funds for Asia, Africa, and Latin America.[62] Also watching Johnson's post-Sputnik performance, the much younger Kennedy admitted that the party owed the majority leader the nomination. "But it's too close to Appomattox for Johnson to be nominated and elected. So, therefore I feel free to run."[63]

Divided by many things, including regional biases, Johnson and Kennedy agreed that the Democrats had to emulate Roosevelt, but without all the footloose experimentalism and ideological fervor of the New Deal. Neither man thought the New Deal experience ought to be repeated. Indeed, they believed it *must not* be repeated. The New Deal legacy was not simply golden memories of Franklin Delano Roosevelt, it was also a legacy of highly charged political beliefs that had divided the country ever since. Now quiescent, there were all sorts of signs that these were gathering force behind the bland face of Eisenhower-era politics, especially in the schools and churches of the South.

Inevitably, these movements would find their focus in the Democratic party. Whether this was because insurgent views sought their natural home in the party of Wilson and Roosevelt, or, as Johnson aide Harry McPherson argued, because Democratic candidates and presidents *believed* that American electoral politics demanded they undertake such a mission, the resulting burden for the party was the same: how to shape the politics of protest without losing control.[64]

"The biggest danger to American stability," Johnson told Doris Kearns, "is the politics of principle, which brings out the masses in irrational fights for unlimited goals, for once the masses begin to move, then the whole thing begins to explode."[65] Democrats were better off—as the party out of power—developing a consensus around achievable goals, with the agenda limited to the reforms necessary to those goals, as Johnson had suggested in his January 1958 speech to the Democratic conference.

Looked at this way, Johnson's (and Kennedy's) espousal of the space program invoked memories of government intervention in the economy in the century past, offering a possible solution to a liberal sense of malaise as the cold war dragged on, and a preferred alternative to an ideologically charged politics of principle. But fascination with technocratic solutions to political problems brought risks of its own. If one could go to the moon, and if one could help grandma with new medical miracles, surely it should be possible to convince Ho Chi Minh to accept a dam on the Mekong River instead of a residence in Saigon.[66]

T W O

Liberal Anxiety in the
Eisenhower Years

IN THE 1950s AMERICAN LIBERALS felt obliged to inform the nation about the perils of prosperity. Not all groups in any age understand exactly what it is that should worry them. Liberals knew. Their concerns, it turned out, sounded very much like traditional conservative fears of a declining nation losing out to a more disciplined enemy. Liberals fretted throughout the Eisenhower years about all sorts of things, about American affluence, the cultural wasteland of television, the false utopias of suburbia—until the Russians sent Sputnik aloft. Then they insisted there really was something to worry about.

By itself American failure to beat the Russians in placing a basketball-sized object in orbit might not be enough to put a Democrat into the White House, as Lyndon Johnson knew, but in combination with a string of apparent foreign policy failures in Eisenhower's second term and the distressing economic slowdown at home, Americans were becoming more than a little uneasy about their future. While they still liked Ike, they had mixed feelings about Republicans, and especially about the likely nominee in 1960, Vice-President Richard Nixon.

"We seem becalmed in a season of storm and drifting in a century of mighty dreams and great achievements," declared Adlai Stevenson, who hoped for a third chance at the Republicans. While Stevenson loyalists responded to his eloquence as always, even they were doubtful about submitting his name once more to an electorate that had twice turned him down. Of course, both times he had been up against the immensely popular Eisenhower, author of victory in Europe, but there was no clear indication that voters would now reward Stevenson, or that the party would risk a third consecutive defeat to vindicate a noble cause.[1]

Less ardent admirers of the former governor from Illinois thought that was just as well. Foreign policy demanded a more "muscular" liberalism. Ever since they took their stand for Harry Truman during the 1948 presidential campaign, and signed on for the cold war, liberals in the Democratic party had agonized over their proper stance toward foreign policy. For the most part they had chosen to give unstinting support to Washington so as not to incur the charge of isolationism. Indeed, they seized upon Eisenhower's "New Look" defense policies as evidence of Republican yearnings for a simpler world, making it clear that they preferred involvement at ground level to massive nuclear retaliation from the air.

Stevenson seemed perhaps too fastidious for the job of convincing Americans that the Democratic party had the toughness to meet the Soviet challenge—especially after Sputnik. "Few persons think," began Daniel Patrick Moynihan's dour commentary on the liberal predicament in the 1950s, "and fewer still take notice of those who do. But within the limited circles involved there was at mid-century a perceptible and almost precipitous turning from received liberalism." Enthralled by a populist anticommunism promoted by a still virulent streak of right-wing capitalism, he continued, the American mass was drifting toward "the same condition of hysteria and fear born of insecurity and rootlessness which provided the setting for the onset of totalitarianism in Europe." The nineteenth-century faith in rational thought and secular individualism, the fundamental basis for liberalism, had simply not dispelled the demons confronting Western civilization. Instead it had "brought mankind into a zone of disaster from which its eventual emergence was problematic at best."[2]

There could be no all-out war against communism like the victory over the Axis powers. The challenge of the Russian Revolution had to be met in the so-called developing world, and in the willingness of the American people to meet that challenge. To do that meant adopting a Manichean view of the world. Moynihan's pessimistic commentary was perhaps best understood, therefore, as an expression of frustration at liberals' constricted role under cold war politics. Having envisioned themselves as tutors to the postwar generation of American leaders, following the precedent set by Roosevelt's use of the "Brains Trust," liberal intellectuals now concluded they must first convince the "masses" of their worthiness as cold warriors, lest the insecurities Moynihan spoke about become the driving force in American political life.

In the wake of Sputnik, congressional legislation to address national needs, such as education and highways, was assured of passage only by putting the label "national defense" somewhere in the bill's title. Democrats saw little chance of winning in 1960 unless their candidate demonstrated how he could best the Russians and restore American preeminence not only in scientific and technical fields but in competition for the favor of the emerging states of the third world. "In 1957," observes Barbara Ehrenreich in a study of the troubled psychology of the middle class in those years, "Sputnik confirmed the suspicion that the Russians were striving in a disciplined, purposeful way, while Americans had been 'meandering along in a stupor of fat.' " The solution was not to go on a starvation diet but to consume more of the right things. "Like conservatives, liberals believed that economic growth was the key to domestic well-being and that military strength was the guarantor of peace—only liberals wanted more of both. 'Russia,' [Arthur M.] Schlesinger observed sternly in 1960, 'more than makes up for its smaller annual output by its harder sense of purpose.' " Thus even the shortage of consumer goods in Russia, once thought to mark the inferiority of the Communist system, now appeared instead as a source of strength.[3]

As the Eisenhower administration appeared to run down like an unwound grandfather clock, liberal intellectuals thus busied themselves trying to find the right candidate to get America moving again. Historian William O'Neill concluded that the American mood turned curiously ambivalent, almost hostile, to its previous celebration of the good life, because "Russia's Spartan vigor exposed American affluence for the enfeebling thing it was."[4] It all meant the candidate must be someone who could do more than stand up to Soviet leader Nikita Khrushchev in a debate over refrigerators and electric can openers.

ONLY A FEW YEARS BEFORE, of course, Eisenhower had also campaigned for the presidency on a promise to pursue a more vigorous cold war policy. Liberation, not containment, would be his watchword. But once in office his priority became to extricate the nation from the Korean War. It was hinted that Ike had threatened the Chinese with the atomic bomb in order to end the conflict. That threat, whether actual or not, provided a basis for launching the so-called "New Look" military policy that emphasized "a bigger bang for a buck"—heavier reliance on technology and fewer men in uniforms. Secretary of State John Foster Dulles trumpeted the policy, declaring that henceforth the United States would retaliate massively against Communist threats, at times and places of its own choosing.

Behind a benevolent Norman Rockwell countenance, Eisenhower fought the cold war by using the CIA in creative ways to restore the shah of Iran to his throne, to oust a leftist regime in Guatemala, and to support the French in Indochina. As the decade wore on, nevertheless, it appeared that the "New Look" meant "Look the Other Way" or "No Look at All." The

United States had sacrificed flexibility to bluster, complained army Chief of Staff General Maxwell Taylor, who resigned in protest to write books about the shortcomings of American military policy. At the battle of Dien Bien Phu in 1954, where the French fell to the Viet Minh, Taylor averred, the United States was left with no option but atomic bombs. "This event," he insisted, "was the first, but not the last, failure of the New Look to keep the peace on our terms."[5]

Taylor's assertion that the French bastion could somehow have been rescued, or the first Indochina war won, if not for the muscle-bound New Look defense policy, rested on flimsy ground. What Sputnik did, however, was to offer powerful evidence that the New Look hypothesis rested on even flimsier ground. It swept away the aura of Eisenhower's military genius with one orbit around the earth. Hip comedian Mort Sahl quipped that after Sputnik was launched, Ike proposed sending Strategic Air Force bombers around the world so that the Russians would be impressed with American power. "I'm sure they will," said Sahl, "if they bother to look down."

Vice-President Richard Nixon made a more sober assessment of the post-Sputnik situation, obliquely commenting as well on his chances for succeeding the general as the next occupant of the White House:

> The Kremlin has offered us a direct challenge. It proclaims to the world that a slave economy can outproduce a free economy. It promises to the developing areas of the world that the Communist system can do more for them in a shorter time than the system of free enterprise which is the economic basis of the free world. And the spectacular success of the satellite project is being held up as proof of the superiority of the Communist system.[6]

Eisenhower bristled at accusations of a missile gap, which, he knew from American U-2 superspy planes, was simply not true. But Nixon sounded very much like Lyndon Johnson or the emerging challenger, John F. Kennedy, in decrying American laggardness in the space race. Meanwhile, a plea for a military strategy to replace Eisenhower's discredited "massive retaliation" made the reputation of a young Harvard professor. In *Nuclear Weapons and Foreign Policy*, Henry Kissinger argued that American defense policy was falsely premised upon the notion that if war came it would come as a sudden surprise attack, a nuclear Pearl Harbor. Kissinger agreed with Nixon that Sputnik's real challenge was Moscow's enhanced prestige, emboldening it to take greater risks to secure its long-term goals. Inhibited by the psychological burden of atomic warfare as an immoral act—as it was under the doctrine of massive retaliation—Americans risked losing everything because they refused to consider the possibilities of "limited" nuclear war as a deterrent.

Each successive Soviet move is designed to make our moral position that much more difficult: Indo-China was more ambiguous than Korea; the Soviet arms deal with Egypt more ambiguous than Indo-China; the Middle Eastern crisis more ambiguous than the arms deal with Egypt.[7]

While the president refused to be drawn into a direct debate with his critics, Vice-President Nixon made sure he was photographed carrying a copy of Kissinger's book under his arm.[8] Critics faulted Kissinger for not offering evidence that nuclear war could remain limited under such circumstances, but not for the argument that the greatest danger Russia posed was "internal subversion and limited war." At the nearby Massachusetts Institute of Technology, two other professors, Walt Whitman Rostow and Max F. Millikan, combined Kissinger's geopolitical musings with moral philosophizing about the new white man's burden. "We need the challenge of world development," they asserted in *A Proposal: Key to an Effective Foreign Policy*, "to keep us from the stagnation of smug prosperity." The United States was now within sight of solutions to a range of issues that had dominated national political life since the Civil War. As a consequence, it must now look abroad for reenergizing experiences:

> The farm problem, the status of big business in a democratic society, the status and responsibilities of organized labor, the avoidance of extreme cyclical unemployment, social equity for the Negro, the provision of educational opportunity, the equitable distribution of income—none of all these great issues is fully resolved; but a national consensus on them exists within which we are clearly moving forward as a nation. . . . If we continue to devote our attention in the same proportion to domestic issues as in the past, we run the danger of becoming a bore to ourselves and the world.[9]

To escape boredom was not the only reason, of course, for going abroad in search of new challenges. "I decided when I was 18," Rostow later told a congressional committee, "that when I learned enough I was going to do an alternative to Marxism because I knew a lot of people in the world were taken in by this theory, and I finally took my shot at it."[10] Should we go on ignoring the underdeveloped world, Rostow and Millikan predicted, Americans would eventually find themselves isolated and forced to seek security in a "garrison state," which would undermine American democracy.

> We have, in short, a major and persistent stake in a world environment predominantly made up of open societies; for with modern communications it is difficult to envisage the survival of a democratic American society as an island in a totalitarian sea.[11]

This old American credo went as far back as Jefferson's quarrel with English restrictions on American trade before the War of 1812, but it was never more popular in liberal circles than in the late 1950s. At meetings of groups like the Democratic Advisory Council, founded by Democratic party chairman Paul Butler after the 1956 election to provide a forum for policymakers-in-exile, former Secretary of State Dean Acheson took on all comers from the ranks of Stevenson loyalists. The latter attacked the Eisenhower administration as inflexibly moralistic and economically old-fashioned; Acheson admonished them to consider that the Chinese might be right—the Republicans had allowed America to become a paper tiger, whose snarl the Reds mocked while they took over his domain bit by bit.[12]

"You know, Dean," John Kenneth Galbraith sighed on one occasion, "I don't agree with your declarations of war."[13] What troubled Galbraith as well was the almost total absence of a domestic "vision" in the manifestos of the cold warriors on the council. "Here, early and in miniature," Galbraith wrote of those meetings, "were the fatal politics of Vietnam."

> It was not that the issue was debated and the wrong decision taken; it was rather that there was no debate. The old liberal fear of being thought soft on Communism, the fear of being attacked by professional patriots and the knowledge of the political punishment that awaits any departure from the Establishment view . . .[14]

While Acheson and Galbraith squabbled around the seminar table, Jack Kennedy and Lyndon Johnson were taking instruction from yet another would-be counselor to the American elite, British economist Barbara Ward. Critics dismissed her *The Rich Nations and the Poor Nations* as lacking sophistication, but its prescription for proving Marx and Lenin wrong in former colonial areas struck a resonant chord.[15] Humankind knew only one method so far of raising up the poor, she elaborated on her arguments in a private memo to Johnson.

> It is the method used in the last century inside *domestic* Western society. By increasing the skills of the poor, by investing in their health and housing, by improving their chances in the market and by financing a part of all these improvements out of taxation, the West has turned its restive proletarians into fine upstanding consumers.[16]

Here indeed was a prescription that promoted the liberal agenda at home as the safest and surest route to victory in the cold war abroad. Whenever a Johnson aide was asked about LBJ's favorite books, there was only one answer (and one book) offered in reply: *The Rich Nations and the Poor Nations*.[17] Johnson read it "over and over again," claimed George Reedy, who added that LBJ's predilection for the underdog led him to take a poorly digested version of Ward's arguments about what America could do—and was obligated to do—to raise standards of living in the third world as justification for what he would do in Vietnam. "I read it like I do the bible," Johnson said of Ward's book. And she returned the compliment: "His profound and compassionate understanding of the roots of poverty gives a unique dimension to the leadership he offers the world."[18]

WITH ALL HIS EXPERIENCE in dealing with domestic issues, and his alacrity in seizing the Sputnik crisis to demonstrate command of the defense problem, LBJ was nonetheless startled by the sudden rise of Jack Kennedy. "It was the goddamnedest thing," Johnson recalled. Kennedy "never said a word of importance in the Senate and he never did a thing. But somehow . . . he managed to create the image of himself as a youthful leader who would change the face of the country. Now, I will admit that he had a good sense of humor and that he looked awfully good on the goddamned television screen . . . but his growing hold on the American people was simply a mystery to me."[19]

In part it was accomplished with a promise to deliver liberals from doubt and division. "We have allowed a soft sentimentalism to form the atmosphere we breathe," Kennedy lectured—and many liberals nodded their agreement.[20] It was hard to establish any causal relation, but after Sputnik had come Castro's revolution in Cuba, renewed tension in Berlin, and, most unnerving for what it suggested about both American efforts to counter the missile threat and Eisenhower's personal leadership, the Russian downing of the U-2 spy plane in early May 1960. In its wake, Eisenhower's forlorn attempts to salvage a Paris summit meeting with Khrushchev only worsened the situation.

Kennedy, meanwhile, had already seized the missile-gap issue from Johnson's grasp, warning that unless a strenuous effort were made to provide funds for missiles and Strategic Air Command forces, the United States would soon be at Russia's mercy. "Would my able friend from Massachusetts agree," wondered another air power advocate, Senator Stuart Symington, "that the situation which the United States faces in the late 1950s may have considerable comparability with the situation faced by the British in the late 1930s?" Kennedy replied, "The Senator is absolutely correct."[21]

All this was very flattering, in a backhanded fashion of course, to the Soviets, whose post-Sputnik boasts about the superiority of communism gained credence from the consternation they caused in the West. "Our job," declared Walt Rostow, "was to deal with an automobile with weak brakes on a hill. It was slowly sliding backward. If we applied enormous energy, the car would begin to move forward, and in time we would get it to the top of the hill."[22]

Kennedy's most famous phrase—"I think it's time America started moving again"—certainly fit the campaign he ran for the nomination and then for the presidency. Johnson had hoped to head him off at the convention. He had stayed away from the presidential primaries in 1960, where Kennedy locked up the nomination, because he believed the prize depended instead on securing the support of congressional "whales," the insiders who controlled the legislative process. He wrongly assumed they would also determine the nominating process. "There I was," Johnson said of the outcome, "looking for the burglar coming in the front door, and little did I know that the fox was coming through the fence in back. When I woke up, the chickens were gone."[23]

But one was left, a scrawny bird not considered worth much—the vice-presidency. Johnson's initial reluctance to consider Kennedy's ambiguous offer of second place on the ticket—supposedly until Sam Rayburn and others persuaded him—appears to have been a calculated move to convince fellow Southerners he was "obligated" to agree for the sake of the party. After all, he had eagerly sought the vice-presidential nomination in 1952 and 1956, when he also would have been running with a Northern liberal.[24]

The offer and the way it was handled fueled an already smoldering dislike between LBJ and Jack's brother, Robert, that would burn steadily over the next eight years and, it can be argued, directly affect the course of the Vietnam War. Speculations about this dispute and about Johnson's "unnatural succession" after Kennedy's assassination in 1963 probably increased Johnson's suspicion of the Harvards—his oldest enemies in politics, further convincing him in the mid-1960s that Vietnam War protesters were spurred on by a liberal elite irrationally determined to punish him for not placing himself between Oswald and their fallen leader.

Bobby's last-minute attempt to yank back the offer of the vice-presidency in order to protect Jack's left flank stuck in LBJ's craw forever. When the nominee's brother suggested that Johnson instead consider the chairmanship of the Democratic National Committee, his seconds, Sam Rayburn and John Connally, exploded that Senator Johnson was not "running for anything." If Jack really wanted him he would accept, but in the future the only one of the Kennedys the Johnson people wanted to deal with was Senator Kennedy. Bobby shrugged, "Well, it's Jack and Lyndon."[25]

Johnson was assigned a specific role in the campaign—and told to like it. A Johnson aide assigned to approach Bobby on the delicate issue of the oil depletion allowance met the nominee's brother at the Austin airport and handed him a proposed statement for Jack that would help Johnson soothe disgruntled oil men, among his most powerful backers in state politics. "Now, Bobby," explained John Singleton, "you know this oil and gas issue is very hot in this area, and here's what we'd like for your brother to say when he comes down here." Bobby tore up the statement and threw it on the ground. "We're not going to say anything like that," he snapped. "We put that son of a bitch on the ticket to carry Texas, and if you can't carry Texas, that's y'all's problem."[26]

Johnson had effectively been stripped of his national power, relegated once again to a regional satrap dependent upon the Kennedys for whatever patronage they might wish to offer. Meanwhile JFK centered his campaign on foreign policy issues. "Who lost China?" the Republicans had charged in 1952; now it was the Democrats' turn. "Who lost Cuba?" Kennedy demanded.

"In 1960," he declared, "American frontiers are on the Rhine and the Mekong and the Tigris and the Euphrates and the Amazon. There is no place in the world that is not of concern to all of us. . . . We are responsible for the maintenance of freedom all around the world." Many liberals still viewed Kennedy with various degrees of skepticism. There were enough agnostics to warrant an unusual defense from Kennedy advocate and Harvard historian Arthur M. Schlesinger, Jr., who wrote a campaign book entitled *Kennedy or Nixon: Does It Make Any Difference?*

The principal difference, according to Schlesinger, appeared to be one of style. Nixon's rhetoric was vulgar. He paraded "emotional irrelevances" while Kennedy was "studiously unemotional."[27] Yet it was hard to call Kennedy's description of the Communist threat from Cuba unemotional. "For the first time in our history," he would repeat over and over again during the campaign, "an enemy stands at the throat of the United States."[28] As the campaign went on, Kennedy spoke of Cuba as the jewel of the Caribbean that had been stolen from its rightful place in the dark of the night while the watchman slept. He made it clear there must be no more thefts:

August 24: "Three years ago I went to Havana. I was told that the American Ambassador was the second most powerful man in Cuba. Probably he should not be, but he is not today."

September 2: "I visited Havana 3 years ago and I was informed that the American Ambassador was the second most influential man in Cuba. He is not today. . . . This is the problem that we face in 1960."

September 5: "Three years ago I went to Havana, Cuba, and I was told that the American Ambassador was the second most powerful man in Cuba. I am not saying he should have been, but he was."

September 15: "I was in Havana 3 years ago. The American Ambassador informed me on that occasion that he was the second most powerful and influential man in Cuba. Today the American Ambassador is not."

September 20: Three years ago when I was in Cuba, the American Ambassador was the second most influential man in Cuba. Today the Soviet Ambassador is."[29]

While Kennedy worried about "losing" various parts of the world, his concerns were not determined by geopolitics. Territory only symbolized momentum. "The enemy is the Communist system itself—implacable, unceasing in its drive for world domination." The United States stood precariously positioned, he believed, between greatness and decline. "I think there is a danger that history will make a judgment," he said early in the presidential campaign, "that these were the days when the tide began to run out for the United States. These were the times when the Communist tide began to pour in."[30]

Such rhetoric made many traditional Democratic liberals uneasy. They welcomed the candidate's emphasis upon ideas, but too often he sounded more like the strident John Foster Dulles than the nuanced and sophisticated standard-bearer of the past two elections, Adlai Stevenson, whose losses to Eisenhower were seen by many as ennobling defeats. Kennedy never saw defeat as ennobling. And he felt uncomfortable around ideological liberals, even those who quickly joined his cause. They did too much hand-wringing in public for his taste, and wanted too many others to share their endless soul-searching in private. Sometimes he seemed to go out of his way to dissociate himself from "liberals," as for example the haste with which he announced the day after his election that he would keep J. Edgar Hoover at the FBI and Allen Dulles at the CIA.[31]

But with the choice down to Kennedy or Vice-President Richard M. Nixon, anathema to liberals everywhere, they joined ranks with fingers crossed. What changed many minds about Kennedy, Schlesinger would write later in his memoir/history of the Kennedy administration, "was their gradual recognition of his desire to bring the world of power and the world of ideas together in alliance—or rather, as he himself saw it, to restore the collaboration between the two worlds which had marked the early republic."[32]

Kennedy achieved only the narrowest of victories in the 1960 election. He now worried, it was said, that bold initiatives could not be undertaken on slim majorities. Yet if he were to bring the world of ideas and power together once again, JFK would have to take bold initiatives. After all, he had made Republican mishandling of the Cuban revolution his rallying cry, and had described Fidel Castro as part of a worldwide plot that demanded a dramatic response.

That response, when implemented, only deepened liberal anxieties about the future and the young president they had helped to elect. But if the Bay of Pigs episode triggered a sequence of events that had its final denouement in Vietnam, there were powerful underlying factors that would ultimately determine the limitations of the Pax Americana, factors that were already evident when Kennedy took office.

On the threshold of the New Frontier, Kennedy faced two issues that posed more danger to American stability than Castro's Cuba. If he did not resolve the balance-of-payments problem, American leadership in the world economy would be undermined, and that in turn would make it far more difficult to come to terms with both economic and social problems at home, above all the collection of issues under the heading of civil rights. That these were connected no one doubted; how to deal with them was another matter.

Kennedy was impatient with the specifics of domestic issues. "Who gives a shit about the minimum wage?" he asked privately. Drop the "domestic stuff," he ordered writers working on the inaugural address. "It's too long anyway."[33] But both he and his advisers realized he had to say something about unemployment, if not in his inaugural then in his first State of the Union message. There were 5.5 million unemployed in 1961, the largest number since the Great Depression. "We take office," he said, "in the wake of seven months of recession, three and one-half years of slack, seven years of diminished economic growth, and nine years of falling farm income."[34] But there was no New Deal public works plan on the New Frontier agenda. The New Frontier remedies were Keynesian tax cuts and more exports to correct the difficulties in the balance of payments. "A lagging economy," explained Chester Bowles, Kennedy's chief foreign policy adviser in the campaign, "creates clashes between labor, management and farmers, further complicating our efforts to assure civil rights to all Americans, increases the political pressure for higher tariffs, reduces economic assistance abroad, and dangerously encourages isolationist thinking."[35]

The economic issue that bothered Kennedy most—more than his discovery of poverty in the West Virginia primary—was the international balance of payments. "Above all," Walt Rostow told an interviewer after Kennedy's death, "he felt impaled on our balance of payments deficit—next to the nuclear problem the balance of payments, I think, worried him more than anything." He had begun worrying about it in the 1950s and was determined to solve the problem by unilateral measures, especially increased exports. He also saw the balance-of-payments problem as a major hindrance in domestic policy, limiting his options for dealing with poverty.[36]

President Eisenhower had pondered the balance-of-payments issue and come up with a "solution" that had little chance of being adopted but that nicely illustrated the perceived inseparability of domestic and foreign questions in the minds of American leaders as the 1960s began. Perhaps, he suggested to the chairman of the Atomic Energy Commission, John McCone, the United States could develop an export market for uranium. If the radioactive metal became a popularly traded commodity, "we could place some of it [in] our stockpile at Fort Knox and announce that uranium, as well as gold, will be used to back up our currency."[37]

This conversation took place on the day Kennedy and Johnson were elected. Walt Rostow, who with Under Secretary of State George Ball, now headed the president-elect's task force on foreign economic policy, did not recommend selling uranium for gold, but he agreed with Eisenhower that the United States could not sustain its world position without solving the balance-of-payments problem.[38] At then current levels American exports simply could not cover the costs of U.S. forces abroad, creating a serious gold drain. Europe had recovered economically, but the need for maintaining American forces on the Continent as a psychological barrier to supposed Soviet expansionist dreams, as well as containing fears about the rise of neonationalist urges within the Western community, was an increasingly expensive aspect of the Pax Americana.

Testifying before Congress, economist Jacob Viner chided the legislators for not realizing sooner the importance of the balance-of-payments question. Americans had lived in an exclusive gold-rich utopia for about two decades, not realizing that the hoard buried at Fort Knox had sustained cold war policies. "That gold at Fort Knox was not at all idle during that period. It was working strongly for us all the time. It gave us a freedom from balance of payments restraints in our foreign and other policy. Without Fort Knox there would have been no Marshall Plan. . . . Without Fort Knox, we would not have dared to undertake our foreign military and foreign aid programs on the scale which we planned and executed them. *Those happy days are over.*"[39]

Already the restless General Charles de Gaulle, chafing under what he deemed the NATO protectorate, threatened to multiply economic difficulties by restricting American access to the French-led European Economic Community (EEC). De Gaulle's irritating behavior eventually became a major concern for Washington, as he made effective use of the Vietnam War to promote the idea in Europe that America was not to be trusted with either economic or political leadership. U.S. policymakers called it the Atlantic Community, but the general disparaged it as a new word for hegemony. Alfred Neal, chairman of the prestigious Committee for Economic Development, testified at these same congressional hearings that the gross national product of the EEC countries was growing at an annual rate of 4.5 percent "while we are having a little bit of trouble keeping up to 3 percent. Everybody knows it is easier to grow in a growing market; you get pulled along with it."[40] The key question for Neal was whether the United States would gain access to the "vast new markets" of the EEC. Kennedy tended to personalize the EEC matter as a test of strength between himself and de Gaulle, but he was certain of the stakes: "If we cannot keep up our export surplus, we shall not have the dollar exchange with which to meet our overseas military commitments. We must either do a good job of selling abroad or pull back."[41]

Kennedy gave his new secretary of defense, Robert McNamara, a major assignment to improve exports by selling American arms to both industrial and developing nations. Here was a way to build a dual constituency for funding the Pax Americana: arms manufacturers at home and their foreign customers. McNamara would even argue that American arms sales served a vital purpose in channeling the resources of the underdeveloped world into productive areas. Under his direction, a special office in the Pentagon, International Logistics Negotiations, was established, headed by Deputy Assistant Secretary Henry J. Kuss. Kuss proved a good salesman. Between 1962 and 1965 U.S. manufacturers received $9 billion in orders and commitments, offsetting almost 40 percent of the dollar costs of maintaining U.S. forces abroad during those years. The sales served American interests in developed countries, McNamara averred, by promoting the orientation of defense programs toward the United States, and they enabled the U.S. to increase its influence over the domestic policies of underdeveloped nations, thereby pointing them toward a supposedly more rational approach to economic and social questions:

> Our first objective is to use the influence that we gain through the military assistance programs and occasionally through the military export sales program to work with them to reduce the share of their resources devoted to defense and to increase the portion of their human and material capital that is allocated to economic and social programs.[42]

Kuss found it difficult to understand why certain American companies proved reluctant to go "international." Such behavior harmed American interests from every standpoint: it risked losing all the "major international relationships" built up by foreign aid; it threatened "the stability of the dollar in the world market" by neglecting the balance-of-payments problem; and it added to economic pressure in both "the international and in the domestic spheres."

> From the political point of view international trade is the "staff of life" of a peaceful world. With it comes understanding; the lack of it eliminates communications and creates misunderstanding.[43]

If increased arms sales thus appealed as a large part of the solution, not only to balance-of-payments problems but also to issues associated with what would soon be called "nation-building" abroad, they became an even larger part of the problem of future policymakers in dealing with destabilizing arms races in the third world.

At best, moreover, arms sales were only a limited and temporary remedy. The object of the 1962 Trade Expansion Act was to head off "bloc" trading systems, such as the EEC might become, and establish a negotiating framework for lowering tariffs and reducing barriers to freer trade. There would be some losses to specific American interests, but overall the administration counted on the nation's manufacturing sectors to demonstrate their superior efficiency in gaining compensating markets. One Kennedy adviser argued that the only way to overcome domestic opposition would be to sell TEA as an anti-Communist measure. George Ball felt, however, that the way to put it across was to say that "this is what we need to raise the standard of living at home."[44]

Like the arms sales program, if less contradictory, the trade bill was seen as essential to the role America had assumed in the world. Kennedy therefore decided to adopt a Churchillian stance in urging its passage:

> One answer to . . . [the economic] problem is the negative answer: raise our tariffs, restrict our capital, pull back from the world—and our adversaries would only be too glad to fill any gap that we should leave. This Administration was not elected to preside over the liquidation of American responsibility in these great years.[45]

Fear that Moscow might outbid the United States in the former colonial areas—cited here as a reason for the Trade Expansion Act—became a rationale for whatever question was before Congress and the nation. Sometimes it was a real stretch. "Who can say that people who have always been slaves to hunger will not put food before freedom?" wrote two former State Department officials, Democrat Will Clayton, a former assistant secretary of state in the Truman years, and Republican Christian Herter, who had succeeded John Foster Dulles in 1959 as Eisenhower's secretary of state. That could happen, they warned, unless America recast its trade policies to meet the totalitarian methods the Soviet bloc could mobilize to divide the industrial nations and subvert the "poorer, underdeveloped countries."[46]

The TEA would presumably counteract Soviet designs by promoting harmony between the industrial nations and former colonial areas. Otherwise, Clayton and Herter warned, general disaster loomed ahead:

> There will probably be no shooting in Khrushchev's war. The Communists have a cheaper, shrewder way. They plan to take us alive, with all our assets intact. If they can encircle us, our grandchildren will live under communism, as Khrushchev has said.[47]

The president needed new powers to adjust trade policy, Clayton and Herter argued. The European Common Market, for example, represented an entirely new challenge, while high-tariff policies against the raw materials of the underdeveloped countries forced those areas to choose between food and freedom. The crisis in the underdeveloped world was made all the worse by the population explosion that doubled growth at Malthusian rates every twenty-five years. "Overt social conflict is a commonplace affair in the Malthusian world."

Bringing Malthus into the discussion led Clayton and Herter to offer a glancing look at the changing situation in the United States:

The United States has been aware of the effects of population change right at home. The rapid migration of the rural population to the cities in the wake of an irresistible technological advance in agriculture has had grave effects on the urban areas. "Exploding cities" are a matter of concern. The situation may become much worse as the increasing younger generations disperse into the suburbs.[48]

Almost an afterthought to the discussion of the Soviet threat, this prediction was the one that "came true" before the end of the decade. Kennedy had realized the potential of civil rights concerns and protests to disrupt the New Frontier's plans, and he had pondered the seemingly intractable "pockets of poverty" like the one he had found in West Virginia. Like that of most other national leaders, however, his education in this area lagged behind his perceptions of a supposedly deteriorating world situation.

During the campaign he did speak out for "executive action" in attacking problems such as segregation in federal housing programs, which, he said, could be changed by a stroke of the pen. Indeed, the most dramatic moment of the campaign may have come when the candidate called Mrs. Martin Luther King to express his concern about her husband's imprisonment after a protest march in Georgia. Certainly black voters turned out in large numbers to support Kennedy. In office, however, President Kennedy hesitated to sign the order eliminating discrimination in federal housing, waiting for a safe moment when it would not cost him support for the trade expansion bill. He also rejected the idea of submitting a new civil rights bill as a priority item in the first list of New Frontier proposals to go to Capitol Hill.[49]

The New Frontier brought considerable optimism (if not great understanding of the depth of the problem) that poverty would yield to the forces of rational planning, and that racial bitterness and struggle would give way to moral suasion—both without undoing the work Kennedy hoped to accomplish in foreign affairs. Where Robert McNamara hoped to influence the underdeveloped countries, through arms sales, to adopt better economic and social policies, Walter Heller, chairman of the Council of Economic Advisers, proposed tax cuts and Keynesian management techniques as weapons against poverty and racial injustice. When the cost of fulfilling a people's aspirations could be met out of a growing horn of plenty, Heller wrote, "ideological roadblocks melt away, and consensus replaces conflict."

> In the battle against discrimination, prosperity adds economic rights to civil rights. Thus economic liberty can grow—indeed, is growing—simultaneously with governmental power.[50]

Heller's optimism did not take into account, however, the dramatic consequences of what Clayton and Herter had noted, albeit as an addendum of sorts to the world problem. The wave of black migration out of

America's rural South totaled nearly three million in the twenty years 1940 to 1960, producing a social and political dilemma off the scale of previous experience with racial issues. "The Negro problem," Republican strategist Kevin Phillips later observed, "having become a national rather than a local one, [thus became] . . . the principal cause of the breakup of the New Deal coalition. . . . More than any other Northeastern religious group Catholics tended to inhabit the socio-economic 'combat zone,' confronting the Democratic Party with the cruel dilemma of aborting its ideological thrust or alienating the loyalties of its largest bloc of longtime supporters."[51]

There was much indeed to concern liberals and the rest of the nation as Kennedy entered office. But Inauguration Day was not a time for pessimism. A heavy snow had fallen on Washington the night before. It was still bitter cold the next day, but bright sunshine filled the Capitol plaza— an appropriate setting for the youthful president's first speech to the nation. Outgoing President Dwight Eisenhower sat muffled and expressionless, only partly visible to the crowd behind a white scarf. Bareheaded and coatless, John Kennedy rose to take the oath of office. "Let every nation know," he said, his clipped words visible for an instant in the crystalline air, "whether it wishes us well or ill, that we shall pay any price, bear any burden, meet any hardship, support any friend, oppose any foe, in order to assure the success of liberty."

THREE

After the Bay of Pigs

SCANNING BULLETINS THAT DETAILED THE ROUT under way at the Bay of Pigs, President Kennedy paced the floor in the family quarters of the White House. Everything that could have gone wrong, had gone wrong. He knew better, he said ruefully, than to trust the "experts." "How could I have been so stupid to let them go ahead?"[1] Even before the first hundred days of the New Frontier were out, he had given his critics all they could want to ridicule his bold inaugural promises to bear any cost or fight any foe to safeguard freedom. The bungled invasion attempt against Fidel Castro was a costly mistake, and the repercussions from the Bay of Pigs would be felt around the globe to Southeast Asia. Vows taken in the aftermath of the Bay of Pigs became due bills that one day would be paid in Saigon.[2]

Kennedy felt abashed. The whole operation looked amateurish from start to finish. On Capitol Hill, administration explanations were greeted with scorn and dismissal. "Are you gentlemen telling us today," Republican Senator Homer Capehart asked of CIA and Pentagon officials in the aftermath, "that . . . our high military people who fought in World War I and World War II . . . approved this, what would appear to me to be a Boy Scout operation?"[3]

During the recent campaign Kennedy had charged that the cold war was being lost because American leadership had faltered in response to Khrushchev's successful campaign in the third world. The Bay of Pigs intensified Kennedy's concern about Soviet support for so-called wars of national liberation—worsened it actually, because it now appeared *he* was failing to meet the challenge. A confused signal had been sent to the world. Especially painful to the White House were the reactions of traditional internationalists. Where an old New Deal stalwart like Adolf Berle was embarrassed only by the botched planning, Walter Lippmann—who had been in Russia at the time—saw an ill-advised and self-defeating adventurism that hardly impressed Soviet Premier Khrushchev with the president's grasp on essentials, and undercut American prestige and influence in the third world.[4]

It did no good to say that Kennedy had inherited the Bay of Pigs plan from President Dwight Eisenhower; he had made the crucial decision to go ahead with the attempt to land a force of CIA-trained Cuban exiles. True, planning for the invasion had begun in the Eisenhower administration, overriding Havana embassy officials' warnings that Fidel had charged Cuban nationalist batteries to the full; but JFK could not shrug off responsibility for neglecting to inquire more deeply into the purpose of the invasion.[5] It was not Republican Richard Nixon, after all, but Democratic candidate Kennedy who had called for military aid to Cuban exiles during the televised presidential debates.

How much Kennedy knew about the planning has never been made entirely clear, nor, indeed, what he thought the objectives of the mission were. Did he believe that CIA Director Allen Dulles had promised an uprising that would topple Castro, or only that the invaders were to make their way into the mountains, there to provide a focal point for anti-Castro activities? When Dulles presented the newly elected president with the Bay of Pigs proposal, Kennedy seemed taken aback by the director's warnings about the consequences of not going ahead. What would he do to keep the exiles from talking about what they had been up to, the director pressed the president? We have a disposal problem, Dulles went on, making it clear it was time to put up or shut up.[6]

Whether it was his own campaign rhetoric or Dulles's pointed warning about a public uproar should it be revealed the CIA had trained Cuban exiles, Kennedy plunged ahead.[7] Only a few New Frontiersmen questioned the scheme. Most, like Kennedy, were itching to get going. "At this point," National Security Adviser McGeorge Bundy quipped to a friend before the Bay of Pigs, "we are like the Harlem Globetrotters, passing forward, behind, sidewise, and underneath. But nobody has made a basket yet."[8]

Secretary of State Dean Rusk had misgivings but did not wish to be a naysayer. His deputy, Under Secretary Chester Bowles, did voice objections—with severe consequences for his career. "If I had been President when Allen Dulles first presented the plan," Bowles later observed, "I would have told him, 'Allen, go back and take a cold shower, have a drink, and go to bed. You're crazy.' " When Bowles tried to communicate his misgivings through a memo, Rusk hesitated to deliver it to the president. Kennedy had assured him the plan had been scaled down, the secretary reported to Bowles.[9]

That certainly did not appear to be the case in the event. "Fifteen hundred Cubans waded ashore on the morning of April 17," relates historian Walter LaFeber, "only to find that one key air strike had been canceled because of clouds, that other naval and air supporting units had been immobilized by Castro's small air force, that the beachhead was indefensible, and that they had no hope of reaching the mountains."[10] As the invasion disintegrated into a roundup of disorganized rebel forces, there were pleas that Kennedy intervene with air strikes. He refused. He would not turn a mistake into a far more grievous error. "All my life I've known better than to depend on the experts," Kennedy chastised himself.[11]

Worst of all, Castro trapped nearly the entire rebel force and was soon demanding ransom from the United States in tractors and medical supplies. If the president's aides resented Fidel's cigar-smoking defiance, they had little charity for those who had voiced objections to the operation. Newspaper reports of Chester Bowles's skepticism were especially irksome. Bowles was "yellow-bellied," growled press secretary Pierre Salinger, and "we're going to get him." Despite his service to Kennedy as foreign policy idea man during the presidential campaign, he was soon moved out, to be succeeded by George Ball.[12]

Himself a secret dissenter, Ball worried that the fiasco had taught the wrong lessons—"loyalty" was the highest value while skepticism brought banishment. Ball also worried about New Frontier fascination with "that intriguing new invention of the professors, 'nation-building.' "[13] Immediately after the debacle, Kennedy told Walt Rostow:

> The British could have a nervous breakdown in the wake of Suez, the French over Algeria. They each represent six to seven percent of the free world's power—and we could cover for them. But we can't afford a nervous breakdown. We're forty percent, and there's no one to cover for us. We'd better get on with the job.14

It would not be easy. "Gentlemen," the president told a group of policy advisers in September 1961, "if we can get through the first year of the administration without losing the Dominican Republic or the Congo to the Iron Curtain Countries, I shall consider it a good year in the foreign field."[15] Out of the Bay of Pigs debacle emerged more powerfully than ever before in the cold war a "crisis management" mentality that was perhaps the most fateful "lesson" of all. General William Westmoreland, who would command a force of half a million in Vietnam, had strong views about crisis management and the war he had to fight. "Many of the errors" in Vietnam, he wrote, "could be traced to strong control of the conduct of the war from Washington, a policy born jointly of the failure of the Bay of Pigs invasion of Cuba in 1961, which demonstrated the perils of decentralization, and of the successful outcome of the Cuban missile crisis in 1962, which seemed to indicate that command from the White House was the only way to handle crises and war in the nuclear age." The Kennedy team, which Lyndon

Johnson then inherited, had deceived itself at the outset into believing that "crisis management" techniques won wars.[16]

WESTMORELAND'S REFLECTIONS on how the crisis management worldview played itself out during the Vietnam years have considerable merit as a military critique, but the full implications of the analysis go well beyond the question of White House insistence on having the command post in the basement situation room. Crisis management, as a political strategy, presupposes the validity of the agent theory of revolution, i.e., that revolutions are manipulated from a central source. Twenty years later it underlay Ronald Reagan's vision of the "evil empire," whose poisonous tentacles stretched out to the far corners of the earth. The Soviet Union's attitudes toward the United States during the cold war were scarcely benevolent, its aspirations global, its techniques as manipulative as situations permitted; but crisis management assumptions predisposed policymakers to deny historical legitimacy to any actors on the world stage except in roles written for them in Moscow or Washington.

Crisis management notions also predisposed policymakers to fixate on the lack of national discipline at home. Kennedy had brooded about democracy's weaknesses in the face of totalitarian regimes since before World War II. His senior thesis at Harvard, published in 1940 as *Why England Slept*, argued that British appeasement in the 1930s was a symptom of national disunity. Disunity appeared to be endemic in a democracy, Kennedy had mused, where class and personal interests took priority over national concerns. Thus democracy and capitalism would always stand at a disadvantage in the struggle with totalitarianism. To win that struggle required a supreme effort, perhaps even the temporary renunciation of democratic privileges. It meant, indeed, a "voluntary totalitarianism" to match the discipline of an enemy whose essential strength was a national purpose that would not permit "group interests to interfere with its fulfillment."[17]

Not surprisingly, such themes dominated Kennedy's postmortem speech to the American Society of Newspaper Editors on April 20, 1961, three days after the Cuban invasion collapsed. The president accepted responsibility for allowing the ill-fated venture to go forward, but he expressed remorse only because it had failed. And he called upon his audience to witness that foreign criticism of the Bay of Pigs on moral grounds had its origins in Communist capitals. Protesters in foreign cities, Kennedy asserted, had been instructed—presumably from Moscow—to stage "riots" against American policy. But their behavior would not deter those who recalled the "long roll call of refugees" from communism:

We dare not fail to see the insidious nature of this new and deeper struggle. We dare not fail to grasp the new concepts, the new tools, the new sense of urgency we will need to combat it—whether in Cuba or South Viet-Nam. And we dare not fail to realize that this struggle is taking place every day, without fanfare, in thousands of villages and markets—day and night—and in classrooms all over the globe.

The message of Cuba, of Laos, of the rising din of Communist voices in Asia and Latin America—these messages are all the same. The complacent, the self-indulgent, the soft societies are about to be swept away with the debris of history. Only the strong, only the industrious, only the determined, only the courageous, only the visionary who determine the real nature of our struggle can possibly survive.[18]

"Let me then make clear as the President of the United States," he ended, "that I am determined upon our system's survival and success, regardless of the cost and regardless of the peril."[19] One Kennedy aide suggested the speech had gone a little too far, stirred emotions a little too deeply. "We should scare people a little," the president replied. "I did it to make us appear tough and powerful." Then he shrugged. "Anyway, it's done. You may be right, but it's done."[20]

Mac Bundy's principal lieutenant in the National Security Council, Walt Rostow, on the other hand, feared not that Kennedy had gone too far but that he might not go far enough, soon enough, to dispel any "perception that we are up against a game we can't handle." As he saw it, the problem was to pick the best place to start afresh. Current arguments suggested Laos might be it. Rostow hoped not. Simple anger could "lead us to do unwise things or exert scarce national effort and resources in directions which would yield no significant results." There was one area, on the other hand, where success against Communist techniques was not only conceivable but "desperately required." "That area is Viet-Nam. A maximum effort—military, economic, political and diplomatic—is required there; and it is required urgently."[21]

> It is not simple or automatic that we can divert anxieties, frustrations, and anger focused on a place 90 miles off our shores to a place 7,000 miles away. On the other hand, I believe that the acute domestic tension over Cuba can be eased in the short run if we can get the OAS [Organization of American States] to move with us . . . ; and a clean-cut success in Viet-Nam would do much to hold the line in Asia while permitting us—and the world—to learn how to deal with indirect aggression[22]

The only real peril in going to Vietnam's rescue, Rostow concluded, was delay. Should Communist China come to believe we were not going to act, things could deteriorate to a point "where nothing short of a substantial war with Communist China would redress the balance."[23] A similar plea on

Vietnam's behalf came from the Senate's scholarly Far Eastern ex
Montana's Mike Mansfield, who joined Rostow in cautioning agains
involvement in a dubious battle to sustain a right-wing regime in neighboring Laos.

Like the Cuban freedom fighters of Brigade 2506, Laos was another
Eisenhower legacy. In a moment of ill-advised enthusiasm, cloak-and-
dagger agents in Laos had encouraged a rightist coup against a "neutralist"
government. But that regime was now in deep trouble. Aligned against it
were not only the neutralists but the Communist Pathet Lao force as well.

Of the three new states that had once made up French Indochina—
Laos, Cambodia, and Vietnam—Laos easily took first place among lost
causes, or, better put, insufficient causes. Kennedy was not anxious to stake
much on Laos. A few weeks after the 1960 election he had confided his
doubts to Theodore Sorensen. "Whatever's going to happen in Laos, an
American invasion, a Communist victory or whatever, I wish it would happen before we take over and get blamed for it." But when the president-
elect came to the White House for a meeting with Eisenhower the day
before the inaugural, Kennedy pressed Ike to tell him what to do. It may
have been an effort to get the general to concede that nothing could be
done. According to Sorensen, more time was spent on Laos than any other
subject. "You might have to go in there and fight it out," were Eisenhower's
last words.[24]

Whether the outgoing president was trying to force Kennedy's hand,
or vice versa, the situation was fast spinning out of control. One thing the
Bay of Pigs did was to slow the momentum. "Thank God the Bay of Pigs
happened when it did," Kennedy quipped. "Otherwise we'd be in Laos by
now—and that would be a hundred times worse."[25] Kennedy feared public
reaction, nevertheless, about the "loss" of another country to communism,
even a place so remote as Laos. Crisis mentality thinking was contagious. At
the time of Kennedy's inaugural only a very few Americans could have
found Laos on a map of Southeast Asia, fewer still could have named the
rival factions struggling to control the former French colony. Policymakers
who were in the know had little to cheer about. The American-backed
Royal Laotian Army was particularly inept against the Communist Pathet
Lao Army, supported by the North Vietnamese. A State Department briefing for new Kennedy officials ended with the wry observation that there
had been real improvement recently: "Only a few months ago, the Laotians
used to retreat without their weapons; now they take their weapons with
them when they run away."[26]

Kennedy moved American seaborne forces into the area while publicly
declaring his desire to see a "neutral and independent Laos."[27] In one way
he was not bluffing: he ordered American military advisers in Laos to put
on their uniforms to show U.S. resolve in the aftermath of the defeat at the

Bay of Pigs. "A new urgency" was injected into "Kennedy's concern for counterinsurgency . . . ," recalled General Maxwell Taylor, who would become the president's closest military adviser on guerrilla warfare.[28]

Mansfield's warning against going into Laos was a timely intervention in a situation drifting toward a dangerous rapids. By cutting losses in Laos, argued the senator, greater funds could be diverted to South Vietnam, where they would be needed to meet the anticipated increase in sabotage and terror. "It will take great astuteness to make this adjustment and we ought to assign to Viet Nam an exceptional diplomatic mission and an aid team in a dedicated effort to foster rapid economic development of the country and the improvement of its political institutions. *Viet Nam, in my opinion, has the greatest potential in leadership, human capacities and resources for a stable freedom in the region.*"[29]

To Kennedy's relief, it turned out the Russians had no appetite for confrontation in Laos either. He and Khrushchev both seemed happy to dump Laos on the Laotians. Agreement on troop withdrawals and a genuinely neutral Laos proved to be the one issue that Kennedy and the Soviet leader could agree on at the Vienna summit in early June 1961. Kennedy was careful during these discussions to distinguish between Laos and Vietnam. Laos, he said, was "relatively unimportant from the strategic standpoint." American policy, he then admitted, had not always been wise. But in Vietnam there were some seven thousand to fifteen thousand guerrillas fighting against the Saigon government. "We do not believe that they reflect the will of the people. . . . The U.S.S.R. may believe so. The problem is to avoid getting involved in direct contact as we support the respective groups."[30]

After a good deal of bluster, Khrushchev accepted Kennedy's suggestions that they work out a solution for Laos. He did not take up Kennedy's suggestions about Vietnam, however, warning instead that the United States had allowed itself to be deceived by its great wealth and power. It could neither delay the quest for national liberation nor prevent the Soviet Union from extending aid to peoples struggling for independence. "The U.S. has no right to distribute indulgences," he said, "and to interfere in the various areas of the world."[31]

As things turned out, the 1962 Geneva conference on Laos that codified the solemn agreement to support a neutral government only reduced the danger of a direct Russian-American confrontation, allowing the two nations plausible deniability while a low-level civil war raged on. The result of all this LeCarré-style "Looking Glass War" worked to Washington's disadvantage, for while the Laotian rightists ended up controlling the capital, Vientiane, a key area of Laos remained open to North Vietnam to aid the National Liberation Front in the south.[32]

Soviet Premier Khrushchev had wanted the Vienna summit to concentrate on the German question. When no progress was made on discussing a peace treaty to "normalize" the Berlin situation, Khrushchev threatened to sign such a treaty with East Germany. In the American view, this endangered the Western position in Berlin and, by extension, the rights of peoples everywhere to whom the United States had given a commitment. The Berlin crisis that began that summer thus overshadowed events in all other parts of the world. It did not ease until the Soviets built the infamous Berlin Wall and accepted the onus for inflicting further pain on the divided country.

Events in Vietnam, nevertheless, would not await the outcome of the Kennedy-Khrushchev test of wills over Berlin. It was all tied together, said Kennedy. "So I've got a terrible problem," he told reporter James Reston. If Khrushchev imagined the Bay of Pigs revealed that he had "no guts . . . we won't get anywhere with him. So we have to act." To disabuse the Russians, he would increase the military budget and send reinforcements to Germany. But that was not enough. The only place in the world where there was a real challenge at the moment was Vietnam. ". . . We have a problem in trying to make our power credible, and Vietnam looks like the place."[33]

Thus did a desire to redeem the Bay of Pigs, to stay clear of Laotian entanglements, and to stand fast in Berlin, all drive the New Frontier in the direction of Vietnam. How to save Vietnam had engaged policymakers in a series of debates since World War II. Roosevelt had vowed to kick the French out and place the area under an international trusteeship. FDR eventually gave up on the idea, and Truman had no inclination to revive it. Eisenhower and Dulles fretted and fumed about French mishandling of the war against the "Commies" but finally turned down suggestions that the United States intervene to save Free World interests at the 1954 battle of Dien Bien Phu. Paris had invoked American aid to save that outpost, but when it was over and the struggle shifted to the conference table, the French bitterly resented American "interference" in their attempts to settle affairs and maintain French influence in whatever political regime succeeded the truce period.

Cochaired by Russia and Great Britain, the 1954 Geneva Conference brought the first Indochina war to an end by establishing a temporary truce line at the 17th parallel. The key provision in the final declaration provided for all-Vietnamese elections within two years. No one came away from Geneva feeling very sanguine about the ultimate commitment of the two sides to settle their differences at the ballot box. But one outstanding fact had been made clear: the United States had replaced France as the obstacle to Ho Chi Minh's quest to create a unified Vietnam.

A longtime Communist and nationalist, Ho had proclaimed Vietnamese independence at the end of World War II. There ensued an eight-year war that had just ended with a temporary partition of Vietnam, and two putative national capitals, Hanoi and Saigon. Against Ho's nationalist appeal, the United States had supported a returned exile Ngo Dinh Diem, whose anti-French credentials had given reason to hope he might be the answer. Acclaimed in the United States as the George Washington of his country, Diem had used the premiership to maneuver the French puppet Emperor Bao Dai out of power; he then held elections to solidify his hold on South Vietnam as its first "president." But could he prove himself enough of a vote-getter to thwart a Communist triumph in the scheduled all-Vietnamese elections?

Diem's supporters in Washington had encouraged him in his resistance to that provision in the Geneva settlement. His government had not signed the final declaration of the Geneva Conference, said Diem, and hence the coerced promise of the Bao Dai regime could not be binding upon his government. This was particularly so, he argued, because there was no chance that the government in Hanoi, the Democratic Republic of Vietnam, would agree to genuinely free elections.

Washington applauded Diem's forthrightness. No Old World trickery or appeasement there, only plainspoken words of the sort Andrew Jackson or Teddy Roosevelt might have used to defy the polite norms that Europeans used to cover their chicanery.

With large infusions of U.S. economic aid, Diem had established an "independent" Republic of Vietnam. His regime had pretensions of democratic legitimacy but was narrowly based on a Catholic minority in a largely Buddhist population. Diem and his brother, Ngo Dinh Nhu, tightened their grip on power by rewarding the landlord class, a policy made possible through American largesse. Rather quickly, moreover, it became apparent that President Diem did not take much notice of what Washington thought about how he spent such funds, nor did he intend to take instruction from his new benefactors in how to run a government. During one visit to Washington, Diem talked on and on at his meeting with Secretary of State Dulles—then abruptly left before anyone could comment. "Wouldn't you think that here in Washington," Dulles mused to an aide, "he might be interested in what our Secretary of State had to say?"[34]

Diem's aloofness left Americans in a quandary. Still, by the end of the Eisenhower years the United States had provided South Vietnam with nearly $2 billion to help keep this new Republic of South Vietnam healthy. Despite this subsidy, there were nagging questions about how well Diem was managing things. In 1958, to take but one index, South Vietnam imported $232 million in American, French, and Japanese goods, but sold only $57 million abroad. The ruddy complexion that the South Vietnamese economy displayed to casual observers was in fact the flushed appearance of a failing tuberculosis patient.[35]

Outside the cities, Diem's ordinations were carried out by security forces and roving military tribunals. Anyone charged with acts against the state could be tried and executed within three days. As in the days of French colonial rule, heavy taxes bent the peasant population down to the lowly status of "natives." In response the peasants joined with rebel forces, the Communist-led National Liberation Front, to fight for national unification or simply to resist Diem's oppressions. Saigon labeled the NLF with the derisive name Viet Cong, or Vietnamese Communists, and claimed that the uprisings were all directed from Hanoi.[36]

In the northern capital, meanwhile, the Democratic Republic of Vietnam, led by Ho Chi Minh, had its own troubles trying to overcome early post-Geneva "mistakes" in implementing land reforms. It was not easy: somewhere between five thousand and fifteen thousand landowners were sentenced to death by local courts, and nearly twenty thousand imprisoned.[37] Hanoi was still recovering from these mistakes late in the 1950s. So Ho Chi Minh was not spoiling for a war with the United States, even to reunify Vietnam under his leadership. Nor could he know how much aid he could expect from Moscow or Beijing.

But Ho's decision to open a guerrilla war against Saigon showed that he was not reluctant to fight, nor had he merely responded to desperate NLF appeals. In the best scenario, from Hanoi's point of view, a combination of political organization and terrorist activity against unpopular Diemist local officials would alter the balance of forces, leading to a general uprising in South Vietnam. Faced with an obviously popular revolt, the scenario continued, Washington would wash its hands of the whole affair, perhaps even act as Saigon's "executioner" in the final denouement of Vietnam's long struggle for independence. The worst scenario, on the other hand, saw Hanoi being forced to rescue the NLF from Saigon's campaign to eradicate the core of the resistance, and finding itself also confronted by American arms, a situation that would indefinitely postpone the day of independence.

Saigon's perception of the two scenarios was essentially the same, and this partly explained why Diem and his successors never trusted Washington. Of course, Diem's unwillingness to take advice had other sources, such as his belief that Vietnamese should decide Vietnamese affairs, and his arrogance that his way was the only way.

Between 1959 and 1961 the number of assassinated South Vietnamese officials soared from twelve hundred to four thousand a year, evoking a repressive reaction from Saigon. Communist tactics also produced an American commitment to bolster military aid to Diem beyond the limits imposed by the 1954 Geneva Agreement. The situation was fast deteriorating. Americans on the scene in Vietnam during the first year of the New Frontier reported that more than half the country was now controlled by the National Liberation Front. In a remarkably revealing paragraph on

Saigon's difficulty in meeting the challenge of the Viet Cong, the head of the United States Information Service in South Vietnam, John Mecklin, wrote:

> The problem that confronted the government forces in areas penetrated by the V.C. might be compared with the police problem in the slum district of a large American city, say, some parts of Harlem. Like the police in Harlem the government forces could go freely wherever they wanted throughout the countryside, as long as they moved in sufficient force. But a single Vietnamese Army vehicle, or a small patrol, invited sudden ambush, just as a single patrolman in Harlem risks being attacked in a dark alley. Also as in Harlem, reinforcements would arrive to find a neighborhood of blank faces. Nobody saw it happen. Nobody heard any shooting. Nobody ever, ever knew anybody who conceivably might be a Viet Cong.[39]

One of Mecklin's principal assignments—indeed what became almost his only assignment—was to convince an increasingly skeptical American press corps in Saigon that the Diem regime had the capability and the will to enlist the support of the peasants in the countryside. What could Diem do about the Viet Cong, American officials were asked, when he could not control the excesses of his brother, Ngo Dinh Nhu, and his sister-in-law, Madame Nhu?

Diem suspected that at least some Americans were already scheming to oust him. He was particularly incensed at Ambassador Elbridge Durbrow for suggesting that brother Nhu and his wife could best serve their country in a high-ranking mission abroad. In September 1960 Durbrow had in fact raised the question of Diem's removal with his Washington superiors. Exasperated by Diem's refusal to consider American advice, the ambassador cabled: "If Diem's position in country continues [to] deteriorate . . . it may become necessary for US government to begin consideration [of] alternative courses of action and leaders in order [to] achieve our objective."[40]

While rumors about American plotting began to circulate in Saigon, a coup attempt by South Vietnamese air force officers nearly succeeded. Durbrow had not been part of the conspiracy, but his general views were well known to President Diem. At a critical moment during the affair, the ambassador had urged negotiations with the rebels, presumably looking toward fundamental changes in the government. The coup attempt proved to be a watershed in Diem's relations with Washington. Henceforth he imagined himself to be expendable to the Americans, just as a difficult ally in Korea, Syngman Rhee, had been "disposed of" to make room for someone more amenable to Washington's wishes. Diem became even more stubborn in resisting advice about reform. Madame Nhu, an elected delegate to the Republic of Vietnam's legislature, soon began making speeches blaming everything wrong with her country on the Americans.

As if this were not enough, when Kennedy came into office an incipient struggle over Vietnam policy had divided the State Department and the Pentagon. The Joint Chiefs wanted to end all discussion about distancing the United States from Diem by putting combat troops into South Vietnam. When State produced its draft policy paper arguing the need for "solid and widespread support" among key political groups in Vietnam— code words for dumping Diem—General Edward Lansdale, a long-time Diem supporter and self-imagined mentor, commented sourly, "The elected President of Vietnam is ignored in this statement as the base to build upon in countering the communists. This will have the U.S. pitted against Diem as first priority, the communists as second."[41]

Lansdale's protest highlighted Washington's counterscenarios for the war and the central dilemma that attached to them. In the best scenario, Saigon undertook a series of reforms that, with American military and economic aid, enabled the regime to win the hearts and minds of its people, then unite for victory over the Viet Cong and its allies. In the worst, America had to send troops to fight for Vietnam, delaying the process of nation-building until military security was sufficient. In either case it was essential not to give Saigon a veto over U.S. policy. Therein lay the dilemma.

Kennedy tried hard to dispel Diem's fears and heal the rift in his administration by replacing Durbrow with Frederick Nolting, who quickly let it be known that he wished to hear or speak no evil of Diem. Removing Durbrow, it was hoped, would make Diem more amenable to American suggestions, specifically a comprehensive counterinsurgency plan designed to woo the peasants away from what Secretary of State Dean Rusk called the Communist "promise."[42] The hope went unrealized. "How do we get Diem's indispensable cooperation," queried a sarcastic NSC staffer, "or to put it another way, how do we properly motivate Diem? We have not done too well on selling him those aspects of the CIP [Commodity Import Program] which call on him to do something instead of us to spend money."[43]

What the Pentagon and the State Department could agree on was that the struggle in Vietnam was too important to leave to the Vietnamese. State wanted to make sure that Diem carried out social and economic reforms to win back the countryside; Defense wanted no less than to prove it could win this new kind of war. But Diem had to be motivated to accept American guidance. Kennedy gave the assignment to Lyndon Johnson.

When he first asked the vice-president to go to Southeast Asia, Johnson balked. "Don't worry," Kennedy gibed. "If anything happens to you, Lyndon, we'll give you the biggest funeral they've ever seen in Austin, Texas."[44] What worried Johnson was not mortal peril but his political future. Eisenhower had used Nixon as a roving ambassador, Johnson reminded the president, "with sometimes disastrous results." He stalked out of the Oval Office mad as a hornet. Kennedy wondered why, but the vice-president's reaction suggested that Johnson feared Vietnam was a losing bet—particularly after the decision to "compromise" in Laos.[45]

Johnson's mission turned out to be something of a conversion experience. While he continued to have certain doubts about President Diem, it was during this trip that LBJ found the rationale for America's new manifest destiny in Asia—a discovery that shaped his thinking ever afterward. It turned out to be the old New Deal faith in the power of government to create economic opportunity.

The discovery process actually began before LBJ's plane took off from Washington. Hearing about Johnson's trip, an old friend from those New Deal days, Arthur Goldschmidt, now an economic specialist at the United Nations, asked for an appointment to show him plans for a project to finance a series of dams on the Mekong River. When they met, the economist went over the history of the Mekong project, explaining how it fit into still larger plans for the long-range economic development of the region, and its equally important potential as an example of how four countries, with differing political views, could work together effectively "even in a period otherwise characterized by a lot of fussing."[46]

Johnson was intrigued. "It's a great thing," he told Goldschmidt, "when people of such different cultures can get together on power."[47] Johnson was still learning about the Mekong proposals when he met in Saigon with President Diem in mid-May 1961. He was the highest-ranking American official to visit South Vietnam since Diem had come to power. Working the crowds, shaking hands, Johnson treated the mission as he might a local campaign in Texas, continually praising Diem as the "Winston Churchill of Southeast Asia." As if trying to top himself with such iconography, at one point he declared, "Your people, Mr. President, returned you to office for a second term with 91 percent of the votes. You are not only the George Washington, the Father of your country, but the Franklin Roosevelt as well."[48]

Johnson carried with him a long letter from Kennedy, offering, in effect, a partnership. "If you concur," read the paragraph on economic assistance, "I will send to Viet-Nam a group of highly qualified economic and fiscal experts who would meet with your experts and work out a financial plan on which our joint efforts can be based."[49] What Diem wanted to hear, however, was what kind of military commitment the United States was prepared to make. The Laotians, Diem charged, felt they had been left in the lurch. Would the vice-president's government agree to provide funds to increase his army to 270,000 men—nearly double its present size? Johnson countered by asking why it was not possible to deal with a Viet Cong force of not more than ten thousand with an army already ten times larger than the enemy? Did South Vietnam want American combat troops to come in to do the job? No, said Diem immediately, he did not want American troops unless North Vietnam actually attacked in force. But he did want an increase in training personnel.[50]

With some effort, Johnson managed to keep Diem's attention focused on the issues raised in Kennedy's letter. He suggested that the Vietnamese leader combine his requests for an increase in support for an additional 100,000 men with a positive response to American proposals on economic and social aid.[51] Such a letter was sure to be favorably received in Washington, Johnson assured Diem, and he, personally, could be counted on to be a strong supporter back in Washington. But even Ambassador Nolting had to admit that despite Johnson's "stress" on economic and social measures, Diem had sidestepped the key issues. In negotiating the joint communiqué, the ambassador reported to Washington, the Vietnamese leader had succeeded in "watering down language which called for more rapid social, political, and economic-liberalization measures." Diem would remain insistent, Nolting concluded, upon governing in his own manner despite what foreign critics might say about his methods.[52]

"I don't know about this fellow, Diem," a less than fully satisfied Johnson confided to an aide after these "negotiations." "He was tickled as hell when I promised him forty million dollars and talked about military aid, but he turned deaf and dumb every time I talked about him speeding up and beefing up some health and welfare projects. I spent two hours and forty-five minutes with him; tried to get knee-to-knee and belly-to-belly so he wouldn't misunderstand me, but I don't know if I got to him."[53]

He left Vietnam feeling unsure whether he had got across to Diem Kennedy's concern about the need for serious economic and administrative reforms, a feeling that continued to trouble him even as he moved to deepen the American commitment.[54] In Bangkok a day or so after leaving Saigon, Johnson followed up Goldschmidt's suggestion that he seek out U Nyun, executive secretary of the UN Economic Commission for Asia and the Far East, to talk about the Mekong. The conversation went very well as Nyun declared that the project envisioned not only dams and conservation plans but highway construction "to span the Asian continent from Saigon to Singapore to Istanbul and Ankara," linking "old caravan routes and existing roads to provide an international highway that eventually will connect Asia and Europe." At this point the vice-president interrupted U Nyun, "rose from his chair, put his hands into his pockets, jingled some silver coins, and then said: 'You know, Mr. Executive Secretary, I am a river man. All my life I have been interested in rivers and their development.' "[55]

On the flight leaving Vietnam, reporter Stanley Karnow had asked Johnson if he really meant it when he compared Diem to Churchill. "Shit," he drawled, "Diem's the only boy we got out there."[56] Such comparisons, it thus appeared, aside from their immediate service in supposedly elevating Diem's stature with his own people, were an exercise in self-affirmation. Diem was neither Winston Churchill nor Franklin Roosevelt, and Lyndon Johnson never believed he was; but, for the present at least, he had to be endowed with the qualities of both—or what prospects were there for saving Vietnam?

Johnson's formal report on his mission bristled with cold war images— lines drawn, battles joined—fully reflective of the temper of the times. "The basic decision in Southeast Asia is here," it read. "We must decide whether to help these countries to the best of our ability or throw in the towel in the area and pull back our defenses to San Francisco and [a] 'Fortress America' concept." About Diem personally, however, the report strained to set aside doubts. He was, it explained, a "complex figure beset by many problems." A man of many admirable qualities, he was remote from the people and surrounded by persons less admirable and capable. In any case, there was no other alternative. "We must decide whether to support Diem—or let Vietnam fall."[57]

If there was no alternative to Diem, Johnson's private comments on the situation in Vietnam revealed little confidence that either the military or the political side of the war could be won without close American supervision. If the present trend in Vietnam continued, he wrote in a memorandum that accompanied the formal report, there was a real danger that the government would become a "glittering façade." "It will come to rest in the end, not on its people, but on a modern military establishment and an oriental bureaucracy both maintained for the indefinite future primarily by the United States Treasury. The power which is inherent in the ordinary Vietnamese people will be left to others to organize." The ordinary people of Vietnam, starved for a leadership with understanding and warmth, would respond with great enthusiasm. "But it cannot be evoked by men in white linen suits whose contact with the ordinary people is largely through the rolled-up windows of a Mercedes-Benz."[58]

The administration should think in terms of a three-year aid program, military and economic, but the Vietnamese would have to commit themselves beforehand to specific "techniques" for improving the livelihood of their people. It should be made clear, in private, furthermore, that barring a massive invasion from without, the United States had no intention of using combat forces—or even naval or air support, which would be the first step in that direction. Then came this tragically prophetic warning:

> If the Vietnamese government backed by a three-year liberal aid program cannot do this job, then we had better remember the experience of the French who wound up with several hundred thousand men in Vietnam and were still unable to do it. And all this without engaging a single

Chinese or Russian. Before we take any such plunge we had better be sure we are prepared to become bogged down chasing irregulars and guerrillas over the rice fields and jungles of Southeast Asia while our principal enemies China and the Soviet Union stand outside the fray and husband their strength.[59]

Johnson's first major speech after returning from Asia was at Howard University, where he addressed the graduating class at that predominantly black institution. He had just completed a "long and grueling journey," he said, "over a vast area of the world where the future of civilization hangs in the balance." After declaring that the United States could not be blind to the strivings of the "teeming masses for human rights and personal dignity," lest America "be swept aside by this great human revolution instead of helping to create a world of liberty under law," Johnson turned to the situation at home. The United States had committed itself to helping nations and peoples less fortunate than Americans, just as it had committed itself to "vast social programs" for those Americans who had been thrust into economic backwaters, and to equality before the law for all its citizens.

Then, in an indirect reference to the civil rights struggles and the "Freedom Riders," the vice-president began drawing a parallel between the conflicts in Vietnam and the United States. There was no constitutional right to mob rule and mob violence, he said. "We have orderly processes of law which determine just what our constitutional rights are." All in the audience would know injustice and unfairness in their lifetimes, not only because they were black but because that was the human condition. Being black college graduates meant, nevertheless, that they had a special responsibility. "What really counts is whether we live in a system that seeks to perpetuate injustice and unfairness or a system which seeks to eliminate these evil sores from the body politic. The world today is a vast battleground between two systems of thought and two philosophies of society.... Throughout history mankind has been confronted with a choice. Either the groups who live in misery and degradation pull down their fellow men to their level; or the more fortunate nations extend the helping hand of friendly cooperation that raises the standards of those in a lowly status.... And you and your fellow graduates of every university in the land can help to prevent what would be the tragedy of the 20th century if Communism were to overwhelm the world."[60]

The speech was remarkable for several reasons. It stressed what would later be called the "other war"—for economic development in Vietnam—as the ultimate answer to the Communist challenge. The object in Vietnam was to sustain the anti-Communist philosophy of society because, Johnson implied, the outcome there would have an impact on what kind of society

America would ultimately become. Concern about Communist influence in the civil rights movement, and later in the antiwar movement, given the assumptions of Johnson's Howard University speech, was a logical conclusion. "The world today is a vast battleground between two systems of thought and two philosophies of society," Johnson had said. In Vietnam the battleground required new techniques of counterinsurgency; in the United States, new legislative initiatives. Failure in Vietnam, moreover, would encourage the enemies of democratic process at home.

Finally, one comes away from the Howard University speech convinced that the vice-president was not trying to rally support for the Vietnam War by emphasizing such connections. As the war expanded at the expense of the Great Society programs later in the decade, similar sentiments would be expressed, and then a case could be made that the purpose was to rally liberals for an unpopular war. But it would be a mistake to read those arguments back into the earlier period. What Johnson was reaching for was, in some sense, a field theory of politics, a way of enabling him to make sense of all his experiences from the beginning of the New Deal. Only in that way could he integrate Vietnam into his understanding of the world.

Even as Johnson spoke, there were warning signals in the 1961 "Freedom Rides" to secure civil rights in the Deep South. As Kennedy prepared to meet Nikita Khrushchev in Vienna early in June, the president was preoccupied with reestablishing American "credibility" in the wake of the Bay of Pigs. So were many of the reporters covering the Freedom Rides. "Reverend Abernathy," a reporter yelled through a car window in Montgomery, Alabama, "President Kennedy is about to meet with Premier Khrushchev. Aren't you afraid of embarrassing him with these demonstrations?" Abernathy replied in his slow vein, "Man, we've been embarrassed all our lives." [61]

As the Freedom Rides demonstrated, forces were already at work fully as powerful as those that separated former colonies from the industrialized nations, rending the fabric of national unity. The moment of truth, as seen by historian Taylor Branch, came in the summer of 1963, with the March on Washington led by Reverend Martin Luther King, Jr. King and Kennedy met briefly in a tense atmosphere, with the president expressing his concern that charges of Communist influence in King's inner circle would weaken the administration's ability to conduct national and international affairs. "If they shoot *you* down, they'll shoot *us* down, too," he said. "So we're asking you to be careful." [62]

King's responses did not fully relieve the president's concerns about the future direction of the civil rights movement. But both men understood that the heart of the matter was white America's ability to sustain and absorb black demands for true equality. After King delivered his "I Have a

Dream" speech at the Washington Monument, the two men left the capital, each in pursuit of a vision. Taylor Branch's description of the impending clash of assumptions well captures the situation:

> In those few days, a president of Irish descent went abroad to Germany while a preacher of African descent went inland to Detroit, both to stir the divided core of American identity. The proconsul defended the empire of freedom while the prophet proclaimed its soul. They inspired millions of the same people while acknowledging no fundamental differences in public. Together, they traced a sharp line of history. Where their interpretations of freedom overlapped, they inspired the clear hope of the decade. Where incompatible, they produced a conflict as gaping as the Vietnam War.63

In 1963, still less in 1961, did these forebodings of future tragedy in Vietnam or in the cities at home shake confidence in policymakers' assumptions. Writing to a private citizen about his Asian trip, Johnson scoffed at the idea that he had been "taken in" by President Diem. Time would tell if the South Vietnamese leader intended to live up to his agreement to institute far-reaching steps to improve economic conditions. "Certainly, I don't think that Vietnam need be—or should be—abandoned to the Communists."64

In mid-October Kennedy sent General Maxwell Taylor and Walt Rostow to Vietnam to evaluate "what could be accomplished by the introduction of SEATO or United States forces. . . ." He wanted them to investigate the situation because the Joint Chiefs had recommended sending forty thousand troops to Vietnam, a "suggestion" he did not favor—at least "at this time." "It was a hell of a note," the president told *New York Times* columnist Arthur Krock, "to try to handle the Berlin situation with the Communists encouraging foreign aggressors all over the place." He was concerned about sending troops onto the Asian mainland, and especially skeptical about the falling-domino theory for Southeast Asia. He doubted the theory had much point any more, because, he told Krock, "the Chinese Communists are bound to get nuclear weapons in time, and from that moment on they will dominate South East Asia." Taylor and Rostow found Diem to be as cagey about American combat troops as when Johnson had tried to pin him down. Without a commitment in the form of a bilateral treaty, Diem insisted, American troops might be withdrawn if the situation deteriorated, and Vietnam "abandoned." What he meant, of course, was that *he* might be abandoned, even if the troops were not withdrawn.65

The Taylor/Rostow report nevertheless recommended the introduction of eight thousand American men into Vietnam under the guise of humanitarian flood relief. Taylor did not deny that the eight thousand might not be enough to halt the NLF from expanding their control over the countryside, but he denied that the course he advocated could lead to a major war. North Vietnam was "extremely vulnerable to conventional bombing," he asserted, a weakness that could be exploited when push came to shove to persuade Hanoi to "lay off" South Vietnam. When Kennedy expressed the hope that the American mission could be accomplished without introducing combat troops, Taylor immediately made the issue into one of courage and credibility. It was necessary to do something to repair South Vietnam's sagging morale, "shaken by our seeming weakness in Laos." A government had to be prepared to do the unpalatable when essential for the national interest. "Certainly President Truman had derived no pleasure from sending American soldiers into Korea," Taylor ended, "only the satisfaction of what he conceived to be his duty."[66]

Kennedy remained doubtful. And it is unlikely that the Korean analogy helped him to resolve his fears. Rostow argued as well for a contingency plan for retaliation against the north, graduated to match the intensity of Hanoi's support for the Viet Cong. They told him it was to restore morale, Kennedy said to another White House adviser. But where would it lead? "The troops will march in; the bands will play; the crowds will cheer; and in four days everyone will have forgotten. Then we will be told we have to send in more troops. It's like taking a drink. The effect wears off, and you have to take another." The war could be won in South Vietnam only as long as it was *their* war.[67]

Nor did the Taylor/Rostow report go down well with other Kennedy advisers. Hearing of the recommendation, Ambassador Nolting, Diem's leading advocate in the policymaking group, warned Washington it would lead to a shifting of responsibility from the Vietnamese to the U.S. army. It reminded him, he went on, of the country doctor who gave all his patients a medicine to bring on fits—because, he said, he was "hell on fits."[68] Even more upset by the Taylor recommendations, Under Secretary of State George Ball called attention to sentences in the report warning that the initiative should not be undertaken unless "we are prepared to deal with any escalation the Communists might choose to impose."

But Ball found McNamara and his chief aides unwilling to listen to anything except how to stop South Vietnam from being taken over. Kennedy may not have subscribed to the falling-domino theory, but it was a palpable presence in the Pentagon. Ball then took his concerns to the White House, despite his memory of what had happened to Chester Bowles after the Bay of Pigs. "Within five years," he said, "we'll have three hundred thousand men in the paddies and jungles and never find them again. That was the French experience. Vietnam is the worst possible terrain both from a physical and political point of view." Kennedy brushed him aside with a dismissive comment: "George, you're just crazier than hell. That just isn't going to happen."[69]

Meanwhile, McNamara submitted a report that supported the Taylor/Rostow recommendations. The defense secretary was more candid about the prospects for a prolonged struggle, however, and set out what he regarded as a realistic upper limit on what might be needed to win. Maximum forces, he predicted, would "not exceed six divisions, or about 205,000 men." Kennedy turned to National Security Adviser McGeorge Bundy for advice, suggesting that he might delay a decision on troops while going ahead with Taylor's and Rostow's other recommendations for stepped-up assistance, such as helicopters, reconnaissance aircraft, and naval patrols. Bundy was troubled by that approach. Whatever the reason, he said, a troop commitment had become "a sort of touchstone of our will." Our willingness to make this commitment, Bundy went on, might well obviate the actual need to send the troops. It was a paradox of sorts: "I think without the decision the whole program will be half-hearted. *With* this decision I believe that the odds are almost even that the commitment will not have to be carried out."[70]

McNamara's and Bundy's initial positions are important indicators of the road to full-scale intervention: McNamara calculating troop needs, Bundy examining paradoxes—both advocating commitment. Likewise, Kennedy's initial reluctance foreshadows similar doubts that later perplexed LBJ. The key debate on the recommendation before Kennedy took place later that same day, November 15, 1961. It was evident from the outset that the president had not been convinced by his advisers' arguments. He could even make a rather strong case, he said, against intervening in an area ten thousand miles away against 16,000 guerrillas with a native army of 200,000, where millions had been spent for years without success. No support could be expected from the French, and the British tended to take the same view. The issues in Vietnam were obscure compared with the clarity of positions regarding Berlin.

Rusk and McNamara picked up on the Berlin question. If firmness in the manner and form used in Berlin were also used in Vietnam, protested Rusk, the desired results might be achieved "without resort to combat." Kennedy disagreed. One could not compare the clearly defined situation in Berlin with the "phantom-like" activities of the Viet Cong. McNamara insisted that the situation in Vietnam could best be clarified by committing U.S. forces, "since this power would be applied against sources of Viet Cong power including those in North Vietnam." And where would those forces McNamara was now talking about base their operations, "other than from aircraft carriers?"[71]

Rusk anticipated Kennedy's next question. Hanoi was the most important target in North Vietnam, "and it would be hit." But it was a political rather than a military target, he admitted, and under those circumstances such an attack would "raise serious questions." After more discussion about tactics, Kennedy returned to the central issue. Would McNamara consider taking these actions if SEATO did not exist? He would, said the secretary of defense. What was the justification, then? Chairman of the Joint Chiefs of Staff General Lyman Lemnitzer produced a page from the usual cold war rationale. "Communist conquest would deal a severe blow to freedom and extend Communism to a great portion of the world." But how could he justify action in Vietnam on that basis, Kennedy still insisted, while ignoring Cuba much closer to home? Lemnitzer had a ready answer: "The JCS feel that even at this point the United States should go into Cuba." [72]

Kennedy was neither ready to "go into Cuba" nor to send combat troops to Vietnam, but Lemnitzer's riposte hit the president's most sensitive nerve. The specific reminder of failure at the Bay of Pigs did not determine Kennedy's decision to implement the other parts of the Taylor/Rostow report, but the general's argument was an essential link in the process of deepening involvement. If the Communists had not been stopped in Cuba, it became all the more important to draw the line in Vietnam.

The stepped-up aid that Kennedy planned to send to Vietnam, including more than a thousand new "advisers," posed the question of violations of the 1954 Geneva Agreement. On November 16, consequently, the president sent Soviet leader Nikita Khrushchev a long, argumentative letter describing South Vietnam's plight in the face of "a determined attempt from without to overthrow the existing government . . . mounted and developed from North Vietnam." The United States was viewing the situation "in conformity with our pledge made at the Geneva Conference. . . . Our support for the government of President Ngo Dinh Diem we regard as a serious obligation, and we will undertake such measures as the circumstances appear to warrant." [73]

Meanwhile, Kennedy had ordered Rusk to send Ambassador Nolting a set of instructions about new aid for South Vietnam. In much stronger terms than were used in Kennedy's letter that Vice-President Johnson had carried with him to Saigon, Nolting was told that it was "most important that Diem come forth with changes which will be recognized as having real substance and meaning."

> You should inform Diem that, in our minds, the concept of the joint undertaking envisages a much closer relationship than the present one of acting in an advisory capacity only. We would expect to share in the decision-making process in the political, economic and military fields as they affect the security situation. [74]

Nolting's subsequent interview with Diem set the tone for a continuing Vietnamese-American confrontation, and more than bore out George Ball's fears that Kennedy and his advisers had already traveled far down a road paved with good intentions. When Nolting explained what was expected of South Vietnam in return for Kennedy's aid package, Diem replied archly that the ambassador realized that American proposals involved the question of the responsibility of the government of South Vietnam. "Viet Nam," he said, "did not want to be a protectorate." At a later interview, Diem cited several articles in the American press that talked about the need to "take charge" if Vietnam were to be saved. These demands of Kennedy "played right into the hands of the Communists." Diem argued, reported Nolting, "that we are pressing him to give a monopoly on nationalism to the Communists."[75]

Diem's initial objections to the American proposals prompted renewed attention in Washington to "possible contingencies" in Vietnam. There was even talk of a coup, but that "option" always ran into difficulty whenever one tried to posit a successful transition to a government headed by any other civilian or a military junta.[76] Eventually Diem agreed to a "memorandum of understanding" that detailed the many things his government would do to improve the military command structure of South Vietnamese forces and to win the hearts and minds of the people. The memorandum ended:

> While continuing vigorously to develop the infrastructure of democracy in Viet-Nam—in which the United States will do its utmost to help— the Government of Vietnam [GVN] recognizes also the importance, in relation to its fight with international Communism, of developing at all levels its democratic institutions, and will take all practical and feasible steps to this end. While the determination of such steps rests of course with the GVN, the GVN will continue to consider suggestions of the U.S. Government in this regard in the spirit of the new partnership.[77]

Kennedy was immensely pleased with Nolting's success. "The President would like you to know that he believes you have 'done a good job,' " Rusk cabled. And Kennedy hoped that Diem would "keep him informed of any thoughts" he might have "as our common effort goes forward."[78] Diem's concessions to the American point of view were really far less than had been demanded, even in earlier proposals. But U.S. helicopters were already en route to Vietnam, and the United States had "informed" Khrushchev as well as its cold war allies that the expanded aid program was under way. Under those conditions, forcing a showdown with Diem was not yet a real option, for the ultimate sanction, abandoning South Vietnam to the enemies—the National Liberation Front, Hanoi, Beijing, Moscow— was unthinkable.[79]

For a time it did not matter. The war appeared to be going extremely well over the next several months. American helicopters and napalm proved effective against the NLF. "Roaring in over the treetops," Roger Hilsman, an assistant secretary of state for the Far East in the Kennedy years recalled, "they were a terrifying sight to the superstitious Viet Cong peasants," who in the first months "simply turned and ran—and, flushed from their fox-holes and hiding places, and running in the open, they were easy targets." On the internal "front," the strategic hamlet program which resettled villagers in fortified areas which, it was hoped, could be kept secure against guerrillas, also seemed to be gaining momentum. A delighted Secretary of Defense McNamara described the strategic hamlets as "the backbone of President Diem's program for countering subversion directed against his state."[80]

In late August 1962, however, Vice-President Lyndon Johnson's military aide, Colonel Howard Burris, summed up the situation as it had developed over the past year. The vice-president's recommendations as set out in his report had been adopted as the administration's policy. But "on the practical side" there was concern over what the new measures had contributed to winning the war or reversing the trend. "While confidence in eventual victory is generally accepted, only General Harkins has said that 'we are on the winning side.'" Despite the State Department's view that the "trend against the U.S. in South Vietnam was halted last November, . . . presently we are just about holding our own and an upward trend in our favor is not yet clearly in sight." The next sentence in Colonel Burris's letter raised the crucial issue that was to haunt American policymakers from this time forward. "Politically, Diem is, if anything, weaker than he was when you met him, but the U.S. is determined to work with him in the absence of a reasonable alternative."[81]

For the time being there was no "reasonable alternative" to Diem. But what if things grew worse? Near the end of the year Senate Majority Leader Mike Mansfield gave Kennedy an updated report on the situation when he returned from a trip to the Far East. Once a strong supporter of Diem, Mansfield was appalled by what he now saw in Vietnam—the corruption, the political deterioration. He prepared a mild cautionary report for public consumption, but on board the president's yacht he was much blunter. As Kennedy read the report, his face grew redder and redder. "Do you expect me to take this at face value?" Mansfield replied, "You asked me to go out there."[82]

American military observers reported, on the other hand, that "attrition" was wearing the enemy down to a point where it could not continue fighting. Pentagon computers toted up the numbers of combat operations, search-and-destroy missions, air sorties, bombing tonnages, and weapons captured. "Every quantitative measurement we have," Defense Secretary McNamara declared at a press conference, "shows we're winning the war."[83]

Kennedy preferred McNamara's statistics to Mansfield's impressions. On December 12, 1962, a reporter asked the president to comment about the number of discouraging reports coming out of Vietnam:

Well, we are putting in a major effort in Viet-Nam. As you know, we have about 10 or 11 times as many men there as we had a year ago. We've had a number of casualties. We put in an awful lot of equipment. We are going ahead with the strategic hamlet proposal. In some phases, the military program has been quite successful. There is great difficulty, however, in fighting a guerrilla war. You need 10 to 1, or 11 to 1, especially in terrain as difficult as South Viet-Nam.

So we don't see the end of the tunnel, but I must say I don't think it is darker than it was a year ago, and in some ways lighter.[84]

Perhaps it was too soon after the Cuban missile crisis, but Kennedy's remarks went unchallenged, despite all they implied about what "we" were doing in Vietnam and the not-so-gradual transformation of the struggle into an American war. There was no follow-up; reporters asked instead whether Kennedy could be sure all Russian offensive weapons had been taken out of Cuba. No one took special notice of what had been said—"You need 10 to 1, or 11 to 1, especially in terrain as difficult as South Viet-Nam." No one asked where the 10 or 11 would come from.

For more than a year after the Bay of Pigs, Kennedy had worried about American "credibility." He had fretted that Khrushchev would misunderstand him, that the Soviet leader would take his offer to neutralize Laos as another sign of weakness. While the Cuban missile crisis of October 1962 ended with Castro still in power, and while the Soviet Union's decision to remove the missiles addressed none of the larger causes of Kennedy's anxiety about the outcome of the cold war, it provided a powerful boost to the president's self-confidence. Kennedy's image had been forever changed from a rash young man who rushed into battle at the Bay of Pigs as if it were a touch-football game on the White House lawn, into the sagacious president who had demonstrated both courage and restraint in nearly perfect measure to outflank his Communist adversaries during the missile crisis.

The missile crisis revealed something else besides Russian adventurism and Kennedy coolness under fire, however: how little the superpowers really cared about the opinions of their clients. Fidel Castro had asked Russia for protection against a new invasion from the United States. Khrushchev put missiles on the island, then removed them according to his needs. Accordingly, to Washington the goal of preserving South Vietnamese independence had become too important to be left to Diem. There was not the slightest trace of irony in what Americans said about Vietnam's right to self-determination. "In effect," wrote John Mecklin, "what the U.S. did in Vietnam was to set up a shadow government—though it would have been heresy to describe it that way publicly because of Vietnamese sensitivities."[85]

When rumors reached Washington that Diem had sent feelers to Hanoi, the search for a "reasonable alternative" to him became an imperative necessity. It was highly improbable that Diem could come to terms with his enemy, but his actions suggested a willingness to "blackmail" the United States, a tactic that could produce all sorts of difficulties. "With the administration's now mounting fear that Diem might actually come to terms with Hanoi and the NLF," concludes a close student of the origins of American intervention, "planning for the possible deployment of U.S. combat forces was revived in anticipation of a range of contingencies that seemed more plausible than before."[86]

There was, for example, always the possibility of a coup d'état.

FOUR

The American Coup

BY MIDSUMMER 1963 the immediate fate of Ngo Dinh Diem's regime in South Vietnam depended on decisions reached in Washington, not Hanoi. Diem's misdeeds were accounted sufficient cause to look elsewhere for others who, some policymakers had convinced themselves, could better represent Vietnamese interests. They took their lead from the president, who replied to a question about the Diem government on September 12, 1963: "What helps to win the war, we support; what interferes with the war effort, we oppose."[1]

Disenchantment with Diem had grown steadily for well over a year, but not all Kennedy advisers agreed he had to be replaced, or that his removal would improve chances for defeating the Viet Cong. The president himself vacillated, not only on what to do about Diem but on whether anything could be done to save the country. He had increased the number of advisers in Vietnam from fifteen hundred to fifteen thousand. He had approved the shipment of additional aid. But he had also expressed forebodings about direct military involvement. At a Palm Beach meeting on January 3, 1962, for example, the president had cautioned the Joint Chiefs and the new American military commander in Vietnam, General Paul Harkins, that he did not want the United States becoming "further involved militarily in that area." "The U.S. military role there was for advice, training and support of the Vietnamese Armed Forces and not combat."[2]

But the dynamics of the situation did not permit stasis. Kennedy knew that; and the ultimate decision to remove Diem may even have appeared to him to be the only way to avoid defeat in Vietnam without a massive American intervention. But by the time that decision was taken, the choice to withdraw was no longer available. One of Walt Rostow's assistants on the State Department's policy planning staff put down on paper what senior policymakers were thinking in early 1962, however reluctant they might be to acknowledge the path they were on:

> We have recently recommitted ourselves to Diem. While this was necessary and proper under the circumstances, we must, if he now fails to perform adequately, give serious consideration to alternatives to him. The situation in Viet Nam is too precarious to permit a prolonged delay in making such an assessment and determination.[3]

And during a visit to Saigon in February 1962, the president's brother, Attorney General Robert F. Kennedy, boldly proclaimed, "We are going to win in Viet-Nam. We will remain here until we do win."[4] When Lyndon Johnson wrote his memoirs, he stressed these vows, along with the more familiar Kennedy statements in support of the "domino" theory Eisenhower had made famous, in order to argue that he had been acting out the heritage left him by three presidents. Whatever ambiguities had once existed in the terms of that heritage, there was no escaping the legacy of the Diem coup. Withdrawal was made unthinkable. It would mean running away not only from the Viet Cong but from the moral responsibility the United States had incurred by encouraging the generals to overthrow Diem. "Vietnam and the consequences of Diem's murder," Johnson wrote, "became mine to deal with."[5]

FROM THE OUTSET of the American buildup in Vietnam, military and political "advisers" chafed at Diemist obstructionism. A formal military assistance command was set up, MACV, to coordinate the new military aid, and, perhaps more important, to put Hanoi on notice. Ten thousand American advisers arrived in South Vietnam to provide the manpower for "Mac-vee," along with a full range of military equipment for the ARVN (Army of the Republic of Vietnam). But despite some striking success with helicopter tactics, and optimistic statements from General Harkins's briefing officers, not much of a dent was made in the enemy's strength.[6]

American political advisers also arrived in great numbers, filled with determination to break "the system which formerly had merely put supplies on the wharf of Saigon at the mercy of the Vietnamese government whether they were or were not distributed. . . ." "Previous to this time," reported an American aid official, "something like less than 2 percent of the total aid going to Vietnam actually got to the people in the countryside, who made up approximately 80 percent of the population." But changing Vietnamese ways proved difficult indeed, militarily or politically, without beginning in the presidential palace.[7]

While he wanted American aid, Diem was both jealous and fearful of the Americans. Following an attack on the presidential palace by two South

Vietnamese pilots in February 1962, Diem saw plots against him every-where. He seemed afraid of losing battles or sustaining heavy casualties that might create discontent and undermine his regime. It appeared that he also did not much like victories, for those might create popular generals who could pose a threat of a different sort. Diem's staunch anticommunism still appealed, however, to MACV headquarters. Adding up various combat numbers for reporters, General Harkins insisted things were going well in this war of "attrition." What was needed was patience—and support for the mission.[8]

The American press corps in Vietnam was not so confident of Harkins's figures and downright disparaging of Diem's capabilities to lead South Vietnam's struggle against the enemy. Reporters were skeptical as well about the "advisory" role Americans were playing. At a March 1962 press conference, Kennedy was challenged to explain what was going on. "Mr. President, I wondered if you could tell us how the subterranean war is going there, because the Pentagon won't put out anything. . . ." There were complaints that the embassy was trying to muzzle reporters who wrote unflattering stories about the Saigon government. "By May the Administration was confronted with two undeclared wars," wrote a former CIA expert on Southeast Asia, "one with the Vietcong, the other with the American press."[9]

Carl Rowan, deputy assistant secretary of state for public affairs, tried to explain to his superiors that attempts to silence criticism of Diem were sure to fail. The reporters could interview Americans who had been in the field and knew the real story, even if they themselves were kept cloistered in the cities. "Doubts as to our ability to win with him are too widespread among newsmen who have spent months on the scene. With good relations, we can get a wide measure of silence by astutely invoking the national interest—but not otherwise."[10]

Rowan's approach only fixed attention again on the Diem "problem." Press criticism later became antiwar criticism, but that was not the case during these early months. Here it was anti-Diemist on the grounds that the quest for victory required a different political strategy. It nevertheless raised the specter of a lost cause, and that was hard to take. "Get on the team," Admiral Harry Felt, the American commander in the Pacific, shouted at Associated Press reporter Malcolm Browne. "Stop looking for the hole in the doughnut." Kennedy even tried to persuade *New York Times* publisher Arthur Hays Sulzberger to remove another reporter, David Halberstam, from Vietnam—to no avail. The president finally had to admit, "The way to confound the press is to win the war."[11]

Smarting at foreign press criticism of her husband, Ngo Dinh Nhu, and her brother-in-law, President Diem, Madame Nhu now made things still worse for the Kennedy administration by launching an anti-American campaign. Ambassador Nolting, always Diem's leading defender (save possibly Edward Lansdale), had to admit that Madame Nhu's public attacks only voiced what the brothers had been known to say in private. The bitter animosity between American reporters and the Nhus now became a constant feature of the Vietnamese situation, made all the uglier because Madame Nhu, South Vietnam's "Dragon Lady," implied that the American government must be plotting against her family—else why did Washington refuse to clamp down on the correspondents?[12]

Madame Nhu's statements eventually became something of a self-fulfilling prophecy. Her tirades provided support for those who wished to destroy the family's power lest the Nhus take the American cause down with them when they fell from power—an increasingly likely (and in some quarters, hoped for) eventuality. At a regional conference of American ambassadors in the Philippines, Assistant Secretary of State W. Averell Harriman was handed a telegram recounting one of Madame Nhu's assaults on all Americans, not just reporters. "Nolting," Harriman growled, "what are you going to do about this bitch?" The ambassador handed it back with the sarcastic comment, "What would you propose, Sir?"[13]

Harriman's antipathy to South Vietnam's ruling family stemmed in part from Diem's complaints that Kennedy was going to turn Laos over to the Communists. Unfortunately, Harriman wrote the president, there was nobody to replace Diem, but we should indicate in all ways we could that American support was for the Vietnamese people, not Diem personally. Could one disengage from Diem without disengaging from Vietnam? Kennedy was not optimistic about the possibility, especially since he had received a memorandum from Ambassador John Kenneth Galbraith in India urging negotiations with the Russians along the lines of a proposed American withdrawal in exchange for Hanoi's restraining the Viet Cong.

Galbraith had flatly suggested a first step of dissociating the United States from Diem. "We cannot ourselves replace Diem. But we should be clear in our mind that almost any non-Communist change would probably be beneficial and this should be the guiding rule for our diplomatic representation in the area." Uncertain of his options, Kennedy told Harriman to be prepared "to seize upon any favorable moment to reduce our involvement, recognizing that the moment might yet be some time away."[14]

Kennedy then gave Galbraith's memorandum to Defense Secretary McNamara for additional comment. In the Defense Department Galbraith's views aroused nothing but contempt. Withdrawal was more risky than military escalation, argued a rebuttal prepared for McNamara. It was tantamount to abandoning South Vietnam to the Communists. What especially angered the generals was Galbraith's attempt to buttress his case for negotiations by drawing a comparison with the 1954 French debacle at Dien Bien Phu. Such a comparison was preposterous. How could he imag-

ine such things? Throughout the Vietnam War, the one thing sure to provoke a violent Pentagon response was the French comparison. McNamara
should say something like this to the president: "The following statement
in your State of the Union address bears on this point: 'The systematic
aggression now bleeding that country is not a "war of liberation"—for
Vietnam is already free. It is a war of attempted subjugation and it will be
resisted.' "[15]

At a meeting with Kennedy on May 1, 1962, Defense and State representatives both pounced on the Galbraith proposal. Let it go for the time
being, the president finally told his advisers, but, he said, he remained
"interested" in another of the ambassador's ideas: using the Indian representative on the International Control Commission to see if there was any
substance to hints that Hanoi would be interested not only in neutralizing
Laos but in opening talks for increased contacts and trade between North
and South Vietnam. Galbraith had been informed that the "Russians have
told Hanoi that we [the United States] are not very comfortable in our situation in the South, that we do not see how we can win with Diem but equally do not see any alternatives."[16]

Hanoi and Saigon had been down that route once before, at Geneva in
1954. Neither was much interested in new negotiations under the aegis of
any of the great powers. Ho Chi Minh was not at all interested in making
the division of Vietnam permanent by accepting trade relations in place of
reunification, though he had indeed dropped hints that direct negotiations
with Saigon were possible as an interim solution. Diem feared being shoved
into a coalition, seeing the American idea of a "neutral" Laos as a precedent
for a safe exit from U.S. commitments to his government.

Diem had already become Averell Harriman's particular bête noire.
The assistant secretary had been put in charge of negotiations leading to
the 1962 Geneva Conference, at which the accords on Laos were to be
signed. Under great pressure, both Hanoi and Saigon sent delegates to the
conference. Harriman wanted to use the opportunity thus presented to
sound out Hanoi's representative about possible negotiations along the
lines of Galbraith's proposed American military withdrawal if "aggression
from the North" ceased. Recalling Franklin Roosevelt's hopes for a postwar
Indochina free from French dominance, Harriman suggested this was a
precedent for Kennedy's attitude toward Vietnam. But this gambit brought
only a response that if the United States had not blocked all-Vietnamese
elections in 1956, reunification would have been achieved. American intervention had grown worse, the North Vietnamese delegate went on, "until it
was now a fact that American forces were mercilessly killing Vietnamese
citizens." "It was a relatively useless conversation," recalled a Harriman
aide. "We got absolutely nowhere."[17]

Frustrated as he was by the North Vietnamese response, Harriman was even more angered by his inability to keep Diem in line. Protesting Laos's decision to establish diplomatic relations with North Vietnam, Diem severed relations with Vientiane. Then he lashed out at Cambodia's Prince Norodom Sihanouk, who had proposed an international conference to neutralize Vietnam. He did not follow the "fashion of neutrality," Diem said, "which seemed to have gained the favor of the free world."[18]

When Ambassador Nolting defended Diem's position, if not his tone, Harriman exploded. The United States had risked atomic war over Russian missiles in Cuba, he cabled Saigon. How dare Diem say America was unwilling to stand up to the Communists! "You and I are not on the same wave length," Harriman rebuked the ambassador. Was it so difficult to see that Diem's behavior was making it more difficult to "cooperate in matters which so vitally affect our efforts to keep South Viet-Nam free?" When Nolting finally conveyed Harriman's demarche to the South Vietnamese leader, Diem answered that while he had no desire to undermine the Laos agreement, he was also determined not to undermine the will of the Vietnamese people.[19]

This game of implied threats and dares could only go so far without a showdown. Interestingly, in the mid-1960s, Robert Kennedy was inclined to blame Harriman for what eventually happened. After his brother's death, Robert told interviewers for the Kennedy Library that Harriman had been wrong. "It became an emotional matter . . . and in fact, his advice was wrong. In fact, he started us down a road which was quite dangerous."[20]

Robert Kennedy's comment was nevertheless a backhanded admission that the road led to a decision at some point to rid his brother of a troublesome native ruler. It was precisely this sort of neocolonialist thinking that Mike Mansfield had been warning Kennedy and his Senate colleagues against since his return from Saigon in December 1962. The Nhus seemed to be concentrating more and more power within their small clique, he told fellow senators. Ngo Dinh Nhu's special project, the strategic hamlet program, was about the only thing the clique had devised, and if it did not work, the only alternative would seem to be "a truly massive commitment of American military personnel and other resources—in short going to war fully ourselves against the guerrillas—and the establishment of some form of neocolonial rule in South Vietnam. That is an alternative which I most emphatically do not recommend."[21]

As long as the illusion of military progress remained, however, American–South Vietnamese relations did not reach a crisis point. Indeed, even when that illusion was shattered, it took the threat of civil disorder in the cities to bring about a final disengagement from Diem.

In early January 1963 military illusions collided with reality at the battle of Ap Bac in the Mekong Delta, only some fifty miles from Saigon. There a Viet Cong battalion was surrounded by an ARVN force four times its size. After suffering moderate casualties, the Saigon troops broke off the engagement, allowing the enemy battalion to escape. Before Ap Bac there had been an American willingness to suspend disbelief, at least at the level of television network news programs. But the stories about this battle, gleaned from accounts by disgusted American advisers who had been with the ARVN units in the field, flatly contradicted General Harkins's bland insistence that Ap Bac had been a great victory because "we had taken the objective"—a vacant piece of territory abandoned by the VC. With victories like that, it was hard to escape thinking, the war might go on forever.[22]

Ap Bac revealed a "cultural lag" at the top echelons of decision-making. In Washington, Ap Bacs were still minor setbacks on the upward curve of military progress, or so Congress was told, along with assurances that the struggle against the NLF was "turning an important corner." Kennedy talked about significant military gains in his 1963 State of the Union address. Saigon's forces, Secretary of State Rusk brushed aside doubters, "clearly have the initiative in most areas of the country."[23]

A Joint Chiefs of Staff team, headed by its chairman General Earle Wheeler, visited Vietnam immediately after the battle and, as expected, concluded that things were going well. The situation had been "reoriented . . . from a circumstance of near desperation to a condition where victory is now a hopeful prospect." Only minor alterations were required in the support program. The real enemy, it appeared from the JCS report, was the press. Reporting on Ap Bac was a prime example. The press insisted, "contrary to the facts, that the battle was a defeat. . . ." While it was true the stories they wrote were derived from American sources, these had been based on "ill-considered statements made at a time of high excitement and frustration by a few American officers."[24]

> Nevertheless, great harm has been done. Public and Congressional opinion in the United States has been influenced toward thinking that the war effort in Vietnam is misguided, lacking in drive, and flouts the counsel of United States advisors. Doubts have been raised as to the courage, the training, the determination and dedication of the Vietnamese armed forces. In Vietnam the backlash of these reports, both in governmental and military circles, is apparent. The Vietnamese resent statements in the American press of such a derogatory nature to their personal characteristics and military habits and objectives.[25]

Readers of the report were hardly prepared, then, for the question its authors posed, and the answers they offered, about the challenge that had to be met: how to call Ho Chi Minh to account for "helping to keep the insurgency in South Vietnam alive?" "We should do something to make the North Vietnamese bleed." Possibilities ranged from an overt attack on targets in the north to minor sabotage forays. The first risked serious implications elsewhere, the last offered no possibility of influencing the progress of the war. What ought to be done, the report concluded, was to attack the north on several fronts in a coordinated program of sabotage, destruction, propaganda, and subversive missions. Kennedy "was quite interested in this," Wheeler recounted later.[26]

On March 20, 1963, General Harkins issued a report on MACV's first year. This "Summary of Highlights" claimed that "barring greatly expanded resupply and reinforcement of the Viet Cong by infiltration, the military phase of the war can be virtually won in 1963." At about the same time, instructions to new personnel assigned to Vietnam told them: "Your approach to the questions of the press should emphasize the positive aspects of your activities and avoid gratuitous criticism. Emphasize the feeling of achievement, the hopes for the future, and instances of outstanding individual endeavor. . . . As songwriter Johnny Mercer put it, 'You've got to accentuate the positive and eliminate the negative.' "[27]

At levels below cabinet secretary, however, Johnny Mercer lyrics were no longer winning the day. The implications of the battle of Ap Bac had finally sunk in. White House assistant Michael Forrestal wondered, for example, if contacts with Diem's opponents were adequate to allow American policymakers to know what was going on?[28] Out in Saigon, Nolting's ears were soon burning. What was this poison brewing back in the little offices on the lower floors in Washington? he wanted to know. He could have introduced "Mike" to any number of his Vietnamese friends when he last visited Saigon, the ambassador cabled. They would, he went on scathingly, "have had a field day criticizing the government in varying degrees and from various angles. But what good this would have done—outside of demonstrating a point and possibly stimulating a coup—I don't know!"

> I should add that, after the unequivocal public pronouncements of Vice President Johnson two years ago, and more recently the Attorney General and other high US officials, which I myself thought right and proper, I would not find it possible to be the agent in a change of US policy away from forthright support of the legitimate government, which happens also, in my opinion, to be the best available at the present time.[29]

Nolting's cable was circulated for comments in the White House and no doubt added to the pressures President Kennedy felt about deepening American involvement with Diem. If his aides *were* thinking about a coup, that made matters all the worse. He had been irritated with Mansfield's growing dissent. But now, in a follow-up discussion with the majority leader, he admitted to having serious second thoughts. He agreed, according to one account, on the need for a complete military withdrawal. But not until after the 1964 election. After their conversation Kennedy turned to an aide: "If I tried to pull out completely now from Vietnam we would have another Joe McCarthy red scare on our hands, but I can do it after I'm reelected. So we had better make damn sure that I *am* reelected."[30]

It is difficult to square such comments with the continuing buildup of American advisers and increasing shipments of weapons. If, on the other hand, Kennedy thought he could achieve what was later called a "decent interval" by extending such aid, it might be possible to argue that he hoped to discover a safe exit before Diem's regime collapsed—or before pressure grew, as Mansfield had warned, to take over the entire war to prevent the collapse of South Vietnam. If so, he was frustrated in the event.

At a meeting on April 1, 1963, Sir Robert Thompson, the British expert on counterinsurgency whose reputation had been made in the effort to preserve Malaya from a Communist takeover, repeated what Pentagon officials had been saying. Saigon's degree of confidence in the American commitment would determine its performance in the war. Kennedy never found a way to answer that admonitory, almost accusatory, argument; neither did his successor, Lyndon Johnson. Much of the Vietnam tragedy was built on that pillar. "This was a matter of making it clear that we were determined to see this through," Thompson pontificated. Harriman, who had now become Under Secretary of State for Political Affairs, wondered whether, on the other hand, it would ever be possible to build Vietnamese confidence in President Diem? Sir Robert responded that confidence was already building in the villages, where it was most needed. Harriman was not convinced. Thompson repeated this comment three days later in a White House meeting with Kennedy. Diem had much support in the countryside, he said, where it counted, and had written off the "Saigon intelligentsia." The president asked vaguely about the political opposition and was told it was "very poor." The question obviously bothered Thompson, having now heard it from both Harriman and Kennedy. He apparently decided to put the idea to rest. "If Diem disappeared," Thompson said, "there would be a risk of losing the war within six months since there was no other leader of his caliber available." After leaving Kennedy, however, Thompson had second thoughts, feeling perhaps he had overdone it, that the impression he had left might be too defeatist. As the result of the war, he sent Kennedy a note, Vietnam was producing a number of competent and experienced officials.[31]

What the British expert said pointed up Kennedy's dilemma with his own advisers. The president could take Thompson's estimate as an argument for sticking with Diem—or, as Sir Robert's reconsideration suggested, as an argument for dumping Diem as a last resort to save Vietnam. Ambivalence reigned as the Kennedy administration picked its way through the spring and summer of 1963, divided in its counsels but edging still closer to a fateful decision.

The first real indications that even Ambassador Nolting was not prepared to leave Vietnam's future to Diem alone came a few days after
Thompson's visit, when President Diem demanded the removal of two
thousand province-level advisers in the field. Diem had complained to the
French ambassador that there were too many Americans around: "All these
soldiers I never asked to come here. They don't even have passports." Nolting was upset. There was no alternative, he cabled on April 6, 1963, but to
show Saigon we meant business by holding up approval of support for
South Vietnam's military budget and other allocations of funds. To be sure,
there were serious risks in such actions. Diem might retaliate in some new
way, worsening relations, or they "might light [a] coup fuse."[32]

Although he hastened to add that a coup would actually weaken South
Vietnam's chances, Nolting had been shaken by Diem's stoic behavior in a
recent conversation. Diem had given the impression he would rather be
right, according to his lights, than be president—or win a war. Nolting had
pointed out that the Americans were popular—even in areas infiltrated by
the Viet Cong. Diem had turned the point neatly. "Yes," he agreed, "that is
often the case. That is what I meant by the colonial mentality of the Vietnamese people. I have complaints from my own officials in those areas to
the effect that the people believe that the Americans are now the government and disregard the authority of my local officials." Nolting warned him
he was "forcing a change in the policy of the U.S. Government towards
Vietnam."[33]

A month later, in the wake of a confrontation in Hue between government police forces and Buddhists celebrating the 2,527th anniversary of
Buddha, triggered by a seemingly minor dispute over whether the celebra-
tors had the right to fly their flag, relations between Washington and
Saigon turned openly antagonistic. The Hue confrontation left one woman
and several children dead. It set off a series of protests against the regime
that Diem met by half-measures that never satisfied the Buddhists, and
eventually by repressive actions that outraged public opinion in the United
States and elsewhere. The Buddhists' list of grievances against Diem recited injustices against their religion and in favor of Catholicism. But these
were only an inkling of what was really a political mobilization against the
Catholic-dominated regime. The Buddhist leader was a monk, Tri Quang,
who met covertly with American officials, warning them: "The United
States must either make Diem reform or get rid of him. If not, the situation
will degenerate, and you worthy gentlemen will suffer most. You are
responsible for the present trouble because you back Diem and his government of ignoramuses."[34]

State Department officials were fully aware of the "grave implications"
if Diem failed to conciliate the Buddhists. "Feeling here," Secretary Rusk
cabled Nolting, "is that GVN must be made to realize extent not only their

own stake in amiable settlement with Buddhists but U.S. stake as well. . . ."[35] And again, two days later: "If Diem does not take prompt and effective steps to reestablish Buddhist confidence in him we will have to reexamine our entire relationship with his regime."[36]

On the morning of June 11, foreign reporters were alerted by telephone to be present at a busy intersection in the heart of Saigon. There, a little after midday, an elderly Buddhist monk named Quang Duc, dressed in a saffron robe, seated himself in the lotus position while his companions poured a can of gasoline over him. What happened next has been best described by the historian Ellen Hammer: "He lit the match himself and sat motionless in the classic Buddhist attitude of prayer as the flames consumed him. There was the smell of burning flesh as a crowd gathered. In three or four minutes it was all over and the blackened lifeless figure toppled over on the pavement."[37]

Pedestrians fell to the ground, prostrating themselves in reverence; trucks and automobiles stopped, snarling traffic. Buddhist monks took advantage of the situation to hand reporters copies of the biography of the suicide. The document included his last words, a "respectful" plea to Diem to show "charity and compassion" to all religions. More immolations followed Quang Duc's suicide. But Diem still refused to retreat from his position that the events at Hue had been caused by Viet Cong agitators who had stirred up the crowd against the Buddhist protest. Never at a loss for the wrong word, Madame Nhu called the immolations "barbecues." "Let them burn," she jeered, "and we shall clap our hands."[38]

Photographs and film of the immolations appeared on world television. "An intolerable image of the Diem regime was set in word and picture, never to be expunged," wrote Ellen Hammer.[39] Kennedy, meanwhile, had decided he must replace Nolting with someone more capable of laying it on the line to Diem. He chose Henry Cabot Lodge, the Republican vice-presidential candidate in 1960. Lodge offered him protective coloration against Republican attacks should he find it necessary to carry out the State Department's threats to withhold funds from Diem; but the Republican was no mere messenger. From the outset the new ambassador behaved in something like viceregal fashion. He expected Diem to come to him with explanations and promises of change, as if the Vietnamese leader was his satrap and South Vietnam simply a disorderly province on the fringes of the empire.

"They can send ten Lodges," Diem proclaimed defiantly, "but I will not permit myself or my country to be humiliated, not if they train their artillery on this Palace."[40] Diem would not come to Lodge, but the South Vietnamese generals had already begun talking to various Central Intelligence Agency operatives, especially Lieutenant Colonel Lucien Conein. After a Fourth of July party at the American embassy, General Tran Van

Don and Conein went off together for drinks at a noisy Saigon nightclub. "What will the American reaction be if we go all the way?" asked Don.[41]

CIA reports of the generals' cautious inquiries about American support set the stage in Washington for efforts to make sure that any coup did not bring a government less determined to carry on the fight against the Viet Cong. Presumably, a government headed by the military would be more anxious to fight the Communists, but the trick was to convince them that *if* they undertook such a radical step, their future depended on U.S. moral and material support. In other words, the answer to the question would have to be that the United States was committed to winning the war. If Kennedy hoped that by removing Diem he would somehow lessen pressure for American intervention, the logic of the coup enterprise pointed 180 degrees in the opposite direction.

The president's statements on the situation in Vietnam over the next several weeks are thus to be understood in the framework of constant and increasing speculation in policymaking circles about the prospects for a coup—not, as is sometimes argued, as indications of his early preparation for an American withdrawal. Assistant Secretary of State Roger Hilsman put it well in early August. American policy at this point was neither to encourage or discourage a coup. "We do not know whether or not Diem can survive. With all that is at stake in Viet-Nam, we obviously cannot afford to back a loser but we are not yet in a position to pick a winner with any confidence."[42]

As the political situation worsened in Vietnam, President Kennedy expressed his determination not to withdraw: "We are not going to withdraw. . . . In my opinion, for us to withdraw from that effort would mean a collapse not only of Vietnam, but Southeast Asia. So we are going to stay there." Such statements could have misled Diem into believing he was indispensable, but probably not, for his own intelligence agents, headed by his brother, Ngo Dinh Nhu, knew of the contacts between the CIA and the generals.[43]

On August 20, 1963, General Don and several of his compatriots proposed that Diem declare martial law so they could prosecute the war more effectively despite the political turmoil. Their real purpose, however, was to strengthen military control preparatory to an attempted coup. To their surprise, Diem acquiesced readily—but because he had another purpose in mind. Nhu had already set in motion a plan to crack down on Buddhist protesters in Saigon and Hue as well as in other cities. The generals' request gave Diem an opportunity to make it appear that the raids and mass arrests that took place the next day were undertaken at the behest of the military, not civilian authorities. Using special forces loyal to the palace, but dressed as regular soldiers, Nhu's men struck after midnight on August 21, surrounding the principal temples. In Saigon some four hundred monks and nuns were arrested; in Hue the Buddhists barricaded themselves inside their temple and fought off the assailants for eight hours as townspeople rioted in protest.[44]

Diem's maneuver failed. The generals' contacts with the CIA had progressed to a point where it was easy for Don to convince Conein that the military had nothing to do with ordering the crackdown. Instead the ploy accomplished exactly what Diem had feared most: it allowed his enemies in Washington to force Kennedy's hand. When information was received in the American capital that the generals were planning to move and needed to know immediately what the American attitude would be, Roger Hilsman drafted a cable that declared, "US Government cannot tolerate situation in which power lies in Nhu's hands. Diem must be given chance to rid himself of Nhu and his coterie and replace them with best military and political personalities available." Diem's attempt to place the onus for the raids on the military was the last straw. "If, in spite of all your efforts," newly arrived Ambassador Lodge was instructed, "Diem remains obdurate and refuses, then we must face the possibility that Diem himself cannot be preserved." The cable went on to offer assurances that if the government fell, the United States would offer "direct support in any interim period of breakdown. . . ." For this dramatic instruction, the drafters had obtained verbal clearances from various under secretaries and from a vacationing Kennedy, but things were moving so fast that there had been no formal National Security Council decision nor any lengthy consideration of the implications.[45]

This was the famous (or *in*famous) "green light" telegram dispatched on a weekend when President Kennedy was at Hyannis Port on Cape Cod. Its authors later claimed that the message had been cleared by the president; indeed, it never was formally rescinded. Opponents of this course protested that the anti-Diem faction had attempted an "end run" around senior administration decision-makers. When Kennedy returned to Washington the two sides were trading accusations and insults. After a stormy session, the president confided to a friend, "My God! My government is coming apart!"[46]

The cable shocked Kennedy's military advisers. As one historian has pointed out, the military might have had a poor knowledge of the political situation in Vietnam, but almost certainly they had a vastly greater understanding of the mediocrity of the generals than Hilsman, and those like Averell Harriman and George Ball who agreed with him. These were the generals who would be counted on to replace the Saigon regime and wage the war.[47]

During the White House discussions of the cable, the president stressed that certain correspondents, especially David Halberstam of the *New York Times*, were actually running a campaign against Diem. It reminded him of another instance when a *Times* correspondent, Herbert Matthews, had influenced public attitudes in favor of Fidel Castro. He did not want that to happen again. Harriman protested that the cable was the result of the people of South Vietnam turning against the government, not a press campaign. Kennedy replied that while Diem and Nhu were indeed repugnant in some respects, they had accomplished a great deal along lines the U.S. desired. "When we move to eliminate this government, it should not be a result of *New York Times* pressure."[48]

That was hardly a repudiation. The rest of the discussion centered on questions from the president and Secretaries Rusk and McNamara about a suitable candidate to replace Diem. Far from disavowing the cable, as Rusk concluded, the discussion revealed that "unless a major change in GVN policy can be engineered, we must actually decide whether to move our resources out or to move our troops in."[49] When the extended deliberation resumed two days later, Kennedy centered the group's thoughts on the issue of "things that can be done in the field which would maximize the chances of the rebel generals." At the moment it looked like the coup forces could not defeat Diem. Treasury Secretary Douglas Dillon interrupted to say, "Then don't go." But Dillon and Ambassador Nolting were about the only ones present to urge against supporting a coup. As the debate went on, Harriman turned emotional about the generals' ability to bring it off. "We have lost the fight in Vietnam and must withdraw if a coup does not take place. We put Diem in power and he has doublecrossed us. Diem and his followers have betrayed us."[50]

Hilsman pleaded that it was impossible to pull back. The war could not be won with Diem. "We can't stop the generals now . . . they must go forward or die." Were they really sure, Kennedy asked, that the generals had the power to overthrow the government? That gave Nolting the opportunity to point out that even if they did succeed, it was likely they would be unable to agree upon a leader. Diem was the only man around who could hold "this fragmented country together." But could he do it without the Nhus? asked Kennedy. Nolting thought he could. At this point Harriman could no longer contain himself. He had disagreed with Nolting from the beginning, he said. It was the ambassador's advice that had led them astray. He was sorry he had to be so blunt about saying so. Hilsman then tried a new tack to put a clinching argument as the meeting ended. Other countries in Asia were watching what we did in Vietnam, he said, and if they saw Washington acquiescing in Nhu's desecration of the temples, it would make our task more difficult throughout Asia. The president would be interested to learn, he concluded, that the Koreans had ordered a special study of U.S.–South Vietnamese relations to determine how much repression the United States would tolerate, to serve as a guide for their actions in upcoming elections.[51]

Kennedy called them all back a few hours later to announce his decision. He would not revoke the cable, but he would send a personal message to Lodge asking for his frank assessment and explaining that he wished to avoid a situation in which a misunderstanding between the field and Washington resulted in a course of action neither desired.[52] The new cable to Lodge put more emphasis, however, on ensuring a successful coup than on learning what the ambassador thought. "We must surely be ready to play every effective card at decisive moments," it read. Hence Lodge was to report what additional actions he and General Harkins expected to take or recommend after a coup began, "to insure its success."[53]

Lodge responded that the only choice was to encourage the generals to act. Even in the short time he had been in Saigon, the ambassador had concluded that the war could not otherwise be won. If riots and violence continued as a result of Diem's actions against the Buddhists, a regime might come into power determined to pursue a pro-Communist or neutralist solution to the war. American prestige was committed to winning the struggle. "We are launched on a course from which there is no respectable turning back: The overthrow of the Diem government."[54]

Lodge's brave words worried the president. There was the shock of seeing where one's speculations led others, but there was something else. He had heard similar assurances once before—at the time of the Bay of Pigs. Kennedy did not question the right of the United States to support or even unleash a generals' coup against Diem. But he feared failure. In a private message to the ambassador, Kennedy said he must reserve the right to change course up to the moment the coup actually started. "I know from experience that failure is more destructive than an appearance of indecision." He would bear the responsibility for changing course, just as "I must bear also the full responsibility for this operation and its consequences. . . . When we go, we must go to win."[55]

After all this soul-searching, the August coup never happened. The generals feared that Nhu had been tipped off and had assembled loyalist forces to defeat any coup effort. They were most concerned as well by an apparent shift in signals from Washington. This occurred when Ambassador Lodge became upset at a Voice of America broadcast that suggested Washington was considering cutting off military aid to South Vietnam, and secured a retraction. Lodge had feared the broadcast might trigger a violent reaction from Nhu before the final coup plans were set, but his intervention only discouraged the generals from moving ahead.[56]

At a "mop-up" meeting on August 31, Secretary Rusk asked a group of advisers which factors had made them think a coup was the answer. Rusk's backing off allowed Secretary of Defense McNamara to reassert the argument for reestablishing relations with Diem. He also put in a word of caution about the assumption—widespread in the press—that the United

States was prepared to change the situation, when in fact it might not have that power at all. Hilsman then set forth the argument for suspending aid to Diem anyway, as a means of forcing him to negotiate with Lodge on all matters of importance. He tried to clinch the point by suggesting that French President Charles de Gaulle's recent call for the "neutralization" of Vietnam had originated in a desperate ploy by Nhu to get rid of the Americans. Rusk was not inclined to pay this much attention. Nor did he now believe other arguments that Diem had only a few months left before he was kicked out by the people—and with him the Americans as well. Such speculations distracted attention from the real situation: first, the United States was not about to pull out of Vietnam, and second, it was not going to effect a coup d'état by itself. "We were making steady progress during the first six months of this year and what we should do is go down the middle of the track and hope to recover that." [57]

Vice-President Johnson was present at this meeting—one of the few top-level discussions he attended. What he heard Hilsman say did not impress him at all. This meeting, at which both Rusk and McNamara stressed staying in Vietnam, left the vice-president with an impression that the argument had been over whether to get out or to support Diem. Johnson had not been informed of recent cables to Saigon, but he had never been sympathetic to the idea of plotting with the generals to produce a change of government. Diem had his evils, but what was the alternative? "Certainly we can't pull out," he said. "We must reestablish ourselves and stop playing cops and robbers." [58]

The anti-Diem factions thus suffered a temporary setback, in Vietnam and at home. But now there was something else to ponder. Rumors of Nhu's flirtations with Hanoi had been filtering into policy conversations for some time. Kennedy had twice reaffirmed the commitment to South Vietnam and the domino theory. What seemed new (and shocking) in the latest reports was Nhu's apparent mocking of American cold war theories, and Vietnam's place in that scheme of things. To justify supporting Diem up to this point, Washington had insisted that Vietnam was part of the life-and-death struggle with "world communism." Following Eisenhower, Kennedy had affirmed that if Vietnam fell, communism would move on to attack the next country, and then the next, and that would "give the impression that the wave of the future in Southeast Asia was China and the Communists." [59]

Kennedy's television interviews also stated very clearly that while the decision had been made to reestablish contacts with Diem, the United States expected changes in policy and "perhaps" personnel. If those did not occur, he could not imagine chances for winning the war would be very good. In the context of everything that was happening, the president's statements were to be taken not as signals of a desire to withdraw, but as a way of letting the generals know what their choices were should Washington-

Saigon relations deteriorate because of Diem's repression—or Nhu's attempts to engage Hanoi in serious talks. "When the spaghetti was pushed," Hilsman cabled Lodge, "it curled; now we must try pulling."[60]

On September 2, 1963, Nhu had a two-hour meeting with Lodge. During the conversation he let it be known that he had been negotiating with Viet Cong representatives, supposedly only over surrender terms. Indeed, that was the key reason why he could not leave the country as the Americans wished him to do. Madame Nhu could leave, and would be happy to tour the United States, but he could not. He would be willing to leave government service "for good," on the other hand, once martial law had been lifted. He would "prefer" to do this after certain American agents who were still promoting a coup against his family left. "Everybody knows who they are."[61]

Nhu's oblique accusations were irritating, but Kennedy decided to treat his comments as a serious gesture toward opening "negotiations" for a truce in the war between Washington and Saigon. Obviously it would be inappropriate for Lodge to discuss the matter Nhu had raised about "American agents." Secretary Rusk did admit, however, that "if the Vietnamese know what we know they would undoubtedly want certain officials to leave." Where did all this leave relations with the generals? They should come to us, Kennedy said. Meanwhile it would be assumed they are not acting, and we should take a diplomatic route. "When they come to us we will talk to them. We should avoid letting the generals think that the U.S. has backed off."[62]

Lodge held no brief for more talks. "They are essentially a medieval, Oriental despotism of the classic family type," he advised Washington, "who understand few, if any, of the arts of popular government." Their only interest was in physical security and survival against any threats, Communist or non-Communist.[63] The ambassador sent word to Nhu that there was nothing to negotiate about his resignation. He must go. A resolution would soon be introduced in the U.S. Senate declaring it a violation of American principles to continue to aid a government that pursued such repressive policies. Lodge's only advice was that Nhu leave the country immediately for at least six months. "It was up to him to take the advice or to reject it. There was nothing to haggle over."[64]

Lodge then went to Diem to warn him that unless Nhu went it was his "personal view" a suspension of aid "would become a very real possibility."[65] In Washington, meanwhile, Nhu's supposed bargaining with Hanoi's representatives had become a central topic in the memoranda circulating around the State Department and the CIA. Those for and against Diem both agreed that Saigon had no right to conduct such negotiations. The unpopularity of the regime provided a rationale for such thinking, but it was all reminiscent of Secretary of State John Foster Dulles's response to a reporter's question at the time of the 1954 Geneva Conference that ended the first Indochina war. Asked what American policy would be if Ho Chi Minh won all-Vietnamese elections and became the head of a reunited Vietnam, Dulles replied, first, that the country was too politically immature as yet for there to be genuine free elections, and then added that "the United States should not stand passively by and see the extension of communism by any means into Southeast Asia. We are not standing passively by."[66]

A decade later Kennedy's National Security Council argued that if Diem, in conjunction with "moves towards France and/or DRV [Hanoi]," demanded an American withdrawal, the administration should be prepared to "intervene with U.S. forces if necessary to protect Americans." Not only to protect Americans but to effect a change in the government so as to go on fighting the war. America was still unwilling to stand by passively and see Vietnam turned over to the Communists because of the folly of the man who had once won Washington's admiration for refusing to put his immature country to an electoral test against Ho's tightly organized Communist regime.[67]

Kennedy sent two missions to Vietnam in September 1963 under orders to clarify both the political and military situations. The first set of reports from a State Department representative and a marine general offered totally opposite estimates. "The two of you did visit the same country, didn't you?" Kennedy asked. General Victor "Buzz" Krulak insisted that his was a "national" viewpoint on the war while State's Joseph Mendenhall's was a "metropolitan" interpretation—implying that little credence could be placed in reports by civilians far removed from the front lines. A heated argument then began over the issue of "paralysis" of the civilian government. There had been earlier similar crises, argued the marine general, supported by former Ambassador Nolting, and the pessimists had always been wrong. Krulak and Nolting were no match, however, for National Security Adviser McGeorge Bundy:

> Mac Bundy said that in 1961 we overcame the paralysis by strengthening the effort against the Viet Cong; now it was the government that was causing the fear and paralysis and it was a little difficult to strengthen a war against the government.[68]

The second mission, headed by Defense Secretary McNamara and Kennedy's special military adviser, General Maxwell Taylor, dismayed Harriman and Lodge, who may have believed Kennedy was backing away from a hard decision. The two arrived in Saigon at the end of September. What they heard apparently convinced McNamara, however, that Diem could not be salvaged.[69] McNamara's biographer, Deborah Shapley, argues, albeit cautiously, that the experience did more than convince him that Diem could not be saved, it persuaded him the war could not be won—and he in turn persuaded Kennedy. The announcement upon his return that the American mission would be completed by the end of 1965 was therefore not more light-at-the-end-of-the-tunnel soothsaying but a decision to start winding down American participation in the struggle. Shapley records McNamara's conclusion as,

> I believed that we had done all the training we could. Whether the South Vietnamese were qualified or not to turn back the North Vietnamese, I was certain that if they weren't, it wasn't for lack of our training. More training wouldn't strengthen them; therefore we should get out. The president agreed.[70]

Whatever Kennedy and McNamara talked about privately, the Taylor/McNamara report itself argued that there had been some progress in the war, enough indeed to permit the beginnings of a troop removal—one thousand men by the end of the year. On the key question it recommended no action be taken to remove Diem, but an "urgent" search should be undertaken "to identify and build contacts with an alternative leadership if and when it appears." Selective pressure should be used to coerce Diem into pursuing steps to reach a situation where the Vietnamese could stand alone.[71]

But how far would the Americans go to bring Diem to heel? The Vietnamese generals had a keen interest in the answer to that question. The Taylor/McNamara report noted: "Any long-term reduction of aid cannot but have an eventual adverse effect on the military campaign since both the military and the economic programs have been consciously designed and justified in terms of their contribution to the war effort."[72] In other words, if the generals simply sat back and did nothing, the cutoff of American aid would wipe out any chance of victory. Could there be a clearer hint? Within days of the announcement that funds for certain projects would remain in suspension, the generals once again began probing their American contacts about Washington's attitude toward a coup.[73]

From their point of view, any cutoff of American aid was a signal not only that the United States was displeased with Diem, but that unless the generals were willing to see their country disintegrate, they must act. And that conclusion was precisely what the anti-Diem faction in the U.S. government hoped for. Hence on October 5, 1963, General Duong Van Minh, who would head the generals' revolt, met with Lieutenant Colonel Conein. He must know, Minh said, what the American government's position would be toward a change in the government of Vietnam "within the very near future." Conein replied that he could not give him a specific answer. Minh asked for another meeting when, he hoped, the American could supply the assurances.

In Washington, CIA Director John McCone advised the president that his agency had reviewed all the possible candidates to replace Diem and could see no one who would improve the situation. "Mr. President," he remembered telling Kennedy, "if I was manager of a baseball team, and I had one pitcher, I'd keep him in the box whether he was a good pitcher or not." What McCone feared, he would testify before Congress, was that if Diem were removed, "we would have not one coup but . . . a succession of coups and political disorder in Vietnam."[74] After this meeting Kennedy instructed Lodge that Conein should try to draw Minh out, to see if his plan had any real chance of success—yet without encouraging him or giving him tactical advice. "While we do not wish to stimulate a coup, we also do not wish to leave impression that U.S. would thwart a change. . . ."[75]

Over the next two weeks, nevertheless, Lodge used these ambiguous instructions to encourage the plotters, even ordering the MACV commander, General Harkins, to reverse himself after he told General Don not to seek out members of the American military for counsel.[76] Don had told Conein, meanwhile, that he could not reveal the "coup committee's" specific plans until just before the uprising. Lodge's eagerness to go off the diving board began to worry Mac Bundy. "We are particularly concerned," he cabled the ambassador, "about hazard that an unsuccessful coup, however carefully we avoid direct engagement, will be laid at our door by public opinion almost everywhere." President Kennedy wanted the option of "judging and warning on any plan with poor prospects of success." Yet even here the ambassador was given considerable leeway to act on his own: "We recognize this is a large order, but President wants you to know of our concern."[77]

How seriously Lodge took this caveat can be judged from his behavior at the Saigon airport early on the morning of October 28. He was preparing to fly with Diem at the latter's invitation for a brief trip to Dalat, apparently planned as a sort of opportunity for the two of them to talk over their differences. The ambassador had been waiting for Diem to come to him, holding back his calls at the presidential palace as yet another sign of American displeasure. As Lodge and Diem said their goodbyes to the assembled officials, General Don took the ambassador aside. Whatever was about to happen, Don stressed, it must be "thoroughly Vietnamese." The United States must not interfere or stimulate a coup. Lodge assured him he agreed. The United States wanted no satellites. But how soon could action be expected? They were not ready yet, Don replied. "We must win before you Americans leave. We cannot do it with this government, we must, therefore, get a government with which we can win now." Keep me informed, Lodge said, as he turned back to join Diem getting onto the airplane.[78]

Don's comments jolted Secretary Rusk, whose composure melted away in a White House conference called to discuss the status of the coup plans. If we support Diem, he worried, the war effort will be disrupted because we will be acting against the generals; if we support the rebels, we will have to guarantee the success of the coup. "We should put our faith in no one, including General Don. We should caution the Generals that they must have the situation in hand before they launch a coup. We should tell them we have no interest whatever in a long civil war in South Vietnam."[79]

Vice-President Johnson was present but offered no comment as the usual lineup of those pro- and anti-Diem spoke their pieces. General Taylor objected that they were treating the situation as if it were a football game. The only big switch was Dean Rusk. After long agonizing, he finally came down on the side of a coup. "If we say we are not for a coup, then the coup-minded leaders will turn against us and the war effort will drop off rapidly."[80] This intriguing comment penetrated to the heart of matter, for it was the logical outcome of what the Kennedy administration had begun by indicating it would continue to suspend aid to the Diem government. The generals had no doubt (even if some in Washington did) what the administration's action meant to their future prospects.

More pleas went out to Saigon for details of the generals' plans and Lodge's assurances that they would succeed. "If we miscalculated," Kennedy fretted, "we could lose our entire position in Southeast Asia overnight." Lodge should be told that from "here we can see that a disaster could take place...." He wanted no repeat of the Bay of Pigs.[81] General Harkins responded to these various messages with his own review of events, essentially a long recital of his differences with Lodge over how Washington's previous instructions should be interpreted, and how he was being kept in the dark. "After all, rightly or wrongly, we have backed Diem for eight long hard years. To me it seems incongruous now to get him down, kick him around, and get rid of him. . . . Leaders of other under-developed countries will take a dim view of our assistance if they too were led to believe the same fate lies in store for them."[82]

Lodge had a very different view of these last-minute qualms. Referring to his instructions and to General Don's conversation at the airport, the ambassador said he did not think "we have the power to delay or discourage a coup. Don has made it clear many times that this is a Vietnamese affair." Having turned the point back on Washington, Lodge spun around to claim credit for what was about to take place:

My general view is that the U.S. is trying to bring this medieval country into the 20th century and that we have made considerable progress in military and economic ways but to gain victory we must also bring them into the 20th century politically and that can only be done by either a thoroughgoing change in the behavior of the present government or by another government. The Viet Cong problem is partly military but it is also partly psychological and political.[83]

"Heartily agree," he closed, that a miscalculation could jeopardize the American position in Asia. "We also run tremendous risks by doing nothing." General Harkins had seen this message, read Lodge's final sentence, "and does not concur."[84] The ambassador thus laid out how the need for success in Vietnam had been created, and how Washington must now respond to the demands of that need. Bundy's rejoinder against taking the initiative sounded a fatalistic note: "But once a coup under responsible leadership has begun . . . , it is in the interest of the U.S. Government that it should succeed."[85]

Two days later, on November 1, the coup began in the middle of the day. Late that afternoon Diem called Lodge to tell him that some of his military units had rebelled. What was the attitude of the United States? Lodge replied that he had heard shooting but was not acquainted with all the facts. Besides, it was 4:30 a.m. in Washington, and the American government "cannot possibly have a view." "But you must have some general ideas," said Diem. The ambassador replied only that he was worried about Diem's physical safety. Although he had claimed not to be acquainted with the facts, Lodge said he had "a report" that those in charge of the "current activity" had offered Diem and his brother safe conduct out of the country if they resigned. Had Diem heard this? No, he replied. And then, "You have my telephone number." Lodge repeated that if he could do anything for his physical safety, Diem had *his* number. Diem said, "I am trying to reestablish order." The last words between Diem and Lodge thus left the dialogue where it had begun: at an impasse.[86]

Diem and his brother fled the palace and were trapped in another section of the city. They offered to surrender in exchange for safe conduct out of Vietnam. General Minh agreed to these terms, but once the brothers were placed in the rear of an armored personnel carrier they were both shot and killed. When Kennedy heard about the deaths, he was deeply shaken. General Taylor saw on his face "a look of shock and dismay . . . which I had never seen before."[87]

Hilsman and Mac Bundy had sent Lodge instructions about how the generals should treat the public relations aspects of the coup so as to make sure the new regime got off on the right foot with the American public:

> If coup succeeds, acceptance and understanding of its purpose here will be greatly increased if generals and their civilian associates continue to develop strongly and publicly the conclusion reported in one of their broadcasts that Nhu was dickering with Communists to betray the anti-Communist cause. High value of this argument should be emphasized to them at earliest opportunity.

The ambassador replied: "Point has been made to the generals."[88] Only the highest crime, treason, could justify what they had done. A few days later Lodge sent Kennedy a report of his behavior since he arrived in Vietnam. "In a country like this," he began, "exhortations, argument, rhetoric, and facial expressions mean very little. Actions apparently are an international language." But then he added that these had not been "colonial" actions, "only the kind of pressure which partners can put on each other." And he repeated, as if to convince himself, "Our actions were not 'colonial' and when Madame Nhu accused me of acting like a Governor General of Indochina, it did not ring true." He was convinced as well that things would now go much better in the war: "The prospects are for a shorter war, thanks to the fact that there is this new government, provided the Generals stay together. Certainly officers and soldiers who can pull off an operation like this should be able to do very well on the battlefield if their hearts are in it."[89]

If, on the other hand, as Lodge and those opposed to Diem had been arguing, the deposed regime had been so unpopular and inefficient, the coup really proved only that the generals had knocked over a rickety structure. Recovered from his shock, Kennedy replied to Lodge that his report made a "fitting ending" to the weekly summaries he had been sending since the final crisis began in August. "Your own leadership in pulling together and directing the whole American operation in South Vietnam in recent months has been of the greatest importance, and you should know that this achievement is recognized here throughout the Government."[90]

It was a neat piece of double entendre, whether intended as such or not. Less than three weeks later Kennedy too was the victim of an assassin. At his first meeting with Lodge and other advisers, the new president disputed optimistic reports about the future in Vietnam. He approached that situation, said Lyndon Johnson, with considerable "misgivings." Many people throughout the country had questioned the American course of action in supporting the overthrow of Diem—a direct comment on Lodge's attempt to suggest that the United States had no responsibility for the coup. On the other hand, strong voices in Congress "felt we should get out of Vietnam." Both facts gave him considerable concern. Johnson then repeated his doubts about whether "we took the right course in upsetting the Diem regime . . . [but] now that it was done, we have to see that our objectives were accomplished." Bill Moyers heard him put it in strongly personal terms: "I am not going to lose Vietnam. I am not going to be the President who saw Southeast Asia go the way China went."[91]

Kennedy's death had sealed the matter, not because Johnson changed Vietnam policy from a planned withdrawal to massive intervention. Rather, Kennedy's death left Vietnam, it was already apparent, on the edge of chaos. Johnson rightly compared his situation with that of Harry Truman. Roosevelt had overcome the Depression, according to legend, and whipped the Axis in World War II. What was left for Truman was to lose the peace. Similarly, what was left for LBJ was to lose Vietnam "the way China went." Even more than his uncertain predecessor, Johnson needed to win in Vietnam.

Robert McNamara would say later that he was sure Kennedy planned to withdraw; but one of the more interesting aspects of the situation in the aftermath of the deaths in November was McNamara's firm determination to see the war through to victory. He was ready, for example, to plunge ahead with a series of actions against North Vietnam, "all designed to make clear to the North Vietnamese that the US will not accept a Communist victory in South Vietnam and that we will escalate the conflict to whatever level is required to insure their defeat." To Johnson directly, the defense secretary stated his belief that the United States must "give the Viet Cong and their supporters early and unmistakable signals that their success is a transitory thing." And again, "The survival of an independent government in South Vietnam is so important to the security of all Southeast Asia and to the free world that I can conceive of no alternative other than to take all necessary measures within our capability to prevent a Communist victory." [92]

Transitions

A FEW WEEKS BEFORE the Johnsons left the White House in 1969, Lady Bird wrote about Jackie Kennedy's remarriage in her diary: "One of the oddest things is that as a result of the wedding which will happen tomorrow on a Greek island, I feel strangely freer. No shadow walks beside me down the hall of the White House or here at Camp David. . . . I wonder what it would have been like if we had entered this life unaccompanied by that shadow."[1]

Many Kennedy loyalists never forgave Lyndon Johnson for being vice-president, for being from Texas, and for succeeding their martyred hero. "George," Ted Sorensen burst out to Johnson aide George Reedy the night of the assassination, November 22, 1963, "I wish to hell that God-damned State of Texas of yours had never been invented."[2] There had been bad blood between the Kennedy aides and their Johnson counterparts on the flight back to Washington. Once back in the capital city, however, not even the most sensitive New Frontiersman had reason to complain about Johnson's treatment of Kennedy's family and close friends.[3] Even so, speech-writer Richard Goodwin remembered, within weeks of the assassination, small groups of Kennedy liberals were meeting to see if there was some way to deny Johnson the Democratic nomination in 1964. "Not only had Camelot dissolved, but Mordred was in command—or at least so it seemed, and was often expressed in those early words of incoherent grief and shock."[4]

"I always felt sorry for Harry Truman and the way he got the presidency," Johnson told a close associate soon after the assassination, "but at least his man wasn't murdered."[5] Murdered in Texas, moreover, murdered in a city filled with Kennedy-haters. Kennedy had gone to Dallas to try to force a truce in the long-standing feud between liberal and conservative forces in the Texas Democratic party. With white voters in other Southern states alienated by the administration's civil rights proposals still pending in Congress, Texas was once again a key battleground.

Little wonder Johnson feared the nation would look upon him as an "illegitimate" successor. These fears were heightened by continuing rumors that Kennedy had planned to drop him from the ticket in 1964.[6] The vice-presidency had not been a happy time for Johnson; that he felt isolated had been no secret. Bill Moyers said that during this time he appeared to be "a man without a purpose . . . a great horse in a very small corral."[7] Another close Johnson observer, Harry McPherson, agreed: "By the late summer of 1963, Johnson had grown heavy and looked miserable." If Johnson looked miserable, however, the "Administration's program was moribund." "If Kennedy hoped," McPherson added, "as Arthur Schlesinger wrote, to 'redeem American politics by releasing American life from its various bondages to orthodoxy,' he was light-years away from achieving it."[8]

Johnson loyalists were particularly irked by the easy way Kennedy partisans had influenced elite opinion-makers, and what they saw as the continuing denigration of LBJ's achievements after he proved he could make the political system work. "The press, to be sure, recorded those achievements," noted Harry McPherson, "with dutiful appreciation, but as Grand Prix drivers might appreciate a good tractor. . . . I could understand how reporters might have enjoyed Kennedy's deft banter more than three hours of self-justifying stream-of-consciousness by Johnson. It was hard to be fair in a climate spoiled by hurt feelings."[9]

In part to establish his "legitimacy," Johnson stressed the theme of continuity. But he retained all the key Kennedy policymakers for two additional reasons. He often remarked in later years that without the Kennedy people he would have had no links to the media or to Eastern intellectuals. "And without that support I would have had absolutely no chance of governing the country."[10] Second, he was quite simply awed by the team Kennedy had put together. Riding back to the White House from Andrews Air Force Base the night of the assassination, Johnson turned to Bundy and McNamara and George Ball. "You're men I trust the most. You must stay with me. I'll need you. President Kennedy gathered around him extraordinary people I could never have reached for. You're the ablest men I've ever seen. It's not just that you're President Kennedy's friends, but you are the best anywhere and you must stay. I want you to stand with me."[11]

Johnson hated the constant comparisons with Kennedy, yet he sometimes yearned to be seen in the exact same poses—even in the same dress. In the summer of 1965, writes historian Paul Henggeler, a men's fashion magazine, *GQ*, contacted the White House about featuring the president on its cover, wearing "the Western casual dress he usually wears during weekends at the LBJ ranch." *GQ* enclosed a 1962 cover photo of Kennedy in a two-button suit. The idea appealed to Press Secretary Bill Moyers, and photo sessions were arranged. When the photographers showed up at the ranch, they found the president ready for them—decked out not in Western dress, but in a dark, two-button suit similar to the one Kennedy had worn.[12]

Over the years of his presidency—indeed, almost from beginning to end—Johnson sometimes referred to the White House in odd terms, as if it were a punishment inflicted on him. "I came back to the White House" the night of Kennedy's assassination, he told a campaign audience in 1964, "and got behind that lonely, black, iron fence, and the Secret Service turned the gate lock on me, and there I have been most of the time for 11 months and 3 days." Four years later, in October 1968, Johnson referred to himself as the resident prisoner of the "big white jail house." "I do anticipate the very great pleasure," he told the audience at a dinner attended by both candidates, Hubert Humphrey and Richard Nixon, "of saluting one of you soon with the greeting, 'Fellow convict.' "[13]

Despite his ongoing fear of adverse comparison to John Kennedy, and his ambiguous attitude toward the presidency itself, much testimony claims LBJ felt a great sense of freedom in the White House. He was reprieved from the past—from his own record of conservative votes on civil rights issues, for example. One evening, talking with friends and staff, Johnson gestured broadly about the mansion and said, "Eisenhower used to tell me that this place was a prison. I never felt freer."[14]

Johnson was a moody man. No doubt he could feel mixed emotions and experience constantly varying degrees of satisfaction and frustration. The country had suffered a terrible shock, he asserted just after the assassination, severe enough to throw it into a serious crisis. The thought that the Soviets might have ordered Kennedy killed to induce a panic preparatory to some grand strategic cold war move was quickly discounted, but the new president remained convinced that malign forces would seek to take advantage of the confusion to attack the American "system." "I entertained grave fears for our future," Johnson told Hugh Sidey. "I didn't know if this was part of a Communist conspiracy or plot against our system. . . ."[15] Watching NBC news the night after the assassination, Johnson glared at the screen and started talking back to reporters Chet Huntley and David Brinkley, who he feared were exciting the people. "Keep talking like that and you'll bring on a revolution just as sure as I'm sitting here."[16]

"This is the time when our whole system could go awry, not just the Republican Party and the Democratic Party but the American system of Government," he told state governors who had come to Washington for the funeral. Kennedy's death was a challenge to the nation's inner strength, another test of wills like the missile crisis. In the struggle of philosophies with the Soviet Union, he went on, what would determine the outcome was how well the American system worked. "I think continuity without confusion has got to be our password."[17]

"Let us turn away from fanatics of the far left and the far right," Johnson then told a joint session of Congress on November 27, 1963. "This nation has experienced a profound shock, and in this critical moment, it is our duty, yours and mine, as the Government of the United States, to do away with uncertainty and doubt and delay, and to show that we are capable of decisive action. . . ." And, he vowed, "This nation will keep its commitments from South Viet-Nam to West Berlin."[18]

From his aides Johnson heard that the speech had struck exactly the right note in all quarters. One of the protagonists in the intraparty struggle among Texas Democrats, liberal Senator Ralph Yarborough, declared his full support for Johnson—because his speech to Congress "was a strong reaffirmation of the goals of the Kennedy Administration." At the bottom of the memo he received quoting Yarborough's words, Johnson scrawled his signature ten times. Now the presidency was his.[19]

Johnson made telephone calls to literally hundreds of citizens in public and private life in the first hours and days after the assassination, asking their support. He had a profound sense that national equilibrium must be restored, that there was a real danger things might come apart. To corporate leaders he argued that labor-management "feuds" should come to an end, that the economic pie was big enough for everyone; to labor leaders he pleaded for help in passing social legislation and asked them to open their ranks to black workers.

As he wrote in his memoirs, *The Vantage Point*, Johnson linked the assassination to a dangerous "crisis of confidence in our system of government." But the source of that crisis was *not* really the trauma of the assassination, however shocking; it was the stalemate that had existed since the Kennedy administration took power in 1961. "An entire program of social legislation proposed by President Kennedy—from aid to education to food stamps to civil rights—remained bottled up in committee, while the Congress defiantly refused to budge or act in any way."[20]

His analysis of the stalled New Frontier program was perhaps overdone, and certainly drawn to contrast his own success in driving Great Society legislation through Congress. "The agenda Lyndon Johnson confronted," explained Walt Rostow years later, "was unique in a particular respect. Aside from the urgent need to unify the nation and establish his legitimacy in the wake of Kennedy's assassination, he faced simultaneous protracted crises at home and abroad: a crisis in race relations and a disintegrating position in Southeast Asia where the United States was committed by treaty and a decade's action by two immediate predecessors and Congress."[21]

MCGEORGE BUNDY AND ROBERT MCNAMARA did not allow themselves to become part of the movement to restore Camelot. They were loyalists to the presidency. In soliciting their advice Johnson erred, if he did err, in not realizing that perhaps they were *too loyal* to the presidency, and were rarely able to offer advice without trying to anticipate Johnson's desires. Perhaps that was why Richard Russell, Johnson's original mentor in the Senate, came out of a meeting with the new president shaking his head. "Missy," he told Juanita Roberts, Johnson's private secretary, "it's a mistake; he ought not to keep them. It's a mistake and I've told him so."[22]

A transition from a martyred leader was very different from a change in administrations. "During those months," observed George Reedy, "it would have been entirely possible for him to interpret the Kennedy staffers as believing that JFK would have *pressed* the war in Vietnam and for the Kennedy staffers to interpret LBJ as *wanting* to press the war in Vietnam."[23] In other words, despite the hurt, despite the feelings of some that Johnson was somehow "illegitimate," the real problem was not that Kennedy staffers wanted to see Johnson fail, but that they tried too hard to make a "mission impossible" in Vietnam work.

A few days after the assassination, Hamilton Fish Armstrong, editor of *Foreign Affairs*, the premier establishment journal, wrote to National Security Adviser McGeorge Bundy to urge him to prepare an article for the journal reassuring the world that the American course remained steady. Kennedy's objectives had appealed to world statesmen, explained Armstrong. But he had won them over with "imponderables" as well, and those were now at risk.

> It was not just the loss of the intellectual Kennedy and the Kennedy in action that has been so deplored; it was the loss of what I can't describe better than by calling it the Kennedy style. . . . Let us take this moment to tell them that the Kennedy style lives on, that we are as sensible, as helpful, as imaginative as ever about the things that concern us all. The very fact that it was you who wrote an article of the sort I have in mind would be the assurance that this was so.[24]

Armstrong's nudging was all Bundy needed. He also felt that too many on the NSC staff looked down on Johnson. While LBJ might not have the elegance of his predecessor, he got things done. Besides, being less familiar with foreign policy questions he would need their advice all the more.[25] The article, originally titled "Of Presidents and Peace," was drafted on Antigua, where Bundy took a short midwinter break. Retitled with the more suitable "The Presidency and the Peace," it appeared in the April 1964 issue. "I am particularly concerned," Bundy explained to Secretaries Rusk and McNamara, "that this article should be useful to the President we have, as well as a tribute to the one we have lost. . . ."[26]

Mac Bundy's background represented generations of service to presidents and secretaries of state. Boston patricians, the Republican Bundys never spoke of partisan politics in the same breath with matters of national security. His father had served as a special confidant of Henry L. Stimson; Bundy himself had edited a collection of Dean Acheson's speeches, entitled inevitably *The Pattern of Responsibility*. The essay he wrote for *Foreign Affairs* began with an assertion that Kennedy's death had revealed his greatness, and now the world was grieving at having lost its Chief Executive for Peace. Moving on to the "most important single event" of the Kennedy presidency, the Cuban missile crisis, Bundy suggested that while the late president had "a taste and style of his own, I think it is right to claim that the office as well as the man was embodied in the resolution, restraint, and responsibility that governed in these weeks."

Thus Bundy's tribute to Kennedy, with its sophisticated effort to transfer some of JFK's charisma to his successor, implied, albeit unintentionally, that Kennedy had transformed the American presidency into a crisis management "team" which could be relied upon to operate successfully under the guidance of a more calloused hand. "The youth, the grace, and the wit were wonderful, but they were not the center. There lay courage, vision, humanity, and strength, tested on the path to the office, and tempered by the office itself. It is these qualities, applied to the greatest issues, that belong not only to the man but to the job."

However Bundy phrased this plea to separate the complementary from the essential, it still sounded as though the nation, having been set on course by Kennedy to achieve greatness, could now carry on, no matter who sat in the Oval Office—even someone lacking JFK's extraordinary gifts of grace and wit. But, once again, one should pay close attention to the crisis management trope that Bundy put forward as the three r's of successful foreign policy—resolution, restraint, and responsibility.[27]

There was also a brief comment on Vietnam in Bundy's essay, easily passed over by his readers, but in the event portentous: "The new kinds of forces designed for South Vietnam have not finished that hard job, but they have prevented an otherwise certain defeat and kept the door open for victory which in the end can only be won by the Vietnamese themselves. And never in any country did President Kennedy leave it in doubt that Communist subversion is always the enemy of freedom, and of freedom's friends the Americans."[28]

Johnson knew full well, even in the first days after Kennedy's assassination, that the situation in Vietnam was much worse than Bundy's comment implied, and that the late president's advisers had been bitterly divided over what course to follow. George Ball, who would become the leading opponent of expanding American participation in the war, nevertheless saw no other choice for Johnson in those first days of his presidency. Had he acted at once to begin to pull out, Johnson would have been subject to all kinds of attacks, Ball noted later, for turning his back on Kennedy's policy and giving something to the Communists. But Vietnam was only one of Johnson's worries at that moment. "It's easy to forget now, but at that time it was almost a constitutional crisis as far as President Kennedy's program was concerned. There was a kind of constipation on Capitol Hill that was really very serious, and the President turned immediately to the problem of how could he get the Kennedy program through."[29]

Ball never believed, on the other hand, that Johnson irrevocably committed himself on Vietnam in the transition period. "There was always a time when a basic change could have been made. I never subscribed myself to the belief that we were ever at a point where we couldn't turn around."[30] Perhaps that was so. Yet if the emphasis was on continuity, these early weeks—even days—were crucial. Alone with an aide on Sunday afternoon, two days after Kennedy was shot, Johnson reflected on what he had just heard Ambassador Henry Cabot Lodge say about the real situation in Vietnam. "It's going to be hell in a handbasket out there," he told Bill Moyers. Swiveling back and forth in his chair, clinking the ice cubes in his glass, Johnson stared at a corner in the ceiling and compared himself to a catfish. "I feel like I just grabbed a big juicy worm with a right sharp hook in the middle of it. . . ."[31]

It was an apt description of what Kennedy's situation would have been as well. But, as Walt Rostow argued, it was a double hook, connected at the center by an ideological weld between the cold war vision of the world and American beliefs about the capacities of their society. Already the hook pierced too deeply to be dislodged without serious damage to both creeds. Kennedy had learned he could not go forward with his foreign policies without confronting the issues of civil rights and poverty; Johnson believed he faced losing the Great Society without going forward in Vietnam. It was not just a matter of votes in Congress for either man. The weld held things together in a powerful ideological grip.

By 1963 the civil rights movement could be classified as an insurgency. Over the next five years the war in Vietnam and the struggle to contain the domestic insurgency exerted countervailing pressures on the White House and the nation. When black leaders complained that Vietnam absorbed resources better used in the inner cities at home, for example, they were talking not simply about material expenditures, although the butter ration had to be cut to pay for guns, but about the nation's spiritual resources. And there were other disturbing crossovers. If Vietnam set financial limits on what could be done to win the War on Poverty, the civil rights movement put limits of a different sort on the war in Southeast Asia. Riven along such fault lines, American society threatened to fragment as old alliances came apart. One can argue whether the Vietnam War would have had such an impact on the nation's moral sensibilities without the spectacle (and spectrum) of black protest movements, and whether the antiwar protest movement would have had nearly the influence it did without the moral authority lent it by guilt feelings over the black struggle for equality.

None of these complex relationships could be fully predicted at Kennedy's death, nor fully grasped even now except in speculative terms. But there were warning signs. Alerted to the danger of a firestorm spreading across the South, Kennedy had nevertheless been surprised by the violence of the "Birmingham Summer" of 1963. Black demands for an end to discrimination at lunch counters and other public facilities grew into massive protest marches for equal rights in other cities across the Deep South. Clearly, civil unrest had entered a new dimension. One of those closest to the situation, Burke Marshall, head of the civil rights division in the Department of Justice, asserted, "We felt this was an experience like . . . like a galaxy which accelerates when it explodes." In the weeks following the beginning of troubles in Birmingham, there were 758 demonstrations in 11 Southern states, and 13,786 arrests.[32] Lyndon Johnson put it in very similar terms. "The biggest danger to American stability," he later told Doris Kearns, "is the politics of principle, which brings out the masses in irrational fights for unlimited goals, for once the masses begin to move, then the whole thing begins to explode."[33]

In Birmingham itself, Reverend Martin Luther King, Jr., had begun to mobilize schoolchildren to produce a confrontation between moral authority and police power. "School children participating in street demonstrations is a dangerous business," declared Attorney General Robert Kennedy. "An injured, maimed or dead child is a price that none of us can afford to pay." King's response was a caustic comment that such tender solicitude for black children had never produced much concern over their miserable schools or segregation in general.[34] As the wave of protests and confrontations produced daily headlines around the world, Kennedy was told that the Soviets had seized on the events to broadcast nearly fifteen hundred anti-American commentaries. And when the president sent greetings to an African summit conference, the prime minister of Uganda responded with an official protest at the fire hoses and "snarling dogs" of Birmingham.[35]

Richard Neustadt's famous study of "presidential power" and the politics of leadership deftly pictured how the civil rights demonstrations were to Kennedy a revelation. "He eventually came to see the risks of social alienation as plainly as he saw the risks of nuclear escalation, and he sought to steer a course toward integration that could hold inside our social order both impatient Blacks and reactive whites—as tough a task of politics as any we have known, and one he faced no sooner than he had to."[36]

"Miscalculation of the moment of truth which is upon us," threatened a prophetic black minister from Brooklyn, "could plunge New York, Brooklyn, Philadelphia, Chicago, Detroit and Los Angeles into a crimson carnage and blood bath unparalleled in the history of the nation." Kennedy had briefly considered seeking legislation to set "a reasonable limitation on the right to demonstrate," but he quickly switched to the idea of new federal civil rights legislation. On June 11, 1963, he introduced his proposed bill with a speech on television. It ought to be possible for every American to enjoy full rights as citizens, he said, but "in too many parts of the country wrongs are inflicted on Negro citizens and there are no remedies at law." Then came the warning: "Unless the Congress acts, their only remedy is in the street."[37]

During a White House meeting to discuss the details of the administration's proposal, Kennedy's concern about the political perils of the legislation was obvious. One who attended the meeting noted, "I had never seen President Kennedy so nervous as he was at that particular meeting. . . . I got a real sense of tension in him."[38] When the civil rights bill came before Congress, Secretary of State Dean Rusk argued that racial discrimination had a deleterious impact on the conduct of American foreign relations. Rusk confronted South Carolina Senator Strom Thurmond's accusations of Communist influence in the civil rights movement and turned them to his best advantage by demonstrating that discrimination gave America's enemies the opportunity to drive "a wedge between people who believe in freedom. . . . I want to reiterate most emphatically that in the fateful struggle in which we are engaged to make the world safe for freedom, the United States cannot fulfill its historic role unless it fulfills its commitments to its own people."[39]

Congress was prepared to be convinced to vote funds for, say, Eisenhower's National Defense Education Act in the wake of Sputnik, or even more readily for the National Defense Highway Act to counter the 1957 recession. Here, however, the issue was redistribution—of social standing and even of economic standing if blacks took higher-paying jobs normally reserved for whites. If assuring civil rights was essential to unify the nation in the cold war, Johnson recognized equally that he must put to rest doubts among conservative Democrats that he would fight communism in Vietnam.

Partly, of course, these concerns were symbolic—but that is what politics is about, symbols. Johnson could both argue that discrimination hurt the nation's foreign policy to win votes for civil rights, and call for the legislation simply as a way to get liberal support for the foreign policy agenda. The permutations on these themes were nearly endless. It is essential to understanding Johnson's approach to Vietnam to explore some of them.

To begin with, Johnson hoped, in Tom Wicker's insightful analysis, to complete as president what he had begun as leader of the Senate. He hoped to find a way to convince Southerners to take off the Jim Crow collar that had constricted Southern politics since the Civil War and kept the region segregated from the rest of the nation and from economic progress. Ruminating one day after his old friend Richard Russell had visited the White House, Johnson told Bill Moyers, "God damn it. Jim Crow put a collar on more smart men as sure as if they were sentenced to a chain gang in Georgia. If Dick Russell hadn't had to wear Jim Crow's collar, Dick Russell would be sitting here now instead of me." [40] In sum, Lyndon Johnson believed he could not run away from Vietnam without giving conservatives, who did not really care much about the little brown freedom fighters in Southeast Asia, the opportunity to deny him the Great Society. When Johnson was faulted for attempting to take the Great Society to Vietnam, critics failed to add that he believed the battle for his domestic agenda turned on the outcome in Southeast Asia.

Johnson had watched the Kennedys struggle with civil rights, but his approach would be different. He was in a position, as they had not been, to offer promises to Southern leaders of an end to the region's "colonial status." In exchange for ceasing to obstruct civil rights measures, they were at last to be reintegrated into the union. "They were not immoralists or degenerates or colonial subjects," he would assure them, notes Wicker, "but men who had lost a struggle." [41]

But none of that would be possible if he could not first keep the country's promises about Vietnam. Southern leaders of the 1960s, blind to their opportunity, might defeat the Great Society with tactics similar to those once used to destroy the Populist movement. Only this time the fight against civil rights could not be fought on the same terms as it had been then, to divide white and black. This time it would be fought over the "Communist" issue. When Johnson heard Ambassador Lodge's first report to him as president, as we have already noted, he said, "I am not going to lose Vietnam. I am not going to be the President who saw Southeast Asia go the way China went." Lodge wondered if he would have the support he needed to fulfill that pledge. The president replied, "I don't think Congress wants us to let the Communists take over South Vietnam." [42]

Whether Johnson meant that *Congress* would demand victory in Vietnam, or that *he* would put the issue in such a way that Congress could not refuse him the support, it probably comes down to the same thing. Johnson fully shared the cold war vision of the world held by Southern conservatives and Kennedy liberals alike in those years of the Berlin crisis and Cuba. After all, it had been the liberals who criticized Eisenhower's foreign policies, and John Kennedy who had declared that Richard Nixon waving his finger under Khrushchev's nose at a Moscow exhibition had not stopped the Soviets from gaining control of Cuba. [43]

At the same time he was meeting with foreign policy advisers on Vietnam, the new president was conferring with Walter Heller, chairman of the Council of Economic Advisers, and other domestic policy advisers. The principal subject was the budget and the Kennedy-proposed tax cut. Johnson knew the country needed federal programs that cost tax dollars, and that the economy needed more money pumped into it. He could not sell a tax cut if the budget came in much over $100 billion. He could try to take it to the country, but FDR had tried that route with his tremendous majority and gotten licked. If anything was going to get done, you had to have the conservatives in Congress. "You had to give something to buy off [Senator Harry] Byrd."[44]

When Heller discussed the tax cut with Kennedy, he had encountered similar objections. Deficit financing, especially if pursued by Democrats, always called up certain unfortunate memories of New Deal fights. Heller had persisted with Kennedy, and he would continue pushing the argument with Johnson, that the remedy for sluggish economic growth was a tax cut, which, he insisted, would also make it less difficult to pass social legislation with high price tags. "When the cost of fulfilling a people's aspirations can be met out of a growing horn of plenty—instead of robbing Peter to pay Paul—ideological road blocks melt away, and consensus replaces conflict."[45]

At another meeting with Johnson, Heller stressed Kennedy's developing interest in a complementary antipoverty program, putting more conviction into his recital of the dead president's views than was perhaps warranted by the degree of JFK's enthusiasm for the economist's ideas. But the Kennedy reputation was already in the hands of the memoir writers, a process that would continue over the next several years until the keepers of the flame gave way to less passionate accounts.[46] There could be no doubt, on the other hand, that the ethos of the Kennedy years infused government with new thinking about what was now possible, and how to go about getting there. "In domestic policy as in foreign policy," writes Nicholas Lemann, "there was a strong bias toward doing things through lean, action-oriented agencies—the Peace Corps, the Green Berets—rather than through the clumsy, slow-moving traditional bureaucracies and their friends in Congress."[47]

Over the next several weeks, as planning went forward for an antipoverty program, Heller saw Johnson as the kind of New Dealer who wanted people working out in the clean air, creating visible accomplishments. "He had this sort of *concrete* idea. Bulldozers. Tractors. People operating heavy machinery."[48] Whatever final shape the program took, Johnson was determined it would be his own. "I have to get reelected in a year and a half, so I have to have something of my own."[49]

Fond memories of the National Youth Administration inclined Johnson toward local community action programs centered in the cities, impact-

ing directly upon urban blacks; at the same time, bad memories from the
New Deal led him to oppose Labor Department proposals for huge public
works programs. Johnson knew well that even ardent supporters of the
New Deal had looked upon the WPA and PWA with mixed feelings, as
"make-work" schemes barely removed from a direct dole to the unemployed. How would such schemes look as a central feature of a program
called the Great Society? When he appointed Sargent Shriver to head the
War on Poverty, he issued one key instruction through Bill Moyers. "You
tell Shriver, no doles."[50]

Like the dole, the New Deal public works programs had suggested a
permanent situation, a stagnant economy, a system that had ceased to provide meaningful employment for its citizens. Toward the end of the 1930s,
when war mobilization provided a powerful stimulus to the economy, New
Dealers reversed their earlier convictions that the United States could make
capitalism in one country work. Adolf Berle, for example, declared that the
war would change the world. "There is no need to fear. Rather, we shall
have an opportunity to create the most brilliant economic epoch the U.S.
has yet seen. It is entirely feasible to make the country at once more prosperous and more free than it has ever been. And . . . without sacrificing any
of the essential freedoms."[51]

Government public works programs were from a different era, when,
everyone remembered, capitalism was on the defensive before the supposedly depression-proof fascist and Communist states. No one wanted to
replay the 1930s. When Johnson talked about being a New Dealer, it
was about faith in government to carry out public power projects, about
TVAs, about picking up stragglers in the march of progress. For him, as for
others, the cold war meant the internationalization of *that* New Deal. Johnson was adamant about removing anything from reports on the War on
Poverty that could be "construed as a reference to putting cash in the hands
of poor people."[52]

The New Deal had been, for both conservatives and liberals, a dare-
devil ride to the outer boundaries of capitalist ideology. Everyone came
back safely after the war. But while New Deal successes left a heritage for
Lyndon Johnson to celebrate, other aspects of that era left a divisive legacy
not far beneath the cold war consensus. The early New Deal, with its
emphasis on intranationalism, still conjured up fears of "socialism"—or
something worse. In that sense, too, a retreat from Vietnam would stir
memories of the isolationism of that period. Johnson wished to bury that
part of the legacy once and for all with the Great Society. He was out to
end poverty, not come to terms with systemic failures—and their political
fallout. "I loved Jack Kennedy, just like you," Johnson told Richard Goodwin, "but he never really understood the Congress. I do. And I'm going
to pass all these bills you care about. It's a once-in-a-lifetime oppor-

tunity, for you, for me, for the country. . . . I'm going to get my War on Poverty."[53]

One final permutation on the theme of the interrelationship of Vietnam and the War on Poverty needs to be noted. Even before Lyndon Johnson assumed the presidency, a powerful theoretical explanation of poverty had gained ascendancy among liberal intellectuals (later it would also become the basis, ironically, of the conservative critique of the Great Society). Social science researchers identified the persistence of indigence with a "culture" that promoted patterns of individual behavior. These were then transmitted from generation to generation within ghettoized communities. Obviously, massive public works programs were not the answer to an imagined "culture of poverty." A memo developed in Heller's Council of Economic Advisers in October 1963, entitled "Program for a Concerted Assault on Poverty," set forth the need to overcome the poverty cycle almost entirely in terms of the individual—whose "cultural and environmental obstacles to motivation" led inevitably to poor health and education, and thus to low mobility and earning power. Here, of course, was an argument for programs like Operation Head Start and the Job Corps, which Johnson had associated with the New Deal National Youth Administration. In this later view, however, the emphasis was on strategies for acculturating the poor to middle-class behavior patterns.[54]

The crucial difference between the War on Poverty and earlier New Deal relief programs was not the absence of the WPA or PWA public works projects, nor the degree of government paternalism. The Great Society was more ambitious, in some ways even more paternalistic, than the New Deal. But by the 1960s planning was no longer Malthusian in mood, observes James Patterson. Continuing economic growth was assumed. "This affluence made people confident, indeed cocky; they congratulated themselves on the professionalism of social science. The precision of modern economics (so it seemed) had resuscitated western Europe and was 'modernizing' the 'underdeveloped countries.' "[55]

The culture of poverty theory thus also helped to undergird the belief that what America could do for its ghettos, it could do in the third world as well. "Without the assistance of liberal intellectuals, dependent people would remain mired in their own degradation. These views also fit easily into the chauvinistic assumptions of the Cold War and American penetration of the Third World."[56]

An aide to Mac Bundy explained why the National Security Council was so confident at the outset of the Vietnam War:

first, our unsurpassed military might; second, our clear technological supremacy; and third, our allegedly invincible benevolence (our "altruism," our affluence, our lack of territorial aspirations). Together, it is argued, this threefold endowment provides us with the opportunity and the obligation to ease the nations of the earth toward modernization and stability: toward a full-fledged *Pax Americana Technocratica*. In reaching toward this goal, Vietnam is viewed as the last and crucial test. Once we have succeeded there, the road ahead is clear.[57]

With all these weapons at hand it was impossible to believe that the War on Poverty would not succeed at home—or abroad. Dean Rusk had lived the reality in rural Georgia, as Johnson had experienced the triumph in the Texas hill country:

> I've been able to see in my lifetime how that boyhood environment has been revolutionized with education, with technology, with county agents, and with electricity—all that helping to take the load off the backs of people who live there. Now I can see that this can happen in one lifetime, I disregard those who say that underdeveloped countries still need two or three hundred years to develop because I know it isn't true. Because I've seen it with my own eyes.[58]

Johnson fully shared Rusk's enthusiasm for the task. Warned against becoming more deeply involved in Vietnam, that it was not like bringing power and enlightenment to the hill country, LBJ made it clear to old friends that he thought otherwise. "I told him he ought to get out," George R. Brown recalled of a conversation at the LBJ ranch at Christmastime 1963. "He couldn't help people that couldn't help themselves." Others around the table disagreed, as did Johnson himself.

> He got very upset with me and got up from the table and walked around and put his finger in my face and wanted to know what I meant when I said he couldn't help people who couldn't help themselves. He said, "You mean you wouldn't help Sam Houston [LBJ's brother] and he is an alcoholic." I said, "That doesn't have anything to do with this. I said you can help him, but you won't do him any good." And he got very upset over it. But I kept repeating that's what he ought to do, he ought to get out. We finally decided we'd best get off on some other subject and so we did. This was after dinner, sitting there at the table, about six men as I remember. The women were all somewhere else and we were in there alone.[59]

Johnson had told high-level policymakers that he would not be the president to lose Vietnam, but here, with this discussion, we look even deeper into LBJ's personal convictions about the New Deal, his political heritage, and the inseparable connections. Later, during a 1966 trip to Asia, he recalled how hard it had been to get Roosevelt's favored adviser, Harry Hopkins, interested in that part of the world during the war. Johnson told companions he had been convinced from that time that America's destiny was in Asia, where history had reached a turning point. "There's where the people are," he said looking out a window of Air Force One. "American interests are where the bodies are."[60]

Roosevelt had taken the country through the valley of the shadow to the postwar era. Johnson would go farther—beyond the New Deal at home, beyond V-J Day in Asia. "We've got to use the Kennedy program as a springboard," Johnson told Moyers, Ted Sorensen, and Richard Goodwin, as they paddled around the White House pool (at LBJ's command) in early 1964. "We've got to use the Kennedy program as a springboard to take on the Congress, summon the states to new heights, create a Johnson program, different in tone, fighting and aggressive. Hell, we've barely begun to solve our problems. And we can do it all. We've got the wherewithal. This country was built by pioneers with an ax in one hand and a rifle in the other."[61]

The Two Wars

"THERE WAS A FATEFUL SYMMETRY between Lyndon Johnson's War on Poverty and his War in Vietnam," wrote Charles Morris, a once-eager foot soldier in the struggle to vanquish poverty. Both wars were products, Morris argues, of rationalist misconceptions and overreaching; both defined their goals primarily in terms of psychological objectives. Sleeves rolled up, can-do metaphors on their lips, Johnson's armies went forth on his command to vanquish the "culture of poverty" in the inner city and to win the "hearts and minds" of the South Vietnamese for democracy.[1]

"I got a lotta problems," LBJ interrupted the lighthearted table banter during a small luncheon hosted by two friendly reporters in late January 1964, two months after he came into office. "I've got a brazen Communist attempt to conquer Asia on my hands. I've got Negroes revolting in America. . . . I got troubles in Central America that the people don't even know about. I gotta figure out how to pay for these fucking wars and keep my commitment to feed, educate, and care for the people of this country."[2]

Johnson always turned serious after a couple of scotches and some wine, noted Carl Rowan, who was present that day. He needed all the help he could get, the president went on, to stave off attacks from the "know nothings on social policy" and the "goddam liberals" on foreign policy.[3] As was often the case, Johnson's plea sounded self-pitying. He was ready to "figure out" all those things he said threatened his presidency. "When I looked inside myself," he recalled on another occasion, "I believed that I could provide the . . . [final] ingredient—the disposition to lead."[4]

"This administration today, here and now," Johnson proclaimed in his first State of the Union message on January 8, 1964, "declares unconditional war on poverty in America." It would not be a short or an easy struggle, but it was a war the nation could not afford to lose.[5] He had already promised that the United States would keep all its international commitments. And in a New Year's message to General Duong Van Minh, head of the military junta that had replaced Ngo Dinh Diem, Johnson called for victory in another "long and arduous war," assuring the general that the U.S. government "shared" Minh's view "that 'neutralization' of South Viet-Nam is unacceptable."[6]

The basic strategic decision in the War on Poverty rejected massive government intervention to create jobs in favor of Community Action Programs (CAP). The Labor Department plan for public works jobs would have cost $3 to $4 billion; the CAPs were estimated at only a third of that figure. CAP recalled Johnson's early days in Texas.[7] He kept referring, Walter Heller recalled, during conferences down at the Johnson ranch in December 1963, "time and again to his NYA—National Youth Administration—experience in the thirties. He liked the idea of learning while doing, learning through doing."[8]

He had listened closely to the economists who assured him that it could all be done without pain by manipulating fiscal policy. When Barbara Ward came to the White House for dinner in April, for example, Lady Bird noted in her diary that Ward talked and Lyndon listened—"something he doesn't always do, especially to women." Ward added one more reassurance that, because of America's great wealth and natural resources, "at last we have it in our grasp to build a really new society, offering more for everybody. . . ."[9]

When he asked for a $1 billion appropriation to launch the War on Poverty, the president declared, "Congress is charged by the Constitution 'to provide . . . for the general welfare of the United States. . . .' Now Congress is being asked to extend that welfare to all our people." But it was touted as something close to the miracle of the loaves and fishes, a program that would create new consumers and reduce welfare costs. Not a dole or federal handout, read one White House memorandum, this program would preserve and enhance capitalist values. "It is one of our most effective tools in the war against Communism," it continued. "Democracy can grow neither at home nor abroad in the shadows of hopelessness and deprivation."[10]

Still more miraculous, it was to be done with a tax cut. Johnson launched the War on Poverty at the same time he persuaded Congress to enact a huge reduction in taxes. It was, said *Newsweek*, "a whale of a big tax cut, and a minimum of reforms."[11] Heller could claim parenthood of this *tour de force* of modern Keynesianism. The idea had not immediately appealed to JFK. "Walter," Kennedy had protested, "it's simply not consistent with my pledge of calling for sacrifice to get the country moving again." Heller had thrown back the challenge. You pledged to get the country moving again, he said, and old-fashioned Keynesian remedies of government spending and welfare projects were not going to get the job done.[12]

The economist then presented Kennedy with a four-page memorandum explaining why a tax cut had to take priority over tax reform. Failure to take this stimulative action, it read, would confirm the "world's image of the U.S. economy as tired and weak."

> The political and economic consequences of this outcome are predictable—extremism will grow in strength on the right and on the left, labor unions will become disenchanted and uncontrollable, a Democratic Administration will be tagged with the worst postwar record of unemployment.[13]

You sold me on the tax cut, Heller remembers Lyndon Johnson telling him, with assurances it would stimulate the economy and help balance the budget. "After you leave me and go back to Minnesota, I'll come out there and haul you back and . . . ," Johnson paused, staring at him, and then added something like "publicly horsewhip you if it doesn't come through."[14]

It was a politician's dream come true. "Whatever tides run in the world," Johnson told a business audience on August 17, 1964, "there is no tide of nationalization or socialization running in the United States. Your Government is determined to support our private sector—not subjugate it. . . . Some may talk of radical changes in our policies—of greater governmental intervention in the economy or abrupt governmental withdrawal from our commitment to our own people. For myself, I do not believe the American people are interested in economic radicalism and recklessness."[15]

The Republican national chairman, Len Hall, groused that Lyndon Johnson was the only president ever to have both poverty and prosperity going for him at the same time. Until recently it had been assumed there was only so much pie, and the social question was how to divide it, wrote America's favorite pundit, Walter Lippman. But in this generation a revolutionary idea had taken hold: you could make the pie bigger with fiscal policies—"and then a whole society, not just a part of it, will grow richer."[16]

Another admirer, the famous head of IBM, Thomas Watson, Jr., wrote the president a confession: ". . . I suppose that even the most optimistic of us did not feel, even knowing your skill as a legislator, that you could accomplish so much. Furthermore, you have completely won the confidence of business and you have made businessmen feel that they are respected members of the American community, as indeed they should."[17]

As the bills enacting the Great Society rolled through Congress at a near assembly-line pace, Johnson seemed strangely dissatisfied. "Johnson lived his presidency in a race against time," a White House aide, Joseph Califano, later wrote, looking back after a quarter of a century.[18] Richard Goodwin, the holdover Kennedy speechwriter who produced the "Great Society" speech for Johnson, reveled in this atmosphere. "As I labored over

Johnson's speech in May of 1964," Goodwin would write, "the country was alive with change: ideas and anger, intellectual protest and physical rebellion. Without this ferment the formulation of the Great Society would not have been possible, not even conceivable." [19]

Having lived through the Great Depression, Johnson was considerably more leery of untamed forces. The tax cut might work the way Heller and the CEA assured him it would; and if it did, the War on Poverty would have a secure financial basis. But, as he said, he wanted it to have as well a "bedrock content." Even as polls showed he would sweep the 1964 election, the president sensed one issue that could not be overcome by pushing the right buttons or pulling the right levers on the GNP machine. Race was the central issue that cut across Lyndon Johnson's vision of the future. John Kennedy had mused to a Democratic poll-taker at the time of Martin Luther King's March on Washington in the summer of 1963, "You know, I never dreamed that the central issue of this decade, of my time in the White House, would be the race question." [20]

Kennedy's less than all-out support for a civil rights bill left it up to his successor to move Congress to act. Johnson had forebodings about the destruction of the old New Deal alliance. On the day the 1964 Civil Rights Act passed, Bill Moyers found him in a gloomy mood. Trying to shake him loose from his melancholy Moyers held up the *Washington Post:* "Johnson Signs Civil Rights Act." The president looked at the headline but did not rejoice over having righted a terrible wrong in American society. "Yes," he said. "And we had to do it and I'm glad we did it, but I think we just delivered the South to the Republican party for your lifetime." [21]

The 1964 Civil Rights Bill had been presented by its Republican cosponsor in the House, Representative William McCulloch, and Democrat Emanuel Celler as something that had to be done. McCulloch began his testimony on its behalf with a warning that "No people can gain liberty and equality through storm troop or anarchistic methods." Over the long run, he went on, such behavior would only undermine all of society. "After the tragic death of President Kennedy, one would assume that certain uncontrolled groups would recognize the futility of riotous behavior." [22]

Such a statement came close to saying that citizens challenging a century of segregation and discrimination, and Lee Harvey Oswald, shared a faith in violent action to achieve their ends. The liberal Celler was scarcely more generous. He understood the wrench from tradition involved in the new law. "I wish, truly, it could be otherwise, but unfortunately it cannot. The die is cast. The cries of pain, humiliation, and anguish must be answered." Celler quoted President Johnson: "Today Americans of all races stand side by side in Berlin and Vietnam. They died side by side in Korea. Surely they can work and eat and travel side by side in America." [23]

The venerable Mississippi representative William Meyers Colmer, following an even more venerable tradition established by John C. Calhoun, warned his liberal colleagues that, knowingly or unknowingly, they were rushing headlong toward a confrontation with individual property rights. "I would be opposed, as I have said many times here, to this legislation or this type of legislation if there were not a Negro in my State." The restaurant owner in Podunk, New York, would come to suffer right along with the one in Yazoo, Mississippi. Celler listened, but, he said, attempts to prevent passage of the bill were useless, "just as useless as trying to make a tiger eat grass or a cow eat meat."[24] Perhaps, Colmer mused, but he had a sense liberals would not always feel so sure of their ground. "I wonder if you do not find yourselves kind of coming back sometimes."[25]

It happened even sooner than Colmer might have predicted. Although Congress passed the 1964 Civil Rights Bill, Joseph Califano would recall, "During all my years on President Johnson's staff, I cannot remember a single personal call from a member of Congress asking us to step up civil rights enforcement for blacks; I remember scores of pleas to blunt such enforcement."[26]

Johnson knew what Colmer was talking about. He had many qualms. After he signed the bill, Johnson called black leaders together and told them there had to be an understanding that "these rights Negroes possessed could now be secured by law, making demonstrations unnecessary and possibly even self-defeating."[27] As it turned out, the danger appeared in the least likely place. Neither Johnson nor Congress imagined that the Community Action Programs would, by establishing federally funded rival power centers, set in motion forces to challenge local government. "What they looked like," wrote two social scientists, "was nothing less than the old political machines." But instead of providing support for the "system," they threatened its stability.[28]

All the safeguards that Congress built into the War on Poverty to make sure that radicalization did not occur, wrote Daniel Patrick Moynihan, had the opposite effect, just as Johnson's choice of CAPs to supply the "bedrock content" of the program instead set the Great Society on quicksand. By various contemporary accountings, the War on Poverty was going well; by others it became a classic case of too little, too late. "The initial desire to facilitate entry into . . . [the] system by outsiders," wrote Moynihan, "was supplanted by a near detestation of the system itself."[29]

One of LBJ's oldest friends from early New Deal days, Elizabeth Wickenden, a prominent consultant on social welfare issues (and, interestingly enough, wife of Arthur Goldschmidt, the UN economist who had first brought the Mekong Valley project to Johnson's attention), expressed grave doubts about the strategy behind the War on Poverty. The CAPs would, she wrote privately to the White House on January 4, 1964, raise expectations out of all proportion to their possible impact. Inevitably they would become subject to attacks from Republicans as a "slush fund," and from other critics who would complain about the localized nature of the program.

> This would be further compounded by the fact that a federal agency would be short-circuiting the normal channels of relationship to states and localities in their own areas of responsibility. This could lead to charges of federal usurpation of power, as well as diluting and obscuring responsibility for initiative and action.[30]

As the program went into operation in the summer of 1964, Wickenden repeated her warnings. Local political leaders would not take kindly to being shunted aside in this fashion. ". . . It is quite a different problem from the Peace Corps since Nigeria does not have a delegation in Congress."[31] The riots that began that summer in Harlem and Rochester and Philadelphia, even as Johnson was being nominated by his party in Atlantic City with an accompanying fireworks display, presaged much more serious disturbances to come.

By the time Office of Economic Opportunity funds began flowing to local community action boards, activists were determined to take charge of the money and continue the challenge to local authorities. The mayors of San Francisco and Los Angeles accused OEO of "fostering class struggle." The most famous boss of them all, Mayor Richard J. Daley of Chicago, told a House committee that involving the poor as leaders was like "telling the fellow who cleans up to be the city editor of a newspaper." OEO's withholding of funds to CAPs whose plans failed to give the poor "maximum feasible participation" galvanized Congress into acting to redesign the programs to include one-third local elected officials and one-third private groups, and to earmark a greater portion of War on Poverty funds to safe projects like Operation Head Start, the program for providing supervisory care and education for the very youngest of poverty's victims.[32]

In the cities themselves, meanwhile, battle lines of a sort were being drawn as whites set out to protect property and contain the black surge. Theodore White, chronicler of American elections, described the situation in 1964 in precisely such terms. America, he wrote, was witnessing one of the great population explosions of all times.

> Something has to give. And what gives is the neighborhood pattern in big-city living as Negroes, fleeing the smell and the rats . . . of inhumanly crowded slums, burst out like flood waters under pressure, spurting and spilling into adjacent neighborhoods. Street by street, block by block, neighborhood by neighborhood, solid black precincts crunch their way year by year through the hearts of our cities.[33]

In response, wrote another contemporary observer, Garry Wills, city governments relaxed their residency rules for the police force.

> Suburbs supply mercenaries to the inner city. The white army of occupation is maintained. That is what the country wants, but it does not want to know that it wants it. The white man does not think of this country as white, but he is careful to keep it that way.[34]

By 1965 Johnson realized that he had not established the War on Poverty on a solid footing.[35] "I should have listened to Wicky," he lamented to another old friend.[36] Whether Johnson had listened to Elizabeth Wickenden or to the Labor Department's plan for creating jobs before choosing his overall strategy for the War on Poverty, it turned out to be less important than the analytical framework for changing the structures of American society. On the one hand, that framework encouraged policymakers to believe in vigorous action and state intervention to overcome both ancient wrongs and meet contemporary needs; on the other, it encouraged false hopes that economists and government experts had discovered the philosopher's stone politicians had been seeking to decode the mystery of poverty amidst plenty.[37]

Johnson's hope of keeping the country united behind either the War on Poverty or the Vietnam War rested on the false assumption that the commitments were mutually reinforcing, instilling confidence in his leadership and thus ensuring the triumph of the Great Society at home and abroad.

"Ultimately," Walt Rostow would assert,

> President Johnson's view of Asia was closely related to his view of the race problem and of social reform in the United States. I remember his telling me once of the visit to his little office outside the Oval Office where he saw visitors in private, of a Senator . . . who, arguing against his position on Vietnam, leaned over and put his hand on the President's knee and said, "But Lyndon, they're not our kind of people." President Johnson said that in thinking about that statement and responding to it, he realized how deeply he did disagree because he felt they were our kind of people in Vietnam and Asia.[38]

But there was another "domestic" front in the Vietnam War. If it ever appeared that the war was being lost, the argument went, Johnson and the Democrats would find themselves in a worse predicament than what befell Harry Truman after the "loss" of China and the Korean War. History would snap into reverse; all that had been gained in educating the world and the American people would be lost, followed by the inevitable decline of the American Century.

Secretary of State Dean Rusk also urged doubters to see that the Vietnamese were "our kind of people"—some of them. Ever since Woodrow

Wilson had explained that he would teach America's neighbors how to elect good leaders, U.S. policymakers had regarded revolution as a special educational opportunity. Rusk was fully in that tradition, sometimes casting Ho Chi Minh in the role of a suspicious warlord whose calculations defied all reasonableness, sometimes simply as the agent of sinister forces whose ultimate goal was world conquest. But Rusk always focused on the differences between a normative worldview and Hanoi's distorted vision. In a 1966 exchange with Senator Frank Church, for example, Rusk averred, "I do believe there is a fundamental difference between the kind of revolution which the Communists call their wars of national liberation, and the kind of revolution which is congenial to our own experience, and fits into the aspirations of ordinary men and women right around the world."[39]

It was North Vietnam's distorted version of reality that explained the origins of the trouble in Vietnam. Unsuccessful in the territory they controlled, the North Vietnamese had launched the war in the south not simply for conquest but to disguise their failure to provide a decent life for the people who lived under communism's harsh rule. Once again Rusk talked with the Senate Foreign Relations Committee about the two revolutions. One was the revolution of "modernization, economic and social development, education and all these things, the rising expectations, that kind of thing." South Vietnam had been doing very well, he argued, "was in the full stream of that revolution" until all the trouble started. The other revolution was "the Communist world revolution, . . . the dynamic force that concerns us all."

> Now, we have reason to believe from intelligence sources that progress with that revolution in South Vietnam was one of the reasons why North Vietnam decided in 1959 and 1960 that they had to do something about it, that they were being outstripped by the south, and that this was of concern to them.[40]

Destined to fail, the Communist system had turned to war to solve its domestic problems—a conclusion supported by those ubiquitous "intelligence" sources that provided the answers to all mysteries throughout the cold war.

North Vietnam's estimates of U.S. actions and attitudes mirrored, in a way, Secretary Rusk's arguments that failure produced aggressive behavior—but the failure here was the south's. At the Ninth Plenum of the Central Party Committee in Hanoi during December 1963, it was decided that it was "within our grasp" to create a basic change in the balance of forces in the wake of the collapse of the Diem regime. Such would not be the case, however, if the "U.S. imperialists" sent large numbers of troops to Vietnam. If that happened, the struggle for final victory would be "stronger and harder."[41]

Where the Johnson administration was willing to intervene to maintain faith in the credibility of its world commitments, the Central Committee believed it would win because it could count on the support of forces in
the socialist bloc and in Asia, Africa, and Latin America to isolate the United States in world opinion. Whatever they said about the war's causes, the
Americans were not so irrational as to allow the war to spread outside Vietnam, "because the purpose and significance of this war cannot generate
conditions leading to a world war."[42]

On one point Washington and Hanoi agreed. At the beginning of 1964
American policymakers concluded that it would not take much to change
the balance of forces decisively in favor of the National Liberation Front, a
belief fully shared by Communist leaders. Even those who had discounted
the optimistic reports from Diem's government to his American "allies"
were shocked by reports of a four-to-one ratio of weapons lost to the
enemy. "It showed not only something about military trends," recalled
William P. Bundy, assistant secretary of state for Far Eastern affairs, "but
something about underlying morale, which was in the end bound to be
more crucial."[43]

While Johnson and his advisers struggled to see the true situation,
Senator Mike Mansfield sent the president a memorandum warning that
"We are close to the point of no return in Viet Nam." Unless Johnson
wanted another Korea on his hands, with all that implied politically, a great
deal of thought ought to go into the question of a peaceful solution—
especially about the ideas of other nations as well as our own.[44]

Not surprisingly, Secretaries Rusk and McNamara and National
Security Adviser McGeorge Bundy all sent Johnson negative responses to
Mansfield's memo. He had the Korean analogy all wrong, Bundy insisted.
Truman and Acheson suffered because most Americans believed more
could have been done to save China. "This is exactly what would happen
now if we should seem to be the first to quit in Saigon." As for the outcome
of the Korean War, it ended with a very solid anti-Communist base in
South Korea and a continuing American presence. Mansfield's support of
proposals for "neutralization" would amount to a forced withdrawal—an
intolerable outcome.[45]

Rusk and McNamara agreed. The secretary of state advised Johnson
that he had talked personally with French president Charles de Gaulle, the
most prominent of those who had advanced the nebulous neutralization
proposal now seized upon by Mansfield and others. Rusk learned that the
French leader had no interest in any Communist-supported neutralist solution. Defense Secretary McNamara argued that Mansfield's proposals
would destroy any chance to prove that the United States could deal with
so-called wars of national liberation. Mansfield was challenging the supposed "gross imbalance between the extent of our involvement in Southeast

Asia and our narrow self-interests in the area." But that was the wrong way to calculate the stakes. His own assessment, concluded McNamara, was that America's security interests "unquestionably call for holding the line against further Communist gains."[46]

Putting Mansfield's memorandum aside, Johnson approved a new program of covert action against North Vietnam, the 34-A plan recommended by a Pentagon committee and the Central Intelligence Agency for "progressively escalating pressure . . . to inflict increasing punishment upon North Vietnam, and to create pressures, which may convince the North Vietnamese leadership, in its own self-interest, to desist from its aggressive policies." Directed by the U.S. military, Op Plan 34-A was designed ostensibly to be a South Vietnamese retaliation against the north for its support and direction of the NLF in the south.[47]

The ultimate object, of course, was to increase Hanoi's learning curve. McNamara was enthusiastic about the idea, though CIA director John McCone and Secretary Rusk cautioned against hoping for great results "from this kind of effort." Rusk reminded Johnson that 98 percent of the problem was in South Vietnam; but it would help, he thought, to persuade Hanoi that "we have no intention of quitting."[48] When Ambassador Lodge explained what was afoot in Washington to General Minh and his colleagues in the military junta that had overthrown Diem, however, he pictured for them a series of daring strikes that would cause "immense destruction" to the economic and military installations of North Vietnam should Hanoi continue its reckless policies.[49]

Minh's reaction disappointed Lodge. His lack of enthusiasm, coupled with the apparent alarm in Saigon about the French diplomatic recognition of Communist China, deeply disturbed the American ambassador. Yet while the junta members complained that de Gaulle's actions stimulated defeatist thinking, they were themselves engaged in various efforts to "shift the contest for power from the military to the political level," including direct negotiations with the NLF—the scariest thing imaginable from Washington's point of view, and the ultimate precipitator of the coup that had deposed President Diem.[50]

The reluctance shown by the Minh-led Military Revolutionary Committee (MRC) toward accepting more American advisers in the rural pacification programs added to Washington's growing disenchantment with its errant protégés. On January 30, 1964, a second coup took place. Headed by General Nguyen Khanh, this group promised to wage the war more effectively—and to have nothing to do with the proneutralist forces in South Vietnam that, Khanh charged, had lately infected the MRC's upper ranks. What role American "advice" played in the coup remains a matter of debate, but the South Vietnamese who figured in these events surmised that Washington would not object and acted accordingly.[51]

However great his surprise, Ambassador Lodge hastened to explain to Khanh the rules of the game. He would rise or fall, Lodge told the general, on the basis of results against the Viet Cong—nothing else. No more fumbling around, no more delay because of "reorganization." He should apply a "few kicks in the rear end where necessary to see that the whole effort against the Viet Cong went ahead in all phases—military, political, psychological, economic and social. . . ." What he hoped for, Lodge concluded, was not rhetoric but concrete results. Khanh played up well, asking the American ambassador for advice about whom to appoint prime minister. "I said I did not feel I knew the personalities in Vietnam well enough to give him a worthwhile answer, as I had not yet been here seven months, but that I would consult people who knew this country much better than I did, and that if I had a valuable suggestion, I would let him know."[52]

This was an oddly modest response, given what he had just told General Khanh. Khanh continued to please Lodge over the next several weeks, beginning with his enthusiastic support for Op Plan 34-A, and by involving Americans in the Vietnamese government at all levels. The American military commander in Vietnam, General Harkins, had been a big fan of Khanh's even before the coup. But Harkins was not sure what it all meant. "One thing is for sure with this coup," he cabled his superiors in Washington. "We've gone through all the eligible general officers."[53]

Lyndon Johnson also felt less than confident about this latest turnaround in Saigon; in fact, he was damned upset. The old generals were sloppy and pro-French, the president had been told. Khanh was our kind of officer—pro-American, a real doer who would get on with the recommended program. Maybe so, Johnson grunted, but he told his staff, "no more of this coup shit." It would kill him with Congress and the newspapers. "If they had to plot, he said, let them plot against the Vietcong."[54]

William P. Bundy, who moved into the State Department from Defense to replace Roger Hilsman as assistant secretary of state for the Far East, delivered the harshest verdict on the events of early 1964:

> In hindsight, most students of the tortured political history of South Vietnam would today agree that the Khanh coup was a disastrous event. It removed, for a long time to come, any chance of a true government of unity, or of all the available talents, or with any claim to the crucial element of legitimacy.[55]

What Bundy could bring himself to say only "in hindsight," Mike Mansfield said at the very moment of the coup. Referring to his earlier warnings, the Senate majority leader now predicted that the Khanh takeover would not be the last. On the contrary, now that the slim cord of political legitimacy had been severed, the likelihood was for a whole series of coups as military leaders jockeyed for control of the power that resided in

American aid. "If these are in fact the grim prospects, our present policies will be drained of any constructive significance for the political future of Vietnam. We will find ourselves engaged merely in an indecisive, bloody and costly military involvement, and the involvement will probably have to increase just to keep the situation as it is." [56]

As before, Mansfield urged the president not to reject out of hand the "faint glimmer of hope" Charles de Gaulle's initiative offered for a "solution at a cost to us somewhere commensurate with our national interests in Southeast Asia." Once again, however, Johnson acted exactly the opposite, opening his press conference the same day he received the senator's memo with a statement that in effect put Paris in the enemy camp. "In view of the French recognition of Red China," he said, "we have been discussing with the free nations of Asia the necessity of resisting any further temptations to reward the Peking regime for its defiance of world peace and order." [57]

Reporters came back to de Gaulle's "neutralization" proposal several times during the press conference. And they were told over and over again that while the French leader had a right to his opinion, "We think the course of action that we are following in Southeast Asia is the only course for us to follow. . . ." A few days later, in extemporaneous remarks to government officials, Johnson made a veiled reference to Mansfield's defection. When he became majority leader in 1955, the president said, he had taken the position that "we had but one President and one Commander in Chief—that I would support his policies and give him strength and comfort, and that I would not be aligning myself with any enemies of the United States in criticizing him." [58]

Here, early on, could be seen the pattern of dealing with dissent that would continue throughout the Vietnam War. It was already evident in the summer of 1963 when American policymakers turned against Diem, half-convinced he was plotting to surrender South Vietnam to the enemy rather than accept American guidance. His successor, General Minh, lost Washington's support for his reluctance to endorse the Pentagon's plans for "covert" action against the north. Mike Mansfield's warnings about the meaning of the Khanh coup were tainted—even if he had not actually placed himself in the enemy camp—because the Senate majority leader looked favorably upon Charles de Gaulle's proposals.

Already de Gaulle was more than a nuisance to American policymakers. It might be, as Ambassador Lodge told the Vietnamese, that the French leader had no stack of chips to push into the game in Southeast Asia, but he was a serious threat nonetheless: de Gaulle's skeptical attitude, even more than his nebulous proposals, caused trouble. It incited doubts like those Senator Mansfield voiced, first in private and then in a speech on the floor of the Senate that warned of another Korea and even a war with China; it stirred up influential columnists, like Walter Lippmann, who echoed de Gaulle's calls for neutralizing the south. At perhaps its most dangerous level, de Gaulle's attitude challenged the fundamental cold war assumptions that had summoned Americans to Vietnam to hunt down the dark forces that disguised themselves as nationalists and played upon the ignorance of "our kind of people" there.

De Gaulle's public utterances "and the work of French agents," Lodge complained to Washington, had turned the Vietnamese community against itself and prevented it from wholeheartedly supporting initiatives against an enemy that was in many ways having a very hard time. Here another pattern revealed itself: the enemy was always about to collapse, asserted policymakers, were it not for the psychological support he received from well-meaning (and not-so-well-meaning) foreign sources. Would de Gaulle have called for a conference to "neutralize" France in the middle of World War II? asked Lodge. Why now, then, "does he speak of neutralism at the worst possible time from the standpoint of a truly just solution," thereby directly helping the Communists? Lodge thought Johnson should ask de Gaulle for a statement "as a man of good will," making it clear that his comments about neutralism did not apply to the present. The neutralism issue was always equated, and properly so, with internal changes in South Vietnam, though de Gaulle never openly admitted that would be the result, preferring to leave to the realm of speculation what would happen to Vietnam after the Americans left.[59]

We entirely agree, Johnson cabled Saigon, speaking for Secretary Rusk and himself. The problem was to find the right way and means of getting the French to understand the damage they were doing.[60] One way, the president's advisers thought, was to step up the rhetoric and reinforce the cold war foundations of American policy. He did so at a speech in Los Angeles in late February. Those engaged in the external direction of the war in Vietnam would do well to remember, he said, that "this type of aggression is a deeply dangerous game." The speech was a warning shot across Hanoi's bow, remembered William Bundy, but it was aimed to land near the Eiffel Tower.[61]

Various motives were suggested for de Gaulle's behavior—a desire to increase French trade throughout Southeast Asia, a broad-ranging deal with China, or simply a penchant for making trouble for the Anglo-Saxons. Vetoing British membership in the European Economic Community and extending diplomatic recognition to Communist China at virtually the same time certainly seemed calculated to add to Washington's burdens. When they looked even harder at de Gaulle's proposals, intelligence officials thought they could detect a conspiracy linking his call for a new conference on Vietnam to a plan devised by Red China, North Vietnam, and the National Liberation Front. French encouragement of such schemes only increased the danger of war with China, it was argued, because it emboldened Peking's rulers to take the very risks the president had warned about in Los Angeles.[62]

Johnson thought Lodge himself should go to Paris to help Ambassador Charles Bohlen present the American case for French restraint. Your mission, Johnson cabled Lodge, "is precisely for the purpose of knocking down the idea of neutralization wherever it rears its ugly head. . . . Nothing is more important than to stop neutralist talk wherever we can by whatever means we can. I have made this point to Mansfield and Lippmann and I expect to use every public opportunity to restate our position firmly."[63]

While the precise instructions for Bohlen's next "chat" with de Gaulle were being drafted in the State Department, Johnson sent McNamara and General Taylor to Vietnam to demonstrate American support for Khanh. In a meeting beforehand with the Joint Chiefs of Staff, the president declared that he wanted to proclaim for all and sundry that General Khanh was "our boy." Taylor's notes of the meeting read, "He wants to see Khanh in the newspapers with McNamara and Taylor holding up his arms."[64]

Yet Taylor's own discussion with the Joint Chiefs struck an uncertain note about the military follow-up to this political offensive. Taylor had begun the meeting by advocating a progressive program of air and naval attacks against the north, "using means beyond those employed in the past." The other chiefs expressed themselves in accord. They doubted China would intervene in strength—but if it did, the United States would have to carry on the military attacks to ultimate success, "cost what may." Johnson blinked at that. There was no question that Hanoi had to be punished, no debate at all, but there were some "practical difficulties" to consider, particularly political ones. "It is quite apparent," Taylor recorded, "that he does not want to lose South Vietnam before next November nor does he want to get the country into the war."[65]

It was not that a group as sophisticated as the Joint Chiefs were so naive as to think politics never entered into military calculations. Even in World War II, when American arms were fully engaged, politics had been a factor on such fundamental questions as where and when a second front would be opened against the Germans. What raised doubts was the nature of this war, where, it already had become apparent, the question of "national security" was far more abstract. Were they fighting Communist ideology or military aggression—or something still more nebulous? The Joint Chiefs never put the issue in those precise terms, but their growing anger at playing the "fall guy" for military failures in Vietnam, and their insistence that political leaders define the mission in a way that military power could be successful, reflected the dilemma.

Meanwhile, McNamara returned from Vietnam in March 1964 prepared to make a gloomy report to the National Security Council, and to recommend stepped-up military pressures against the north. Worried about what the secretary of defense would recommend, Johnson instructed McNamara beforehand *not* to recommend a bombing campaign. The president's intervention produced an oddly bifurcated document. The preamble set forth the familiar premise that the whole world was watching to see if the United States could meet the challenge of a "Communist" war of national liberation. It went on to assert that the U.S. had thus far limited itself to a "very modest" covert program against the north. Viet Cong control of the countryside in various provinces ranged from 40 to 90 percent, and the situation was growing worse. "Large groups of the population are now showing signs of apathy and indifference, and there are some signs of frustration within the U.S. contingent." The greatest weakness in the situation, the report went on, was the questionable viability of the Khanh regime. A constant threat of a new coup hung over the scene. "Whether or not French nationals are actively encouraging such a coup, de Gaulle's position and the continuing pessimism and anti-Americanism of the French community in South Vietnam provide constant fuel to neutralist sentiment and the coup possibility." If that happened, morale and organization would drop to zero.[66]

On the positive side—or what McNamara called a positive side—it could be said that while the regime's "top layer is thin, it is highly responsive to U.S. advice, and with a good grasp of the basic elements of rooting out the Viet Cong." Yet in the succeeding paragraphs the argument was repeatedly made that until that regime established itself on firm foundations, "an overt extension of operations in the North carries the risk of being mounted from an extremely weak base which might at any moment collapse and leave the posture of political confrontation worsened rather than improved."[67]

Aiding Khanh to establish himself on such a basis, McNamara estimated, would cost no more than $50 million to $60 million a year. A list of proposed actions suggested, however, that "holding the line" was all that could be expected in the foreseeable future. If the Khanh government took hold "vigorously," or if it could be shown that the north had increased its aid to the Viet Cong, "we may wish to mount new and significant pressures against North Vietnam." Contingency plans that could be implemented on thirty days' notice for initiating a program of graduated overt military pressure, the report ended, should now be put in train.[68]

The gist of McNamara's argument was that bombing should be used as a morale booster for the south, the same argument that had been made for Op Plan 34-A, and a "crisis management" way of signaling the north. The Joint Chiefs did not like the idea then, nor again a year later when Johnson finally ordered a sustained bombing campaign against the north, Operation Rolling Thunder. This disagreement widened as the war went on and on without a clear military definition of the problem.

McNamara's prerequisites for offensive action against the north—either a stronger government in the south or evidence that Hanoi was preparing a final blow—made little sense militarily, however much they appealed to the White House. The day after McNamara made his report, and the recommendations were solemnly approved by the NSC, White House aide Michael Forrestal reported to Mac Bundy that the Joint Chiefs were unhappy. They felt that "if we couldn't make the high jump in South Vietnam, . . . we should pole-vault into the North." Worse, Forrestal had heard about grumbling in the Pentagon that "the strong forthright actions called for may not be taken because some advisers close to the President are telling him his decisions should be determined by their impact on his chances for re-election, rather than by what is required in terms of the 'national interest.' "[69]

Johnson was well aware of the military's unhappiness. "They're trying to get me in a war over there," he told aides. "It will destroy me. I turned them down three times last week."[70] At the same time he was complaining to civilian aides about the military, however, the president was instructing Ambassador Lodge to knock down the idea of neutralism wherever it reared its "ugly head." Clearly, Johnson did not wish to have his hand forced during the election, but given McNamara's gloomy report, he did not want to rush into something that had unforeseen complications. A Republican candidate, Nelson Rockefeller, spoke to the central issue in a semirueful comment after losing the California primary to the eventual nominee, Barry Goldwater. "There are things that you don't have to worry about anymore," he said, "like do you have to take the country into war over Vietnam."[71]

Johnson had said repeatedly that he would not be the president who lost Vietnam. But neither did he wish to be the president who got the United States into a war with China. He expressed the dilemma in far more colorful terms. "We're not going to have any men with any umbrellas," he told *Life* reporter Hugh Sidey. On the other hand, he shook his head, "We can't let Goldwater and Red China both get the bomb at the same time. Then the shit would really hit the fan."[72]

The margin was getting pretty thin, Secretary McNamara warned the National Security Council in late April. He could not guarantee that "we would still be there six months or twelve months from now." His recommendation, therefore, was to pour in resources, even if the Khanh government wasted some of them, because that was preferable to the "terrific cost . . . involved if we had to use U.S. forces." This was scarcely unambiguous counsel. A few days later an old Democratic "pro," who had not attended the NSC meeting where McNamara delivered this judgment, sent word to Johnson that he should *not* consider the defense secretary for his vice-presidential candidate in the 1964 election. "It would be suicide for

President Johnson to pick the one man as his running mate who can be held responsible for Viet-Nam," James Rowe wrote a White House aide. "Whatever his virtues or defects in other matters, McNamara is the architect of Viet-Nam policy. It is irrelevant whether this is good or bad policy." [73]

It was not irrelevant, but what Rowe really meant was that thus far no one could call it a successful policy. Efforts to persuade de Gaulle to withdraw his call for a new conference to "neutralize" Vietnam met a strong rebuff and the pointed comment that France and the United States had never coordinated their policies in that part of the world—especially during World War II, when Washington seemed to be working against French efforts in Indochina. Ambassador Bohlen countered that while such might have been the case late in the war, soon afterward the United States did everything it could to help—including, he said, giving serious consideration to using atomic weapons to relieve the siege of Dien Bien Phu in 1954. But de Gaulle waved all that aside. What was important now, he lectured Bohlen, was that the only alternative to his neutrality policy was for the U.S. to engage in "a major hostility against North Vietnam and China." [74]

Bohlen's cable detailing this dialogue was sent direct to President Johnson, who already had sufficient reason to believe that de Gaulle might be right. In Saigon, for example, Secretary of State Dean Rusk encountered a somewhat surprising challenge from General Khanh. Contrary to what had been agreed upon earlier with McNamara, Khanh was now insisting that a move north could not wait upon a more secure base of operations in the south. Rusk responded that such a move risked war with China, which meant nuclear war, because the United States could not repeat the Korean experience. Khanh agreed—that was what made the decision so urgent. Rusk's record of the conversation showed that the general had long since crossed the border in his mind:

> As far as he was concerned we could use anything we wanted against China. As long as Communist China remained, "you will never have security." Communist China was Vietnam's hereditary enemy, and the issue must be resolved. [75]

Talk of hereditary enemies was nothing Rusk cared to hear, for it did not fit the cold war scenario, in which such old-fashioned items as nationalism and geography faded into the deep background. It was, in fact, evidence to support the kind of argument de Gaulle had been making for a new conference at which China would have to be a leading participant. Rusk did not wish to hear it because it thus implied, as well, that South Vietnam's goals were not entirely synonymous with American proposals for dealing with the Chinese threat. From the beginning of the American escalation of its role in Vietnam, the major obstacle to success had seemed to be Saigon's persistent inattention to the ideological dimension of the war: first Diem's mishandling of the Buddhist crisis and his general lack of understanding of the need for political reform; then Minh's unfortunate fixation on reconciliation; now, at the opposite end, Khanh's perturbing notions about hereditary enemies and such.

At a meeting with congressional leaders, Johnson summed up the situation: "Even with increased U.S. aid the prospect in Vietnam is not bright."[76] It was mid-May, and the election campaign was just around the corner. Pentagon skeptics were right, up to a point: Johnson did not wish to lose the election, or, more likely, all those additional seats in Congress he hoped to gain so that he could push through his domestic programs without kowtowing to conservatives. But that was not the real issue. Johnson was waiting for his advisers to give him a plan that would assure American control of events in Southeast Asia—protection against a war with Communist China being at the top of the list—and also assure him of support at home.

Several put their minds to it, but where to begin? As McNamara complained to his colleagues on the National Security Council, "Where our proposals are being carried out now, the situation is still going to hell. We are continuing to lose. Nothing we are doing will win." "Somehow we must change the pace at which these people move," Rusk had cabled Lodge in frustration, "and I suspect that this can only be done with a pervasive intrusion of Americans into their affairs." What did the ambassador think? Lodge's candid response stripped away layers of ambiguity and self-deception from Rusk's query.

> This unhappy country emerged from colonialism ten years ago and has been trying to get along since then with help from us that is, in all truth, advisory and not at all colonial. The question clearly arises as to whether this "advisory" phase is not about to be played out and whether the United States will not have to move into a position of actual control. This time has clearly not arrived yet, but it may be approaching. Whether it means that we will have a High Commissioner or a Commissioner General, or a man who really gives the orders under the title of Ambassador, will have to be determined in the light of circumstances as they develop. It appears to me now that such a relationship can only succeed if we are invited in.[77]

McGeorge Bundy submitted a full set of basic recommendations from Rusk and McNamara to President Johnson on May 25, 1964. To begin with, Bundy's memorandum averred, his top advisers had agreed that the president must decide on a gradual increase in military pressure on the north. Such actions should not be carried out, however, without first preparing the way with appropriate diplomatic and political warnings—and not at all if such warnings, "in combination with other efforts," should produce an improvement in South Vietnam's prospects. The phraseology scarcely disguised the hard facts of the situation: there were real risks of war with China, no matter what diplomatic reassurances were delivered to Beijing, and taking the war north did not solve the issue in the south. Bundy admitted as much in a covering letter: "There are several holes in this discussion, most notably on action in South Vietnam and on precise U.S. objectives, but there is more thinking on these topics than this particular paper shows."[78]

The basic recommendations included a brief comment on something that had been discussed and refined since early in the year: a congressional resolution that would authorize President Johnson to use American military force directly.[79] The final "vote" was against submitting such a resolution, because its existence would tend to "determine the decision in the direction of military force."[80]

Evidently Johnson still had not heard what he needed to hear from his advisers. If anything, during the early summer he was pulling back from a basic commitment to expand the war to the north. Arguments that a congressional resolution was needed, precisely because the electoral hiatus in the United States would make it more difficult to obtain such authorization until early 1965, were unavailing in the Oval Office.[81]

The president began to work his way into a decision from a very different direction. Ultimately he would allow it to appear that his hand had been forced by the North Vietnamese, on the basis of supposedly unprovoked attacks on U.S. warships in the Gulf of Tonkin in early August. But while Johnson would not allow himself to be fully convinced by the Rusk/McNamara/Bundy arguments in favor of crisis management techniques modeled on the tightening-ring concept of the Cuban missile crisis, he began to develop a supporting rationale along the lines that the conflict in Vietnam and the War on Poverty were indeed joined together symbiotically.

First, there was a letter from Ambassador Chester Bowles in India. Bowles had been "demoted" from his post as under secretary of state, presumably for not being tough enough to suit the Kennedy image. He had often cautioned against deeper involvement in Vietnam. In this letter, however, Bowles described in detail how the Communists had come to power in Russia and China on the basis of promises of land reform; and how, in the postwar era, the United States had successfully blunted the Communist appeal in Japan, the Philippines, and Taiwan, by force-feeding land reform in the old American Populist tradition of "Vote yourself a farm."

It could work in Vietnam, Bowles insisted, but we had not tried there. "It is particularly tragic when we realize that not only have we rooted our own American society in the concept of individual land ownership (the Homestead Act) but that wherever possible (except in Viet-Nam) we have applied this policy effectively abroad." Bill Moyers replied to Bowles that he had discussed the letter with Johnson, who greatly appreciated his thoughts. "I might add," Moyers wrote, "that I thought your ideas concerning the American Populist tradition and our foreign policy excellent."[82]

Then there was an interview with David Lilienthal, former head of the New Deal power project, the Tennessee Valley Authority, and later chairman of the Atomic Energy Commission. Lilienthal had come to report on his company's activities in Iran. "The Shah thinks a lot of you," the president began. "I guess he means business about land reform." Lilienthal had been told by a White House aide that the president only had a few moments to spare before an NSC meeting on Southeast Asia. He leaped right in with a comment sure to catch Johnson's attention: "I don't say that . . . [Iran] is like South Viet Nam, but there is a resemblance: what we have been doing is giving the peasants—they use that word though I prefer farmer—a stake in the country. . . ." It was like Vietnam, too, in that there was an "infiltration" effort in the poorest regions. Hopefully, Lilienthal's work was making it less likely that some day soldiers would have to be sent there.

"Using troops is the very last thing we want to do," Johnson said, putting his head back and looking at Lilienthal through the lower part of his glasses. Then Johnson got up and strode toward the door—or getting stuck with "the responsibilities of a sink-hole kind of 'war' in Laos [Vietnam?] just before an election here." "He looked at me hard," Lilienthal noted, "his head cocked; I haven't seen such close, intense listening in that room, ever."[83]

Next were two memos from idea man Douglass Cater, a former journalist, now a White House aide, who regularly sent Johnson suggestions on both domestic and foreign affairs. "As a step in preventative action in Southeast Asia," he wrote to the president through Bill Moyers, perhaps it would be feasible to send UN technical personnel into Vietnam to begin preliminary work on the Mekong River Valley project. It could provide "heartening evidence" of a project "to bring future bounty rather than bloodshed." Having UN personnel there might give the Communists pause and would certainly provide world opinion with "a more solid reason for U.S. intervention to protect the peace."[84]

Encouraged by Moyers to elaborate on his idea, Cater came back with a lengthy memo on June 23, 1964, that repeated what both Bowles and Lilienthal had been saying about the need for land reform. In addition to the Mekong Valley project, he wrote, there might be other worthwhile undertakings to consider, and perhaps the Soviets could be asked to join in. "What reform measures—land, tax, credit system, etc.—could we persuade General Khanh to pursue vigorously as signal of a new deal in Viet Nam?"[85]

New Deal! That was a phrase Johnson *really* understood. "We need more diplomatic ingenuity," the president lectured the "big three" advisers, Rusk, McNamara and Bundy, "more diplomatic ingenuity, not more hardware." Looking at the reports in front of him, he warmed to his theme. "Why can't we bring in more civilian governors and administrative advisers to help improve the civil problems. Why not get AID, Agriculture, and Peace Corps people in there to help their farming." He stood up, roved the floor, jingling keys and coins with one hand in his pocket, gesturing fiercely with the other. "Dammit, we need to exhibit more compassion for these Vietnamese plain people. . . . We've got to see that the South Vietnamese government wins the battle, not so much of arms, but of crops and heart and caring, so their people can have hope and belief in the word and deed of their government."

Abruptly shifting back to the military problem in Vietnam, Johnson cautioned his advisers that he was not yet ready for a full commitment. "What I am saying is if I have to turn back I want to make sure I am not in too deep to do so." His meaning was plain, concluded another person present during this recital, Jack Valenti. He wanted to do all he should short of provoking reprisals from China and Russia. "No one," the president said about bringing the superpowers face to face, "would be a winner."[86]

Johnson was determined to put down speculation that any fundamental decision had been made about Vietnam. In response to a memo from Cater about press conjectures, the president urged him to explain to reporters that all this talk about a tough line one week, a soft line the next, was just that, unfounded speculation. "We are where we were Nov. 22."[87] Did he really believe that? While Johnson had found McNamara's recommendations too one-dimensional, he was undergoing a process of ratiocination that permitted him to see the war in Vietnam as integral to the success of the Great Society, but not simply because it would affect conservative or liberal votes in Congress. When he first discussed Vietnam as president, the weekend of Kennedy's assassination, Johnson left the strong impression on listeners that too much emphasis had been placed on social reforms. "He has very little tolerance with our spending so much time being 'do-gooders,' " John McCone had recorded.[88] Johnson was "in deeper" now, if only because he was close to convincing himself that being a do-gooder was the right thing to be. He had listened to Heller and the Council of Economic Advisers, moreover, and had "learned" that winning the War on Poverty was a matter of turning dials and pushing buttons in fiscal policy. That fit in with his New Deal faith in government intervention. And so it was with Vietnam. The gaps in McNamara's and Rusk's and Bundy's advice were now being filled in by Bowles and Lilienthal and Cater. He could now have a New Deal faith in America's attempt to remake the landscape of another troubled "hill country."

When Henry Cabot Lodge resigned as ambassador to South Vietnam in early summer 1964, Johnson had several offers from "volunteers" to go there to fulfill the American mission, including even Robert F. Kennedy. Lodge had cabled that he believed the "advisory" period was fast coming to an end, that the next envoy would have to fill the role of proconsul. One man Johnson approached about the ambassadorship was John J. McCloy, former high commissioner in Germany after World War II. Such an appointment would be loaded with the implicit comparison of the stakes of the cold war in Europe and Southeast Asia. McCloy would not have to have the formal title of high commissioner, but the president talked to him about the assignment in precisely such terms. "We're organizing for victory out there, McCloy," Johnson declared, leaning over the famous banker-lawyer who had sat at the right hand of power and was now being summoned again to put on his armor, "and I want you to go out there and help in the organization." McCloy tried to decline, but Johnson turned up the volume. "I want you to go out there, McCloy, because you're the finest." Look what you accomplished in Germany, the president went on. "You're the greatest proconsul the Republic has had."[89]

He almost got me at that point, McCloy recalled. "I saw myself with a Roman toga with a laurel wreath around my head." But he managed, in the end, to resist the president's blandishments and cajolery. Lodge was replaced by General Maxwell Taylor and a political "deputy," U. Alexis Johnson. Together they did not carry the symbolic weight of a John J. McCloy, but Taylor's letter of instruction gave him more authority than any previous emissary. "What it does," Bundy affirmed to the president, "is to give Max full control over everything in South Vietnam."[90]

It remained to be seen, of course, how the South Vietnamese would react to this enlarged authority of the American ambassador to Saigon. In early May, Doug Cater had sent Johnson a memorandum about a possible address to the nation after the passage of the Civil Rights Bill. He had reviewed the tragic events in the United States between 1832 and 1860, Cater noted, and concluded that while the British and Spanish colonial empires had dealt successfully with the slavery issue in that period, the United States had not. It had failed because the politicians abandoned the struggle to the nonpoliticians, the abolitionists and the slaveholders. Cater's model appeared to apply to the present—and not only in domestic affairs. For the Spanish and British, all one had to do was substitute Russia and China, and for the abolitionists and slaveholders, those who would withdraw from Southeast Asia and those who were anxious to go north. However that might be, Cater's final comment reminded Johnson of the need to take charge:

> There are moments in history when politics must act or the forces of anarchy take charge. America does not want another civil war even if it is

confined to the streets of Birmingham or the expressways of New York. Lasting progress cannot be won by zealots. It takes the skill and dedication of those who have been elected by the people to build the great society toward which we must be constantly moving.[91]

When the Republicans nominated Barry Goldwater for the presidency, it became all the easier to believe in the absolute necessity of a well-controlled middle course between extremes of zealotry, and to believe that Lyndon Johnson embodied in his person those skills and that dedication. The flaws in the War on Poverty strategy had not yet surfaced, and his handling of the Gulf of Tonkin "crisis" convinced all but the last few holdouts that it was possible to meet the challenge in the jungles of Southeast Asia with equivalent measures.

Part Two

VISIONS

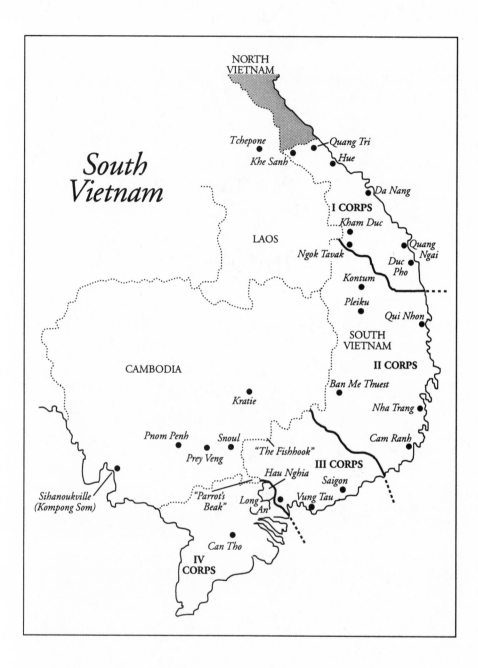

NORTH
VIETNAM

*South
Vietnam*

Tchepone

Quang Tri

Hue

Khe Sanh

Da Nang

I CORPS

Kham Duc

LAOS

*Quang
Ngai*

Ngok Tavak

*Duc
Pho*

Kontum

Pleiku

Qui Nhon

SOUTH
VIETNAM

II CORPS

CAMBODIA

Ban Me Thuest

Kratie

Nha Trang

Pnom Penh

Snoul

Cam Ranh

Prey Veng

"The Fishhook"

III CORPS

Hau Nghia

Saigon

*Sihanoukville
(Kompong Som)*

*"Parrot's
Beak"*

*Long
An*

Vung Tau

Can Tho

**IV
CORPS**

The Peace Candidate

"IT IS A CHOICE between the center and the fringe, between the responsible mainstream of American experience and the reckless and rejected extremes of American life." Barry Goldwater's supporters talked of changing the world, Johnson told a convention of electrical workers, but what "they" really wanted to do was change America. Before Vietnam was a name, before the Congo was a map, before there was a NATO, or even before atomic weapons, the president asserted, these were the people who opposed the minimum wage and all the other legislation on behalf of workers through the years. "I would like to feel," he said, that when he returned to the White House, to that place "surrounded by a big, black iron fence, that whatever I do, wherever I go, wherever my decisions may lead us, I will have your prayers and support."[1]

Johnson portrayed himself throughout the 1964 campaign as the peace candidate, the man who would use only the minimum force necessary to ensure national security. Americans were not faced with a choice between liberalism and conservatism, but between fringe and center. "Come let us reason together," Johnson said as he went to the electorate, sometimes quoting this passage from the Book of Isaiah several times in one speech. Then, after insisting he was not going to brag about it, the president would go on, "We have more strength than any other nation, more strength than all nations put together, and we are going to keep it."[2] At a stop in Ohio, Johnson said his daughter Luci had told him there was no point in his coming to Dayton because she had already been there, and he was going to win the state. But, the president told his audience, he came because "Wouldn't it really be better for us, wouldn't it really be better for the Soviet Union, wouldn't it be better for Great Britain, wouldn't it be better for all the people of the world who are looking to us for leadership if we carried Ohio by 400,000 instead of 300,000?"³

Civil rights leader Bayard Rustin feared it might not, that an overwhelming victory might prove to be a curse instead of a blessing. But he was very much in the minority. Nearly everyone else on the Democratic side believed that the electoral landslide so obviously in the making would provide the momentum needed to establish the Great Society program as the ruling paradigm of American politics for a long time to come. Rustin worried instead that Johnson's Great Society would be undermined by a great temptation—to expand the center until it included even the fringes. Yielding to the temptation to be the president of all the people all the time would dissipate a very real mandate for liberal action. In the guise of consensus would come political confusion. "Goldwater's capture of the Republican party forced into the Democratic camp many disparate elements which do not belong there," Rustin wrote, especially "Big Business." Not even Johnson's considerable political genius, he predicted, "will be able to hold together a coalition so inherently unstable and rife with contradictions. It must come apart."⁴

Johnson's chief concern, on the other hand, he later insisted, was to pile up a sufficient majority in the popular vote or in Congress to overcome the handicaps, as he would have it, imposed upon him by the "opinion molders" in the press and television. So great was the onus he bore as a Southerner, Johnson tells us, he considered withdrawing from the 1964 race.

> The burden of national unity rests heaviest on one man, the President. And I did not believe, any more than I ever had, that the nation would unite indefinitely behind any Southerner. One reason the country could not rally behind a Southern President, I was convinced, was that the metropolitan press of the Eastern seaboard would never permit it.⁵

Lyndon Johnson's fear and dislike of the "Eastern Establishment" were constant companions throughout his political career. He often hid these feelings with exaggerated displays of contempt for the denizens of Martha's Vineyard, that "female island" where they gathered to ridicule anyone not of their own upbringing and style. In another mood, Johnson believed that all he had to do was remove one individual from his path. He would never be president in his own right if Bobby Kennedy somehow finagled himself onto the ticket. "Bobby Kennedy thinks I'm an ignorant Texas hayseed," Johnson roared. "But I know more about what the little people of America need than he does. When did that sumbitch last miss a meal?"⁶

The Robert Kennedy / Lyndon Johnson feud was a special case, of course, but certainly a large part of its continuing intensity was its defining role in LBJ's picture of himself as national leader. When he had finally found a clever way, however transparent, to deny Robert Kennedy the vice-presidential nomination, Johnson chortled about what he had accomplished: "Now that damn albatross is off my neck."[7]

LBJ understood the paradox of political riches—that with huge majorities came huge expectations—but he railed against his fate anyway. Challenged by black leaders who asserted that the war in Vietnam drained the country of material and intellectual resources needed for the War on Poverty, Johnson protested that greed was the problem. "It isn't the war," he insisted after meeting with black leaders. "We're the wealthiest nation in the world. . . . We need to appeal to everyone to restrain their appetite, to stop running around after everything like dogs chasing their tails. We're greedy but not short of the wherewithal to meet our problems."[8]

Even during the 1964 campaign, however, there were occasions on which he leveled with himself. And when he did, he did not blame his Southern background, the media, Robert Kennedy, or greed. Speaking spontaneously and with deep feeling at the end of a long day of campaigning, the president gave his audience in Manchester, New Hampshire, a candid picture of the Vietnam dilemma, ending with a statement that caused him much trouble in later years:

> Some of our people—Mr. Nixon, Mr. Rockefeller, Mr. Scranton, and Mr. Goldwater—have all, at some time or other, suggested the possible wisdom of going North in Vietnam. Well, now before you start attacking someone and you launch a big offense, you better give some consideration to how you are going to protect what you have. . . . As far as I am concerned, I want to be very cautious and careful . . . when I start dropping bombs around that are likely to involve American boys in a war in Asia with 700 million Chinese.
>
> So just for the moment I have not thought that we were ready for American boys to do the fighting for Asian boys. What I have been trying to do, with the situation that I found, was to get the boys in Vietnam to do their own fighting with our advice and with our equipment.[9]

There are several things to say about the Manchester speech. First, although the press focused on the statement about not sending American boys to Vietnam to do the actual fighting, the president's remarks did not indicate an intention to withdraw from the American "commitment" to Saigon. Second, the speech offered a good indication of the debate going on within the administration over the question of a bombing campaign, and of Johnson's hesitance to commit himself to expanding the war in any direction.

AT ONE POINT IN THE CAMPAIGN, both Henry Ford II and UAW leader Walter Reuther appeared with the president at an airport rally, one on each side hoisting an arm. "Did you see that?" Johnson declaimed. "I never had it so good."[10] In his memoirs, however, Johnson looked back on that summer and argued that he had been filled with a sense of foreboding about the "dark days of trial ahead." Only a few days after the signing of the 1964 Civil Rights Act, he wrote, "Negro rioters went on a rampage in Harlem and Brooklyn." Then, in early August, U.S. navy ships "were attacked in the Gulf of Tonkin."[11]

No sooner had Johnson's new envoy to Saigon, Maxwell Taylor, arrived in Vietnam to replace Henry Cabot Lodge than he found himself having to fend off General Khanh's revived interest in a "March North." American opinions about Khanh's chances to mount such an unlikely endeavor had not changed. He had no business thinking he could pull off such a feat alone, or in trying to "blackmail" the Americans into contributing to his folly. State Department officials let it be known to the press that they were exceedingly unhappy with Premier Khanh for his insistence that expanding the war was now official policy.[12]

They were even more unhappy, however, with having to fend off France's Charles de Gaulle, who chose this moment to renew his call for a great-power conference on Indochina. De Gaulle's "press conference" of July 23, 1964, covered many topics, not just Southeast Asia. The division of the world into two camps led by Washington and Moscow, he began, no longer suited actual conditions. "The Europe that must be built must be a European Europe." It must have an independent voice and policy. At the head of such a Europe, of course, would be an atomic-armed France. Some Frenchmen disagreed, he admitted, with this vision. On the one side were the Communists. On the other were "the partisans of the American protectorate," who feared "the prospect of a France which would be its own master."[13]

Indochina, it became obvious as he went on, was one of the places where Europe should have its own voice and policy. De Gaulle's review of what had happened since the 1954 Geneva Conference flowed from this general premise. When the French left that country, the Americans came in.

> They had a conviction that they were following a sort of vocation, and also that they felt an aversion toward any colonial performance which was not their own, and last, the desire—very natural in such a mighty people—to install themselves in new positions led them to occupy France's place in Indochina.[14]

President Diem had tried to extricate himself from American control, he went on, and was replaced after a military putsch. Another putsch followed, one closely connected to military actions supported by the United States. Guerrilla warfare now extended over more Vietnamese territory than ever before, and the population felt less inclined than ever to support an authority—whatever their opinions about communism—that seemed to them indistinguishable from a foreign state. Under such conditions there could be no military solution. It was true that some people thought a military solution "could be reached by the Americans elsewhere by carrying the war as far north as necessary—and certainly they have all the means for doing so." But that would only lead to a generalized conflict. "So, since war cannot get things done, the only alternative is to make peace." All those who had been or were now militarily involved would have to sit down at a peace conference. They must resolve together to remove all military forces and aid, and, once peace was achieved, to agree to supply massive economic and technical assistance to Indochina as a whole. France was ready to observe both of these conditions. What of the others?[15]

De Gaulle's press conference was a closely observed affair, if for no other reason than it represented a direct challenge to American leadership of the Free World. One could also anticipate that the French leader would not stop with calls for an Indochina peace conference: he was committed to a vision that excluded Americans from the final say about Europe's future. While Europe-firsters in the administration worried about taking up de Gaulle's challenge over Indochina, the general had left them no alternative, at least for the time being.

CIA director John McCone advised Johnson that de Gaulle's recital of the ten years since the Geneva Conference was "reasonably accurate," but his interpretation of those events was "often unjustified."[16] Anyway, Americans should avoid doing battle over past history; more relevant was France's seeming determination to make Vietnam a testing ground for American leadership of the Western alliance. Russia and China apparently wished to make Vietnam a testing ground for wars of national liberation; France posed a separate issue, which, in the long run, might be the greater danger. To accept de Gaulle's call for a new "Geneva Conference" would be to defer to Paris, over and above the fate of South Vietnam.

"We do not believe in a conference called to ratify terror," President Johnson declared. But he was in a predicament. The United States was supposed to be fighting Hanoi and Moscow/Beijing; instead it appeared to be struggling with Saigon and Paris. Johnson advised Ambassador Taylor that he had decided to increase American forces in Vietnam to 21,000. Beyond that, Khanh was to be told that talks could begin about what "might" be done against North Vietnam, so long as it was made clear that no decisions had been made "to carry out such plans." Khanh needed visible support from Washington, Johnson had been told, if he was to hold dissident generals in line. Truth was, Americans did not believe South Vietnam could survive either another Geneva Conference or a "March North."[17]

Maybe there was a solution, however, both to Khanh's worry and Lyndon Johnson's problem with Charles de Gaulle. Viewed this way, the events of August 1964 in the Gulf of Tonkin and in Congress cannot be explained simply by domestic politics and the desire to strip Barry Goldwater of all but the lunatic fringe. Ambassador Taylor met with Khanh on July 27, 1964, to ask him to elaborate on his reported dissatisfactions with American policy. Was he really as unhappy as had been reported? Taylor asked. His people were suffering from war-weariness, Khanh answered. There had to be some way to bring pressure on the north, some way to bring hostilities to an end. But it "came out clearly," Taylor reported, that General Khanh had no desire to send a large ground force against the north or engage in massive bombing. What he wanted, rather, was "reprisal tit-for-tat bombing" to encourage his people and convince Ho Chi Minh to stop supporting the Viet Cong.[18]

Near midnight, a week later, on August 4, 1964, President Johnson appeared on television to inform the nation that renewed hostile actions against United States ships "on the high seas in the Gulf of Tonkin" had required him "to order the military forces of the United States to take action in reply." Two attacks had taken place, one on August 2 against the destroyer *Maddox* by North Vietnamese torpedo boats and a second two nights later against the *Maddox* and its companion ship, the *Turner Joy*, "by a number of hostile vessels attacking . . . with torpedoes." Such repeated attacks must be met with a positive reply. American warplanes were on the way to attack torpedo boat bases and related facilities—the first direct attack on North Vietnam by U.S. forces. "Firmness in the right is indispensable today for peace. That firmness will always be measured. Its mission is peace."[19]

Three days later, after a brief hearing before the relevant committees and a short debate on the floors of the Senate and House, Congress passed the "Gulf of Tonkin Resolution," approving "the determination of the president to take all necessary measures to repel any armed attack against the forces of the United States and to prevent further aggression." Another section, worded somewhat differently, stated that the *United States* was "prepared, as the President determines, to take all necessary steps, including the use of armed force, to assist any member or protocol state of the Southeast Asia Collective Defense Treaty requesting assistance in defense of its freedom."[20]

Despite later complaints that Johnson had hoodwinked Congress into surrendering its constitutional prerogatives, the president had not yet gone beyond "crisis management" (Cuban-missile-crisis style) thinking about Vietnam. Drafts of a proposed congressional resolution had been floating around since early in the year, and the option for a large-scale bombing campaign was on the table. But at this stage the civilian leadership of the administration was still looking for a proper way to signal Hanoi—and Paris.

Some hours before Johnson went on television, Dean Rusk explained to congressional leaders, "For months and months we have been trying to get to them a signal." Rusk spoke in tones of restraint and diplomacy, but his approach was the modern equivalent of a whiff of grapeshot to send the wogs a message they would understand. While the military never thought whiffs would do it—you would have to rub their noses in it—they shared the common view of the Vietnamese as an especially primitive variation of Communist irrationality. "Asiatics," the *Maddox* commander John J. Herrick shook his head when asked why he thought the attacks had happened, "Asiatics. They don't think of the consequences the way we do. We've been softened in some ways." And when NBC asked Rusk what he thought, he replied, "I haven't been able, quite frankly, to come to a fully satisfactory explanation. There is a great gulf of understanding between that world and our world, ideological in character. They see what we think of as the real world in wholly different terms. Their very processes of logic are different." [21]

Now, perhaps, de Gaulle would cease his carping, now that it was understood that you don't invite such people to peace conferences except to impose terms; now, also, perhaps those who had been listening to de Gaulle in other countries, including the Walter Lippmanns and their ilk in this country, would take notice of what the real stakes were—and they were not confined to Vietnam.

Secretary McNamara and Mac Bundy worried, meanwhile, about what Congress might do when news of the second attack on the *Turner Joy* reached Capitol Hill. The legislators must be carefully handled lest the reports set off an "orgasm of outrage . . . and some of the right-wing hawk Republicans might take such action that would be in effect a declaration of war or would put the administration in a position where we had to do things which we thought would be very unwise, that might involve bringing the Chinese in or offending somebody else." [22]

Indeed, McNamara reportedly told his colleagues after the attack on the *Maddox* that it might be a good idea to leak the information that there had been an Op Plan 34-A attack by the South Vietnamese on islands near North Vietnam. While the *Maddox* was not involved in that attack, the other side might have thought they were related, and retaliated. That might defuse congressional passions. [23] The secretary of defense did the leaking himself at a congressional leadership briefing on August 3, between the first and second attacks. And Senator Richard Russell duly repeated the story to waiting reporters. But the next day a State Department representative told the press it was unlikely the North Vietnamese could have made such a mistake.[24]

Appearing before the Senate Foreign Relations Committee, McNamara fell in behind the State Department line: "Our Navy played absolutely no part in, was not associated with, was not aware of, any South Vietnamese actions, if there were any. I want to make that very clear to you. The *Maddox* was operating in international waters, was carrying out a routine patrol of the type we carry out all over the world at all times. . . . I say this flatly; this is the fact." The admission that South Vietnamese attacks had indeed taken place was not made public for several years. Even the general testimony McNamara and Rusk gave that day was to remain unpublished for two years.[25]

McNamara's original notion to hint at North Vietnamese confusion had been cast aside. Instead his testimony made it sound as if the *Maddox* could just as well have been sailing in the Gulf of Mexico when it was attacked, carrying out one of those "routine" patrols he spoke about. Much of what he said that day was, to put the kindest interpretation on it, a misrepresentation of the facts. The *Maddox* was not just engaged in a routine patrol but was taking part in a series of specially named "De Soto" patrols, "aggressive" intelligence-gathering missions to discover the location of shoreline radar defenses and, by so doing, shake up their owners. Indeed, Dean Rusk appeared delighted with the results. "We believe that present OPLAN 34A activities are beginning to rattle Hanoi," he cabled Ambassador Taylor the day after the first attack, "and *Maddox* incident is directly related to their effort to resist these activities. We have no intention yielding to pressure."[26]

These "activities" Rusk spoke about went beyond intelligence missions and included raids by South Vietnamese PT boats on islands near the coast of North Vietnam. They were pinprick attacks, but in conjunction with the De Soto patrols they were aimed at demonstrating that an American shield had been placed around South Vietnam. Not surprisingly, Admiral Thomas Moorer rejected Commander Herrick's request that the *Maddox* break off its mission to get out of harm's way. To terminate the patrols so soon after the incident, said Moorer, did not "adequately demonstrate United States resolve to assert our legitimate rights in these international waters." The Pacific Fleet commander did order Herrick to move away from the area where the 34-A activities were going on—another South Vietnamese attack occurred on the night of August 3—and sent the *Turner Joy* to join the *Maddox* for the rest of its mission.[27]

Whether the attack on the *Turner Joy* ever actually took place became a matter of controversy almost immediately, long before Vietnam War critics or historians raised the question. Commander Herrick first reported that the *Maddox* and the *Turner Joy* had come under assault in heavy seas by

North Vietnamese PT boats firing torpedoes and automatic weapons, and were returning fire. A few hours later he sent an urgent "flash message" to CINCPAC (Commander in Chief, Pacific Fleet) that the sightings were doubtful. "Freak weather effects on radar and overeager sonarmen may have accounted for many reports. No actual visual sightings by Maddox. Suggest complete evaluation before any further action taken." Herrick never retracted his original contention that the North Vietnamese had set up an "ambush," only that he could not confirm the torpedoes. In one report he suggested that what the sonarmen had tracked on their screens might instead have been the PT boats as they feinted close to the American warships.[28]

Commander Herrick's musings were not welcome in Washington, where near-frantic preparations were under way for a retaliatory strike against the PT boat bases. Secretary McNamara, meanwhile, continued his efforts to confirm a definite attack with real torpedoes streaming toward American warships, but his results proved less than definitive. The commander in chief in the Pacific, Admiral Ulysses Grant Sharp, would not yet commit himself. "How do we reconcile all this?" McNamara pleaded. Wait for a definite indication it took place, replied the admiral.[29]

It never came. At CINCPAC, Sharp's headquarters in Honolulu, efforts were made to correlate all the reports from the scene with other intelligence information. Sharp's memoirs describe only vaguely what happened as McNamara waited impatiently in the Pentagon to give the word to President Johnson.

> After a few hours, Admiral Moorer and I decided that there was enough information available to indicate that an attack had, in fact, occurred. Accordingly, I called McNamara and informed him of our evaluation, indicating that, while reports from the ships were not conclusive by themselves, the weight of evidence (including some radio intercept intelligence) supported our conclusion.[30]

Sharp talks about the "weight of evidence," and, almost casually, includes a parenthesis about some "radio intercept intelligence." But for McNamara the intercepts were everything. He seized hold of the precious sheets stamped TOP SECRET on August 4, 1964, and never let go afterward.[31]

Only a few days after the attack, a CIA analyst took a careful look at the intercepts and concluded that North Vietnamese radio communications cited by McNamara as proof of the second attack were actually messages about the *first* attack. Even a casual examination told him the timing was all wrong. When he reported the discrepancies to the president's Foreign Intelligence Advisory Board, Ray Cline warned them not to push the second attack too far. It was "probably just a technicality," Cline explained, but anyway they could justify American policy on the basis of the first attack. "I never heard any more about it from them," Cline told an interviewer. "I don't know whether they reported it to the President. I doubt it."[32]

Probably they didn't. But Johnson seemed almost blithely unconcerned about whether sailors on the *Maddox* and the *Turner Joy* were shooting at torpedoes or sharks. When he first met with congressional leaders to "counsel with you" about the proper response, on August 4, the president cautioned them against leaks. "Some of our boys are floating around in the water. The facts we would like to present to you are to be held in the closest confidence and are to be kept in this room until announced."[33]

Having set such a tone for their "counseling" session, Johnson and his two briefers, Rusk and McNamara, spent much of the discussion damping down enthusiasm for a stronger response. Despite the exaggerations, then, despite the misrepresentations, despite even the untruth about "our boys . . . floating around in the water," despite all these, Congress was not really bamboozled by Lyndon Johnson. He led them where they wanted to go. Presidential initiatives in the cold war had always had the blessings of Congress. McNamara would not have forwarded "evidence" of the attack had he thought this was anything more than another crisis management situation; Johnson would not have gone ahead had he thought otherwise. But this time policymakers were storing up terrible troubles for the future.

Only Senate Majority Leader Mike Mansfield dissented from the "count me in" response voiced by Republican Charles Halleck when Johnson went around the room counting noses. Halleck's senatorial counterpart, Everett Dirksen (who had been instrumental in passing the Civil Rights Bill), sounded off exactly the way Johnson wanted: "If I had it to do I would put our references to the word 'limited' in deep freeze." Virtually every statement by the legislative leaders boosted Johnson's hopes that he would have the votes to spare to demonstrate American unity before all. His old mentor, J. William Fulbright, later his strongest congressional critic, wanted to know if American bombers would hit Haiphong harbor near Hanoi. McNamara appeared shocked: "No, we will not destroy any in the Haiphong area." This was not war, it was crisis management, and they were all being tutored in its finer points.[34]

The final word was pronounced by Vermont's George Aiken. By the time the White House sent a resolution to Capitol Hill, he quipped, "there won't be anything for us to do but support you."[35] Steered through by a reassuring Fulbright in the Senate, the Gulf of Tonkin Resolution passed with but two negative votes. In the House the vote was unanimous. Johnson had sent his signals. He had outflanked Goldwater on both the left and the right. And it is not hard to imagine the president's delight at the didactic cable drafted for his signature to de Gaulle. "As I am sure that you will agree," it read, these attacks could not go unanswered. The response we are making is, however, limited and fitting. I hope that it will make clear to the North Vietnamese regime the dangerous character of the course they are following in Southeast Asia.[36]

The French president's answer was expectedly standoffish: "I have . . . taken careful note of the considerations which guided your decisions, and I thank you for having informed me so promptly about them." "Old De Gaulle is pretty reserved, isn't he?" Johnson chortled. "Didn't make any commitment."[37] The president had all the commitments he needed, including, apparently, private indications that the Chinese would not go beyond supplying material resources to North Vietnam short of an American invasion threatening their borders.[38]

Smiling, Johnson leaned over as if to confide something important to a reporter the day after the American raids. "I didn't just screw Ho Chi Minh, I cut his pecker off."[39] Perhaps McNamara fretted about the president's performance at the congressional leaders' meeting—fretted especially about "our boys . . . floating around in the water"—for he knew the intelligence reports would not bear that load on top of all the rest; but the president waved all that aside. "Hell," he told George Ball, "those dumb, stupid sailors were just shooting at flying fish!" He couldn't trust the military, Johnson repeated to Carl Rowan. "The only ones who make my belly rumble more with doubt is the intelligence bunch. You don't know what they know for sure, or what they are pulling out of the fog and handing to you."[40]

But Johnson had no qualms about using the FBI to provide him with intelligence about potential disruptions at the Democrats' Atlantic City convention. Although the celebration was marred by a dispute over the seating of the Mississippi Freedom Democratic Party's delegation, it seemed but a small cloud that passed over the convention hall. Bayard Rustin, in fact, played a key role in the compromise that pushed the MFDP to the sidelines.[41] Serious riots in Harlem caused Johnson some anxiety at convention time, but he had reason to feel almost as good about chances for taking control of the civil rights struggle as he felt about his handling of the Gulf of Tonkin. "Those Negroes go off the ground," he said during the campaign. "They cling to my hands like I was Jesus Christ walking in their midst."[42]

Still, there were hints of a dangerous crossover attitude, as when the funeral of murdered civil rights workers in Mississippi took place on the same day as the retaliatory raids on North Vietnam, and trainees at a voter registration center asked federal officials, "How is it that the government can protect the Vietnamese from the Vietcong, and the same government will not accept the moral responsibility of protecting the people in Mississippi?" Other storm signals were visible that day in Chicago. Representative Dan Rostenkowski told Jack Valenti that polls showed 78 percent of his constituents in a heavily Polish district opposed the Civil Rights Bill because of black demonstrations. "They are mostly Catholic but in spite of the Church's emphatic stand on civil rights, they are very much opposed to the Negro advances. The Polish people are real estate conscious and worry about the value of their homes." But these flash-forwards did not yet divert attention from Lyndon Johnson's vision of a Great Society.[43]

His was a unique opportunity, Barbara Ward assured him as the presidential campaign began:

> Yours is the first Presidency to be able to make use of America's astounding abundance. Roosevelt had the ambition to build a great society. But he lacked the means. Kennedy would no doubt have conquered business distrust and Congressional obstruction. But you have from the start the physical resources, the confidence of the business community, and the magic hand with Congress! No other Presidency has ever been launched under such exhilarating conditions.[44]

He was the master of his fate, the captain of his soul. Unfortunately, the same could not be said for Nguyen Khanh's bid to control his situation in South Vietnam. On August 14 Khanh told Ambassador Taylor of his plan to proclaim a new charter for South Vietnam. Taylor thought it might cause trouble, but Khanh was determined and so the ambassador cabled, "We see no alternative but to make the best of it."[45] But when Buddhist and student protesters denounced the proposed constitution as a return to Diem's methods, General Khanh caved in and retreated to the resort city of Dalat, where he did nothing but receive medical treatment and sit in the sun. "He seems oblivious to the need to get his government going again," complained Taylor. Where this was all leading disturbed the ambassador, for he foresaw an unhappy sequence, a faltering of will in Saigon, the creation of a "popular front" government, then demands for negotiations with the Viet Cong.

> This amalgam, if it takes form, may be expected in due course to become susceptible to an accommodation with the Liberation Front, which might eventually lead to the collapse of all political energy behind the pacification effort. . . .
> We may, therefore, expect to find ourselves faced with a choice of (a) passively watching the development of a popular front, knowing that this may in due course require the U.S. to leave Vietnam in failure; or (b) actively assuming increased responsibility for the outcome following a time-schedule consistent with our estimate of the limited viability of any South Vietnamese government.[46]

Henry Cabot Lodge had predicted that his successor would have to assume the responsibilities of "high commissioner" if the situation was to be saved; now Mac Bundy had to brief Johnson about this unfolding situation when the president returned to Washington from Texas after celebrating his fifty-sixth birthday. "We just do not know whether Khanh still has it in him to resume full control," said the national security adviser. There were several things to think about, several military steps to take that might improve morale in the south, but these were more to "show our strength of purpose than to accomplish anything very specific in a military sense. . . ."

> A still more drastic possibility which no one is discussing is the use of substantial U.S. armed forces in operations against the Viet Cong. I myself believe that before we let this country go we should have a hard look at this grim alternative, and I do not at all think that it is a repetition of Korea. It seems to me at least possible that a couple of brigade-size units put in to do specific jobs about six weeks from now might be good medicine everywhere.[47]

Everywhere? Sending American troops into Southeast Asian jungles two weeks before the election certainly would not be good medicine at home. Having made his point in the Gulf of Tonkin, Johnson did not feel the need to show more muscle. And he was more than a little uneasy with the notion of trying to save a bad situation in the south by provoking the north to knock more chips off Admiral Sharp's shoulders. The Joint Chiefs split on what action should be taken, but those who favored an extensive air campaign against North Vietnam had to be content with the president's agreement that any new attacks on American units would be met tit-for-tat.[48]

The answer to those who wanted immediate and extensive action, the president told his advisers, was that we could not do this until "our side could defend itself in the streets of Saigon." De Soto patrols and 34-A operations could begin again after the short hiatus he had imposed on such activities following the Gulf of Tonkin events, along with some ground operations on the Laotian border, but that was all. But while that was the consensus among his close advisers, as well as Ambassador Taylor's view, there was no sentiment at all for calling it quits. At the end of a long discussion during which Johnson posed that possibility in different ways several times, the president turned to General Wheeler and asked him to "explain to his colleagues in the JCS that we would be ready to do more, when we had a base."

> The President did not wish to enter the patient in a 10-round bout, when he was in no shape to hold out for one round. We should get him ready to face 3 or 4 rounds at least.[49]

Johnson's doubts about the next escalation, his somewhat uncertain response to the question of where matters rested, and his fears about the situation in Saigon all attest to LBJ's concern that he had been bamboozled by the Vietnam "hawks" instead of the other way around. Circling the skies over Washington, carrying position papers back and forth from the White House to the Pentagon, from the Pentagon to State, the hawks were a different breed of bird than Johnson had encountered in the Senate. Put alongside his public campaign statements, Johnson's private statements at NSC meetings and elsewhere begin to display a certain wariness. The argument has been made that John Kennedy was only awaiting the 1964 election to begin implementing a withdrawal plan, and that Lyndon Johnson sabotaged that plan even while he was still vice-president. But it was Kennedy's advisers who now pushed the president toward deeper commitment, starting with Mac Bundy's two brigades.[50]

As Johnson considered his Vietnam policy options, he received recommendations that campaign speeches should stress the peace theme. He should treat Goldwater with ridicule, particularly on foreign policy issues. "We must make him ridiculous and a little scary," said Bill Moyers, "trigger-happy, a bomb thrower, a radical...."[51] From the State Department's policy planning council, however, came a strong dissent against "permitting the guarantee of peace to become too equivocal." The president's speeches, and the way prominent opinion-molders were treating them, warned Walt Rostow, could create an atmosphere which hindered taking the necessary steps "in a future tough situation." If the president did have to act with force soon after the election, "this could reopen charges of alleged Democratic campaigning deceit, against the background of 1916 and 1940."[52]

Johnson was well aware of such historical precedents. Admiral Sharp had geared up for a decisive showdown in the Gulf of Tonkin, going well beyond the September 9 decisions to resume the De Soto patrols. The admiral ordered aircraft cover for all patrols and directed that the planes illuminate any vessels that approached within five nautical miles of the destroyers. He also ordered a submarine stationed in the gulf. Sharp's forces were prepared to win any naval battles, above, on, or below the surface—and even, Johnson soon suspected, fantasy encounters.[53]

Just five days after the De Soto patrols resumed, American destroyers fired at several boats presumed to be attacking North Vietnamese torpedo boats. The president was unhappy with Pentagon leaks to the press about the supposed encounter, which he saw as an effort to force him into making a public statement. At a series of meetings to discuss the official reaction to the reported attack, Johnson found both McNamara and Rusk surprisingly eager to seize upon this new affront to hit back at targets in North Vietnam. This despite the recent agreement that resuming the patrols should not be considered as a prelude to a major campaign against Hanoi, at least not until the situation in the south was more clearly defined. Reminding his advisers of the agreement, Johnson declared that he "was not interested in rapid escalation on so frail evidence and with a very fragile government in South Vietnam."[54]

Where he had accepted all the "evidence" about the early August events (though later joking about dumb sailors shooting at flying fish), the president now challenged every piece, even the "clincher" intercepts that had played a key role in the original presentations. Disturbed by the apparent drift in the president's thinking, Dean Rusk said that he put the probability of hostile vessels in the area at 99 percent. The secretary of state also argued that it was important not to seem to doubt "our naval officers on the spot." They were convinced, he said, that they had been facing the enemy. Expressions of doubt in Washington "would be damaging." But Johnson replied "somewhat sharply" that he would not make a radio broadcast, conceding only that it was important to continue trying to find out exactly what had happened.[55]

Arguments that Johnson's chief advisers attempted to anticipate what the president wanted to hear obviously do not explain this exchange, or Secretary McNamara's persistence in suggesting that further De Soto patrols be carried out "to show the flag and prove to Hanoi and the world that we were not intimidated." Johnson seemed about to agree with that more moderate response, but Under Secretary of State George Ball spoke up: "Suppose one of those destroyers is sunk with several hundred men aboard. Inevitably, there'll be a Congressional investigation. What would your defense be?" Everyone knew, Ball went on, that those patrols had no intelligence mission that could not be accomplished by planes or small boats at far less risk. "The evidence will strongly suggest that you sent those ships up the Gulf only to provoke attack so we could retaliate." When Ball finished, no one spoke for a long moment. The president broke the silence. "We won't go ahead with it, Bob. Let's put it on the shelf."[56]

But Johnson still wanted to find out what General Wheeler thought of Ball's argument. What was the military value of the De Soto patrols? Wheeler hedged. Well, no, the patrols were not essential, and, yes, aerial surveillance could do most of the job. But something more important was at stake: "We should not allow ourselves to be denied free movement on the high seas." Indeed not, Rusk eagerly jumped in, anxious to return discussion of Vietnam to first essentials, which were, in his mind, to demonstrate to the "bandits" in Hanoi that "we were in the area and had no intention of being driven out." These arguments had force, Johnson agreed, but they did not fully respond to the thought Ball had planted in his mind. Some time in the future, he said, "a brutal prosecutor like Tom Dewey might be asking how we got into these troubles, and he wanted to be sure the answers would be good." He reminded them all of the Pearl Harbor hearings and the ugly suggestions that the Roosevelt administration had been unpre-

pared with its top military out horseback riding or playing tennis when critical decisions had to be made. Johnson did not mention, however, the
charges that FDR had connived to provoke a Japanese attack on the American fleet, though it is impossible not to believe it was very much on his
mind.[57]

The meeting concluded with the president issuing instructions to
McNamara to prepare a brief for additional De Soto patrols, and to Ball to
prepare a list of arguments against resumption. In the event, Johnson did
not order the patrols resumed until five months later. And it was after these
meetings that Johnson made his strongest "antiwar" statements of the political campaign, as if he were carrying the debate with his advisers into the
public arena, not simply challenging Barry Goldwater. In Oklahoma on
September 25 Johnson explained that he would not listen to those who
urged either escalation or withdrawal:

> There are those that say you ought to go north and drop bombs, to try to
> wipe out the supply lines, and they think that would escalate the war. We
> don't want our boys to do the fighting for Asian boys. We don't want to
> get involved in a nation with 700 million people and get tied down in a
> land war in Asia.
>
> There are some that say we ought to go south and get out and come
> home, but we don't like to break our treaties and we don't like to walk off
> and leave people who are searching for freedom and suffering to obtain
> it, and walk out on them. . . .
>
> We are not about to start another war and we're not about to run
> away from where we are.[58]

In New Hampshire three days later, Johnson referred to the shaky
government in Saigon: "When a brigadier general can walk down the
streets of Saigon the other day, and take over the police station, the radio
station, and the government without firing a shot, I don't know how much
offensive we are prepared to launch."

> As far as I am concerned, I want to be very cautious and careful, and use
> it [airpower] only as a last resort, when I start dropping bombs around
> that are likely to involve American boys in a war in Asia with 700 million
> Chinese.[59]

Other considerations weighed on Johnson in late September as he
made these cautious statements about the Vietnam situation he now confronted. The biggest imponderable was China. A large part of the justification for not "going south" and "running out" was concern about
Communist China's supposed bid for hegemony over Southeast Asia. Yet
the determination to send Hanoi a signal by retaliating for the "attacks" on
the destroyers, and lining up congressional approval by means of the Gulf
of Tonkin Resolution, also carried with it an obligation to signal Beijing

that the United States had no wish to renew the land war in Korea or in any other location. In the midst of the Gulf of Tonkin crisis, UN Secretary General U Thant conferred with Johnson and Mac Bundy. The gist of Thant's remarks was that the Chinese Communists had informed his country, Burma, even as they assumed power in Beijing, that they would not aid Burmese Communists as long as Rangoon prohibited "Western bases." If Burma went the other way, they had warned, and accepted "foreign installations," the Chinese would have to "destroy" them.[60]

Thant hoped to encourage direct talks between Hanoi and Washington, using the Burmese example as evidence that there was no Moscow/Beijing/Hanoi "conspiracy" to spread communism across Asia. What Johnson took away, however, was something different: a reason for reassuring Beijing that American actions were limited to holding the line in South Vietnam. This need became still greater in the wake of China's first test of an atomic bomb a month later, just as Admiral Sharp's battle-ready destroyers and airplanes cruised around the Gulf of Tonkin looking for, and finding, something to shoot at. China's atomic test was the subject of two White House meetings on September 15, 1964. It was decided that there would be no "unprovoked unilateral U.S. military action against Chinese nuclear installations at this time." But if military hostilities with China occurred, action would have to be considered, possibly in cooperation with the Soviet Union. And a decision was taken "to explore this matter very privately with Ambassador Dobrynin as soon as possible."[61]

What went on in Johnson's mind as he listened to this discussion and heard arguments about hostile military action in the Gulf of Tonkin? Did he wonder if he might have secured too much freedom of action with the congressional resolution, not for himself, but for his advisers to push arguments for expanding the war? What had originated as a way to force de Gaulle to back off, to caution Hanoi, to one-up Goldwater, had already grown into something much bigger—and obviously not better.

U Thant's discussions in Washington on August 6 had included a separate meeting with Dean Rusk and UN Ambassador Adlai Stevenson. That talk had been concerned more specifically with the possibility of direct negotiations between the United States and North Vietnam to bring about a cease-fire. Thant apparently left the capital with the impression he had been given a green light to try to arrange such an exchange. On September 23 the secretary general told Ambassador Stevenson that he now had a favorable reply from Hanoi. Three weeks later Stevenson told Thant that Johnson was too preoccupied with the election, and that it would be best to shelve the initiative for the time being.[62]

Thus began a game of diplomatic blindman's bluff that produced recriminations and acrimony, but no negotiations. It remains unclear whether Johnson ever heard about Thant's response from Hanoi, or whether he gave instructions to say he had not heard about it. It is also not clear whether Stevenson's response to Thant, in turn, was based upon anything other than a vague hope that after the election Washington would look more favorably on the idea. In any event, the Thant initiative was as unacceptable to Johnson as going north with a bombing campaign. It was generally agreed that Saigon could not survive if word got out that the United States had even entertained a proposal to talk with Hanoi.[63]

Dean Rusk seemed put out with U Thant's efforts to inject himself into the dispute as a would-be peacemaker. "Who does he think he is?" Rusk would ask. "Does he think he's a country?" U Thant reciprocated in kind. Exactly what government, he asked Stevenson, did the United States think it was protecting by refusing talks—Minh, Khanh, or the string of would-be saviors who kept popping up in Saigon?[64]

American policymakers had a point, certainly, that Thant's initiative sent Hanoi a mixed signal at a time when Johnson and his advisers clearly hoped their diplomatic and military warnings would give the North Vietnamese pause. Did Hanoi believe, for example, that despite all the drum rolls and bugles Washington was sounding, the secretary general's probes indicated a faltering will to carry on in support of an obviously disorganized regime? Rusk later suggested that the tenor of Johnson's statements during the campaign might have influenced the north to believe it could make a wider war without encountering an American response. At this stage, moreover, the North Vietnamese did have more concrete plans than Washington for "escalation" in the event of failed negotiations.[65]

The middle ground, so seemingly solid once the Gulf of Tonkin Resolution had passed, now seemed hardly more so than the Okefenokee swamp in Georgia. Trembling ground, the Indians called Okefenokee, and LBJ was finding out what that meant. Between his advisers and U Thant was a treacherous space of deceptively solid-looking terrain. George Ball, meanwhile, had taken the president's instructions to prepare arguments against resuming the De Soto patrols as an opportunity to develop a full-scale critique of the dangerous drift toward disaster. Ball worked on the paper at home late at night during the last two weeks of September, increasingly fearful that the Pentagon was itching for an opportunity not only to slap down Hanoi's impudent challenge to American power in Asia, but more than willing to find a reason for going after China's nuclear weapons facility.[66]

Entitled "How Valid Are the Assumptions Underlying Our Vietnam Policy," Ball's paper restated the basic argument that no matter what the United States did or how it saw its role, Vietnam was still too much like a colonial war—white men fighting a native insurgency. He reserved his strongest comments, however, for those who argued that American air power changed all the political equations. Citing a CIA finding that disputed the assumption that the South Vietnamese yearned for Americans to start bombing the north, Ball said there was "little evidence to suggest that the South Vietnamese would have their hearts lifted by watching the North suffer a sustained aerial bombardment."[67]

> It is in the nature of escalation that each move passes the option to the other side, while at the same time the party which seems to be losing will be tempted to keep raising the ante. To the extent that the response to a move can be controlled, that move is probably ineffective. If the move is effective, it may not be possible to control—or accurately anticipate— the response. Once on the tiger's back we cannot be sure of picking the place to dismount.[68]

Although Johnson had said practically the same thing himself in campaign appearances, the Ball paper drew sustained fire from Rusk and McNamara and Bundy. It caused a furor. "McNamara, in particular, was absolutely horrified," recalled Ball. "He treated it like a poisonous snake. The idea that people would put these kinds of things down on paper!" The paper did not reach Johnson until some months later, long after it might have had its greatest impact.[69]

Probably it made no difference, for the under secretary's arguments were well-known heresies, especially the hated French comparison. Despite the rampant disorder in South Vietnam, it was argued, the inability of the Viet Cong to seize control of the government "proved" that the Communists could not win without massive aid from the north. Hence the absence of a stable government in Saigon should not be taken too seriously, and certainly not as an indication that the United States was repeating France's mistakes. China's atomic bomb suggested, furthermore, that the struggle involved critical questions about the "rules of the game" in world politics. The Russians had been taught how to behave in the Cuban missile crisis, and the Chinese must not be allowed to believe that because of temporary American difficulties in Vietnam the rules did not apply to them. Adding a point of emphasis to this last was the news from Moscow in mid-October of the fall of Nikita Khrushchev. How would his successors see their "obligations" to the Communist movement worldwide? If Khrushchev had been sent packing because he had neglected Soviet interests in East Asia and allowed China's bolder line to win Beijing friends and influence, that might portend unwelcome changes. Even a period of uncertainty might move the Chinese comrades to demonstrate their more energetic support for local parties, with all sorts of troublemaking for Western interests.

Such imponderables weighed heavily in the calculations of the man assigned to answer the theses Ball had tacked on the doors of the National Security Council. "With Khrushchev," recalled William Bundy, "many Americans had come to have a real feeling for his attitudes: crude as he might be, you knew where you stood, and much about his underlying views.... Khrushchev had come to symbolize extreme Sino-Soviet friction ... and ... a general reduction in Soviet interest and influence in Southeast Asia. Had these positions been major causes of his removal?" Throughout the whole period 1961–1965, America's China watchers had eyed Beijing's return to the world scene behind dark-tinted glasses.[70]

When Ambassador Anatoly Dobrynin came to the White House on October 16 to inform the president of the changes in the Soviet Union, Johnson launched into a lengthy disquisition on peace, including a fascinating glance back at the Cuban missile crisis as if alluding to events many years ago, and as if the two stood together looking at a monument to the moment the world stood on the brink of nuclear war. "It was an embarrassing business for both sides," Johnson began his recital, "for us because of the presence of these missiles so near to us, and for the Soviets because they were obliged to remove them."

> The point, however, was that in this situation we had been a little flexible and, for that matter, so had the Soviets. The President did not question that the Soviets wanted peace as we did, but we both had problems. The Soviets would have to bend a little bit and so would we. . . .
>
> When our destroyer had been shot at in the Gulf of Tonkin, we had responded, but had done so responsibly. We could not allow ourselves to be shot at on the high seas. The President said a good many people wanted him to go north in Viet-Nam and he mentioned Nixon, Rockefeller, and other Republican leaders and said there were some in his own Party. What the President wanted in Viet-Nam, however, was for the people there to be left in peace. We wanted to get out but he would not turn these people over to someone attempting to dominate them by force. The independence of this area was our aim and he thought this was what we had agreed to. He said he thought the Soviets had even greater problems than we with the trouble-makers in this area.[71]

Johnson's constant reiteration of his desire neither to go charging into the north nor run away to the south became a general claim that his leadership stood between a world of order and justice, and chaos. Such a claim, of course, was the theme of the Democratic campaign that year, while Barry Goldwater provided a perfect foil with his casual remarks about lobbing missiles into the Kremlin men's room. It was a role that Johnson had essayed throughout his years as Senate majority leader, and it would have been unusual had he stopped thinking that way. This was no bad thing in itself. Certainly Johnson's leadership in the civil rights struggle was a manifestation of his belief that he was *the Southerner* who had to stand up to the heritage that had imprisoned his region in backwardness and a semicolonial status. It probably made him more prone as *the president*, however, to arguments that world events in 1964 required him to stand firm in Vietnam.

Johnson's role as the peace candidate had been defined for him by the Goldwater candidacy. One observes in the aftermath of the Gulf of Tonkin crisis in August, nevertheless, a growing reluctance to commit the nation to further escalation—or to engage in risk-taking or overly provocative actions. Even though Rusk and McNamara and Bundy all joined in one proposal or another for strong action, Johnson appeared to use public statements to limit what he was willing to agree to. What he "gained" in the Gulf of Tonkin Resolution, in other words, he "gave back" in campaign speeches. So much so, indeed, that Rusk felt the president himself was guilty of sending mixed signals to Hanoi.[72]

Khrushchev's fall and the Chinese atomic bomb may have had little real impact on the course of American policy. Other arguments could be found to refocus Johnson's attention on what had to be done in Vietnam. Certainly the NLF attack on the U.S. air base at Bien Hoa on October 31, during which five B-57s were destroyed and thirteen badly damaged, with five Americans killed and thirty more wounded, convinced the president that he needed to rethink the "crisis management" assumptions gleaned from the Cuban experience. Hanoi did not scare easily. Johnson decided not to respond in kind, now considered futile. Rusk informed Ambassador Taylor, accordingly, that in "this one case" election considerations were important reasons for delaying a response—to avoid accusations of manipulation for political gain. "I want to leave you in no doubt that highest levels feel we are reaching point where policy hardening must be acutely considered."[73]

Weeks earlier, while aloft on Air Force One, Johnson had exclaimed, "Look around the world. Khrushchev's gone. Macmillan's gone. Adenauer's gone. Segni's gone. Nehru's gone." A pause. "Who's left—de Gaulle?" When he mentioned the French leader it was with a sneer. Then, leaning back, Johnson thumped his chest. "I am the king!"[74] On November 2, 1964, Johnson wound up his campaign with an evening speech at the state capitol in Austin that struck a semireligious, Christmas Eve–like tone. "Around the world tonight," he began, "millions watch and wait. A stillness is on the earth tonight, in London and in Moscow, in Peking and in Cuba, in humble huts and in mighty palaces around the world. Yes, millions enslaved and millions free await to hear your decision tomorrow. On that decision rests our future, and largely theirs, and the future of our children, and largely theirs." It seemed to him, he said, that he had spent his whole life getting ready for this moment. On election day Johnson named William Bundy to chair an interdepartmental study group to provide him with new recommendations. The president was thinking, Bundy recalled, "in terms of the maximum use of a Gulf of Tonkin rationale. . . ."[75]

Throughout the presidential campaign Johnson had struck several different poses. His hesitations in September and October may be accounted for simply by domestic politics. But perhaps there was more. Bayard Rustin may have been right. Had Johnson's victory been a little less overwhelming, would he have pursued the same course in Vietnam?

EIGHT

Groping Toward a Decision

NEAR THE END of his Thanksgiving holiday, President Johnson held a press conference at his Texas ranch. No longer a successor, elected in his own right, LBJ felt ready to play a new role. And the ranch was the perfect place to start. He knew he could never banter with reporters like Jack Kennedy or tease them with clever evasions à la FDR. So he would try something else. Johnson constantly groused about "leaks," but in fact he needed the press in order to establish himself as the unmoved mover. He relished opportunities to make it appear the newsmen had "guessed" wrong. From the outset there was a truculent edge to these performances that only grew sharper and cut deeper as Johnson's worst fears about the Vietnam War and racial conflict became nightmarish reality.

But here, in this first postelection news conference, he displayed an appropriately benign demeanor. "I have just been sitting here in this serene atmosphere of the Pedernales for the last few days reading about the wars that you have involved us in and the additional undertakings that I have made decisions on or that General Taylor has recommended or that Mr. McNamara plans or Secretary Rusk envisages." Then the edge showed, just a bit. All this speculation was premature. "When you crawl out on a limb," the president lectured the reporters, "you always have to find another one to crawl back on." [1]

Without realizing it, perhaps, LBJ was describing his own predicament. The "working group" Johnson had assigned the task of reformulating Vietnam alternatives had spent the month of November developing options. They all looked like pretty shaky limbs. At the outset the chair, Assistant Secretary of State William Bundy, and John McNaughton, the

's chief civilian representative, thought about including an option
~~u "fallback objectives." If the South Vietnamese government sim-
~ollapsed and in some fashion made peace, they suggested, it was essential to manage the situation "so that we emerge from it, even in the worst
case, with our standing as the principal helper against Communist expansion as little impaired as possible."[2]

That "option" went undiscussed. Instead Ambassador Maxwell Taylor
took over the worst-case scenario. It made no difference, he cabled,
whether there was an effective government in Saigon. "If the government
falters and gives good reason to believe that it will never attain the desired
level of performance," Kennedy's former chief of staff declared dramatically, "I would favor going against the north anyway. The purpose of such an
attack would be to give pulmotor treatment for a government in extremis
and to make sure that the DRV [North Vietnam] does not get off unscathed
in any final settlement."[3]

A defeat sometime in the future was *possible*, Taylor allowed, but not
until all that could be done had been done. The "pulmotor treatment"
became a favorite image for policy planners. It substituted action for thinking, and it implied that the American obligation was to the Vietnamese people, whether or not they were able to decide on a government to represent
them, and whether or not they wished to continue the war. So it was not
beyond the realm of the possible, in Taylor's vision, to continue a war
against the north even after Saigon fell to the National Liberation Front.
An absurdity? Put that way, yes, but not far short of such thinking were
arguments already being made for a bombing campaign against North
Vietnam to bolster Saigon's sagging morale. Johnson, in fact, constantly
worried about something like that. All the Joint Chiefs did every morning,
he complained to a White House visitor, was come in and tell him, "Bomb,
bomb, bomb"—and come back in the afternoons and repeat, "Bomb,
bomb, bomb."[4]

Meanwhile, Taylor had been ordered home to take part in final deliberations on the working group's report. Withdrawal under any guise had
been ruled out. And with everyone agreeing that Option A—continuing at
roughly the current level of American assistance—was slow defeat, the logical remaining choices came down to rapid or gradual expansion of American intervention, and whether or not to send in combat forces to go with a
bombing campaign. The military argued strongly for Option B—heavy
bombing of North Vietnamese military bases with a possible ground invasion to follow. Civilian planners hovered uneasily around Option C—a
more moderate military escalation accompanied by hints of negotiations to
save face for Hanoi.[5]

While the president remained at his ranch in Texas for a few days after
Thanksgiving, his senior advisers met to reshape the final version of the

report. Taylor dominated these discussions. The situation in Vietnam did not permit a delay in initiating action against the north, the ambassador contended. Perhaps this would help to unify the south, perhaps not, but at the very least such measures would buy time, "possibly measured in years." The debate over Options B and C was simply bypassed in favor of new formulation that incorporated both into a two-phase program of gradually escalating bombing attacks. During Phase I, expected to last for thirty days, the United States would intensify its activities along North Vietnam's borders and launch retaliatory strikes for any "spectacular Viet Cong action in the south," thereby "foreshadowing still greater pressures to come." Phase II would see a steady increase in American bombing raids, a marching forward with air power farther and farther into North Vietnam and ever closer to Hanoi. Meanwhile, Washington would listen carefully for any signs North Vietnam was ready to yield. But Max Taylor's fateful imagery had found its way into the final list of policy recommendations. A moribund government in Saigon could not be allowed to do damage to the image or substance of the American Century. "The US would seek to control any negotiations," read the report, "and would oppose any independent South Vietnamese efforts to negotiate."[6]

Billy Bundy was an easy convert to the Taylor view. Much later he wrote that such attitudes could be "caricatured as simple Occidental 'face' "—but early in January 1965 he had come to the conclusion that the great danger in the immediate future was that "key groups" in South Vietnam might start negotiating with the NLF or Hanoi behind American backs:

> The situation in Vietnam is now likely to come apart more rapidly than we had anticipated in November . . . the most likely form of coming apart would be a government of key groups starting to negotiate covertly with the Liberation Front or Hanoi, perhaps not asking in the first instance that we get out, but with that necessarily following at a fairly early stage. In one sense, this would be a "Vietnam solution," with some hope that it would produce a Communist Vietnam that would assert its own degree of independence from Peiping and that would produce a pause in Communist pressure in Southeast Asia. . . .[But] the outcome would be regarded in Asia, and particularly among our friends, as just as humiliating a defeat as any other. . . .[7]

Johnson had returned to Washington in early December. It was expected he would set in motion the policy of graduated escalation. Instead the president let his advisers know he was unhappy about almost everything. Above all, he declared at the outset, he was not going to send Johnson City boys out to die if the South Vietnamese kept on acting the way they were. All through the "discussion" he jabbed at the planners' conclusions, poking holes in their assumptions. Where were all the other nations that were supposed to be America's allies in these things? They had to do more than send chaplains and nurses. And why was it the South Vietnamese army of 200,000 could not whip 34,000 guerrillas? A day of reckoning was coming, he warned. It could start with a DRV strike at Saigon. When it did, they would be off to the races, and he did not want to have to send a "widow woman to slap Jack Dempsey." If it came because the United States hit Hanoi first, were we really ready? "When I send a man to sock another man—I've got to be ready for them to strike back." Aroused by Johnson's challenge, Ambassador Taylor responded that he did not think the DRV would be very eager to strike back. Johnson had been waiting for that answer: "Didn't MacArthur say the same?" [8]

Before Phase I could begin, Johnson lectured his advisers, Ambassador Taylor was to put some home truths to the South Vietnamese. Nothing could be done without progress toward unity. Indeed, said Johnson, this was the last chance he would give the South Vietnamese. Stop fighting one another, Taylor was to tell the generals, and get on with the war. "If more of the same, then I'll be talking to you, General." [9] This last was probably a more friendly admonition than it sounds from notes of the meeting. But Taylor's instructions commanded the ambassador to say that it was a matter of the utmost difficulty to talk about requiring "great sacrifices of American citizens when reports from Saigon repeatedly give evidence of heedless self interest and short sightedness among all major groups in South Vietnam." [10]

Before he returned to Saigon, Taylor met with the Senate Foreign Relations Committee in executive session. There he reasserted the case for bombing attacks against the north:

> I cannot believe they will sacrifice their economy, that they will sacrifice the society they have constructed at great pains over the last 10 years. It just shouldn't be worth it to them. If we can get that message across and organize that scenario, I would have hopes we can come out of it. [11]

Should the present government fall, Taylor asserted, a "military dictatorship" could provide the necessary stability the U.S. needed as a precondition for the attacks. Peering over his eyeglasses at Taylor, Senator Fulbright expressed deep concern about a decision to send in American troops. "MacArthur said never get into a land war in Asia," Fulbright reminded the general, echoing the president's concern without knowing about the earlier exchange. "I don't care whether it all goes Communist. . . . I don't give a damn what the provocation is. I am not going to vote to send a hundred thousand men, or it would probably be 300,000 or 400,000. The French had 500,000." Yes, the French had tried and failed. But we were not the French, Taylor said. Besides, he was not for sending troops either, he assured Fulbright. "We should respond with our air, punish them appropriately, and let it go at that." The senator worried that if air attacks failed, "they will just go all out." Taylor assured the chairman that the world was too dangerous a place for uncontrolled actions. "I think we have more maturity now."[12]

Despite the doubts he had found in Washington, Taylor returned to Saigon in a sanguine mood about his ability to persuade the Vietnamese to pull together. How could they turn down what the United States had to offer for cooperation—not only the benefits promised from a bombing campaign but a pledge to pay for increasing the South Vietnamese army by 100,000 men, with new opportunities for promotion and patronage? Yet none of Taylor's inducements produced results. Worse, the Buddhists seemed determined to oust the latest Saigon government, while the Young Turks in the military seemed determined to do their best to demonstrate that no matter how outrageous their behavior, Washington had no choice but to support them or face defeat.[13]

Johnson had also demanded an all-out effort to secure more support from NATO and SEATO allies. But Secretary of State Dean Rusk's attempt to coax aid from them drew a blank. As expected, France's de Gaulle, while remaining affable and friendly throughout a long discussion of Vietnam, insisted that the United States could never build a position of strength in that country. "Everything was different there, even Communism." France preferred peace. Whatever the consequences of that choice, he told Rusk, they would be better than war. Should we forget about our great sacrifices in the Pacific in World War II, retorted the secretary of state, and our even greater security interests now? The United States could never accept such reasoning. De Gaulle only shrugged. Of course, he said at length, it was within the power of the United States to keep things going for quite a long time. It could supply arms and technical support. It could wage war against the north, or attack China. Or even go to world war. But what would the final outcome be?

Rusk refused to go down that path with the French leader. Instead he concentrated on what de Gaulle had said earlier about America having inherited French responsibilities in Southeast Asia, without acknowledging the intended irony. The problem would be with us for some time to come, he agreed, given the announced doctrine of Hanoi and Beijing. What the West faced were precisely the same pressures the Communists had exerted against Western Europe earlier in the cold war. "We believed that if the edges of the Free World were eaten away then we at the center would sooner or later feel these pressures on ourselves."[14]

De Gaulle was hopeless. That had been clear for some time. But Rusk's conversations with the Italian foreign minister suggested that even the least independent-thinking of the NATO allies had serious qualms about a policy that seemed to them to be pushing China back toward Russia, instead of exploiting differences. Certainly Rusk's language in the interview suggested a consequences-be-damned determination to "win" in Vietnam. Beijing must change its policy, he began. "We are on a collision course. China must not feel she is reaping a harvest from her present behavior. The American people have the impression that our Atlantic allies are just standing by and watching developments in the Far East."[15]

Frenchmen or Italians fighting in Vietnam was not the issue here. But strong evidence of allied support for the United States might convince the Russians that the American government had moral backing for its actions and therefore enough staying power to outlast the NLF *and* the troubled situation in Saigon. Johnson did not wish to go it alone in Vietnam for another reason: domestic opinion. A decision to escalate was sure to produce a potentially divisive public debate. Longtime political adviser Horace Busby had drafted a memorandum about the "image" problem, the first of several cautionary memos on the implications of the election. He and other staff aides, noted Busby, believed that a "watershed" had been crossed in the Lyndon Johnson image. All the old questions about LBJ had centered on the man himself; now the interest of the media and the public centered on what the man stood for. "For all of us, this is a profound change."[16]

Two weeks later Busby submitted a "background" memorandum for the president to use in developing his remarks to a meeting of leading businessmen. It was essential to keep both feet on the ground. "Because we [have] peace, because we have friends and allies in every part of the world, because we are a nation whose use of its strength is trusted, we are in a climate now which permits us to think ahead, plan ahead, act for the future. Given the blessings that are ours in the world, we must conserve and utilize our potential at home by maintaining a spirit of unity in this country—rather than allowing a spirit of division to grow between labor and management, between white and black, between liberal and conservative, etc."[17]

Douglass Cater submitted a similar memorandum on themes for the State of the Union message Johnson would deliver in January 1965. "There is no longer a neat dividing line between domestic and foreign policy," it read.

> What we do to safeguard the civil rights of all our citizens has a fundamental effect on what we try to do abroad. How well we support freedom's cause in the far corners of the world plays a basic part in how we maintain our well-being in the city and on the farm. Neither the President nor Congress can any longer judge a policy or a program in the abstract.[18]

Cater had also forwarded excerpts from a memorandum by NSC staffer Mike Forrestal. "It represents the feeling of frustration by some of those working on the Vietnamese crisis," wrote Cater, "that we are increasingly becoming trapped by the military problem there." Forrestal had suggested to Rusk that the president deliver a speech about regional economic development, "just about the time that military activities in the area are stepped up." Forrestal wanted to see if somehow it was not possible to "convey to our own people and to the rest of the world more of a sense that the U.S. is thinking in constructive political and economic terms with respect to Southeast Asia."

> We are now on the verge of decisions which will tend to heighten rather than moderate this military image of ourselves. There is no doubt that such decisions have been made necessary and we are right in facing up to them. But it seems to me that their adverse political effects can be moderated if, at the same time that we take new military actions, we can announce our readiness to embark upon an international effort to make rapid and dramatic contributions to the economy of Southeast Asia as a whole (including North Vietnam).[19]

Johnson, meanwhile, was confiding his troubles to various persons and friends outside the official policymaking group. On December 5 *New York Times* editor Turner Catledge received a summons to the White House. "We are in bad shape in South Vietnam," Johnson told him. "We must find some way to bring the job off even if we have to set it up so that a withdrawal would have a better face." But there was no intention of withdrawing—not now at least. It was crucial to broaden the base of participation. He wanted moral support all the way from West Germany to India. He had just told Ambassador Chester Bowles to go back to New Delhi and say to Prime Minister Shastri that "he'd better get off his can, and indicate at least some moral judgments in favor of our position. . . . It won't cost 'em anything, but they'll be in better shape to call on the United States if they should happen to get in more trouble with Red China."[20]

On another occasion Johnson met for three hours with a small group of three reporters. He likened his situation to a man standing on a copy of a newspaper in the middle of the Atlantic Ocean, one of them recalled. " 'If I go this way,' he said, tilting his hand to the right, 'I'll topple over, and if I go this way'—he tilted his hand to the left—'I'll topple over, and if I stay where I am, the paper will be soaked up and I'll sink slowly to the bottom of the sea.' As he said this, he lowered his hand slowly toward the floor."[21]

"If we get into this war," he told still other visitors, "I know what's going to happen. Those damn conservatives are going to sit in Congress and they're going to use this war as a way of opposing my Great Society legislation. People like Stennis and Gross. They hate this stuff, they don't want to help the poor and the Negroes but they're afraid to be against it at a time like this when there's been all this prosperity. But the war, oh, they'll like the war. They'll take the war as their weapon. They'll be against my programs because of the war. I know what they'll say, they'll say they're not against it, not against the poor, but we have this job to do, beating Communists. We beat the Communists first, then we can look around and maybe give something to the poor." One of Johnson's listeners said it was eerie listening to the president—like being with a man who has had a premonition of his own death.[22]

LBJ was behaving as he had in the campaign, dropping hints to the press and other White House visitors that he was being forced against his will into an ever tighter corner. The president had many reasons for playing this game. He had tried to make sure that Vietnam did not hurt his chances for an overwhelming mandate in the election. Now he wanted to make sure it did not deprive him of votes in the new Congress for Great Society programs. But Lyndon Johnson's continuing crablike approach to Vietnam also tells us about American history and the ambiguous (if not contradictory) urges in twentieth-century reformism. LBJ's whole sense of himself, his understanding of the cold war, the convictions he shared with key advisers, were now tightly wrapped around Vietnam.

America found itself in Vietnam *in medias res*, as it were. The nation's supposed manifest destiny took it beyond the narrow imperialist policies of the European era to establish what LBJ called the Great Society and George Bush would later call the New World Order. Like Wilson and Roosevelt before him, each step Johnson took to preserve his options actually narrowed future choices. And, more than his predecessors, Johnson feared the outcome. Conspiracy theorists see only deception by the president. There *was* deception involved, and probably more self-deception; but Johnson and his advisers played out their roles convinced that the stern voices that spoke to them from the nation's past permitted no other course. What was most remarkable about the Vietnam War was that, with the exception of Charles de Gaulle, George Ball, and a handful of others, so few challenged the fundamental assumptions of the American vision. In part this was true precisely because Johnson felt his way ever so cautiously. Later military critiques of the war faulted the strategy of gradual escalation as a sure way to lose a war. Hawkish analysts complained that it gave the enemy a chance to prepare for each new American step. But Johnson knew he would never have gotten away with an all-out bombing campaign, much less an invasion, without first protecting the moral authority of the United States. He could not fool all the people all the time, but he could force doubters to support him out of fear their dissent would weaken American positions elsewhere in the world. After all, Vietnam would be over some day, wouldn't it? Meanwhile, no one wished to contribute to a perception that the nation had lost its way, morally as well as militarily. What strikes post-Vietnam observers as an amazing failure of nerve, or simple stubbornness or stupidity, was not so clear in the event. It became a case of trying not to allow Vietnam to undermine policy in the rest of the world.

Ambassador Taylor, meanwhile, had to deal with a fresh crisis. Young

Turks in the Vietnamese military aligned with General Khanh had decided to depose the civilian government of Tran Van Huong, a sixty-one-year-old schoolmaster. Huong and a new body, the High National Council, had been attempting to write a constitution and schedule elections. Americans in Saigon prayed Huong would be allowed to succeed and that his efforts would put a solid foundation under civilian rule. The leader of the Young Turks, Nguyen Cao Ky, branded Huong a disaster. "He had no drive, no foresight," Ky wrote in his memoirs, "and, worst of all, no guts when dealing with the thousands of rioters fighting in the Saigon streets against his weak and ineffectual government." The High National Council simply multiplied Huong's weaknesses. "The council was so senile that it was called the High National Museum in the bars of Saigon."[23]

Prodded by General Khanh, the Young Turks soon worked themselves into a wrath over the supposed determination of the HNC to return General Duong Van Minh to power. "Big" Minh had been overthrown several months earlier by Khanh, it will be recalled, ostensibly because he had been plotting with French agents to hold negotiations with the NLF and Hanoi. When Khanh met with the Young Turks and revealed this new "plot," one of the latter cried out, "Who the hell do they think they are?" A quick vote was taken to arrest the members of the HNC to put an end to the chicanery. "It's getting late," said one of Ky's lieutenants as dusk fell. "It's time to round up the chickens and put them in the coop."[24]

Ky commanded the air force, so it was easy for him to have Minh and several others arrested and spirited off to Pleiku in the highlands early Sunday morning, December 20. Ky had scarcely issued the orders to fly the "prisoners" north, however, when the telephone rang at general staff headquarters. It was Ambassador Taylor. Khanh listened to the ambassador for some time, occasionally saying "yes" or "no." When he put down the phone, he turned to the others present. "Taylor wants to see us all at the American Embassy right away." Khanh refused to go. But he wanted someone to represent him. No one volunteered. "Come on Ky," he urged, "you are the leader of the Young Turks, you had better go."[25]

Taylor was himself in a bit of a quandary about what to say or do. He had told the Senate Foreign Relations Committee that, if it came to that, Washington might eventually have to accept a military dictatorship to hold things together, or even to carry out the "pulmotor treatment." But not this way, or at this time. When the Vietnamese arrived at the embassy, Taylor dressed them down like West Point plebes who had gotten into trouble in New York City. "I told you all clearly," he began in English, "we Americans are tired of coups. Apparently I wasted my words. Maybe this is because something is wrong with my French because you evidently didn't understand. . . . Now you have made a real mess. We cannot carry you forever if you do things like this."[26]

Ky claimed they had simply forced the civilian government to clean house. "If we have achieved it, fine. We are now ready to go back to our units." Exasperated by such naiveté, Taylor shot back, "You cannot go back to your units, General Ky. . . . You are up to your necks in politics." After some discussion about how to get things back on track, Taylor started thinking out loud about things Johnson had said back in Washington and where matters stood: "I have real troubles on the U.S. side. I don't know whether we will continue to support you after this. . . . You people have broken a lot of dishes and now we have to see how we can straighten this out."[27]

Khanh was the main obstacle, the ambassador had decided. One way or another he must be gotten out of the way. It was obviously getting easier and easier, even for Taylor who had opposed overthrowing Diem, to think about removing such obstacles to the American mission. Over the next several days Taylor and the Vietnamese general carried on a debate waged both in private and in the newspapers. Taylor declared that Khanh had outlived his usefulness. Khanh retorted that Taylor had interfered in Vietnamese affairs "beyond imagination" for an ambassador. "We make sacrifices for the country's independence and the Vietnamese people's liberty, not to carry out the policy of any foreign country."[28]

General Khanh may have made a most unconvincing "nationalist" figure to be prating on about American intervention in Vietnamese affairs, but each of his predecessors—and his successors as well—ultimately took refuge in that stance. In truth they needed protection against the Americans as well as against the NLF if there was to be anything substantive to the Saigon regime. Khanh's *cri de coeur* rang hollow, but that was because he had put himself in Washington's service since the overthrow of Diem. Now he was being discarded. The new American military commander, General William Westmoreland, watched the melodrama unfold at close quarters. "Khanh was obviously trying to demonstrate how well he could resist the role of puppet, thereby hoping to regain control over the generals; but in the process he inevitably revealed that the American mantle was slipping from his shoulders. Men as astute as Thieu and Ky could hardly have missed noting that."[29]

For a time matters remained in flux. Khanh did not dare go as far as to declare Taylor persona non grata; and neither the ambassador nor Washington dared to suspend American military actions against the NLF. On Christmas Eve an NLF sapper unit placed explosives in the American officers' billet in the heart of Saigon. When the bomb went off, two Americans were killed and thirty-eight injured. Taylor recommended an air strike against North Vietnam. This was the very sort of "spectacular" demanding retaliation that had been envisioned when the advisers drew up the Phase I plan earlier in the month. Johnson rejected the appeal. The plain fact was that the situation in Saigon was so bad that reprisal bombing would be certain to produce a "strong reaction in US opinion and internationally" that the administration was "trying to shoot its way out of an internal [Saigonese] political crisis."[30]

He had no intention of being drawn into a war against North Vietnam because "our own people are careless or imprudent," the president declared. "I have not yet been told in any convincing way why aircraft cannot be protected from mortar attacks and officers quarters from large bombs." This was a curious way of putting his doubts. Ever since the second series of Gulf of Tonkin "incidents" the previous September, the president had expressed skepticism about American intelligence and security efforts. Here he came close to implying that someone was in fact plotting an incident. In a scorching rebuke to Taylor, the president said, "If we ourselves were uncertain for several days about the source of the Brink's [i.e. the officers' billet] bombing, we cannot expect the world to be less uncertain." But then he startled the ambassador by seeming to call for a land war in Asia:

> Every time I get a military recommendation it seems to me that it calls for large-scale bombing. I have never felt this war will be won from the air, and it seems to me that what is much more needed and would be more effective is a larger and stronger use of Rangers and Special Forces and Marines, or other appropriate military strength on the ground and on the scene. I am ready to look with great favor on that kind of increased American effort, directed at the guerrillas and aimed to stiffen the aggressiveness of Vietnamese military units up and down the line. Any recommendation that you or General Westmoreland make in this sense will have immediate attention from me, although I know that it may involve the acceptance of larger American sacrifice. We have been building our strength to fight this kind of war ever since 1961, and I myself am ready to substantially increase the number of Americans in Vietnam if it is necessary to provide this kind of fighting force against the Viet Cong.[31]

Johnson's message alarmed Taylor. He replied with a sharp warning against any plan to introduce U.S. combat forces. Here began a "debate" that raged throughout the Vietnam War and continues to figure largely in memoirs and studies of American strategy. On one level the argument concerns the wisdom of gradual escalation versus a relatively quick passage to whatever was needed to "win." Military critics of the Johnson administration have argued that the pace of American escalation, and the micromanagement of the war from Washington, practically assured what Admiral Ulysses S. Grant Sharp called *Strategy for Defeat*.[32] At a second level, however, the Johnson/Taylor disagreement was about the "lessons" of the Cuban missile crisis, and which variations should be tried in Vietnam. This was a particularly tricky business because, as LBJ said, the Kennedy administration had inaugurated a program of counterinsurgency training to deal with situations like Vietnam. Yet the Cuban missile crisis suggested to others that the most effective signals—the best deterrents—were those that demonstrated American capacity and will to use its technological superiority, if necessary, to destroy, as Taylor had put it to the Senate Foreign Relations Committee, "the society they have constructed at great pains over the last 10 years. It just shouldn't be worth it to them."

Although the Taylor position later became the basis for bombing advocates, the general had in mind a variation on "crisis management" techniques. Taylor tried to elaborate on this point at some length in his January 6, 1965, reply to the president's objections to reprisal bombing. He agreed, he said, with Johnson's feeling that a war against guerrillas could not be won—"if we are thinking in terms of the physical destruction of the enemy."

> The Phase II program is not a resort to use bombing to win [per] Douhet theory (which I have spent considerable past effort in exposing) but is the use of the most flexible weapon in our arsenal of military superiority to bring pressure on the will of the chiefs of the DRV. As practical men, they cannot wish to see the fruits of ten years labor destroyed by slowly escalating air attacks (which they cannot prevent) without trying to find some accommodation which will exercise [sic] the threat. It would be to our interest to regulate our attacks not for the purpose of doing maximum physical destruction but for producing maximum stresses in Hanoi minds.[33]

Taylor's logic suited the thinking used in the Kennedy administration when it devised its flexible response strategy. And it suffered from all the flaws in that logic concealed by the praise (and *self*-praise) heaped on Kennedy and his "crisis managers" in the aftermath of the Cuban missile crisis. Taylor now declared once again (as if to convince himself) that as "practical men," Hanoi's leaders would not wish to see the fruits of their "ten years labor destroyed by slowly escalating air attacks." But Secretary Rusk, at the time of the Gulf of Tonkin crisis, had argued that he could only explain the DRV's action as the aberrant behavior of people who thought about things quite differently from the men who manned strategy centers in the basement rooms of the White House or the Pentagon. Rusk's pejorative labeling of the North Vietnamese as semirational creatures aside, the secretary's comment went to the heart of the problem: American bombs could destroy buildings, but they could not "take out" the adversary's nonmaterial foundations.

However selectively and precisely Taylor wanted to increase the "maximum stresses in Hanoi minds," if the bombing technique proved to be futile and costly, pressure to go straight for saturation bombing was likely to prove irresistible. Taylor's messages were composed as if from some European capital, not Saigon. For all the supposed sophistication of his argument, the former army general, like his compatriots still in the Pentagon, had either not absorbed or not accepted much of the counterinsurgency thinking that the Kennedy planners had gone to such pains to develop. The army "concept" for fighting the Vietnam War was to treat it as a mid-level contest, of the sort that had been expected to break out some day in Europe. Taylor differed with this concept in believing that the bombings could substitute for American soldiers. If the DRV could be dissuaded from helping the insurgents in the south, enough time could be bought to enable Saigon to get on its feet and win the war.[34]

Taylor also opposed the president's desire to withdraw American dependents from South Vietnam. It was a matter of timing. The situation was so bad, he feared, that to withdraw American dependents would indicate that the United States was abandoning the fight, getting ready to clear out altogether. It would cause panic in South Vietnam and adversely affect "our ability to obtain third country assistance from our *less sturdy friends.*" But if other action—the bombing, he meant—were taken first, such a decision to withdraw dependents could "reinforce the tonic effects" of such action. "I have, for example, in mind the successful way in which we used the evacuation of our dependents from Guantanamo during the Cuban crisis to reinforce the signals that we were seeking to communicate to both Havana and Moscow."[35]

As for Johnson's complaint that lax security could not be a reason for going to war, Taylor found a way to turn the argument. He had consulted with General Westmoreland, Taylor said, and found the "startling" news that complete protection would require at least 75,000 American troops. These troops sitting in static positions would hardly speed up the conclusion of the war. Still worse, they would represent an occupying force. If the advisory effort had failed to instill the South Vietnamese with the proper motivation to carry on the fight, there was little reason to believe the situation could be rescued with American troops. Instead, as the Americans took on the burden of the fighting, said the ambassador, the likelihood was that the majority of Vietnamese would "actively turn against us . . . until, like the French, we would be occupying an essentially hostile country."[36]

None of the challenges Johnson had put to his advisers in December, nor indeed any he would put later in the war, ever received adequate answers, not in Taylor's cables and not in anything he heard elsewhere. Yet how long could matters go on as they were? The president might rail at columnist Joseph Alsop for his attempts to force his hand—and suspect that the Bundys were feeding their friend information about high-level deliberations—but he accepted Alsop's estimate of the stakes:

For Lyndon Johnson, Vietnam is what the second Cuban crisis was for John F. Kennedy. If Mr. Johnson ducks the challenge we shall learn by experience about what it would have been like if Kennedy had ducked the challenge in October, 1962....[37]

Oddly enough, General Westmoreland was one of the few who believed that domestic and foreign opinion would have understood a decision to leave Vietnam to its fate. He later wrote of the situation in early 1965:

> Whether the United States would, in fact, have pulled out of Vietnam in 1965 if the political instability showed no signs of abating is problematical. I think it likely that Washington was already too deeply committed in word and deed to do other than more of the same. Yet so obvious was the bickering, the machination, the inefficiency, the divisiveness among the Vietnamese that I suspect few in the world would have faulted us at that point had we thrown up our hands in despair. When we failed to renege on our commitment under such blatantly exigent conditions, the time when we could have withdrawn with some grace and honor had passed.[38]

The more perilous the situation inside Saigon, the harder Johnson tried to make it appear that South Vietnam had powerful friends around the world. German Chancellor Ludwig Erhard and the Japanese prime minister were persuaded, for example, to close their visits to Washington with strong public endorsements of American policy in Vietnam from the portico of the White House. Erhard was said to have impressed on Johnson during their talks "the importance of mutual solidarity in dealing with communist aggression," while the Japanese prime minister supposedly "agreed that continued perseverance would be necessary for freedom and independence in South Vietnam."[39]

LBJ was steadily building up arguments that he would find it impossible to ignore; still he hedged about a bombing campaign against the DRV. Down deep he may have understood the biggest flaw of all in Taylor's argument: bombing North Vietnam could never win the war in the south. In any event, the ambassador was instructed to allow it to become known that the United States had decided to adopt a reprisal policy. It was left to Taylor to handle this without making it seem a definitive change. "We would prefer that this indication be given by inconspicuous background briefings rather than formal public statement...." Targets selected for reprisal bombings should be in the southern section of the DRV. All air attacks were subject to the president's review before the execute order could be given. Meanwhile, the ambassador and General Westmoreland were urged yet again to seek better cooperation from the South Vietnamese in planning and executing military actions inside South Vietnam. "A few solid military victories achieved by use of U.S. military command judgment and energy would be worth all the rest of this program put together."[40]

Washington's latest instructions puzzled the ambassador. They seemed to add new conditions, not remove obstacles to a clear-cut policy. They could even be regarded as a step backward. Could he not say to the Vietnamese, plain and simple, Taylor cabled, that a firm decision had been made to go ahead with Phase II, with the understanding that no commitments had been made as to timing or scale? The message produced no clarification. The president would go no further. And there matters stood.[41]

While Taylor fretted about Washington's dillydallying, rumors of an impending change had reached Congress. Questioned closely by Senator Fulbright in executive session, Secretary Rusk coyly refused to say if the Foreign Relations Committee would be consulted. "I myself feel that strikes against the North are a part of the problem on which the leadership and President would be in consultation, because this would be a significant development of the situation."[42]

Taylor had convinced McGeorge Bundy and Robert McNamara, however, and they were determined to move the president into Phase II of Operation Vietnam—a steady escalation of bombing—before things finally fell apart. In Saigon, General Khanh was once again scheming to gain power. The worst aspect of his maneuvering was his surprise "alliance" with Buddhist factions. At least the Young Turks were anxious to continue the war. Even if Khanh thought he would be able to use the Buddhists, there was always the chance he would be the one to be used. "I'm convinced," Vice-President Hubert Humphrey was heard to say, "that we don't have to worry about this [whether to escalate] because, before this bombing can be undertaken, there will be a neutralist government in Saigon and we will be invited out."[43]

Alerted to the possibility that Khanh was about to seize power, Mac Bundy asked for a meeting with Johnson to discuss whether "this back-and-forth in the government in Saigon is a symptom, not a root cause of our problem."[44] Even to phrase the issue in this fashion helped to predetermine the answer to the question. Meanwhile, Bundy promised, he would prepare a paper explaining the president's options. On the morning of January 27, 1965, Bundy and McNamara met with the president to receive his decision. General Khanh had staged his expected coup during the interim. But Bundy had successfully reversed, as he hoped to do, symptoms and root causes. Khanh's coup was no reason to think about getting out. "Both of us are now pretty well convinced that our current policy can lead only to disastrous defeat," the national security adviser began, referring to McNamara and himself. The continuing difficulties in Saigon arose, he went on, from the spreading conviction that "the future is without hope for anti-Communists." "More and more the good men are covering their flanks and avoiding executive responsibility for firm anti-Communist policy." Such a novel reading of Vietnamese politics obscured practically all the major forces at work in favor of an imposed history constructed according to cold war exigencies, but Bundy had little patience with those unable to perceive the higher truth. "Our best friends"—not presumably the Vietnamese living in the countryside where the war was going on—"have been somewhat discouraged by our own inactivity in the face of major attacks on our own installations."

> The Vietnamese know just as well as we do that the Viet Cong are gaining in the countryside. Meanwhile, they see the enormous power of the United States withheld, and they get little sense of firm and active U.S. policy. They feel we are unwilling to take serious risks. In one sense, all of this is outrageous, in the light of all that we have done and all that we are ready to do if they will only pull up their socks. But it is a fact—or at least so McNamara and I now think.[45]

Given the determination he and other policymakers had exhibited in denying Diem or Minh and now Khanh any opportunity to follow a policy except in accordance with the war aims of the United States, Bundy's ability to speak about what frightened the Vietnamese people, and what would bolster their spirits, seems suspect. But there was more. This time around, he and McNamara had determined, there would be no other choice for Johnson but "honest" commitment.

This uncertainty that "pervades" the Vietnamese people, stated the national security adviser, was increasingly visible "among our own people, even the most loyal and determined." Again, a curious phraseology, why "even the most loyal and determined"? It could mean several things, all of which presumably spelled trouble for Lyndon Johnson's ability to hold his administration together if he did not decide to go forward. The ground raked smooth, all the clumps of doubt broke up, Bundy set out the two alternatives: "The first is to use our military power in the Far East and to force a change of Communist policy. The second is to deploy all our resources along a track of negotiation, aimed at salvaging what little can be preserved with no major addition to our present military risks."[46]

"Bob and I," he said, "*tend* to favor the first course, but we believe that both should be carefully studied and that alternative programs should be argued out before you." Rusk did not agree with their recommendation, Bundy noted, because he feared the consequences of veering off in either direction. He felt the present policy had to be made to work. "This would be good if it was possible. Bob and I do not think it is."[47]

"A topic of this magnitude," Bundy's memorandum read, "can only be opened for initial discussion this morning, but McNamara and I have reached the point where our obligations to you simply do not permit us to administer our present directives in silence and let you think we see real hope in them." Was there the slightest hint here that they could not administer their present directives in silence—period? Did this sentence go with the phrase about doubts among "even the most loyal"? A president a good deal less sensitive concerning his origins, or a good deal more secure in his grasp of foreign policy questions, would have paid more than casual attention to the wording of this memorandum. Johnson was neither. Summed up in a few sentences, the memo read: We are losing the war. The Vietnamese are now incidental to the outcome. But you need Vietnam to save your administration. If we lose because we have withheld our military power, you will be blamed, and nothing can undo the damage.

By the time Johnson finished reading Bundy's memorandum he hardly cared any more about the ups and downs of South Vietnamese politics: the implicit warnings in the second half of Bundy's memorandum—backed by McNamara's presence at the meeting on the morning of the 27th—were enough. "Stable government or no stable government," Johnson declared, "we'll do what we have to do—we will move strongly. I'm prepared to do that." That same evening the president cabled Ambassador Taylor, "Once we get the dependents out of there, I am determined to make it clear to all the world that the U.S. will spare no effort and no sacrifice in doing its full part to turn back the Communists in Vietnam." [48]

Bundy himself cabled the next day that even on the question of getting the dependents "out of there" the president had relented. Now he only demanded a "decision" to remove the dependents. The timing and method could be worked out when the national security adviser arrived in Saigon to talk about the general political situation. Taylor had asked earlier for a Bundy visit, but now it took on special meaning because the ambassador was having his own quarrel to settle with General Khanh. If Taylor had his way, Khanh would be sent packing to some place close to the North Pole. But the national security adviser had little desire to carry on a time-wasting vendetta against the errant general with the odd-looking goatee. See him, Bundy instructed Taylor. Find out if he was willing to carry on the war. If he indicated he was—as Washington expected—then "we think you should certainly respond that U.S. is equally determined to go on supporting Vietnamese government and people." As proof of American determination, Taylor was to tell Khanh that the De Soto patrols in the Gulf of Tonkin would be resumed the following week. "Object of meeting should be to establish firmness of both sides and create atmosphere that would begin to bury past problems." [49]

Bundy's cables left no doubts about the new firmness in Washington's attitude, nor about *his* new role. Deputized by LBJ to act on his behalf, Bundy was coming to Vietnam to see that things got done. No more shilly-shallying. "Intense, abrupt, at moments a bit arrogant," General Westmoreland noted his impressions of Bundy, "like numbers of civilians in positions of some government authority, once he smelled a little gunpowder he developed a field marshal psychosis."[50]

Bundy's first impression of the political situation in Saigon could scarcely have encouraged the president to believe he had made the right decision. "The current situation among non-communist forces gives all the appearance of a civil war within a civil war." The main stumbling block was the Buddhist leadership. There was "no present prospect of a government acceptable to us which would also be acceptable to the leaders of the Buddhist institute," Bundy reported. But that gave him no pause. "In this situation, the construction of a government of national unity may well require sharp confrontation with Buddhists before, during, or after the construction job."[51]

Given the current success of the NLF on the battlefield, the prospect of a "sharp confrontation" with another faction in the tangled world of Vietnamese politics was not something Lyndon Johnson cared to think about. The next news out of Vietnam was something altogether different. At 2 a.m. on February 7, Viet Cong soldiers launched an attack against a U.S. helicopter base and barracks at Pleiku in the Central Highlands. Eight Americans were killed and 126 wounded; ten planes were destroyed and many others damaged. Other South Vietnamese installations were attacked that day, ten in all, but Pleiku was the only place where Americans were involved. Two Americans had been killed in late December by the bombs placed in the Brinks barracks in Saigon. Johnson had stayed his hand on that occasion, but not now—not when he had been told it might be his last chance to send what he hoped would be an unmistakable signal to Hanoi— and Saigon.[52]

There was only one difficulty. Soviet Premier Alexei Kosygin was in Hanoi at the head of "an unusually strong delegation." To bomb North Vietnam while Kosygin was meeting with Ho and his lieutenants risked forcing the Russians to play a deeper role in the conflict. On the other hand, not to retaliate risked giving the impression that the United States was a paper tiger. "We cannot put ourself in the position of giving the Russians control over our actions," declared the unabashed Mac Bundy, "by their moving Soviet diplomats from one place to another."[53] That Alexei Kosygin ranked somewhat above a diplomat apparently made no difference.

Johnson wrote in his memoirs that CIA Director John McCone told him the Kosygin visit to Hanoi "promised only more trouble." The new Soviet leaders had decided to reverse Khrushchev's policy of relative inaction, Johnson recorded McCone's opinion. They had concluded Hanoi was about to win and desired to "move in to share credit for the anticipated victory."[54] As Communist leaders toasted one another in Hanoi, preparing to celebrate the fall of yet another nation on the border of the Free World, the president of the United States—in this accounting—had to act or face humiliation.

Johnson did act. While members of the National Security Council listened, the president read a list of proposed targets. Pentagon estimates indicated that if four barracks complexes were hit, as proposed, casualties could run as high as 4,500. No one dissented. "We are all in accord that action must be taken," began Under Secretary of State George Ball, sitting in for Rusk, even though he could not have been happy contemplating what it meant to send 132 carrier-based jets over North Vietnam. Only Senate Majority Leader Mike Mansfield objected, and then only obliquely. "The North Vietnamese attack has opened many eyes," he said. "We are not now in a penny ante game. It appears that the local populace in South Vietnam is not behind us, else the Viet Cong could not have carried out their surprise attack."[55]

In the event, bad weather prevented the American planes from hitting more than one of their selected targets. This gave Johnson the opportunity to put off for a few more days a decision to do more than launch reprisal raids. "We all felt," Johnson wrote, "that a second-day strike by U.S. planes might give Hanoi the impression that we had begun a sustained air offensive. That decision had not been made."[56] At a briefing for congressional leaders, however, the president declared that the Gulf of Tonkin Resolution "plus the legal power of the Presidency made it possible for him to carry out at a manageable level an effort to deter, destroy and diminish the strength of the North Vietnamese aggressors and to try to convince them to leave South Vietnam alone." As the meeting ended, Johnson repeated that "our actions will be kept at a manageable level."[57] No one challenged his interpretation of the Gulf of Tonkin Resolution. And why should they? He had promised to keep things under control. Yet in conversations outside the formal setting of an NSC meeting, Johnson portrayed himself as under enormous pressure from the military. "Just between you and me," he told Carl Rowan, "all I want to do is bloody their noses a little bit and maybe they'll leave their neighbors alone." He had to approve the bombing "because that damn cigar-smoking [Air Force General] Curtis LeMay is pushing me, and I gotta let him know that I'm as tough as he is."[58]

So Johnson launched what soon became Operation Rolling Thunder to show that he was just as tough as Ho Chi Minh, Alexei Kosygin, General Curtis LeMay, and, equally if not more important, former Kennedy advisers Robert McNamara and McGeorge Bundy. It was launched, even more fatefully, in a confused atmosphere of what the bombing was supposed to accomplish. Since the December meetings in Washington, Ambassador Taylor and other advocates of the "pulmotor treatment" had been arguing for bombing the north to pull the south together, and to punish Hanoi. Bundy and McNamara had likewise claimed that the U.S. was headed for defeat because the South Vietnamese lacked any feeling of confidence about American willingness to use its power against the enemy. Now the McNamara/Bundy position began to shade off into a dangerous self-delusion that air power could "win" the war, ultimately the most dangerous policy quagmire Vietnam presented.

Thus where Taylor's unstated premise had been that America held Vietnamese national self-determination in trust for some future Saigon government, Bundy's report on his return from Saigon stressed that American policy must do something immediately to fulfill that responsibility, that Washington had yet to provide an adequate response to the yearning and groping for a genuine revolution. "This is the overriding reason for our present recommendation of a policy of sustained reprisal. Once such a policy is put in force, we shall be able to speak in Vietnam on many topics and in many ways, with growing force and effectiveness,." [59]

Bundy once quipped, "Pleikus are like streetcars." One came along every ten minutes or so.[60] Yet the timing of the Pleiku raid was highly important in providing a receptive audience for the report he presented upon his return from Saigon. As pressure built from December onward for a bombing campaign, other pressures were also mounting for a new diplomatic initiative. Public opinion divided, as might be expected, expressing a desire for negotiations but not wanting a defeat. State Department aides discounted serious public opinion difficulties over Vietnam, because they imagined that the president's huge approval ratings in general would carry the nation along whatever course he chose. Yet the mood was shifting in many places, noted William Bundy, nationally and internationally, that pointed "quite markedly in the direction of seeking a negotiated outcome."[61]

Public opinion against the bombing might also bring pressure on Hanoi by focusing world attention on the war. Johnson had declared at the congressional briefing on the retaliatory attack that he would not allow the views of a "few senators" to control his actions. The next day, however, he received a memorandum from Mike Mansfield urging him to see if the cochairs of the 1954 Geneva Conference, Russia and Great Britain, could not reconvene that forum—or some other group—to seek some way to end the fighting.[62] But the attack at Pleiku and the retaliatory raid had made it difficult for Mansfield, let alone lesser figures, to argue for a conference that could only end either with a concession to the political legitimacy of the NLF, or a walkout and the likelihood of rapid escalation with the danger of war with China. Even Mansfield ended his letter with a pledge that regardless of his "individual" views he would do whatever he could to support the president "in the exercise of your grave responsibility."[63]

American officials had rightly concluded that *any* negotiations would mean the failure of the rescue mission they had set for themselves. Confident that Hanoi was ready to deliver the death blow to Saigon, Moscow and Beijing were both jockeying for position. Thus China had launched a psychological warfare campaign against Thailand while Russia sent Kosygin to North Vietnam to promise greater support from Moscow. Certain Asian leaders had chosen sides already. Cambodia's Prince Sihanouk had made a trip to Beijing and had then refused to accept a new American ambassador. Indonesia's Sukarno menaced Malaysia and indicated his preference for Mao over any Western leaders. If this nightmare scenario played out as indicated, the loss of Vietnam would reduce the American role to observer while the Communist rivals vied for supremacy across Asia.[64]

From Laos, Ambassador William H. Sullivan cabled a warning against negotiations on the basis of the 1954 Geneva Agreement. Washington's public position, albeit stated ambiguously most of the time, was that all the Communists had to do was to return to the 1954 agreements. The DRV (and now the French) had been insisting for some time that those agreements had been violated when "free general elections" were not held in 1956, as stipulated in paragraph seven of the final declaration. Sullivan admitted as much. "This, of course, would merely be non-violent means of achieving subversion," the ambassador said, "which DRV would have been unable [to] carry out by force of arms." What was needed was a "codicil" to the 1954 agreement, providing for the "indefinite existence of two separate entities north and south, postponing elections sine die and perhaps including certain economic clauses tempting to [the] DRV."[65]

Sullivan's candor was unusual, even in cable traffic between Washington and diplomatic posts abroad. The United States had supported Diem's rejection of Hanoi's efforts to hold all-Vietnamese elections in 1956, a clear violation of the Geneva accords, but not one American official talked about it, even in private.[66] There were no indications, however, that the North Vietnamese wanted anything so chancy as a return to the 1954 accords. What did seem to be emerging was a possible North Vietnamese ploy, as related by French sources, to allow South Vietnam to remain nominally independent and "neutral" but controlled by the NLF, as part of a two-stage process leading to eventual reunification. All this supposedly would be worked out at a new conference convened by the Soviet Union and Great Britain.[67]

This explanation might account for the Hanoi-Moscow rapprochement of recent weeks, both in terms of Soviet promises and Russian concern that the North Vietnamese not do anything to force the United States into an irrevocable escalation of its role in the war.[68] In that case, the Pleiku attack had been a mistake, or possibly a miscalculation. More likely, however, the North Vietnamese were showing their independence of *any* foreign control (so as not to alienate China) as well as a lot of self-confidence. Thus even if the French sources were correct, all the Americans were being offered was an opportunity through "negotiations" to make a graceful exit.

If American policymakers hoped that the retaliatory bombing of North Vietnam, and a second strike a few days later in response to a similar attack at Qui Nhon that killed twenty-three American enlisted men, would quiet calls for an international conference or bilateral negotiations, such expectations went unrealized. In the United States there was a rally-round-the-flag response to events in Vietnam, but the bombing raids intensified international efforts to bring about peace talks.

UN Secretary General U Thant tried to prod Washington toward peace talks with Hanoi, and, when rebuffed by Secretary Rusk, disclosed the background of his effort at a news conference. "I am sure," he said to startled reporters, "that the great American people, if only they knew the true facts and the background to the developments in South Vietnam, will agree with me that further bloodshed is unnecessary."[69] U Thant's "meddling" was especially hard to take, based as it was on an accusation that the American government was not telling its people the truth. Upon his return to Moscow, Alexei Kosygin issued an appeal for peace in Vietnam. He denounced the American attacks as a "personal insult" and again promised greater aid to North Vietnam; but he was also quick to support both U Thant's initiative and to second Charles de Gaulle's call for reconvening the Geneva Conference.[70]

In London, Prime Minister Harold Wilson faced a sharp reaction to the bombings from Labour back-benchers, many of whom did not usually join in left-wing America bashing. Wilson proposed to take the heat off himself by going to Washington for a talk with LBJ, just as Clement Attlee had flown over to reassure his back-benchers that Harry Truman was not going to start throwing atomic bombs during the Korean War. Johnson was furious at the idea. "I won't tell you how to run Malaysia," the president fairly shouted into the telephone, "and you don't tell us how to run Vietnam. . . . If you want to help us some in Vietnam send us some men and send us some folks to deal with these guerrillas. And announce to the press that you are going to help us."[71]

Wilson's efforts to get cooperation from the Russians in calling for a reconvening of the Geneva Conference did not bring an immediate response. By the time Moscow finally replied to the British effort, the tit-for-tat bombing had become Operation Rolling Thunder, the Phase II plan for bringing steadily increasing pressure on North Vietnam. And Hanoi's response had become what it would remain over the next three years: the bombing must stop before there could be any talk of negotiations.[72]

Dean Rusk put the administration's position on negotiations very succinctly to congressional leaders:

If Hanoi and Peking bring themselves to a point where they are prepared to leave these people alone, there are a dozen channels which could register that very quickly, and this whole situation could move very fast. But thus far there has been no indication that that is their purpose, and therefore, there arises the great issue as to what a negotiation would be about, and against the background that a negotiation . . . failed, [that] could add immeasurably to the danger.[73]

The "negotiations" problem was vastly more complicated than simply inviting the other side to talk about the terms of its surrender, however, as Rusk understood only too well. The secretary had built his case for American intervention in Vietnam on recitations of Communist perfidy in breaking solemn agreements. This was a cold war staple, going back to Harry Truman's day. President Johnson had stated many times that he would be only too happy to withdraw American forces from Vietnam as a result of a peace settlement. And what then? There had been nine changes of government since Diem's death, as Rusk himself told the congressional leaders. Now fully confident that he had Johnson with him all the way, Mac Bundy pointed out to French Foreign Minister Couve de Murville that aside from de Gaulle's assessment of Chinese motives, there was another difference between Paris and Washington. "France seems to think that there can be no solution to the problem of stable government in South Vietnam while the United States remains there, while we think that there can be no solution if we leave."[74]

Dean Rusk liked to invoke the Greek civil war of the late 1940s when he discussed negotiations. There were no negotiations in that case, just disengagement when the Communist guerrillas realized that the United States would not be driven out of the Mediterranean. Bundy preferred the situation in Berlin as his model. American policymakers from Truman to Johnson had refused to "negotiate" a change in Berlin's status as a divided city. "I saw a message the other day from President [James] Conant of Harvard," Bundy told congressional leaders, reminding them that Conant had been the American high commissioner in Germany at the height of early cold war tensions in Europe. Conant was not a belligerent man, the national security adviser continued, but "the burden of his message was that the defense of Berlin, right now, is in Vietnam."

And I believe this to be true, gentlemen. This is a test of our ability to take and deal with the most difficult and dangerous challenges, proudly stated by the Communists in their doctrine of wars of national liberation. The frustrations which you gentlemen feel are frustrations which we all feel. The point is that we have to get beyond them and have the courage to stay with the task.[75]

And to Johnson in a private memorandum, Bundy added the logical conclusion of all he had been saying since returning from Saigon:

> The pressure for negotiations is coming mostly from people who simply do not understand what the word means in Asian ears right now. If the U.S. proposes negotiations or even indicates a desire for them, the word in Saigon will be that we are getting out. And the consequences of that rumor would be very severe for our whole position.[76]

Former President Dwight D. Eisenhower was equally opposed to the idea of negotiations. His analogy was the American Civil War. Seeking bipartisan support to ward off expected criticism once Rolling Thunder began, Johnson had invited Eisenhower to a well-publicized meeting in the White House. Eisenhower held practically the same views as Johnson's key advisers: bombing the north was essential to the morale of South Vietnam and to the weakening of morale in North Vietnam. He would put the importance of morale, the old soldier-politician said, even higher than Napoleon had rated it at 3 to 1 over the material element. When Johnson said that some of his advisers were pushing for negotiations, Eisenhower answered with a rumination about Lincoln and the Emancipation Proclamation. Lincoln had had the proclamation ready for a long time, he began, and he yearned to put it out. But he had to wait through long, dreary months of military reverses before he could seize upon a Confederate defeat as the occasion to issue it. Negotiations from weakness could only be disastrous. His answer to all those who wanted negotiations would be, "Not now boys."[77]

The Greek civil war, Berlin, the American Civil War—Johnson found himself surrounded by analogies that all but walled off the reality of the situation in Saigon and the countryside. A disturbing fragment of that reality, nevertheless, provided yet another complication to the negotiations conundrum. At a press conference on February 4, 1965, the president was asked about rumors that the north and south were negotiating behind the scenes. Would the United States leave if asked by South Vietnam? "I would not anticipate that we would receive such an invitation," Johnson shot back. He would cross that bridge *if* he ever got to it, but he did not expect to get to it. What about the suggestions of certain senators that Washington should explore the negotiations path? "You will find from time to time that Senators from both . . . parties will have different viewpoints, to which they are entitled, and they will express them, as I have expressed mine."[78]

Johnson's testiness, it can be argued, stemmed from a concern that while the bombing might be "manageable," as he kept telling congressional leaders, the pressure for negotiations might easily get out of hand. In the aftermath of the first bombing raid on North Vietnam, a Committee to Defend the Peace was established in Saigon. A petition campaign gathered thousands of signatures denouncing the attacks on the north and calling for negotiations. The leader of the group was arrested, but it managed to stage a press conference anyway. More arrests followed. Those detained constituted a substantial proportion of Saigon's professional and business classes. The police station, quipped one of the committee members, suddenly looked as if "the city's elite had somehow mistaken the address of an upper-crust social gathering."[79]

It was terribly important, Johnson told the National Security Council, that the government in Saigon not get the impression that the United States was seeking negotiations prematurely. "Under these circumstances Saigon might begin its own negotiations quickly and without our knowledge or participation."[80] Despite his abrupt dismissal of unverified reports from Paris about General Khanh's contacts with Hanoi and the NLF, the president and his advisers had in fact been alerted by the CIA to the general's ambition to "make himself the 'Prince Sihanouk' of Vietnam by negotiating a deal with the Viet Cong's National Liberation Front to neutralize South Vietnam."[81] Johnson told French Foreign Minister Couve de Murville that "we might have to leave South Vietnam for some reason but we hoped not." One wonders what the Frenchman made of the president's next statement:

> We have no ambitions, but if we were to abandon Vietnam, we would be forced to give up Laos, Thailand, Burma, and would be back to Hawaii and San Francisco.[82]

Perhaps he was reminded of former Secretary of State Dean Acheson's statement that American policy was to enable peoples who thought the way Americans did, to live the way they wanted to. In any event, the president committed himself in principle to a sustained bombing campaign against North Vietnam on February 13, 1965. He reserved for a final decision the timing and implementation of the campaign. As each day passed, Bundy and McNamara grew more restless. "We have waited many months to put it into effect," the national security adviser wrote in as near exasperation as one dared to use with LBJ. "There is a deep-seated need for assurance that the decision has in fact been taken."

> When you were out of the room yesterday, Bob McNamara repeatedly stated that he simply has to know what the policy is so that he can make his military plans and give his military orders. This certainty is equally essential if we are to get the necessary political effects in Saigon.[83]

Ambassador Taylor and General Westmoreland, meanwhile, had been wrestling with the problem of getting rid of Khanh, whose maneuvering between the Young Turks and the Buddhists had kept alive fears that America would be "invited" to leave. After a complicated set of countermaneuvers, U.S. officials managed to secure a "vote" in the Vietnamese Armed Forces Council in late February dismissing Khanh from all power and authority and leaving him with an empty title, "roving ambassador." When his plane took off from Saigon, the final obstacle to Rolling Thunder had been removed.[84]

The nominal prime minister under Khanh, Pham Huy Quat, remained nominal under the new regime, closely controlled by the Armed Forces Council. On March 1, 1965, Air Marshal Ky, speaking for the council, declared that it would replace any government that in its judgment "threatened to betray the country." The next day American planes began the sustained bombing of North Vietnam.[85]

"The policy of gradual but steady reprisal against North Vietnam for its continuing aggression in the South had been put into action," Johnson wrote in his memoirs. "The decision was made because it had become clear, gradually but unmistakably, that Hanoi was moving in for the kill."[86] A few days after the bombing began, however, Johnson was in a dark mood. Outside the White House, blacks were marching for the right to vote. Preoccupied with his many problems, Johnson mused about his predicament. He was not optimistic the bombing would prove the answer. "I can't get out. I can't finish it with what I have got. So what the Hell can I do?"[87] His advisers were urging him to announce a Johnson Doctrine, a promise to undertake the "other" war in Vietnam, to bring the Great Society to Southeast Asia.

The Johnson Doctrine

WHEN THE BOMBING CAMPAIGN BEGAN, Richard Goodwin and Bill Moyers drafted a prophetic memorandum. The most threatening consequence of Rolling Thunder, they wrote, was that it had "escalated the war to the front page of every newspaper," diverting public attention from the Great Society and endangering the "consensus on which domestic progress depended."[1] Johnson had himself predicted that congressional conservatives would seize upon the war to block his legislative program. His top advisers were nonetheless surprised by the sudden appearance of a full-fledged "antiwar" movement, and pretty much at a loss as to how to respond to the Teach-in movement that spread rapidly across college campuses in opposition to the bombing. Dismiss the protesters as they might—uninformed young academics parading their little bit of learning in front of still younger students looking for a cause—here was something that could not be ignored.

Although the bombing campaign itself was having a hard time getting under way, given the cloud covers of a typical Vietnamese spring and—military leaders groused—Washington's severe limits on what targets could be hit, domestic and international opinion was aroused and seeking answers.[2] McGeorge Bundy had tried his hand at a speech addressed to "Fellow Americans—and Fellow Citizens of the World." For too many years, it began in an appropriately somber tone, the people of South Vietnam had had to endure guerrilla assaults on their peaceful villages, terroristic acts in their cities, and thousands of assassinations—all of these conceived and directed from the north. Now, our patience exhausted, the time had come for America to respond. "The aggressor will no longer be allowed to export death and destruction at no cost to himself. . . . We have been patient with your calculated use of fear against your neighbor and we fear that you have misunderstood us."[3]

Bundy's proposed speech promised that a full account of North Vietnam's crimes would be presented to the world, and new evidence submitted to the UN each time the United States found it necessary to launch another attack. "These actions will stop when the aggression stops." To "all the people of the world," Bundy had some special words:

> The United States knows that in any action which requires the use of force, there is need for care and prudence. We have shown that care and prudence throughout the last twenty years. We have had to deal with threats to peace in many parts of the world, and we have had to prove our good sense under many provocations. Through all that time we have been the world's strongest power, and through all that time we have been first in the responsible search for peace. As we now take resolute but limited action against a particularly destructive form of aggression, we feel it right to call attention to our claim upon your confidence. We have nothing to hide and we are eager for talks—our purpose is peace.[4]

The speech was not given. Johnson told his advisers he wanted no formal "announcement" of a change in policy. Something else Bundy said about American leadership eventually did appear in print. It sounded much different in tone, less like Old Testament prophecy and more like a former Harvard College dean. "What he had learned from Dean Acheson," the national security adviser explained, was that "in the final analysis, the United States was the locomotive at the head of mankind, and the rest of the world the caboose."[5] The promised evidence of North Vietnam's sins against its "neighbor" appeared in a State Department White Paper, *Aggression from the North: The Record of North Viet-Nam's Campaign to Conquer South Viet-Nam.* But its principal author, Chester Cooper, a Bundy aide, almost wished it had not appeared. "The White Paper proved to be a dismal disappointment." While certain data critical to the case were too highly classified to be divulged, Cooper would write, "the actual findings seemed pretty frail." Certainly they were not strong enough to provide support for a bombing campaign. Quite the opposite. "Three 75-millimeter recoilless rifles of Chinese Communist origin, forty-six Soviet-made rifles, forty sub-machine guns and one automatic pistol of Czech origin had been captured. This was hardly the kind of arsenal to lead many people, especially those who were initially skeptical, to feel it was necessary to bomb North Vietnam in order to stop the flow of men and equipment. The fact that since 1961 we had given the Government of South Vietnam over $860 million in military assistance made Hanoi's aid to the Viet Cong hardly seem consequential."[6]

The White Paper only satisfied the already convinced; it did nothing to make converts. "Page after page . . . of minuscule detail," a rueful Cooper quoted from the usually friendly *New York Times*, "merely raises anew the question of whether massive air strikes would accomplish anything except large-scale civilian casualties."[7] If the White Paper provided—at best—a shaky underpinning for the air campaign, it left Johnson's advisers and the president himself in an exposed position. Everything they now said was put in the context of an unequivocal condemnation of Hanoi and a commitment to redress the wrongs. A judgment had been rendered, punishment would be meted out. In Saigon, Ambassador Taylor was quoted as saying that "no limit existed to the potential escalation" of the war. On that same day, March 22, 1965, the Defense Department was reported to be using a variety of gas in Vietnam.

Where was it all leading? British Foreign Secretary Michael Stewart had just arrived in Washington and now found himself in the middle of the controversy. Stewart told both Dean Rusk and President Johnson that he would have to comment on these developments in a speech he was scheduled to deliver at a luncheon at the National Press Club. Whether he told them what he would say as he left the White House for the luncheon is another matter. "In the choice of measures everyone should consider not only what is militarily appropriate for the job in hand but the effect on people around the world. What I am in fact asking the United States to display," Stewart's blunt speech concluded, "is what your Declaration of Independence called 'a decent respect for the opinions of mankind.' "[8]

Hearing Jefferson's words thrown back at them by—of all people—a servant of the British crown was a galling experience. Johnson eventually replied to Stewart's ironic accusation with a curiously phrased statement that only highlighted the difficulty of the search for an effective answer to such criticism. "We have—as our forefathers had—a decent respect for the informed opinions of mankind," the president told an audience at Catholic University, "but we of this generation also have an abiding commitment to preserve and perpetuate the enduring values of mankind. And we shall keep that commitment."[9]

Introducing the qualifier "informed," and suggesting thereby that critics were ignorant of the true facts, became a staple of the Johnson administration's public response. But the persistent attempt to go beyond the White Paper to square the Vietnam War with America's idealized image of itself suggests that neither Lyndon Johnson nor his advisers were ever comfortable with the terms of the debate. And all too soon the original argument for starting the bombing campaign—to revive South Vietnam's faltering will to resist—was overtaken by an urgent need to demonstrate that the attacks could produce real military benefits. Deep down both the president and his advisers had shared a conviction that a steadily mounting air offensive would persuade Hanoi to cease, or at least curtail, its support of the guerrillas. Johnson had gone along with the bombing because he thought it would produce something like a traditional military victory—in the shortest time possible.

"Bomb, bomb, bomb. That's all you know," he was already complaining to General Harold Johnson, army chief of staff, only a day or so after Rolling Thunder began. "Well, I want to know why there's nothing else. You generals have all been educated at taxpayer's expense, and you're not giving me any ideas and any solutions for this damn little pissant country. Now, I don't need ten generals to come in here ten times and tell me to bomb. I want some solutions. I want some answers." The president then gave General Johnson orders to go to Vietnam to find those answers. As the two men descended in the White House elevator after their meeting, the president turned and stared closely at the general with a finger pointed at his chest. "You get things bubbling, General." [10]

Later that same day, however, in extemporaneous remarks he delivered during a congressional briefing session, LBJ revealed just how precarious he believed his position was. All those "fuzzy folks," he began, the people who were pushing for negotiations, they were "happy [go] lucky fellows that smoke a little marijuana and drift down the streets after they've had a drink or two." Good thing they never had any responsibility. Former President Eisenhower had told him, Johnson went on, about how he had conveyed to the North Koreans a "signal" about negotiations. What Ike had conveyed was that he would not feel constrained about using weapons—any weapons—anywhere, anytime. Within a week the Communists said, well, maybe we can work this thing out. [11]

But having invoked Eisenhower's example as a precursor for his own actions in Vietnam, Johnson backed away from its implications as fast as he could. "Now I'm not going to say that we are going to use all kinds of weapons." He might not even go as far as some of those present wanted him to go. But he was going to defend against aggression "out there . . . just as long as I can, and I think I can." This statement brought applause, but whether for Eisenhower's supposed threat to use atomic weapons or Johnson's promise he would not is impossible to say. Perhaps the congressmen clapped out of simple relief that the president had consulted with Eisenhower and seemed to know where he was going with the bombing campaign. [12]

Later on in the briefing, however, one of the legislators asked a key question: "Have we communicated to them informally, formally or otherwise, our indication or our willingness to use whatever force may be necessary?" Defense Secretary McNamara suggested that we had "by the very fact that we have not indicated the contrary policy." Johnson then joined in to say that that was the approach Eisenhower had found effective in Korea. The bombing was to persuade Hanoi to stop sending infiltrators into South Vietnam. "We're trying to take their temperature. I guess as they're taking ours. . . . Any damn fool can lay a bomb on Hanoi in four hours. It's just a question whether that is the wise way to do it. . . . Now we're hoping that they keep on coming and we keep on killing them and we touch them up here and touch them up [t]here and we hit them up here—that in time they will say, well, we want to try to work this thing out and we will try to buy an agreement. That's all we hope."[13]

What had begun as a confident recitation of how strength of purpose had been passed on from one president to another thus trailed off into vaguer territory. It appeared, after all, that LBJ had not put to rest the questions and doubts, whether from "hawks" or "doves." When General Johnson returned from Saigon, the terms of the debate shifted to the question of American ground forces in Vietnam. In his formal report the general recommended deploying a division of U.S. ground troops to free South Vietnamese army units from security duties and shift them to combat, as well as a four-division ground force, made up of either American troops or an international force, to stand guard at the 17th parallel "border" across Vietnam. General Johnson submitted twenty-one other recommendations about bigger and better bombing missions and such, but ground forces were the new element. The general introduced this part of his report with a blunt statement: "The time has come to decide how much the United States is willing to commit to the security of South Vietnam within South Vietnam."[14]

In a conversation with the president, the general was blunter still: to win the war could take 500,000 U.S. troops and five years. According to an aide, this statement "sent a shock wave through the administration because they hadn't been talking in those terms or even facing up to that kind of a possibility."[15] Ever since Korea, army leaders had been more than dubious about involving the United States in another land war in Asia. A "Never Again" club had been formed to prevent a repetition of that situation. General Johnson had himself expressed the view in February 1965 that Vietnam could be Korea all over, "only worse, an enemy using sanctuaries, the United States unable and unwilling to use its full power, all the old frustrations again." Yet here he was ready only a month later to send up to four divisions to help Vietnam remain a nation. "The alternative was that Vietnam fell to North Vietnam," he later explained his about-face.[16]

Max Taylor remained loyal to the "Never Again" club. He argued vehemently against troops.[17] If the administration resisted the blandishments of "our friends" who, by their constant pressure for negotiations, gave Hanoi reason to believe the air strikes were "meaningless," and if it carried out the Phase II campaign as envisioned back in December to convince the Communists that they faced the prospect of "progressively severe punishment," all would come out well—and sooner rather than later. "I fear that to date Rolling Thunder in their eyes has been merely a few isolated thunder claps."[18]

But Taylor knew he was up against a powerful force in Washington, "flogged to a new level of creativity by a President determined to get results." He moved with that force, reluctantly, and with considerable misgivings about the future.[19] If he had not moved, McGeorge Bundy was ready to shove him out. Bundy had leaped out ahead of General Johnson in suggesting to the president that a decision would have to be made about sending ground troops, perhaps a force made up of Australians, Filipinos, Thais, Koreans, and conceivably even Pakistanis. This, he said in his March 6, 1965, memo, "would give real international color to the defense of South Vietnam and would also have a substantial braking effect on any possible Communist escalation."[20]

Taylor was doubtful about the idea, Bundy went on, but Rusk and McNamara agreed with him that it was worth "serious" exploration. "Max has been gallant, determined, and honorable to a fault," he wrote elsewhere in the memorandum recommending a change in ambassadors, "but he has also been rigid, remote and sometimes abrupt." Although Bundy congratulated the president on his decision not to make the bombing appear to be a major new departure, and although he said the air actions had caused "somewhat less international reaction than we expected," the most surprising thing about the memo was its gloomy prognosis. After all, Rolling Thunder had begun only a few days earlier. Johnson's "noisiest advisers," as Bundy labeled himself, Rusk, and McNamara, had worked on the president for four months to get him to commit himself to the bombing. Already the national security adviser had apparently decided it would not work. Last night, he told Johnson, Bob McNamara said for the first time what many others had been thinking for a long time: "The Pentagon and the military have been going at this thing the wrong way round from the very beginning." The key to victory was not in military engagements with the guerrillas but in pacification programs from the village up.[21]

What accounts for this sudden reassessment? While Bundy congratulated Johnson on the quieter than expected international reaction, he could not feel serenely confident that as Phase II moved the bombers steadily closer to Hanoi, opposition to administration policy would not escalate as well. At the same time McNamara was discovering that the Pentagon had been going at the thing the wrong way round from the beginning, the *New York Times* was calling the bombing a "One-Way Street strategy." "There is inherently a tacit admission of failure in this new American strategy," its lead editorial read. "Even if American strategy in North Vietnam is successful there is no reason to suppose that the Vietcong in South Vietnam will end their internal war against whatever government happens to be installed in Saigon." What prospect was there for winning a war in the north gradually being lost in the south? The major prospect, instead, was for Russian and Chinese involvement. "And how far is this country prepared to pursue the one-way street in which it is letting itself be trapped?"[22]

Similar criticisms from college faculty—even Harvard faculty—failed to dent Bundy's resolve. The Teach-in movement was not something he could take all that seriously, like an uproar over some perceived slight to faculty prerogatives of consultation. But editorials like the one in the *Times* made him uneasy. Within a few days he was sending Johnson another memorandum, no less gloomy, about the prospects for victory through air power. In it he paid special attention to General Johnson's recommendation for sending four divisions to Vietnam to establish the line at the 17th parallel. Defense and State were studying the recommendation, he said. "Preliminary analysis suggests that such deployment may soon be necessary for both military and political reasons." The argument here seemed to be that whether or not the Americans could halt the infiltration, their presence would signal to Hanoi that victory would be denied the Communists—no matter the cost.

Three outcomes had emerged as possibilities for an eventual settlement, Bundy wrote. The most desirable, but the least likely as matters stood, was a wholly non-Communist Vietnam. After that came a "somewhat Laotian solution," a coalition government that would include members of the NLF and would accept de facto Viet Cong control of large parts of the countryside. "This is what the French and the Lippmanns have in mind, and . . . this solution would be acceptable only if some significant U.S. presence remained" to hold substantial areas, especially Saigon. The third choice was an explicit partition of South Vietnam. It would provide for a rapid deescalation, but VC ambition made it the least tenable of the three. It was not necessary to choose right away. "What does appear quite likely is that our eventual bargaining position with respect to all three possibilities will be improved and not weakened if the United States presence on the ground increases in coming weeks." [23]

Bundy also proposed that Johnson now deliver something on the order of the speech he had declined to give when the bombing started: "a more detailed exposition of our conditions for peace, and our view of the future in Southeast Asia." The object of the speech would be to gain time to improve the American bargaining position. That would also be the object of increasing the American ground presence. "Our object must be to trade off our own trumps in return for enemy actions which will give us advantage in the South. This will not be easy." [24]

It would not be easy to gain time with critics, nor to use that time to finesse the Pentagon's desire to combine troops and heavy bombing to "win" the war. Bundy may have thought his recommendations provided effective answers to criticism like that offered in the *Times* editorial. But the sudden reassessment of the bombing campaign suggested that for all the preliminary planning and debate, the Phase I and Phase II plans had never really been thought through.

Ambassador Taylor may have had little firsthand knowledge of the subtleties of this emerging dialogue at the highest level, but he knew that General Johnson had taken back to Washington Westmoreland's plea for ground troops. Taylor pointed out that while introducing a division of U.S. troops would end talk of a possible withdrawal, it would also mean greater involvement in the counterinsurgency. And that would mean greater losses and the introduction of sensitive questions. It might, for example, encourage an attitude of letting the United States do it. "It will increase our vulnerability to Communist propaganda and third country criticism as we appear to assume the old French role of alien colonizer and conqueror."[25]

Taylor often came close, as in this instance, to an implicit concession that the bombing would not win the war. He had originally advocated it as a "pulmotor treatment," a final effort to get the South Vietnamese out of their lethargy and to punish the north. He had then argued that the bombing would bring a favorable political solution. So had Johnson's other advisers—if not with Taylor's apparent conviction. The ambassador's exaggerated claims for the bombing perhaps discredited his views on sending American troops, or perhaps he failed to present the views of the new government in Saigon effectively enough. In Vietnam the first contingent of American marines assigned to guard the air base at Danang had arrived on March 8, 1965. General Khanh had been removed from the scene, to be replaced by the more pliable Pham Huy Quat. But even Quat was alarmed at the peremptory manner in which Washington demanded a "communiqué" from him announcing the landing, as if it had come in response to a formal request. "I think Taylor himself was taken by surprise by a quick decision from Washington," Quat told a colleague. "This morning he tried to present it to me as a strictly limited military move that had to be taken because conditions were bad around the base." Quat and Taylor shared the view that American troops were dangerous—to South Vietnam's chances. "To be openly accused of being puppets was not just personally insulting," wrote Bui Diem, Quat's associate, "it was a wedge that would be driven between the government and the people."[26]

Taylor understood the point. But in Washington Mac Bundy was preoccupied with figuring out what President Johnson should say to the nation to blunt criticism of the bombing and prepare opinion for the next steps in Vietnam. At lunch with the man who had originally recommended him to Kennedy four years earlier, the national security adviser listened to Walter Lippmann repeat his advice that the United States should settle for a "Titoist Vietnam" as the best available outcome. The idea still seemed "foolish" to Bundy, but Lippmann said something else that he felt deserved the president's attention: "the need for a Wilsonian 14 points on Southeast Asia." He had drafted an opening statement for Johnson to make at his next press conference that would incorporate much of what Lippmann proposed.[27]

Meanwhile, Bundy prepped himself on the essentials of the Vietnam question as they now appeared. The "cardinal" interest of the United States was "*not* to be a Paper Tiger." While this meant a willingness to fight China if necessary to prove the nation stood by its commitments, it probably would not come to that if the administration focused attention "where it belongs: on the South." This implied, among other things, a change in ambassadors. If the United States did enough in the south, whatever that might be, then failure would be considered "beyond our control." Bundy then engaged in a series of private conjectures. "Question: in terms of domestic US politics, which is better: to lose now or to lose after committing 100,000 men? Tentative answer: the latter." But was this political issue real or fancied? "A tentative conclusion is that: the whole game is less than it today appears because the level of open conflict is and will probably stay low—and because the result elsewhere would not be earthshattering—win or lose." Both sides would be able to claim special circumstances whenever they wanted. Yet, perhaps surprisingly, that did not lead him to conclude that getting out via the French/Lippmann route was best for everybody. He turned briefly to the question of how to get out *after* having put in x number of divisions. He thus raised the key question, but did not answer it. Instead he ended with something like a shrug that everyone was stuck with the situation. "A hasty glance suggests that in very large measure this analysis is reciprocal for US and USSR (and now China to a degree). This means the battle in the South must go on. (And of course that *is* what is happening.)"[28]

Bundy's agenda for the March 23 "Tuesday Luncheon," a new White House mechanism for intimate discussion with only a few regulars, listed several items on Vietnam. "Where are we going?" Johnson demanded, tossing the agenda aside. According to Bundy's sketchy notes, McNamara and Rusk did not have much to report. The message that America was in to stay *might* be getting through to Hanoi, said the defense secretary. Johnson wondered if Hanoi knew he was willing to talk? Then he said that the bombers could revisit once-hit targets. "I don't wanna run out of targets and I don't wanna go to Hanoi. I was a hell of a long time getting into this. But I like it."[29]

Johnson's new enthusiasm for the war is not further explained in Bundy's notes of the Tuesday Luncheon. Two days later, however, the president issued a "statement" on the war. "It is important," it began, "for us all to keep a cool and clear view of the situation in Vietnam." There were seven points in Johnson's statement, not the Wilsonian fourteen. But in several places it echoed Woodrow Wilson's statements on world order from the time of the Mexican Revolution to the intervention in Russia. "We threaten no regime and covet no territory. . . . But the aggression from the North must be stopped." Point 5 was the most Wilsonian of all:

The United States looks forward to the day when the people and governments of all Southeast Asia may be free from terror, subversion, and assassination—when they will need not military support and assistance against aggression, but only economic and social cooperation for progress in peace. Even now, in Vietnam and elsewhere, there are major programs of development which have the cooperation and support of the United States. Wider and bolder programs can be expected in the future from Asian leaders and Asian councils—and in such programs we would want to help. This is the proper business of our future cooperation.[30]

Johnson's young assistant, Bill Moyers, who would replace George Reedy as press secretary, was ecstatic about the "hole you opened up today." "There could be developed the 'Johnson Plan' for Southeast Asia equivalent to the Marshall Plan for Europe." The perfect place had been suggested by Jack Valenti—a speech celebrating the University of Virginia's 222nd anniversary on April 13. The time and place would be perfect. "You could widen Thomas Jefferson's dream for America into a dream for the world." In the meantime, thought Moyers, "we ought to continue to sustain our pressure militarily . . . while developing this approach."[31]

Whether he "liked" the war better now because he enjoyed the role of commander in chief, or because Bundy had supplied him with the seven points, LBJ was in his element. He was on the verge of putting his opponents, domestic and foreign, back on the defensive. He had faced down Governor George Wallace of Alabama on the question of the voting-rights protest marches in Selma, and had quoted Martin Luther King—"and we shall overcome"—in a speech to Congress calling for passage of the Voting Rights Act, both to tremendous expressions of approval. From United Auto Workers president Walter Reuther he heard it was "reassuring" that the historic task of ensuring full citizenship was in good hands. "Under your dedicated and inspired leadership, I am certain that we shall overcome." A former black aide to President Eisenhower wrote, "This is a better country and a better world today because of your Christian conviction."[32]

The crisis in Selma demonstrated that Johnson would not back away from his domestic commitments, the crisis in Vietnam that he would not back away from the U.S. commitment to the world. The promise he had long held out to the South, the promise of again playing a leading role politically and economically, that promise he now had on the tip of his tongue for Southeast Asia. On March 26, the day after he issued his seven-point statement on Vietnam, the president went on television to announce the arrest of Ku Klux Klan members for the murder of a Detroit civil rights worker, Mrs. Viola Liuzzo, who had been shot as she was transporting blacks for the march between Montgomery and Selma. "We will not be intimidated by the terrorists of the Ku Klux Klan any more than we will be intimidated by the terrorists in North Vietnam."[33]

Johnson declared himself ready to go on the political offensive in Vietnam as he had with the Voting Rights Bill in the United States. He was tired of being on the defensive over things like the use of tear gas to control riots in Saigon, he said, a somewhat ironic counterpoint to his condemnation of local Alabama officials' use of fire hoses and truncheons. "An overall policy speech on Vietnam should be prepared," he instructed the National Security Council. "We should enlist new brain power in drafting the things which need to be said."[34]

That same day future Vietnam critic Senator George S. McGovern came to the White House to talk about the situation. McGovern had carefully prepared for this meeting. He brought with him a formal presentation that began by commending the president for his March 25 statement, especially his offer to go anywhere, at any time, to meet with anyone if there were a promise of progress toward an honorable peace. Building on that announcement, the senator went on, "would it be wise for you now to issue a more detailed policy statement, along the lines of Woodrow Wilson's Fourteen Points or Franklin D. Roosevelt's Atlantic Charter, or even the very effective Red Chinese Panch Shila of 1955 (pledging non-intervention in its neighbors' affairs)?" American policy had to go beyond vows to stop aggression from the north, or not to withdraw from Southeast Asia. The Alliance for Progress had wider goals than merely to stop Cuban subversion. "Likewise, your magnificent efforts to stop the injustice against Negroes have been combined with the promise of a 'great society' for all Americans." That was the right approach in Asia, even though the practical difficulties of carrying it out were great.[35]

McGovern believed a beginning could be made by encouraging the north and south to negotiate a trade agreement, somewhat on the order of the economic arrangements between East and West Germany. As Johnson had indicated, the basis of a settlement probably should be the 1954 Geneva accords. McGovern's use of the German example indicated, however, that he understood and shared the administration's qualified view of the free general elections clause. Free elections in Vietnam, like reunification of the two Germanies, was something far off—an ultimate goal that no one expected would be realized, at least not soon. "I strongly favor . . . a Mekong River regional development effort, perhaps modeled on our own TVA, to promote not only economic growth, but also a sense of regional community."[36]

"I was a hell of a long time getting into this. But I like it," Johnson had told the Tuesday Luncheon. Bundy was spreading the word, meanwhile, "to a number of people" about paragraph five of the Vietnam statement, "on economic development in Southeast Asia." He had gotten a good response from White House reporters and television commentators. "Walter Lippmann called me to send thanks for your courtesy in having a copy of the Vietnam statement sent to him." There was only one hitch with Lippmann. "He asked whether in our view the essentials of the Geneva Accords included reunification. I told him we did not see it this way. . . ." Bundy was alerting the State Department to be ready for a Lippmann column pushing that argument.[37]

Meanwhile, the national security adviser went to work on a draft of the proposed policy speech. It rehearsed all the arguments for the American position, reaching, not surprisingly, the standard conclusion that "Vietnam [is] the best place" to meet "this type of challenge." The speech should contain a section "along the lines of paragraph 5 of the President's statement of yesterday, but with more concreteness." This section would spell out "the true future of Southeast Asia." Meanwhile, the effort to defend South Vietnam must continue. "We should speak of the reality of South Vietnam's own revolution . . . , and we should make plain once more our own stamina, and determination, and control, and good heart."[38]

Suggestions for the policy speech came to Bundy from a number of White House aides. Chester Cooper, for example, thought it should be framed in terms of the "human spirit" everywhere.

> The issue goes well beyond Vietnam or Southeast Asia. Free men everywhere must oppose by every possible means the stifling of the human spirit in any part of the world. We are determined that no more doors be slammed, no more windows be shut, on the free flow of ideas and peoples and goods. For it is on this that the promise of twentieth century man depends—whatever his color, wherever his home.[39]

Another memorandum from Bundy's office elaborated on these same themes, providing perhaps the best summary of New Frontier / Great Society policymakers' views of the evolving relationship between social forces inside and outside the United States. Historians of the future, it began, might designate the 1960s as the decade when "our civilization fashioned so painfully since the Reformation could be said to have reached its end." If that happened, it would likely not be because of nuclear cataclysm but as a result of a new polarization of the world between the poor, the restless, and the nonwhite peoples, led or pushed by China, as opposed to Europe and North America.

"We will find ourselves in a virtual state of siege," predicted the writer:

> The West, of course, still can survive as a political grouping and even as a culture. We will still maintain overwhelming military power in the sense that we could at any time reduce the land mass of Asia and of Africa to ashes. But this would provide us with slim comfort. . . .

In the last analysis, the West must preserve (or at least not willingly and voluntarily default) its access to, communications with, and benign influence on the peoples of Asia and Africa. We have much that is worthwhile to offer and much to gain. Our society and theirs can be enriched and nourished by the two-way flow of ideas and goods and peoples. China has chosen to slam its doors, at least for the present. We and the other peoples of the world cannot afford to see any more doors close, for every door that closes quickens the pace of rich-poor, colored-white, North-South division of the world.[40]

Bundy had also called upon his aide Walt Rostow for advice as to how the question of American aid to Southeast Asian economic development could be given concreteness, as the national security adviser had put it. Rostow's suggestion was to convince "U Thant to seize this idea and make himself the Ernie Bevin of the exercise." Bevin's crucial role as Labour foreign secretary at the outset of the cold war had given American policy a useful shield from leftist criticism in the development of the Marshall Plan and NATO. "Having launched the concept in the context of the South Vietnam crisis, we should seek now (via U Thant or otherwise) to detach it operationally from the crisis so that it may go forward on a parallel track with the widest possible Asian and Free World support."[41]

Like the Marshall Plan and NATO, the major political purpose of the proposal, whatever final form it took, was to dramatize the seriousness of America's long-term commitment to Asian development and unity. It would thus offer ways to convince Hanoi that American policy had not isolated itself from the mainstream of Asian political and economic life.[42] Rostow had sent Dean Rusk, meanwhile, a proposal for a "Johnson Doctrine." America's world position required a foreign policy with clearly stated objectives. In a nutshell, he wrote, the major conclusion was this:

> It is our interest in each of the regions of the Free World to assist in the development of local arrangements which, while reducing their direct dependence on the United States, would leave the regions open to cooperative military, economic and political arrangements with the U.S. This requires of us a systematic policy designed to strengthen the hand of moderates in the regions and to reduce the power of extremists— whether those extremists are Communists or ambitious nationalists anxious to take over and dominate their regions. We are for those who, while defending legitimate national and regional interests, respect the extraordinarily intimate interdependence of the modern world and pursue policies of development and peace rather than aggrandizement.[43]

Bundy picked up on Rostow's suggested idea of drafting U Thant to play Ernie Bevin's role in what was now being called a Southeast Asia Economic Development Plan. Modeled as closely as possible on the Marshall

Plan, on which the national security adviser had originally cut his teeth in government service, the project would enable the United States to separate its larger goals from Vietnam, just as the European recovery scheme had been separated from the Truman Doctrine of military aid to Greece and Turkey. The more policy planners looked at the situation this way, the more striking the parallel became to them. "We do not want it thought that we are interested in economic development," Bundy wrote to the president as the idea took shape in his mind, "only because we are trying somehow to get out of our mess in Vietnam. The Marshall Plan was helpful in dealing with Soviet pressure on Europe, but it was not designed or presented to the *Europeans* in those terms."[44]

It would not be necessary or wise, however, to offer a precise description of the form this development organization would take, or to make a commitment in dollar terms. "A long forward pass would probably be incomplete, if we do not line up some receivers downfield. This could make us look quite silly." Hopefully U Thant could be persuaded to "pick up the ball and organize some Asian responses." Averell Harriman should then be asked to take charge on the American side, "because of his history as a Marshall Plan leader, his international prestige and his position as a liberal."[45]

Despite Bundy's warning against getting too specific at the outset, Johnson had been in contact with his old friend, UN economist Arthur Goldschmidt, about putting into the speech a recommendation for a $1 billion contribution from the United States to the Mekong River plan to lead off the Asian development scheme. He did not want Harriman to head up the American side, preferring Eugene Black, former head of the World Bank. "Bundy agreed this was fine and would neutralize Fulbright," recorded White House aide Jack Valenti.[46]

Time was becoming a crucial factor. Operation Rolling Thunder, the bombing campaign, had begun on March 2, 1965; plans were being made for stepping up the war with more ground forces. The first Vietnam teach-in was held at the University of Michigan on March 24. A week later a conference of "nonaligned" nations meeting in Belgrade called upon the interested parties to begin negotiations "as soon as possible, without posing any preconditions."

Interestingly, Defense Secretary Robert McNamara felt that Bundy needed to come out "a little stronger" on economic development to go with the theme of unwavering resistance to aggression. "I have also wanted to include enough history," Bundy wrote the president when he submitted the results, "to keep us straight in the line started by Eisenhower and continued by Kennedy. The Kennedy quotations are designed to give us protection and encouragement with some of the 'liberals' who are falsely telling each other that your policy is different from his."[47]

Also attached to Bundy's draft were some final words of encouragement—and caution: "This may well be the most important foreign policy speech you have yet prepared." Johnson read over Bundy's effort and told another close aide, Jack Valenti, and speechwriter Richard Goodwin, the principal author of the 1964 Great Society speech, to convert it into a presidential-style address. Get more into it about American willingness to commit large sums to the economic development of Southeast Asia, he instructed, and specifically something about the "Mekong River project," a proposed system of dams to rationalize irrigation patterns and bring electrification to a broad area across national boundaries that reminded the president of the New Deal TVA.[48]

Valenti's research discovered that the Mekong project, under United Nations supervision, was still progressing despite the war in Vietnam and strained relations between Saigon and the cooperating nations, Cambodia, Laos, and Thailand. Fourteen million dollars had been spent thus far on preliminary work needed to design a program of managing water and land for the population of twenty million, mostly rice farmers, who lived in the regions through which the lower Mekong flowed. But the American contribution, Valenti emphasized, had been only about $5 million, less than the cost of four days of military aid. "Send to Goodwin this a.m.," Johnson scrawled on Valenti's report.[49]

Goodwin was ambiguous about his assignment. Uneasy about the drift toward deeper involvement in Vietnam, he nevertheless turned his hand to what the president had asked for—and came up with a billion-dollar proposal for the Mekong plan—because he wanted to believe that Vietnam was but a "transient aberration," a temporary diversion from the Great Society domestic programs that were still to be the "centerpiece and overriding goal of the Johnson administration."[50] In early 1965, with administration aides storming Capitol Hill almost daily armed with White House proposals, Vietnam did still appear if not a "transient aberration," certainly less central than the Great Society. Given Johnson's instructions, Goodwin could even have argued himself into believing further that the speech was about taking the War on Poverty to Vietnam.

That was indeed something of what the president intended. But Goodwin's draft gave him the phrases and wording he wanted to commit the United States to a fateful mission in Southeast Asia. The "principle" at stake, began the final version, was the same as that "for which our ancestors fought in the valleys of Pennsylvania." Changes in successive drafts made the speech an entangling policy declaration. In an early version, for example, this opening reference to the American Revolution was followed by a series of somewhat uncertain disclaimers: "Vietnam is a strange and distant place. Most of us know little about the land or its people. We have no territory there, nor do we seek any."[51] These were not suitable at all. The final version replaced the first two sentences in this sequence with: "Vietnam is far from this quiet campus."

The change was significant. The president's purpose was to put Vietnam into a familiar framework, not emphasize the physical distance that separated that country from North America, or its culture from Western assumptions. If the North Vietnamese ceased their aggression, Goodwin's speech promised midway on, linking both the promise of the Great Society and the liberal heritage of the New Deal to American objectives in Vietnam, they would find the United States eager to help them to overcome "the bondage of material misery." "The vast Mekong River can provide food and water and power on a scale to dwarf even our own TVA."

"In the countryside where I was born," the speech continued, now in the form of an emotional reminiscence about what the New Deal had accomplished with the Tennessee Valley Authority,

> and where I live, I have seen the night illuminated, and the kitchen warmed, and the home heated, where once the cheerless night and the ceaseless cold held sway. And all this happened because electricity came to our area along the humming wires of the REA.[52]

As in Europe where the Marshall Plan followed the Truman Doctrine, Johnson was pledging the nation to do something, in fact a lot more, than merely contain the Communists. Above all, he had deemed it essential to show that what had worked in America would work in Southeast Asia. Nebulous plans for a series of dams on the Mekong River, and the proposed offer of $1 billion, alarmed the State Department, which argued with White House advisers for taking out that section because "we didn't have a plan for using it [the money.]"[53] That missed the point, the White House replied, and restored the billion-dollar offer. The president was pleased with his advisers: "I see you put this back in—that's good."[54]

As this final draft was being completed, Bundy aide Chester Cooper reported on reactions to point five in the president's March 25 statement on aid for Southeast Asia. Hanoi claimed this "bait" only exposed more plainly than ever the "stupid and aggressive colonialist nature" of American policy. Beijing added that the United States apparently had "suddenly thought of the carrot as a hopeful complement to the big stick. . . ." Outside the immediate region, India had shown no real reaction. "The Embassy attributes this to the fact that the proposals did not emerge clearly and a dramatic setting for giving them the necessary weight was lacking." On the other hand, U Thant had spoken warmly of the president's initiative. He would take no action until he had discussed detailed possibilities with American officials. "The Mission impression was that U Thant was amenable to taking a lead if he could find a line of approach which had some possibility of involving the DRV."[55]

The whole point of the president's speech was to recast the war as a prelude to a new era of Asian economic and political development. "Tonight," the speech would begin, "Americans and Asians are dying for a world where each people may choose its own path to change." If only Hanoi and the rest of the Communist world would understand that American goals were limited to the preservation of South Vietnam's freedom of choice, all the killing could stop, and so forth. Then all nations could get back to making the ancient dream of world order come true. "We have the power and now we have the opportunity to make that dream come true." Even now, before the fighting ended, the United States was ready to engage in a "massive effort to improve the life of man in that conflict-torn corner of the world." Then came the call for U Thant to take the lead in developing a plan for economic cooperation with all the countries of Southeast Asia.[56]

All this and more was possible. What was not possible was any change in the American position about dealing with the NLF—just, for example, as there had never been room for compromise over the status of Berlin. The United States, Johnson was to say, would never be second in the search for a peaceful solution. But negotiations or the "unconditional discussions" he promised were to be between only "the governments concerned." This, in essence, was the full Truman Doctrine / Marshall Plan / NATO scenario as imagined for Southeast Asia, and reduced to a single speech.[57]

The section in the speech that referred to the specifics of negotiations or discussions was squeezed in between a discussion of American military power and the promise of economic development—the war had become simply an awkward bulge blocking passage from the strife of the past into the promised world of the future. "Every night," began Johnson's peroration, "before I turn out the lights to sleep I ask myself this question: Have I done everything I can to unite this country? Have I done everything I can to help unite the world, to try to bring peace and hope to all the peoples of the world? Have I done enough?"[58]

Satisfied with what his aides had prepared, the president read the final product to a delegation of twenty-five Americans for Democratic Action. They "received it with enthusiasm." As the ADA delegation started to leave, Johnson asked members of the National Security Council to come into the cabinet room. "It would be good for them to rub shoulders with the ADA."[59]

But while invocations of the New Deal spirit were a sure bet to provide a palliative for nervous ADAers, there was more to it than a need to calm queasy liberals. Johnson's whole career *was* the politics of economic development. His decision to focus on the proposed Mekong River project, a plan that had been bouncing around UN agencies for some time, had evolved, in the first place, from what he remembered about the project as vice-president when he made the 1961 tour of Vietnam and Asia for President Kennedy. But the Mekong resonated with Johnson's earliest political memories and for that reason added to the confidence (and urgency) he felt about Vietnam. Far more than Kennedy, Johnson's political career had been intimately entwined with the positive role of government in the economic development of "backward" regions, whether as a newly elected Roosevelt stalwart in Congress in the 1930s, or as Senate majority leader in the cold war calling for more spending on space projects.

Johnson took Goodwin's draft to Camp David the weekend before the speech, now scheduled for delivery at Johns Hopkins University on April 7. He invited his old friend from New Deal years, economist Arthur Goldschmidt, now director of special funds at the United Nations, to join him at the presidential retreat. Goldschmidt had been the first to call the Mekong project to Johnson's attention in 1961, as the vice-president was preparing to leave on his mission to Southeast Asia.

What Goldschmidt reemphasized to Johnson during that weekend at Camp David before the Johns Hopkins speech was probably along the lines of what he had written in a more recent article on the U.S. government's role in the development of the American South and Southwest in the New Deal years. At that time "Tex" Goldschmidt and Johnson had both been interested in the Lower Colorado River Authority, Goldschmidt as a planner, Johnson as a politician. In those days they would meet in Washington on Goldschmidt's porch in Georgetown to discuss a report on economic backwardness in the South that Roosevelt had requested. Writing later about that report, Goldschmidt noted that the South in the 1930s had existed as "a kind of colony of the U.S." But the traditional antidote to colonialism was obviously not available to the region. "Only economic integration with the nation as a whole could cure the South and close the North-South gap. And this integration could only be accomplished by Federal action. There is a direct parallel today in the economic development of the former colonial regions of the world."[60]

The two most important government interventions, asserted Goldschmidt, had been in "land reform" (broadly conceived to include improvements in farm credits and marketing) and irrigation programs, all the way from the TVA down to micro-management of small streams in hills and gullies. "Water conservation and development projects, led by the pace-making Tennessee Valley Authority program, brought navigation channels, flood control projects, and power to the region." The South also provided an example of what the third world was undergoing, as economic development there had been accompanied by social upheaval and the shattering of traditional patterns of living. "In this situation fear of the future and nostalgia for the past occasionally outweigh courage and eagerness for progress."

It was ironic, he continued, that the region which had presented to the world such a disturbing picture of human relations should also hold out such an important message to the emerging nations.

> Economic development is too important to leave to the blind play of economic forces; it can be hastened or hindered by the intervention of policies designed to increase production and promote welfare. And the process is strengthened by outside assistance. The rich nations of the world will have to do for the poor nations what the Federal Government of the U.S. did for the South.

Johnson had thanked Goldschmidt for sending him the article on the South, writing, "We are in a better position to handle some of the problems of the developing countries because of the problems we faced so recently in developing our own."[61]

The president returned from Camp David on Monday, April 5, confident he was in a better position to head off defections and that he had the right mix for this speech that McGeorge Bundy had suggested could be his "most important foreign policy speech." Johnson knew he had a tough sell. A few days before he was scheduled to deliver the speech at Johns Hopkins, Canadian Prime Minister Lester Pearson had spoken at Temple University in Philadelphia suggesting a cease-fire to give negotiations a fair chance. Johnson was incensed by Pearson's performance. He took it out on Mac Bundy, recorded Jack Valenti. Why Bundy should be blamed for not muzzling Pearson seemed beside the point. What the president was really angry about, one suspects, was the evidence of discontent within NATO about American policy, and, still more, the refocusing of attention on the specifics of the war.[62]

Bundy warned him the day before the Johns Hopkins speech that he must be careful in talking with Walter Lippmann about the phrase "unconditional discussions." Lippmann had become infected, it appeared, with a virulent strain of "neutralism" transmitted to North America from Paris. Bundy arranged for the pundit to have a private audience with Johnson Tuesday afternoon, the day before the speech. "A part of our purpose, after all," argued the national security adviser, "is to plug his guns. . . ."[63]

Bundy was concerned only that Lippmann might catch on that Johnson's offer of "unconditional discussions" did not mean accepting the non-aligned nations' proposal for negotiations, nor any willingness to talk about the composition of the government of South Vietnam or reunification. "While I recommend these words myself and believe that they put us in a strong, balanced position, there is no doubt that some commentators will think that they are not so much a clarification as a softening of the position. My own view is the opposite, as you know." The best way to approach Lippmann, he said, would be "to slide gently past the words 'unconditional discussions.' " Later in the same memo, Bundy seemed to change his mind.

Lippmann should perhaps hear it straight from the president himself that the United States was not ready for a cease-fire.[64]

> You may also want to make it clear to Lippmann that when we say we are ready to talk, we do not at all mean that we are ready for a cease-fire. The fact is that we expect our own military action to continue unless we see a prospect of a better situation in the South than we have now. Walter needs to understand this, and if he gets it straight from you, he is likely to be less objectionable about it. Under pressure he will admit that the Secretary of Defense is excellent, but he will still think him wrong. He has a useful tendency to think the President himself is right.[65]

Lippmann arrived at the White House late that afternoon and was ushered into an anteroom of the Oval Office, where the president sat perched on a stool, posing for a sculptor. "Walter, I'm going up to Baltimore tomorrow to give a speech," Johnson began, "and I'm going to hold out that carrot you keep talking about." Nodding to Bundy, he went on, "Now Mac here is going to show you the speech, and I want to know what you think of it." Lippmann had hardly gotten through the first page, however, when the president began bellowing, telling it straight, as Bundy had suggested he do. "I'm not just going to pull up my pants and run out on Vietnam," he declared. "Don't you know the church is on fire over there . . . ?" Using General Curtis LeMay and Senator Wayne Morse as the unacceptable extremes of bombing and surrender, Johnson lectured the famed columnist about the middle way. "You say to negotiate, but there's nobody over there to negotiate with. So the only thing there is to do is to hang on. And that's what I'm going to do."[66]

After about an hour of this, the president sent Lippmann off to another room to discuss the speech with Bundy. For some time Lippmann had believed that Mac Bundy was a reluctant hawk, though he had begun to express doubts as a result of previous conversations. "This isn't going to work, Mac," Lippmann said when they were alone. "It's just a disguised demand for capitulation." The only thing that could bring a favorable response was an unconditional cease-fire. Bundy argued the point but suggested he would do what he could about the speech.[67]

Lippmann's fear that Bundy's years in the White House had "coarsened" his method of analysis, and his growing conviction that LBJ's advisers were pushing him into making Vietnam an American tragedy, were only momentarily assuaged by the Johns Hopkins speech. There was something in it for everyone. When he confronted Bundy afterward, disappointed that there had been no mention of a cease-fire, he was told that Johnson had no intention of negotiating as long as Saigon remained so weak.[68]

At 9 p.m. on April 7, 1965, President Johnson stepped to the podium in an auditorium at Johns Hopkins University and into the glare of television lights. The first real stirrings of uneasiness about Vietnam had brought him there, and he was determined to place the war into a proper cold war framework. "We will not be defeated. We will not grow tired. We will not withdraw, either openly or under the cloak of a meaningless agreement." What fateful vows these were, underlined in the slow cadence Johnson always used to convey resolve: "We *will not* be defeated. We *will not* grow tired. We *will not* withdraw. . . ." These were warnings, moreover, not only to the enemies of the Saigon regime but also to Americans. "We must stay in Southeast Asia—as we did in Europe—in the words of the Bible: 'Hitherto shalt thou come, but no further.' "

White House aides were satisfied the president had succeeded in turning things around. Listeners could hear what they wanted to hear: a plan for the Mekong Valley, or a warning that the United States was in Vietnam to stay. The speech had brought a "sharp reversal in the heavy flow of critical mail" to the White House. From four or five to one against the administration's policy, letters and telegrams were now running four or five to one in favor. In particular, Johnson's offer of economic aid had brought strong expressions of approval, albeit mixed with some concern about paying what Republican Senator Everett Dirksen had called "tribute" to an enemy. Dirksen's response, however, only helped ensure liberal support for the war. "Significant numbers of writers," concluded the report, "note the pride they felt in the President and the country while listening to the address. Others mentioned a new feeling of optimism and relief—of new hope for the future." All in all, a more than satisfactory result.[69]

On the helicopter ride back to the White House after the speech, the president told press secretary and confidante Bill Moyers, "Old Ho can't turn me down."[70] Moyers marveled at Johnson's continuing faith that such assumptions had anything to do with ending the war in Vietnam. "He'd say," Moyers recalled other conversations, " 'My God, I've offered Ho Chi Minh $100 million to build a Mekong Valley. If that'd been George Meany he'd have snapped at it!' "[71] But as the war deepened from misadventure into tragedy, Johnson clung all the harder to an abstract vision of Vietnam transformed, just as the Texas hill country had been transformed. "I want to leave the footprints of America in Vietnam," he said in 1966. "I want them to say when the Americans come, this is what they leave—schools, not long cigars. We're going to turn the Mekong into a Tennessee Valley."[72]

White House aide Douglass Cater telephoned several prominent columnists immediately after the speech to see what they thought. Philip Geyelin, foreign policy expert for the *Wall Street Journal*, was the most enthusiastic. "He thinks it definitely puts the cat on the Communist back for awhile," reported Cater.[73] The *New York Times* heralded the speech as a serious shift toward peace. "Washington Is Reported Shifting Stand in Effort to Tempt North Vietnamese Away from Aggressive Course," read the headline over Max Frankel's front-page article. The pressures on the president to say what he said, that the United States would discuss the war as long "as no conditions were set by any party," Frankel wrote, had been immense.[74] *Washington Post* columnists Rowland Evans and Robert Novak were delighted with the craftiness of the president in pulling the teeth from his critics—and delighted with themselves for being privy to how it was accomplished—by inviting Senators George McGovern and Frank Church to the White House to hear LBJ swear on a draft of the Johns Hopkins speech that "negotiations were what he really had in mind. . . ."[75] Senator McGovern was more than pleased, and anxious to put his spin on the speech. "It represents a significant part of the course some Senators have been urging for many months," he said on the floor of the Senate. "It sets forth America's willingness to explore the possibility of a peaceful settlement without preconditions."[76]

As Bundy feared, however, once the speech was delivered, Lippmann picked up on the differences between "unconditional discussions" and "unconditional negotiations." Washington had very definite views about what could be negotiated and what could not. It was willing to discuss how to get negotiations started, or, less ambiguously, how to get Hanoi to take itself out of the war and to dismantle the National Liberation Front in exchange for promised participation in a regional economic development plan. Lippmann was angry because he felt Bundy and the president had tried to use him (which they had) and to patronize him (which they also had). But there was some honest self-deception as well. American policymakers were now acting as if they really believed Hanoi could stop the war if it chose.

Bundy talked with Lippmann again and found him in a mood very different from how the president found him the day of the speech, when LBJ had portrayed himself as under the gun from the mad bombers in the military. Lippmann complained that the speech as delivered was "very different" from the draft he saw. Bundy admitted that was so, but his recollection was that the term "unconditional discussions" was already in the draft. Lippmann then complained that either way the continued bombing made it difficult to achieve a settlement. "I had to say firmly that continuing air action was a necessary part of your policy, as I understood it." But he should not think Johnson was in any hurry to "escalate"—and the president "constantly emphasized the importance of acting on every front in *South* Vietnam." Lippmann thanked Bundy "warmly" for that assurance.[77]

But Lippmann's experience with presidential loopholes went back to Wilson's time and the Paris Peace Conference. He may not have caught the nuance in Bundy's phrase "on every front in *South* Vietnam," but he was not to be taken in a second time. The national security adviser wrote Johnson how the conversation had ended:

In closing, Walter said he thought he would write now on the difference between the two sides on the ways and means of working out a settlement—and particularly on our differences over letting the Viet Cong or Liberation Front join in the discussions. I fear that Walter will gradually line himself upon the pro-Communist side on this one, but we will keep working on him. It really would be very bad for our whole position to allow the Viet Cong to have a separate presence in any negotiations—at least at this stage of the game.[78]

Lippmann's anticipated column, "The Baltimore Address and After," appeared a few days later. It was perhaps less pro-Communist than Bundy had feared. After brief comments about his disappointment that "unconditional discussions" meant nothing like a prelude to a halt in the bombing or serious negotiations, balanced later by his view that the other side wanted nothing to do with negotiations either, Lippmann considered the likely future course of the war. There were those, he wrote, who knew that the bombing (even increased to include cities) would not save South Vietnam, and who were now arguing and putting pressure on the president "for the commitment of a huge American army to another Korean war on the ground." He thought it more likely, apparently following Bundy's lead, that the president would escalate slowly, hoping for a military miracle, and when that did not happen some future government in Saigon would undertake to end the fighting itself. Of course, that was precisely what Washington had acted to prevent since November 1963, but Lippmann apparently had taken Bundy's assurances at face value—either that or he was trying to head off what he feared would be the next step.[79]

The editor of the *Saturday Review*, Norman Cousins, meanwhile, had encountered the Soviet ambassador, Anatoly Dobrynin, who delivered the "pro-Communist" view that Bundy had feared Lippmann would adopt. "Didn't you think the President made himself clear in his talk at Johns Hopkins last night?" the famous liberal asked. "I don't know what to think about it," Dobrynin grunted. "Quite honestly, I am confused." Cousins's efforts to convince him that America had no military objectives beyond Vietnam and was "genuinely interested in stabilizing the area" did not succeed. Those who favored the "coexistence feeling" in his country were having second thoughts, said Dobrynin. Protest meetings against the bombing raids had sprung up all over Russia. "Frankly, they trouble us because they are having a very bad effect on public opinion. Many times I have read in your press that it would be a good thing for a real public opinion to exist in the Soviet Union. Well, now there is such a public opinion." Dobrynin was worried that all the work of recent years to improve relations was being torn down. "And it is even worse than that. I believe that we are moving into military action ourselves in Vietnam. I don't see how we can avoid it. A Socialist country—a very small country—is being bombed by you. We have to respond. The Socialist world is looking to us to respond. We know how dangerous this can be, but we have to do it. This is what your bombing has to mean. And so you will step up your military effort when we get more involved and then we will step it up and what has been gained?" Cousins countered that things were not really as black as the ambassador painted them. Because of the president's speech, there was room to maneuver. "It would be a shame if this new opening were to be lost because it was not even perceived."[80]

"I hope you are right," sighed Dobrynin. "I would like to believe you are right. And two months ago I was saying what you are now saying. But there has been a change. I wish I could believe there has not been a change."[81] Vice-President Humphrey also wanted to believe there had not been a change, perhaps even more than Dobrynin. As Johnson began to let members of Congress in on what he meant by "on every front in the *South*"—American ground troops—worries grew. After one session at the White House, Senator Gaylord Nelson told Humphrey as they drove home that it looked bad. Johnson was talking about forty thousand to fifty thousand men. The nation was being pulled into a big war. "You know, Gaylord," said the vice-president, "there are people at State and the Pentagon who want to send *three hundred thousand* men out there." Humphrey paused. "But the President will never get sucked into anything like that."[82]

TEN

The Demanding Dream

IN LATE APRIL 1965, a day or so after he returned from a conference in Honolulu, Defense Secretary Robert McNamara invited the venerable *New York Times* columnist Arthur Krock to the Pentagon for a "background session." According to the ground rules, Krock could use any of the information, but it had to be attributed to "high government sources."[1]

McNamara started off by pressing the case that the guerrilla war was "NOT merely an indigenous rebellion, that in fact the Viet Cong do depend on outside power for weapons, strategy, tactical doctrine, daily operational control." There were 45,000 to 50,000 VC regulars, and perhaps 100,000 additional irregulars. They all needed weapons. In the previous four years the South Vietnamese had lost 39,000 weapons and recaptured 24,000. "Therefore," McNamara concluded, "more than 100,000 of the VCs must be armed by outside assistance."

McNamara, a former Ford Motor Company head, ticked off such statistics with the agility of a skater leaping a row of barrels. The North Vietnamese, he sped along to the next jump, had seized the opportunity presented by the continuing turmoil in Saigon following Diem's assassination to raise the level of infiltration. Given the total numbers of VCs and irregulars, which he had put at 150,000, the current strength of the South Vietnamese armed forces, 525,000, was not enough to provide "the accepted ratio of 10-1 needed in Greece, Philippines, Malaysia, elsewhere, to overcome well-led guerrillas."

To remedy that situation, several steps would be taken in the near future. It had been decided, for one thing, to "add to SVN forces at rate of 8-10,000 monthly for next 12 months." If North Vietnam would shut down its aid to the VCs, McNamara claimed, the south could control the guerrillas without long-continued American aid. But the "ultimate settlement would have to be guaranteed," complete with a "legal opening to go back" if South Vietnam was threatened again from without.

Having pinpointed the specifics of the "local" issues in Vietnam, McNamara reached out to paint the "global" concerns at stake in the war. He described for Krock two visions of the future:

> If the U.S. withdrew from SVN, there would be a complete shift in the world balance of power. Asia goes Red, our prestige and integrity damaged, allies everywhere shaken (even those who publicly ask us to quit bombing, etc.). At home, he foresees as a result of these calamities a bad effect on economy and a disastrous political fight that could further freeze American political debate and even affect political freedom.

On the other hand,

> If U.S. achieved in SVN the objectives stated by LBJ in Baltimore, there would be substantial political and economic and security gains. Way then open . . . to combine birth control and economic expansion techniques in gigantic arc from SVN to Iran and the Middle East, bringing unimaginable developments to this region, proving worth of moderate, democratic way of growth for societies.

In spelling out the "options," McNamara had carefully avoided telling Krock about the most critical decision of the Honolulu conference—a recommendation to increase the ground forces to nearly 100,000 U.S. soldiers. Johnson had been worried about Ambassador Taylor's opposition to using American combat troops, on which his Washington advisers now insisted. In mid-April the president sent McNamara to Honolulu to talk things out with Taylor and others from Saigon. When the defense secretary returned, his April 21 recommendation for a troop increase sounded as if he were proposing only a stopgap measure until South Vietnam reached full mobilization. But his conversation with Krock revealed clearly that McNamara's vision of the future was, as historian Christopher Thorne has suggested, a demanding dream.

"If we can just get our feet on their neck," Johnson had beseeched his advisers a week before the Baltimore speech. He liked their notions concerning a super TVA on the Mekong. But what he heard about the military situation suggested there wasn't going to be time enough for a Vietnamese New Deal. "We are losing the war out there," General Wheeler, chairman of the Joint Chiefs, said bluntly. The Joint Chiefs proposed sending General Westmoreland two divisions before it was too late. Johnson winced at that prospect. He had just told a press conference that he knew of "no far-reaching strategy that is being suggested or promulgated." Throughout the meeting with his political and military advisers LBJ rambled back and forth. One minute he mused about coaxing the Viet Cong into giving up the struggle with promises of New Deal–style reform programs like "rural electrification"; but the next he was barking at McNamara and Wheeler to get more planes, as "damn many planes" as were needed "to find 'em and kill 'em."[2]

When he was finished ruminating and scolding, Johnson agreed only to a change in the mission of American marines already stationed at Danang and other locations. Henceforward they would be permitted to seek out the enemy and engage him in combat in the surrounding areas. CIA Director John McCone quickly pointed out to the president that he could not get away with thinking he had solved his problem, even temporarily. McCone thought it was just about the worst half-decision LBJ could have made. "We will find ourselves mired down in combat in the jungle," he predicted, "in a military effort that we cannot win, and from which we will have extreme difficulty in extracting ourselves." If Johnson wanted to change the ground combat mission, he would have to change the Rolling Thunder rules. "A bridge here and there will not do the job. We must strike their air fields, their petroleum resources, power stations and the military compounds . . . and with minimum restraint."[3]

Senator William Fulbright, meanwhile, had heard about the idea of sending two or three divisions to Vietnam, and was equally unhappy, if for different reasons. Fulbright feared it would start with 10,000 one time, and then another 10,000, and another, until one day Americans woke up to discover there were 300,000 soldiers in Vietnam. "You won't put 300,000 all at once, you can't do that," he told Ambassador Maxwell Taylor, who had come to the Foreign Relations Committee. But when Taylor talked all the time about Vietnam being vital to American security, "it seemed to me the only conclusion you can draw is that you are going to do this."[4]

Fulbright then tried to raise the issue of the Tonkin Gulf Resolution, suggesting he did not think the president could stretch it wide enough to cover large numbers of American soldiers spreading out into Vietnam's heartland. Taylor offered vague comments about consultation, and, as usual, neither Fulbright nor any other committee member could get anything more from an administration witness. In truth, the ambassador had his own reservations about sending combat forces into Vietnam. He had taken Johnson's decision to mean that the president wanted to try an "experiment" with the marines, nothing more.

Within a few days of his return to Saigon, however, Taylor was cabling his alarm about the "eagerness in some quarters" to deploy large-scale forces in Vietnam. "The mounting number of foreign troops," he repeated his earlier advice, "may sap the GVN initiative and turn the defense of the GVN homeland into what appears a foreign war."[5] "I am sure we can turn him around," Bundy wrote Johnson about Taylor's doubts, "if we give him just a little time to come aboard. . . ." The national security adviser also thought the president needed a little time himself to come aboard. "It is not clear that we now need all these additional forces."[6]

The next day, however, Bundy cabled Taylor and General Westmoreland, informing them that the "highest authority" believed that the deteriorating situation in Vietnam required not just military experimentation with the marines but the introduction of additional battalion-level forces at two or three new locations along the coast, as well as something close to the kind of "guidance" the United States had provided during the postwar occupations of Germany and Japan: "An experimental introduction into the provincial government structure of a team of US Army Civil Affairs personnel (or similarly qualified personnel) to assist in the establishment of stable government in the provinces and to initiate and direct the necessary political, economic and security programs." The ambassador was "urgently" instructed to obtain Saigon's agreement to all these "experiments."[7]

Bundy added a personal message to Taylor explaining that President Johnson was "very eager to see prompt experiments in use of energetic teams of U.S. officials in support of provisional [provincial] governments under unified U.S. leadership." As for troops, the president had seen no evidence of a negative result of new deployments—and he did not want to wait "any longer than is essential for genuine GVN agreement."[8]

While Washington waited impatiently for its ambassador to secure Prime Minister Quat's approval, Bundy took time to draft an eleven-page letter to the editor of the Harvard *Crimson*. It began, as one might expect a former dean to begin, by situating his critics as dissident faculty members or overexcited undergraduates. "Occasionally," Bundy wrote with the nicest touch of wit academic deans reserve for those groups, "my own activities have been criticized with a cheerful undergraduate superiority which reminds me happily of what I used to read about 'the Administration' when the phrase meant University Hall to me because that was where I worked."[9]

The main body of the letter, however, provided a fascinating look at Bundy's thoughts as the United States moved to the cusp of an all-out decision on Vietnam. The historical parallels that counted for Bundy were the American decision to resist Germany before World War II and the Cuban missile crisis. "We are not paper tigers," Bundy wrote to the editor Donald Graham (and to convince himself once again), "and it would be a very great danger to the peace of all the world if we should carelessly let it be thought that we are. This is the lesson that we learned in failure and redeemed in triumph by John F. Kennedy over Cuba." What was wrong with the Bay of Pigs, according to this reconstruction, was not the mistake of trying to overthrow Fidel Castro but the carelessness of allowing the world to think the United States had become a paper tiger.

If Professor John Kenneth Galbraith pointed out that strategic bombing was a clumsy instrument in the 1940s in order to criticize Rolling Thunder, he simply did not understand either the purposes or the sophistication of today's bombing techniques. If other critics pointed to the failed French attempt to reconquer Indochina after World War II, they simply did not understand either. America's purposes were different. "We simply are not there as colonialists." He reworked this section of the draft many times, more than any other part of the letter. The changes reveal his difficulty in reaching exactly the right phrasing: "Our innate lack of imperial zeal is visible ~~to all~~ *to any observer in Vietnam and to the Vietnamese people.* The French never earned a similar reputation, *and as a consequence they were* ~~not~~ ~~able to generate~~ *the inevitable target of Communist and non-Communist nationalists alike. The situation today is quite different, and as a result* ~~In the current~~ ~~struggle~~*South* Vietnamese forces ~~themselves~~ with sharply limited American troop support, have been able to maintain a balance of strength which the flower of the French professional army could not keep. Only a very ~~ill-informed and~~ casual ~~observer~~ *commentator* would compare the two experiences as if they were parallel." What thus emerges from the emendations and additions to this paragraph is Bundy's difficulty in reconciling what he wrote to the *Crimson* editor with what Johnson had demanded in the way of "experiments" in South Vietnam. We might still be Wilsonian self-determinists in the national security adviser's mind, but he had to be careful about claims that the South Vietnamese forces "themselves" were fighting very hard to make their nation-building a success.

Ambassador Taylor, meanwhile, had capitulated on the troop issue during the meeting in Hawaii. The civilian contingent—McNamara and assistant secretaries McNaughton and William Bundy—fashioned something of a compromise. The Joint Chiefs had wanted approval for two divisions, but what emerged was a recommendation for three battalions—an increase from 33,000 Americans currently in Vietnam to nearly 82,000. This 150 percent expansion breached the invisible wall between support and active participation in the actual fighting.[10]

Taylor's counterpart in Vientiane, Laos, William H. Sullivan, a career diplomat who had assisted in much of the policy planning for Southeast Asia, was much alarmed by the rumors of extensive troop deployments. The Laotians, he reported, would interpret such a decision as evidence of panic. "Despite many earlier misgivings and in the face of Communist and French propaganda to the contrary, Lao accept the idea that we have no, repeat no, colonial or neo-colonial ambitions here. A massive occupation of South Vietnam by U.S. forces except *in extremis* would . . . cause this assumption to be re-examined." The practical consequences would probably include, Sullivan thought, much less cooperation with American military operations and even a "headlong rush" to embrace the French policy of negotiated neutrality.[11]

Sullivan's dissent went unnoticed. But McNamara wanted the president to inform Congress about the proposed deployment and the changed mission. This Johnson specifically refused to do, instructing Secretary Rusk not to talk about numbers with the Senate Foreign Relations Committee. At the subcabinet level the prospect of sending American troops to do the actual fighting set off a flurry of memo-writing. Under Secretary of State George Ball wanted to see if Hanoi's recent four-point declaration did not offer a diplomatic opening.

A week after Johnson's speech at Johns Hopkins, Hanoi had responded with a "counterproposal" in the form of a four-point declaration. Point one demanded recognition of the basic national rights of the Vietnamese people. According to the Geneva accords, that meant the United States must immediately cease its military activities and dismantle all its bases on Vietnamese territory. Point two declared that, pending the peaceful reunification of Vietnam, the two zones "must refrain from joining any military alliances with foreign countries." Ball perhaps hoped he could parlay that into a pledge that Hanoi had no intention of linking up with Russia or China, and was here promising neutralization of a type more acceptable to Washington. However that may be, point three—the one seized upon by the president's other advisers to justify the escalations—declared that the internal affairs of Vietnam had to be settled by the Vietnamese "in accordance with the program of the NFLSV [National Liberation Front] without any foreign interference." The phrase might be read two ways, depending upon where one put the emphasis. It might mean that the NLF program called for a settlement free from foreign interference, or, alternatively, that the settlement must accord with the NLF program. Point four reiterated that reunification was for the Vietnamese to settle themselves. Ball wanted to probe the ambiguities before making a commitment that he thought would later be regretted. "If we are to settle this matter short of a major war," he wrote, "we must be prepared for a settlement that falls somewhere short of the goals we have publicly stated, but that still meets our basic objective."

Assistant Secretary of State William Bundy prepared a memorandum that argued the United States could gain a "propaganda advantage" by offering free elections—"*after* South Vietnam had been freed of external interference"—in both North and South Vietnam to determine the question of reunification. The U.S. and South Vietnam could also think about some method of determining the popular will "*within* South Vietnam" that would allow the NLF to participate as a political party. As he thought more about this idea, however, Bundy decided it might not be a good thing to propose because it would cast doubt on the legitimacy of the current South Vietnamese government. From inside the White House, Johnson received a memorandum from Jack Valenti urging a slowdown of the bombing to allow Hanoi to talk without feeling it was being bombed into submission. Throughout were warning notes about deeper involvement. Escalating the bombing only meant "less and less result for more and more noise." "This kind of approach will bring with it a substantial chance of Chinese intervention. Even Ho Chi Minh will probably prefer Chinese intervention to surrender. We should . . . make a real peace effort before putting in many more ground troops. It is a lot easier to disengage planes than ground troops."[12]

"All right, George," Johnson told Ball. "If you can pull a rabbit out of the hat, I'm all for it."[13] Bill Moyers was also told to start looking around for hidden rabbits. Johnson wanted them, Moyers then told Averell Harriman, "to do some quiet thinking on ways out of Viet-Nam . . . without anybody knowing about it."[14] Harriman apparently took Moyers's phone call as an indication that he would soon be "back in the saddle" as America's premier Russia-tamer, a role he had zealously guarded for himself since World War II when he had served as Franklin Roosevelt's ambassador to Moscow. More recently, of course, as assistant secretary of state for Far Eastern affairs, he had been the principal negotiator of the 1962 Laos accords, and he firmly believed that the ultimate settlement of the Vietnam War would come in great-power agreements imposed on the squabbling lilliputians. He had been reassigned to African affairs in a State Department reshuffle, and there he had waited ever so impatiently to be recalled to the serious work of Soviet-American diplomacy. Perhaps to remind Johnson of his lineage in cold war "problem-solving," and where he now languished out on the edge of things, Harriman wrote the president on the day of the Moyers phone call to tell him about seeing former President Harry Truman at a celebration of the twentieth anniversary of the San Francisco UN Charter Conference.

Truman "spoke warmly" of what his Democratic successor was doing, and specifically on Vietnam said, "The President is dead right—and I'm 100% back of him." If Communist aggression were not stopped in South Vietnam, it would spread and become far more difficult to deal with. "For my part," Harriman recounted the conversation, "I told him you were acting on the principles that guided Churchill in his warnings in the 30s against appeasement of Nazi aggression."[15]

The next day Johnson opened his press conference with a prepared statement that began, "We are engaged in a crucial struggle in Viet-Nam." Defeat would mean that all nations within reach of would-be conquerors were in danger.

Our own welfare, our own freedom, would be in great danger. This is the clearest lesson of our time. From Munich until today we have learned that to yield to aggression brings only greater threats and brings even more destructive war. To stand firm is the only guarantee of a lasting peace.[16]

Johnson knew very well what Truman would say without having Averell Harriman report the details. Johnson probably hoped, furthermore, that when he told Moyers or George Ball (or anyone else) to do some thinking about ways out of Vietnam, and in admonishing them all to silence, he was actually assuring leaks about his anguished quest for peace—none of which could be pinpointed. However that may be, Ambassador Taylor had now undergone a remarkable conversion. "In essence," McGeorge Bundy informed the president, "Max says he thinks we can get a favorable settlement in a matter of months rather than in 'perhaps a year or two' if we keep up our bombing and introduce substantial U.S. and third-country forces."[17]

Max Taylor's promises seemed better than a couple of loose rabbits, which, once out of the hat, might run off in the wrong direction. Rusk already had to busy himself chasing down a number that had skipped away. A SEATO foreign ministers' meeting was scheduled for early May in London, where difficult questions were going to be asked. Cambodia's Prince Sihanouk had informed the secretary general of the organization that his country "cannot allow certain member countries of SEATO to continue to consider it, or pretend to consider it, to be under the protective shield of the treaty." Earlier requests that the organization recognize Cambodia's desires had been ignored, he complained, which seemed "very much like an attempt to force an inadmissible protectorate status upon it." "I wish to emphasize on this occasion that the only aggression and threats which Cambodia must face come from member countries of SEATO or countries which are closely linked to SEATO."[18]

A bold challenge to the very raison d'etre of SEATO, but Rusk was also having to deal with the possibility of a New Zealand defection from SEATO orthodoxy.[19] And then there were de Gaulle's continuing antics—potentially far more troublesome. People like Walter Lippmann and Mike Mansfield paid attention to everything the old Frenchman contended about the fool's errand Washington seemed determined to pursue through the jungles of Southeast Asia. France's defection from SEATO was already a fact. At the moment, to add injury to insult, the general was entertaining Soviet Foreign Minister Andrei Gromyko. A communiqué issued after their formal talks stated the two countries were agreed on their opposition to "foreign interference" in Southeast Asian "domestic affairs." London looked to be a real trial for Dean Rusk.[20]

What troubled Lyndon Johnson most at this moment, however, was not Sihanouk's outbursts or de Gaulle's studied aloofness, but the unpleasant prospect of "consulting" with Congress. McNamara had cautioned that before he went ahead with the Hawaii recommendations for increasing American ground troops to 82,000, the president ought to inform congressional leaders about the new deployments and the new combat mission they were to carry out, or face serious trouble in the future. Johnson had not followed that advice; indeed, he had instructed Secretary Rusk not to discuss numbers or even a promise to consult in advance of any major decision. "He considered that to be a matter for him to decide," Rusk said many years later in a television interview, "under the Gulf of Tonkin Resolution, and, indeed, independently in his own role as Commander in Chief."[21]

Senator Fulbright pressed Rusk hard on this point. During an executive hearing on April 30, the chairman of the Senate Foreign Relations Committee declared that there had been an understanding at the time of the Tonkin Gulf Resolution that Congress was reaffirming the limited mission and role of the United States in Vietnam. Now it appeared evident that "we are waging war on North Vietnam." If the president planned to send up to 100,000 troops to fight in Southeast Asia, Fulbright lectured Rusk, it did not seem "out of order" for Congress to "have the say about it." He added, "This operation in Vietnam has obviously become quite controversial. A lot of us have been quiet. We do not want to embarrass the administration ... because we realize this is a very difficult situation."[22]

William P. Bundy would suggest in an unpublished manuscript on Vietnam that LBJ was getting ready to consult with Congress in the last days of April, and that was why he asked various people to put together some thoughts on "new peace tactics" and such "for an intensive consultation with Congress during May, and perhaps a reaffirmed Resolution of some sort. . . ." But a crisis in the Dominican Republic intervened, "and whatever chance there might have been of a careful Congressional review went by the board."[23]

The Dominican crisis has often been discussed in terms of what Fulbright was to call the "arrogance of power." It is better understood as an event that permitted the Johnson administration to slip around a very awkward corner. That Johnson wanted a "reaffirmed Resolution of some sort," that indeed he ardently desired such a resolution, can scarcely be doubted. That he wanted anything like a "careful Congressional review" can hardly be credited. The Dominican situation allowed him an opportunity to recreate the atmosphere of August 1964 and thus to get the resolution without the review. The president apparently did not realize at first what an opportunity had been laid at his feet—but when he did, he made the most of it to confound his Vietnam critics.

Briefly explained, the crisis in the Dominican Republic originated in 1961 after longtime dictator Rafael Trujillo was gunned down by assassins.[24] The Kennedy administration supported Juan Bosch's provisional government. Bosch then won more than 60 percent of the popular vote in a national election. Just ten months later, however, the liberal leader was overthrown by an army coup. Behind the soldiers stood a phalanx of conservative landholders, businessmen, and church leaders. This time Washington did not intervene. The State Department had become disenchanted with Bosch, dismissing him as a mere "literary figure." But the Reid Cabral junta which assumed power proved unable to win any new friends among the Dominicans. In fact, no one liked it except Washington. Reid Cabral announced, nevertheless, that he would be a candidate for president in the June 1965 elections. He had a "donation" from Washington to start him off, a $5 million loan for his regime, but it was not nearly enough.

A rebellion that began on April 24 saw army officers fighting on both sides. For a day or so the Cabral loyalists gained the upper hand. But on April 28 General Wessin y Wessin, commander of the pro-Cabral forces, sent word to the American embassy that he could not guarantee the safety of American citizens. By nightfall six hundred U.S. marines were ashore. Landed from a nearby task force, the marines established a safety perimeter around the Hotel Embajador, where Americans and other foreigners had taken refuge.[25]

Eventually more than 23,000 American marines came ashore to complete a larger mission: to save the Caribbean country from communism. The Wessin camp asserted that the rebel forces had been infiltrated by Cuban-trained agents who specialized in taking over such movements. The American embassy tried hard to locate these infiltrators and released a list of fifty-eight such individuals, "prominent Communist and Castroite leaders." Salvaged from the Trujillo archives, the list was pretty unreliable. Some of those named turned out to be deceased. American reporters on the scene scoffed at the crude propaganda and agreed with Bosch's assessment that "this was a democratic revolution smashed by the leading democracy of the world."[26]

Lyndon Johnson also scoffed—at first—at the charge that the Bosch movement concealed a dangerous Communist element that would, if given a chance, love to turn over another Caribbean country to Havana and Moscow. George Ball was with the president when he made the decision to send in the first marine units. "There is absolutely no doubt whatever that the initial decision was made," Ball said later, "with only one consideration in mind . . . that we damned well had to get some troops in there in one hell of a hurry or our people would have been killed." Ball has given somewhat different answers about whether the president should then have also sent in a "mass of troops" to ward off a supposed Communist takeover. In this same interview he talked about the "clamor" that would have arisen had the Dominican Republic become another Cuba. "I think this very deeply concerned the President; that, plus the fact that he was getting a lot of what I thought were highly dubious reports from J. Edgar Hoover about the number of communists." On another occasion Ball emphasized the Vietnam connection. "We were just on the verge of committing large numbers of American combat forces to Vietnam and the President feared that a disaster close to home might lead more Americans to challenge our adventure ten thousand miles away."[27]

As the Dominican plot thickened, it occurred to Johnson that he had been offered an opportunity to put the world Communist menace to work for him as in the heroic days of the cold war. He could use it to recapture the initiative in the Vietnam debate at home. No one was going to handle the Dominican crisis except Johnson. As Ball put it, "The President became the desk officer on the thing. He ran everything himself."[28]

Charles Mohr of the *New York Times* met for two hours alone with Johnson late in the afternoon of April 29, 1965. The president had just awakened from a nap before their "chat" began, and may not have had a chance to put on protective armor. In any event, he was exceptionally candid. Mohr started off with a semiapology for not including the Communist angle in his first story on the Dominican crisis. He had not given enough emphasis to Assistant Secretary of State Thomas Mann's "guarded report" that there were some Communists among the rebels. "Johnson disagreed, saying it was hopeless to think that anyone would ever believe him but that he had not landed marines to put down a communist threat." When he met with congressional leaders, he had not given them a scare story, but that was what they wanted to hear. The CIA director, Admiral Raborn, had spoken only briefly and identified only two leaders of the rebel forces believed to be Communists, and perhaps there were seven or eight more. Out of how many, asked Mohr? "How would I know," said Johnson, "for all we know there are 800 leaders."[29]

The congressional questioner may have been Senator Everett Dirksen. In his conversation with Mohr, Johnson acted out almost all the parts of his meeting with legislative leaders, not hiding his amusement. "Ev Dirksen had gotten up," Johnson said, at the end of the briefing, "and given a strong rah-rah speech praising Johnson and telling him not to let himself be pushed around by communists." Reminding Mohr this stuff was all off the record, Johnson said "he thought Ev might have been just a bit drunk."[30]

LBJ continued in this vein for several more minutes, declaring at one point that all the emphasis in the press on communism had caused him trouble with Bosch. "We don't regard Bosch as a communist at all...."[31] But the very next day Johnson issued a public statement that asserted, "People trained outside the Dominican Republic are seeking to gain control."[32] And three days later he made a dramatic appearance on television. There were times, he began, when great principles "are tested in an ordeal of conflict and danger." The Dominican crisis presented such a challenge. The hopes and concerns of the entire hemisphere were focused on that

Caribbean nation. "What began as a popular democratic revolution, committed to democracy and social justice, very shortly moved and was taken over and really seized and placed into the hands of a band of Communist conspirators." After a lengthy recital of his actions and efforts to coordinate with the Organization of American States so as to assure the Dominican Republic its opportunity for self-determination and freedom, Johnson closed as he had begun, with a ringing peroration.

> I want you to know and I want the world to know that as long as I am President of this country, we are going to defend ourselves. We will defend our soldiers against attackers. We will honor our treaties. We will keep our commitments. We will defend our Nation against all those who seek to destroy not only the United States but every free country of this hemisphere. We do not want to bury anyone as I have said so many times before. But we do not intend to be buried.[33]

Two days later Johnson sent to Congress a request for $700 million to pay for American efforts in both Vietnam and the Dominican Republic. "This is not a routine appropriation," read his accompanying message. "For each Member of Congress who supports this request is also voting to persist in our effort to halt communist aggression in South Vietnam. Each is saying that the Congress and the President stand united before the world in joint determination that the independence of South Vietnam shall be preserved and communist attack will not succeed." During a White House meeting with selected congressional leaders, the president elaborated on the reasons for the request and justified the bombing policy against its critics. "Our firmness and the action that we have taken in the last few weeks may well have already brought us much closer to peace."[34]

As William Bundy noted, Johnson had successfully made the appropriation of a relatively small sum into a new "small-scale Tonkin Gulf Resolution." He had substituted the Dominican rebels for the North Vietnamese PT boats. In fact the president had done more. He had loaded the issue, for anyone voting no on the special appropriation could be depicted as having voted to deny help to American soldiers already in the field.[35] Only eight in the House of Representatives took that risk. In the Senate only three negatives were cast, by Wayne Morse, Ernest Gruening, and Gaylord Nelson. The Oregonian maverick, Morse, was scathing about the "reservationists" who voted for the bill, all the while claiming they did not support the Vietnam policy. "Whom do they think they are kidding?" "I think the White House must be laughing at their 'reservation.'"[36]

McGeorge Bundy had been dispatched to calm one of the "reservationists," Senator Joseph Clark of Pennsylvania. Clark was furious about the supplemental appropriation, Bundy reported, but thought he would have to vote for it. He did not buy into any of the reports that the Dominican Republic was about to go Communist, and he was unhappy about Vietnam policy. "I see no chance whatever of changing his mind on any of these issues," concluded the national security adviser, "but I think he can be kept moderately quiet by the simple fact that he is not ready to break with you—though emotionally, he would certainly like to."[37]

Arthur Krock, who had no use for the "professional" liberals in the Senate, watched Johnson's performance with a mixture of admiration and apprehension.[38] His column for Sunday, May 9, 1965, was titled "Pandora's Heir in the White House." When he signed the appropriation measure granting him $700 million to fight communism in the Dominican Republic and Vietnam, Krock noted, the president had dealt with the reservationists exactly the way Morse predicted. "It is not the money but the message that matters," LBJ had declared, "and that message . . . is clear: 'We will do whatever must be done to insure the safety of South Vietnam from aggression.' " In the last fortnight, Krock went on, the president had astonished Washington with an exhibition of energy and loquacity never before displayed by a White House occupant. "It was a continuous mixture of a Broadway production and a TV documentary." Congress was constantly being summoned to the White House to create the atmosphere of unending emergency. Day after day, as well, the president walked and talked the press into physical exhaustion. But having proclaimed this new mission to use whatever means necessary to establish the United States as the "policeman of peace" around the globe, how could even the inexhaustible Lyndon Johnson, Krock wondered, escape Pandora's fate?[39]

In Paris, General de Gaulle contemplated America's future difficulties with a serene sense that the "Yalta system" of dual hegemony was coming undone. Ambassador Charles Bohlen asked if de Gaulle did not agree that since the Johns Hopkins speech it had become clear that the French and American positions were really not very far apart? A great many things had happened in the past year, the general said, dismissing Bohlen's argument. The United States was now bombing North Vietnam. It was his impression that the Chinese and the North Vietnamese were no longer interested in negotiations but accepted the inevitable escalation of the war with oriental fatalism—and believed that in the end, however long it took, their view would prevail. De Gaulle brought up the Dominican Republic. The U.S., he said, as with all countries that had overwhelming power, was coming to believe that force could solve everything. But this was not the case, and Americans would soon realize it. Bohlen recited the arguments for the intervention, all of which de Gaulle waved aside. He had met Bosch and found him a reasonable man, certainly no Communist. "He said Bosch had been overthrown by his own military, and with an ironic smile, 'Perhaps with the help of some of the American services.' "[40]

The ambassador denied there had been any such chicanery involved in

American dealings with the former Dominican leader. What would be the situation in Southeast Asia, Bohlen challenged, returning to the previous question, if the United States had failed to respond to Vietnam's request for aid in the face of Communist aggression? It should never have come to that, de Gaulle responded. He had been prepared at the end of the war to negotiate the road to independence for the Vietnamese, he claimed, "with the various elements of Vietnamese national life which would have, of course, included Ho Chi Minh." This had been impeded by American and British opposition. Then he left power and could assume no responsibility for what happened afterward, which he merely found lamentable.[41]

Johnson never ceased telling anyone who would listen that he had inherited the Vietnam War, mentioning it again when he met with congressional leaders to secure their support for the $700 million supplemental appropriation. Like de Gaulle, LBJ thought what had happened since World War II was lamentable, but negotiations with Ho Chi Minh could take place only on the basis that there would continue to be two Vietnams. Having secured his new congressional "mandate," the president sought once again to strike the pose of a reflective statesman to foil efforts to paint him as a blusterer, hostage to the Pentagon. He knew it wouldn't work, he said later, but he would go that extra mile liberals always expected of him just because he wasn't Kennedy. So, on May 10, Johnson sent Ambassador Taylor a personal cable, informing him that he was ordering a bombing suspension to take effect in the near future. "You should understand that my purpose in this plan is to begin to clear a path either toward restoration of peace or toward increased military action, depending upon the reaction of the Communists."[42]

Code-named Mayflower, the bombing pause was a tightly held secret in the United States. Johnson doubted it would secure him much credit with either liberal or conservative critics. The Bundy brothers drafted the message that Johnson wanted delivered to both Moscow and Hanoi. It was a truculent statement that the "the cause of trouble" in Southeast Asia was armed action against the South Vietnamese by forces "whose action can be decisively affected from North Vietnam." Only by ending those attacks could North Vietnam secure a permanent end to the bombing. The North Vietnamese refused to receive it—but, as in the way of diplomacy, made a copy before they sent it back.[43]

"I don't think it was well handled," William Bundy later admitted. For Hanoi to acknowledge that its forces were fighting in South Vietnam would only give the Americans more reason to step up the bombing. Better to maintain the diplomatic fiction and deal with such questions at the peace table. But if the United States was not interested in negotiations, which it was not, it is hard to see how gentler language would have made any difference. If the purpose was to put the squeeze on Hanoi, the language was proper.

Mayflower marked the end of the "crisis management" phase of the Vietnam War. Yet some still believed that once American power was arrayed in all its technological majesty, the enemy would begin to adjust to the inevitable. Bundy's aide Walt Rostow, for example, wrote a memo explaining this variation. Hanoi was staring defeat in the face. But North Vietnam's leaders would not accept that reality until "they are convinced time has ceased to be their friend. . . . Victory . . . is nearer our grasp than we (but not Hanoi) may think." [44]

Former President Eisenhower's reaction to the briefing he received on Operation Mayflower from Johnson's emissary, General Andrew Goodpaster, was more pointed than Rostow's oblique recommendation. Johnson had invoked Eisenhower's aid in selling his Vietnam policy to congressional critics, and Goodpaster was sent to explain the political reasons behind the bombing pause—"it will be helpful to him in dealing with elements opposing or criticizing his policy within our own country, as well as helping internationally." Eisenhower understood. But if the "Communists" failed to respond, he told Goodpaster, we should hit them with "everything that can fly." He reiterated once again how he had passed the word to the Chinese that if they failed to stop the Korean War, they were liable to be attacked with nuclear weapons. As for the president's critics, "too much attention need not be given to these people." [45]

McGeorge Bundy agreed with that point. He was scheduled to present the administration's case at the National Teach-in in Washington on May 15, 1965. Instead Johnson ordered his national security adviser to go to the Dominican Republic to preside over efforts to restore order in the wake of the failed rebellion. Perhaps that was Johnson's way of showing that he did not give "too much attention . . . to these people." Or perhaps he hoped to use the Dominican crisis with academics as he had with Congress. All day long, however, television cameras at the teach-in focused on the empty chair behind Bundy's nameplate. Walt Rostow did attend some of the teach-in sessions and reported to Dean Rusk that the critics were a sanctimonious lot and represented "in American academic life a minority of no great distinction." [46]

Rostow's dismissal of Hans Morgenthau and George McT. Kahin, along with other well-known scholar-critics such as William Appleman Williams and China expert Mary Wright, as "a minority of no great distinction," revealed much about his capacity for rationalizing unwelcome intrusions into the serene atmosphere of unchallenged assumptions. It also suggested a new mood of prickly defensiveness. Certainly that was the atmosphere at a meeting in the president's office in the White House the day after the teach-in. Johnson was impatient to start the bombing again. "No one has even thanked us for the pause," he complained. "We tried out their notion and got no result. . . . My judgment is the public has never wanted us to stop the bombing. We have stopped in deference to Mansfield and Fulbright, but we don't want to do it too long else we lose our base of support." Defense Secretary McNamara was equally truculent: "Mansfield ought to know Hanoi spit in our face."[47]

Nevertheless, resuming the bombing at a higher level was sure to cause trouble with critics. So Johnson moved to position himself once again as a prisoner of circumstance, bound to obey the congressional mandate set forth in the Tonkin Gulf Resolution. The ploy was beginning to sound Uriah Heepish, as in an interview with a favored *Washington Post* correspondent. The president, wrote Edward T. Folliard, was "distressed and perplexed" by North Vietnam's failure to understand his motives. "It pains him to know that he is pictured in North Vietnam as a wheeler-dealer, a sort of emperor who wants to conquer that country when his true goal, as he says, is the very opposite of conquest." It was a shamelessly maudlin performance by both the president and the reporter. "Mr. Johnson doesn't see how any man in the Presidency could do anything except what he has done and is doing in Viet-Nam. This is because of the Southeast Asia resolution adopted by Congress on Aug. 7, 1964, five days after the North Vietnamese attacked American destroyers in the Gulf of Tonkin."[48]

Gone were the hedges Johnson had scattered throughout his comments on the war in the preceding year, replaced now by a tendentious fatalism. He had prodded Congress into reaffirming the Tonkin Gulf Resolution by using the Dominican crisis to substitute for North Vietnamese PT boats, but all these efforts to fashion a "containment" policy against critics would fail—as he probably knew beforehand. More and more dependent on Republicans and conservative Democrats for support on Vietnam, he began to blame dissenting liberals for the way the war was going in Asia. "The professors believe you can get peace by being soft and acting nice," he would later say. History had proved that theory wrong. It had caused the nation all kinds of trouble before: World War I, World War II, and Korea. "And now we're really up for grabs. We're the richest nation in the world. And the minute we look soft, the would-be aggressors will go wild. We'll lose all of Asia and then Europe and we'll be an island all by ourselves." When that happened, he ended his lecture on the fecklessness of Eastern intellectuals, "I'd sure hate to have to depend on . . . that Harvard crowd to protect my property. . . ."[49]

Johnson found inspiration for staying the course in Vietnam in Walter Prescott Webb's book on the Texas Rangers, just as he had discovered in the historian's writings about the West during the Depression intellectual precedent for a Great Society. "Captain McNelly repeatedly told his men," Johnson wrote in a May 1965 preface to Webb's book, "that 'courage is a man who keeps on coming on.' Dr. Webb would explain to me, 'You can slow a man like that, but you can't defeat him—the man who keeps on coming on is either going to get there himself or make it possible for a later man to reach the goal.' In the challenging and perilous time of this century, free men everywhere might profitably consider that motto. . . . We can . . . be the kind of people who 'keep on coming on.' " [50]

The bombing attacks resumed in the spirit of Captain McNelly's admonition to his sturdy band of rangers. "Air Force planes today smashed military barracks within 55 miles of Hanoi," read the first paragraph of an Associated Press report from Saigon dated May 22, 1965, the day Folliard's portrait of a saddened but stalwart president appeared on the same page of the *Washington Post*. It was "the closest strike so far to the capital of Communist North Viet-Nam." In the next paragraph, however, the AP story illustrated Johnson's predicament:

> Aground, the Viet Cong inflicted a major defeat on a Vietnamese force in an ambush near Beancat, 30 miles north of Saigon, killing 55 government troops and a U.S. military adviser, an American spokesman said. Two other Americans, an officer and an enlisted man, were killed in a Viet Cong ambush at Songbe, 74 miles north of Saigon. . . . The guerrillas allowed the first truck in a convoy to pass unmolested and then raked the following vehicles with heavy small-arms fire. [51]

Captain McNelly might recognize the tactics from Indian-fighting or cattle-rustling days, but these fellows had modern weapons and would not be rooted out by bombing the north. William Fulbright watched his old colleague—who had stood with him against John Foster Dulles when Eisenhower's secretary of state wanted to intervene to try to prevent a humiliating French defeat at Dien Bien Phu—mystified at Johnson's willingness to consider sending American soldiers by the thousands to get mired down in Southeast Asia. "When it comes to domestic things," Fulbright told an old New Dealer, "he is a wizard, he works miracles. . . . Hell, we have tried for 20 years to get an aid to education bill through, and he gets it through just like that. . . . But he is in real trouble in Vietnam. . . . The President is in trouble around the world, no doubt about it. He listens only to military people, I'm afraid." [52]

Mac Bundy thought the president ought to make a new statement about what would soon be called the president's "other war" in Vietnam. At the end of May he sent Johnson a draft message to Congress asking for an appropriation of $89 million for a Southeast Asia economic program. Harvard professor, and most recently ambassador to India, "Ken" Galbraith had been called in to help with the speech. "The use of Ken is our response to your desire for good liberal rhetoric in this speech. . . . You may want to consider giving it some dramatic treatment in the light of the unprecedented measures we took with the military request. A television pitch for this one might help with the wider purpose of getting the Fulbrights on board for our whole policy."[53] Johnson liked the idea. "I propose we start *now*," read his message to Congress, "to make available our share of the money needed to harness the resources of the *entire* Southeast Asia region for the benefit of all its people." It would be an international venture in which, he hoped, all the industrial nations, including the Soviet Union, would take part. "Now," his message went on, "this is just part of the beginning." With this statement, the ambiguity of the Vietnam policy darkened into a grim vision of the future. "This appropriation today calls for only $89 million, but in the future I will call upon our people to make further sacrifices because this is a good program. . . . This is the only way that I know in which we can really win not only the military battle against armed aggression, but the wider war for the freedom and progress of all men."[54] Here was a demanding dream indeed.

ELEVEN

The First 100,000

GENERAL WESTMORELAND'S CABLE from Saigon on June 7 1965, told Washington that the enemy had at last declared his intentions in classical military terms. There was no mistaking the evidence. New units of North Vietnam's army had already crossed over into the south, and more were on the way. Jet fighters and light bombers from Russia and China had arrived in Hanoi, presumably to prepare for the onslaught. Captured documents and prisoner interrogations, Westmoreland concluded, confirmed other intelligence that a "campaign is now underway to destroy government forces. . . ." The Communists believed final victory was within their grasp.[1]

But if Washington responded as it ought—as it now *must*—Westmoreland was ready to show the enemy what war was all about. He needed combat troops, not just advisers and security forces—and a different attitude about the war. "I am convinced that U.S. troops with their energy, mobility, and firepower can successfully take the fight to the V.C." Everyone understood that what Westmoreland was asking had to do not with numbers, or at least not simply with numbers, but with a conception of what the Vietnam War was all about. The June 7 cable was an attempt to uncomplicate the war by presenting Hanoi as an enemy state mobilizing all its resources for offensive warfare.

Figures were juggled, but the Joint Chiefs told their civilian superiors that Westmoreland needed ten new battalions to increase American forces to nearly 125,000 men.[2] Putting large numbers of combat troops into Vietnam meant something altogether different qualitatively, even more than quantitatively. Westmoreland and the JCS wanted a bigger say in how the war was being run. But that was still not all of it. While the Johnson administration had dismissed war critics as uninformed or unduly alarmist, its own management of the war was disturbing many military leaders. Out in the Pacific, for example, Admiral Ulysses S. Grant Sharp at CINCPAC headquarters in Hawaii fumed about the delay in responding to Westmoreland's cable. He was upset that Washington did not seem to understand that even if the troops were eventually sent, precious time was being lost by not striking the enemy homeland with air power. "The logical course would have been to unleash that air power against the homeland of the aggressor," he complained. "Instead we wasted our air strength on inconsequential targets while planning to commit still more of our men to the ground battle."[3]

Previous Vietnam decisions had been premised, first, on the crisis management model, and, since the bombing began, on a punishment squeeze model. The object had been to convince Hanoi that the war was not worth what it would have to sacrifice to secure a victory in the south—that it could not win anyway. It was against these supposedly overintellectualized scenarios, dreamed up by the civilians in the Pentagon and the National Security Council, that plainspoken men like Admiral Sharp and air force General Curtis LeMay were in revolt. Now, with Westmoreland's cable, Johnson was being asked to choose.

LBJ's immediate reaction to the Westmoreland cable was that it provoked thoughts of a new Korean War. More troops and then a call to go north—and what if China responded to cries for help from Hanoi? Yes, what then would the generals say? Until now the president could count on public opinion to back him. Dissident intellectuals had made a lot of noise late at night on college campuses. But they wouldn't count, McGeorge Bundy predicted, not when stacked up against the "people." "It is not the White House," Bundy argued to *Times* columnist "Scotty" Reston, "but the academics who are currently out of step with the main line of American conviction and purpose." "I went on to tell Reston," Bundy then reported to Johnson, "that any President who was asked to choose between understanding and support of the American people, and the understanding and support of the intellectuals, would choose the people."[4]

While he was always glad to hear negative comments about the Harvards, especially from one of their own, what Johnson now faced was a decision that called forth unhappy memories of the last time the U.S. had gone to war in Asia. And he had only to recall that it had not been the intellectuals but the man in the street who had rejected Truman's war in Korea and voted for Eisenhower. Bundy's sudden new admiration for the *vox populi* could not alleviate Johnson's growing concern that Vietnam was another Korea in the making. Mike Mansfield and Bill Fulbright had confronted him on that ground. Even Dick Russell was getting restless. What if they were right? Over and over again during the seven weeks between Westmoreland's cable and the final decision, Lyndon Johnson challenged his advisers: Where are we heading? Is this another Korea?

It is variously argued that LBJ knew precisely what he would do from the very moment Westmoreland's message arrived, and then skillfully brought his advisers around to accepting his version of how it was to be done; or that the president's extended deliberations with his closest advisers ultimately convinced him there was no other course to follow.[5] Whether the force lines ran from Johnson to his advisers, or the other way, the president's dismay that the carefully calibrated steps of previous models, the Phase I and Phase II bombing schemes, all of it, had led to this point, was obvious to those around him. In the midst of this troubled period before a final decision, Johnson walked in on a White House staff meeting one day. "Don't let me interrupt," he began, sounding like the Ancient Mariner, neck bent under the weight of his albatross. "But there's one thing you ought to know. Vietnam is like being in a plane without a parachute, when all the engines go out. If you jump, you'll probably be killed, and if you stay in you'll crash and probably burn. That's what it is." Then he turned and left without another word.

That day, or one like it, Johnson took his dogs for a walk around the Rose Garden back of the White House. Alerted that LBJ was on the prowl, reporters joined the parade, puffing to keep up. His shoulders drooped, recalled Hobart Rowen, and his eyes betrayed fatigue as he launched into a discourse on Vietnam troubles. The reporters peppered him with questions: Where was it all heading? What would it really cost? Suddenly Johnson jerked the dogs to a halt. "I don't know what the fuck to do about Vietnam. I wish someone would tell me what to do." He strode away from the startled reporters.[6]

For several days before Johnson's decisive press conference on July 28, newspapers speculated about the *size* of the expected troop commitment. "I have asked the Commanding General, General Westmoreland, what more he needs to meet this mounting aggression," Johnson ended the suspense. "He has told me. We will meet his needs." American fighting strength in Vietnam would be increased immediately from 75,000 to 125,000 men. "Additional forces will be needed later, and they will be sent as requested."[7]

Finished with his opening statement, the president nodded to Nancy Dickerson, an old friend and reporter from NBC. How did he feel about making this decision, "particularly in the context we always hear that your Office is the loneliest in the world?" He could not have asked for a more perfect prompt. Nobody in the country, Johnson smiled, had as much help and understanding, as many experts and good advice, and people from both parties eager to help, than he had. "Nancy, I haven't been lonely the last few days—I have had lots of callers."[8]

WESTMORELAND'S FAMOUS CABLE calling for American troops was not the first notice that Americans in Saigon, at least, had made up their minds about the issue. Ambassador Taylor had sent a similar message earlier. "The cumulative psychological impact of a series of significant ARVN defeats could lead to a collapse in ARVN's will to fight," he had warned. "To ward against the possibility of such a collapse it will probably be necessary to commit US ground forces to action."[9]

McGeorge Bundy had gone to Dean Rusk's office on a Saturday, June 5, 1965, to talk informally about Taylor's cable and about South Vietnam's obvious inability to meet the threat on its own. There was no formal agenda. Bundy's handwritten notes are filled with doodles as the conversation drifted from topic to topic.[10] Rusk and Robert McNamara, who was also there, talked for a time about likely attitudes on Capitol Hill. Well, they agreed, at least Congress was still "comfortable" with the idea of 75,000 troops in Vietnam. Unexpectedly, Johnson walked into the room. He was alone in the White House, he said, "and I heard you fellows were getting together, so I thought I'd come over." The doodles stop. "LBJ" (underlined ten times in Bundy's notes) formulated an agenda for the rest of that day— and for other meetings to follow—in a series of sharply pointed questions:

Who sees our purpose and means of achieving it, out there?

Will it be so costly?

How do we expect to win? Shocked by skill of VC—hit and run successfully.

How do you expect to wind things up?

Before anyone could answer, Johnson told them what wrong guesses would mean: "You'll get 'I'll go to Korea.' " Memories of the 1952 presidential campaign and Ike's promise to go to Korea haunted all Democrats.

Secretary Rusk was the first to take up the challenge. America's purpose, he said, was to get back to 1958, the year before—in Washington's chronology of the war—North Vietnam had intervened in the struggle. To get there required demonstrating that the latest Communist effort in the cold war could not succeed. McNamara said something that sounded almost the same but actually concealed a potentially significant disagreement among advisers. "We're looking for no more than a stalemate in the South." Then Hanoi could be led to the conference table.

There was not much here to feel good about. Rusk's reassertion of the containment worldview and McNamara's military estimate foretold another agonizing era of talk and fight. To think about debates over atomic weapons, sanctuaries, about a new Korea, was more than a little unsettling. Not surprisingly, the meeting ended with Johnson's urgent plea, "We are trying to do everything we know how to do, aren't we?"

The president was furious a few days later when a State Department press officer took it upon himself to discuss some of the things Westmoreland was already authorized to do. Backed into a corner by reporters, Robert McCloskey explained that while the primary mission of the forces already in Vietnam was to maintain the security perimeter around American installations, General Westmoreland had the authority to send these troops into combat in support of ARVN units. The White House did what it could to "clarify" the State Department report and to deny there had been any change of mission. Press Secretary George Reedy insisted that the issue here was simply the inherent obligation of a military commander to do all that was necessary to defend his men and his position, but White House correspondents already had their lead paragraphs. They knew, even if the president was still deceiving himself, where it was all heading.[11]

They were helped along, moreover, by a "deep background" luncheon with Secretary Rusk that same day. Rusk began by telling reporters he was "surprised" that anyone ever thought that American troops would not go into combat when needed. And that need would be determined first and foremost by what Hanoi did by way of infiltration and Viet Cong attacks. The secretary did not leave it at that, but pushed the argument that the real decision had already been made.

> Rusk said [recorded a *New York Times* reporter] the principle change in American strategy was the decision to begin bombing the north on Feb. 7. He said that was a truly major development and a change (something, of course, which Johnson denies). He asserts that the contemplated use of combat troops is small beer compared with the bombing decision.[12]

Asked about the dangers of escalation, Rusk said there was always "the possibility of a big war in any crisis but that if you blink at this danger the communists will drive you out everywhere in the world." Yet in the very next sentence the secretary effectively undercut his own argument, without a "blink" at the contradiction.

> He went on to say that the Soviet Union had no real interest in confronting the U.S. in Southeast Asia, but that the Russians had no influence with Hanoi and Peking to cool down the situation. He said the Russians are being "dragged along" by Hanoi, which is not much comfort to the U.S. because we don't know how far Hanoi will be able to drag them.[13]

Deeply troubled by the momentum that was building—even without knowing about Rusk's extra shove—Senate Majority Leader Mike Mansfield tried once more to stem the tide. He had already sent Johnson a desk drawer full of memos, as the president quipped once, but he tried again, first on the telephone and then in a new three-page memorandum that posed the very same questions Johnson had just directed at his advisers dur-

ing the informal conference at the State Department. "The formal delegation of authority to Westmoreland to commit American combat troops
comes at a time when the last semblance of constituted government (the
Quat group) in Saigon is disappearing," the Senate majority leader began.

> It raises again the question, and it is a crucial one: In what direction are
> we going in Viet Nam? We can talk of negotiations, conferences and
> peace. We can talk of independence and welfare of the people of South
> Viet Nam. We can talk of unconditional discussions. But the question is
> going to be asked increasingly: What do we mean when we say we are
> going to stay in South Viet Nam and for what specific United States or
> Vietnamese ends are we going to stay there? The question will be asked
> increasingly at home no less than abroad.[14]

As Mansfield said, the final breakdown of civilian government in South
Vietnam was at hand. Between sandwiches and beer, Premier Quat's fate
was decided during a meeting in the premier's office on June 12, 1965. After
three hours of prodding Quat, General Nguyen Cao Ky whispered to an
aide, "Go out into the next room and write out a declaration announcing
Quat's desire to hand over power to the Armed Forces Council. Bring it to
me. Try and find a tape recorder and bring that along too."[15]

After the civilians resigned, the generals went home, dead tired. "The
question of electing a new prime minister could wait until the morrow,"
said Ky. To no one's surprise, he himself accepted the burden of the premiership, and Nguyen Van Thieu became chief of state. They would rule in
tandem for the remainder of the war, trading positions under the new constitution of 1967, when Thieu became president and Ky vice-president. No
one in Washington particularly mourned the passing of the Quat "group."
Unlike earlier episodes, when Ambassador Taylor had upbraided Ky and his
coterie for staging a coup d'état against civilian rule, this time he merely
shrugged: "There will always be a straight military government."[16]

George Ball really didn't care either. But like Mansfield and a few others, he hoped the collapse of the Quat government would persuade Lyndon
Johnson he had room to backpedal around his own past statements citing
America's obligations to South Vietnam. Kennedy and Johnson had both
cited Eisenhower's famous 1954 letter of support to Ngo Dinh Diem. But
Eisenhower had, in fact, conditioned American support upon Diem's ability to use the aid effectively and to reform his programs. "The Government
of the United States," Eisenhower had written Diem on October 23, 1954,
"expects that this aid will be met by performance on the part of the Government of Viet-Nam in undertaking needed reforms."

When Ball tried to convince Dean Rusk that Quat's demise effectively
ended American responsibility for what now befell South Vietnam, he got
nowhere. "Look," Ball argued, "You've got no government. It's impossible

to win in a situation where you've got this totally fragile political base. These people are clowns." Rusk would have none of it. "Don't give me that stuff," he retorted. "You don't understand that at the time of Korea that we had to go out and dig Syngman Rhee out of the bush where he was hiding; there was no government in Korea either, and we were able to come through. We're going to get the same breaks down the road. One of these days something is going to happen, and this thing is going to work, just as it did in Korea."[17]

Few could match Rusk's confidence that something positive was going to happen; fewer still—certainly not the president—wanted it to happen "just as it did in Korea." "Why must we do it?" Johnson questioned Westmoreland's troop request at the next meeting of his advisers. "What if we don't do this?" He put Mansfield's memorandum on the table. They were going to have to answer it "line by line," he said. And he had brought Senator Richard Russell with him to hear the answers. Ambassador Taylor gave him a military answer: we could lose a province, lose territory, lose towns. A confused dialogue followed, as Bundy recorded it in his notes:

LBJ: Will this lead to more? How do we extricate ourselves?

MDT: If we can stalemate monsoon & go back in strong?

Taylor wanted to know, apparently, if Johnson meant, How do we extricate ourselves from defeat? But the president was fixated on Korea and long lists of casualties. "What kind of losses?" he asked. "400-4000." McNamara estimated four hundred by October. The president kept on asking questions—and getting the same answers. What were other governments doing? Not much. Beyond the Koreans (who were being paid by Washington) and a few others, hardly anything. Someone pointed out that Harold Wilson's Labour government would not survive if he tried to send troops. "But this is a U.S.-GVN commitment," protested the ever serene Rusk, who could match McNamara's facility for rattling off numbers and statistics with his own calculus of cold war truisms.

What about the DRV? queried Johnson. Any sign of a response there? "No," said Rusk, "and we don't expect 'em." George Ball feared the president was getting himself deeper into a corner with these questions instead of gaining flexibility. "We need to be careful," he said, "not to regard this decision as defining or predeciding what we do after we see what happens in [the] monsoon." Russell also tried to help. Wasn't the real issue "how to get out and save face?" But then he reconsidered. What "little knowledge I have, I'd send division in and . . . " Bundy's notes of the senator's rumination end abruptly there. Russell may have given it up. Several days later, indeed, he gave a speech indicating the involvement had been a terrible mistake, and a full-scale land war in Asia the ultimate folly. But there was a commitment. "The flag is there. U.S. honor and prestige are there. And, most important of all, U.S. soldiers are there."[18]

The president and his advisers eventually turned toward a moderate troop increase, a wait-and-see attitude, until a new reckoning could be made after the expected Viet Cong offensive during the monsoon season.[19] Secretary Rusk had his own reasons for not wanting to go up the escalation ladder too fast. A full-fledged national debate on sending troops, he said, would get out of hand. "The Commies would use their whole apparatus to stir up trouble—which might have serious international results." In Rusk's tightly framed Manichean worldview, Satan never rested. Bundy's notes of that day's meeting end cryptically with arrows drawn at two points Johnson made, as if he were recording Kurtz's last words in Conrad's *Heart of Darkness*:

The freedom of choice.

The Korean trauma. Was it too much? No. But.[20]

At the next day's formal National Security Council meeting, the president suggested his position was designed to preserve his freedom of choice—and to avoid another Korean trauma.

We must delay and deter the North Vietnamese and Viet Cong as much as we can, and as simply as we can, without going all out. When we grant General Westmoreland's request, it means that we get in deeper and it is harder to get out. They think they are winning and we think they are. We must determine which course gives us the maximum protection at the least cost.[21]

White House aides were anxious, meanwhile, to demonstrate how smoothly the decision-making process was going, how firm was Johnson's grasp of all the essentials. To get that word out to the public, the president's special assistant, Bill Moyers, invited Columbia University historian Henry Graff to come to Washington from June 9 to 11, 1965, to interview members of the "Tuesday Cabinet," the "informal" group of Johnson's advisers who met with the president each week for a luncheon discussion of foreign policy issues. As Graff had recently published articles decrying the trend toward neoisolationism he perceived lurking behind criticisms of the Dominican Republic intervention and the administration's policy in Vietnam, it was thought he could write articles with a better perspective than some journalist caught up in the day-to-day happenings of the war. Even though the article the historian published in the Sunday *New York Times Magazine* left out many of LBJ's most telling comments, what it revealed was a president nearly obsessed with self-image as he approached his most fateful decision of the war.[22]

Moyers had welcomed Graff to his office by assuring him the president gave careful attention to all his "options." At the last meeting, for example, by actual count Johnson had asked forty-one questions. It was obvious, Moyers went on to say, that the "drama of working on the tip of a volcano" affected the president, but he was in complete command. He took his example, the president's trusted young aide said, from FDR who had successfully "walked the line between lack of Congressional support and the necessity of providing moral and material help to the British people in 1940–41." In this crisis he was determined not to abandon American responsibility nor to risk World War III. "He is determined to avoid large-scale war." Neither did he maintain that the United States had all the answers, Moyers said, only that the outcome of events was "not beyond our influence."[23]

When Graff talked with Defense Secretary Robert McNamara, Korea came up in an interesting fashion. What analogy did Johnson draw about Vietnam, the historian asked? Korea was more important than Munich as an analogy, McNamara volunteered, not for any logical reason, but it was "significant in psychology." There would be no sanctuaries in this war, neither would there be war with China, the secretary of defense reassured Graff, because "we are not moving in that direction."[24]

McNamara's cool balancing act was not repeated in Dean Rusk's office. The secretary of state redirected attention to Munich and the prewar world's failure to meet the Nazi challenge. "The underlying conflict," he averred, "is between a U.N. kind of world and those trying to build a world revolution." The leaders of "the other side" had laid plans for Vietnam, the Dominican Republic, the Congo. "Their declared doctrine of the world revolution ought to be as credible as *Mein Kampf*."[25]

Graff then asked McGeorge Bundy what he thought about the historical antecedents and particularly the importance of Korea in shaping Vietnam policy. That experience might cause "pain" for Congress, came the reply, but "Johnson is not terrified by Korea." He knew it "shakes the party." As for the intellectuals, he had now come to appreciate what John Foster Dulles had once said during a visit to Bundy's seminar on foreign policy at Harvard. Professor Bundy and his students voiced their opposition to the Eisenhower administration's determination to prevent Red China from seizing two tiny islands in the Taiwan Straits, Quemoy and Matsu. Dulles was not disturbed. Despite what Harvard seminarians thought, he had replied, he was confident about the response of the American people.[26]

What he had learned from Dean Acheson, Bundy added, was that in the final analysis the United States was "the locomotive at the head of mankind, and the rest of the world the caboose—explaining that he was not expressing chauvinism but simply passing judgment on the usefulness to the world of American energies." When Graff published this exchange, the White House rushed off a letter of protest to the *Times*. Actually he opposed such views, Bundy explained. He had not meant to say anything, he claimed, that could be construed as believing in anything other than the importance of "responsible energy" in foreign policy.[27]

Graff found Johnson in a somber mood. "The worst mistake we ever made was getting rid of Diem," he said. Expressing resentment at what the Kennedys had left on his plate, and what he saw as their snide insinuations about his ineptness in foreign policy, Johnson's bitter remarks to the professor were hardly what White House aides had hoped for—though the worst of them were not published until he left the presidency.[28]

He had been deeply involved in foreign policy questions, Johnson began, since before American entry into World War II, when he helped to save the draft law from defeat. What followed this assertion did not appear in the original 1965 magazine article. "Now they say I am not qualified in foreign affairs like Jack Kennedy and those other experts. I guess I was just born in the wrong part of the country." He had carried on through the 1950s serving on key congressional committees dealing with foreign policy; he had gone through the Dien Bien Phu debacle; he had served as majority leader—all this "while Kennedy was on the Labor Committee." Graff noted, "The sarcasm was deep and biting."[29]

Another key editing change came when Graff recorded Johnson's impressions of predecessors. FDR was his model, of course. But he had worked well with Eisenhower on all his foreign policy problems. "He had also 'tried to comfort' Kennedy after the Bay of Pigs." That was enough of a slight, but Graff left out of the magazine article an even nastier ending for the sentence about the 1961 fiasco: "He had also 'tried to comfort' Kennedy after the Bay of Pigs *when 'he and Bobby thought they were right.'* "[30]

The final cuts from the 1965 article were perhaps the most revealing, as Johnson one last time tried to show how his World War II heroism fitted him for the job of commander in chief in this new crisis. "As if to complete his account of his previous experience, he reminded me that he had won the Silver Star in the Second World War for helping shoot down 20 Zeroes." LBJ's exaggerations were famous, but this one seemed like an attempt to convince himself as well as others around him of his ability to do the job in Vietnam.[31]

He needed such bolstering. During early discussions about Westmoreland's troop request, Johnson had countered one proposal for deploying an air mobile division to operate inland with an idea for adding instead a brigade for use in coastal base areas. The president then asked General Andrew Goodpaster to take this idea to Gettysburg to see what Eisenhower thought. Ike delivered a judgment that probably made Johnson wince when he read Goodpaster's report. "A first question to consider," Eisenhower began, "is what the end of all this can be." Having "appealed to force," there was no option, "we have got to win." Simply holding on or sitting passively would not suffice. The only reason you build bases is to make it possible to take the offensive "and clear the area."[32]

Johnson publicly thanked Eisenhower for his advice at a press conference, though he carefully avoided saying what that advice was. "I applaud and appreciate the assistance that General Eisenhower, who is the only President of the other party that is living, has given me." At this same meeting with reporters, LBJ related the story of the farmer who was being kept awake at night by frogs barking in the pond. "Finally he got irritated and angry . . . the way you all describe me—those of you that never come around here—and he went out and drained the pond and killed both frogs." The story was meant to illustrate that the frogs that "keep us awake sometimes," like critics of the war, were few but just made a lot of noise.[33]

At the same time he praised Eisenhower's advice, Johnson was soliciting a memorandum from George Ball on possible alternatives to escalating with ground troops. Perhaps he knew that sooner or later it would be leaked that the president was considering alternatives, thereby lending credence to Moyers's assurances to Henry Graff and others that Johnson was asking lots of questions of his advisers before he made up his mind on anything so important. Or maybe he was simply trying to ensure that everyone felt there had been a fair hearing. "He wanted a united front," Johnson told Ball on the telephone, he did "not want to be a dictator."[34]

In any event, the president was anxious for Ball to get going on a memorandum to summarize what had already been done to negotiate a peace. He particularly liked what the under secretary had been doing, "raising the red flag and saying we ought to give thought to different approaches, etc." Johnson did not think he could sell the idea of an Asian Tito to the country, but he seemed interested in an idea for UN-supervised elections to "let the people have a choice."[35]

Ball took his cue from Johnson's general uneasiness about Vietnam rather than any specific indication the president wanted to hear more about alternative A or B. He was also encouraged by Johnson's allowing Bill Moyers to serve as a principal funnel for his ideas and memos, rather than insisting that the under secretary go through Mac Bundy.[36] Ball titled his next memo "Keeping the Power of Decision in the South Viet-Nam Crisis." It began with a quotation from Ralph Waldo Emerson: "Things are in the saddle, and ride mankind." The president's most difficult problem, the under secretary wrote, was to prevent "things" from getting control of policy. Playing directly on the president's frequent expressions of concern about maintaining freedom of choice, Ball told him the only way to do that was to limit commitments to a certain time and a certain magnitude. The use of combat troops should be explicitly labeled a test for no more than three months' duration. The president's key advisers should understand that at the end of that test period, after the monsoon season, "we will take a serious look at our accumulated experience and decide whatever long-range course of policy or action is indicated."

> For the fact is—and we can no longer avoid it—that, in spite of our intentions to the contrary, we are drifting toward a major war—that nobody wants.[37]

Ball developed his ideas in the remainder of the memorandum that went on for nine pages, but it all boiled down to one point: despite our best intentions we were repeating the French experience. As carefully as he could, the under secretary tiptoed around Johnson's frequent claims that he had made serious overtures for negotiations. It was taboo to talk about that subject except to express regrets that the bombing pause had brought no response. During recent weeks, Ball wrote, "we have concentrated on seeking a political solution that would fully meet our stated objectives. . . . Since we cannot yet be sure that we will be able to beat the Viet Cong without unacceptable costs, we would be prudent to undertake an additional study of the political means to achieve less than a satisfactory solution—or, in other words, a solution involving concessions on our side as well as the Viet Cong."[38]

The day he read Ball's memorandum, Johnson wrote a note to "Scotty" Reston, praising the reporter for a column that "was to the point, and from the facts." Inspired apparently by one of those "key advisers" whom George Ball cautioned the president about, the column was in fact a rehearsal of arguments that would be used *against* the under secretary's proposals for thinking about the unthinkable. The heart of the Bundy-Rusk-McNamara case against Ball was that America could not yield to a demand for a humiliating withdrawal of its forces. "Sure it's an awkward and dangerous situation, he says," Reston explained the president's view, "but what would you do? What are your specific proposals to deal with the facts as they are? And what would be the consequences of your proposals in the rest of Asia and the world?"[39]

The message Bill Moyers conveyed to George Ball, on the other hand, was that the president had read the under secretary's memo over the weekend at Camp David and agreed "in substance" with what it said—"one or two slight changes possibly." Johnson, like Franklin Roosevelt, was a master dissembler. But that does not really explain LBJ's turmoil as he came to a decision on sending troops to Vietnam. FDR faced easier choices. He laid the groundwork for the "American Century" in World War II, when all the world looked to Washington for salvation; LBJ faced the burdens of the "imperial presidency," when much of the world resented American presumption. Johnson desperately wanted a way out of Vietnam. If George

Ball could buy him time, he would take it. He knew better than all the others that once the troops went in it would be "Mr. Johnson's War."

Johnson instructed Bill Moyers to tell Ball he should keep working on possible alternatives to follow the monsoon season. "I don't think I should go over 100,000," Johnson said, "but think I should go to that number and explain it. . . . I am not worried about riding off in the wrong direction. I agree that it might build up bit by bit. I told McNamara that I would not make a decision on this and not to assume that I am willing to go overboard on this—I ain't. If there is no alternative, the fellow here with the program is the way I will probably go."[40]

Two Soviet officials in London, meanwhile, had sought out American newsmen and engaged them in long discussions about Vietnam. Both professed to be deeply worried about the potential for a Russian-American confrontation in Vietnam; and both expressed an understanding that the United States could not tolerate a defeat in the "classic sense." As they saw it, Moscow could help only if the United States agreed to end the bombing and negotiate with the Viet Cong. As matters stood, Hanoi was rapidly moving away from Moscow toward the "Chinese camp." More than 95 percent of the leadership of the DRV was already there. What was remarkable about these conversations, however, was a statement by the Russians that the United States should *increase* its military force by five divisions, "seal off the 17th parallel, cut off the Viet Cong from their northern logistics, then ignore the north and wait for [the] Viet Cong to come to terms because 'starved' by lack of northern support." Here was a serious hint that Moscow's interest in Vietnam actually ran parallel to Washington's, at least in terms of keeping China out of the picture. And what was really being argued here was that a stronger regime in Saigon could only be constructed with the participation of the National Liberation Front.[41]

On the London telegram detailing the Russian contacts, someone on the National Security Council staff had written, "There is an element of the frantic in this." Who was frantic? If the Russians, it was largely because they were unable to get it across that U.S. policy was destabilizing Asia. The irony was that the cool, conservative, geopolitical arguments were coming from the Soviet Union while fevered ideological concerns preoccupied Washington. Bundy in fact told the president that the Russians were "floating the notion" that "we can do anything we want as long as we do it in South Vietnam."[42] Who to believe? And even if these officials spoke with Moscow's authority, friendly Communists, an old British World War II saying went, "were like cobras being matey." He could not pull out, the president told a *New York Times* reporter, without giving up everywhere. No one would count on the United States honoring its commitments. He knew it would be the "easiest thing in the world to get into a war with Red China."

Peking just wanted an excuse. Only 10 percent of the American people would support going north—but likewise only a few would pull out. *Times* editorials criticized him, Johnson complained, but they gave him no alternative. The reporter's notes continue, "Says he wishes Johnny Oakes [editorial page editor] would come down to Washington and tell him how to solve the problem. Best generals, best diplomatic brains working on it and they haven't been able to figure out what to do. Appears genuinely concerned about Times editorial policy. 'I can't fight this war without the support of the NY Times.' " Johnson rambled on about what mothers of soldiers in Vietnam said about the newspapers, about how only 168 Americans had been killed so far and he was trying to keep the zeros off it, about his instructions to U.S. troops to shoot. "What am I supposed to ask them to do? Sit there and dodge?" As Johnson perhaps expected, the reporter came away concerned about the president's travail: "Overall impression: The man is deeply worried about Vietnam and sees no way out. Desperate for a workable plan. His wife is worried about him."[43]

Having defined the National Liberation Front as nothing more than "agents" of a "foreign" country, North Vietnam, there *was* no way out for Johnson. Like Woodrow Wilson who defined the Bolsheviks as "agents" of a foreign conspiracy, he had set for himself the mystical challenge of reimagining (and *r*econstructing) Vietnamese nationalism. Negotiating with the Vietnamese about the American mission thus became unthinkable. And that was true, it needs to be reemphasized, whether with the NLF or any Saigon regime. The enemy, as one State Department draft statement put it, exhibited "a brand of behavior which would be unthinkable for a civilized people"—plastic bombs in Saigon restaurants, terrorist tactics in the countryside, and now the execution of a captured American soldier. But none of this would "deter us from our task."[44] Neither, however, would America's shaky Vietnamese allies, the presumed beneficiaries of Washington's determination. As Henry Cabot Lodge, about to replace Maxwell Taylor for his second tour as American ambassador, put it during the troop debate:

> There is not a tradition of a national government in Saigon. There are no roots in the country. Not until there is tranquility can you have any stability. I don't think we ought to take this government seriously. There is simply no one who can do anything. We have to do what we think we ought to do regardless of what the Saigon government does. As we move ahead on a new phase, we have the right and the duty to do certain things with or without the government's approval.[45]

Preoccupied with the *New York Times* editorial policy and suffering premonitions about a Kennedy "fifth column" in his midst, Johnson did not credit his own doubts about whether "white men" could win a war on such an unfriendly terrain. Lodge's assertions about Vietnamese malleability thus went unchallenged. And if the president fretted that China was only looking for an excuse to come into the Vietnam War, he agonized more over the loyalty of the Kennedy holdovers. One obvious reason why the loyalty question became so pressing just at this time was that the major proponents of sending troops were Kennedy men. Johnson loyalists, ironically, were more skeptical.

The more he had to rely upon the judgment of the Bundys and McNamaras, and to turn away from the Fulbrights and Mansfields, the deeper ran his fears of betrayal. He dreaded most of all finding himself alone. Johnson's obsession with Robert Kennedy began to shift from resentment at past slights and retribution to forebodings about failure in Vietnam. Johnson later told Doris Kearns about a repetitive dream sequence he experienced during this time.

> There would be Robert Kennedy out in front leading the fight against me, telling everyone that I had betrayed John Kennedy's commitment to South Vietnam. That I had let a democracy fall into the hands of the Communists. That I was a coward. An unmanly man. A man without a spine. Oh, I could see it coming all right. Every night when I fell asleep I would see myself tied to the ground in the middle of a long, open space. In the distance, I could hear the voices of thousands of people. They were all shouting at me and running toward me: "Coward! Traitor! Weakling."[46]

However much LBJ embellished this recollection, there is good evidence that in the days before he made the decision to send combat troops to Vietnam, the president's mind was filled with suspicions that Robert Kennedy was actively promoting disloyalty among his chief advisers. In an odd fashion, LBJ thus transferred his own doubts about Vietnam into a Kennedy plot to destroy his presidency.

White House aide Harry McPherson tried his best to dispel such fears in a thoughtful memorandum that portrayed Robert Kennedy as a power-seeker to be watched carefully, but whose greatest threat to the Johnson presidency was that he distracted the president from seeing the true situation. "You have the office, the policies, the personal magnetism, the power to lead and inspire, and above all the power to put good ideas into effect. An obsession with Bobby and with the relationship of your best people to him may, I believe, distort policy and offend the very men you need to attract."[47]

Johnson had apparently singled out Defense Secretary McNamara, who was preparing a crucial paper on combining military and political approaches to the Vietnam problem, as one of those whose contacts with Kennedy worried him most. McPherson's memo offered the argument that the New Frontiersmen had shown a degree of loyalty that was sufficient to insure effective operation of the government. "We cannot afford to lose them. Neither, in my opinion, can we afford to give them a polygraph-loyalty test to determine whether they would go to the wall for you against Jack Kennedy."[48]

> It is possible, in my opinion, for people to work hard for you, maintain confidences, and still find the Kennedys (including Bobby) attractive and adventurous. The Kennedys are handsome and dashing, they support fashionable artists, and they can pay for almost anything. They support a great many good causes. And to some people even their rudeness and ruthlessness is exciting. They were the most "in" of all families for three years. There is an air of tragic loss about them now. They are still rich and powerful and liberal. People who knew them and admired them when Jack Kennedy, their most winning member, was alive, no doubt still feel attracted to them. But this does not imply disloyalty or real danger for you, particularly in the case of McNamara.[49]

Johnson had considerable reason, nevertheless, to wonder about the purpose of McNamara's June 26, 1965, paper, "Program of Expanded Military and Political Moves with Respect to Vietnam." Years later McNamara maintained that he wanted to open up political options by confronting Hanoi in similar fashion to Kennedy's stance in the Cuban missile crisis. In other words, to force the North Vietnamese to negotiate on American terms. Yet he also claimed he was aware, even at this early date, that military victory "in the narrow sense of the word" was impossible. According to a biographer, however, McNamara appeared to have "stapled together all the Joint Chiefs' suggestions" for waging war against North Vietnam.

The memo proposed a troop level of 175,000. And that was only for 1965, to stabilize the situation. To cause the enemy to back off would require "substantial" additional forces as yet undetermined. The paper argued for a call-up of 100,000 reservists and extended tours for those already on active duty. Expanded air and sea actions would include mining harbors, destroying rail and highway bridges, and cutting off all supply lines with China. The goal was to "destroy the war-making supplies and facilities of North Vietnam wherever located."[50]

So much for the military steps. In a second section, entitled "Political Initiatives," McNamara proposed direct contacts with the National Liberation Front, "making clear a readiness to discuss ways and means of achieving settlement in Vietnam." What the United States should offer (or accept) in those discussions was not spelled out, but the idea of face-to-face negotiations with the Viet Cong was a forbidden subject. The "official" position was that the VC could have their views represented by the DRV, all in accordance with the American interpretation of the war's origins. Only a week earlier, for example, Lyndon Johnson had told reporters, "I don't believe we'd ever agree to someone negotiating that is not a government. I am not aware of any government the Viet Cong has. What would you think about the State of Mississippi negotiating for us in this matter? Although it is a State it is not a sovereign government." [51]

McNamara's memorandum suggested, nevertheless, another bold departure: opening a dialogue with Beijing. While all this was going on, McNamara wrote, the Soviets should be kept informed, all in the hope of finding "common ground to work with them" instead of an increasing risk of confrontation. Such political initiatives would cement support for U.S. policy within the nation and from its allies, he said, and "keep international opposition at a manageable level." "While our approaches may be rebuffed until the tide begins to turn, they nevertheless should be made." If it is almost impossible today to determine from available evidence whether McNamara meant simply to restate cold war clichés as Washington escalated its forces, in order to keep opposition at manageable levels, or whether this was a serious departure, what must Johnson have thought? [52]

Mac Bundy's reaction to the McNamara paper only adds to the difficulty. "This program is rash to the point of folly," Bundy declared in a sharply worded rejoinder he sent to the Pentagon. He objected to almost every military proposal McNamara had recommended as unwarranted and likely to be ineffective; but then, in confusing fashion, Bundy listed "additional possibilities" the paper had supposedly omitted. These included an Eisenhower-style ultimatum to Hanoi, but not, however, a threat to use nuclear weapons. Bundy thought a "realistic threat" to deny North Vietnam aid from its outside suppliers might do the trick. There was also the possibility of "stronger interdiction" of north-south traffic. And so on. What it really came down to, for all the searching questions, was the national security adviser's alarm at the prospect of an open-ended troop commitment, which he apparently singled out as the central issue. [53]

Bundy did not speak directly to the proposed political initiatives, but the final paragraph of his rejoinder appeared to address the subtext of McNamara's paper as if it were (as perhaps it was) a proposal so outrageous as to force a reconsideration of the entire Vietnam policy. McNamara's military recommendations, in this reading, were either too much—or too little.

> Any expanded program needs to have a clear sense of its own internal momentum. The paper does not face this problem. If US casualties go up sharply, what further actions do we propose to take or not to take? More broadly still, *what is the real object of the exercise? If it is to get to the conference table, what results do we seek there?* Still more brutally, do we want to invest 200 thousand men to cover an eventual retreat? Can we not do that just as well where we are? [54]

Did the national security adviser fear others would see the defense secretary's proposals the same way, and the critics would seize upon them to
push for disengagement, for "peace at any price"? The Munich analogy had
never seemed so complicated. When George Ball presented his own memorandum "proposing a plan for cutting our losses in South Viet-Nam,"
Bundy began a determined search for a way to regain full control of the
decision-making process lest the president find himself squeezed between
the all-outers and the disillusioned. Already it was being reported by *Washington Post* columnists Rowland Evans and Robert Novak that Republican
leaders had smelled out a plot to "get a negotiated settlement including
Communists in a 'neutralist' government in Saigon," and that McNamara
had made a pilgrimage to Capitol Hill to dispel that notion.[55]

Of those closest to the president, however, only George Ball openly
urged a withdrawal—and then in the most careful language, so as not to
break the surface tension that held cold war assumptions together. He was
no more eager than Bundy to see a full-scale debate about cold war tenets
focusing on Vietnam as a test of their validity. Johnson should invoke
Eisenhower's 1954 letter not as a justification for deepening American
involvement with what had become a "travesty" of a government in Saigon,
Ball wrote, but to justify an honorable withdrawal. Since Americans were
dying in South Vietnam, he argued, the United States was fully within its
rights and duty to demand that Saigon "fashion a stable Government of
National Union." Ball proposed giving the South Vietnamese a month to
accomplish this feat. Even if they were somehow able to bring it off, which
he did not think likely, "The President should make the firm decision that
he will *not* commit United States land forces to combat in South Vietnam."

> The position taken in this memorandum does not suggest that the Unit-
> ed States should abdicate leadership in the cold war. But any prudent
> military commander carefully selects the terrain on which to stand and
> fight, and no great captain has ever been blamed for a successful tactical
> withdrawal.[56]

Ball was correct on one point, as Bundy had confessed to Johnson in
his comments on an earlier memorandum from the under secretary: there
was no "legal" commitment to South Vietnam under any treaty Washington had signed. The commitment was primarily political.

> My own further view is that if and when we wish to shift our course and
> cut our losses in Vietnam we should do so because of a finding that the
> Vietnamese themselves are not meeting their obligations to themselves
> or to us. This is the course we started on with Diem, and if we got a
> wholly ineffective or anti-American government we could do the same
> thing again. With a "neutralist" government it would be quite possible
> to move in this direction.[57]

Yet when confronted by Ball's arguments for recognizing that such a situation already existed, the national security adviser drew back as if he had mistakenly opened the lid of a snake charmer's basket and released the cobra. Thus confronted, Bundy scampered behind the oldest defense— America's unique mission to the world. It was being suggested "in some quarters," he wrote Johnson, that the United States now occupied the same position vis-à-vis Vietnam that France had found itself in at the time of Dien Bien Phu. France in 1954 was a colonial power seeking to reimpose its rule, he went on, out of tune with Vietnamese nationalism and divided at home. "The U.S. in 1965 is responding to the call of a people under Communist assault, a people undergoing a non-Communist national revolution; neither our power nor that of our adversaries has been fully engaged as yet." Here was the grand theme of the cold war. It was possible, apparently, to muse about a way out of Vietnam only as long as everyone understood the game. In the cold war a "place" was important if one of the major players, the United States or Russia, said it was, however difficult it might be to explain that logically.[58]

Bundy's aide, Chester Cooper, also admitted that Ball's picture of the situation in Saigon was justified. He had painted a pessimistic and "God help us, perhaps realistic account of what we confront in Vietnam." "A more ebullient artist might have cast the situation in somewhat less somber tones, but there is not much point here in determining how dark a grey or how deep a black to use." By setting impossible conditions for Saigon, Ball was providing a flimsy cover for American withdrawal. Before the administration adopted that "unsavory" course, Cooper advised, it could wait to see what happened at the end of the monsoon season. "If we can come out of it in the fall with a situation in which the VC is not much better off than it was in May, we may be over the hump."[59]

In the end, Cooper's temporizing position prevailed. It was not his alone, of course, and the NSC aide was a lesser player than even George Ball at the subcabinet level. In the end it prevailed because thinking about the unthinkable was too much for policymakers who depended on the cold war vision for their understanding of the world. Ball performed a service, nonetheless. Nothing concentrated the mind so powerfully, it seemed, than his picture of a waiting gallows. Bill Bundy took particular umbrage, for example, at the supposed insensitivity of Ball's memorandum and elaborated yet a new variation on what losing "face" would cost. "After all the political confusion and ineptitude the US had put up with for two years past, it would have seemed absurd to insist on a new perfection just as the going was at its worst; to Asian eyes, it would have been the most cynical exit method possible."[60]

To avoid a choice between McNamara's extremes and Ball's too hasty retreat, Bill Bundy drafted his own " 'Middle Way' Course of Action" memo. "In essence," he wrote, "this is a program to *hold on* for the next two months, and *to test* the military effectiveness of US combat forces and the reaction of the Vietnamese army and people to the increasing US role." There was little in the assistant secretary of state's memo to force readers to think about fundamental issues presented by Vietnam. Military pressures were to be kept at the same level, with most escalatory decisions deferred until the fall. American troops should not engage in major operations beyond easy reach of their bases. The Ky government should be "galvanized" to act in the "direction" of "maximum revolution and reform, but minimum repression." Discreet contacts with Hanoi, and possibly even "cut-out" contacts (not identified with the U.S.), should be encouraged as well with the NLF. "These would not be with any serious negotiating expectations, but to open channels and to soften up both by playing on Hanoi's fear of Peiping and the possible Liberation Front fear of being totally under Hanoi's domination."[61]

In a rare personal memorandum, Dean Rusk tried to clear Johnson's field of vision so that he could once again see the forest. The only reason for the United States to stay in Vietnam, he intoned, "must be to insure that North Viet-Nam not succeed in taking over or determining the future of South Viet-Nam by force. We must accomplish this objective without a general war if possible." After the DRV gave up its dream of conquest, everyone in the south could sit down to work out local problems, including the "indigenous" Viet Cong. But there could be no "serious debate" about the American obligation.

> The integrity of the U.S. commitment is the principal pillar of peace throughout the world. If that commitment becomes unreliable, the communist world would draw conclusions that would lead to our ruin and almost certainly to a catastrophic war. So long as the South Vietnamese are prepared to fight for themselves, we cannot abandon them without disaster to peace and to our interests throughout the world.[62]

Filled with near-apocalyptic phrases—"principal pillar," "our ruin" "catastrophic war," "disaster to peace"—Rusk's memorandum slipped by the issue of the "indigenous" Viet Cong as a minor matter to be somehow resolved afterward. It breathed the very spirit of Old Testament prophecy. In spirit and language it was not terribly different from what the evangelist Billy Graham wrote Johnson:

> It is my prayer that you will continue to face the somber realities of this hour with faith and courage. The Communists are moving fast toward their goal of world revolution. Perhaps God brought you to the kingdom for such an hour as this—to stop them. In doing so, you could be the man that helped save Christian civilization.[63]

The well-known affinity between Rusk and Johnson, both "dirt-poor" Southerners by heritage, risen to the pinnacle of national leadership—"Perhaps God brought you to the kingdom for such an hour as this"—deserves special attention. Given Johnson's suspicion of McNamara and Bundy as Kennedy men, if Rusk had dissented, LBJ's own skepticism would no doubt have weighed more heavily in his decision-making. It might have reopened his mind to the dissents of old friends like Fulbright and Mansfield, and doubters like George Ball.

Harris Wofford, a War on Poverty aide, witnessed a remarkable Johnson recitation of how he approached the crucial Vietnam decision. It began during the signing of the 1965 Peace Corps Act at the White House. Suddenly Johnson plucked a letter from a pile on his desk. It was from a mother whose son had died in Vietnam. "Believe me, my heart breaks when I read this mother's letter," he told those who had been invited to the ceremony, "and I want you to know there is nothing more important to your President than peace. . . . That's all we're fighting for in Vietnam. I lay awake nights asking myself if there is anything more I can do for peace. Just last Sunday at the ranch, I took Billy Graham and Bill Moyers down to the banks of the Pedernales and we sat there talking and thinking and praying for peace."

Then, after a pause, "the President's eyes began to close and his arms went out and up as if for a laying on of hands. He waved them and shook them, tremblingly, as he went on: 'And I want you to know that no matter what my problems and my worries are, when I think of you, when I think of the Peace Corps, when I think of all those Volunteers around the world, helping the poor, healing the maimed and curing the blind, then my heart lifts up and I know that peace is on its way.' " Wofford and several others present were stunned by the intensely emotional way Johnson had spoken. "At points he was almost whispering, with his eyes squinting or shut, then, eyes bulging, he would rant and almost bellow."[64]

Wofford wondered if Johnson had tried to mesmerize himself by this "act." It was an insightful observation. All the praying together over Rusk's and Graham's "messages," the seance on the Pedernales, had not completely resolved LBJ's crisis of faith. Far from it. Thinking about Peace Corps volunteers doing God's work helped—"my heart lifts up and I know that peace is on its way." McGeorge Bundy, meanwhile, was fully back on an even keel. His brother Bill's memorandum offered a reasonable counter to McNamara's impetuosity and permitted debate to return to safer, or at least more familiar, ground. "My hunch is that you will want to listen hard to George Ball," he wrote the president, "and then reject his proposal. Discussion could then move to the narrow choice between my brother's course and McNamara's." A decision could be made, then, in about ten days.[65]

A meeting to discuss the "narrow choice" was scheduled for July 2,

1965. Shortly before it began, Johnson received a phone call from Eisen-hower. When LBJ outlined the position, Ike admonished him not to pay attention to critics. "When you once appeal to force in an international sit-uation . . . you have to go all out! This is a war. . . ." The situation was not hopeless, not at all. "We are not going to be run out of a free country that we helped to establish." Yes, Johnson replied, but he was being told that stronger action would cause us to lose the British and the Canadians—and we will be alone in the world. Eisenhower shot back: " . . . We would still have the Australians and our own convictions." [66]

Johnson's next question was not so easy for the old general. "Do you really think we can beat the Vietcong?" This time there was no talk about how he had ended the Korean War with atomic threats. Instead Eisenhow-er hedged. "This was hard to say because we cannot find out how many are imported and how many are rebels within the population of South Viet-nam." [67] Indeed, that was the crux of the matter. When he met with his advisers, it was clear that Bundy's proposed ten-day countdown did not give Johnson enough time to find out everything he wanted to know—as if there was really anything significant more to know. He had allowed himself to be steered into the narrow channel between brother Bill's memorandum and McNamara's program, where the questions and answers were predictable. Nevertheless, Johnson wanted McNamara to go to Saigon to examine the situation firsthand. He also ordered Averell Harriman to go to Russia to probe Soviet intentions, and George Ball to continue looking into negotia-tion possibilities. [68]

It was also decided to convene the so-called "Wise Men," a group of sixteen prominent Americans whom Johnson had called on for advice dur-ing the 1964 presidential campaign. They assembled on July 8 and 9 and were presented with quick briefings on the Vietnam situation. Whether Johnson expected to hear anything negative about the proposal to send combat troops may be doubted, but he was apparently surprised at the near unanimity and vigor of their enthusiasm for Vietnam as the place to hold the line against communism. Not surprisingly, on the other hand, the views of this group, the cold war genro, focused largely on the worldwide impli-cations, as they saw them, of Vietnam, and very little on the internal situa-tion there. Losing in Vietnam could not be contemplated. To avoid bringing Russia into the war with both feet, on the other hand, U.S. strate-gy should center not on dramatic air strikes against Hanoi and other DRV cities but on increasing combat troop strength in the south. "To carry out this role with some prospect of success," Roswell Gilpatric, a former assis-tant secretary of defense and, like many others of the Wise Men, an East Coast lawyer, summed up their conclusions, "calls for the application of whatever amounts of military power may be needed, perhaps as much as brought to bear in Korea fifteen years ago." [69]

The Wise Men's spirit of noble sacrifice called for President Johnson to reprise Harry Truman's brave stand in Korea. He was to emulate Sidney Carlton in a modern rewrite of *A Tale of Two Cities*. LBJ was not sure he liked the idea. When he met with the Wise Men at the end of the second day, he began ruminating out loud. As he rambled on about how mean everyone was to him—Fate, the Press, Congress, the Intellectuals—the acknowledged leader of the Wise Men, Dean Acheson, fidgeted impatiently. Finally he could stand it no more. "I blew my top and told him he was wholly right on Vietnam," Acheson wrote his old boss, President Truman, "that he had no choice except to press on. . . ."[70]

Before this outburst Acheson had reserved his opinion on Vietnam. In fact, he and George Ball had teamed on a proposal for a political solution by encouraging the Saigon government to plan for local elections that would include VC participation—an idea promptly dismissed by Ambassador Taylor and others as "a giveaway program of the worst sort."[71] Acheson's bitter memories of his travail during the Korean War as Harry Truman's beleaguered secretary of state apparently led him to forget his doubts and to seek vindication anew by getting Lyndon Johnson to stand up to his responsibilities. Something of that nature was at work, anyway, stimulated in this instance by LBJ's peevish whining about the slings and arrows of his critics.[72]

Knowingly or not, Johnson had pushed the right button to goad a powerful response from Acheson. But what the episode also told the president was that *he* could not make a case for getting out that would satisfy the still dominant cold war worldview that kept Americans steady in their purpose. He shared that outlook fully, but precisely because he was better informed—at least about the battlefield situation—than any of his critics on the left or right, and because he was a very intelligent man, he had premonitions about where it was all heading. What if American power proved useless in Vietnam? What if it all came apart in that pissant country because his soldiers couldn't find that bandy-legged Ho Chi Minh?

Johnson's dilemma was perfectly summed up in two "estimates" he received as McNamara landed in Saigon for talks with Westmoreland and the Vietnamese. The first was a quantitative estimate of what could be expected with 200,000 to 400,000-plus American troops in Vietnam. The author of this study, Assistant Secretary of Defense John McNaughton, thought chances of victory with that number of troops would be 20 percent throughout 1966, 40 percent in 1967, and still only 50 percent by election year 1968. How did one value-scale the desirability of various outcomes? McNaughton asked himself. "Is a collapse at a 75,000 level worse than an inconclusive situation at 200-400,000 level? Probably yes." If a "compromise" was more likely at that level—70 percent by 1968—McNaughton was unable to describe what it might be. In a final paragraph headed "Prognosis," McNaughton confessed the difficulty: "It is not obvious how we will be able to disengage our forces from South Vietnam. It is unlikely that a formal arrangement good enough for the purpose could possibly be negotiated—because the arrangement can reflect little more than the power situation." He thought a "compromise" solution might require a large number of American troops in Vietnam, as many as two divisions, for "a period of years." The only "compromise" McNaughton could envision was therefore a return to some imagined time in Vietnamese history, an era American policymakers had made up to suit both domestic and international cold war requirements.[73]

The other "estimate" was a qualitative statement by Russ Wiggins, an editorial writer for the *Washington Post*. Wiggins was a big supporter of Lyndon Johnson's domestic policies, the Great Society and civil rights. He was also an avid champion of the president's foreign policy. In Moscow to see the "top brass," the *Post* representative had to be satisfied instead with a Soviet press chief. They argued about Vietnam. Unable to make a dent by talking about the merits of American policy, Wiggins fell back to basics. "Look," he explained, "if you think a great world power is going to let itself get pushed out of Asia by a 10th rate country like North Viet-Nam, you're crazy."[74]

McNamara's formal report on his findings in Vietnam was an odd mixture of candor and conjecture. It opened with a frank statement that the situation in South Vietnam was worse than a year earlier, when it was worse than a year before that. It ended with the promise that if the military and political moves he recommended were executed with vigor and determination, there was "a good chance" of achieving an acceptable outcome within a reasonable time. Further on, however, the report cast doubt on the survival of the Ky government, on the bombing campaign's ability to shut down the flow of supplies to the NLF, on the success of Saigon's rural pacification programs, on ARVN morale and fighting capability. Against these depressing facts McNamara placed the potential of American fighting men, 100,000 now and another 100,000 in the next year. Even that number would perhaps not be sufficient to reach the "approved" guerrilla fighting ratio of ten to one, but great enough to make a significant difference in the "third stage" or conventional warfare the enemy was apparently ready to fight. In the "third stage" it would be easier to identify, locate, and attack the enemy. As in jujitsu, the enemy's supposed strength could be turned to your advantage.[75]

The defense secretary admitted that his recommendations meant heavier casualties, as many as five hundred a month, and envisioned a willingness to see a fighting war clear through. Once adopted, indeed, it would make any later decision to disengage much more difficult. "The South Vietnamese under one government or another will probably see the thing through and the United States public will support the course of action because it is a sensible and courageous military-political program designed and likely to bring about a success in Vietnam." Henry Cabot Lodge added a dubious footnote to McNamara's written report at this point: "We may face a neutralist government at some time in the future and . . . in those circumstances the US should be prepared to carry on alone." [76]

Even more remarkable, perhaps, and especially given the other contradictory opinions scattered throughout, McNamara simply took John McNaughton's disquieting "Prognosis" almost word for word in the penultimate paragraph of his report. McNamara's version read:

> It should be recognized also that, even in "success," it is not obvious how we will be able to disengage our forces from Vietnam. It is unlikely that a formal agreement good enough for the purpose could possibly be negotiated—because the arrangement can reflect little more than the power situation. A fairly large number of US (or perhaps "international") forces may be required to stay in Vietnam. [77]

No professional gambler would wager much on the odds offered by McNamara's report. And Johnson did not—or he convinced himself that he was not. While the defense secretary was still engaged in the Saigon briefings, the president sent word that his "current intention" was to approve a troop buildup, but it was "impossible" to ask Congress for more than $300 to $400 million in supplementary funds before January. If a larger request were made, he feared it would kill his domestic program. "I can get the Great Society through right now—this is a golden time. We've got a good Congress and I'm the right President and I can do it. But if I talk about the cost of the war, the Great Society won't go through." Johnson also demanded that Mac Bundy prepare a memorandum detailing all the reasons why a billion-dollar appropriation had to be avoided.

Discussion of the ten-page McNamara report had already begun when Johnson entered the cabinet room at 11:30 a.m. on July 21, 1965. [78] As was his usual procedure during these debates, the president fired off a series of questions: "What has happened in [the] recent past that requires this decision on my part? What are the alternatives?" It was all old ground—so much so that the meeting seemed scripted, everyone reading lines long since committed to memory. George Ball suggested once again that McNamara's plan assumed the Viet Cong would accommodate American preferences for fighting a large-unit war. But what if they didn't? What if they played it like they did against the French, and avoided direct confrontation? General Earle Wheeler was not worried about that, neither was Secretary McNamara. "They will have to fight somewhere," Wheeler said. "If [the]

VC doesn't fight in large units," McNamara elaborated, "it will give ARVN a chance to re-secure hostile areas. We don't know what VC tactics will be when VC is confronted by 175,000 Americans."

Ball persisted. "I can foresee a perilous voyage—very dangerous." He felt "great apprehensions that we can win under these conditions." Johnson reacted as before: "But is there another course in the national interest that is better than the McNamara course? We know it's dangerous and perilous. But can it be avoided?" Yes, said the under secretary, but it meant letting the current Saigon regime fall and allowing its successor to negotiate on terms that probably would mean a Communist takeover.

Johnson repeated his plea: "I feel we have very little alternative to what we are doing. . . . Right now I feel it would be more dangerous for us to lose this now, than endanger a greater number of troops." Nevertheless, he wanted Ball to present the full case against the McNamara proposal at another meeting that afternoon. When they reassembled, Ball argued that what loomed ahead was a protracted struggle. It would be Korea all over again—only worse. World opinion this time would not be on the American side:

> I think we have all underestimated the seriousness of this situation. Like giving cobalt treatment to a terminal cancer case. I think a long protracted war will disclose our weakness, not our strength.

As the discussion continued, Johnson wrestled with cold war images. "Wouldn't all these countries say Uncle Sam is a paper tiger—wouldn't we lose credibility breaking the word of three presidents. . . . It would seem to be an irreparable blow. But, I gather you don't think so." "The worse blow would be that the mightiest power in the world is unable to defeat guerrillas," the under secretary replied. Mac Bundy allowed that Ball's arguments had "a great many correct elements" in them, but also two major weaknesses:

> The difficulty in adopting it now would be a radical switch without evidence that it should be done. It goes in the face of all we have said and done.

> His whole analytical argument gives no weight to losses suffered by [the] other side.

What the national security adviser was really saying, however, was that neither case was provable. Thus the issue had to be decided on merits other than arguments pro or con. In this case, the highest merit was being assigned to protecting "all we have said and done." From Dean Rusk came another Old Testament lesson: "If the Communist world finds out we will not pursue our commitment to the end, I don't know where they will stay their hand."

Rusk would say later that he understood the importance of the Sino-Soviet split but that America's position in Vietnam encouraged the "peaceful co-existence" wing of the Communist movement and discouraged the "wars of national liberation" wing headed by the Chinese. In his sweeping statement during the July deliberations, however, there was little of such nuance. He did not refer, for example, to Averell Harriman's conclusions from his trip to Moscow that the Russians were deeply concerned about Vietnam escalations and Chinese gains because of American actions.[79] Be that as it may, Johnson ended the meeting with an oblique admission that what they were contemplating would be a hard sell; and he admonished them to think about how to deal with that problem.

> How can we get everybody to compete with McNamara in the press? We are trying to do so many other things with our economic and health projects. Constantly remind the people that we are doing other things besides bombing.

If the president yearned to remind the people of the good things America was doing in Vietnam, Mac Bundy worried that he was storing up trouble for himself by not being ready to admit what the war would cost. McNamara was carrying out "your orders to plan this whole job with only $300- $400 million in immediate new funds," Bundy advised Johnson that same evening.

> But I think you will want to know that he thinks our posture of candor and responsibility would be better if we ask for $2 billion to take us through the end of the calendar year, on the understanding that we will come back for more, if necessary. . . . Cy Vance told me the other day that the overall cost is likely to be on the order of $8 billion in the coming year and I can understand Bob's worry that in the nature of things, these projected costs will be sure to come out pretty quickly, especially if he looks as if he was trying to pull a fast one.[80]

Still later, at 10 p.m., White House aide Horace Busby offered the president his impressions of the day's debate. Like Bundy, he found George Ball an impressive advocate: "Given his point of view, Ball is impressively clear-headed and well-organized. . . ." Certainly he was more impressive than the "academic intellectuals." But he was too much a prisoner of past experiences—Korea, the French "fiasco."[81]

> What we are considering is not whether we continue a war—but whether we start (or have started) a new war. The 1954–1964 premises, principles and pretexts no longer apply. This is no longer South Vietnam's war. We are no longer advisers. The stakes are no longer Vietnam's. The war is ours. We are participants. The stakes are ours—and the West's.

One had to forget about what he called "the fixation about working with the Vietnam government." That too was a holdover from the past. The U.S. had "to run its own effort rather than stand by seeking permission from a government-that-is-not-a-government."

Clearly, the acceptable objectives in Vietnam—acceptable in proportion to U.S. sacrifice required—are world-size, not country-size. It is hard to define an acceptable objective in Vietnam: To seek one there leads inevitably to Ball's conclusion and thesis. The objectives—the acceptable objectives—must be in terms of Southeast Asia, the Pacific or even the broad-East-West relationship. Rusk sees it in this dimension—and his logic prevails over Ball's.

Busby's admiration of Dean Rusk's ability to finesse concrete reality into abstraction came at a particularly crucial moment in the Vietnam debate, but it was perhaps not as important in shaping the president's mind as less glowing estimates of Rusk from Kennedy exiles. Johnson had faced questions at a recent press conference about the secretary of state's performance and had called him "one of the most able and most competent and most dedicated men I have ever known." Then, as the Vietnam deliberations continued, the *Washington Post* reported that the historian Arthur Schlesinger, Jr., said President Kennedy planned to replace Rusk after the 1964 election. Seeking confirmation, the *Post* asked JFK's brother, Senator Robert Kennedy, to comment. He refused to confirm or deny the statement, saying only that he could not "speculate on what might have been."[82] If anything would persuade Johnson to listen to Rusk over all others, Kennedy interference would do it.

Johnson met with his top military advisers at noon on July 22. At that meeting the process of defining the mission of American forces in Vietnam came no closer to concrete reality than had the political discussions a day earlier.[83] Perhaps the most interesting aspect of the meeting was the byplay between civilian Pentagon officials and the Joint Chiefs. At times they seemed to be trying to convince one another that Vietnam really was vital to American national security, even given cold war assumptions about a monolithic Communist enemy. Secretary of the Navy Paul Nitze, a cold war theoretician from the Truman years, for example, argued that in the beginning, when international communism threatened Greece and the Philippines, it had been shown that guerrillas could be beaten. After sending Westmoreland the soldiers he wanted, American forces could advance from the secure positions they held and gradually turn the tide. But to walk away from this challenge, Nitze said, would be "to acknowledge that we couldn't beat the VC, [and] the shape of the world will change."

The uniformed officers around the table struggled with the geopolitics of cold war military strategy, hedged on predictions of "victory" on this specific battlefield, and, like Nitze, fell back in the end on the domino thesis. It was an uncomfortable resting place, as air force General John P. McConnell's response to Johnson's direct questions made plain.

> If you put in these requested forces and increase air and sea effort—we can at least turn the tide where we are not losing anymore. We need to be sure we get the best we can out of SVN—need to bomb all military targets available to us in NVN. As to whether we can come to satisfactory solution with these forces, I don't know. With these forces properly employed, and cutting off their supplies, we can do better than we're doing.

Well, what about the chances China would come in with "volunteers," just like Korea in that cold November of 1950? Over and over again Johnson asked this question. Would China shove in its stack? At one point the president pushed army Chief of Staff Harold Johnson as hard as he could.

PRESIDENT: If we come in with hundreds of thousands of men and billions of dollars, won't this cause them to come in (China and Russia)?

GEN. JOHNSON: No. I don't think they will.

PRESIDENT: MacArthur didn't think they would come in either.

GEN. JOHNSON: Yes, but this is not comparable to Korea. . . .

PRESIDENT: But China has plenty of divisions to move in, don't they?

GEN. JOHNSON: Yes, they do.

PRESIDENT: Then what would we do?

GEN. JOHNSON: (long silence) If so, we have another ball game.

Yet the president failed to follow up in a similar manner comments by the chairman of the Joint Chiefs, General Earle Wheeler, earlier in the meeting. "We are not proposing an invasion of NVN," Wheeler had said. "Secondly, on volunteers—the one thing all NVN fear is Chinese. For them to invite Chinese volunteers is to invite China's taking over NVN." Wheeler's ambiguous comments went unremarked. Johnson might have asked him to explain why, if we were fighting an international conspiracy, the North Vietnamese were more afraid of China than losing the war in the south?

Instead Johnson asked about George Ball's "alternative" of setting forth conditions Saigon could not meet, and then clearing out. Could we make a stand in Thailand? With that question the president had put the needle back down in familiar cold war grooves, where it went spinning around to 1947 and the original formulation of the Truman Doctrine. Greece and Turkey must be sent military aid, Truman had said then, or the forces of subversion and Communist revolution would spread unchecked across Europe and Asia, and even through Africa. On this day Secretary McNamara explained why there was now no exit from Vietnam, except to repudiate the Truman Doctrine.

> Laos, Cambodia, Thailand, Burma, surely affect Malaysia. In 2-3 years Communist domination would stop there, but ripple effect would be great—Japan, India. We would have to give up some bases. Ayub would move closer to China. Greece, Turkey would move to neutralist position. Communist agitation would increase in Africa.

Almost immediately after this meeting, the president had yet another discussion of the impending decision. In attendance were two key members of the "private" sector, John McCloy and Arthur Dean, intermediaries between the administration and the most powerful banking and legal firms in the nation.[84] Dean raised the big military question. "If this carries on for some years," he worried, "we'll get in the same fix we were in Korea and the Yalu." McCloy asked the big political question. "What do we have to negotiate?" He was not satisfied with any of the answers he got from Dean Rusk. "When do the troops get withdrawn?" he pursued. When we had proof the infiltration from the north had stopped, repeated the secretary of state. But Mac Bundy realized McCloy's point: there really was no basis for negotiation with the NLF except about South Vietnam's political future. "If we really were the ones for free elections, it would be good," he said. "It is difficult for Saigon to sign on." That was precisely where McCloy was heading: "Would we be willing to take a Tito government or a VC victory?" Bundy was candid: "That's where our plan begins to unravel."

Lyndon Johnson had listened to this dialogue without interrupting. Finally he said, "It's like a prizefight. Our right is our military power, but our left must be our peace proposals." It was a meaningless statement, as he surely realized. The discussion left Johnson rattled. Bundy had put it so matter-of-factly—"That's where our plan begins to unravel." He and Bundy talked on the telephone later that day. They must be ready for "deep trouble" in the Vietnam situation, the president said. Then almost immediately he started talking about the way the elite regarded him—"a high-handed buffoon—no class or style." It was up to Bundy, he implied, to save the situation. Somehow he must get Ball and Rusk and McNamara and himself on all fours with a "position that doesn't go beyond first 100,000. Then we're going to have peace."[85]

Johnson was not the only one rattled by the day's discussions. Jack Valenti, who had taken careful notes on all that was said, wrote to Johnson about his fears of what the "ordinary citizen" might feel. "We might wave mightily as the flag goes by now, but later, when the passions have faded, we will grow weary and cynical. . . . And soon, there will come a time when the liberal hand-wringers and the now-warlike Republicans will be joining down the road denouncing the President and the war." What can we do about it, because we are all agreed we just can't pack up and leave? He suggested some military moves, but without much conviction. "What I have gotten out of these meetings these two days is a terrible compassion for the President, who has to make this decision. It is such an awful duty I want to weep because the options are so narrow, and the choices are so barren."[86]

On Friday afternoon, July 23, Johnson decided to go to Camp David to think it all out. He was unhappy with where the position stood. At the discussions that day he had informed McNamara and the others that while he agreed with sending the troops, he would not agree to a call-up of the reserves or to pushing Congress for anything more than a $1 billion appropriation—far below even the most conservative estimate of what the war might cost. "I've got just a little weak spot in my stomach," he told his advisers.[87]

Sunday afternoon he assembled a very small group of kitchen cabinet advisers at Aspen Lodge. The principal speaker was Clark Clifford. Like Jack Valenti, Clifford had been present at several of the discussions, and, like him, he was deeply worried about the president's narrow options. He had seen George Ball's memoranda against expanding the war dating back several months, and he thought they made a whole lot more sense than what Rusk and Bundy and McNamara were telling Johnson. He had been somewhat encouraged by what had occurred Friday afternoon. Ball had told him that his, Clifford's, private conversation with the president after the others had left had made an impact.[88] The first thing to do, Clifford urged the president at Camp David, was to tell everyone to stop talking so much about Vietnam. Gain some time. Wait until January before deciding finally. Valenti's notes record in terse fashion what Clifford said:

> Don't believe we can win in SVN. If we send in 100,000 more, the NVN will meet us. If the NVN run out of men, the Chinese will send in volunteers. Russia and China don't intend for us to win the war. If we don't win, it is a catastrophe. If we lose 50,000+ it will ruin us. Five years, billions of dollars, 50,000 men, it is not for us.[89]

Even if the United States should "win," he added, there would have to be a long military occupation with constant troubles. While Johnson sat sipping on a soft drink, McNamara repeated what he had said before in the other meetings. The president cut short the discussion and left to walk around the Camp David woods. Clifford knew he had lost the "debate," because, he believed, Johnson had so personalized the issue.[90]

But Clifford had undercut his own case by stressing that Russia and China were not only supplying Hanoi with aid but were behind the war and intended to win. McNamara did not feel like a winner, on the other hand, because Johnson had chosen to go to war without making it plain that it really was a war. There was to be no reserve call-up, no budget request, no tax increase to pay for the war. McNamara's biographer writes, "Johnson would make them fight not as past wars had been fought, with the public fully aware of the commitment and behind the fighting men; they would tiptoe into war."[91]

Neither Clifford's nor McNamara's perceptions exhausted the possibilities of what Johnson thought might happen as a result of his decisions. Back at the White House, he explained to the National Security Council that he had decided to do what was necessary to meet the present situation, but not to go all out, or brag about what the U.S. was doing, or thunder at the Chinese or Russians. "We will hold until January. The alternatives are to put in our big stack now or hold back until Ambassadors Lodge and Goldberg and the diplomats can work."[92]

At that point the deliberations finally ended, and congressional leaders were ushered into the cabinet room. Before getting down to specifics, the legislators—with one exception—delivered impassioned Fourth of July speeches to one another, warming up for what was to come. Ambassador Lodge kept temperatures high by declaring that backing out of Vietnam would be "worse than a victory for the Kaiser or Hitler in the two World Wars."[93] Going over the options once more, just as he had for the National Security Council, Johnson explained, "I want to use this period [until January] to show them they can't run us out."[94] He also said he planned to do everything he could, with honor, to keep Russia and China out of the war. Senator Everett Dirksen raised questions about the financing. Some worried, he said, that the nation was stripping its forces in Europe to send more to Southeast Asia. "Baloney on stripping," McNamara interrupted. "We are *not* stripping. It is not necessary." The defense secretary had obviously reconciled himself to Johnson's way of handling the finances. "When you come back in January," the president assured Dirksen, "you'll have a bill of several billion dollars." Congress, at least, was not being deceived about the price tag on escalation.

Then Mike Mansfield spoke. He would not be true to himself if he did not say what was on his mind. The only pledge the United States had made was to "assist" the government of South Vietnam. But now there was no legitimate government to assist:

> We are going deeper into war. Even total victory would be vastly costly. Best hope for salvation is quick stalemate and negotiations. We cannot expect our people to support a war for 3–5 years. What we are about is an anti-Communist crusade—escalation begets escalation.

According to a press leak, the president looked at Mansfield and said quietly, "Well, Mike, what would you do?"—the standard response to anyone who urged such a course. The Senate leader supposedly had no answer.[95] But that was not true. As the notes of the leadership meeting record, Mansfield's remarks pointed toward negotiations about the future government of South Vietnam.

Mansfield's dissent annoyed Johnson, no doubt about that. But there were indications even at this meeting that LBJ had not dismissed Clifford's warning. He was well aware, too, of Republican eagerness to substitute patriotism for social conscience at the top of the nation's political agenda. Republican Bourke Hickenlooper, whose passion for a non-Communist South Vietnam knew no bounds, warned that the president's proposed course only treated symptoms. There was a great danger of an Asian "Yalta" ahead, a sellout like all the others since World War II. Wearily, Johnson told Hickenlooper he should talk to Mansfield and Fulbright and see what the three could work out. "I supported the decisions in 1954," he said, "but did not approve of them. I opposed going in then, but we're there now."[96]

Johnson would go to 100,000, he had told Bundy privately, and then seek peace. He was not putting in the big stack—yet. To some, indeed, it appeared that the skeptics had won this round in the Vietnam debate! Howard Margolis in the *Washington Post* and Hanson Baldwin in the *New York Times* both reported the Pentagon's disappointment that the president had not ordered a reserve call-up, an indication, they agreed, that Johnson was not yet fully committed to Westmoreland's strategic plans for building a fortress Vietnam. Margolis went further: "The Administration since February has been engaged in the delicate task of escalating the war while de-escalating war aims." He professed to see in the president's decision a carefully plotted maneuver to convince the NLF to accept a political victory by raising the odds against an easy military takeover.[97]

War hawk Joseph Alsop worried about the president's demeanor at the news conference where he announced the troop buildup. Alsop saw Johnson wrestling with Vietnam, trying to find a course that promised progress yet minimized controversy, his usual way of tackling domestic problems. No one could tell, the columnist concluded, whether that phase was over. Walter Lippmann, on the other hand, fairly rejoiced at what he called the president's "realism and prudence." "Although he repeated the grand formulae of a great war, in fact his decision as of now is to fight a limited war." He also felt that Johnson had sent Hanoi a real signal by accepting the principles of the 1954 Geneva Agreement as a basis for negotiations.[98]

Had he got it right, Lippmann asked George Ball on the telephone? Just about, the under secretary responded. "The president is still in control of the situation," Ball said. He felt very good about the way the situation had developed. "Things were not yet in the saddle."[99]

Ball was an obvious source for many of the stories that characterized Johnson's decision as an effort to continue, and indeed to intensify, the search for peace through diplomatic means. When another newspaper correspondent telephoned him to ask directly if the "limited commitment" had any connection to the search for a negotiated solution, the under secretary said "he did not think it was unrelated." [100] One reason for encouraging Ball's dissent, on the other hand, was precisely because Johnson expected such leaks—however much he bellowed and raged about them—and wanted the leeway that stories about his keenness for a negotiated settlement offered him both at home and abroad. Above all, he wanted time to get the Great Society in place before he had to face either the political fallout from a defeat in Vietnam or the consequences of a split in party ranks over escalation. In July 1965 he could not be sure which fate would befall him. Labor leader Walter Reuther had expressed his faith in Johnson's vision of the Great Society. "Communism is morally bankrupt and historically obsolete," he wrote the president. "There are no problems in America too large or too difficult for free men to solve. We have the scientific, technological and productive know-how; we must now work together to develop a comparable human and social and moral know-why." [101] If Vietnam was too large to solve, what would happen to the Great Society? Thus Johnson wrote back, "The promised land is in sight but it has been a long trek and until we are on the other side I hope no one will relax." [102]

TWELVE

A Fearful Symmetry

ON THE SAME DAY, July 28, that Johnson announced the troop buildup, Doug Cater, the White House aide who had once edited the *Reporter* magazine, an outstanding liberal journal, invited McGeorge Bundy to a meeting to discuss the government's information program, "primarily as it pertains to the domestic audience." The "home front" was a real front line in this war, said Cater, and he attached an outline of what was to be discussed. The basic assumption they would work from, he wrote, was that "we are going to have a 10 to 20 year period of 'twilight war.' " That situation required a "sophisticated consensus of the American people" to avoid the dangers of "polarization and extremism."[1]

Hence they would consider ways to communicate complexity as against simplicity, including how to achieve a "partial mobilization" of the home front over long periods of time without falling prey to the dangerous "syndrome of frustration, hostility, etc." Above all, it was a "philosophical" challenge they faced: the need to "communicate the uniqueness of the United States experiment and accomplishments." "Our chief weapon" in this battle for the hearts and minds at home, Cater asserted confidently, "is an honest quality dialogue and a search for the truth (we are not afraid of discussion)."[2] Vietnam, it seemed, required a convincing reaffirmation of American exceptionalism.

One week later Cater's group met for dinner in the White House mess to begin work on this critical assignment. Besides Bundy, it included John Chancellor, the former radio and TV commentator, Chester Cooper from Bundy's staff, Joe Califano, and several others from USIA and State. Cater opened the discussion with a frank statement that as matters stood "our public posture is fragile." Instead of being offered an understanding of the "broader aspects" of the situation, the American people were being asked to rely on specific facts. In other words, the steady stream of military reverses,

goof-ups, and corruption reported out of Vietnam were not being effectively countered by government explanations of the larger issues at stake. "And
with this situation, we are extremely vulnerable to rumor, gossip, and quick
reverses."[3]

One of those present, James Greenfield, said there was little time to
think about the philosophical. "We only plug holes and run as fast as we
can to stay even." There were several reasons for this situation, including
the presence of more than three hundred accredited correspondents in
Vietnam who were reporting on everything from Saigon to the smallest
village. That statement brought general agreement. But then Greenfield
went off on a different tack that did not receive a favorable response
around the table. "We are involved in too many clichés," he said. "For
example, we should look again at 'Our country's honor is at stake.' One day
we may be sorry that we are tied too closely to this stand. Another cliché
we ought to examine is 'Our friends won't trust us if we desert the Vietnamese.' This one gives us trouble when foreigners say publicly that they
want us out of Vietnam—in effect, pulling the rug out from under us." That
was too close to the bone for Mac Bundy and Chester Cooper. They disagreed and said that more had to be made of statements from foreign leaders "which support our argument." What Bundy and Cooper saw, of
course, was that Greenfield's direction undercut the argument for exceptionalism.

A few minutes later, however, John Chancellor turned the discussion
to the issue of how to stimulate an "honest quality dialogue." His comments
also undercut the exceptionalist premise, but in a fashion much more congenial to notions of American responsibilities for the world's safety and
well-being. Perhaps, he said, we ought to recognize that for the first time in
the nation's experience we have "a non-packageable commodity." "Most of
the people have very little to say to us." Therefore, "we should try to emulate the 19th Century British and try to get a sort of general commitment
and support. . . ." What was wrong with telling the people, "We are a world
power and are stuck with this sort of thing . . ."? In Bundy's notes this was
abbreviated to "all mess + necessity," a phrase that covered the same basic
set of self-imposed obligations that nineteenth-century statesmen had
proudly called the "white man's burden."

An "honest dialogue" about the specifics of American intervention in
Vietnam was, Chancellor pointed out, a less promising alternative—indeed,
"a non-packageable commodity," involving inconclusive arguments with
people who "have very little to say to us"—than to emulate the attitudes of
the Pax Britannica in Disraeli's or Lord Salisbury's time. If that did not
square with Cater's original idea that the government must get across how
Vietnam fit into the unique American experiment since 1776, it was at least
a better solution than constantly trying to "plug holes." Soon enough,

another member of the group brought up the biggest hole: the American people really did not understand how we got into Vietnam in the first place. "Mr. Bundy agreed that there is a problem here, but thought that this particular piece of exposition might simply not be manageable. Our best posture may be to say simply that somehow we are there and that we have to stay."

After this remarkably preemptive comment by Bundy, set up by Chancellor's exposition, the discussion bounced back and forth over the mechanics of getting across to the public the issues at stake on "the whole chessboard." "The point is that there is a vacuum," observed one discussant. "If we don't fill it, then it will be filled against us." All that "makes our present posture swing," commented Greenfield, "is that the people have confidence in the President." Cater agreed: "This is evidence of how fragile our posture is. . . ." But where were they to find other spokesmen to take the burden off President Johnson? Greenfield suggested Rusk, McNamara, and Bundy. John Chancellor interrupted, "Bundy is probably not good for the housewife in the back yard; unfortunately, Bundy appeals to the sophisticated and the sophisticated are already rigid in their confusion or in their position pro or con the Administration in Vietnam."

The discussion ended, not surprisingly, on a highly uncertain note. Cater suggested that the meeting had revealed the need for a tsar outside official government circles to coordinate efforts in the private sector, "a man with great prestige, preferably from New York. . . ." Bundy agreed that finding the right man was always a problem. "He went on to say, however, that the private sector would probably not sit still for a ringmaster. He also suggested that perhaps we do not want to get so heavily organized either in the Government or in the private sector in the area of public information."

The Cater group had begun with the premise that victory on the "home front" depended upon convincing the public of the essential relationship between the unique American experiment in democracy and successes achieved abroad. These successes, in turn, reaffirmed the uniqueness of the American experiment. A few days later former President Dwight Eisenhower pushed that point to the next level. "He stressed the overriding importance of Viet Nam wanting to be free," Henry Cabot Lodge reported his conversation with Eisenhower. "We should do everything to inculcate such a desire. They must have 'heart' or, after we have achieved a successful outcome, they will slump right back. It would be tragic if a successful outcome were followed by an election in which the people voted for the Viet Cong."[4]

Eisenhower imagined that such a desire might be instilled by relief projects modeled after UNRRA (the United Nations Relief and Rehabilitation Agency) at the end of the war in Europe. American help for the war-weary citizens of the devastated lands once occupied by Hitler's army was something else to emulate besides the Pax Britannica. It was also a surprisingly naive notion about Vietnamese realities. But the idea of stimulating Western ideas of political freedom preoccupied Johnson as well. One day a phone call took USIA Director Carl Rowan away from a lunch at the German embassy. He picked up the telephone to hear Johnson say, "John McCone has been talking to me. He says we could win this goddam war by winning over the people of Asia if we could just get a place to put a million-watt medium wave transmitter in that region." Rowan was astounded at the CIA's credulity. "Sir," he replied, "they've [the CIA] tried for five years to find a place for that transmitter. India, Thailand, everybody has turned the U.S. down because they think this is a war of rich, powerful white people against poor Asians. Did McCone tell you how to change this fact of life?" Johnson ignored Rowan's protest. "McCone and Rusk and Bundy and the other white boys," he went on, could not talk to Asians the way Rowan, "being colored," could. Disturbed by the absurdity of the idea, Rowan nevertheless promised he would try his "damnedest." Returning to the table to finish his lunch, the USIA director thought about what he had agreed to do—and what he had already done to contribute to the growing madness. "I thought about how I was relaying 'surveys,' 'reports,' and 'analyses' to Johnson, suggesting that the people of South Vietnam were supporting the United States and whichever scoundrel happened to be in power in Saigon at the time, even when I felt queasy about those analyses."[5]

Early in September, President Johnson answered a letter from a woman whose son had been killed in Vietnam. Her letter asked the president to explain why American boys were in Vietnam. In the first paragraph of his reply, Johnson called the situation a dilemma. In the remainder of the letter, however, he tried to establish the symmetry between the search for freedom at home and abroad. "We must maintain the commitment we have made. For if we do not we shall have little chance to devote ourselves to the nourishment of freedom in America. *It is that certainty that impels us onward in a conflict we abhor.*"[6]

It was a fearful and a fateful symmetry. Fearful because it did indeed impel Johnson onward; fateful because it drove liberal assumptions back on themselves when Vietnam came to America in antiwar protests and turmoil in the cities. Throughout the cold war, the notion that containing communism abroad was required by American "national security" had been crucial to the rationale for NATO and the Korean War. The letter Johnson signed to a grieving mother put new emphasis, however, on the symmetry policymakers saw between the Great Society and the war in Vietnam. Defeating the enemy in Vietnam had become essential to the confidence policymakers had in their domestic solutions, not simply out of concern for sustaining legislative momentum, but from something much deeper in political life that was quite apart from fear about a conservative backlash.

One week after the Vietnam troop decision, Congress passed the Voting Rights Act of 1965. Johnson was elated. That evening he went to Capitol Hill to celebrate by having a drink with Senate leaders Mike Mansfield and Ev Dirksen. The next day he talked with Martin Luther King, urging him to devote his energies to voter registration. To satisfy all those who crowded around him at the formal signing on August 6, 1965, the president used a different pen not just for each letter of his name, but even for parts of letters. As he handed pens to Reverend King and other black leaders, the president repeated that he hoped they would shift their energies "from protest to politics."[7]

Johnson had staked a great deal on passage of the Voting Rights Bill. In February he had watched King direct the protest marches in Selma, Alabama, in an effort to force local authorities to register black voters. The plan was to walk from Selma to Montgomery, the state capital, to call the nation's attention to Alabama's refusal to grant blacks full citizenship rights. After hearing the civil rights leader report on his efforts, the president told King he thought the public pressure generated would help to pass a voting rights bill. The first attempt to start the march was halted by club-swinging state troopers. Johnson then sent word that he hoped a second try would be canceled. An informal bargain of sorts was struck between King and the president's emissary. Johnson had already told the civil rights leader that he intended to introduce a voting rights bill; King now agreed to lead the two thousand marchers to a point directly in front of the Alabama state police blocking their way on Edmund Pettis Bridge, but to go no farther. After kneeling in prayer, the marchers would disperse. There was more violence in Selma involving attacks on individuals in the protest movement, but no immediate "showdown" with Southern "law and order."[8]

King's willingness to back off in anticipation of federal action did not sit well with many in the civil rights movement. But Johnson moved swiftly to vindicate King's faith in the federal government and to secure his own position on the domestic front. On March 15, 1965, he appeared before Congress to plead for the Voting Rights Bill. "Should we defeat every enemy," he declared, "should we double our wealth and conquer the stars," and still deny equal rights to blacks, "we will have failed as a people and as a nation." Then he startled everyone present by promising, in King's own words, "And . . . we shall . . . overcome."[9]

Alabama Governor George Wallace reacted strongly to Johnson's next step, the federalization of the state's National Guard. The march from Selma to Montgomery took place in safety, but Wallace went on television to deliver a dark prophecy. The march was typical of Communist street warfare, he declared, of the sort that had "ripped Cuba apart, that destroyed Diem in Vietnam, that raped China—that has torn civilization and established institutions of this world into bloody shreds."[10] Many would soon agree with the governor's reformulation of the symmetry between what was going on in Vietnam and the inability of the government to protect its citizens at home against a social revolution led by blacks and counterculture war protesters. "In the spring of 1965," writes one historian, "the dominant symbol was a petitioning black voter being brutalized by Sheriff Jim Clark in Selma. By 1966 this had been countered if not displaced in the volatile world of *Time* and *Newsweek* by the rampaging ghetto rioter in Watts, or the black racist harangues of H. Rap Brown." [11]

But Wallace's denunciation of the protest could not stop the march to Montgomery, could not silence Reverend King's speech to a crowd swollen to 25,000 from the steps of the state capitol, nor, finally, block passage of the Voting Rights Bill. For the moment Johnson felt very good about the nation's response to the challenges it faced, and about himself. "We are a country which was built by pioneers who had a rifle in one hand and an ax in the other," he exulted to White House aides.

> We are a nation with the highest GNP, the highest wages, and the most people at work. We can do both. And as long as I am president we will do both. I am tired of people who talk about sick societies. Our country is being tested with a war on two fronts—a war on poverty and against aggression. [12]

Johnson had warned Defense Secretary McNamara that he was not to propose anything more than a $1 billion to $2 billion increase in the budget to cover the expenses of the troop decision. But the new chairman of the Council of Economic Advisers, Gardner Ackley, was considerably more bullish on Vietnam. His own review of Department of Defense figures, Ackley reported to the White House, indicated only a modest buildup of expenditures. And that was just fine. The stimulus provided by the 1964 tax cut had about run its course, and something more was needed. "We are certainly not saying that a Vietnam crisis is just what the doctor ordered for the American economy in the next 12 months. But on a coldly objective analysis, the over-all effects are most likely to be favorable to our prosperity." Certainly no new taxes would be needed to finance the war unless costs got into the "$10 billion" range, a possibility Ackley regarded as remote. Because of the economy's rapid growth, Ackley foresaw ample room "for both more butter, and if needed, more guns." [13]

Things appeared to be shaping up well in all directions. Johnson was still savoring his successful campaign for the Voting Rights Bill when a white policeman in Los Angeles pulled over a black driver in a black neighborhood of the city, Watts, triggering a riot that lasted five days. Thirty-four people died and more than a thousand were seriously injured before it was brought under control. Johnson secluded himself at the ranch in Texas during the riot, almost as if he could not bring himself to consider what it foretold for his administration's future. "He just wouldn't accept it," recalled an aide. "He refused to look at the cables from Los Angeles. . . . He refused to take calls from the generals who were requesting government planes to fly in the National Guard. . . . We needed decisions from him. But he simply wouldn't respond."[14] Just as government was moving to help them, Johnson told one of his intimates, the "Negroes" were starting riots out of frustration and anger. "Negroes will end up pissing in the aisles of the Senate," he exclaimed to Joe Califano, and making fools of themselves the way they had after the Civil War during Reconstruction. If that happened, everything that had been gained would be placed in jeopardy.[15]

After the Watts riot finally ended, California officials appointed former CIA director John McCone to head an investigatory commission to look into its causes. Not surprisingly, the McCone Commission reported that the riot had been a "senseless" explosion caused by a handful of alienated blacks. No one who knew anything about conditions in the Watts ghetto believed the commission. From years of cold war conditioning, McCone had a well-developed "agent" theory of revolution at hand to apply to domestic unrest; he simply had to alter a few words about Communist operatives in third world countries.[16]

Johnson's own investigator, Under Secretary of Commerce LeRoy Collins, a former governor of Florida and, most recently, his chief emissary to Martin Luther King during the Selma crisis, ended his confidential report with a grim prediction:

> . . . the biggest and most dangerous ingredient is a feeling on the part of the Negro community that they are "out of it." They will continue to risk riots . . . until [they have] a genuine example of participation in the affairs of the community at large.
>
> And, what is even more sobering, this problem to one degree or another is multiplied in every city in this country.[17]

In the wake of the Watts riot, Martin Luther King went to Los Angeles. The issue was economic, he said, jobs were the answer. And then he pronounced what had happened in Los Angeles "a class revolt of underprivileged against privileged." For him, as for Lyndon Johnson, Watts had altered visions of the future. It was permissible in liberal circles to talk about "discrimination" against blacks, and even to discuss the underprivileged, but to mention "class" made people uneasy. Worse, King now began to link Vietnam and the domestic crisis. Even those who opposed the war preferred to keep the focus on terms like "quagmire," "wrong direction," "Mr. Johnson's War," and the like. King was talking like a radical. He asserted that the intervention was likely to endanger "the whole of mankind," and then he declared that Red China should be admitted to the United Nations and ought to be included in any Vietnam negotiations.

King was moving toward his own version of the fearful symmetry: Vietnam and black poverty both stemmed from the common heritage of capitalist materialism. When the minister urged the president to pay more attention to antipoverty efforts in Los Angeles and elsewhere, Johnson reacted with a peevish lecture about criticizing the war. "He's making me look like a fool," LBJ complained to Carl Rowan. "He's got a goddam nest of spies around him. And he's starting to oppose his own country on Vietnam. Whata you think I oughta do?"[18]

At the end of the year King moved into an apartment in Chicago, from which he directed a crusade to desegregate housing. He had moved the civil rights campaign north, and he had moved it philosophically much farther to the left. Perhaps the stimulus came from rivals like Malcolm X and the Young Turks who formed the Black Power movement, but his speeches now rang with denunciations of "our vicious class system." The Chicago problem existed, he averred, because someone profited from the slum, which was itself "a system of internal colonialism." "The purpose of the slum is to confuse those who have no power and perpetuate their power-lessness.... The slum is little more than a domestic colony which leaves the inhabitants dominated politically, exploited economically, [and] segregated and humiliated at every turn."[19]

King's "nonviolent" campaign did not prevent him from seizing an apartment building owned by a notorious slumlord, and declaring that henceforth his group would collect the rents and use the money for repairs. Nor did it abjure him to stop preaching massive-resistance tactics: "If 100,000 Negroes march in a major city to a strategic location, they will make municipal operations difficult to conduct . . . and they will repeat this action daily, if necessary."[20]

Mayor Richard J. Daley was already in a wrath about King's "visit" to Chicago. The black leader had refused to meet with him at the outset of the housing campaign, and, unlike other "ethnic" leaders the mayor dealt with, seemingly had little interest in personal gain or palliatives. Daley got so worked up that one of his protégés, Congressman Dan Rostenkowski, requested a personal meeting with Lyndon Johnson to recommend that the president send King out of the country for a while on some pretext or another.[21]

Mayor Daley had seen what was coming, had smelled out trouble with the OEO's Community Action Programs. It was no part of Johnson's intention to promote a "leveler" movement in the United States nor to tolerate anything that resembled New Deal versions of the dole. The president stood amazed, nevertheless, as the Great Society's War on Poverty faced almost simultaneous counterattacks from both left and right. "How is it possible," Johnson wailed, "after all we've accomplished? How could it be? Is the world topsy-turvy?"[22]

Traditional Democratic party stalwarts like Mayor Daley accused him of conducting guerrilla war against local authority. The OEO had no sooner gotten under way in 1965 than it came under attack from other big-city mayors as well. At their annual conference that year, the mayors narrowly defeated a resolution attacking OEO and the Community Action Programs for "creating tensions" in the cities and failing "to recognize the legal and moral responsibility of local officials who are accountable to the taxpayers for expenditures of local funds."[23]

Community Action Programs had received 45 per cent of the original appropriation for OEO, $658 million that year. A good portion of the money went into teaching the poor how to take action against landlords and lackadaisical city bureaucrats. If OEO had distributed its funds through city government, in the correct tradition of urban Democratic politics, all would have gone well—supposedly. There would be something for everybody—supposedly. But those in charge of the CAPs, operating under the charter of OEO to achieve "maximum feasible participation" of aid recipients, directed their efforts toward organizing the poor for political action. Accept this state of affairs, and one day you wake up and there is no machine. Daley complained, Washington listened—and tried to redirect OEO's efforts in safer directions. "For God's sake," Johnson exclaimed to Bill Moyers, "get on top of this and put a stop to it at once."[24]

But this genie had got loose, and others were popping out all over the place. Another escaped right under Johnson's nose in the Labor Department. When an assistant secretary of labor, Daniel Patrick Moynihan, drafted a report entitled "The Negro Family: The Case for National Action," favorable reactions in the black community quickly did an about-face as their attention was directed to the supposed "blame the victim" nature of the report. Moynihan had asserted that the black family was abnormal, that it suffered from a "pathological matriarchal" syndrome that held back the black community as a whole. When Labor Secretary Willard Wirtz forwarded a summary of the report to Johnson, he called it "nine pages of dynamite."[25]

How one felt about the Moynihan Report became a means of defining political outlook. At Howard University, Andrew Billingsley wrote that the family was a creature of society. "And the greatest problems facing black families are problems which emanate from the white racist, militarist, materialistic society which places higher priority on putting white men on the moon than putting black men on their feet on this earth."[26] Before 1965 the white liberal agenda on poverty and civil rights had been solidly integrationist. From now on the agenda itself was under challenge. A renascent white left sought to substitute a totally different agenda. "It seemed to many on the left," commented one close observer of the changing mood in

New York City, "that capitalism's two most durable struts, racism and anti-communism, might at last be exposed and then shattered."[27]

Such calculations, continued Jim Sleeper, figured in the creation of the National Welfare Rights Organization. Traditionally the objective of welfare had been to provide a bridge until the unemployed could find the means to become productive members of society. War on Poverty programs from Operation Head Start for preschool children to the Job Corps for training young adults fit well into that tradition, but the National Welfare Rights Organization, like the Community Action Programs, posed a direct challenge. NWRO activists planned to flood the system with claims, forcing it to collapse under the strain—to be replaced by a guaranteed minimum income for all. They failed in the attempt, but meanwhile welfare rolls increased to over one million, and the traditional Democratic urban coalition started to crack under the pressure.[28]

It was becoming difficult to determine the driving force behind such protests. Was it the stimulus given to rising expectations by the gap between the promise of the Great Society and the continuing reality of inner-city life? Or was it mounting rage at something that could not even be defined until the Vietnam War provided a focus for reexamining basic assumptions about the structure of American society and how it had developed since the Civil War and perhaps even earlier?

Alarm bells were going off inside government, certainly, but the reaction was to the supposed harm that protesters were doing to their own cause, especially the blacks. Even as—*especially as*—challenges to the legitimacy of the war policy grew, policymakers feared that war protesters, not the war itself, would alienate groups crucial to the success of the Great Society. In late November 1965 a White House aide fretted, "I am increasingly concerned over the involvement of the civil rights groups with the anti-Vietnam demonstrators. The anti-Vietnam types are driving the middle class to the right. This is the key group that is slowly being won over to the civil rights cause. Negro leadership involvement with the anti-Vietnam groups will set their progress back substantially."[29]

A few days later this same aide suggested that it was urgent to have labor leader Walter Reuther "talk turkey" to Martin Luther King. He had seen a new public opinion poll taken in Newark, New Jersey, that showed a very high figure, 28 percent of the respondents, believed the U.S. should "get out now" from Vietnam. Since other recent polls tallied only 8 to 13 percent favorable to the "get out now" option, the pollster ran his cards again, this time by race. He found that the strength of the "get out now" group came largely from blacks, low-income "virtually the same people," and young women. "As I mentioned before, it is not only in our interest, but in the Negroes' interest as well to disassociate from the anti-Vietnam movement. The demonstrations are driving precisely the group—the

American lower and middle classes—that the Negroes need most to persuade, away from the 'pull-out' sentiment. For the civil rights groups to join the anti-Vietnam demonstrations will severely hurt their cause."[30]

This came close to saying that if the war did not end with a "victory," blacks would be blamed and progress in civil rights reversed. Watts had already started the rumor that military troubles in Vietnam and unrest in the cities stemmed from the same "liberal" mollycoddling of society's enemies. At various times even Johnson attempted to work a twist on this theme, arguing that both his nemesis on the Senate Foreign Relations Committee, Arkansas's Bill Fulbright, and hypocritical Northern liberals opposed the war because they cared little for helping the colored peoples of Asia. The Eastern Establishment also came in for criticism as Europhiles who lacked sympathy for the plight of those from a different culture. Thus, too, Dean Rusk's later bitter comment about Dean Acheson's lack of interest in that part of the world: "Acheson was a superb secretary of state, and yet he really didn't give a damn about the brown, yellow, black and red peoples of the world."[31]

It now appeared that both prowar and antiwar groups saw a common failure of nerve in the handling of the twin crises. Daniel Moynihan had his own interpretation of what took place beginning in the middle of the decade as the Great Society was being launched simultaneously with the escalation of the war in Asia. He later attributed Johnson's ultimate undoing to a contest between the cultural and political capitals of the nation, between New York and Washington.

> The twin issues of the Negro revolution and the war in Vietnam were at the base of it, but also the personality of Lyndon Johnson. . . . Johnson, in effect, drifted into a Washington–New York confrontation. And he lost. His administration was toppled by the literary reviews, the salons, the intellectual elite. . . , the cultural arbiters of New York who, during this period, determined that his course in foreign policy was a disaster. Simultaneously, for reasons that may or may not be connected, the Negro slums of the nation erupted in violence. Desperately committed to Vietnam, Johnson had no funds with which to respond to what was manifestly a problem of poverty. He responded instead with commissions of enquiry of various kinds. Repeatedly his commissions would tell him he had to spend more, just as repeatedly his Secretary of the Treasury told him there was no money. The war went badly; violence spread to the middle classes; the country was approaching instability; the President resigned.[32]

Moynihan's analysis exaggerates the power of the "literary reviews, the salons, the intellectual elite," but it catches well the frenetic scramble to push through enough legislation, send enough troops to hold at bay Blake's tiger burning bright in the forests of the night.

OEO Director Sargent Shriver, meanwhile, had promised to reduce the prominence of the CAPs in the War on Poverty, but he argued that if the government was serious about its intentions, it would have to raise his budget from $1.75 billion to $10 billion. Shriver's proposed plan to eliminate poverty also included the negative income tax. To Johnson, direct payments to the poor meant the dole, and he would have none of it. But there was to be no $10 billion for OEO. When Shriver claimed they could actually eliminate poverty, the president responded, "Well, Sarge, we can't spend that kind of money. . . . Congressional elections are coming up. After that we'll be out of this Vietnam thing, and I'll give you the money."[33]

Such statements only increased accusations that Vietnam and the War on Poverty were linked, and that Johnson would always yield to conservative demands to cut spending at home to finance the war—even when these demands were made out of dislike for the purposes of the federal programs rather than the costs. Shriver knew the "jig was up" for OEO, that there would never be a $10 billion appropriation; therefore the War on Poverty would decline into skirmish activities that guaranteed failure. Given Gardner Ackley's predictions, Johnson presumably should have been more responsive to Shriver's proposals—except that he knew the true costs of the war were being kept from the public and the Council of Economic Advisers, and he knew that powerful forces were mobilizing against federal initiatives like the Community Action Programs.

By the fall of 1965 even Gardner Ackley, who had promised plenty of room in the economy for guns and butter, had changed his mind as the military buildup began to trigger inflationary pressures.[34] Johnson still had plans for expanding the Great Society and for introducing more civil rights legislation aimed at equal opportunities in housing and other objectives, but not for giving Sarge Shriver a tenfold increase in funds. When Treasury Secretary Henry Fowler submitted a speech to the White House that sounded a warning note about federal expenditures, he got back a message from Bill Moyers that the president thought it was a "little too hard on Vietnam." What the president didn't want to do, Moyers instructed Fowler, was to say to the "business community that we have declared war in Viet Nam." And that there was no longer enough for guns and butter too. "You don't say that. That is what he is trying to avoid."[35]

Budget Director Charles Schultze then cautioned White House aide Harry McPherson against a "travelling circus of senior officials" going around the country explaining all the new Great Society programs. Such a tour would stimulate interest in programs "we cannot adequately finance." "Raising hopes and then crushing them because of budgetary limitations," Schultze warned, "is worse than leaving the public in the dark about new programs." McPherson conveyed the budget director's concerns to Moyers, adding, "The only counter-argument I can make is that we are not closing the door on the Great Society; we are just muting our welcome to it because of Vietnam." Moyers was not sure the president even wanted to give that impression. Hold everything in abeyance, he told McPherson.[36]

William McChesney Martin, chairman of the Federal Reserve board of governors, wielded power outside Johnson's command structure. When Martin, Fowler, and Schultze met with Johnson in early October, the Fed chairman wanted to know how much was going to be spent in 1966, particularly by McNamara on the war? He wanted the information to help him decide whether to raise interest rates that the Fed charged to member banks in order to rein in the forces of inflation. Johnson pretended he really had little idea how much Vietnam would cost: "It could be $10 billion, it could be $3 to $5 billion." Martin promptly showed which figure he believed by raising the discount rates. Unless he could make enough appointments to the board to put Martin in a minority, the president could not prevent the Fed from making Vietnam "the" issue. But Johnson still would not listen to Ackley's plea that a $5 billion tax increase was needed to cool down an economy that was now heating up like a nuclear reactor.[37]

In defiance of all the warnings from Ackley and the other economic "specialists," Fowler, Schultze, and Martin, Johnson plunged ahead with a "pedal-to-the-floor" approach to the Great Society. He gave his blessings to a massive second-year program, wrote Joe Califano, "that would astound the Congress and the country when he unveiled it in his State of the Union message on January 12, 1966."[38] Johnson refused to include a tax increase, not because he imagined he knew better than the specialists but because he did not wish to make the central issue Vietnam or the Great Society. As it happened, a variety of factors held inflation in check—at least for a time. The president offered a budget based upon unreal expectations, the most unreal being the assumption that Vietnam spending would be no more than $10 billion. This fanciful estimate required Secretary McNamara to inform Congress that Defense Department figures assumed the war would be over by June 30, 1967. No one believed that, least of all McNamara himself. As it turned out, Vietnam expenditures for the fiscal year 1966–1967 were almost $20 billion, twice the estimate. But consumer spending leveled off, and even the president's economic advisers relaxed.[39]

Nevertheless, Johnson's dilemma in trying to maintain the symmetry was there for all to see in his 1966 State of the Union message. Vietnam "must be at the center of our concerns," he began, but he would not permit those who forced the war on us to "win a victory" over the desires and intentions of the American people. "This nation is mighty enough, its society is healthy enough, its people are strong enough, to pursue our goals in the rest of the world while still building a great society at home." But, then, after listing all he expected from Congress, he said, "Because of Vietnam we cannot do all that we should, or all that we would like to do." A strange passage followed, a sort of dare to critics to risk denying him what the "people" wanted. Johnson challenged those who did not believe the nation could carry on both wars to take the sacrifice from those "who live in the fullness of our blessing, rather than try to strip it from the hands of those that are most in need."

It was "against all the most inward pulls of my desire," he launched into what sounded like an apologia, that he had given orders for our guns to fire. "For we have children to teach, and we have sick to be cured, and we have men to be freed. . . ." Then the final appeal:

> Yet as long as others will challenge America's security and test the dearness of our beliefs with fire and steel, then we must stand or see the promise of two centuries tremble. I believe tonight that you do not want to try that risk. And from that belief your President summons his strength for the trials that lie ahead in the days to come.[40]

The immediate trial he faced was how to convince South Vietnamese leaders that his ability to carry on the war depended upon their ability to respond to his wishes. Accordingly, the president's advisers prepared remarks for him to deliver to South Vietnamese leaders at a February 1966 "summit" meeting in Honolulu. Johnson was to say that "the struggle in your country can finally be won only if you are able to bring about a social revolution for your people—while at the same time your soldiers and ours are beating back the aggressor." Washington could not disengage from this "other" war in Vietnam and could not "separate our responsibility for the Americans who are dying there. We want to make sure that the measures which must be taken assure our men don't die in vain."[41]

As the conference concluded, Johnson reiterated that it had not been about growing military effectiveness. "You don't want to be like the fellow who was playing poker and when he made a big bet they called him and said, 'What have you got?' He said, 'Aces,' and they asked how many and he said, 'One ace.' " "We have been talking about building a society. . . ." The outcome of the struggle in Vietnam—and at home—would depend on what he and his aides now called "The Other War." Meeting alone with President Ky, Johnson first asked if he would like to have an autographed picture of himself to take back. Then he said he wanted to send Vice-President Hubert Humphrey back with him to "start the policy ball rolling."[42]

> *On what wings dare he aspire?*
> *What the hand dare seize the fire?*

Johnson previews his civil rights proposals for Martin Luther King, Whitney Young, and James Farmer. LBJ later tried to mesh the Vietnam War into a worldwide struggle for civil rights.

Already on the agenda at the LBJ ranch in December 1964 was a proposed bombing campaign. McNamara pressed the need to demonstrate American power in order to strengthen Saigon's will to continue.

McGeorge Bundy reports on his trip to Vietnam during Rolling Thunder, February 1965, beneath John Quincy Adams's portrait. "America goes not abroad in search of monsters to destroy," Adams had warned.

The president with aide Harry McPherson near the end of the thirty-seven-day bombing pause in early 1966. McPherson later sought to give the president a "peace" speech in the wake of Tet and King's assassination.

George Ball's dissents allowed Johnson to claim that he had truly considered all alternatives, including withdrawal.

The search for peace in mid-1966: Johnson, National Security Adviser Walt W. Rostow (left), and Secretary of State Dean Rusk sought answers for a war that had long since overwhelmed "crisis management."

At Hawaii in February 1966, South Vietnamese Prime Minister Nguyen Cao Ky took his cue from Johnson to declare that the war could be won only by also addressing political questions and "social defects."

Troubled hawks: In September 1966, Clark Clifford, a once and future opponent of escalation, joined former Ambassador Henry Cabot Lodge and General William Westmoreland to consider how to increase outside support for the war.

Slipping away from the Manila Conference in October 1966, Johnson reviewed troops at Cam Ranh Bay, the huge facility constructed to receive the massive U.S. buildup in Vietnam.

War protesters and civil rights veterans at the White House gates in May 1967. The administration feared this joining of forces would damage the war cause as well as support for the Great Society.

In mid-1967 Robert McNamara's doubts were growing. Averell Harriman (second from left) was also a closet skeptic who would try to find a way out of Vietnam through Moscow. Rusk (right) never doubted ultimate success.

No photograph better captures Johnson's agony over the war: he listened to a tape from son-in-law Marine Captain Charles Robb, serving in Vietnam.

Despite the official rationale for the war—to halt the spread of communism—Soviet Premier Alexei Kosygin was almost as eager as LBJ to ensure great-power management of the conflict. At the 1967 Glassboro, New Jersey, "mini-summit," Kosygin told Johnson he thought the North Vietnamese were ready for talks.

The March 31, 1968, speech did not end debate within the administration. It stimulated Clark Clifford's efforts not only to halt the troop escalation but to convince Johnson that a total bombing halt was the only path to serious negotiations.

As he had on the road to escalation, Johnson pushed his advisers again and again to make the case for a total bombing halt. He was not surprised at Saigon's refusal to go along with negotiations.

To pay the price for Vietnam, Johnson finally had to sacrifice the Great
Society coalition. He left his successor, Richard Nixon, an opportunity to
use the war differently so as to open the door to détente.

Part Three

THE WAR COMES HOME

THIRTEEN

The Pause That Failed

SOON AFTER THE DECISION at the end of July 1965 to send the first 100,000 men to Vietnam, Secretary of State Dean Rusk sent for the South Vietnamese ambassador, Bui Diem. "When we want to do something we do it," Rusk assured him.[1] With an equally self-confident Defense Secretary Robert McNamara managing the logistics, the buildup was indeed accomplished with stunning speed and efficiency. "After July 1965, the American build-up was so massive, so irresistible," Ambassador Diem would write, "and so fast that it simply left no room for doubt or second thoughts of any kind."[2]

Only a few doubters persisted. In early October 1965, Under Secretary of State George Ball tried to persuade McNamara to scale back the bombing raids in the Hanoi area. One plane had apparently gone down over China, and there were known instances of Chinese MiGs being scrambled. We are getting into a Russian roulette game with the Chinese, Ball argued, at an especially bad time with the president scheduled to go into the hospital for a gall bladder operation. McNamara dismissed Ball's worries in his most impatient you-don't-know-what-you're-talking-about fashion. He doubted the story about the downed plane in China, he told the under secretary, nor could he see any evidence the attacks were causing great risks. Well, Ball rejoined, that was exactly what Truman's advisers said in 1950, "and then suddenly the 'boys' appeared." McNamara assured him he only wanted to keep the pressure on North Vietnam, not take on Red China.[3]

In November things began to change. First came the battle of Ia Drang near the Laotian border. More than two thousand enemy soldiers were killed during the fighting while "only" two hundred Americans died. The American military immediately pronounced Ia Drang a great victory. Westmoreland's new army had routed the enemy in their first encounter.

Army Chief of Staff Harold Johnson went so far as to declare that "the worst is behind us." Westmoreland's men, confirmed JCS chairman General Earle Wheeler, had exploded the myth that a ten-to-one ratio was required to defeat guerrillas. "We can achieve the preponderance of force required with less than that ratio."[4]

While the celebrating continued, McNamara took a second look at what Ia Drang suggested and was not so sure he liked what he saw. Exaggerated body counts were not yet an issue; but he was disturbed by the battle site—so far from Saigon. True, American forces had prevailed, but the North Vietnamese had stood and fought. True, also, the premise of the July 28, 1965, decision had been that the buildup would force the enemy into the open for "decisive" battles like Ia Drang. McNamara was no "enclave" strategy man, but neither was he really comfortable with the search-and-destroy, "attrit"-the-enemy-and-win plan that Westmoreland now seemed determined to carry out. During his next trip to Vietnam, moreover, McNamara was apparently shocked at estimates of what the strategy would require. Westmoreland wanted 400,000 troops by December 1966 and an additional 200,000 in 1967, or double most previous estimates. One must say "apparently shocked," because such figures had been bruited about earlier.

Greater infiltration numbers from the north had also been predicted as a response to the American escalation. There were still no indications, moreover, that the bombing had slowed the process or sapped the will of the North Vietnamese. Ia Drang was a costly victory. What did it foretell? What would Americans read in the newspapers or see on television after the next "victory"? General Ky seemed more realistic than American commanders when he told the defense secretary that the strategy would take a long time—years—and, McNamara now fully realized, many American lives.[5]

McNamara also began to fret that Ball might be right, not because of some errant American bomber straying across the border, but because the number of troops the generals wanted would finally cause China to intervene. A stalemate at 600,000 or more, and then war with China. Grim prospects indeed! While he had been careful to restrict such musings to private memoranda and inner-office conversations, the tension he felt began to emerge in more public settings. Sixty-eight Labour MPs wrote British Prime Minister Harold Wilson, for example, about a rumor that the American secretary of defense had told a NATO council meeting that war with China had become a "near certainty." The prime minister should press the Americans to end the bombing.[6]

Even before the battle of Ia Drang, McNamara had suggested a bombing pause to give Ho Chi Minh a chance to reconsider his course of action. He now urged a pause to satisfy public opinion that there was no alternative to further escalation of the war. Before sending more men and increasing the bombing pressure on North Vietnam, he argued, Washington should have a final go at diplomacy.[7]

At first neither Mac Bundy nor Dean Rusk agreed. Rusk in particular feared that if a pause actually led to talks, Hanoi would take advantage of American restraint to conduct a fight-and-talk strategy indefinitely. By threatening to leave the talks if the bombing resumed, the Communists could hold the Americans hostage. Rusk actually feared talks under any conditions, for he saw no way to keep the National Liberation Front outside the door. "If the Viet Cong come to the conference table as full partners," Rusk kept reminding his colleagues, "they will in a sense have been victorious in the very aims that South Vietnam and the United States are pledged to prevent."[8]

Inside the inner circle it was all right to say blunt things like that, despite Johnson's frequent public assertions that he desired "unconditional" discussions and recent comments that the NLF would have no difficulty finding a way to be "represented, or have its views presented." Such contradictions were not yet open secrets. What a hubbub arose, then, when the respected journalist Eric Sevareid reported that Adlai Stevenson, who died in July as the troop question was being finalized, had believed Washington ignored an opportunity to pursue peace negotiations. The outlines of the story of U Thant's thwarted efforts to bring about a face-to-face meeting were already known, if not what Stevenson had thought about Washington's lack of interest in the secretary general's plan for bilateral conversations in Rangoon. Hanoi had apparently signaled a willingness to attend such a meeting, but the plan was nixed in Washington. Sevareid's account caused the State Department to admit, for the first time, that there had indeed been a formal proposal and an American rejection. Its spokesman, Robert McCloskey, tried his best to dismiss the whole episode as much ado about nothing. Dean Rusk's "antennae is [sic] sensitive," McCloskey said, and if Hanoi "was prepared for serious talks . . . he would recognize when it came." Everyone jumped on that one. The *New York Times* editorialized, "This comment reminds one of the ancient Roman practice of drawing auspices from the flight or the entrails of birds. It would be a shuddering thought that the fate of nations and thousands of young Americans depended on Dean Rusk's antenna."[9]

A *very* unhappy Lyndon Johnson demanded to know about "this midnight brandy conversation between Stevenson and Sevareid that got us turning down a poor North Vietnamese desire to make peace." George Ball was put in charge of cleaning up the fallout from McCloskey's gaffe, but some sticky bits were not easy to get rid of. It was embarrassing, for example, that the president had not been kept informed of the U Thant business. Much worse, it was impossible to reveal that Rusk's decision to turn down the approach was based on fear that the South Vietnamese would learn of the negotiations—even if he was only willing to talk about a North Vietnamese withdrawal. To explain Rusk's reasoning would suggest that Saigon held a sort of veto over American policy, even if it stemmed from weakness. The main thing right now, Ball told the president, was to prevent Thant from saying "we were liars again and blowing this thing up." Johnson wondered how many other people "were going around telling stories over brandy to Sevareid." "Ball said he realized this is one of the problems."[10]

It was also a reason why Rusk began to feel more sympathy for McNamara's argument: if they were going to load up the transport planes and the bombers, they needed a pause first to satisfy America's pledge always to give decent respect to the opinions of mankind. The posthumous Stevenson "revelations" caused the most trouble, perhaps, in Europe, where they stimulated calls for a bombing pause. In the United States, public opinion polls the president saw showed increasing support for a "hard line" in Vietnam. Commenting on these polls, one White House assistant observed that, yes, the antiwar demonstrators were succeeding in putting pressure on the government, but it was exactly the converse of their hopes. "Rather than 'awaken the American conscience, etc.,' they are driving the great American middle ground sharply to the right. This is going to make it much more difficult for us when and if we can get to negotiations."[11]

That assessment was certainly accurate about the degree of animosity—even hatred—shown to antiwar protesters that fall. The Teach-in movement on college campuses the previous spring had given way to marches in several cities. Prowar crowds jeered and threw things. But they were not the only ones upset. The elder generation of liberals, conditioned by the cold war, hardly knew what to make of the marches. Most stood on the sidelines, taking notes for articles that expressed concern at the "simplistic" solutions offered by the marchers, and for their lack of concern about Communist "infiltration" of the movement.[12]

But neither sticks and stones nor name-calling halted the growth of the antiwar movement. A big reason, of course, was the draft. More than 36,000 men received draft notices that fall, the largest number since 1952 at the height of the Korean War. But while draft resisters held rallies at which they burned their draft cards, by far the most dramatic protest of the war occurred on November 2, when a Quaker well past draft age poured kerosene over himself and struck a match. Instantly he was engulfed in flames—scarcely fifty yards from Robert McNamara's office in the Pentagon. The defense secretary saw an agitated crowd, ambulances, and smoke. Years later he called it "a personal tragedy for me."[13]

The man who immolated himself, Norman Morrison, lived in Baltimore. He had been an antiwar activist. That morning he read an account by a French priest in Vietnam describing American use of napalm, a form of jellied gasoline, against suspected Viet Cong hiding places. "I have seen my faithful burned up in napalm," the priest wrote. Morrison also read an appeal for more letters to legislators. "What else can we do?" he asked himself. A week later a second man, Roger LaPorte, a Catholic Worker, followed Morrison's example, setting fire to himself on Dag Hammarskjold Plaza outside the UN buildings.[14]

Thirty thousand marchers came to Washington on November 27, 1965, carefully instructed by SANE (the National Committee for a Sane Nuclear Policy) organizers not to engage in provocative behavior. Scheduled speakers included the famous "baby doctor," Dr. Benjamin Spock, and, with one or two exceptions, other "highly respectable" Americans. The longtime Socialist party candidate Norman Thomas, now accorded almost elder statesman status, told the crowd, "I'd rather see America save her soul than her face." For the first time a taunting chant was heard from a small contingent of those who circled the White House on the way to the grounds of the Washington Monument for speeches and songs. "Hey, hey, L.B.J., how many kids did you kill today?"[15]

Newspapers and columnists not yet known to have any sympathy for the antiwar movement were beginning to sound a little fidgety about it all. James Reston, who could usually be counted on for a sophisticated defense of administration policy—all the more effective for its independent stance—now wondered about how the path to involvement had been charted in quiet little talks, not bombastic pronouncements. Now, he said, McNamara was home from Saigon for another quiet talk about increasing American troop strength. "Maybe it is unavoidable, but at least this time it should be explained . . . something is out of kilter. A policy of more troops and more profits, draft the poor and reward the rich, more Social Security at home and less security in Vietnam is not easy to explain, but somebody who knows ought to try. . . .The impression is gaining that everybody is trapped by events and not quite sure of what to do, and it is this sense of stumbling deeper into the bog that is frustrating and dividing the people."[16]

Reston's paper, the *New York Times*, then ran front-page stories, side by side, one datelined Washington, the other Hong Kong, under a large, italicized headline, "*Some U.S. Aides See Risk of Direct Clash with China.*" Both stories talked about Chinese preparations for war and the "grave questions" McNamara and Rusk were posing in terms of the possibility of a wider war. Max Frankel's report from Washington closed with a statement from an informed official that the bombing of North Vietnam had become so widespread that Hanoi and Haiphong were left as mere "islands." Attacks on those cities were no longer being ruled out, the official went on, and he would "not now buy real estate" in the North Vietnamese capital. In an adjoining article, Cuban Premier Fidel Castro declared that if asked, his country would send volunteers: "There are many in this country who gladly would volunteer to go there to fight against the criminal soldiers of Yankee imperialism."[17]

The *Times* leader that day declared that escalation had failed; more escalation could bring a war with China, even a world war. Alternatives had not yet been tried. "The most obvious alternative, despite the failure to get any advance promise or concession from Hanoi and Peking, is to try a reasonably long pause in the bombing of North Vietnam—more than the token five days of last spring." Reports from Moscow "strongly indicate," the editorial asserted, a desire to see the war ended; but the Russians could not be expected to yield their leadership in the Communist world to China by abandoning North Vietnam. If the Soviet leadership was to have any influence on Hanoi, it appeared to the *Times* that it could only be in a face-saving context.[18]

Whether the "usually well-informed" *Times* knew what had passed between Soviet Ambassador Anatoly Dobrynin and McGeorge Bundy during a quiet luncheon ten days earlier is an interesting speculation, because "sides" were being chosen up for another "great debate" among the president's top advisers. Bundy was in the process of switching to the McNamara position. Fallout from the Stevenson "revelations" and the "antics" of the antiwar movement were not enough to work such a change, though they certainly contributed. At the luncheon with Dobrynin, the national security adviser used public speculation about a pause to inquire "whether the Soviet Union had any useful thoughts on the matter."[19]

Bundy had good reason to expect a substantive reply to his apparently casual inquiry. The editor of *Foreign Affairs*, Hamilton Fish Armstrong, had forwarded comments made to him by an *Izvestia* "correspondent" to the effect that the only way to bring about negotiations was for the U.S. to stop the bombing "for a considerable period." It should be a long enough pause so that pressures could build on Hanoi "from all sides." There must be no hint, of course, of "anything like collusion," and there should be a cover story to protect both Moscow and Washington. Otherwise the Soviet Union could not act without opening itself to attacks and jibes from Beijing, and the common interest they shared in erecting a barrier to China's expansion southward would go unrealized.[20]

It was no surprise, then, when Dobrynin replied that if the United States were to stop the bombing for twelve to twenty days, the Soviet Union would exert its influence toward constructive action by Hanoi. He could give no assurances of a favorable response, of course, but Moscow would try.[21] Bundy came away from the luncheon convinced that he must persuade Johnson to reconsider his early opposition to a pause. What Dobrynin said had not convinced him that a pause would lead to fruitful negotiations, not at all, but several things had now combined to require a fresh look at the pros and cons. The outlook was for a "pretty grim year" ahead. Westmoreland had increased his troop recommendations, and McNamara was now convinced that the budget figures he had previously given the president, already alarming, "may turn out to be an understatement." Even if the Soviets failed to produce Hanoi at the conference table, a pause would certainly intensify dissension between Moscow and Beijing. "We should expect that it will not lead to negotiations, but it will strengthen your hand both at home and abroad as a determined man of peace facing a very tough course in 1966." [22]

Bundy had assured Johnson that hard-line critics could be answered by actions taken after the pause. A second memorandum a week later told the president, who was still recuperating from a gall bladder operation in Texas, that opinion in favor of a pause continued to grow. Dean Rusk had come around, and Russian expert Llewellyn "Tommy" Thompson thought it would strengthen Soviet resolve to stand clear of the fighting in Vietnam. If the pause should lead to the conference table, moreover, it would mean that Hanoi had given up its insistence that the United States accept the NLF program for peace. "Thus such a move by Hanoi would drive a sharp wedge between Hanoi and the Communists in South Vietnam. We know that it is just this kind of sell-out that the Southern Communists fear." Bundy did admit that a pause would very likely lead to increased international pressure to extend some sort of recognition to the NLF, people who "control one-half the country."

This is exactly what we must not do if we do not wish to lose the whole game in South Vietnam. But sooner or later we are going to have to face this music, and perhaps it is not so bad to face it now during a pause. [23]

"There is no trap we cannot manage in deciding when and how to end the pause." If anything, however, Bundy's memorandum would raise new questions for the president to brood about. He understood very well that pause advocates did not expect negotiations to result, for there really was nothing to negotiate. What bothered him was the defensive tone throughout Bundy's messages, suggesting, he believed, that his advisers themselves were having doubts. Beneath all the "tough-minded" talk about putting up a good show to satisfy well-meaning but ill-informed critics, the president sensed feelings that could lead to disloyalty. A pause might well indicate confusion, not firmness of purpose.

Johnson returned to Washington in mid-December in a truculent mood. At 9:15 a.m. on the 17th he met with his advisers. The mood in the cabinet room during these discussions was completely different from the feisty, almost triumphant attitude around the table when the decision was made to jump in with both feet back in July. Nothing was being written about Viet Cong atrocities, Johnson complained by way of an opening, nothing to make you hate them. "Everything that is being written is done to make the world hate us." He needed someone to construct another Baltimore speech, the president went on, not something written out of desperation but an appropriate speech. He leaned forward. "I am willing to take any gamble on stopping the bombing if I think I have some hope of something happening that is good." [24]

Bombing never wins a war, George Ball began, but it did risk escalation in Vietnam. The only chance to avoid that danger was to stop the bombing of the north and redouble the ground effort in the south. Everyone in the room agreed that a bombing pause was necessary, though none was willing to go as far as Under Secretary Ball. The main obstacles to be overcome were the Joint Chiefs and the selling of the public. For the remainder of the session, the president and his advisers worked on those problems. "Let McNamara say to the Chiefs: we've got a heavy budget, tax bill, controls, danger of inflation, kill the great society." The diplomats had to have their chance before more troops were sent, and they claim they can't talk with bombs dropping.

Jack Valenti believed the president was ready to decide for a pause. As the two men left the meeting, Johnson murmured, almost to himself, "God, we have got to find a way to end this war, we've got to find a way." But the next day the president invited two old Democratic "pros," Clark Clifford and Abe Fortas, to the follow-up meeting that was supposed to consider only the specifics of the decision. He had been talking with the chairman of the Joint Chiefs, he began, and had got an earful about why a bombing pause would make it impossible to attack the enemy. "The military say a month's pause would undo all we've done." [25]

"That's baloney," McNamara protested sharply, "and I can prove it." But Johnson had to be convinced all over again. "I don't think so," he said, "I think it contains serious military risks." Then he challenged Rusk to go all through the litany of why the American people needed the pause. "They are isolationists at heart," said Rusk, and had to be convinced there was no alternative. Why, then, were the Russians so interested? "The Russians don't want China's policy to win." And so on.

When it came to risks, however, Rusk did not mention the Joint Chiefs' concern. Instead he talked about failure and pressure to go all out. At that, Johnson leaped in:

> That is the most dangerous aspect. Don't we know a pause will fail? If we are in worse shape then, won't we be bringing a deadly crisis on ourselves? The Republicans are looking for an exit. When we suffer reverses, it will be attributable to this. The support we have will be weak as dishwater.

After more discussion along these lines, Secretary McNamara started listing the reasons he found compelling. All but the last had been heard before. And it drew the president's full attention as he fixed a mournful gaze on McNamara. "Military solution to problem is not certain," the defense secretary said. He put the odds at "One out of three or one in two. Ultimately we must find solution, we must finally find a diplomatic solution."[26]

"You mean that no matter what we do in the military field, you think there is no sure victory," the president said. "That's right," McNamara replied in the same crisp tone he had used all through the war, only now it snapped off the light at the end of the tunnel. "We have been too optimistic. One in three or one in two is my estimate." Rusk broke in to say he was "more optimistic than that, but I can't prove it." McNamara was not ready to let it go at that. "I'm saying: we may not find a military solution. We need to explore other means."

After the war, McNamara reiterated that he had thought it unlikely the war could be won militarily "at times in 1966, if not earlier . . . and I believed considerable emphasis should be put on developing what was called a political track, which would lead to negotiations with the North Vietnamese. . . ."[27] With the *North Vietnamese*, he remembered—but the sticking point was always the role of the NLF at a peace conference. McNamara's genuine fears of a long war leading to stalemate did not yet force him to consider withdrawal, or to reconsider his own commitment to escalation. "This seems a contradiction," he admitted during the discussions on December 18, 1965. "I come to you for a huge increase in Viet-Nam—400,000 men. But at the same time it may lead to escalation and undesirable results. I suggest we look now at other alternatives." But not dealing with the NLF.

The meeting adjourned for lunch. When it reassembled, Fortas and Clifford ticked off their objections in lawyerly fashion. Both men agreed with Johnson's comment that if the pause failed, the pressure for an all-out effort would be all but irresistible. A pause could prolong the war, on the other hand, by encouraging Hanoi to believe Washington was losing heart. Clifford, especially, went down the line of the various arguments in favor and came to the heart of the matter: did anyone present really feel a pause would bring serious negotiations? "If you accept the hypothesis that there is no chance of success, others will know it too, and I don't like the president to take a posture that is clearly unproductive. It might end up being viewed as a gimmick."

Obviously dismayed by these comments, McNamara repeated arguments Clifford had made back in July in opposing the first 100,000 troop decision. "If we put in 400,000 men, what will they do?" he asked rhetorically. And then answered himself:

They will match us. We are going to be bombing assets of North Vietnam dearer to them than the ones we are bombing. China is beginning to ready planes to meet us in the skies. It appears that MIGs are being introduced into North Vietnam. They are getting ready for escalation—and will call on Russia. They don't want to confront us in Vietnam—they want a way out.

At the end of the day a very weary Lyndon Johnson sighed and stood up, stretching himself to his full height. "We'll take the pause," he said, looking at McNamara. "With a slight wave of his hand," recalled Valenti, "he strode from the room."[28]

No bombing pause was announced, however, except as part of a one-day Christmas truce. When the bombing did not resume at once with the fighting on the ground, press speculation grew about the peace offensive. There was no peace offensive yet. Johnson was still playing it on a day-to-day basis. Rusk had no intention of extending the pause for more than a few days. He urged ending the pause quickly and trying a longer pause later on, after informing the Russians. Mac Bundy confronted the secretary on these grounds and had to take the argument to Johnson, as did McNamara, who pleaded with Johnson that a decision to send out special peace emissaries meant that the bombing pause had to continue at least past New Year's Day. In a telephone conversation with George Ball, the defense secretary went about as far as he had allowed himself to go in thinking about a settlement. "Mc said he realizes as well as Ball that it is unlikely that this is all going to end with unconditional surrender by NVN. They both agreed there had to be face savers."[29]

Bundy and McNamara won the debate. Johnson telephoned Rusk from his Texas ranch to instruct the secretary of state that he wanted the emissaries to go out—immediately. And he telephoned Averell Harriman to say that he was to go wherever he wished in Eastern Europe and then report direct to Johnson. The president made it plain that Harriman's usefulness would not end when he returned home if the trip failed to bring tangible results, for then he would have a role to play convincing antiwar senators and "New York Times(men)," all those who thought that if "we were only willing to have peace, we ought to give it the old college try," that they had given it their all. "Don't you let Dean talk you out of it," he said, and hung up.[30]

Rusk did try to talk him out of it. And was taken aback when Harriman told him there would be no time for the secretary to present his arguments to President Johnson because he had been instructed to leave that afternoon. Harriman did go to see Llewellyn Thompson, however, and found himself in a debate over whether Saigon would be upset by this diplomatic extravaganza. "Tommy, this is the President of the United States, not South Viet-Nam, whom you are working for. South Viet-Nam we can protect as much as possible, but the President has the job of convincing Congress he has made the last effort."[31]

Rusk's concern, shared also by less "pro-Vietnam" aides, that the whole thing would look gimmicky (as Clark Clifford had predicted), was not unjustified. Johnson's newly designated "Ambassador for Peace" was on his way across the Atlantic in an executive jet with two flight crews before the American embassy in Warsaw, his first stop, was even informed he was coming. Others were sent speeding on their way as well—for example, UN Ambassador Arthur Goldberg to Rome, because the president especially wanted to send a Jew to talk to the spiritual leader of the Catholic world. Even George Ball was more than a little queasy about all the drums and bugles. But Johnson gave him a pep talk about how he was depending on him "as his lawyer and his devil's advocate." Ball was not to "let 'them' talk him out of anything." He should "stay right on it until we are sure we have bled it for all it is worth."[32]

Ball probably winced at that statement—and what was to come. "We have . . . made it clear—from Hanoi to New York—that there are no arbitrary limits to our search for peace," Johnson proclaimed in overdrawn fashion in his State of the Union message on January 12, 1966. "We stand by the Geneva agreements of 1954 and 1962," he went on. "We will meet at any conference table, we will discuss any proposals—four points or fourteen or forty—and we will consider the views of any group."[33] Johnson's search for peace in the winter of 1965–1966 had a frenetic quality, with emissaries rushing to and fro like pigeons pecking at imaginary pieces of food on a piazza. Yet however clumsy the attempt to implicate Wilsonian objectives in his fourteen-point "peace offensive," LBJ's willingness to open discussions under the general rubric of the 1954 Geneva Agreement, and the offer to consider the "views of any group" constituted a change in American policy, if only the slightest grey tinge on what had been an adamant black-and-white refusal to consider serious negotiations that would include the NLF. In Saigon, Ambassador Henry Cabot Lodge had in fact taken issue with such an offer. He did not like the idea of suggesting a new Geneva-type conference. It would be packed with governments like the British, motivated by wishful thinking, and France and China, who actively wanted the U.S. to fail. "We could get into horrible and unnecessary complications."[34]

There was no real expectation in Washington, on the other hand, that Hanoi was ready to retreat to Geneva to renegotiate agreements that Ho's government felt had been violated—else Lodge's view would have prevailed. From Hanoi's point of view, it was the Saigon government that was illegitimate. The only thing worth negotiating, therefore, was how that regime might be allowed to disappear. With a new government in the south, it would then be possible to set the terms for reunification.

As Johnson said in his letter to Australian Prime Minister Robert Menzies, the real purpose of the various missions, which included a series of one-night stands by assistant secretaries in Latin America and Africa, was to negotiate for world opinion—to bring pressure on Hanoi and New York.

Among the important effects of our total activity is surely a far greater understanding of the merits of our position, so that, as we move ahead with our reinforcement in the South and if and when we decide to resume bombing, we shall do so with greater support and understanding than would otherwise have been the case, and with some hope that worldwide support for our total position will be stronger than ever in the past.[35]

The serious danger in all this, the president confided to Menzies, was that the Soviets might advise Hanoi to "come up with actions or responses designed to make it difficult for us to resume."

Already there have been indications that they may try to move us on the issue of representation of the so-called National Liberation Front. This is a fundamental issue and we are fully aware of its most serious implications. And other tricks may be tried.

And yet—and yet. When Harriman returned from his halfway-around-the-world magical mystery tour, Bundy instructed him how he was to make it "30% clearer" than Rusk had in all his briefings of congressional leaders that while there had been no response from Hanoi, the tour had been a great success in further isolating Hanoi and Beijing in world opinion. The president also wanted Harriman "to make sure that it was clear he was for self-determination, free elections. He was quite ready to have the South Vietnamese make their own choice." All the indications were, of course, that "they would choose independence."[36]

Other hints during the pause showed that American officials had begun to realize the NLF would have to be taken into account. Although he remained unwilling to go beyond his statements at the prepause meetings in the White House, Robert McNamara was, aside from George Ball, the most open to considering face-to-face negotiations with the NLF. While in public he continued to insist the NLF was nothing more than a fictitious front for North Vietnam's aggression against an independent country, he was now saying in private that he "would jump at the chance at getting in contact with them . . . we should find out as much as we can about NLF—we do not know who they are, whether they are operating from Hanoi, etc."[37]

McNamara apparently hoped the private diplomacy going on beneath all the showy displays might produce such a contact; then, perhaps, serious negotiations might somehow evolve out of the studied ambiguity American (and North Vietnamese) spokesmen had practiced when talking about the 1954 Geneva Agreement.[38] Yet only a few days after a heart-to-heart with George Ball, McNamara took the lead in arguing for resumption. Unless we do, he admonished the others, "we will give [a] wrong signal to Hanoi,

Peking and our own people." Saigon's morale would suffer. "They don't understand why we don't punish those who foster the war."[39]

Even as he argued these points, however, the defense secretary dismissed claims that the bombing would slow infiltration. McNamara knew he had put himself in a tough spot. More than anyone, he stood by quantitative measurements to determine who was winning and who was losing. How did one measure morale? If the bombing did not slow infiltration, what gauge of its success was there? McNamara had already admitted that his proposals for sending more troops seemed contradictory—and he had confided a desire to seek contacts with the NLF. The muddle in strategic thinking reflected, it can be argued, the intrusion of "illicit" thoughts policymakers did not want to admit to one another: thoughts about inviting the NLF to the peace table.

Even Mike Mansfield drew back from openly advocating seating the NLF. At a White House meeting of legislative leaders where he and Senator Fulbright were a minority of two against seventeen favoring resumption, Mansfield did have something to propose, an idea he hoped the president would take up before ordering the bombers back into the air over North Vietnam. The Senate leader suggested Johnson say something like: "I favor a cease-fire now and I call for a meeting of all the interested parties. I call for free elections within three to six months. I contemplate withdrawal of our forces after a secure amnesty. I favor reunification in accordance with the Geneva agreements."[40]

Left out of his oral presentation was a statement in the written version that declared explicitly, "We recognize the National Liberation Front as a participating element in the proposed elections."[41] Even without this sentence, Mansfield's proposal was too disorienting to be considered. Except for Fulbright, no one wanted to talk about anything except resuming the bombing. At one juncture Johnson suggested that they look at Mansfield's proposal point by point. In remarkably self-assured language, McNamara asserted that the lever to negotiations was continued military action. None of those present felt a need to pursue the matter further.

Instead the defense secretary's certitude encouraged pleas from the group that Johnson resume bombing—and somehow make Vietnam look like World War II! Thoughtful critics of the decision to suspend the bombing had foreseen such a trap. You could not insist, on the one hand, that North Vietnam was fighting a war of aggression, on behalf of a system as inherently evil as Nazism, and on the other hand engage in behavior that in any way implied disbelief. Those who had opposed the bombing suspension were not all screaming hawks. Some realized the trap—Johnson certainly did—and that a likely result would be to put off serious negotiations, not improve the chances for peace. Some of this was said in coded fashion by

Richard Russell, Johnson's old mentor in the Senate. "This is the most frustrating experience of my life," he began. "I didn't want to get in there, but we are there. I don't think the American people take this war seriously (enough). I don't credit the polls on Vietnam." Many American boys were going to die, "casualties of our care for peace."

> For God's sake, don't start the bombing half way. Let them know they are in a war. We killed civilians in World War II and nobody opposed. I'd rather kill them than have American boys die. Please, Mr. President, don't get one foot back in it. Go all the way.[42]

A lesser figure in the Senate, Republican Bourke Hickenlooper, squirmed a bit but settled back firmly into orthodoxy. "If only Vietnam were concerned," he said, "I'd get out. But we are confronting the Communist world. Either get out or lick them. I've been restless with our light bombing. If we win, we must take out their ability to make war." All wars involved risks. There was no other choice.[43]

But Johnson was not yet sure how to play out the string. More meetings followed. At one, several of the cold war Wise Men heard McNamara and Rusk describe the war as at an impasse, and, without challenging the logic of a policy that promised more of the same, nodded their heads that, yes, the bombing must be resumed.[44] The sterility of these "consultations" was summed up in McNamara's final argument for resumption. "Universal opinion of our estimators," he said, was that "cessation of bombing would cause the enemy to believe their cause was right."[45]

At the end of each of these meetings Johnson would aver that *now* he was ready to resume—then schedule another session. He constantly fretted about defections in Congress, about risking war with China, about what he knew would break loose when the first bombs started falling:

> I think if you stop bombing they will go for something else. If you let them run you out of the front yard, they'll run you out of the house.
> I don't want war with Russia or China. I feel less comfortable tonight than I felt last night. I don't want to back out—and look like I'm reaching to the Fulbrights.
> We must realize the price we pay for going back in. We will lose a good part of the Senate. *I thought of chucking that resolution back to them.*[46]

Washington Post columnists Evans and Novak declared they were getting fed up with "leaked stories from the White House about how agonizing and lonely it is to be President of the United States." After all, it was pretty clear, wasn't it, that the Soviets had not shown the slightest disposition to play the peacemaker's role? And hadn't Johnson produced "irrefutable evidence" that the Communists used the pause to increase the flow of supplies and men down the Ho Chi Minh trail through Laos into

South Vietnam? Johnson might think he was softening up the peace bloc by all his public agonizing, but he only encouraged more dissent that way. Thus the trouble he now faced from critics on Capitol Hill was at least partly of his own making.[47]

Johnson decried the enemy's supposedly perfidious behavior in using the pause to build up its forces—a staple of all cold war argumentation, going back to Harry Truman's citation of the scores of agreements broken by the Soviets—but there had been no understanding that Ho would show such restraint, nor, moreover, any American intention to slow its own buildup. The president nonetheless used the complaints of his military about North Vietnamese reinforcements to convince himself of the need to pursue the "tough" road to peace. "Was Clifford right?" he asked his advisers. "Was Clifford right about talking about peace as a deterrent to peace?" McNamara and Bundy defended the pause. No, Clifford was wrong, they said. General Wheeler thought differently. "I agree with Clifford."[48]

On January 28, meanwhile, Washington made available the transcript of a radio broadcast from Hanoi giving the text of a letter Ho Chi Minh had sent to "some heads of state and others interested in the Vietnam situation." Ho complained about the intensified and "extremely barbarous methods of warfare" the Americans were now employing, including "napalm bombs, poison gases and toxic chemicals," all the while "clamoring about their desire for peace. . . ." As for peace terms, the DRV stood by its four-point plan, "which is an expression of the essential provisions of the 1954 Geneva agreements on Vietnam." But before any talks could begin, the U.S. would have to end "unconditionally and for good all bombing raids and other war acts against the D.R.V."[49]

See, American policymakers argued, waving Ho's latest pronouncement: Hanoi demanded capitulation. Commenting on Johnson's bombing-pause diplomacy, Dean Rusk would later assert, "We put everything into the basket except the surrender of South Vietnam." Outside Washington, however, Ho's reassertion of the four-point plan appeared to leave the door open a crack. Secretary Rusk's assertions did not command universal agreement even within the administration. NSC aide Chester Cooper mused about how Johnson's appeal might have looked to Hanoi, and suggested the North Vietnamese had as much reason to doubt the president as Rusk had to dismiss Ho Chi Minh's open letter to the world.

> Instead of maximizing the effect of our fourteen point package, we buried it in the razzmatazz of sudden, noisy, and florid VIP trips. In short the President was acting like a ringmaster of a three-ring circus, rather than as the focal point of a carefully worked out exercise in diplomacy.

> But still he wondered.

More to the point, however, Washington was unprepared for negotiations. Little work had been done in blocking out a negotiating strategy, very few position papers on the key negotiations issues had been prepared.[50]

One of the great mistakes of the war, Johnson later called the bombing pause. He had allowed himself to be talked into something he had always known wouldn't work. Wouldn't work in what way? Washington had made no serious preparations for negotiations because the only question to discuss was South Vietnam. Johnson had allowed himself to be convinced against his best instincts that the pause could work to alleviate pressure from war critics, hence his complaints about Hanoi's deceptions were an integral part of the original rationale. What really angered LBJ was his allowing himself to fall in with the self-deceptions of the Bundy-McNamara arguments for the pause. He had sensed from the beginning that hawks would never forgive him for suspending the bombing and that doves would never forgive him for resuming it.

As soon as the resumption was announced, the president rushed forward with plans for a summit conference with South Vietnamese leaders Ky and Thieu in Honolulu. The theme of this meeting was the launching of the "other war." "The struggle in your country," LBJ lectured them, "can finally be won only if you are able to bring about a social revolution for your people—while at the same time your soldiers and ours are beating back the aggressor."[51] The president then described what he wanted done in the next three months, the next six months, and so on. He would send them the experts to tell them how to accomplish the social revolution, and the money to make the wheels turn.

Dean Rusk accompanied the president to Hawaii, where he posited his most likely scenario for an end to the war. In all the cold war confrontations, he reassured Johnson and the South Vietnamese, from Iran through Korea, the Russians had backed off. There could come a moment when the Viet Cong position and Hanoi's position began to unravel very fast.

> At some point, if things go well, if we keep the pressure on, on the military side, and it is clear that you and your people are moving to build the kind of society which is indestructible, as you put it, that decision could come sooner rather than later.[52]

Rusk's imperturbable confidence in his own exegesis of past cold war crises stood him in good stead when he had to face the penetrating questions put to him by the Senate Foreign Relations Committee during two days of televised hearings. Lyndon Johnson was not nearly so confident everything would turn out the way his secretary of state predicted. At Hawaii, General Westmoreland observed a changed president, despite all the displays of confidence in the "other war." He "seemed intense, perturbed, uncertain how to proceed," recalled the general. How long would the war last? he kept asking. "General," Johnson leaned toward him, "I have a lot riding on you."[53]

For Lyndon Johnson the war was a contract he couldn't escape. And he bitterly resented never having had a say in its making. Or so he complained to historian Henry Graff after the bombing was resumed. "I didn't make this contract, SEATO," he lectured Graff in a rambling harangue. "Eisenhower told Kennedy, 'Vietnam and Laos will be your biggest problems.' After Kennedy became president, people began to say, 'Whatever happened to Lyndon?' I was the number two man, of course, but the real number two man was Bobby Kennedy." Lest the historian somehow miss this point, LBJ put it again. " 'It was President Kennedy'—the meaning being Kennedy-without-Johnson—'who said, "We're here till we win." ' "[54]

Graff was also the recipient of a lecture on how Senator Fulbright had acquired a taste for appeasement while studying at Oxford University before the war, and had not abandoned his racist inclinations while serving in the Senate. Both these traits, Johnson claimed, now showed up in Fulbright's criticism of the war. Anything the president could do to cast doubts on the hearings Fulbright had scheduled in the wake of the bombing resumption, he would do. Nothing like these hearings, which began at the end of January 1966 and continued through the middle of February, had ever occurred during the cold war.

No chair of the committee had challenged the White House's version of events as Fulbright and others now did—at least not in public hearings. Johnson had tried to drive Fulbright off the front page by dramatically summoning Ky and Thieu to Honolulu, but the breach was out in the open. The damage was done, and not undoable. Everyone could see that the policymaking consensus handed down from the time of the Truman Doctrine was broken wide open.

Fulbright had seized upon a minor matter—a supplemental request attached to the foreign aid bill to provide South Vietnam with an additional $275 million in economic aid—to use as his lever to force open a debate. Dean Rusk was slated to appear as the opening witness. The secretary seemed as calm as Sir Thomas More confronting an errant Henry VIII. The American commitment to protect South Vietnam from "Communist aggression," he implied in his opening statement, was no mere legal obligation. It was a pledge that involved the validity of the American Revolution itself. It was beyond debating. Fulbright was not dissuaded from pressing on: "I need not tell you that many of us are deeply troubled. . . . Could you tell us very briefly, when did we first become involved in Vietnam?"[55]

"Very briefly" went on, back and forth between Rusk and Fulbright, for the next several minutes. The secretary of state kept insisting this was not the first time Congress had explored the Vietnam issue, trying to get across the point that commitments had been made, as it were, in open court, and what was now happening was a somewhat petulant response to admittedly unpleasant developments—understandable, perhaps, but not, in the end, worthy of the American people. "It seems to me, sir," Rusk addressed one of the waverers, "that we have to reflect upon how one builds a peace. Do we build it by standing aside when aggression occurs, or do we build it by meeting our commitments?" [56]

The issue was drawn in its most dramatic form in an exchange between Senator Frank Church and Rusk. Church began by saying that he interpreted the secretary's explanations of the origins of the war to mean that whenever a revolution occurred against an established government, and was infiltrated, as most doubtlessly would be, by Communists, the United States would intervene to prevent a Communist success. Rusk objected to such a characterization. "We are stimulating, ourselves, very sweeping revolutions in a good many places," he said, for example the Alliance for Progress. Those were changes sought without violence, Church replied, but did the secretary believe that American foreign aid programs could avert violent changes in poor countries in future years?

SECRETARY RUSK. Not necessarily avert all of them, but I do believe there is a fundamental difference between the kind of revolution which the Communists call their wars of national liberation, and the kind of revolution which is congenial to our own experience, and fits into the aspirations of ordinary men and women right around the world.

There is nothing liberal about that revolution that they are trying to push from Peiping. This is a harsh, totalitarian regime. It has nothing in common with the great American revolutionary tradition, nothing in common with it.

SENATOR CHURCH. The objectives of Communist revolutions are clearly very different indeed from the earlier objectives of our own. But objectives of revolutions have varied through the centuries. . . .

Now, the distinction you draw between the Communist type of guerrilla war and other kinds of revolution, if I have understood it correctly, has been based upon the premise that in Vietnam the North Vietnamese have been meddling in the revolution in the south and, therefore, it is a form of aggression on the part of the north against the south.

But I cannot remember many revolutions that have been fought in splendid isolation. There were as many Frenchmen at Yorktown when Cornwallis surrendered as there were American Continentals. [57]

Rusk had another chance to take up the issue in response to a question from Senator Albert Gore. "I think that the doctrine of an unlimited world revolution by militant means is a doctrine that is so incompatible with the peace of the world and the system of international society that we are trying to build on the United Nations Charter, that is certainly one of the largest questions, if not the largest question."⁵⁸ The assault upon world order was at the heart of cold war beliefs, and there Rusk rested his case. And it was right there as well that his congressional critics found American policy in Vietnam least effective, and, for some, least credible. Retired General James Gavin, for example, won wide praise for his testimony in favor of an "enclave" strategy in Vietnam, and for his warning about the dangers of overextension.

> What we are doing is terribly important, but I have the feeling that it is time that we stop and take a look at where we are, in terms of our total global commitments, and realize that if we are going to really do well in this confrontation in the long run, we had better be restrained and wise in what we do in South Vietnam.⁵⁹

Critical as he was of overextension, Gavin's testimony did not really challenge Rusk's premise that the war exemplified an assault via world revolution on the entire structure of the "Free World" and the network of alliance systems the U.S. had created to bind it together. The fate of Vietnam itself was only incidental to such enormous questions. General Gavin might decry the loss of a sense of proportion, and recommend a means for returning things to balance by abandoning the countryside to the enemy, but he could not abandon belief in "this confrontation in the long run."

Neither could the "author" of the containment doctrine, George Frost Kennan, who testified after General Gavin in support of the enclave strategy. "No one is more unhappy than I about our government's present involvement," Kennan wrote privately, a few days before his appearance, to the editor of *Foreign Affairs*, Hamilton Fish Armstrong. This was the journal where his famous containment article, "The Sources of Soviet Conduct," had been published in 1947.⁶⁰ Ever since, Kennan had been engaged in a long reevaluation of both the Russian situation after Stalin's death and the wisdom of the globalization of containment.

How difficult was Kennan's journey became apparent during the hearings when conservative Democrat Frank Lausche took him back over his career as the original theorist who described the ideological basis for Soviet foreign policy and forcefully advocated a containment policy until that ideology, and with it Soviet power, either mellowed or collapsed internally.⁶¹

> SENATOR LAUSCHE. Ambassador Kennan, it has been said frequently that you were the designer and architect of the policy of the United States that we cannot suffer the expansion of communism, and, therefore, there must be adopted a plan of containment. Were you a participant in the design of that plan?

MR. KENNAN. Senator Lausche, I bear a certain amount of guilt for the currency this word "containment" has acquired in this country. I published an article, an anonymous article, in 1947, written actually in 1946, in which this word was used, and the article got much more publicity than I thought it would get. It is true that in this sense I am guilty of the authorship, or at least of the use, of this word with regard to our policy toward the Soviet Union.

SENATOR LAUSCHE. Right.

Isn't it a fact that when this policy was announced, it was predicated upon the belief that the security of our country required that there be a stoppage of the aggressive advancement of communism into areas of the world other than those in which it was already prevalent?

MR. KENNAN. Yes, sir. At that time—

SENATOR LAUSCHE. If that is so, has your view changed then?

MR. KENNAN. No, the situation has changed. There was at that time—

SENATOR LAUSCHE. Well, if there has been a change in the situation, has your view changed in that it would now be within, let's say, the general security of our country to permit an expansion of Communist aggression?

MR. KENNAN. It would certainly not be in our interests to encourage it. But I did not mean to convey, in the article I wrote at that time, the belief that we could necessarily stop communism at every point on the world's surface. There were things I failed to say, I must admit, in that article, which should have been said, and one of them was that certain areas of the world are more important than others; that one had to concentrate on the areas that were vital to us.

But in addition to this, I must point out that at that time there was only one center of Communist power, and it was to this that I was addressing myself.

Today there is more than one, and that makes a great deal of difference.

SENATOR LAUSCHE. Right.

There is now more than one, and with that I agree. But the nation included now is Red China, and Red China does not believe in peaceful coexistence, but urges the expansion of communism by whatever means are necessary. Do you agree with that?

MR. KENNAN. I agree with that.

SENATOR LAUSCHE. The split between Red China and Russia has come about because Khrushchev believed in peaceful coexistence, thinking that by ideological combat, communism would be triumphant, but the Chinese did not subscribe to that theory. Is that correct?

MR. KENNAN. I think this could stand as an explanation of one of the reasons for the Russian-Chinese conflict, but by no means all of them.

SENATOR LAUSCHE. All right.

If China is the real aggressor now, doesn't the policy of containment become more demandable than it was when you announced it back 20 years ago?

MR. KENNAN. Senator Lausche, the policy of containment certainly has relevance to China, but it is a question of what and where and what lies within our resources. If we had been able, without exorbitant cost in American manpower and resources and in the attention of our Government, in the emphasis of our foreign policy, if we had been able to do better in Vietnam I would have been delighted, and I would have thought that the effort was warranted.

SENATOR LAUSCHE. That brings us down to this plateau. Do you advocate pulling out of Vietnam?

MR. KENNAN. If by that you mean an immediate and sudden and unilateral withdrawal without any sort of a political arrangement and simply permitting to happen what will in that area, I do not advocate it.

SENATOR LAUSCHE. Under present conditions, you would not advocate pulling out. Would you advocate allowing the people of South Vietnam by open, free elections—supervised either by the United Nations or by an international body authorized to hold elections—to determine whether they want a Communist government or a government leaning to the free world?

MR. KENNAN. I think it would be very fine if one could have such a test of opinion, but I doubt that it would be possible in the conditions that prevail today.

SENATOR LAUSCHE. Who stands in the way of it? Does the United States or Red China or Hanoi? Who stands in the way of it? Are not the President and the United States urging that course?

MR. KENNAN. Senator, it seems to me that the whole situation stands in the way of it. You could not have such an election in a civil war situation.

SENATOR LAUSCHE. All right, if that is your answer, I ask you: Have not the U.S. Government and the people of the United States probed every avenue through which there could be discussion toward reaching a settlement, and has there not been constant rebuttal of those efforts by China and by Hanoi?

MR. KENNAN. It is correct that we have gotten nowhere.

SENATOR LAUSCHE. All right. Who is to blame if that is the effect?

SENATOR GORE. He didn't complete his answer.

SENATOR LAUSCHE. But he says that it is so—that we have tried. Who is to be blamed? Is it our Government or is it the Chinese and the North Vietnamese?

MR. KENNAN. Perhaps the reasons go deeper than a mere question of blame on either side. Obviously, it seems to me, the other side have much more blame for this than we have.

SENATOR LAUSCHE. Our Government has stopped bombing, it has stopped fighting. Can you point out a single act on the part of the North Vietnamese and Hanoi, which collaborated with this policy of stopping activities—point out one act of the North Vietnamese and Red China where they have tried to help toward bringing the subject to the negotiating table?

MR. KENNAN. They have shown to my knowledge no interest whatsoever in negotiations at this time.

I must say that I did not expect that they would, and I believe that I said in the article which was written at the end of November, before this bombing pause was announced, that I saw no interest on their side in negotiations and did not think that in the immediate future they would be interested.

SENATOR LAUSCHE. All right.

In addition to what the President has done, what would you propose that we do now to bring this to a settlement without damage to our prestige and without danger to our security. What would you propose?

MR. KENNAN. I would propose that we limit our aims and our military commitment in this area, that we decide what we can safely hold in that region with due regard to the security of our forces, that we dig in, and wait and see whether possibilities for a solution do not open up. I am fully prepared to agree that I do not see the possibilities for a peaceful solution today. But I have seen too many international situations in which they were visible at another time if one showed a little patience and had a reasonably strong position.

SENATOR LAUSCHE. There are many, many people who believe that this is exactly what our Nation is trying to do—the recommendation that you have just made.

You don't propose pulling out precipitously, then.

MR. KENNAN. That is correct, Senator.

SENATOR LAUSCHE. If we do pull out—let's assume that we were determined to—would that be the end of our troubles, or would we be confronted with new troubles in Thailand and Burma and Malaysia and Indonesia and other places?

MR. KENNAN. I think it is likely that we would certainly be confronted with new troubles because this is a very troubled part of the world and conditions there generally are not favorable from our standpoint.

SENATOR LAUSCHE. In other words, the desire of the Communists would not come to an end after a surrender of South Vietnam?

MR. KENNAN. Certainly not their desire, but I think, Senator, that when one speaks of the Communists these days, if it is to be meaningful, one really has to be specific, and state exactly which Communist regime one is talking about.

SENATOR LAUSCHE. I understand that. There is supposed to be the beneficent Communist Tito, and the torturous and brutal Communists in Red China—but we are dealing now with Red China, and the question is, What do we do there? I want to advocate pulling out, but I can't bring myself to that conclusion—and you agree with me.

MR. KENNAN. Yes, I think I have indicated my position here.

SENATOR LAUSCHE. You did, in your paper today, point out the misdeeds of Hanoi and the Vietcong. I appreciate that very much. I think it is wrong to leave the image throughout the world that the Communists have been gentle in this matter, and that we have been the brutal perpetrators. That is not the fact. We tried with all our might to go to the point—in my judgment, practically on the border—of appeasement.

What is the alternative, if you have one, to the course which our Government is now following? I would like to explore the alternatives, and I know the people of the country would like to know.

Lausche had the best of the argument—at least when one granted, as Kennan did, the major premises. What, indeed, was his alternative? The author of the "X" article had tried his best to provide policymakers with a rationale for disengaging Vietnam from the category of needed "things"— and had failed, as the courtroom-style dialogue with the Ohio senator demonstrated. Perhaps for that reason it made the defense of the war against critics all the more determined. Writing privately to himself, for example, Mac Bundy's argument with what he called the "Lippmann Thesis" took on a brittle harshness seemingly at odds with his and McNamara's prepause musings. It was contended that the United States "didn't belong there," he noted at the outset, but for twenty years "we have been the dominant power" and had already accomplished a great deal. "The truth is that in Southeast Asia we are stronger than China. It is *not* the mass or imperialism of China which creates our problem. It is a particularly vicious and skillful form of attack upon all order that is not Communist." The casualties were terrible, but the "danger to one man's life, as such, is not a worthy guide." "If the basic questions of interest, right, and power are answered, the casualties and costs are to be accepted." As for the argument that France had tried and failed, Bundy was especially brutal: the truth was that France had been a failure on the world scene. "There has been no serious proof of French political effectiveness since 1919."[62]

George Ball had apparently undergone an even more profound transformation. Readily admitting to an interviewer that he had held out to the last against resumption of the bombing, the author of all those papers against escalation, going back to the days of the Gulf of Tonkin, declared, "As far as we are concerned today, we haven't got any options. . . . I am greatly concerned over the hand-wringing I see. . . . The one thing we have to do is to win this damned war."[63]

Ball's despair was genuine: "We haven't got any options." Clifford had been right: the pause came at the wrong time, whatever one thought about the tragedy of the involvement. Certainly after the pause, positions everywhere hardened. The New York "business community," it was reported by one of the Wise Men, Arthur Dean, was in a "complete and total state of confusion." "Rusk says we are fighting for a free and independent SVN and then others say we should have a coalition with the Communists. As Dean puts it, the President will be 'in real trouble' if he has to call for 200,000 more men and billions in outlays and then agrees to a coalition takeover and to get our Army out even before any elections. The thrust of Dean's interlocutors is 'why don't we get out now, if all we are going to have is elections which the Commies will win?' "[64]

Outside Congress other groups were calling for America to get out of Vietnam. The antiwar protests had not been quieted by the pause. As Clifford and others had predicted, Johnson gained no ground with the critics. He lost ground. One evening late in February, Clifford and Mac Bundy came to dinner at the White House. The discussion came around to letters from mothers of men serving in the war. "There's not a mother in the world who cares more about it than I do," Johnson said, "because I have two hundred thousand of them over there—and they think I am in charge, and if I am not, God help them—who the Hell is!"[65]

The pause over, it was back in the soldiers' hands. McNamara soon announced that thirty thousand more troops would be sent to Vietnam. The path ahead had become darker and more uncertain. For thirty-eight days Rolling Thunder operations had been suspended while American diplomats flew peace sorties instead, trying to convince both friendly countries and skeptics that the United States desired negotiations on a reasonable basis. Johnson had foreseen the outcome. "If we should stop for a while and Hanoi did nothing in return," he asked his advisers, "would we not have trouble resuming the bombing?" They assured him it was not a serious problem—and they could not have been more wrong. "As it turned out, of course," Johnson wrote in his memoirs, "we received little credit for stopping the bombing and heavy criticism for renewing it." [66]

Samplings of congressional opinion had revealed a majority in favor of more bombing, not less, and the decision to resume brought forth hawkish demands for using whatever it might take to blast Hanoi into submission. White House aides had recommended the "summit" in Hawaii as a way to slip out of this nutcracker. If the president went to Hawaii to meet with Prime Minister Ky and General Westmoreland, suggested Jack Valenti, he could regain the initiative. "Such a meeting could serve as a focal point for showing how bright the future for South Vietnam could be—and indeed a future for all of Southeast Asia." [67]

Valenti's upbeat suggestions belied his real feelings about what the future would bring. "Gloomily," he wrote about the discontents of this first winter of real war, "it was apparent that Vietnam was a fungus, slowly spreading its suffocating crust over the great plans of the president, both here and overseas. No matter what we turned our hands and minds to there was Vietnam, its contagion infecting everything that it touched, and it seemed to touch everything." [68]

FOURTEEN

Rostow Takes Over

WHEN VICE-PRESIDENT HUBERT HUMPHREY returned home from the special tour of Vietnam and Asia he had undertaken at President Johnson's behest after the Honolulu Conference, he had become a solid supporter of the war and eager to make converts. For Humphrey—as for others—the revelatory experience was not what he saw close up but what he now understood about the commitment's centrality to the inner core of cold war beliefs. Both political parties had shared in the construction of those beliefs, but the Democrats were in power and stood to lose the most if things finally collapsed. Furthermore, the ties that bound Democrats together as a national party were already dangerously strained to the breaking point by powerful forces pulling from right and left.[1]

In an unintended double entendre that perfectly illustrated the predicament, the always ebullient vice-president told his staff as they left Vietnam, "This just happens to be the place where we are caught."[2] The fighting in Vietnam was center stage today, he went on, but this was only "act one in a three-act play in which we all know what the plot is." The Communists thought they had written the final scene already, but they were in for a surprise. The Vietnam drama would change the world. This was the message that had to be gotten across to the intellectuals as well as to the public. Yes, mistakes had been made, but the biggest mistake of all, Humphrey admonished his half-skeptical staffers, had been to allow the *New York Times* "to box us in on Vietnam." If you argued details with critics under those conditions, you stayed boxed. "I do not want to look at fly specks," he groped for a different metaphor. "I want to show the big picture." Out there beyond Vietnam, all Asia looked to the United States for leadership to turn back the Chinese bid for hegemony. It was the old Communist pattern, he rambled on, and now there was the U.S.-backed "social revolutionary movement to uplift man." That was what the whole thing was about. Everyone must be allowed to see there were two wars being fought in Vietnam. "Must lift this whole thing out of the quagmire of Saigon. Must prove that we have to do it. We've been fighting Russia since 1945 in order to contain them. . . . Get this in the proper background—find an environment and then come to Vietnam. . . . The real message of Vietnam is that they are capable of performing a social revolution."[3]

At a luncheon for newspaper executives after his return, Humphrey simply brushed aside all questions about peace negotiations. "We're not the French, with all respect to that fine nation. We are not colonialists. We have no empire to save. We are not fighting against a whole people. We are fighting for the freedom of that people." Thus it was a waste of time to go on talking about how America got involved, and a dangerous heresy to entertain proposals for a coalition government in Saigon, for these came "right out of the book of Communist conquest." It was wrong, too, to believe that meeting the nation's obligations in Southeast Asia would force the administration to abandon its commitments to creating the Great Society. America would have both guns and butter—just as the president had promised. You could bet on it. He was even willing to wager, he told the editors and publishers, that Johnson would *not* ask for a tax increase to pay for it all![4]

As the commitment deepened, the dream demanded more. It could be no other way. The "Johnson Doctrine," Humphrey exclaimed, promised victory over social misery and a viable structure of peace, now truly linked in a global politics. It guaranteed nothing less than the full realization of the "dream of the Great Society in the great area of Asia, not just here at home."[5]

Thus did the Vietnam challenge stretch backward into early American visions conjured up by Thomas Paine, and reach forward to the far reaches of contemporary liberal imagination and ingenuity. It propelled Johnson ever faster along a narrow path fraught with dangers no cold war president had confronted. To intimidate his foes, the war critics, Johnson blandished public opinion polls showing high levels of support for escalating the war—"clobbering" the enemy with whatever it took to win. But the same polls also revealed steadily mounting disenchantment with the war itself. The key issue in LBJ's overall standing, moreover, was Vietnam. From South Carolina to California, the majority of respondents said they did not approve of the way he was handling the war, by a margin of about 53 percent to 47 percent. Bill Moyers reported this bad news to the president, along with pollster Lou Harris's conclusion that "the people are in a foul mood over Vietnam: there is no getting around that fact." Both Gallup and Harris also agreed, said Moyers, that the problem was "the isolated island in the middle on which the President is now standing, will shrink smaller and smaller."[6]

As that island shrank, moreover, so would public confidence in the legitimacy of liberal postulates about both the cold war and the Great Society. Secretary McNamara's efforts to launch a civil rights program from the Pentagon perfectly captured, if in an extreme example, the essence of the liberal promise. The first results were in, he explained to Johnson on March 2, 1966, of an experiment begun some months earlier. He had ordered changes in qualification standards for enlistment and induction. Approximately fifty thousand men "who would otherwise have been denied an opportunity to improve themselves and serve their country" had been enrolled. Indeed, the experiment, soon dubbed "Project 100,000," had proved so successful that further changes were being introduced to waive requirements on arithmetical and verbal tests—as long as the individual possessed acceptable aptitudes in two military occupational areas. "We will continue to search out still other revisions," McNamara promised, "in order to make military service available to a maximum number of young men in the 19 to 26 year old age group."[7]

Was it fear of allowing Lyndon Johnson to think about failure that produced such extravagant claims? Liberal loyalists were now, as Hubert Humphrey put it, "caught" in Mr. Johnson's War, and there was nothing for it but to construct images that would see them all through the dark passage to the other side. Self-protection and boosting the president's ego were related in complicated ways to a genuine concern for the nation's well-being. An isolated president feeling besieged was a dangerous situation in the nuclear age. "I can't trust anybody," LBJ burst out to an aide. "What are you trying to do to me? Everybody is trying to cut me down, destroy me."[8]

How much had changed from the days when courtiers made the king's mood their first duty? It is worth considering that *both* Johnson and his chief advisers were acting out a masquerade, each concerned not only to conceal his own doubts but *not* to discover the other's doubts. Certainly much otherwise unexplainable behavior can be accounted for in this fashion. However much he expatiated on great-day-a-comin' themes, for example, Vice-President Humphrey confessed in private that he would be happy with less. Gradually, he told aides, "this thing will stand. We'll steal out of the situation like Korea. We'll have a demarcation line, and that will be it."[9] When he stepped out of the helicopter on the White House lawn after his return from Asia, however, Humphrey proclaimed, "The tide of battle has turned in Vietnam in our favor."[10] A few days later he forwarded a "suggestion" to Johnson that, he wrote, merited the president's consideration. Social reform in Vietnam was the "real Achilles' heal [sic] of the Commie push." Eighty-five percent of the Vietnamese were landless tenants, yearning for their own plot of land. "Tell the President that he can cut the Gordian Knot by a stroke of history as significant as the Emancipation Proclamation by a massive land reform program." Take some of the dollars earmarked for a military buildup and buy up landlord rights and redistribute the land to peasants. "This would leave the Viet Cong without a cause and would provide an economic underpinning for a democratic government." [11]

Humphrey was not the first to draw LBJ's attention to the Lincoln parallel. It may have been Robert Kennedy. Writing to the president in early January 1966, the New York senator said he had been thinking of him while reading one of Bruce Catton's volumes on the Civil War. Catton had related how lonely Lincoln felt in the late spring of 1864:

> Of course the situation improved a few months later but it does show how terribly distressed even he must have been at times. Actually it was clear that the division within the North was much greater during various periods of time in that war though I recognize that there are not exact parallels and you face problems and situations that he did not have to meet.
>
> In closing let me say how impressed I have been with the recent efforts to find a peaceful solution to Vietnam. [12]

Kennedy's letter was apparently intended to give Johnson support against the generals who were clamoring to resume the bombing, yet it was curiously ambivalent, particularly as JFK's brother added that the president should not be discouraged about what "columnists and . . . my colleagues in Congress (including myself)" were saying about the war. [13] Thus Johnson could take it as support against war critics. And that was precisely what he did. The letter had arrived at an appropriate time, he wrote Bobby. "It was one of those hours when I felt alone, prayerfully alone." He read the suggested paragraphs in Catton's book and then went into the cabinet room to talk with congressional leaders. "I read them that passage where Lincoln told a friend that all of the responsibilities of the administration 'belong to that unhappy wretch called Abraham Lincoln.' I knew exactly how Lincoln felt." [14]

This exchange marked the last "friendly" words the two men had to say to each other on the subject of Vietnam. However cautiously, Kennedy was moving into the war critics' camp. In a statement on February 19, 1966, the senator had said that "to admit [the Viet Cong and other discontented elements] to a share of power and responsibility is at the heart of the hope for a negotiated settlement. . . ." [15] He later tried to climb down a bit from such an exposed limb, for he was certainly not yet a dove, but even the hint of an open defection by JFK's brother put new pressure on Johnson to escalate the promise that there would be not simply light but the "birth of a nation" at the end of the tunnel.

Having spent two days in Saigon, Humphrey believed he knew enough about coalitions with the Communists to nip RFK's apostasy before it infected other liberals. It would be like "putting a fox in the chicken coop," he asserted.[16] At one of Johnson's meetings with his advisers in late February, the acting national security adviser, Robert Komer, observed that Senator Kennedy's proposal had upset the "New York business community," which felt that "if we are going to spend $10 billion—let elections take place—and then bug out, then we ought to get out now."[17]

Heading into what he rightly expected would be the most difficult days of the war, Johnson had to choose a new national security adviser. McGeorge Bundy had departed to become head of the Ford Foundation. It was the first major "defection" from a member of the original Kennedy team—and no matter how many letters of support Mac sent to LBJ over the next months, his leaving just at the end of the bombing pause rankled.

Komer had hoped he would be the one to succeed Mac Bundy. Instead he got Vietnam and the "other war." As Komer recalled it, LBJ told him one day, "Bob, I'm going to put you in charge of the other war in Vietnam." ". . . What's the other war in Vietnam?" Komer replied. "I thought we only had one." "That's part of the problem," Johnson shot back. "I want to have a war that will build as well as destroy. So I want to put you in charge of a massive effort to do more for the people of Southern Vietnam, particularly the farmers in the rural areas, and your mandate will be a very extensive one. In fact I wrote it myself."[18]

Johnson's Baltimore offer—a $1 billion pledge to develop a Mekong River Valley system "to dwarf TVA"—had been stillborn. Hanoi had not responded to his appeal that North Vietnam join with the other states of Southeast Asia to exchange bombs for electric power plants and irrigation canals. The Asian Development Bank was off the ground, but the crisis in South Vietnam was a series of localized issues that authorities in Saigon preferred not to comprehend, let alone do anything about.

The urgency for getting on with the Vietnamese "social revolution" arose at this moment because of the stir caused by Robert Kennedy's sudden "call" for a coalition government in Saigon. But LBJ would have gone in this direction anyway. In late March he told congressional leaders, "You have to go back to the Civil War to find this public dissent." The "VC" were illegitimate claimants to power, he implied, just as the seceded Southern states had formed an unlawful regime. To treat them as a legitimate government "would disintegrate all that we have in Vietnam." But the Honolulu Conference had focused attention on the "other war." Now eyes had been opened to an ongoing major campaign dedicated "to ending poverty." "Newspapers in Saigon are full of comments on the social revolution going on in Vietnam."[19]

Two days after that, the president told his advisers of his plan to name a special assistant to head this "other war" in Vietnam, in other words, to take charge of the social revolution. This man would report directly to him or perhaps to the secretary of state. He hadn't decided finally on that point.

He was thrilled, Johnson said, to hear about the work being done by American marines on health, reconstruction, and schools. But he still needed someone special right in Washington to carry out plans for the peace. Leonard Marks, head of the USIA, said that money was now available to "get TV going in Vietnam." Johnson asked, "What about TV sets?" TV sets would have to be part of any social revolution. Perhaps the Japanese would help with plans to assemble TV sets in the country.[20]

But while Johnson discussed the problem of getting enough TV sets into Vietnam, the "social revolution" went off track again in Saigon. In early March 1966 Premier Ky tried to dismiss General Nguyen Chanh Thi, who was in charge of ARVN forces in the area near Saigon. Accused of scheming to overthrow the Ky regime and replace it with one that would eventually seek neutralization and "possibly federation" with the north, Thi was regarded as a dangerous man, not only in Saigon but in Washington as well. Even so, he was popular with some Americans who thought him the best of a mediocre lot. When Thi refused to accept his dismissal, a political movement suddenly rose up around his "cause," composed in the first instance of disaffected Buddhist groups happy to seize upon a new opportunity to demand radical changes.[21]

Washington was caught off guard by these events. McNamara reported Ky's move to oust Thi at a meeting on March 11, 1966, with a brief comment that he thought it would all turn out all right. CIA Director Richard Helms noted, however, that there had been demonstrations in Saigon by paratroopers loyal to General Thi. McNamara then acknowledged that the affair had left "some bad taste in mouths of our people." Puzzled, Johnson asked if "our people wanted him to leave?" "I do," McNamara affirmed. And former Ambassador Maxwell Taylor chimed in, "He's a bad character and good riddance."[22]

But there was not to be an early end to the protest marches, which soon spread to other South Vietnamese cities. Calling their organization the Struggle Movement, the dissidents enlisted Catholic leaders to march with them as they paraded through the streets of Saigon halting in front of the American Embassy. Stop the killing, the demonstrators demanded, raising banners that proclaimed, "Foreign Countries Have No Right to Set Up Military Bases on Vietnamese Land." If nothing else, the rally revealed that the Vietnamese "social revolution" might not be manageable on any terms except its own.[23]

One of the president's advisers, probably Jack Valenti, prepared an "eyes only" memorandum for Johnson arguing that the Ky government simply was not on a political footing to win the war. The Thi affair had seriously weakened the American-backed regime. It lacked popular support, could not risk elections especially in rural areas, and was totally unprepared to combat growing inflation. Instead of more troops, what was needed was a quest for negotiations. Put forward in cautious language so as not to arouse Johnson's ire at a disguised "coalition" proposal, the memorandum closed with a recommendation for the further study of a "covert approach to NVN or even to more moderate elements in contact with the VC. . . ."[24]

Johnson did seem to waver at this point. "We ought to preserve him if possible," he said of Ky, but at the same time there had to be some thinking about a fallback position—even getting out.[25] Jack Valenti tried his best to get the president to think about seizing the moment to call it halts, sending him several additional memos on the theme that it was impossible to force someone to be free. In one, he cautioned against both military and ideological escalation. Johnson's achievements would mark him as an all-time great president—unless a large-scale war ruined everything. "All that you strive for and believe in, and are accomplishing is in danger, as long as this war goes on. *If* there were a way out, some hint of the end with honor, I would believe it best to stay there till the bitter conclusion. But there is no reasonable hope."[26]

Oh yes there was, insisted Walt Rostow, who had succeeded to Bundy's post as national security adviser. He could see "a little light—only a little," but it was enough. If the Vietnamese could put their minds to the task of writing a civil constitution, he advised the president, "we will have passed a great turning point." Troubles aplenty remained, but the Communists would understand what agreement on a constitution would mean and the setback it represented for their hopes.[27]

Rostow had a whole stack of silver linings in his office. He would pluck one to fit the crisis of the moment. None held up very long. A much publicized constitution was written, but all the fanfare could not disguise who really ruled and the truth that the government existed only to fight the war. Any doubts on that score were put to rest by Ambassador Lodge's encouragement to Ky to use whatever methods he needed, including force and deceit, against the Buddhists and the so-called Struggle Movement. That it took nearly three months to put down the dissidents scarcely encouraged hope that the ruling junta would succeed in the ultimate struggle for control of South Vietnam.[28]

When Ky struck at the Buddhist stronghold in Danang, the American commander in the area, Marine General Lewis Walt, felt aggrieved and tried to rein in the Saigon operation. Walt came to Ky demanding to know why he had not been informed of the operation ahead of time. "In normal military operations, perhaps, General," Ky replied, "but not in this kind of operation. This is an internal problem—the people versus the government." After he had "quelled" the Buddhists, Ky explained later, he could get on with the business of government. Promises were made that elections would be held in the fall for a constituent assembly, supposedly the first step in restoring a civilian government.[29]

In Washington, General Earle Wheeler, chairman of the Joint Chiefs, pondered the meaning of the Buddhist revolt and its impact on support for the war. He was not optimistic. "I think I can feel the first gusts of the whirlwind," he warned General Westmoreland. It was a truly sickening situation, and no matter what Ky did from now on, the support of some Americans was "lost irretrievably . . . many people will never again believe that the effort and sacrifices are worthwhile."[30]

But Rostow repressed such gloomy thoughts. He had been thinking positively about what progress toward a civil constitution should mean for the American war effort, he explained to the president on April 5, 1966. *"Then will be the time to pour it on* and see if we can't force, in the months ahead, a resolution of the conflict. *The strain on our political and economic life and the strain on the South Vietnamese is all but intolerable."* On the diplomatic front, it would also be time to "begin to get word to the VC that their destiny is: to sit on the Hanoi delegation at the international conference; and to talk to Saigon about how to end the war and get back into the national life of South Vietnam."[31]

Publicly, and privately too, Walt Rostow was about as far from Robert Kennedy on the "coalition" question as it was possible to be. But what is one to make of this recommendation about talks between Saigon and the NLF, surely a recognition that the latter did indeed have a legitimate role to play? In an accompanying memo, Rostow went further than any previous administration figure in actually imagining a way out along a two-track line of negotiations, in which the Geneva Agreement powers would seek the restoration of the 1954 and 1962 accords, and an "internal negotiation" would take place between Saigon and the NLF to end the war "and create the conditions for absorbing the South Vietnamese now caught up in the VC insurrection into the life of the Country." *"The surfacing of a two-track policy is a delicate matter,"* Rostow confessed, for there was strong opinion against ever talking with the VC.[32]

Yet for all the apparent flexibility in these two documents, the second memo concluded with a prediction that the war would end only when Hanoi had had enough militarily, and when the lines between North Vietnam and the guerrillas had been effectively shut down. "There will probably still be some last-ditch VC to mop up; but, if other guerrilla wars carry any lesson, it is that when the organizational structure cracks, it cracks pretty well down the line."[33]

Rostow constantly stressed that Hanoi's only hope was the failure of American will. The will he worked on most was LBJ's self-image, which, like others, he now tried to fashion into a modern-day likeness of Lincoln. He worked harder at this than Hubert Humphrey or anyone else. In early June 1966 Rostow proposed that the president go to Notre Dame to deliver a short speech on the theme of reconciliation. "It would be, in effect, your Gettysburg Address of the Cold War." Johnson could draw back from the day-to-day struggles to underline that this was a time when three enormously complex processes of reconciliation were under way. There was the reconciliation of the races, the reconciliation of the religions, and the reconciliation of ideologies. Absorbed by superficial incidents that captured newspaper headlines, people needed to hear about these vastly more important tectonic shifts underlying global politics. He had a feeling, moreover, the new national security adviser wrote, that this was a moment of thought and reflection in Hanoi. The American buildup and Johnson's continued pledges "to see it through" must have impressed Communist leaders with the same thought.[34]

The president turned down the idea for a new Gettysburg Address, but Johnson was attuned to what Rostow had to say about Vietnam and most everything else. Some of the president's aides regarded the former MIT professor, who had once set himself the task of disproving Marx, to be a terrible influence in the White House. Rostow was, said one, "like Rasputin to a tsar under siege." George Ball, soon to resign out of a sense that nothing more could be done to halt the momentum leading to ever deeper involvement, saw Rostow playing to Johnson's weaker side, convincing him that he was indeed just like Lincoln in the Civil War—abused by everyone but triumphant in the end. "He spent a good deal of time," Ball bitterly recalled of Rostow, "creating a kind of fantasy for the president."[35]

But in fairness, the Lincolnization of LBJ was a group effort in which the president was an active participant. In early May, Johnson looked back over nearly three years and struck a Lincolnesque pose for the National Security Council. "We are committed and we will not be deterred. We must accept the fact that some will always oppose, dissent and criticize. We want results." And, referring to the recent Ky-Thi struggle, he approved what had been done. "It is acceptable that we referee some of the fights between General Ky and others in the Saigon government." Bob Komer was at this meeting, and Johnson turned to him for the first report on his survey of the strategic issues in the "other war." Komer was not shy about spelling out the issues. The American military effort, he asserted, had produced three harmful effects: anti-Americanism, rampant inflation, and neglect of the pacification program.[36]

Johnson's "Mr. Vietnam" assured the president that he and his aides could get things turned around in the political struggle, but he faced as many obstacles on the American side as in Saigon, where Ky seemed to have forgotten all about the pledges he made at the Honolulu meeting to initiate a "social revolution" while the war continued. Never shy, Komer pressed Ky to remove a few corrupt officials, to build more schools, to do all those things Johnson wanted done.

He never lost faith in the president's promise to take the Great Society to Vietnam, especially not in the prospects for pacification, but he knew the reports coming out of Vietnam, including those over his signature, usually bore little resemblance to reality. The galloping inflation problem, a direct result of the American buildup, threatened to undermine the military effort. "Sooner or later," Komer wrote privately, "the Vietnamese will get around to blaming the US presence for the disastrous rise in [the] cost of living."[37] At first the American way of waging war simply amazed the Vietnamese. "They stared at the great PX warehouses stocked full of appliances whose uses they could only guess at, and they wondered what kind of army this was that trailed such opulence with it."[38] It did not take long for the Vietnamese to figure out what to do with the appliances, and the cigarettes, whiskey, hair spray, and other consumer goods, as well as rifles, ammunition, helmets, flak jackets, and so forth. Instead of a smaller replica of the Great Society, American expenditures were fueling an "epic black market" that turned Saigon into a bazaar of stolen goods pilfered from PXs and warehouses.[39]

Efforts to extend aid to the villages produced, in turn, tiny replicas of the Saigon bazaar, particularly near American military outposts, where bar-brothels competed with beer and soft-drink stands for GI business. Too expensive for ARVN soldiers, these establishments thrived from noon to 5 p.m., because the countryside after dark still belonged to the enemy.[40] Bemused by these scenes, a reporter approached Komer with a cynical proposition. "The way we're squandering money here, we could probably buy off the Vietcong at five hundred dollars a head." "We've staffed it," he snapped back. "Twenty-five hundred dollars a head."[41]

Komer scarcely believed that was the solution, but he found himself confronting the basic contradiction on which both the "other war" and the military effort were foundering. As late as 1967, General Creighton Abrams was still calling the half-million American soldiers in Vietnam an "in-depth U.S. advisory network" that supplied the "glue" to hold things together at the local level. American commanders thus resisted the "colonial" notion that they establish a joint command with the Vietnamese. Komer replied to such arguments with total disdain. "Hell, with half a million men in Vietnam, we are spending twenty-one billion dollars a year, and we're fighting the whole war with the Vietnamese watching us; how can you talk about national sovereignty?"[42]

Robert McNamara was "boiling mad" when he heard about Komer's complaints. "I want you to run your war, not run my war," he shouted over the telephone. But then he calmed down. "You know, I recommended this once before, and they turned me down." McNamara's confused response to what he perceived as unfair criticism perfectly reflected the constraints that crippled the American military effort in Vietnam. These were not of the sort that postwar revisionist critics talked about. Neither McNamara nor

Lyndon Johnson, nor indeed some mythical dybbuk of embittered imagination, decreed that the United States would not be allowed to win the war.
Consider instead the tenuous logic (and its implications for strategic clarity)
of a war that prevented the administration from admitting anything but an
"advisory" role for U.S. forces. So while the North Vietnamese continued
to deny (for their ideological reasons) that their army was engaged in a
struggle against the Americans, U.S. spokesmen had an even worse time
avoiding the accusation that the South Vietnamese government was a puppet regime. The stated goal for both sides was a legitimate South Vietnamese government that could stand on its own—long enough, on the
North Vietnamese side, to carry out the reunification of Vietnam, long
enough, on the American side, to do what? The American pledge to withdraw its forces precluded the only possible "winning" strategy. "American
policy in Vietnam was called imperialistic," wrote Jonathan Schell in a ret-
rospective look at what happened. "But it is a strange, crippled sort of imperialism that foresees departing its colonial possession even before it has
seized it. At best, it is imperialism on the cheap, in which the colony is supposed, in a manner of speaking, to colonize itself."[43]

But the American military did not resist Komer's pleas only out of sensitivity to charges of "colonialism." In another revealing comment about
the logic of the American position, Maxwell Taylor would complain that
there had been altogether too much emphasis on the civil field before a
state of security had been reached. "We should have learned from our frontier forebears that there is little use planting corn outside the stockade if
there are still Indians around in the woods outside."[44]

While Komer soldiered on to try to break through such notions and
get the corn planted before the stockaders starved, the "other war" at home
became an issue of "Vietnam or Brownsville," as critics put it, decrying the
money supposedly being taken away from civil rights and antipoverty programs to pay for the war. The scene of these attacks, Johnson aide Harry
McPherson warned, was going to be the civil rights conference that the
president himself had called for a year earlier. And the assault was to be led
by New York Mayor John Lindsay, along with Senator Kennedy "and some
of the far-out Negro leaders. . . ." McPherson worried that they would succeed only in driving a wedge between the poor and the rest of the nation—
a standard response as noted earlier, based upon the high public support for
doing everything short of nuclear war to win in Vietnam. McPherson wanted Johnson to order Rusk and McNamara to talk about the reciprocal relationship between meeting commitments to social programs and meeting
international obligations.

> We should express our shock that some politicians are trying to drive a
> wedge between the poor and the rest of the country. . . . This is demean-
> ing to the poor. It suggests that they have no stake in maintaining free-

dom in the world. In the second place, the continued commitment of the nation to expensive social programs depends on our unity as a people. It can be destroyed by pitting the poor against the rest.[45]

Secretary McNamara was in Montreal at this very moment, delivering a speech to the American Society of Newspaper Editors. The core of his remarks had to do with the challenge of modernizing societies—a challenge that McNamara suggested came mainly from within those societies. His tenor was very different from the hard line Johnson was pushing, and he closed with a plea for taking risks in opening relationships with Communist China, the nation he had seen promoting Hanoi's aggression and outlaw behavior. He even pointed out that Communists had been involved in only 58 of the 150 serious insurgencies of recent years—at least an indirect contradiction of the notion that Vice-President Hubert Humphrey had used as the basis for American intervention in Vietnam since his return from the Asian tour. There were practical alternatives to current relationships, or nonrelationships, with Russia and China, McNamara said. And there were many ways to build bridges even to those countries that would cut themselves off from meaningful contacts with the United States.

> There are no one-cliff bridges. If you are going to span a chasm, you have to rest the structure on both cliffs.
>
> Now cliffs, generally speaking, are rather hazardous places. Some people are afraid even to look over the edge. But in a thermonuclear world, we cannot afford political acrophobia.[46]

McNamara went as far here as he would ever go publicly to hint at his growing disillusion with the policy of escalation in Vietnam: "Certainly we have no charter to rescue floundering regimes, who have brought violence on themselves by deliberately refusing to meet the legitimate expectations of their citizenry." The speech took everyone by surprise. Writers who had attacked McNamara for his lack of candor and cold body-count calculations to determine progress in the war now fell over themselves to praise this new public philosopher in the Pentagon. Johnson was furious. The Montreal speech not only upstaged his recent efforts to "clarify" the stakes in Vietnam, it set up a situation that made McNamara the reluctant warrior—a role the president had zealously kept for himself since the 1964 election campaign. There was the hint of Bobby Kennedy's influence floating in the air.[47]

To administration insiders, moreover, the Montreal speech identified McNamara as possibly a secret sympathizer with the doubters. What these cognoscenti knew that the columnists did not know was that a plan to extend the bombing to oil storage facilities around and near Hanoi and Haiphong had been under serious consideration since early that month. Averell Harriman had sent Secretary Rusk a memorandum on May 10 opposing such an extension of the bombing as harmful to the cause of any possible peace negotiations and damaging to world opinion. The arguments on the other side were the usual ones that the North Vietnamese had a breaking point, and the problem still was to convey to the Communist leadership that the United States was determined to find that point.

Harriman talked with McNamara a few days before the Montreal speech and repeated to the defense secretary what he had told Rusk. McNamara seemed to be of two minds. "He admitted that [the bombing extension] was a dramatic step and didn't argue against my position," Harriman noted down, "but did indicate that he felt it would create further difficulties for the North Vietnamese government." Two weeks later, after the Montreal speech, the two men spoke again about Vietnam, though not specifically about the proposed bombing strikes. This time McNamara gave Harriman "the impression that he didn't see any value in escalation," and said that "we should agree . . . to let the South Vietnamese decide their own future even if it meant a coalition government with the Viet Cong, which might or might not take over."[48]

When push came to shove in discussion of the planned attacks within the administration, however, McNamara came down firmly on the side of going ahead—despite UN Ambassador Arthur Goldberg's strong dissent, and despite knowledge that British Prime Minister Harold Wilson would formally dissociate himself from the new American bombing policy. Strikes on those storage targets and facilities had been opposed "by me for months," McNamara explained, but the situation had changed. The military importance of the targets could not be disputed, and now was the time to strike because the North Vietnamese were seeking to disperse their supplies. "Our guess," he said, is that the attacks would limit infiltration and cause concern among North Vietnamese troops in the south. But McNamara's ultimate reason appeared to be that the raids would exert political pressure on Hanoi's leaders. "This bombing program seems to be the least costly way to tell them of our serious intentions."[49]

And at another meeting five days later, McNamara found himself again in the old role of advocate trying to persuade a reluctant president to seize this opportunity to bring home American determination to save South Vietnam from Communist aggression. And there was Johnson, once again, closely questioning everyone in the room—each one nodding assent except for Goldberg and Ball. At one point, indeed, the president sounded as if he were speaking lines from an Elizabethan tragedy:

> People tell me what not to do, what I do wrong. I don't get any alternatives. What might I be asked next? Destroy industry, disregard human life? Suppose I say no, what else would you recommend?[50]

General Earle Wheeler, chairman of the Joint Chiefs, took the question literally. Mine Haiphong harbor, he said. Max Taylor agreed: press hard all the way. "Personally I would mine Haiphong at the same time and get the political flak over with."[51] That far the president would not go. The bombers flew north to attack the oil storage sites on June 29, 1966. When Johnson was shown the photographs of the raid he was ecstatic, remarking to Rostow that "them sons-of-bitches are finished now."[52] He was presumably much less happy about polls reported in the *Los Angeles Times* that same day showing him running behind Senator Robert Kennedy as the choice of California Democrats for their presidential nominee in 1968. The article accompanying the poll could not have made it any plainer: "Mr. Johnson's popularity has been declining steadily, according to nationwide polls, largely because of the situation in Vietnam."[53]

On June 30 Johnson traveled to Des Moines to speak at a Democratic dinner and ended by ad-libbing a war-rally type of answer to the polls. No man in an American uniform that he had ever met, he began, wanted to come home with his tail between his legs. Then he read off a roll call of former presidents, all the way back to Herbert Hoover, with whom he had counseled about foreign affairs. Eisenhower was the most important, of course, and he had been in communication with the World War II hero more than thirty times in twenty-six months, receiving the wisdom that Ike had offered from his years as a cadet at West Point all the way through his illustrious career.

> I called him and talked to him. I sent a general to see him. Then I put on my hat and went to his hospital room and talked to him for more than an hour before I issued the order that sent our men in to destroy the petroleum dumps near Hanoi and Haiphong.[54]

The president had a hidden asset, however, one great strength that he had seen on the faces of the people in Omaha earlier in the day, and now on the cheeks of people in Des Moines:

> Prosperous, yes. Healthy, yes. Happy, yes. Happy, God-fearing, freedom-loving people. Fight if they must, ready to negotiate if they can, but let no would-be conqueror ever doubt us. We shall persist, and America shall succeed.[55]

Other polls showed the apparently paradoxical impact the war was having on voters' opinions of Johnson. In Vermont, for example, seven of ten Americans favored the present course or doing more, but less than three of ten gave the president a favorable rating. The Quayle Organization conducted this poll, and it concluded that there would be no great defection in 1968 over Vietnam. "Those who wish to get out of Vietnam will have no place to go in 1968," predicted Quayle, "they are mainly Democrats and are more likely to line up behind the President on domestic issues than to vote for a Republican who will be as firm, if not firmer, on Vietnam." Johnson's efforts to mobilize the nation to stand firm in Vietnam were successful, then, but it did not like his way of conducting the fight.[56]

Harry McPherson took a vacation in late July and conducted his own poll of middle- and upper-middle-income Rhode Islanders and summer people. They were Republicans, for the most part, but not of the Goldwater stripe. One Wall Street lawyer surprised the White House aide by saying that the nervousness in the market was caused by the Vietnam War, because the longer it went on the more difficulty Johnson would have getting his domestic program through Congress. "Why should Wall Street care about a social welfare program?" McPherson asked. "Because," came the answer, "getting it through is an indication that the President controls Congress. We look on the President as our protector. He believes in the profit motive." McPherson reported to Bill Moyers that the Wall Street lawyer was shrewder, perhaps, than the others, but they were all well-informed, internationalist supporters of nearly every foreign policy initiative since World War II. "Their support is vital, and we don't have much of it right now."[57]

In August 1966 Johnson drew attention to the "Lincoln parallel" in somewhat odd fashion, again to comment on the polls. During a speech dedicating a new federally aided hospital in Ellenville, New York, and with Robert Kennedy sitting on the platform, the president quoted what the entertainer George Jessel had written him: "You may feel that you do not have the capacity or the great character that some of our other Presidents have had that have borne these burdens. . . . But you and Lincoln have one thing in common. You both had many problems, you both had dissents, you both had diversions, and you both had distractions and frustrations among your people. Remember that almost half of the people of the country were against Lincoln when he was so right in the war that was right. So be patient, be tolerant, be understanding." He had replied to Jessel, Johnson recounted, that all presidents want to do what is right—the problem came in determining what that was. Then he ended with an even stranger comment. He was going to campaign in the fall midterm elections, though his name was not on the ballot. "Some of you may wish you could retract what you have done, but I'm there until January 1969."[58]

At his next press conference Johnson was asked about the polls that showed Democrats would rather have Bobby Kennedy as their candidate in 1968. "Could you tell us, how do you explain this?" "No," said Johnson, "I don't have an explanation for it." "Are you surprised, sir?" There was no answer. Later in the press conference he was asked about the Communist argument that the United States military was building a permanent bastion in South Vietnam, and whether he believed, as others argued, that this was a factor in holding up negotiations. "Yes, I can understand their doubt. I have made it as clear as I know how to make it, that we do not intend to maintain any bases in South Vietnam or Thailand, that we have no desire to keep our men there." [59]

Later amplified in the "Manila Communiqué," Johnson's answer became central to several connected controversies. Ambassador Lodge, meanwhile, knew very well that back in the Oval Office a sorely pressed Lyndon Johnson anxiously awaited some word of "really smashing results." Lodge sent him a whole list of what these might be: to be able to drive securely from Camau in the south all the way to Quang Tri near the parallel, for example, would be a truly significant psychological victory. "But none of these things are just around the corner." Yet he was far from discouraged, for there was "something tremendously effective about sheer mass."

> On the fifth floor of this building, [the new American Embassy] I can see the port of Saigon, thick with shipping and in the green flat fields through which the Saigon River winds, I see more ships constantly making the sixty-mile trip to and from the open sea. . . . This is American mass, which none can produce as we can. [60]

Lodge's view from the fifth floor looked out on a supposed miracle of American "know-how," something, indeed, to match that great moment early in the cold war when the airlift broke the Berlin Blockade. But Vietnam in the 1960s was not Germany all over again; it never had been and never could be. Lodge continued to believe that American "mass" was the answer, nevertheless, despite the appearance in neighboring Cambodia of French President Charles de Gaulle, who, in barely diplomatic language, disavowed the U.S. effort. British Prime Minister Wilson had dissociated his country from the Hanoi-Haiphong air raids in Parliament, but de Gaulle's speech on September 1, 1966, before 100,000 at the sports stadium in Phnom Penh, hammered at Washington's every political justification for the war, and predicted that none of its military strategies would succeed:

> As France sees it, although it is unlikely that the American war machine will be crushed there, there is no likelihood that the people of Asia will submit to the law of a foreigner coming from the other side of the Pacific, whatever his intentions may be. [61]

The passage that particularly angered Lodge had to do with the origins of American involvement. "While your country succeeded in safeguarding body and soul because it remained the master of its own house," de Gaulle praised the Cambodians, "the political and military authority of the United States was seen . . . to take root in South Vietnam, and, simultaneously, the war rekindled there in the form of national resistance." [62] He's calling us the aggressor, an outraged Lodge cabled home. "The aggression here is crystal clear—as clear as was the German aggression against France in

1940." But Lodge promised to refrain from public comment. "I shall resist the temptation to attribute motives and to say that his statement is due to anti-Americanism or a desire to have us fail where they failed or to his extraordinary tendency to try to equate a nation of 40 million with a nation of 200 million."[63]

Lodge's comment "a desire to have us fail where they failed," highlighted the U.S. dilemma in trying to define its role in Vietnam. A large part of the rationale about why it could not lose in Vietnam, aside from the issue of "mass," was a flawed "syllogism" that American policymakers had constructed concerning the outcome of colonial wars. It went like this: The United States did not fight colonial wars; Vietnam was not a colonial war; therefore the United States would win.

At the end of September 1966 American officials thought they detected renewed interest in Moscow in finding a solution to what no one yet said out loud but many believed to be the case—that Vietnam had become a standoff. Low-level chatter with a Soviet official in London, Walt Rostow reported to Johnson, had posed "interesting" questions about "what are we offering the VC for the long pull if they stop their killing?" Rostow had been considering the question since becoming national security adviser. His first answer had been that the "former" VC should be allowed to resume their lives—on an individual basis—in South Vietnamese politics. He now suggested that an offer be made "to let them form a political party and run for office under the constitution, once the killing stops." But he stopped short of saying that they should be offered a place in the government beforehand.[64]

The "negotiations committee" of the State Department, under Averell Harriman's leadership, had come up with similar suggestions for a grant of amnesty to VC willing to lay down their arms. The trouble with any of these proposals was that they required getting Saigon to go along. Not only go along, but initiate the proposals themselves, so that they did not appear to be American mandates. Saigon's leverage over American decision-making had, somewhat paradoxically, grown as the Ky regime became more dependent upon the United States. When everything seemed to hinge on the survival of that government, the handling of such questions became tricky business.[65]

Johnson's advisers began to focus on the Manila meeting of those nations participating in the war, scheduled for mid-October, as a good time for Saigon to issue a new x-point declaration (the number decided upon was six) concerning its peace terms. An amnesty declaration could be postponed until after the conference, but it was especially important that the South Vietnamese, on their own, make a statement about American troop withdrawals. Among the factors here, of course, was the impact that a promise to bring the GIs home would have on November midterm elections in the

Unites States. But there was also what Russian Foreign Minister Andrei Gromyko had told the president during a White House tête-à-tête on October 10.

Gromyko had said that the Soviet Union was eager to promote an international détente but that it found aspects of American policy baffling. Johnson replied in kind that he found the Russian reaction to "keeping our commitment to South Vietnam" equally baffling. Then, upon Gromyko's invitation, Johnson asserted that he had made it plain as early as the Baltimore speech that "we were willing to withdraw from that area and give up a very important negotiating position provided there was self-determination for South Vietnam and that it was not overrun." Exactly what the president was getting at here is not easy to determine from the notes of the meeting. What negotiating position, for example? What form of self-determination, for another example?[66]

Gromyko picked up on these questions and pointed out that his government saw the American terms as essentially calling for Hanoi and the VC to surrender. He then insisted that an end to the bombing of North Vietnam would have to be the first step. The Soviet diplomat thought that ending the bombing should be coupled with a statement giving a definite timetable for the withdrawal of American forces. Johnson promised he would try to make that clear in his next public statement. At the end of the day the American understanding of Gromyko's position apparently was that the Russians were eager to help bring about negotiations and now had the influence in Hanoi to do so, provided the U.S. made a specific commitment to mutual withdrawal within a certain time period. Still, from what is available, it is hard to determine if wish-fulfillment played a large role in this conclusion.[67]

Harriman had another conversation with Secretary McNamara on the eve of the Gromyko visit to the White House, during which he pressed the Pentagon head about one of his favorite subjects. As always, he believed the key to getting negotiations started was to find a way to make it worthwhile for the Soviets to risk a showdown with China to become the "provider of largesse for Hanoi." Something had to be put into the hopper to induce such behavior on their part. Once Hanoi became more dependent on Moscow, things would begin to move in the right direction. And the best inducement Harriman could think of would be American guarantees that West Germany would not get atomic weapons, and completion of a nonproliferation treaty. McNamara was skeptical about such reasoning, even though he also favored such a treaty with Russia. Why couldn't the State Department open up direct channels of communication with Hanoi, he demanded? Harriman replied that there was no problem talking to Hanoi, it was what Washington said that closed them down. "We have nothing of any interest to Hanoi to tell them."[68]

McNamara left for Vietnam on the day Gromyko and Johnson met, to see for himself what the first full year of massive involvement had wrought. There was no question but that American forces had blunted the NLF/NVN military offensive, he reported to the president. Even allowing for possible exaggeration by local commanders, the enemy was suffering at a rate of more than sixty thousand deaths per year. "The infiltration routes would seem to be one-way trails to death for the North Vietnamese." But there were no signs of a break in enemy morale, and it appeared that he could go on replacing his losses indefinitely. His strategy now was to exhaust our national will. "He knows that we have not been, and he believes we probably will not be, able to translate our military successes into the 'end products'—broken enemy morale and political achievements by the GVN." [69]

Pacification was a disappointment. Faint signs that Ky and his people would eventually be able to develop a legitimate civil government were surely welcome, but they did not translate into political achievements at the province level or below. If anything, the situation had gone backward. "As compared with two, or four, years ago, enemy full-time regional forces and part-time guerrilla forces are larger; attacks, terrorism and sabotage have increased in scope and intensity; more railroads are closed and highways cut; the rice crop expected to come to market is smaller; we control little, if any, more of the population; the VC political structure thrives in most of the country, continuing to give the enemy his enormous intelligence advantage; full security exists nowhere (not even behind the US Marines' lines and in Saigon); in the countryside, the enemy almost completely controls the night." [70]

Following this gloomy recitation, the defense secretary had two major military recommendations: first, to place a limit on American forces at 470,000 (there were currently 325,000 in country, and the uniformed chiefs wanted 570,000); second, to spend a billion dollars to erect an electronic barrier near the 17th parallel, from the sea into Laos, to choke off infiltration. McNamara did not recommend a major increase in the bombing program and indeed argued for "terminating bombing in all of North Vietnam, or at least in the Northeast zones, for an indefinite period in connection with covert moves toward peace." [71]

The latter half of his memorandum suggested possible ways for getting a response to American offers of negotiations. These were introduced by a remarkable appeal for the need "to increase the credibility of our peace gestures in the minds of the enemy."

> Analyses of Communists' statements and actions indicate that they firmly believe that American leadership really does not want the fighting to stop, and that we are intent on winning a military victory in Vietnam and

on maintaining our presence there through a puppet regime supported by US military bases.[72]

For the first time McNamara revealed to Johnson the concerns he had been discussing privately with George Ball and Averell Harriman over several months. It was important, he said, to avoid any implication that American forces would stay in Vietnam or guarantee any particular outcome of a "solely Vietnamese struggle." Efforts should be made to contact the VC/NLF, in the first instance to see if sections could be split away from Hanoi. Then there had to be a plan to provide a role for the VC in "negotiations, post-war life, and government of the nation."[73]

McNamara's analysis and conclusions drew heavy fire from the Joint Chiefs. In their memorandum the military situation appeared very different: "Free World military forces have enjoyed an almost unbroken series of successes in combat." It was correct, however, to say that the enemy strategy was to "wait it out." The Communists expected to win the war in Washington, just as they won with France in Paris. "In this regard," began one of the many political assertions that gave the document its caustic tone, "the Joint Chiefs of Staff consider that there is reason for such expectations on the part of the communist leadership."

They argued old questions about the concept of "slowly increasing pressure," as against the "sharp knock" strategy they had wanted from the beginning. Yet even the "restricted air campaign" had been an unqualified success. "The demands of communist leaders and leftist sympathizers for cessation of bombing give strong indication of the impact the bombing is having on the North Vietnamese." The use here of the term "leftist sympathizers" again suggested that the real enemy was not in Vietnam at all. Decisions taken in the next sixty days, the JCS memorandum asserted ominously, could determine the war's outcome, and could therefore affect "the over-all security interests of the United States for years to come." Then came a peroration in which echoed all the many frustrations voiced in the halls and offices of the Pentagon:

> The frequent, broadly-based public offers made by the President to settle the war by peaceful means on a generous basis, which would take from NVN nothing it now has, have been admirable. Certainly, no one—American or foreigner—except those who are determined not to be convinced, can doubt the sincerity, the generosity, the altruism of US actions and objectives. In the opinion of the Joint Chiefs of Staff the time has come when further overt actions and offers on our part are not only nonproductive, they are counterproductive. A logical case can be made that the American people, our Allies, and our enemies alike are increasingly uncertain as to our resolution to pursue the war to a successful conclusion.[74]

At the forthcoming Manila Conference, therefore, the first order of business for the president should be to issue a statement "of his unswerving determination to carry on the war until NVN aggression against SVN shall cease."

As Johnson prepared to travel to Asia to rally support for American policies, he had before him, then, two very different assessments of the military situation and two very different recommendations about what his next steps should be. He also apparently had Gromyko's word that a specific statement of U.S. intention not to stay militarily in South Vietnam would help to create an atmosphere for negotiations.

The lead article in *Foreign Affairs* for October 1966 was by Vietnam expert Bernard Fall, whose voice commanded attention in all quarters. Fall began his piece with a discussion of the military situation since the battle of Ia Drang a year earlier. Quite clearly, he asserted, American intervention had prevented a Communist military victory—at least in the short run. What was the outlook now? The April issue of *Foreign Affairs* had carried the "official" position of the U.S. government on the origins of the war, written by CIA analyst George A. Carver. Carver had developed the argument that the "faceless" Viet Cong enjoyed no status outside the role of agents for the North Vietnamese regime. Such a conclusion spoke to the question of what would follow the present stalemate, and therefore to the dispute between McNamara and the Joint Chiefs. If Carver was right, forcing Hanoi to cease its support for the Viet Cong would mean a victory in something close to a traditional meaning of that word.

Fall thought American policymakers were being misled by their concentration on members of the NLF who also belonged to the Lao Dong, the North Vietnam–based Communist party. As for the origins of the NLF, Fall could cite an American government publication of May 1966 that at last stated candidly "what was a well-known fact all along—to wit, that some of the so-called 'political-religious' sects provided the hard core of the early opposition" to President Diem. Using arguments from World War II situations—for example, the relationship between the British clandestine services and the French Resistance—Fall pointed out that however much aid and guidance London's Special Operation Executive provided, the success of the resistance depended upon popular support. As for the contention that the "faceless" NLF had no leaders of stature, Fall had only to mention the rise from obscurity of General Ky among the conspirators against Diem to make his point that leaders of clandestine organizations are seldom well known to the outside world. Nothing justified Hanoi's claim that the NLF should be the "sole legitimate voice of the South Vietnamese people." But the idea that the NLF without Hanoi's full support would disappear like a desert mirage could not be sustained either. "It must be treated as what it is—a political force in South Viet Nam which cannot be simply blasted off the surface of the earth with B-52 saturation raids, or told to pack up and go into exile to North Viet Nam."[75]

On his way to Manila, Johnson stopped off in New Zealand and Australia. In public and private he sounded old themes and tried to play down the idea that the divisions at home amounted to much. Once again he renewed his Baltimore pledge that if North Vietnam would give up on this war it could not win, the United States would join with Hanoi in a struggle against ancient enemies, hunger and illiteracy.[76] Australian Prime Minister Harold Holt and his cabinet got the full LBJ treatment, including a recitation of how the president first came to realize during World War II that Asia really counted—something the Harvards still didn't understand. The newspapers he read were dominated by Europe. Every morning he got up feeling depressed. The reason was he saw all those "Phi Beta Kappas' commentary" about how we ought "to spend more money on European culture. . . . We ought to spend some of that money on saving lives in Asia."

Collective security had been developed in Europe, he rambled on, but it was a good idea in Asia too. The U.S. entered into all those treaties, and he took them seriously. As a matter of fact, whether you actually signed a treaty or not, any indication, "whether it be a wink of the eye or a nod of the head," committed you. We ought to say about SEATO, "you lick one of us, you have to take on the other six."

Then he really got going. He was disappointed about Harold Wilson's dissociating himself from SEATO over the bombing of Hanoi and Haiphong. "Maybe Wilson never got his copy of the treaty." The Soviets were trying hard to sell the idea that America was all alone in Vietnam—he was amazed at what an impact they had on the world with this line. "About two weeks before they make a move he can see their beginning . . . all over the world . . . over Washington . . . sometimes he thinks they have more influence in Washington than he has."

That was really why he was in Australia. He hadn't come to ask for a man or a dollar. Vietnam is dangerous. "And we want Prime Minister Holt to let the world know that he thinks it's dangerous . . . that this is your war . . . that these people are in your front yard." If the U.S. pulled out, Thailand would fall "in two weeks." "And [we] want you to remember the Chinese would be in Australia . . . would be in Canberra before they would be in San Francisco."

And on and on. "Both Asia and Australia [are] in the goldfish bowl. . . . I think the world is looking at you. . . . I know you've got some peace-niks in Australia—just as I have." They made headway because the media inflated their importance. "I really believe that they dominate two of the networks in the United States."

At the end of what had become a Johnson harangue against familiar

foes, Prime Minister Holt reminded the president that Australia had suffered half a million casualties in two world wars, from a nation of only seven
million. Australia was with you, he went on, but it was necessary to sustain
national growth. "So we have to ask ourselves how far can we go in devot-
ing our resources to Vietnam without stopping this economic growth." In
addition, he said, "we have a political problem." He was explaining the
opposition's attack on Australia's current involvement when Johnson interrupted to say he was perfectly satisfied with Holt's position. He just wanted
him to say it at length and publicly in Manila, "so that the world will know
that position without question and won't think it is just the United States
trying to dominate Asia." [77]

With Australian Labour party leaders, however, Johnson played up the
recent conversations with Gromyko. He felt a "bit more encouraged by
those talks than he was prepared to let on in public."

> First, the Russians appeared more confident of their position in the
> Communist world and of their leverage on Hanoi. Second, the Russians
> would not dispute our sincerity in searching for peace. They understood
> that a contract takes two to make and they are not prepared to say that
> Hanoi is stubborn and stupid; but they did say that it might help if we
> are a bit more explicit about our conditions and negotiations. [78]

The plan had been for Johnson's arrival in Manila to be a low-key
affair, so that he projected the image that the U.S. was just one of seven participants in this common struggle. But thousands of people gathered near
his hotel, and the old campaigner could not resist getting out of his sedan to
press the flesh. American aides watched the scene from the hotel's window,
and shrugged. Harry McPherson thought the plan was ludicrous anyway.
"Like Gulliver, just one of the boys on the beach," he quipped. [79]

The first night of the Manila Conference, protocol chief James
Symington trundled through the halls of the hotel with a cart filled with
gifts from Lyndon Johnson to the other heads of state. The principal gift
for each was the choice of a marble or bronze bust of the president himself.
He had brought two hundred of the busts to give away on this trip. Knocking on doors, Symington got "rather curious looks" from the intended
recipients, who finally caught on that they were to choose which likeness
they wanted. [80]

Johnson also presented two likenesses of himself at the Manila meeting, just as he had in discussions with the Australian politicians. In private
sessions with the various heads of state, the president stressed that he had
come to Manila to focus world attention on "unity" among the nations participating in the war—to make it clear that Hanoi could not win the war in
Washington as the Communists had won the first Indochina war in Paris.
He coached Prime Minister Ky on what he should tell the conference, what

an "enormous opportunity" he had with the whole world listening to his words.

The President's advice was this: lean as far away as you can from the "imperialist" Johnson, from the hard-liner Rusk, and that fellow with stars on his shoulders, Westmoreland. You just hold the Bible in your hand tomorrow. You be a man of good will; love your neighbor; but indicate, of course, that you will not take steps which tie your hands behind your back when they are still shooting.[81]

Johnson wanted Ky to deliver a speech that would do "all of us a great deal of good. . . ." He should "go into the causes of the war—Asian poverty—and to look forward beyond today to the long future of Vietnam and Asia." The president wanted to turn the spotlight of the world on the Asia of today, and tomorrow. "The President is prepared to do this, he said, because he sees the emergence of new leaders, new voices, new institutions, like the Asian Development Bank." "The President's last word was: Don't let the newspapermen divide us."[82]

Johnson wanted more from Ky than simply a great speech on Asia's future, however. He wanted agreement that the Manila Communiqué would contain a pledge that American forces would be withdrawn within six months of a North Vietnamese withdrawal. And he wanted Ky to initiate that offer! Johnson left the negotiations on these points to his aides. Indeed, he never mentioned the idea during his private conference with South Vietnam's leaders. Inside the American delegation, furthermore, there was a division between advocates of this idea (who actually preferred a three-months' pledge) and opponents who knew that not only the South Vietnamese but the Thai and South Korean delegates would object. Eventually something emerged from various drafting sessions that satisfied President Johnson's need to make it appear he had met one of Gromyko's key desiderata. The proposed paragraph would state that "allied" forces were in Vietnam at the request of that government in order to resist aggression. "They shall be withdrawn as the other side withdraws its forces to the North, ceases infiltration, and the level of violence thus subsides."[83] As the president hoped, newspapers did pick up on the "Manila Formula" as the big story out of the conference. "US and Allies Pledge to Leave South Vietnam Within 6 Months After Hanoi Abandons the War," read the *New York Times* headline on October 26.[84]

Leaving the Philippines, Johnson flew to Cam Ranh Bay in Vietnam to see the troops at a huge American supply base. After pinning decorations on several combat veterans, he delivered a highly emotional speech promising his full backing for the duration. A Far East specialist with the president's entourage wrote, "It was quite a day."

No one who was there will ever forget it. It stirred memories of Lincoln visiting the Army of the Potomac, and of Roosevelt in North Africa. Here was the Commander-in-Chief going to a war zone to visit with his men—giving them encouragement—drawing strength from their strength.[85]

At the officers' club, Johnson delivered an off-the-cuff remark that was remembered ever after. "I thank you, I salute you, may the good Lord look over you and keep you until you come home with the coonskin on the wall." And, in a remark the White House managed to cut out of a printed version of a tape prepared for broadcast at home, the president gasped something like, "Do you know that some of these men had just climbed out of their foxholes to be with me. . . ."[86]

Almost at once, criticisms of the Manila Formula caught up with the first headlines. To answer former Vice-President Richard Nixon's charge that the formula spelled disaster for South Vietnam, because it would leave Saigon unprotected against a resurgence of the subversion, Johnson's aides pointed to the clause in the sentence that began, "and the level of violence thus subsides." At a press conference on November 4 the president was asked about Nixon's criticism. It was Nixon's penchant, said Johnson, to find fault with his country during October every two years: "Why would we want to stay there if there was no aggression, if there was no infiltration and the violence ceased? We wouldn't want to stay there as tourists. We wouldn't want to keep 400,000 men there just to march up and down the runways at Cam Ranh Bay."[87]

No, Johnson had made no promise to keep American troops in Vietnam to march up and down the runways at Cam Ranh Bay—but he had now promised to stay until "the violence ceased." It was the most binding pledge of all. Vietnam had become Johnson's world. He had schemed before, during, and after the Manila Conference to write into the communiqué some kind of pledge to withdraw from Vietnam and still leave himself room for maneuver. Like so many other ploys, the effect was the reverse. In the process he had described to the Australians a Communist conspiracy to control major television networks, then, in a speech delivered in Korea, he had created a personal mythical past for his position by inventing the tale of a great-great grandfather who died fighting in the battle of the Alamo; and, finally, he had imagined a brilliant future for America in the new "Golden West." "They have the manpower, the resources—Indonesia and Southeast Asia have everything you need in the world. . . . This is the way of the future . . . unlimited resources untapped . . . two-thirds of the people . . ."[88]

The lilliputians at Manila humored Johnson. Then Gulliver helped them tie him up.

FIFTEEN

Winter of Discontents

BUOYED BY THE RECEPTION he had received throughout the Far East, President Johnson's spirits were high on the return flight home from the Manila Conference. He was especially delighted by the huge crowds that had turned out in Seoul, Korea. "My god," the president recalled the scene later for friends, "I've never seen so many people lining the streets." How many were there? he had asked President Chung Hee Park. Johnson loved to chuckle over what Park's interpreter told him: "President Park, he say population of Seoul is one million. People on the streets is one million. That's all the people we have. So solly."[1]

Maybe the "body count" in Vietnam was exaggerated, and maybe Park exaggerated too, but the stopover in Seoul got Lyndon's juices going. Too bad President Truman never had the opportunity to take his bows in Korea, a reporter quipped to Secretary of State Dean Rusk. "When are you going to have a show like this in Saigon?" someone else asked. "I don't know," came the reply, "it'll be a long haul; but we will, we will." As he turned to walk away, Rusk shook his finger, adding, "And off the record, someday there's going to be a Bay of Pigs Avenue in Havana, too!"[2]

"Looks like you got a good reception everywhere," his old friend Representative Wilbur Mills congratulated the president. "It was wonderful," replied Johnson, "and if we could ever get them where they had any modern means of production and with all that vast manpower it would be a hell of a market for us. Two out of every three people in the world live out there and they die at 40 and have a per capita income of less than $100 a year. . . . But they are making good progress and in some places it is very encouraging." Those Koreans, especially, they were real go-getters! But things looked pretty good generally. "We've got Gene Black out there and he was going country to country right after me," the president rambled on, "and we've got 31 nations in the Development Bank in Asia and they are all participating. . . ."[3]

Johnson later complained in his memoirs that this "whole exciting story of what was happening in Asia behind the shield of our commitment was largely neglected." Pointing to Asian Development Bank loans totaling over $150 million in 1968 and 1969, he argued that he had known from the outset that "our struggle there would make sense only if it were part of a larger constructive effort in Asia."[4]

Vice-President Hubert Humphrey, as usual, went the extra hyperbole. Vietnam stood in the line of Valley Forge and Yorktown and Dunkirk, he had told the embassy staff in Saigon—though Dunkirk hardly supported his point. Vietnam, he puffed on, would be "marked as the place where the family of man has gained the time it needed to finally break through to a new era of hope and human development and justice. . . . This is our great adventure—and a wonderful one it is!"

In Joseph Conrad's classic account of the European "adventure" in Africa, *Heart of Darkness*, the narrator Marlow comments, "What redeems it is the idea only. An idea at the back of it: not a sentimental pretense but an idea; and an unselfish belief in the idea—something you can set up, and bow down before, and offer a sacrifice to. . . ." Regional economic development was the "idea" that made all the terrible things about the war endurable—and necessary. "It isn't winning the war, it isn't the military operations that are closest to the President's mind," Clark Clifford explained to David Lilienthal. "It isn't even South Vietnam. It is a pattern for a kind of life that the people of all Southeast Asia can begin to enjoy that is at issue. So what the President wants is to make a *demonstration*, a demonstration in South Vietnam into which North Vietnam can be persuaded— later, and after difficult problems—can be persuaded to participate because they see it is good for them. . . . The President is prepared to stake *everything* on this vision of what we can help bring about in Southeast Asia."[6]

The president wanted the former TVA head to work with Bob Komer on plans for Vietnam's postwar reconstruction, but Lilienthal had to be assured the "other war" was not "just a cosmetic layer to cover the ugly side of military operations. . . ." "Dave," Johnson took up the wooing, "you give them some of that philosophy, that good TVA philosophy. . . . As much as you want."[7] Lilienthal had been interested in Southeast Asian development problems at least from 1961, but now the former TVA and Atomic Energy Commission chairman had to ponder whether, given attitudes about the war, he could recruit a first-rate staff to work on Vietnam's postwar economic problems. Komer tried to cheer him up: "We are just at the beginning, Dave. Anyway, there is no other place to go except up."[8]

Vietnam perplexed him—but he wanted the challenge. He felt something akin to the mixture of awe and dread, Lilienthal recorded in his diary, as when he first heard the secret facts about atomic weapons. It was a revealing passage. Once the "idea" caught hold of him, the war, nasty as it was, became something to be endured until Hanoi came around. "I have found more fear and timidity at my club in New York than I found in some of the villages that have been exposed to the ravages of attack by the Viet Cong," he reported after his "fact-finding" mission to Vietnam.[9]

Eugene Black also had positive things to say about his post-Manila swing through Southeast Asia. The countries he visited were taking steps to increase foreign investment, and they had "great expectations" for the Development Bank's leadership and what it could mean for economic life throughout the area. There were just a couple of concerns—for example, "The real possibility of misunderstanding and disappointment if we make too much of the $1 billion offer for Asian economic development." The Johns Hopkins pledge to commit $1 billion to the Mekong River project had been contingent on North Vietnamese willingness to participate in a regional plan, a reward for abandoning its efforts to "conquer" South Vietnam. But Johnson was stuck with it. And Congress, which still voted automatically to support the boys with more guns, had become balky about even a pat of butter to spread the ideals of the Great Society into Asia. Black suggested "we think of the offer as an order of magnitude of our intentions, rather than a firm promise for which we will in future be held accountable."[10]

Present accountability was Defense Secretary McNamara's assignment. At the president's first news conference after Manila, McNamara stood at Johnson's side to tell reporters that the scene in Vietnam had "changed dramatically" for the better since the dark days in 1965 when anti-Communist forces faced a potential disaster. "Now, having said this, I want to emphasize that we do face a stubborn enemy." Despite the enemy's heavy casualties—more than a thousand deaths a week, McNamara said— infiltration from the north continued, not only individuals but entire units. The enemy continued to send down these forces, but the victory he had expected was no longer within his grasp. What's more, with sufficient military power in the field to blunt these assaults, the South Vietnamese could now begin the vast reconstruction effort needed to recover from more than two decades of war. "And, finally," McNamara said, "the most vivid impression I brought back from South Vietnam, . . . is of the very high morale and very high effectiveness of all elements of the U.S. Armed Forces there." General Westmoreland had told him they were the best-armed and most efficient combat troops he had ever seen in uniform, with the highest morale to go along with their skills.[11]

Mulling things over after Manila, National Security Adviser Walt Rostow wanted to present Hanoi with a sort of "either . . . or" proposition. South Vietnam's reported progress toward establishing a viable state provided an argument for sending a direct message to Hanoi. The purpose, he said in a curious memorandum to the president, would be to solve a problem he suspected Hanoi's leaders had in figuring out how to get to the peace table. Probably the North Vietnamese still believed they could get better terms sometime in the future, he wrote, although that conviction might be waning. It might also be the case, however, that what kept Hanoi from accepting American terms was a concern about reprisals against Viet Cong guerrillas. After the recent rightist coup in Indonesia, there had been a slaughter of pro-Communist cadres. A guarantee against such a thing happening in Vietnam might be the way to break through to genuine peace negotiations. So far, all the North Vietnamese had been offered was an American withdrawal six months "after they are out and violence subsides, plus a free Viet Cong run at peaceful politics plus the promise of an ultimate plebiscite on unity under peaceful conditions plus economic assistance in reconstruction as part of Southeast Asia if they want it." Rostow had earlier suggested that a place would have to be found for the VC in the political life of South Vietnam as individuals. In this memorandum he advanced that offer to "a right to organize politically and to vote, but only after arms are laid down." The VC had already missed the elections for the constitutional assembly. If they wanted to establish a political base—after they laid down their arms—they had better move fast toward the peace negotiations.

Such an offer to participate in South Vietnamese politics might not be worth much, Rostow confessed, but Hanoi "could be concerned to save some face for their protégés and protect them from the reprisals that could come if they persist in violence once the game from the North is called off." [12] North Vietnam could save more face by accepting an American offer to join with South Vietnam, the NLF, and the United States in a four-part announcement the war was over. In fact, that was the "best facesaver they could have, with symmetrical movements promptly following." Why not test the validity of this concept, Rostow suggested, by a "direct U.S.-Hanoi gambit, with no intermediaries?"

In a bracketed paragraph, however, the proposed gambit was reduced to something like the ultimatum MacArthur had once sent to enemy commanders in Korea:

> [It may, incidentally, be important to communicate to them soon that we do not intend to let the war drag; that we plan to up the ante; and our present offers to them may not hold indefinitely.] [13]

MacArthur had lost his job for confronting the North Koreans with such an "either . . . or" proposition. Either they came to terms, the general had notified the North Korean commander, or his forces would annihilate them. Rostow's proposed warning was not quite so minatory, but neither was his confidence in the south's ability to eradicate the Viet Cong. And Bob McNamara, despite his most recent public affirmation that, yes, he really could see the light at the end of the tunnel, had even less confidence that there really was an "or" to go with Rostow's "either," however high the ante was raised. "Ho Chi Minh is a tough S.O.B.," he told his staff. "And he won't quit no matter how much bombing we do. I'm as tough as he is and I know I wouldn't quit no matter how painful the bombing."[14]

Averell Harriman was another doubter. Johnson had ordered him to go forth once again to take the message to world leaders who hadn't been at the Manila Conference. Tell them he wanted peace, he said. So Harriman went—and came back with *their* message for President Johnson. They appreciated hearing about the Manila Conference and American determination to limit the war's objectives, Johnson's envoy extraordinary reported, but in "almost every conversation" the question of a bombing suspension arose. It was commonly believed that peace talks could be gotten under way "if we would stop the bombing." Whatever his private thoughts, Harriman had dutifully responded that the bombing was "a military necessity" and stressed Johnson's well-known position that there must be a reciprocal action by Hanoi to deescalate the war.[15]

While these explanations helped to clarify the situation, Harriman added, there was no getting around "the fact that bombing was extremely unpopular among the people everywhere."

> I gained the impression that the favorable reaction from the Manila Conference would be dissipated if there was an evident escalation of the bombing. George Brown [British Foreign Secretary], who has done much to keep the Labor Party in line on Vietnam, stated flatly that any further escalation "might well lose you the support of all your friends in Europe like me who are trying to help."[16]

McNamara and Harriman agreed—when they met in private—that the president was deceiving himself by boasting about the importance of his post-Manila reception. McNamara related how he had recommended against certain targets the Joint Chiefs wanted to hit, only to have the president restore them himself. "The President had come back with the feeling that the world was with him, after associating with the Thais and Koreans who were warlike and wanted to finish up China, while we were at it," Harriman responded. Truth was, the world didn't agree. "Of course they don't," the defense secretary sighed. "The world doesn't agree with escalation."[17]

Harriman should tell the president what he was up against, said McNamara. If the war was not settled soon, he would be beaten in 1968. Johnson knew very well what he was up against. And so did Rostow, which accounts for the note of desperation in his memorandum proposing a direct approach to Hanoi. At the end of November, Senator Stuart Symington sent word to the president via Walt Rostow that he was "thinking of getting off the train soon."

> It looks to me that with the restraints on the use of airpower, we can't win.
>
> In 1968 Nixon will murder us. He will become the biggest dove of all times. There never has been a man in American public life that could turn so fast on a dime.[18]

Symington's threatened defection because of the "restraints on the use of airpower" perfectly illustrated the president's unhappy predicament. A former secretary of the air force under Harry Truman, Stu Symington represented all those who, while they would not go as far as General Curtis LeMay in advocating "bombing 'em back to the stone age," believed the U.S. had failed to use air power properly in Korea or now in Vietnam. From its formation in 1947 as a separate branch of the armed services, the air force had carried on a highly successful "public relations" campaign (equaled perhaps only by J. Edgar Hoover's FBI) to establish itself as the Defense Department's "first team." The trouble was, said it champions, the air force had never had a chance to prove what it could do because of political constraints and/or inadequate understanding of aerospace military doctrine.

In Korea there had been the infamous sanctuary across the Yalu River; now, it was argued, the air force was not being allowed to go after the "real" targets in North Vietnam. The July raids on North Vietnamese oil storage facilities had supposedly destroyed 70 percent of Hanoi's reserves, but despite Admiral U.S. Grant Sharp's predictions, neither the enemy's will nor his capacity to resupply his forces was much affected. By the end of the year the air force had flown over 355,000 tactical sorties and close to 4,300 raids by B-52 bombers. More than half a million tons of bombs had been dropped on all targets in Vietnam. Aerial interdiction efforts alone were now costing more than $250 million a month.[19]

Asked for an accounting by Congress, air force Chief of Staff General John P. McConnell testified in early 1967 that the bases and aircraft, the bomb tonnages and sorties, and the men were all "enormously impressive." Then he added, "It is so impressive as to make the question 'Why hasn't air power won the Vietnam war?' a natural one." In a sense, it had, he answered himself. "The effects of air power must be considered in terms of our national objectives." Such an answer gave McConnell's listeners on the Senate Armed Services Committee the opportunity, of course, to raise the issue Symington had put to Rostow. Something was out of kilter.[20]

From the outset of the cold war, thousands upon thousands of businessmen and community leaders had been invited to witness firepower demonstrations at locations like Eglin Air Force Base in Florida. First there might be a drive down the runway, past F-4s and F-100s, shimmering in the bright sunlight, as the buses proceeded to the grandstand. Then the show itself. While the audience watched, eyes shaded against the sun, the fighter-bombers would scream down to carry out their "mission" to destroy an "enemy outpost" with bombs and rockets and machine guns and napalm. Air power was a beguilingly attractive option because it promised to do more than just compensate for an enemy's manpower advantage, whether it be the Red Army in Europe, People's Republic of China "volunteers" in Korea, or Hanoi's PAVN infiltrators. Its theorists had reimagined the globe, mixing geopolitical theory with technological capability to win huge congressional appropriations year after year.[21]

If the war in Vietnam could not be won under present conditions, implied the air force chiefs, the place to look was at the civilians in the Pentagon who had failed the test of leadership. That Vietnam in no way resembled the Potemkin Village stage sets at Eglin Air Force Base eased none of the pressure from hawkish critics who demanded the Joint Chiefs be given full opportunity to demonstrate that a "sharp knock" could bring the North Vietnamese to the peace table. Such euphemistic phrases—"sharp knock" for massive bombing attacks on cities, or "birds" for nuclear-tipped missiles—often threatened to drive out clearheaded thinking (and often succeeded), but Johnson could not afford to lose the Symingtons if he was to retain control of a "centrist" majority in Congress, not simply to conduct the war but also to manage other foreign and domestic questions.

Lyndon Johnson had invited, indeed insisted upon, comparisons of his record with the accomplishments of FDR's New Deal—and let everyone then conclude what they might about how to get the liberal agenda adopted. But Vietnam mocked all his boasts. It even altered the significance of John Kennedy's martyrdom. No one was asking if JFK would have handled Vietnam as badly as he fumbled the New Frontier legislative program with Congress. Instead, Johnson now faced accusations on the left that he had betrayed liberalism, a charge that posited both Vietnam and LBJ as aberrations. Already there were assassination legends and tales of JFK's secret plan to end American involvement in Vietnam.

How much attention would these have stirred if the war had not hung like an albatross around Johnson's neck? As matters stood, however, it took very little to convince opponents of the war that the "accidental president," as muckraker Robert Sherrill called Johnson, had brought on this plague of evils.[22] Barbara Garson's bitter satire, *MacBird*, which portrayed LBJ as Macbeth and John Kennedy as the murdered Duncan, allowed New Yorkers to enjoy a risqué evening at a theater in Greenwich Village without associating themselves too closely with "radical" peace-marchers. Playwright Garson was hardly a Kennedy fan. She spared no one in *MacBird.* In her view they were all—Kennedy, Johnson, Congress—dedicated to spreading a Pox Americana around the world. Indeed, her witches' comments on MacBird's plummeting standing voiced a radical lament that Kennedy's death had allowed liberalism to get off the hook, shifting the blame from the "system" to LBJ:

> How true. MacBird's too easy to attack.
> By now he's scoffed and sneered at left and right.
> He's so despised it's fash'nable in fact
> To call him villain, tweak him by the nose
> Break with his party and jeer him in the press.[23]

Garson and radical leaders might lament that Kennedy's martyrdom got in the way of a conscious understanding of how rotten American society had become, but they too were no less fascinated by it all as a sort of political cognate to chaos theory in the natural sciences. Though immersed in an ideology that drew no distinctions between liberals and conservatives—or Kennedys and Johnsons—Todd Gitlin and his friends were nevertheless drawn to theories that cast Lee Harvey Oswald in an eponymous role of "lurker," a mysterious figure in a history being made "behind our backs." "Late at night, amid our sage analyses of political forces, the thought of lurkers would leap up, and we would muse about the havoc these apparently marginal men had wrought."[24]

A British observer, Louis Heren, recalled reporting that "a great drama was slowly unfolding, the like of which, perhaps, had not been seen since medieval times." Barbara Garson's *MacBird* was an especially cruel and irresponsible rendition of the feud between the Kennedy loyalists, now united behind Senator Robert Kennedy, and the increasingly beleaguered Johnson forces; but this contest between the two "American political princes" was unique in modern American politics. "It mesmerized Washington, where even the war was occasionally forgotten, though it was part of the drama."[25]

More than just part of the drama, however, for without Vietnam—and the implication that John Kennedy's death had changed American policy (or that Vietnam had changed Kennedy, which amounted to the same thing)—Robert Kennedy would not have been thought of as a serious rival to LBJ, except by diehard mourners for the lost kingdom of Camelot. For traditional liberals seeking to rescue their faith from the crushing coils of Vietnam, the effort to enshrine the Kennedy image became part of a necessary redemption process.

Johnson's predicament was obvious. From now on he would have to stress all the more JFK's commitment to protecting South Vietnam from the Communists in order to answer the criticisms that he had taken it upon himself to launch a major war. The more he did that, alas, the more he reduced whatever flexibility he had left for seeking peace negotiations. Little wonder he regarded Robert Kennedy's still hesitant criticisms with special bitterness. The one thing the president did not need during this period, if he was to think clearly about keeping the Kennedy "thing" separate from his reactions to Vietnam developments, was a new aide whose meat and drink was plots and counterplots. Yet that is precisely what he got when he brought to the White House as intellectual-in-residence Brandeis University Professor John Roche, a former chairman of the liberal Americans for Democratic Action (ADA). Neither Barbara Garson nor Louis Heren could have imagined a more fitting Iago than Roche. The new professor in the White House strode through the halls with chips permanently attached to both shoulders, and liked to think of himself as an Irish street-fighter without a single compunction about doing to others more than they could do to you. His major accomplishment in the West Wing was to nurture LBJ's paranoia about the Kennedys, applauding as it grew to ever higher levels of intensity. Reading his memos on infighting at ADA conventions, his responses to "out-of-line" war critics, and accounts of debates with reporters, Johnson could come to no other conclusion but that the antiwar protests were all orchestrated by an elitist corps of pseudointellectuals determined to drive him from the White House so that the Kennedys could return to power.[26]

On November 16, 1966, for example, Roche linked attacks on the Warren Commission report on the assassination (naming Oswald as the lone killer) to a "filthy campaign against the integrity of our society, the quality of our government, and the character of our President." "The Communists and their allies among the New Left and the alienated intellectuals," and the "Kennedy government-in-exile," were jointly responsible for this campaign "designed to erode the faith that Americans have in the integrity of their system . . . and to convince the average citizen that the moral fabric of American society is rotten from top to bottom." "I understand," Roche added, "that the Manchester book on President Kennedy—practically quoting Mrs. Kennedy—asserts that you dragged Kennedy to Dallas."[27]

With the serialization of excerpts from William Manchester's *The Death of a President*, questions began appearing in mainstream publications about Johnson's role before and after the shooting in Dallas. These surface disturbances betrayed the deeper, if often not clearly articulated, sense of things gone terribly wrong in Vietnam. LBJ had declined to talk with the author while the book was being researched, apparently expecting that anything he said would depict the Kennedy/Johnson relationship as terribly distant and lacking trust. He was not surprised when the book did. Here were his old enemies, the Harvards, once again plotting his downfall, seizing upon the idea of Johnson's "illegitimacy" to make an argument for Bobby's right of succession.[28]

Manchester's *cri de coeur* hit the White House like a torpedo amidships.

From every executive office came memos with recommendations about how to seal off the damage. But the impact put a permanent hole in the Johnson presidency, a breach that constantly had to be shored up to prevent further deterioration of LBJ's moral position.

The opening pages of *The Death of a President* did indeed make it seem that Lyndon Johnson had put Kennedy in the path of an assassin's bullet. Still worse, in a way, the trip to Dallas, as Manchester explained it, had become necessary because Lyndon Johnson no longer had any power base—and no political future unless Kennedy willed it so. "Some Congressmen had more influence," wrote the author. Feuding Texas Democrats had ignored LBJ's commands to unite for the sake of the party, and the vice-president had been forced to ask JFK for help even as rumors grew that he would not be on the ticket in 1964. "At 12:29 his career was at a low ebb. He sat sluggishly in the back seat of his convertible, insensitive to the cheers around him, seeking refuge in the blare of a dashboard radio. His prestige had come apart, and for the moment he had apparently abandoned hope of reassembling it. Then, sixty seconds later, the elected President and his lady lay in a welter of blood, and Lyndon Johnson was the leader of the nation."[29]

Those close to the Kennedys might not yet be ready to publish revised accounts of the fallen leader's attitude toward Vietnam, but the work of creating a usable past for a legend that would culminate in Oliver Stone's movie fantasy *JFK* had begun.[30] And John Roche was not the only Johnson aide to find Manchester's book deeply offensive. Bill Moyers, who did not see Kennedy plots behind every antiwar poster, wrote to Richard Goodwin, who had sent him the galley proofs to peruse, "You probably know my reaction before I tell you: that the book is permeated by a malignancy I find dishonest, disgraceful, and distorted. Its effect is to cheapen rather than clarify history."

Moyers urged a delay in publication for "many years to come," until time diminished the possibility of "undue injury to people who will suffer because Manchester became the victim of his own grief."[31] More than injury to individuals may have been at stake. *The Death of a President*, it could be argued, helped to put LBJ in a personal and political bind, and certainly made him more defensive about his Vietnam policy—especially where it touched at all on the Kennedy legend. On at least one occasion during the winter months of 1966–1967, he reacted to a possible "peace move" that involved Robert Kennedy as if he were being maneuvered into acknowledging he had committed grievous sins and errors.[32]

Needing to keep JFK's memory alive as the original author of *his* Vietnam policy, Johnson had to wait until retirement before evening the score on the legitimacy question. "Kennedy was trying to get Castro, but Castro got him first," Johnson then told a startled ABC newscaster, Howard K.

Smith. The Cuban leader had acted in retaliation for the "Murder Incorporated" the U.S. had been running in the Caribbean after the failure at the Bay of Pigs, he told others. Most Americans probably regarded Castro as a legitimate target in the cold war, so JFK's reputation did not immediately suffer much by the revelation. But if Havana was behind the killing, and it was done in retaliation, the insinuation that Johnson had lured JFK to Texas ceased to have any significance at all. What LBJ said in retirement did not suddenly come over him during a television interview. Questions about his "right" to the White House were something he brooded about during most of his presidency, certainly from the time of the Warren Commission report, and they led him in his frustration and resentment to hint at CIA schemes like Operation Mongoose, the code name for Castro assassination plots, to tie Kennedy to a darker side of America's cold war policy.[33]

Whatever one concludes about the impact of Manchester's book, there is no need to speculate about the hurt Bill Moyers's mid-December resignation caused Johnson. LBJ always regarded resignations as personal affronts, but coming when it did, and the way it was explained to Johnson by John Roche and others as something approximating desertion to the Kennedy camp, Moyers's leaving took on a sinister aspect. Robert Komer's carefully phrased aside to Lilienthal about Moyers's decision suggested there was a body-count tally of even greater significance to the White House than Pentagon casualty figures. "Yesterday was a bad time," Komer related. "Hit the boss hard; all of us. Bill is an extraordinarily intelligent man."[34]

People did speculate, of course, about why the president's "protégé" left, as Moyers was much more than a press secretary to Johnson. It proved that Johnson had become impossible to work for, said some, a view that Moyers himself may have encouraged through casual comments. "I thought I could make [Johnson] more like me," he was quoted once, "but I've found in the last several months that I'm becoming more like him; so I got out."[35]

Moyers was replaced by George Christian, Johnson's fourth press secretary in three years. Compared to his predecessor, Christian lacked nimbleness and never enjoyed the respect of the press corps at the White House. But after the post-Manila euphoria was gone, he had little good news to give out. By the end of December the White House was on the defensive again. On Christmas Day the first of fourteen news stories written from Hanoi by Harrison Salisbury, the assistant managing editor of the *New York Times*, began appearing on that newspaper's front page. The articles and accompanying photographs flatly contradicted Pentagon claims that American bombing had successfully avoided residential areas. Efforts to discredit Salisbury's contentions, or to turn his casualty figures around to show how *few* civilians had been killed during attacks on the Hanoi region, only made matters worse. The Defense Department's press secretary, Arthur Sylvester, tried to dismiss Salisbury as a sentimental softie, referring to him in a speech as "Harrison Appalsbury," and, in more inflammatory terms, to the *Times* as "The New Hanoi *Times.*" These efforts only widened the "credibility gap." Large numbers of citizens now began to wonder if the government had lied and was using terror tactics to win an otherwise unwinnable war.[36]

The real "news," as far as Salisbury was concerned, was not the shocking revelation that American bombs had fallen in civilian residential areas but the "message" he had received from North Vietnamese Premier Pham Van Dong. Salisbury believed the premier treated him as an official representative of the U.S. government, whose cover was his position at the *Times*, a conclusion that suggested to the reporter that Hanoi was not very up on developments in the United States. It was convenient for Salisbury to think that, because otherwise he could have found himself accused of encouraging Pham Van Dong to go around the American government to achieve peace talks.[37]

Throughout his interview with Pham Van Dong, Salisbury tried hard to get the premier to respond with a specific statement of what North Vietnam would do if the United States stopped the bombing. He phrased the question in a variety of ways, posing the issue not as a required "condition" but as an indication of goodwill. Once or twice during the conversation, Pham paused as if about to say something specific, but his response always ended up as a generality. If the United States halted the air attacks, he said, "as far as we are concerned we will take an appropriate stand." Salisbury found it encouraging, nevertheless, that the North Vietnamese would not allow him to include even such vague promises in his story about the interview. As he saw it, the hidden meaning behind Pham Van Dong's cautious behavior was a genuine concern about Chinese disapproval of a North Vietnamese move toward peace.[38]

Salisbury gave Secretary Rusk a full typescript account of his interview with the North Vietnamese premier on Friday afternoon, January 13, along with his conclusion that Pham had signaled a willingness to commence peace talks without conditions—once the bombing stopped. Unwittingly, Salisbury had phrased his inquiries about a possible Hanoi response to a bombing halt in much the same fashion as administration policy planners would soon do in what would be called the "A"-then-"B" scheme. The idea was that to spare Hanoi a "loss of face," Washington would not set "condition(s)" for a bombing halt (A); instead the North's reciprocal gesture of halting infiltration and resupply of its forces (B) would simply become evident, to be followed eventually by the beginnings of an American withdrawal. The real sticking point, as in the internal debate over the Manila Communiqué, remained the question of what happened then? Salisbury had told Pham Van Dong that he "thought such a move [a reciprocal gesture] would have tremendous potential for the success of negotiation and bringing about an end of the war and quite frankly for achieving their objectives."[39]

That was precisely what Dean Rusk and other administration policy-makers feared. At a meeting on December 1, several second-level planners had discussed a paper entitled, "A Package Deal for Hanoi." One commented that the paper assumed that substantial American forces would remain for as long as it took to work out a final settlement. It also assumed that Ky would remain in power all that time. Hanoi would hardly go along with what that implied, he said. Bill Bundy objected, on the other hand, to the assumption in the paper that the elections would occur before the VC were disarmed and with the areas under their control still intact. Saigon could not be expected to accept those terms. Discussion then ranged over all the complications of trying to arrive at something that could be sold to both sides. It was like trying to square the circle, said Bundy. "The present government in Saigon would never buy this package even if Hanoi would." The best bet was to continue to encourage the evolution of representative government in the south, and thus to open up new possibilities for a settlement, presumably along the lines of Rostow's memo to the president about guaranteeing the NLF a chance to "participate in the process if they were willing to give up their attempt to seize power by violence."[40]

What came out of the December 1 discussion was the futility of trying even to discuss an American negotiating package, at least for the immediate future. When Salisbury said he believed the North Vietnamese were ready for negotiations, therefore, Rusk's response was to reargue previous American positions. The reporter was puzzled about this "odd circumstance." "The Secretary, whom I've known for many, many years," he told an interviewer, "seemed to feel that this should be a debate between him and me. He kept sort of making speeches about various things, which I didn't answer because I was not interested in debating . . . our Vietnam policy. I was trying to deliver my impressions and the message, because it was very important for him to know this."[41]

Rusk's report to the president about his conversation with Salisbury, on the other hand, dismissed the possibility that there was any real message to be delivered. "Our net judgment is that Pham Van Dong's unreported statements—which the North Vietnamese would not let Salisbury print—are interesting as mood music, but give us no real handle beyond what we already had from similar statements."[42]

Rusk's distracted and at times combative attitude toward Harrison Salisbury was no doubt heavily influenced by his smoldering anger at amateur diplomacy and the damage the articles had done to American credibility. But it also originated in the same ambiguity that had characterized the December 1 meeting of State Department aides. There was no American negotiating position because the only thing to negotiate was the future structure of South Vietnam. That meeting had concluded with a statement that Washington's position must be to encourage the hopeful processes of establishing a constitutional government in place of Ky's military rule. The day after his talk with Salisbury, Rusk met with David Lilienthal. "Once the present violence and fighting wanes," averred the secretary, "—and that may come sooner than one might think—the country will be ready to pick up and move on to a substantial future, with none of its plant, its roads, its agriculture badly damaged." Captured intelligence documents, he went on, showed Viet Cong plans for continuing sporadic opposition. In other words, they were beginning to understand they couldn't win.[43]

Little wonder Salisbury's efforts to obtain an audience with Johnson failed, as did those of another returning "Mission to Hanoi," this one a team of two representatives from the Center for the Study of Democratic Institutions in California. Headed by the former chancellor of the University of Chicago, Robert M. Hutchins, the Center had set itself the task of transforming Pope John's encyclical *Pacem in Terris* into a series of conferences to bring about a thaw in the cold war. Its initial efforts were encouraged by the Johnson administration, but when the Center's Harry S. Ashmore and William C. Baggs took up the opportunity to meet with Ho Chi Minh in Hanoi, the reaction in Washington was considerably less than enthusiastic about the growing number of self-appointed diplomats standing in line to take counsel with Ho and his lieutenants.

Ashmore and Baggs were also journalists. They arrived in Hanoi as Salisbury was leaving. After surveying the scene, they concluded as had Salisbury that the bombing was not nearly as accurate as the Pentagon claimed, or—more cynically—that all that kept the American military from pulverizing the city was the presence of diplomatic missions from friendly countries scattered along its tree-lined streets. When they met Ho Chi Minh, he reminded them that he had once spent a good deal of time in New York City. "Tell me, gentlemen," he opened their discussions with a wry quip, "is the Statue of Liberty standing on her head?"[44]

As they wrote later, there were few such "light moments" during their discussion. Asked why they believed Johnson would be willing to accept a negotiated solution to the war that did not entail an NLF surrender, Ashmore and Baggs suggested that it was now clear the bombing had failed, and that the president faced the only option left—an escalation that risked World War III—or serious negotiations. Johnson was no madman. When they finished, their Vietnamese interlocutors nodded gravely and played back recordings of passages from the president's State of the Union message delivered a day earlier. American forces were achieving major victories, Johnson had proclaimed, and then asked for a 6 percent surcharge on income taxes to finish the job! "We will stand firm in Vietnam," he ended, with nothing less than the determination Americans had always shown in war.[45]

More familiar with the American idiom than Pham Van Dong, Ho was also more specific about North Vietnam's negotiating position. He began a discussion on that question with a sharp rejoinder to the American insistence upon reciprocity for a bombing halt:

> When you ask what would we do in return if you stop the bombing it is like being asked by a Chicago gangster who has held you up at gunpoint what you are willing to pay him not to shoot you. The answer is that when the bombing stops the talks can begin.[46]

Having said that, however, Ho went on to say that the famous "Four Points" were not preconditions for negotiations. Washington had always balked at North Vietnam's point three—settlement of the internal affairs of South Vietnam "in accordance with the program of the National Liberation Front"—as a demand for surrender. Now Ho was telling them that neither point three nor the others were preconditions, simply items to put on the agenda at the conference table. As for eventual reunification of the two Vietnams, that could not be negotiated; but there was no reason South Vietnam could not be governed separately for a while, provided the Saigon regime was a truly representative one and not a puppet government ruled by foreigners. "It could be ten years or longer. That is not important, so long as the Vietnamese people were free to work out their own destiny. They will see to it that Vietnam is again one country. I may not live to see it, but I have no doubt that this will come. All our history demands it."[47]

When Ashmore and Baggs presented their report to State Department officials, they were cautioned by Under Secretary Nicholas Katzenbach that they must be patient, it took time to get readings on such delicate matters. Katzenbach also hinted at other channels that were being explored. Once or twice the two brushed up against Dean Rusk in the corridor outside the under secretary's office, but the secretary kept himself aloof from serious contact, almost as if they had brought back a disease from Hanoi. In a sense, of course, they had. The conversations in Katzenbach's office followed classic lines. Polite and attentive, the State Department officers finally fell back to the line that unless one had read the "secret cables," it was impossible to have a valid opinion about such important matters of state. "This was doubtless true," Ashmore and Baggs replied, "unless he had been out talking to the people the men who send the secret cables ought to be talking to, but can't reach."[48]

It was doubtless true, also, that the administration regarded Harrison Salisbury and Ashmore and Baggs as facilitators of Communist efforts to undermine the hopeful political developments in South Vietnam since the Manila Conference. Long since banished from White House confidences, Senator Fulbright attempted to intercede to gain Ashmore and Baggs a meeting with President Johnson. "I'd like to see them, Bill," LBJ replied, "but you know I can't talk with everybody who's been over there talking with Ho Chi Minh." It was a revealing comment, not simply because, as some pointed out, Ashmore and Baggs made a grand total of three, but because it conveyed a bitter sense of being cornered.[49]

Still, Johnson's unease led him to suggest another interview at State. Rusk could make himself available, added the president, but probably it was better for the two, plus Fulbright as well, to meet again with Katzenbach. Having been a prisoner of war, the under secretary was disposed toward peace. That certainly was a curious way of defining Dean Rusk's position, but as matters turned out it was a clue of sorts to another, far more complicated, set of maneuvers that eventually involved British Prime Minister Harold Wilson, Soviet leader Alexei Kosygin, and Robert Kennedy.

When Ashmore and Baggs joined Fulbright in Katzenbach's office on February 4, 1967, they scarcely expected to hear a tirade from the chairman of the Senate Foreign Relations Committee. But that was the way things began. "I say you're caught in a trap and you can't get out because you won't do the one thing you've got to do," Fulbright wound up, "admit you're wrong and start off in a new direction."

> That's what I mean by the arrogance of power, and I'm prepared to bet that you're going to prove me right by hanging so many conditions on whatever reply you send to Ho Chi Minh you'll make sure he'll turn you down, and then you'll use that as an excuse to step up the bombing even more.[50]

Things calmed down, however, when William Bundy produced a proposed draft of a reply that Ashmore and Baggs could send to Hanoi. Bundy even commented that what they had established was a useful channel for informal communication, "rather than running the risk of direct official contact." It was agreed that the language needed some reworking, but after another drafting session a letter was produced that satisfied both sides. The crucial paragraphs read:

> They [State Department officers] expressed particular interest in your suggestion to us that private talks could begin provided the U.S. stopped bombing your country, and ceased introducing additional U.S. troops in Viet-Nam. They expressed the opinion that some reciprocal restraint to indicate that neither side intended to use the occasion of the talks for military advantage would provide tangible evidence of the good faith of all parties in the prospects for a negotiated settlement.
>   In the light of these concerns, they expressed great interest in any clarification of this point that you might wish to provide through a communication to us.[51]

Ashmore and Baggs added an interpretive paragraph explaining that they believed Washington required an arrangement that neither side would gain an advantage during the period of the peace negotiations. As it turned out, that was not all Washington required. On Sunday afternoon, February 5, Ashmore dropped the letter in a mailbox at Dulles Airport.

When no answer came from Hanoi, the two proposed a return visit through the Mexican intermediaries who had set up the original trip. A terse reply to Luis Quintanilla from Hanoi came in the form of a cable sent by Hoang Tung, editor of the principal party newspaper, *Nhan Dan:*

USA UNDERTAKING NEW SERIOUS STEPS OF WAR ESCALATION AGAINST DRV. VISIT TO HANOI AS REQUESTED BY ASHMORE AND BAGGS NOT OPPORTUNE.[52]

This puzzled Ashmore and Baggs until later, when Ho Chi Minh made public a separate letter he had received from Lyndon Johnson. The president's letter, released by Ho on March 21, 1967, had been received in Hanoi on February 10, 1967—ahead of the Ashmore/Baggs missive. The latter had contained the interpretive paragraph about a suitable reciprocal gesture being a guarantee that neither side would take advantage of the peace negotiations to improve its position. Johnson's letter eliminated any possible speculation about what Washington wanted, and did so by reversing the proposed order not only of the Ashmore/Baggs letter but of the "A" and "B"–phases proposal developed independently by administration policy planners: Hanoi's "reciprocal" gesture would have to come *before* a bombing halt—and it would have to be a complete cessation of "infiltration into South Vietnam by land and by sea. . . ." The tone of the letter, moreover, was peremptory, indeed, almost like a warden addressing a prison riot. "As soon as I am assured . . . ," that Hanoi had stopped these acts of war, Johnson would stop the bombing and "augmentation" of U.S. forces into South Vietnam. It perfectly fulfilled Fulbright's bitter prophecy.

Embittered, Ashmore and Baggs accused Washington of "double dealing," but they had had only a peek at the secret diplomacy of the war. To begin with, the two travelers from the Center for the Study of Democratic Institutions, and Harrison Salisbury, had wandered onto what was already a crowded stage. Amidst all the bustle, rival directors gave cast members cryptic lines to read; they hoped somehow the outcome could be disguised enough to make it easier for the other side to agree to a defeat. After many trips back and forth between Saigon and Hanoi, the Polish representative on the International Control Commission, Januscz Lewandowski, for example, had produced a ten-point memorandum at the end of November 1966, listing what he understood the American position on negotiations to be. Ambassador Henry Cabot Lodge confirmed that the points "seemed to be in order," but the whole matter would have to be approved in Washington. The second point in Lewandowski's ten was the crucial one:

Negotiations should not be interpreted as a way to negotiated surrender by those opposing the U.S. in Vietnam. A political negotiation would be aimed at finding an acceptable solution to all the problems, having in mind that the present status quo in SVN must be changed in order to take into account the interests of the parties presently opposing the policy of the U.S. in South Vietnam.[53]

From the outset of the Lewandowski initiative, code-named Marigold, Secretary Rusk had warned that even if the DRV moved from insistence on its Four Points, what was now proposed could lead to giving the NLF a major, even "fatal" role in South Vietnam's politics. Not surprisingly, then, the response to the Ten Points in Washington was that Lewandowski's Point Two could mean either that the NLF would be admitted to a coalition or allowed to take part in the evolving political process in the South as per earlier American public statements and private memoranda.[54]

Rusk did not wish to "harden" the U.S. position before possible negotiations began, however, so Lodge was merely to tell Lewandowski that Washington had certain reservations. Meanwhile, Rusk had sent British Foreign Secretary George Brown, who was on his way to Moscow in mid-November, a message for Soviet leaders. Without mentioning the Lewandowski intercessions, Rusk put forward the Phase A, Phase B formula as "one way of saving Hanoi's face." Given subsequent events, the message has particular interest.

> You may wish to explore on your own initiative the possibility of a package deal which *in its totality* represented what both we and Hanoi would agree to as a reasonable measure of deescalation, but which would have two separate phases in its execution. Phase A would be a bombing suspension, while Phase B, which would follow, would see the execution of all the other agreed deescalatory actions. Hanoi's actions taken in Phase B might appear to them to be in response to our actions in Phase B rather than to the bombing suspension. Obviously, Hanoi cannot have the bombing suspension without also accepting Phase B. We would, of course, like to hear Moscow or Hanoi's reaction to this admittedly general proposition before we make any specific commitments.[55]

The secretary's language is remarkably unambiguous here, at least about the process he is proposing: the United States would halt the bombing first, then in the second phase *both* sides would take deescalatory actions. Brown reported Soviet interest in the general idea of getting to negotiations via such a preliminary understanding. "Their package," Brown advised Rusk directly, "would seem to be an unconditional stopping of the bombing, some de-escalation in the South and then negotiations" using Hanoi's Four Points as "a basis for discussion."[56]

Back on the Lewandowski front, the Polish diplomat had proposed a meeting in Warsaw between a U.S. representative and someone from Hanoi. It never came about. The North Vietnamese representative failed to show up, the Poles claimed, because Washington had not specified what its objections were to Lewandowski's ten-point memorandum, supposedly after Ambassador Lodge had approved the memo, and because the U.S. had intensified the bombing around Hanoi. While it was true, as Johnson pointed out in his memoirs, that the North Vietnamese had not on their part specified that there must be a bombing halt before such a meeting took place, the raids were certainly an unusual P.S. to Washington's "notes" to Hanoi and Moscow.[57]

To American explanations that the raids had been planned for some time and were carried out when weather permitted, Polish Foreign Minister Adam Rapacki rejoined sharply that policy must come above weather. Rusk confirmed, in a backhanded way, that policy did indeed come above weather. For the immediate future, he cabled the ambassador in Warsaw, the pattern "will remain unchanged." "Present bombing pattern has been authorized for some time and we do not wish to withdraw this authorization at this time."[58]

Secretary Rusk, to keep things straight, was not talking about American rejection of a bombing suspension in this message, but about maintaining the "present bombing pattern"—which was an escalation of the raids on targets near Hanoi. When the first of these attacks took place in early December, North Vietnamese officials had been in Moscow. They were there, in other words, just at the time George Brown conveyed the idea of a package deal. With the Lewandowski initiative on the table as well, it appeared that Washington might be ready to enter into serious discussions. But, a Soviet diplomat later told Assistant Secretary William Bundy, the air raids made it impossible for the Russians to convince their North Vietnamese visitors that the Americans had anything on their minds but military victory.[59]

Bundy rejoined that Washington had recently learned that the Poles had not really been authorized by Hanoi to commit the North Vietnamese to anything at anytime. Even so, "we were definitely aware of Hanoi's sensitivity to intensification of the bombing" and had made a proposal for mutual restraint in bombing attacks near the North Vietnamese capital and Saigon. Here was a good example of the ambiguous scripting of the diplomatic dialogue in these weeks and months. If the Polish initiative was nothing more than a bill of goods Lewandowski tried to sell both sides, why bother to offer to change the bombing policy?

The day after the biggest raid, on December 14, Hanoi cabled a visa to Harrison Salisbury. Concern at what the respected *Times* reporter might send back for American readers no doubt affected what State Department officials said and did, as in Bundy's comment to a Soviet diplomat, but the more important issue was on another level. Salisbury's articles proved to be a big boost for Hanoi's campaign to win over world opinion with "public diplomacy," but behind the scenes the message he conveyed connected to the failed Marigold initiative. The U.S. had refused to "clarify" its reservations about the Lewandowski memorandum. Now, according to Salisbury, the North Vietnamese were clarifying their position: talks could begin only after a bombing suspension. At the same time, the discussions with Salisbury, and then with Ashmore and Baggs, were designed to demonstrate that negotiations could begin without any other preconditions.

National Security Adviser Walt Rostow recognized that the North Vietnamese had handled the situation in an adroit fashion that required an effective response. "Hanoi is in a very different position than it was a year ago," he wrote the president at one point. "It is they who have stirred the hopes of peace; they have been doing the equivalent of sending Goldberg, Harriman, etc. around the world." Enclosed with this memo was a revised draft of a proposed presidential letter to Ho Chi Minh, part of an even more complicated gambit than Marigold.[60]

Marigold became Sunflower when, in early January 1967, Rostow first began playing around with the idea of a presidential message to Ho, based upon his continuing belief that signals from Hanoi indicated they might be "trying to get out of the war but don't know how." Put that way, of course, *any* message to the North Vietnamese leader would have to do with "saving face" rather than with serious negotiations.[61]

Looked at from Rostow's perspective, North Vietnamese willingness to abandon the Four Points as preconditions, along with repeated direct statements of Soviet diplomats that Hanoi was "serious about conversations" and was not demanding that the NLF be put in a dominating position in Saigon, suggested that a little extra push might convince the North Vietnamese to go back to the original 1954 Geneva Conference "rules" for settling the Indochina question. Vietnamese reunification would then take its place alongside German reunification as "goals" of both sides in the cold war.[62]

"As the pre-negotiating dance proceeds," Rostow wrote Rusk, Saigon must soon indicate that it understood the problem of peace was not just an international question but something for the South Vietnamese to settle among themselves. To that end, Ky's government should state its readiness to "discuss" with "any South Vietnamese how all citizens can join in creating a peaceful, constitutionally-ruled nation." Hints during the Marigold probings that North Vietnam would talk separately about the framework for peace discussions without the NLF present no doubt convinced the national security adviser more than ever that Hanoi needed (and wanted) to be helped in its presumed quest to quit the war without more damage, materially and otherwise.[63]

Ambassador Lodge's mission in 1967, Rostow wrote the president, would demand all the wisdom and skill he could muster from a lifetime in politics. Ky was also going to need help in creating first a government and then a party "that can defeat the VC if they give up the war and enter politics. None of us knows when the South Vietnamese may have to face that test. We must help them prepare now." "I would hope," Rostow wrote the ambassador,

> you would use all your great weight and prestige to make the military and civil leaders lift their eyes beyond their current politicking; move rapidly to the formulation of national goals and to building a big national political party that could overwhelm the NLF (and the popular front it will attempt) in any election.[64]

These instructions assumed, of course, that Hanoi could be persuaded to play the game. Accordingly, Rostow's first draft of a letter to Ho Chi Minh, dated January 5, 1967, began with a statement that the conflict had taken a heavy toll in lives and property. "If we fail to find a just and peaceful solution, that toll will certainly rise." The only proposal the letter made was for "direct talks between trusted representatives."

> They should be held in a secure setting and in secrecy, away from the glare of publicity. They must not be used as a propaganda exercise but should be a deadly serious effort to find a workable and mutually acceptable solution.[65]

Instead of sending a personal message to Ho, however, it was decided to try to reach him through North Vietnamese diplomats in Moscow, apparently with the expectation that the Russians would become aware of these "contacts" and their purpose.[66] Johnson explained all this to Senate leaders without using the code name Sunflower, imploring them to keep his confidence and asking that they urge Senator Fulbright to consider postponing any Senate hearings on Vietnam for the next several weeks. This was, he said, "the most important thing I have talked to you about since I became President."

> I considered writing directly to Ho Chi Minh but we decided on another way. Now they have come back asking for clarification. . . . Just give me two or three—or a few weeks.[67]

Johnson's "real" purpose may have been to deflect pressure for negotiations, but it seems more likely that Sunflower originated as an attempt to test the thesis that the North Vietnamese needed guidance to find their way out of a no-win situation. That would explain the use of the Moscow "channel," since the Russians would be put on the alert that something was up— and, hopefully, weigh in with their own influence. Indeed, at one point the British were again asked to pass a message to the Russians, explaining that

Moscow had both a responsibility to offer Hanoi support against any Chinese reactions to peace negotiations, and an opportunity to pursue policies "which would be in tandem with our own and which would be of common benefit in reducing tensions in that part of the world." Working together, in other words, the two superpowers could isolate China.[68]

Finally, the president knew very well that he faced heavy pressure to escalate the war even further, and that all the talk about an evolving constitutional government in South Vietnam was just that, talk. The problem thus simplified became to convince the North Vietnamese that they really were defeated, with the hope that they would, in turn, convince the NLF. While the defense of the bombing continued to be that it was making infiltration and resupply more difficult, and forcing North Vietnam to pay a heavy cost for supporting the war, increasingly the real purpose was to break down North Vietnam's morale and thus set in train the sequence imagined in the Sunflower messages.

Johnson's appeal to Senate leaders for restraint contained poignant reminders of how shaky this balancing act really was. Assertions that everything was going well, better than we have ever done, "if we just don't blow it," were mixed with laments for his fate. "He personally wished he had never heard of South Vietnam; wishes we were not there but we are there. . . . I did not vote on [the] SEATO agreement. I was sick—Dirksen was sick—Kennedy was in Florida."[69]

The essence of Sunflower came out, albeit in odd fashion, during Robert McNamara's startling testimony in early 1967 in support of supplemental appropriations. The war was already costing over $20 billion a year, more than twice the estimates the defense secretary had given Congress a year earlier. Pressed for answers why, McNamara was asked to comment on the effectiveness of the air war. Now he was trapped into an admission that the bombing was largely ineffective as a weapon to turn the tide on the battlefield. "I don't believe that the bombing up to the present has significantly reduced, nor any bombing that I could contemplate in the future would significantly reduce, the actual flow of men and material to the South."[70]

When the chairman of the Joint Chiefs, General Earle Wheeler, hotly disputed this conclusion, the debate appeared to be a Pentagon issue, but what McNamara was really saying concerned the diplomacy of the war. The bombing was the "blue chip," as policymakers called it, to bring Hanoi to the peace table. Meanwhile, North Vietnamese diplomats in Moscow had responded to the American overture for a meeting by asking for clarifications of what was meant by a "settlement," encouraging a belief that Washington's "signals" had gotten through and that it was possible to go on to the next step.[71]

Washington replied by reaffirming previous positions yet suggesting it was willing to discuss "any topic the DRV felt should be included." This brought an angry denunciation of the bombing and a demand for an "unconditional cessation of bombing and all other acts of war" against North Vietnam. Once that happened, there could be an exchange of views "concerning the place or date for contact between the two parties." The North Vietnamese diplomat, Le Chang, also said his government would comment upon the American points at an "appropriate time." Washington was not clear what the diplomat meant to convey. Was this the start of a dialogue, "with the other side staking out an opening extreme position?" Or simply more rhetoric to go with other public and private statements demanding a cessation of the bombing as a precondition?[72]

Perhaps the most important phrase in Le Chang's statement was the phrase "contact between the two parties." Certainly it was the closest approach to a suggestion that Hanoi did not expect the NLF to dictate terms of the settlement in the south, though exactly where that left matters was unclear. But Ho's "public diplomacy" with Salisbury and Ashmore and Baggs, as well as an interview the North Vietnamese foreign minister gave to an Australian journalist, obscured everything else behind demands for a bombing cessation, with only a vague promise of talks. The North Vietnamese thus succeeded in bringing heavy pressure on Johnson, as they hoped, but mostly in the opposite direction.

Worst of all for negotiating prospects was the involvement of Robert Kennedy. It was not in Ho's interest to have Johnson's nemesis brought to the forefront among those who conveyed the message that a bombing halt would bring peace talks. The likelihood that world opinion would force Johnson to stop the bombing "unconditionally" was slim to start with, especially after Pentagon denials about civilian targets and the accusatory Salisbury articles: it was akin to answering yes to the question, "Have you stopped beating your wife?" But if anything could further diminish those chances, it would be a Robert Kennedy challenge.

Kennedy's sardonic comments on the bombing—"We've solved their unemployment problem for them, putting them to work repairing bridges and roads"—ridiculed the very policy his brother's advisers, Bundy and McNamara, had recommended as the way to demonstrate American determination. The war wasn't going to end, Bobby went on in an interview, until there was a civilian government in Saigon willing to negotiate with the Viet Cong. "I don't think the war can end in total surrender, nothing like the business on the deck of the Battleship Missouri."[73] To "insiders," a personal feud with grave implications for the way the war would be settled now approached a level of supposed deceit and betrayal that shook the establishment like the furor caused by Wallis Simpson's uninvited role in British politics. An ironic twist in the Manchester affair, for example, came when Bobby and Jacqueline Kennedy threatened suit to stop the publication of certain remarks in the book, mainly derogatory to LBJ, but also some that could be considered less than adulatory about the dead president. Their efforts brought a great deal of bad publicity but also a series of sketches and revelations about Kennedy clan activities that had relevance for the political situation and, indeed, the Vietnam War. There were, for example, lengthy comments on a birthday party for Jackie on Cape Cod. Among the guests at this glittering gala were Averell Harriman and Robert McNamara. It was called the event of the summer, a simple, uncluttered evening of sheer pleasure. It was hardly that simple or uncluttered for the Johnsons, whose several invitations to Jackie to attend White House parties had all been turned down.[74]

Lady Bird watched uneasily from the visitors' gallery as her husband delivered his 1967 State of the Union message. Her eyes focused on two opponents of the war. "Senator Fulbright sat silent, above it all, the whole evening. Bobby Kennedy was stony-faced. He applauded once, two or three light claps. It was a cold audience."[75] An unnamed Johnson "associate" finally talked about the situation to a reporter for the Knoxville Journal. The entire postassassination series of events had been designed, he said, to enhance the Kennedy image. "With the Kennedys, the White House is still 'their house'—and Jacqueline Kennedy is the widowed queen in exile, awaiting a return of the dynasty to the throne."[76] The associate may well have been John Roche, who wrote directly to Johnson that Mrs. Kennedy was "acting like an arrogant French Seventeenth Century Queen."[77]

There was no letup in December and January and into February of news about revelations in the Manchester book and various comments by and about the Kennedys. Robert Kennedy was traveling in Europe as the administration sought to devise a response to Hanoi through the Moscow channel. All sorts of variations on the A-then-B formula were being tossed around. Averell Harriman's negotiations committee considered ways to work with the A/B formula in a planned Tet bombing pause (for the Vietnamese New Year). "He felt that if we could provide Hanoi advance notice of this and indicate that we would watch very carefully their behavior during the bombing cessation, that we might then have an opportunity for meaningful talks." Discussion centered on the timing of this "notice," but the committee understood very well that no policy decision had been made about the "fairly definite hint" that the North Vietnamese would engage in talks if the bombing stopped.[78]

Harriman set out to get that decision—only to find that Bobby Kennedy had interjected himself into the scene. Worried about the president's ability to remain aloof from all the controversy over Salisbury and Ashmore and Baggs, Harriman had recommended against receiving them in the White House. But just as the veteran diplomat was explaining to Rusk and Johnson his reasons and the value of extending the pause beyond Tet to halt the buildup of diplomatic pressure and to test Hanoi's intentions (meanwhile informing the Russians so that they might bring to bear whatever influence they could), Ambassador Lodge cabled that Kennedy's statements about contacts with the North Vietnamese and the NLF at Oxford University and in a press briefing in Paris had caused a furor in Saigon. Harriman's carefully sculpted arguments, designed to ease the president into a more flexible position, shattered under this constant barrage of Kennedy headlines and fell apart at his feet.[79]

Johnson had revealed the existence of the Moscow contacts in general terms to congressional leaders, it will be remembered, pledging them to secrecy. Here was Kennedy, according to Lodge's report of General Ky's outbursts, making statements that could cause "great difficulty" and work to the Communists' advantage. It looked as if the United States was negotiating behind Saigon's back to achieve something like an agreement on a coalition—or worse. Kennedy's statements, after all the attention given to Ho's willingness to wait for reunification, and Pham Van Dong's indications that Hanoi would accept a separate, Communist, government in the south, had damaged morale. A Saigon newspaper article quoted by the ambassador had charged that "the United States has ignored the voice of free Vietnam and encroached upon the self-determination right of the Vietnamese people."[80]

These were telling shots. Always before, going back to the ouster of Diem, Americans had asserted a right to intervene in South Vietnamese political affairs to prevent negotiations with the enemy, using, however disingenuously, the claim that they were protecting South Vietnam's ultimate right of self-determination against the temporary weaknesses of the new nation's political leadership. Inevitably, the slightest indication Washington was clandestinely meeting with DRV or NLF representatives was bound to cause trouble. All the more so when the author of such "rumors" was none other than Senator Kennedy, the brother of the man who first acted to steer South Vietnam through Scylla and Charybdis.

What had gotten through to Saigon was, moreover, only half the story. Kennedy's off-the-record press conference in Paris had not only scattered hints about secret talks. He had also suggested that unless everything was settled by the time peace delegations sat down at the conference table, there would be no settlement. "I am not a strong advocate of the bombings," he ended, "they do not accomplish any military purpose."[81]

Someone less suspicious than Lyndon Johnson would have pondered Kennedy's motives with raised eyebrows. By revealing the existence of the secret contacts he had placed in jeopardy the Sunflower exercise; at the same time his criticism of the bombing forced the president to up the ante or appear to be yielding to a dissident group within his own party. Either way he was bound to be weakened both in foreign and domestic policy. How dramatically the fear of appearing weak influenced Johnson's Vietnam policy can be seen in the changes made in the text of a letter to Ho Chi Minh. On February 4 Rostow sent the president a redraft of his original letter, now a month old, proposing a meeting of representatives in Moscow or Burma, or some other agreed-upon site. The national security adviser said the new draft contained "slight" changes by Secretary Rusk. But there had been many more alterations and additions to Rostow's original letter. Declassified at last in December 1993, the letter and other documents pertaining to Sunflower finally make it possible to study this Byzantine episode. The key paragraphs of this much longer draft now read:

> In the interest of creating an atmosphere conducive to the success of such talks, I am seriously considering not resuming the bombing of targets in the territory of North Vietnam after Tet. We would make no immediate public statement or explanation.
>
> My hope would be that such action would make it possible for our representatives to meet promptly and to begin serious work on a realistic formula for settlement.
>
> You will realize, I am sure, that the unilateral halt of the bombing beyond Tet would raise serious problems for us. We would be inundated with questions as to the reason for the action. There would be much speculation that secret talks were underway. There would be many Americans who would criticize us for what they see as one-sided and dangerous concessions.
>
> I would be prepared to live with these questions and with the criticism if, by such action, we would have opened the road to peace.
>
> But you will understand, too, that we would not be able to remain silent on these matters for a lengthy period. I would hope, therefore, that by the end of the Tet holidays our representatives would have begun talks and shortly thereafter made sufficient progress to permit some kind of announcement explaining why our bombing had stopped.
>
> If we do end the bombing, I would assume that such restraint on our part would be met with a prompt appropriate gesture of restraint by your authorities. Willingness to take such actions on your part, as I have said before, would permit us to take additional actions to bring about the de-escalation or cessation of hostilities.[82]

Filled with conditionals—"I am considering . . . If we do end the bombing," and so forth—the draft was vague at every critical point. Yet what comes through all the haze is that the first step would be an American bombing halt, followed by the initiation of serious talks, and then reciprocal deescalatory steps. The tone of the draft is still high Tory, and the time periods specified confusing on exactly how long Hanoi had to respond—in one place it appears the bombing halt was to continue beyond Tet, waiting for the agreement for talks, while later the draft stipulates that talks should have begun before the end of the Vietnamese holiday period. But a reader generally familiar with the course of Marigold/Sunflower proposals would conclude that this draft, for all its curiosities, was a form of the A-then-B formula—and even, in some ways, an advance on previous versions.

Chester Cooper, who had seen the drafts floating around and who was a member of the Harriman negotiations committee, was sent to London at this time to brief Prime Minister Harold Wilson and his aides on the American position. He arrived as the Tet holiday bombing suspension started. Somewhat to his surprise, Wilson asked him to stay through the upcoming Kosygin visit to London, because the prime minister intended to make an effort to get a joint appeal for peace negotiations and wanted Cooper standing by as a close liaison for rapid communications. The National Security Council aide wondered how useful he would be in such a role, first, because he was himself now known in Washington as predisposed to getting negotiations started, and second, because he suspected that aside from all other considerations, LBJ wanted the credit, if credit there was to be, for bringing peace to Vietnam.[83]

When Kosygin and his party arrived in London, Prime Minister Wilson was fearful he might not have a chance, for the Soviet premier had brought only one "Far Eastern" expert with him, a specialist on Mongolia. But on the ride back from the airport, Kosygin turned at once to Vietnam— and his main worry, China. The first word Cooper sent back to Washington about the Kosygin-Wilson talks was a request for fuller instructions. It appeared that the Soviet leader had put the Hanoi "offer" on the table: a bombing halt for negotiations. What was new was that Kosygin was willing to underwrite North Vietnam's promise to show up at the peace table. He had been in communication with Hanoi, he would say, and had their agreement. Wilson refused to join in a Russian appeal to Washington to accept the offer, but he wanted Cooper to ask for instructions about what he should reply. Did we have in mind anything concrete, since Johnson had said at a recent press conference the United States was willing to stop the bombing "for almost any reciprocal action"?[84]

Walt Rostow forwarded Cooper's information to Johnson early in the evening of February 6, 1967, explaining, "This is obviously a pressure play which we should take seriously but not react to with excessive haste."[85] For the president that evening, "obviously a pressure play" were the key words. He felt himself squeezed on all sides. In a personal message to Wilson, the president declared that he needed to know "what the military consequences will be—that is, what military action will be taken by the other side," not simply that talks could begin.[86] This message was still in the Phase A, Phase B format. But earlier that day there had been a bitter confrontation with Robert Kennedy. Hard upon Kennedy's return from Europe, the *New York Times* published a report about a story that would soon appear in *Newsweek* magazine concerning a peace offer the North Vietnamese had supposedly made to Kennedy through French intermediaries. Johnson was furious. It turned out that a French official in the Quai d'Orsay had only transmitted *his* interpretation of the well-publicized (at least in diplomatic circles) offer to negotiate if the bombing stopped. But that did not really matter, nor did it matter that Kennedy appeared puzzled by the whole affair. Someone had leaked the story to *Newsweek* reporter Ed Weintel, either someone from the senator's staff or from the State Department.[87]

According to his biographer, the senator thought "the courteous thing" to do would be to report directly to the president.[88] They met the very afternoon, February 6, the *Times* story appeared. LBJ was ready for the visit. He waded right in with complaints about the leak. Bobby replied he had not been aware at the time there was a peace feeler, and still was not sure there had been. "I think," Kennedy went on, "the leak came from someone in your State Department." "It's not *my* State Department, God damn it," Johnson exploded. "It's *your* State Department." A Johnson diatribe about the irrelevance of negotiations followed. The war would be over in six or seven months. "I'll destroy you and every one of your dove friends in six months. You'll be dead politically in six months."

Kennedy then asked if Johnson was interested to hear what he thought the president should do? Johnson said yes, go ahead. "Say that you'll stop the bombing if they'll come to the negotiating table." "There just isn't a chance in hell that I will do that," came the reply, "not the slightest chance." LBJ then told Kennedy that he and his friends had blood on their hands for prolonging the war. "Look, I don't have to take that from you," Kennedy declared, and rose to leave.

John Roche claimed he had seen it all coming. Bobby's efforts to raise private funds for housing projects in Bedford-Stuyvesant, his supposed association with Walter Reuther's attempts to set up a parallel union movement, and his forays into an alternate foreign policy, presaged a "demonic" drive to steal the 1968 nomination.

> What all this adds up to in my judgment, . . . Bobby's "royal visit" to Europe, his dabbling in peace feelers, and his China speech, is a full-court press aimed at discrediting the Administration.[89]

Cooper, meanwhile, had gone out on a limb without realizing he had budged an inch from the tree trunk. In company with British Foreign Office aides, he had developed a new statement of the Phase A, Phase B position, assuming the various earlier versions and the draft of a presidential letter to Ho was still the basis for administration policy. They were not. Cooper and his British co-drafters produced a document that gave the British and the Russians the initiative for "inviting" the U.S. to stop the bombing, and "inviting" the North Vietnamese and the U.S. to halt the augmentation of their forces in South Vietnam, after which there would be a reconvened Geneva Conference. It was then handed over to Kosygin as an authoritative statement of American views.[90]

Washington had been slow to reply to Cooper's messages, not wishing to appear overly eager. Intelligence reports from Vietnam, meanwhile, gave Washington a vivid picture of massive troop movements through the so-called Demilitarized Zone between North and South Vietnam, established by the Geneva Agreement when it was thought the division would be temporary. One pilot reported that traffic proceeding south reminded him of "a Sunday on the New Jersey Turnpike."[91] One is hard-pressed to understand the apparent shock these reports caused. At this point Washington was using the Tet suspension as a ploy to regain support for its war policies after the Salisbury articles. Hanoi could scarcely be expected to play the game that way, Soviet Premier Kosygin pointed out to Wilson. U.S. ships were bringing in troops all the time, he said. "We should get nowhere talking about troop movements—our task was to concentrate on getting the two sides in contact."[92] Nevertheless, Washington felt aggrieved and reacted accordingly. In Johnson's memoirs, the Tet suspension is treated as if it were Phase A, and the troop movements were Hanoi's insolent "answer" to Phase B—a tendentious rendering that glided over a change in American conditions for negotiations.[93]

The key decisions had already been made before Cooper's request for final approval of his document reached Washington. From what is now available, it appears that at a White House lunch on February 7 it was finally decided to send Ho Chi Minh the long-delayed personal letter. In its final form, the first paragraphs varied hardly at all from the original draft of early January. It referred, obliquely, to Kosygin's assurances that the offer to talk in exchange for an end to the bombing was "in fact your proposal."

It then set forth reasons why the U.S. could not stop the bombing as a first step. To do so would produce worldwide speculation that discussions were under way and would therefore impede the privacy and secrecy of those discussions. (Given the outbursts in Saigon at Senator Kennedy's activities, the argument had merit, but it was rather late in the day to change the American position on those grounds.) There would be grave concern as well, it went on, that "your government would make use of such action by us to improve its military position." Then came the new American counteroffer: "I am prepared to order a cessation of bombing against your country and the stopping of further augmentation of US forces in South Vietnam as soon as I am assured that infiltration into South Vietnam by land and by sea has stopped."[94]

Whether it was the military intelligence reports from Vietnam, and the adamant opposition of General Earle Wheeler to any cessation of the bombing for negotiations, or Johnson's fury at Bobby Kennedy, the Phase A, Phase B formula had become Phase B, Phase A—a complete reversal of the American position since November.[95] Johnson acknowledged the change in his memoirs but argued that North Vietnamese troop movements justified his decision.[96] The explanation falls short, nevertheless. When Cooper's message came through informing Washington that the Phase A, Phase B proposal had been passed to Kosygin, Rostow advised Johnson, "We have a problem: real but soluble." Admitting "we virtually reversed the A and B," the national security adviser suggested this was "a good initial bargaining position to be in—if bargaining it gets to be." He also suggested, however, that Secretary Rusk, who was as fully informed on the military intelligence reports as Rostow and Johnson, and who was as committed to the war as they, was confident that if the other side "in fact, buy the A–B formula we can work it out to protect our interests."[97]

The gist of the letter to Ho was sent to Wilson, and the new position was rushed to Kosygin just as he was boarding a train for a brief tour of Scotland. Rostow also sent an additional message elaborating on the precise meaning of Johnson's counteroffer to Ho Chi Minh. Wilson was to be told that the president's letter should be interpreted very specifically:

> You should be clear that the stoppage of augmentation by us would still permit the rotation of United States forces and their continued supply. Augmentation means no net increase. Stoppage of infiltration, however, means that men and arms cannot move from North Vietnam into South Vietnam.[98]

Wilson reacted with a mixture of bewilderment and outrage. He could only conclude, he wrote in his memoirs, that the hawks had gotten to Johnson. In a set of cables to the president, he poured out his complaints that his credibility with the Russians had been undermined. He emphasized that, for the first time in the war, Kosygin had abandoned the position that what happened in Vietnam had nothing to do with the USSR: "He now says he and I must do all we can to get a settlement."[99]

In response to the prime minister's pleas, a new American "formula" was sent to London for Kosygin to transmit to Hanoi. It gave the North Vietnamese twelve hours to provide an assurance that "all movement of troops and supplies into South Vietnam will stop" before 10 a.m. the next day. Then American bombing would stop, and the U.S. buildup would stop within a matter of days. Kosygin snorted that it was an ultimatum. No one could give an answer in such a short period of time. "And he was assuredly right," added Wilson.[100]

In more circumspect fashion, Averell Harriman expressed his exasperation at Washington's maneuvers. It was bad luck, he told an interviewer, that Kosygin was in London that week of the Tet suspension. The implication of his remarks was that the Wilson-Kosygin intervention in Sunflower caused the ever-jealous Lyndon Johnson to change his mind. But there was

also the pressure from the military against ending the bombing. Nevertheless, said Harriman, when the Soviet leader asked for an extension to present the new American position, "We almost gave him an ultimatum—'you
must have an answer within a period of time,' which was quite impossible to
get." [101]

Prime Minister Harold Wilson continued to believe that an historic
opportunity had been missed had it not been for White House advisers surrounding the president. Talking about the episode two years later with a
senior American diplomat who had been involved, Wilson expressed the
view that, "in terms of influence on his master, the more I saw of certain of
the White House advisers the more I thought that Rasputin was a much-
maligned man. There was no dissent." [102]

Ho Chi Minh's reaction to Johnson's letter was certainly predictable,
given all that had transpired in Moscow and London, and elsewhere: total
rejection. The day after he dispatched the letter to Moscow for delivery to
Hanoi, Johnson met with Hugh Sidey of *Time* magazine and gave him a
review of Vietnam policy from 1954 to the present. Opponents of the war
go on "jags," the president said, "which pretty much originate in the Communist world and eventually find their way to American critics." The first
example he gave concerned the first bombing pause in the summer of 1965,
after a Communist diplomat talked to some "influential Americans."
"Bobby Kennedy sat here and told me if we would order a pause something
would happen." This was the same time, Johnson added, that Kennedy recommended Bill Moyers for secretary of state. The last example he gave was
also Bobby Kennedy: "Kennedy in France had gotten an impression from a
Frenchman who had an impression that North Vietnam might talk if the
bombing stopped . . . , there was nothing to this matter." But we follow
these things up, he added, even if it was a whisper in Hanoi. "There is an
absolute lack of a substantive response on anything that [they] would do if
we stop the bombing. We've had maybe 200 flickers . . . but so far there has
been nothing." [103]

A week later Johnson went through a similar exercise with congressional leaders. He did not talk about Robert Kennedy, but his complaints
about the "jags" of the war critics to suit some external line were the same.
Yet the section of the briefing done by Under Secretary of State Nicholas
Katzenbach was at odds with these traditional cold war obsessions. Speaking for Secretary Rusk and himself, Katzenbach began, "I say to you very
confidentially, . . . if we were trying to settle this matter in Vietnam and if
we were settling it with the Soviet Union, we could settle it. And we could
settle it on a basis entirely satisfactory to us." During the questioning that
followed these presentations, Katzenbach was asked several times about the
implications of his remark and about recent newspaper stories about Kosygin's role in the London talks. In response, Johnson said that Ho Chi Minh

was the man who had to say what he would do if America stopped the bombing.[104]

Not surprisingly, several of the congressional leaders confessed they were confused by the events of recent days and by the explanations they had been given. Katzenbach had stressed that the significance of Vietnam "is very fundamental to this business of building a durable peace in this world." And yet in answer to the questions put to him about Russian desires for peace, he stressed that American policy had caused Moscow to worry about a direct confrontation in Southeast Asia over matters of far less importance to it than control of nuclear weapons or China's looming presence as a major rival.

The Vietnam War had always been about matters outside that tortured country, so the apparent contradictions that emerged here were not surprising. What Katzenbach had been saying had been said before: the cold war was a transition stage, and Vietnam was, in this accounting, a final phase of that process. What Hanoi or Saigon wanted had to be subordinated to a vision of world order. Johnson had always resented, on the other hand, the accusations of the Harvards that he lacked the sophistication to carry out a foreign policy designed to achieve those ends. Neither he nor Kennedy had voted for the SEATO pact, he repeated once again at this congressional briefing. But he would not go begging, cup in hand, to Hanoi for peace. Even if the popularity polls showed him at 30 percent approval, he would not raise the white flag.

When Chester Cooper returned to Washington he learned that the letter to Ho had been drafted in haste by Johnson and a few others at two o'clock in the morning, in a state of near panic over North Vietnamese troop movements.[105] Was that the case? In the middle of the night did Lyndon Johnson change policy out of fear that the few days between Phase A and Phase B would award the North Vietnamese such a great military advantage that it was worth scuttling the plan? A better case can be made that Johnson's sudden change of heart actually reflected long-standing fears that antedated Vietnam. Had he accepted Harold Wilson's word that Kosygin now had the North Vietnamese ready to negotiate, he would appear to have surrendered control to Bobby Kennedy. Beyond that fear, moreover, lay the whole burden of Johnson's political career: to bridge the ideological imperatives of American liberalism with the realities of regional politics. However wrong the path taken since Diem's death—and Johnson had hinted several times at that unspeakable truth—things had gone too far to back out now. The New Deal coalition was at stake. In Johnson's memory it had all happened before—in 1948 with Henry Wallace's challenge to Truman. Until now the Vietnam War had been a liberal cause, despite growing defections from the cold war consensus. From this point forward it had become "Mr. Johnson's War."

The letter to Ho Chi Minh marked a dividing point. The president had taken responsibility for refusing an opportunity to negotiate and had thrown down the challenge to his critics. Bobby Kennedy's position had such towering significance in this internal struggle in Johnson's mind that his advocacy of the bombing pause certainly became one of the key factors that crowded in on LBJ late that night when the letter was being drafted. On February 20, 1967, John Roche wrote the president another of his commentaries on RFK. "Whatever the truth may be," Roche commented on rumors that Bobby was planning to go after the presidential nomination, "it seems to me that the best insurance is to plan for the worst—and keep a damn close watch on Democratic Party developments in New Hampshire."[106] The war had come to the heart of the Democratic party.

Four days after John Kennedy's assassination, someone close to Johnson warned him about an already developing situation. "There are several points of misunderstanding that should be cleared up between the Attorney General and the President. Everyone's interest in involved—the President's and Bobby's, the Party's, the country's." No one could have predicted that the Vietnam War would provide the setting for the realization of that prophecy.[107]

SIXTEEN

Wars of Attrition

AT A WHITE HOUSE DINNER in mid-May 1967, Lyndon Johnson asked his old friend Richard Russell to stay later. He needed to talk about Vietnam, the president told the senator. When they were alone, LBJ said he saw only three choices open to him:

1. I can move further in the North—but they tell me that moving further in the north with the bombing will result in only killing civilians and will not accomplish anything that we've not already accomplished.

2. I can concentrate completely on the DMZ.

3. I can concentrate on the areas between the seventeenth and twentieth parallels and make my planes make that a desert. Just destroy anything that moves.

Those weren't choices to end the war, protested the Georgian, they were just ways of dragging it out—and probably toward getting into a big war. "We've just got to finish it soon," said Russell, "because time is working against you both here and there." He'd blockade the ports, he said, and cut off supply lines from China and Russia. Johnson shook his head. That'd get us into a bigger war sooner than anything, he declared, and so would an all-out bombing campaign, his first "option." "The only thing left to take out up there," he went on, "is a power plant which is located ½ mile from Ho's headquarters." After a pause, he added, "Suppose we missed." Whether because he agreed or saw no point to arguing, Russell said no more.[1]

Johnson moved away from Vietnam to ask about Georgia politics. What did Russell think about the surprising victory of white supremacist Lester Maddox in the gubernatorial primary? Just lucky, said the senator. The president complained about prying White House reporters, and they talked on for a while. But there were no more exchanges about Vietnam. At midnight Russell stood up. "Mr. President, it's midnight, and I have to go to bed because I'm an old man, and you have to go to bed because you're President of the United States."[2]

The president's sleep was troubled these nights. Russell had said nothing very helpful. Back at the end of February, Johnson had told congressional leaders a story about his feelings when he sent bombers off to targets near Hanoi and Haiphong. His daughter Luci had come home late that night, he began, just after he had heard from Bob McNamara that the bombers had taken off. "You look more terrible than I've ever seen you," he recalled she said. "The lines are so deep. What in the world's wrong?" LBJ explained to her about the bombers. "In the morning, we may be in World War III." Luci suggested they go and pray at a nearby church where "little monks" kept the vigil all night long. They went. "But I didn't know but what—I just thought it would be my luck for some old Texas boy to be leading an outfit and he'd get right over a Russian ship and drop it down the smokestack. And he'd be from Johnson City, probably, an old family friend. . . ."[3]

Once it hit the press, the story of LBJ and Luci praying for accuracy with the "little monks" occasioned some ridicule, but the president was probably right that the people wanted to hear about the president and his daughter down on their knees praying before Almighty God.[4] And their prayers had been answered—at least that night. All the bombers but one came home safe, and no bombs had fallen on Russian ships. Give me a few more months, he had told the legislators in February. "I think in a few months we'll be proud of what we've done." It was going to be just like Greece and Turkey, just like the Berlin airlift, just like the Dominican intervention. "And they are going to yell. And they are going to cry. Because the bombing is hurting them."[5]

A few months had already passed when the president talked to Russell about the unhappy choices he now faced. True, there had been intelligence reports of North Vietnamese war-weariness under the constant pressure of the air attacks, but no sign of an impending collapse of enemy will. Only a few days after the late February congressional briefing, moreover, Johnson answered critics of the bombing in an open letter to Senator Henry Jackson that denied he'd ever said the bombing would do it: "We never believed aerial attack on North Vietnam would, alone, end the war."[6]

Johnson's worries about a boy from Johnson City, Texas, dropping a bomb down the smokestack of a Russian ship may have kept him awake part of the night, sometimes, but his advisers fretted during the daytime about his being identified as a "war-lover"—worse, one who couldn't win the war! Harry McPherson, who would have a crucial role to play in the final scenes of the Johnson tragedy, warned the president that he was getting pushed into a lineup next to Ky and the generals. "The Russians, the British, the French, the Pope, the intellectual community, the students, Bobby Kennedy—will be the 'peace-lovers.' "[7]

The trouble was that if all Johnson could say was that he had tried everything, and the only thing he could do was increase the bombing, "we may be isolated by world opinion and ultimately forced to yield to it— through a bad bargain that gets us out of the war at any price. The only alternative to that, McPherson wrote, "is to ignore world opinion altogether, and escalate massively in a way that threatens to widen the conflict." Secretary McNamara delivered a similar message to the White House: "There may be a limit beyond which Americans and much of the world will not permit the United States to go. The picture of the world's greatest super-power killing or injuring more than 2,000 non-combatants a month while trying to pound a tiny backward nation into submission on an issue whose merits are hotly disputed, is not a pretty one."[8]

McNamara's closest aide on Vietnam was Assistant Secretary of Defense John T. McNaughton. No doubt they had talked about the "public relations" situation and what it portended. After one meeting in the White House, for example, McNaughton was particularly appalled at what he had heard. A catastrophic loss of proportion had overtaken the military effort in Vietnam. "We seem to be proceeding," he told an associate in barbed tones, "on the assumption that the way to eradicate Viet Cong is to destroy all the village structures, defoliate all the jungles, and then cover the entire surface of South Vietnam with asphalt."[9]

McNamara himself still swung back and forth, however, on the chance that somewhere, somehow, a military formula could be found to avoid a stalemate. Perhaps the most outré scheme he supported for a time was the notion of placing an electronic barrier across the top of South Vietnam to halt infiltration with small mines and other antipersonnel devices. What rationale was there for this science-fiction version of Hadrian's Wall? Was it designed to win the war by stopping the North Vietnamese from coming south, or was it simply a clever ploy to distract the probombing forces in the Pentagon and on Capitol Hill? Walt Rostow, the old MIT professor, was sure to be intrigued by a proposed technological fix, but what about McNamara himself?[10]

When pressed, the defense secretary still denied that Vietnam was a no-win stalemate—sometimes as vigorously as Walt Rostow. The national security adviser had given up on his "hunches" in recent months that Hanoi was trying to figure out a way to negotiate without losing face. The problem, he now believed, was that the North Vietnamese were banking on American war-weariness to save them from certain defeat. They would hang on as long as they thought there was a chance their cause would somehow be rescued by war-protesters in America. He had put an aide to work,

Rostow informed Johnson, "brooding about the analogy between our position and that of Lincoln in 1864." The aide had produced a "first-class memorandum" demonstrating how the fall of Atlanta in September 1864 saved Lincoln and the election—and ultimately the Union cause in the Civil War.

Written by Henry Owen of the State Department's planning council, the memorandum considered the roles of Jefferson Davis and Ho Chi Minh, suggesting a parallel between the Confederates' situation and the one faced in 1967 by the North Vietnamese. The leaps of historical imagination here were fully as fanciful as the technological feats proposed in the "McNamara Barrier." Civil War peaceniks, the policy planner asserted, had made Lincoln so gloomy that he predicted his own defeat and an ignoble end to the war. Despite the assurance of ultimate victory, Lincoln despaired the war would not be won. The Union cause would fail because his political opponents would promise a compromise peace to win the 1864 election. Confederate leaders took heart from Lincoln's bitter predicament and held on, hoping their own similar analysis of the politics of war would permit them to claim a victory not won at Gettysburg or in the Wilderness. But the fall of Atlanta changed the political atmosphere overnight. The Union had been winning all along, of course, but the "process was hard to perceive." When Union armies marched into Atlanta, the very heart of the Confederacy, they threw a spotlight on what was happening. In 1967 the war in Vietnam was being won too, but some way had to be found to bring this fact home. Owen's "first-class" memorandum did not suggest how this was to be done, only the pressing need to do it.[11]

In case the president missed the point, Rostow wrote in a covering note what was the lesson to be learned:

> In short, the analogy would call for our pouring it on in Viet Nam so that our people can see clearly the end of the road in 1968, even if the end is not fully achieved by November.[12]

Johnson's reaction to these meditations, and this new twist on the Lincoln analogies Rostow always found so compelling, is not available in any documentary form. The president had once taught history on the secondary level, a long time ago. He could hardly have found the thought that Vietnam would still be a critical issue in the 1968 election very reassuring. In Saigon, meanwhile, South Vietnamese leaders had discussed the "peace movement" in America and concluded that Washington and Moscow might indeed get together in an effort to impose a coalition government on the warring parties. The new ambassador to the United States, Bui Diem, warned his colleagues, according to a CIA intelligence report, that the Americans did not really have a Vietnam policy but struggled along day to day finding temporary solutions. If the Vietnamese faltered in the effort to achieve a stable government, Washington would cut them adrift—and deal with their enemies.[13]

Johnson might have yearned to cut a deal with Hanoi—if he could get what a Nixon policy adviser later called a "decent interval" before the fall of Saigon—but the risks of exposure were great, ten times greater in terms of backlash, say, than the dangers Allen Dulles had pointed out to JFK before the Bay of Pigs. Bui Diem was therefore correct in predicting that Johnson would put heavy emphasis on "pacification" and the creation of a stable government, to the end of refuting domestic critics. The president summoned Ky and Thieu to a new "summit" meeting at Guam at the end of March. There, his advisers hoped, a way could be found to finesse the whole issue of a "coalition" government through a national reconciliation plan that would allow "defectors" from the NLF to participate in South Vietnamese politics. If that could be pulled off, it would solve a whole lot of problems. Secret reports indicated that Ky had toyed with the idea of admitting VC leaders into comparable positions in the Saigon government, provided they abandoned their party and entered as individuals. But Ky and Thieu had been dragging their feet since Manila the previous October, and were now absorbed in their own struggle for power. If the United States attempted to force the issue of a "compromise settlement" with the NLF, concluded Averell Harriman, "we might have to use our military presence in Vietnam to prevent the situation from deteriorating into chaos."[14]

He was going out to Guam to get some new things started, Johnson told Drew Pearson. And he was thinking of a new team. "I am taking along Dave Lilienthal to work on a sort of a TVA of the Mekong River. If we can get those things started, we'll really be getting someplace." He implied that with him working on Ky and Thieu, and the Russians working on Ho Chi Minh, the prospects for peace were good. "When I talked to Gromyko [before the Manila Conference]," he said, "Gromyko promised to throw his weight on our side for peace, and I am sure he did his best. But he just didn't have the same weight that apparently the Chinese have. When the Chinese get a little weaker and the Russians stronger, we're going to have a peace."[15]

As Saigon feared, an imposed peace was not out of the question, even if it seemed more remote than Johnson's casual remarks suggested. Rostow, meanwhile, reminded the president on the eve of his first conversation with the two generals at Guam that it was up to the Vietnamese themselves to win the crucial battles in the effort at pacification. "It is the highest priority task in the war. Drive, drive, drive, on this." America had put half a million men into Southeast Asia. "You are not going to sell out the people of South Vietnam." Thieu and Ky should remember this; America's friends from Greece and Berlin to South Korea had all emerged well from cold war crises. "We are shedding blood with them on their soil. We do not intend to give away the fruits of our effort at the conference table." But America expected them to "do their job with confidence. On the basis of that confidence they must reach out to draw those with the VC into the society under the constitution. It is much cheaper to defect a VC than to kill him."[16]

It took little insight to see in Rostow's proposed talking points the tiny telltale signs of an appeal to the South Vietnamese rulers to take into the government on their own accord VC defectors—without asking too many questions about the sincerity of their change of heart. Here was a double deception. Ky and Thieu were being asked to do something that went beyond even "plausible deniability," for in the past any hint that Saigon was negotiating with its enemies brought down the severest of sanctions. Johnson fully realized the need to tread softly along this path. On the flight to Guam, he summoned all his aides and advisers to his airborne conference room. "There'll be eighty newsmen there. Most of them leftist and pacifist. . . . So you fellows give them just one opening and they will turn this meeting . . . into a war council. They are writing stories that what we are going to decide here is what other targets we should select. I have got more targets right now than I can use." Ky had screwed up the last Vietnamese-American summit with a belligerent statement about never letting the VC into any government that was coming—"and bang, there went the whole conference down the drain." He wanted no repeats of that performance. Even Rusk and McNamara had given out conflicting statements recently, LBJ went on, using his hog-caller voice, "and only the god Lord saved us from getting hell beat out of us." No one was to go beyond formal handouts; no one except Rusk and McNamara was to answer questions. "No, except Dave Lilienthal—and he can talk all he pleases about the future. . . . Dave, you give them some of that philosophy, that good TVA philosophy. . . . As much as you want."[17]

Like Bob McNamara, David Lilienthal was becoming deeply ambiguous about the whole venture. Moment to moment he would lurch between optimism and admiration for Johnson and the deepest possible questioning, between admiring LBJ's powerfully persuasive efforts to make it seem as though South Vietnam stood on the verge of making itself into a nation, just as the Thirteen Colonies had become states under the Articles of Confederation even during the Revolutionary War, and disgust for a façade got up to fool newsmen into believing in progress. "A strange place, Guam," Lilienthal ruminated, "to select for a peaceful goals conference."

This is the main base for the B-52, the greatest bomber in history; it is from here, on a huge field . . . that these aerial monsters start with their store of bombs to pound North Vietnam. And Guam is as well the home of a fleet of Polaris submarines that patrol the China coast. A modern citadel, extending American power as Singapore once extended the Asian power of the British Empire.[18]

At the end of the conference, Lilienthal added up all the "many pictures" he had seen. "And I find myself sad," he wrote in his diary, "sad, sad, sad. Unutterably sad." These were not war lovers, they bore not the remotest resemblance to war lovers. He saw them as trapped men, trapped by their own power. "We have poured more bomb loads onto North Vietnam than in the whole of World War II," McNamara told him, "and yet we have no sign that it has shaken their will to resist, none."[19]

But the most memorable picture was of General Westmoreland and President Johnson. The general with his jaunty soldier's bearing and burning eyes, the president slouched down in his seat listening with eyes half closed. Then, in answer to a question in the middle of his briefing, came Westmoreland's shocker: "As things now stand it may take ten years." "The look on the President's face! (I was seated to his right, where I could see him in profile.) Ten years, my God! . . . Ten years. I imagined I could read the President's mind: think of the mothers of eight-year-old kids; could they possibly face up to that? And should the bombing be greatly increased, as the soldiers recommended, to avoid that impossible ten-year agony?"[20]

Johnson had gone to Guam determined to make Ky and Thieu understand that the war had to become more than a spectator sport for the South Vietnamese. Not only did he want them to press forward with political reforms, he wanted more South Vietnamese soldiers out there alongside the Americans. Indeed, he had told Lodge's successor, Ellsworth Bunker, who was about to take up his duties in Saigon, that his principal mission as ambassador would be to "wind up the war for American troops as quickly as possible." And here was Westmoreland requesting more troops, a minimum of 80,000 to bring the total to 550,000. The "optimum" new force would be 200,000, he said. That number would permit him to carry the war to the enemy in Laos and Cambodia and really shut down the VC operation![21]

Even with these reinforcements, Westmoreland expected the war to last another three to five years. Thus Johnson came home from Guam to ponder where the politics of war might now lead. The deputy chairman of the Democratic National Committee, Louis Martin, met with Harry McPherson and other White House aides to consider what could be done to counter the "vocal minority which is misleading Ho Chi Ming [sic] regarding the opinions of Americans on the Viet Nam issue. . . ." The "real war," it seemed, was not for the hearts and minds of the Vietnamese but for the American soul. Martin's idea was to organize an "independent group," with no connection to the government, to provide a focus for all the intellectuals and liberals who do not agree with the "ADA types." This would provide a "third force which might be attractive to hundreds of intellectuals and academic leaders. . . ."[22] Martin also wanted the Pentagon to consider promoting a black officer to a position of recognized leadership in Vietnam, a position "sufficiently important to attract national attention." The radical left, he warned, was trying "to make points with the argument that Negroes are merely 'black mercenaries' and 'cannon-fodder' in Viet Nam."[23]

Opponents of the war, meanwhile, were preparing a Spring Mobilization scheduled for mid-April; they hoped to see mass demonstrations in major cities across the nation. What the administration dreaded most had come to pass: marching at the head of the column would be Martin Luther King, Jr. King's leadership in the civil rights movement gave the antiwar movement a special kind of moral legitimacy with liberals. On the evening of April 4, 1967, he delivered his most critical speech yet on the war. Speaking at New York's Riverside Church in his familiar measured cadence, King said: "I could never again raise my voice against the violence of the oppressed in the ghettos without having first spoken clearly to the greatest purveyor of violence in the world today—my own government."[24]

Although prominent black leaders like Ralph Bunche and NAACP director Roy Wilkins disavowed King's speech and the general effort to "confuse" the two causes, Harry McPherson saw real trouble ahead. King had become "the crown prince of the Vietniks," he wrote the president, "and along with the ADA blames the war for our failure to remedy social ills." The argument wouldn't stand up to scrutiny, but it was sure to disaffect people in both movements. It was a lot easier to make Vietnam the villain than face up to problems of managing the new social programs, or the apparent failure of minorities to make substantial gains, or the reluctance of Congress to support existing programs.[25]

McPherson suggested that Johnson deliver a speech at a Job Corps training center to counter King's charges; John Roche proposed a more direct assault to "dispose" of the "King candidacy." "Essentially, the Communist origins of this operation must be exposed, the leaders discredited, and the flag-burners and draft-card burners jailed. This is not McCarthyism—McCarthy could not distinguish a Communist from a giraffe. It is a rigorous defense of what we have built from a bunch of nihilists, commies, and opportunists. It can *not* be done by HUAC—it should be handled by tough-minded liberals."[26]

While Roche liked to prate on about the "Communist origins" of the antiwar movement, his real concern (as always) was with Bobby Kennedy, who, he told Johnson, "has a vested interest in the defeat of the national ticket in 1968." Kennedy himself, meanwhile, thought his recent speeches had only stiffened LBJ's resolve to stay the course and even to escalate the bombing.[27] The Spring Mobilization turned out 200,000 in New York City and 50,000 in San Francisco, but movement leaders also felt discouraged at their seeming inability to reach down to the grass roots where the voters lived who could put sufficient pressure on the administration and Congress to change the war policy.[28]

Nevertheless, the peace movement had forced the administration to use dangerous tactics in its counterattacks on war protesters. The White House pressed the FBI and CIA to produce evidence to support Roche's charges about the "Communist origins" of the movement, without success. But that did not prevent Secretary of State Dean Rusk from asserting that the antiwar demonstrators were at least supported by a "Communist apparatus."[29] Small left-wing groups, writes Melvin Small, did play a disproportionately large role in the planning of many of the largest demonstrations, but they could not manufacture the issues nor persuade people to buy bus tickets to Washington to participate in protest marches.[30] Still, the administration's general tactic was to delegitimize the antiwar movement as un-American, something the House Un-American Activities Committee and FBI Director J. Edgar Hoover had always believed—but, which, John Roche insisted, it was up to "tough-minded" liberals to demonstrate.

The argument was a hard sell. It involved, for example, asserting that the large turnouts in American cities only prolonged the war by encouraging Hanoi to feel that the nation's will to continue the war was weakening, while at the same time arguing that the demonstrators were only a tiny fringe element of American society.[31] In the White House, John Roche and Harry McPherson became the chief strategists for designing the administration's counteroffensive against the protesters. Roche relished the assignment while McPherson accepted it with his usual sense of loyalty to the president. Among the ideas they floated was a proposal to organize a committee of notables, with honorary cochairmen Harry Truman and Dwight Eisenhower, to rally "the Silent Center" to Johnson's side.[32]

To avoid charges that the committee was a White House "front," Roche planned to locate the headquarters in New York—and he promised Johnson, "I will leave no tracks." Several old stalwarts, Clark Clifford and James Rowe, for example, were enthusiastic about the project and its potential for stemming the growing tide of defections. Christened the "National Committee for Peace with Freedom in Vietnam," it began publishing full-page ads in the *New York Times* that fall. James Rowe was delighted he could tell Johnson there would be "at least two Harvard professors . . . on the Committee."[33]

But the heavy-handedness of the campaign against dissenters began to have a boomerang effect and indeed to damage arguments for the war. Thus when Harry McPherson drafted a statement for President Johnson to use at a Medal of Honor ceremony for Staff Sergeant Peter S. Connor, who had died while shielding his comrades from a hand grenade, his harsh words about the cost of dissent alienated Russ Wiggins, the basically prowar editor of the *Washington Post.* McPherson had written that "many" of the dissenters had a genuine concern about the wisest course for their country, but "some" had forgotten important lessons about appeasing aggression. He did not stop there, however, but continued:

> The debate will go on—as long as we are a democracy, so long as men like Peter Connor shoulder their packs and face—not hostile placards and debating points—but bullets and mortar shells of marching aggressive armies. The debate will go on, and it will have its price. It is a price our democracy must be prepared to pay, and that the angriest voices of dissent should be prepared to acknowledge.[34]

McPherson communicated to the president Wiggins's concern that Sergeant Connor's death was being "used" in a disingenuous fashion, acknowledging responsibility for the "error, if it was one." He insisted, nevertheless, that the remarks were "extremely temperate, and to my mind take a fair position on the question." The right to dissent had to be secured by men paying the full price, as Sergeant Connor had, but it was a price that "must be paid." That was not quite the tone suggested in the remarks he had prepared for the White House ceremony, but McPherson was a different sort of partisan than John Roche. Having justified the phrases he had used, McPherson suddenly launched into a remarkable exposition of Walter Lippmann's view that "it is not *dissent* that is costly, but a bad policy."

> In the abstract, that is an arguable proposition. But wars are not abstractions. Either this war is being fought for just purposes, or it is not. If it is, then ideally the country should be rallied behind its soldiers and diplomats as they seek an honorable way to achieve those purposes: i.e. ending the aggression, and bringing peace and stability to South Vietnam. Vehement dissent weakens our capacity to achieve those purposes, because it makes us appear divided, and suggests that our policy may change at any moment in order to satisfy the dissenters.
>
> If the purposes are unjust, then the dissenters are right and it is our policy that serves to prolong the war. Lippmann has made his choice on this question; to him, our purposes are not what we say they are, but are essentially imperialistic.

More remarkable still, McPherson did not close his memo with a strong statement affirming the "just purposes" of the war. Instead he struck an agnostic, if not downright skeptical, note: "In any event, I will lay off the subject in the near future."[35]

Walt Rostow had, as might be expected, an interesting twist on the whole question of how the two wars of attrition were going. Since 1966, he confided to a visitor from the Republican camp, the war had been about

American politics, with Hanoi's military losses balanced by Johnson's decline in public opinion.[36] Hence Rostow's near obsession with Civil War parallels and his search for a dramatic politico-military triumph to match the fall of Atlanta in September 1864. With General Westmoreland's Guam request for 80,000 to 200,000 more men now before the National Security Council, the politics of war in both Vietnam and the United States were certain to become still more centered on the issue of stalemate and desperate measures.

An NSC staffer, James C. Thomson, Jr., had recently defected from administration ranks to take a teaching position in Far Eastern history at (where else?) Harvard. In the May 1967 issue of the *Atlantic Monthly*, Thomson published a mockingly satirical "record of a meeting yet to be held" in the situation room of the White House. Presiding at this session was the "Hon. Herman Melville Breslau." Among those attending was the "Hon. Charles Homer, Special Assistant to the President for Peaceful Reconstruction in Vietnam." Few insiders, or outsiders for that matter, could miss the references to Walt Whitman Rostow and Robert Komer, especially since Thomson had previously circulated the document using real names. The meeting began with Breslau's comments on the latest reports from Vietnam:

> In general, he felt, the events of the previous day were a wholesome and not unexpected phase in South Vietnam's growth toward political maturity and economic viability. The fall of Saigon to the Viet Cong meant that the enemy was now confronted with a challenge of unprecedented proportions for which it was totally unprepared: the administration of a major city. If we could dump rice and airlift pigs at Hue and Danang, he was pretty sure that the other side would soon cave. He cautioned, however, that this was merely a hunch. "It is not the kind of smell you can hang your hat on."
>
> Mr. Homer said that Mr. Breslau was full of crap; Mr. Breslau had never understood Vietnam and should stop trying. Things were very, very bad, but they would get infinitely worse if we dumped rice and pigs.[37]

The "discussion" continued with a Pentagon representative reporting on the success of air raids the previous night. "We had knocked out 78 percent of North Vietnam's petroleum reserves; since we had knocked out 86 percent three days ago, and 92 percent last week, we were doing exceptionally well." Another asked if perhaps it was not time for a bombing pause? Clearly out of the question, said Breslau, "now that the 12,000 student leaders and 3 million housewives had once again called for a pause." "The President did not like to be crowded, especially now that Hanoi was hurting." Finally, someone asked about the fall of Saigon from the "public relations aspect." Breslau said he thought "we could live with that one." "What fascinated him more than Saigon was the reported purge of the assistant managing editor of the *Hankow People's Daily;* in writing his book on Communist China in 1953, he had concluded that the assistant managing editors of riverport newspapers were often the key indicators of policy shifts."

Rostow forwarded a copy of the article to President Johnson with the comment, "Because there is nothing really effective to do about all this, we will limit our responses to pointing out that people have differing ideas about what is 'funny.' "[38] Rostow's penchant for colorful descriptions of his "hunches," and his strained historical analogies, had left him wide open to such thrusts. Thomson's rapier drew blood, but Westmoreland's troop request concerned him more. Beginning on April 27, 1967, the national security adviser sent a series of memoranda to the president warning of the consequences of sending large numbers of additional troops to Vietnam "if we are to do just a bit more of the same."

> We would be creating a major political crisis in the U.S. without being able to promise an early or decisive result. Westy's plan, as presented to us, was accurately defined as "ladling some water out of the bath tub while the tap is still turned on."[39]

Perhaps that was the best to be done, but before committing himself to that plan Johnson should consider possible ways to use military power to turn off the tap, like mining Haiphong and other harbors, landing forces north of the DMZ to clean out the three North Vietnamese divisions still located there, or putting ground forces into Laos to cut off infiltration routes. Rostow acknowledged the risks of Chinese or Russian intervention as a result of any of these steps; but he raised the question because he felt the American people, if they were going to be asked for additional sacrifices of men and money, "would rather do something big and hopefully decisive rather than something small."[40]

General Westmoreland had been brought home at the end of April to deliver pep talks to various Washington audiences to assure them of real progress. There was no hint of a military stalemate in anything he said to a meeting of newspaper editors or to a governors' conference. The enemy was taking "staggering combat losses," Westmoreland claimed, yet he clung to the belief he could defeat us. "And through a clever combination of psychological and political warfare—both here and abroad—he has gained support which gives him hope that he can win politically that which he cannot accomplish militarily." Westmoreland wound up his speech to the newspaper editors by repeating, and amplifying, what Johnson had said at the Medal of Honor ceremony for Sergeant Connor. The enemy "does not understand our democracy is founded on debate, and he sees every protest as evidence of crumbling morale and diminishing resolve....This, inevitably, will cost lives—American, Vietnamese, and those of our other brave Allies."[41]

Besides the attempt to shift responsibility for Hanoi's perseverance to war protesters, the general's depictions of North Vietnam's understanding of the outside world were so obviously contradictory, and fit such old stereotypes of the sinister Asian mind—cleverly evil, yet ultimately lacking any understanding of Western ways—that one had to wonder if he truly had any strategy for using the men he now requested be sent to Southeast Asia, beyond "a little more of the same." Rostow was right to worry. Despite the jut-jawed message Westmoreland was delivering in these speeches, moreover, there were "leaks" about his call for new troops that threatened to become the big story of his visit to Washington.[42]

When the general argued for the troops at a White House meeting, Rostow broached the plan for shutting off the tap nearer to Hanoi. An awkward silence around the table told him the president was not keen on either idea.[43] Before Westmoreland got any more troops, Johnson was determined that the Vietnamese themselves had to show they were ready to do more. "You will understand that before a case can be made for additional US manpower," Rostow cabled the new ambassador, Ellsworth Bunker, "we must have an iron-clad case that the use of Vietnamese manpower is screwed up to the maximum." The president also planned to ask "our present fighting allies" for increments of their manpower on a basis proportional to population. He might even ask the Republic of China (Taiwan) to supply troops, breaking a taboo that had lasted since the Korean War—if it could be done "with minimum noise in the international system." As Rostow was dictating this cable, the president phoned from his ranch. Tell Bunker to get to General Ky, Johnson instructed, and tell him that the president would be grateful if Ky would not discuss any additional manpower requirements in public.[44]

Rostow was more and more concerned, meanwhile, that evidence of a stalemate might surface in yet another way. If we don't try to "close the top of the funnel" by shutting down the ports and rail lines into China, he suggested, it might be necessary to "phase down" the bombing of the north, because there were only fifteen JCS-recommended targets left to hit and only one of those was truly important! The JCS had other lists, Rostow reported to the president, but these "began to foreshadow" attacks on the ports and rail lines. Both Rusk and McNamara were concerned about the risks of involving China and Russia, and during the discussions over what to do about the threat of a bombing pause by default, McNamara had become "increasingly uneasy and felt that rational control over targeting was getting out of his hands."[45]

Journalist Rowland Evans, a steady hawk in the past, lit into Rostow with a sharp challenge: "What are you going to do now that your policy has failed?" What policy? countered Johnson's chief adviser. "The policy of forcing Hanoi to negotiate by bombing. It's worse than the Bay of Pigs."

Rostow protested that in the fourteen months he had been in the job, no one had ever said that bombing alone would end the war. Evans pushed that aside. He had been to the Pentagon, and the military men who had had such high hopes for the bombing now wanted to blockade Haiphong. Rostow answered that he could not be held responsible for what someone was saying in the Pentagon. Only the president could decide such a question, "but it seemed extremely difficult to conceive of operations which would close off imports from abroad to North Vietnam."[46]

Pressure was building for such a decision. McNamara sent Johnson a memorandum a few days later, on May 19, that argued the case against bombing near Hanoi and against sending Westmoreland more than thirty thousand additional troops. It also implied that the military had lost sight of original American objectives, largely obtained already by checking Chinese expansion, out of an intense frustration at being unable to defeat the enemy as in a "regular" war. As for the commitment to defend the Saigon government against its enemies, therefore, that obligation ceased if the country failed to help itself. McNamara's memo came against a background of reports from Ellsworth Bunker that the two leading military figures in South Vietnam, Ky and Thieu, both wanted to be president and were feuding like rival warlords over the spoils.[47]

Johnson had always told the NATO allies that the Unites States was defending their interests as well in Vietnam. He could hardly have expected, however, to be put to the test in the Middle East, where the conflict between Israel and neighboring Arab nations was about to explode into another war. The specific issues that brought about the Six-Day War in June 1967, crucial as they were to understanding later developments in the region (and globally), were less important to President Johnson than the general impression that the Soviet Union was mounting a forward movement into the area on the back of Arab nationalism.[48]

Thus events in another part of the world lent weight to an argument that the United States dare not falter in its purpose in Vietnam. The JCS, as represented by General Wheeler, meanwhile, had begun a full-scale assault on McNamara's memorandum. Wheeler argued that to refrain from bombing in the Hanoi area would "stir deep resentment at home, among our troops, and be regarded by the Communists as an aerial Dien Bien Phu." The very mention of that debacle sent shudders down lots of spines—and was intended to do so. "There are dangerously strong feelings in your official family," warned the national security adviser, "which tend to overwhelm the strictly military factors." Rostow proposed that Johnson seek to take advantage of the increasing deadlock between the civilians and the military on the bombing issue by signaling to Moscow that we were cutting back on the attacks. "The question is what kind of scenario can hold our family together in ways that look after the nation's interests and make military sense." During this interval the whole matter of whether and how to continue the bombing attacks could be considered, as well as what to do about the troop request. At that stage, when he had the reports in on both issues, Johnson could summon a council of Wise Men, as he had recently suggested he wanted to do, to put their imprimatur on whatever was decided.[49]

At his own suggestion, Harry McPherson went out to Vietnam in early June to see firsthand the war he was writing about and defending in Johnson's speeches. He came back, he wrote to the president, neither more of a hawk nor more of a dove. The overwhelming fact was that we were there, and, he assured himself as much as Johnson, "we should be." McPherson's report was nevertheless filled with cautionary statements—warnings about "body-count" figures, about corruption, about General Ky's ambition. At one point McPherson went so far as to say that if he were a young peasant and had suffered none of his family hurt by the VC, if he were offered the possibility of striking at "my Frenchified oppressors and their American allies, and of rising to a position of leadership in the VC, I would join up." His point, he quickly added, was that the NLF had tapped some wellspring of idealism and romanticism, and would continue to do so until the Saigon government found a way to tap it for itself.[50]

Politics were the key. Using another metaphor, McPherson suggested that American forces had created a vacuum by pushing the VC out of a great many places they had controlled. But who was going to fill that vacuum?

> It could be the VC; though they are hurt, I think they are still strong enough to do it. It could be us, with another 200,000 troops. But if it is us, what follows when we leave?

McPherson's report was filled with such questioning, all the while stressing his loyalty to the policy. It ended with a solemn warning, almost a *cri de coeur.*

> One thing you must always insist on is honest reporting by your own people. You must put a premium on candor, and a pox on what is only meant to make you, and other leaders at home, feel confident. . . . There is a natural tendency in the military to feel that things are going pretty well, and will go much better if we only have a few more bodies and bombs. I am not competent to pass on the more-troops question, but I think every eye that passes on it should be somewhat wary of the hungry optimism that is a part of the military personality.
> *Every aspect of our national life and our role in the world is involved in Vietnam. I feel that I am only another of those many men who have part of their souls at stake there.*[51]

The summer of 1967 saw events in American cities as well as in Vietnam try men's souls as perhaps they had not been tried since the Civil War.

Like several others in the administration, McPherson believed that Johnson turned down Rostow's advice—to shut off the flow at the tap by an invasion of North Vietnam—out of concern for the likely domestic outcry. He also rejected military advice about increasing the Rolling Thunder campaign out of a similar concern. "Had we set out to destroy Hanoi and Haiphong," Dean Rusk would recall, "we could have done so with conventional bombing—and there wouldn't have been a Hanoi for Jane Fonda, Ramsey Clark and others to visit." And, added McPherson, LBJ didn't want to become a subject for cartoonist "David Levine or others as the gun-toting, arrogant, unfeeling Texan who didn't even have any sense of the necessary limits of the war."[52]

McPherson's report on what he had seen in Vietnam was on Johnson's desk the same day, June 13, 1967, that the president sent Thurgood Marshall's name to the Senate as the first black nominee for the Supreme Court. Interviewed by Wallace Terry, author of a cover story in *Time* magazine on black soldiers in Vietnam, Johnson produced a list of black firsts his administration had named to key posts in government. Marshall was at the top. He was proud of "the Negro fighting man in Vietnam." They represented the country well. Now, he said, Marshall's appointment demonstrated that "The old fences are coming down."[53]

Terry was, if anything, more enthusiastic than the president about black attitudes toward the war, declaring at one point that black soldiers had a great deal of sympathy for the Vietnamese because they had seen the same poverty and misery in the slums and ghettos where they grew up. Terry believed that the "American Negro would be better for his service in Vietnam." A poll of one hundred black soldiers serving in Vietnam rated Senator Edward Brooke of Massachusetts even higher than Marshall, because the senator had visited Vietnam and "returned with his mind changed" about the war. Black Power leader Stokely Carmichael was at the bottom. Obviously pleased with all this, Johnson responded, "I haven't had a Negro fail me yet. I haven't had one turn on me."[54]

Carmichael had just been arrested in Alabama, allegedly for assaulting a police officer, setting off a skirmish between blacks and police when he elected to remain in jail rather than post a $500 bond. These events in Prattville, Alabama, not only produced a gun battle between officers and Carmichael's supporters but a ringing declaration from H. Rap Brown, the new head of SNCC (Student Non-violent Coordinating Committee), which no longer went along with Martin Luther King's civil rights strategies. "We are calling for full retaliation from the black community across America," Brown declared. "We blame Lyndon Johnson."[55]

"It appears," Brown went on, "as if Alabama has been chosen as the starting battleground for America's race war. This is both fitting and appropriate." Carmichael's arrest and what followed constituted a declaration of war by white America, part and parcel of "gestapo tactics to destroy SNCC as well as to commit genocide against black people." The starting point may have been Alabama, as Brown said, but the real battles of what historian-essayist Garry Wills bluntly called (or predicted would be) *The Second Civil War* were fought that summer in the cities, especially Newark and Detroit.[56]

Speaking to the National Convention of Jaycees at the end of June, Johnson described how bad things were in America back in 1931 when he first came to Washington—and how great things were in 1967. The speech appeared to be an argument from prosperity against war protesters. In a series of convoluted passages, the president seemed also to suggest something like the old Puritan belief that the elect could be identified by earthly well-being. The City on the Hill was doing very well indeed, and must, therefore, be doing right for the world.

> Although we have only about 6 percent of the population of the world, we have half of its wealth.
>
> Bear in mind that the other 94 percent of the population would like to trade with us.
>
> Maybe a better way of saying it would be that they would like to exchange places with us.
>
> I would like to see them enjoy the blessings that we enjoy. But don't you help them exchange places with us—because I don't want to be where they are.
>
> Instead, I believe we are generous enough—I believe we are compassionate enough—and I believe we are grateful enough that we would like to see all of them enjoy the blessings that are ours.[57]

Looked at another way, the way Johnson intended, these passages constituted an appeal for support in spreading the American Dream. But the context clearly implied that the war protesters, by, among other things, challenging the reality of the dream, threatened its validity at home and abroad. Two weeks later the dream was challenged by protesters from the "other America," the inner cities.

New Jersey Governor Richard Hughes called the Newark riot that began following the arrest of a black cab driver on July 12, 1967, a "criminal insurrection." Although there was talk of federal intervention, the situation was ultimately brought under control by local authorities after widespread destruction of property and days of looting. Hughes was a staunch defender of Johnson's Vietnam policy, and a Democrat. Governor George Romney of Michigan was neither. From the beginning of the Detroit riots on July 23—the most destructive in the city's history since the 1943 wartime race riots—Johnson and Romney picked at one another, even as the situation became more and more tense. The president believed he was being set up by Romney and the Republican party, who wanted to force his hand on the issue of sending troops to quell the riots and restore order. Johnson was especially angry when former President Eisenhower endorsed a Republican coordinating committee statement that charged, "Widespread rioting and violent civil disorders have grown to a national crisis since the present Administration took office."[58]

Detroit Mayor Jerome Cavanagh also blamed the federal government, but from a different perspective. "What we've been doing, at the level we've been doing it, is almost worse than nothing at all. . . . We've raised expectations, but we haven't been able to deliver all we should have."[59] In part because of the Romney complication, Johnson's announcement that he was sending federal troops into Detroit sounded cold and unfeeling. McPherson felt the presentation had been unfortunate. There was no point in criticizing everyone including Congress, "unless and until we are willing to go before them in joint session and state the case for America's cities." In other words, Johnson would now have to prove he had not abandoned America's poor, the better to fight a dubious battle on behalf of South Vietnam's generals.[60]

Vice-President Hubert Humphrey headed a cabinet working group that sought the cause of the riots. "I would report to you," the vice-president informed Johnson, "that we are more deeply concerned than ever before. This is so . . . because we believe the character of the riots suggests widespread rejection of our social system and not simply dissatisfaction with conditions." But the group's only recommendation was to do better with Great Society programs, not to initiate new plans. Humphrey's letter sounded a weary and self-defeated note, unusual for the ordinarily ebullient vice-president. "We must convince more of the public that, as is true in fact, strong national leadership is being exercised to eliminate the causes of the disorders."[61]

Reporting from the "front lines," Garry Wills noted the use of commando cars in Detroit like those used by the army in Vietnam. They were effective in knocking down fences, cutting off snipers, and, he was told, perhaps most of all, as psychological deterrents. The Detroit police commissioner also told Wills that the city had called for a "war budget" of $9 million to buy armored vests, machine guns, and more battle cars. "This is a revolution, and people have not become aware of that. Certainly the President hasn't." Philadelphia Mayor Frank Rizzo promised he would be ready if riots came to his city. Unlike Vietnam he would not escalate gradually: "If they fire on us, I assure you we won't use the *least* amount of force. We have to use force just as the army does. It's war. But I don't think we will ever need federal troops. We're becoming familiar with guerrilla tactics, and we have the weapons to fight a war." In Baltimore, Wills talked with the head of the Maryland National Guard. "Riots like that in Detroit are not conventional police action," said the general. "This is guerrilla warfare; these people have been learning the lesson of Vietnam. . . ."[62]

Despite efforts to portray the riots as "Communist" inspired, Johnson feared the white backlash more. The president appointed a commission under the chairmanship of Illinois Governor Otto Kerner in an effort to overcome white fears that the riots did indeed presage civil war, and black concern that nothing was being done to alleviate conditions in the inner city.[63] In announcing the National Advisory Commission on Civil Disorders, Johnson condemned the rioters but warned, "It would compound the tragedy . . . if we should settle for order that is imposed by the muzzle of a gun. . . . The only genuine, long-range solution for what has happened lies in an attack—mounted at every level upon the conditions that breed despair and violence."[64]

How aware Johnson was that his rhetoric about the War on Poverty was becoming more and more like Vietnam, would be hard to say. But it was. More than rhetorically, the riots had put the administration on the defensive against those who now pictured the rioters as "guerrillas," supported by outside agitators who were determined to overthrow the government. It was an opinion not confined simply to besieged mayors and National Guard commanders. At a cabinet meeting later in the summer, Dean Rusk and others wanted Attorney General Ramsey Clark to find some legal way to "take care of" Stokely Carmichael and Rap Brown to stop them from inciting more riots.[65]

As might be expected, Walt Rostow, explorer of Civil War analogies, was now "much struck . . . by the parallels between your formulation of domestic policy and . . . foreign policy."

> The equivalent of domestic law and order on the world scene is that nations forego the use of violence across international frontiers. . . .
> I cite these parallels because it is a fact that we cannot play our part on the world scene unless we do so from a base of order and progress at home; and, equally, we cannot build order and progress at home in a world where U.S. withdrawal from its responsibilities results in an international environment of chaos and violence.[66]

The riots brought some surprising reversals, however, as when the staunchly anti-Communist Bishop Fulton J. Sheen, a charismatic figure with darkly piercing eyes who had shared media attention with famed Protestant leaders Norman Vincent Peale and Billy Graham, took Johnson's call for prayers for racial peace to appeal as well for an immediate withdrawal from Vietnam. "Is this reconciliation to be limited only to our citizens?" he asked in a sermon in Sacred Heart Cathedral in Rochester. "Could we not also be reconciled with our brothers in Vietnam? May we plead only for a reconciliation between blacks and whites, and not between blacks and whites and yellows?"[67]

Sheen used the evidence of the riots in Newark and Detroit to delegitimize the Vietnam War. Turning Walt Rostow's Civil War analogies on their head, the Catholic prelate called the situation at home the real "Civil War II." What had happened in the cities revealed "the disease of national decadence," a sickness caused by the same insensitivity that produced Vietnam. "May I speak only as a Christian and humbly ask the President to announce: 'In the name of God who bade us love our neighbor with our whole heart and soul and mind, for the sake of reconciliation I shall withdraw our forces immediately from South Vietnam.' "[68]

Sheen might ask such things of the president, but if Johnson brought the troops home without some plausible or at least face-saving concession from the other side, the embitterment process would only worsen. Fewer and fewer people thought he had any answers left—for either war.

Searching for some "program" that would be more worthwhile than the make-work government jobs the New Deal had offered, and that Johnson always associated with Roosevelt's failures, the president hit upon the notion of a National Alliance of Businessmen, cooperating with the government—which would put up funds for the extraordinary training costs involved—to put hard-core unemployed to work. At the first NAB executive committee meeting, held at the White House in January 1968, Johnson looked around the table at the top executives and said, "This is no bullshit meeting. We're going to have assignments and commitments for you to deliver on."

> This economy has been so good to you that you can afford to give a little back. You can put these people to work and you won't have a revolution because they've been left out. If they're working, they won't be throwing bombs in your homes and plants. Keep them busy and they won't have time to burn your cars. And you'll be doing something as important for your country as the platoons of Marines are doing in Vietnam.[69]

The program proved to be a "success," with hundreds of thousands of unemployed men and women trained for jobs over the next two decades, but it answered none of the fundamental questions about the persistence of poverty and the decline of the cities. Meanwhile, Johnson continued to wrestle with the Vietnam situation and Westmoreland's troop request.

A visit to the UN by Soviet Premier Alexei Kosygin offered Rostow a chance to pursue his idea for seeking from the Soviets a diplomatic "cover" for restraining the bombing around Hanoi for several weeks while Johnson decided the troop question. Kosygin had made it plain, moreover, that he hoped to see Johnson while in the United States. Since the previous winter and the failed "A-then-B" initiative, Soviet representatives, diplomats and others, had been trying to sell the idea that Hanoi would respond quickly to a bombing halt. The problem the last time around, *Pravda* correspondent Yuri Zhukov told Averell Harriman on one occasion, was that the United States had not understood that patience was needed in dealing with Asians. Johnson's letter had barely reached Hanoi when the bombing resumed, and the angered North Vietnamese decided "to smash all the crockery." [70]

The same message was conveyed to American officials in a variety of ways, sometimes in almost pleading fashion. Johnson's discussion of the Kosygin visit in his memoirs suggests, on the other hand, that he and the Soviet leader recognized they were both confronted with a recalcitrant and difficult bunch in Hanoi. By their stubbornness, the North Vietnamese were holding up important talks on the great issues of nuclear proliferation and what would later be called détente. [71]

The site chosen for the talks between Johnson and Kosygin was Glassboro, New Jersey, a small town halfway between New York and Washington. The Russians insisted that Kosygin could not be seen going to Washington because of Arab and Chinese sensibilities. He had come to the United Nations ostensibly to bolster Arab morale in the aftermath of the Israeli victory in the Six-Day War, but the Middle East discussions at Glassboro were really the least substantive (if rhetorically the hottest) of their exchanges. Harriman had informed Johnson ahead of time not to expect much on the Middle East, and further that Ambassador Dobrynin had called Vietnam the number one subject for discussion. Cooperation with the Soviets was essential if peace talks were ever to get going. "From my talks with Kosygin two years ago and his actions in London last February, it is clear that Kosygin believes that Soviet interests are best served by the ending of hostilities in Vietnam." [72]

On June 23, 1967, the Soviet delegation drove down from New York, arriving late in the morning after delays on the New Jersey Turnpike. At lunch the toasts suggested that little had changed in stated positions on the Middle East and Vietnam. Once Kosygin and Johnson were alone, except for their interpreters, the Soviet premier launched into an impassioned appeal for an end to the bombing with a promise of peace talks within a day or so. He had just received a message from Hanoi within the past hour, said Kosygin. "In substance, it amounted to the following: Stop the bombing and they would immediately go to the conference table." Here was a chance, he went on, to engage North Vietnam directly, "at no risk for the United States." [73]

Kosygin asked Johnson to remember that President de Gaulle had fought in Algeria for seven years and still wound up at the conference table. He was sure the North Vietnamese would continue to fight, even longer if necessary, and what would the president accomplish? America would fight for ten years and kill off the best young people in the nation. American soldiers fought well, as would Soviet soldiers under similar circumstances—because they believed they were fighting for their country. But now was the time to end this war. "This could be the very greatest problem the two of them could resolve here together today: to end this obnoxious war and to let the rest of the world breathe easier because the danger of it spilling over into a bigger war had been removed." Kosygin reminded Johnson that he had told him over the telephone hotline that there were forces in the world that hoped to see a Russian-American clash. Now he wanted to assure the president that such forces did indeed exist.[74]

Johnson's response was to put forward the example of the infuriatingly prolonged Korean peace negotiations, to which the Soviet premier agreed that he could give no promise the war would end quickly. But then he made the point that even in Korea, while the Americans thought they had been fighting China, they had actually been "helping the Chinese in achieving their very worst designs." Please, Kosygin urged, "bear in mind that this meeting between them was of an emergency nature, that time was short. . . ." Previously the United States had sought intermediaries, using the offices of some second-rate countries which carried no weight in the world, "but here and now there was an opportunity to engage in direct negotiations. . . ."[75]

Johnson then raised the perennial question of the five North Vietnamese divisions supposedly hovering in the demilitarized zone, ready to attack American forces at the least opportunity. What would happen if he ended the bombing and the attacks came? He would be crucified, Johnson declared, if that happened. Kosygin repeated that the early response of the North Vietnamese in opening talks would reduce this risk to acceptable levels. Then Johnson pressed to find if the Soviets would "provide assistance at the conference table" to obtain self-determination for the people of South Vietnam. Kosygin offered to transmit the president's political conditions. Johnson repeated the question. Would the Soviets help to obtain an agreement that provided for self-determination by free elections? Formulate the question without reference to the USSR or himself, replied the premier, and he would send it to Hanoi. It was decided they would meet again two days later, on Sunday, to discuss such a message.[76]

The proposed communication was prepared the next day, but, surprisingly, it included no political conditions of the sort Johnson had pressed at the first session. Even more surprising, these were not discussed orally when the two men met for their second discussions, and even though Walt Rostow had counseled the president to try to find out if Russia knew whether Hanoi was willing to make the 1954 and 1962 Geneva agreements the basis for peace.[77] This communication marked a significant softening, moreover, of the terms proposed in the president's letter to Ho Chi Minh.

Instead of insisting that after a bombing halt and the initiation of talks the North Vietnamese cease all aid to the NLF and its forces in the south, the language of this new proposal said, "The United States further anticipates that its own and allied forces in the northern provinces of South Viet-Nam would not advance to the north and that elements of the armed forces of the Democratic Republic of Viet-Nam in the northern part of South Viet-Nam and in the southern portions of North Viet-Nam would not advance to the south." How much of a change this actually marked over the proposals of the previous winter was not clear, but certainly the language used was much less minatory than in earlier communications to the North Vietnamese. Along with this proposal, Dean Rusk suggested Johnson stress that the United States could not stop half the war: if the talks became protracted, or were used to achieve military advantage, the U.S. would have to resume full freedom of action.[78]

At the session on Sunday afternoon, Vietnam was discussed only briefly. In businesslike fashion, Johnson read the document to Kosygin, and the premier promised it would be transmitted at once. The president asked if Kosygin had any comment to offer on the message. It contained a "certain qualification," came the response, but "it looked alright to him on the whole." The discussion could not have lasted more than a few minutes, and the atmosphere was entirely different from the first meeting. In contrast to the lengthy and emotional appeal Kosygin had made when they were first alone, his final laconic comment was that "if and when a reaction was received, the United States would be immediately informed."[79]

There was no reaction. Kosygin's great stress on having received only minutes before his first meeting with LBJ direct word from Pham Van Dong, the DRV foreign minister, that talks could begin within two days of a bombing halt, his references to de Gaulle's experiences, to world anticipation of being able to stop the war before it spilled over, to the urgency of the whole situation—what did all these mean if not a prior understanding with Hanoi? Unlike other highly publicized "peace efforts," this time the language on the American side also suggested movement. Johnson's lament in his memoirs rings all the truer for these reasons:

> No response to our proposal ever came back, either directly or through Moscow. Despite many subsequent exchanges with the Soviets on Vietnam, they never gave us an answer. Nor did anything ever come from Hanoi. The door to peace was still tightly barred.[80]

Soon after the Johnson/Kosygin summit, the president directed McNamara to go to Vietnam to survey the situation, particularly the question of South Vietnamese mobilization. Warned that the secretary of defense would insist on greater evidence of South Vietnam's willingness to fight its own battle before more American troops were sent, General Westmoreland and other MACV officials suggested that progress had been made, but that to push too hard would be "psychologically" difficult for the South Vietnamese government. McNamara exploded. "Psychologically, I can't accept it." He was "sick and tired of having problems in what the GVN will accept when American society is under the strain it is under today. . . . There is no damn reason why we should worry about whether the GVN will accept it psychologically." There would be no troops until Saigon mobilized.[81]

When he returned home, however, McNamara offered the blunt reassurance that "There is not a military stalemate." He also suggested there were ways of squeezing down Westmoreland's troop request to get it well under 100,000. Present at the White House for this meeting, Clark Clifford wanted to hear the defense secretary elaborate on that point. Public sentiment in the nation sometimes called the Vietnamese conflict the war that can't be won, he said. Was that true? McNamara responded that the Americans were wearing down the enemy; there was a limit to what he could send south. For the first time, McNamara said, he felt that "if we follow the same program we will win the war and end the fighting."

Hanoi's continued resistance, he concluded, and therefore its silence after the Johnson/Kosygin meeting, indicated it was still "testing" American patience and unity. As the meeting ended, Secretary Rusk delivered a benediction of sorts. Compared with Greece, Berlin, or the early days of 1942, he said, the Vietnamese War had "passed that stage." "We are going to come through this thing." They were just going to have to get the American people to realize that the war was being won.[82]

Rusk's calm belief in ultimate vindication and victory was not shared by McNamara, despite what he said at this meeting. He did not fool Lyndon Johnson. He may not have been "hanging on by his fingernails," as John Roche claimed, but Johnson could see that his secretary of defense was struggling, fighting to keep the military and human "costs" of the Vietnam War from destroying the nation's soul, and straining to the utmost to control his own inner conflicts. The president had heard from Bill Moyers, moreover, that Kennedy loyalists Arthur Schlesinger and Richard Goodwin were trying to persuade the secretary of defense to resign as a moral protest to the war.[83]

Johnson and McNamara now entered into something of a pact, never spoken of between them, and perhaps not entirely understood by either, to limit the war. The president (as he would with McNamara's successor, Clark Clifford) allowed this to happen by not raising the critical question at the crucial moment. McNamara had determined not to give Westmoreland 200,000 troops, nor half that number, but to work the figures down to a quarter of the number and hold it there. His "promise" of a successful end to the war came from that decision and not from one of his famous mathematical projections. The day after the meeting at which he had declared there was no stalemate, McNamara met with Westmoreland and Johnson. The secretary announced that he and the general had reached full agreement on the troop question. Westmoreland confirmed that was the case. "He was delighted with the outcome of the deliberations." He had not asked for any specific number of troops, he went on, and "asserted that his recommendations have been honored." [84]

In his diary, however, Westmoreland's response was more qualified. "I made the point that I fully appreciated his [Johnson's] difficult position and had made every effort to ease his burden by my conduct and demands. . . ." [85] Westmoreland was put under considerable pressure by LBJ during this visit to Washington. Not only was he "persuaded" that he had made no specific troop requests at Guam, but the president summoned a press conference to hear Westmoreland "testify" that Vietnam was not a stalemate. Johnson introduced Westmoreland to the reporters and explained that he and McNamara would "touch" on this stalemate question. The general did not disappoint: "The statement that we are in a stalemate is complete fiction. . . . We have pushed the enemy further and further back into the jungles." [86]

In the weeks after this headline performance by General Westmoreland, reports out of Vietnam were all upbeat. Rostow told the president he had read "literally hundreds of particular intelligence reports on the situation in the various provinces of South Vietnam." They showed definite strains in VC morale and a weakening of the enemy's military effectiveness, "but no definite break in the resilient Viet Cong structure." [87]

"I'm not distressed," the president told a reporter during a private interview. "There is no truth in the stalemate theory." When Peter Lisagor asked Johnson whether he would oppose an effort by Saigon to try its hand at reconciliation, however, he got this reply: "Confidentially, if that were to be the case, we would encourage it. Ambassador Bunker is there to find the ways and means to get peace." [88]

Only three days later Johnson heard new appeals from the military to increase the bombing around Hanoi. Weary of Pentagon complaints about restraints on the bombing campaign, the president said he would approve the proposed targets only if assured they could be hit "without going into China." "We have got to do something to win," he implored those around the table. "We aren't doing much now." Propaganda about a stalemate "has us wobbling." Rostow was all for hitting the targets. McNamara doubted it would do much to stop infiltration, and the two fell to arguing about the effects of the bombing. Rostow claimed that intelligence reports showed the bombing impeded 50 percent of the infiltration. One percent was more accurate, returned a sarcastic and skeptical McNamara. "Much of the infiltration flow was cut down by disease such as malaria—not by the bombing."[89]

The implications of this casual comment were devastating. Unless McNamara could come up with an effective way of increasing the malaria rate, nothing the United States military could do would bring victory. Talking to labor leaders the next day, the president lamented that "Ho won't talk to anybody. He wouldn't even listen to Kosygin. I'm the guy who's got to ride with this thing. The first thing that comes to me each morning is the list of how many of our men died out there the day before. Remember that every time you criticize me it is just another sack of cement that I must carry."[90]

During another meeting in the White House, Johnson asked yet again, "What is the answer to the stalemate issue?" General Wheeler said there was no stalemate. Not good enough, Johnson shot back. "McNamara gets ridiculed when he says it. I answered it today by saying it was pure communist propaganda. We should have some colorful general like MacArthur with his shirt neck open to go in there and say this is pure propaganda . . . we have no songs, no parades, no bond drives and we can't win the war otherwise." Turning to Walt Rostow, he instructed him to get "a colorful general to go to Saigon and argue with them [the press]. We've got to do something dramatic." He puzzled over numbers. How many people were there in South Vietnam? Fifteen million, said Wheeler, and about four million Viet Cong. "It seems like with all the South Vietnamese and all the American troops," Johnson wondered aloud, "we could whip 'em."[91]

SEVENTEEN

The Last Days of Robert McNamara

NO ONE HAD BETTER REPRESENTED the optimistic spirit of the early 1960s than Robert McNamara, and no one agonized more over the war as things fell apart. During one of his inspection tours to Vietnam at the end of 1965, a marine colonel briefed the defense secretary and his party on progress in pacification. Things were going well, said the colonel. The Viet Cong faded away whenever his men approached rather than risk engaging the Americans. The only problem was, they had a tendency to move back in when the marines left the area. That night in Saigon, McNamara asked Sander Vanocur of NBC News what he thought of the briefing. Vanocur replied that he feared Vietnam was a bottomless pit. "Every pit has its bottom, Mr. Vanocur," said the secretary.[1]

In public, McNamara never let on that he thought anything different about the war. But by the fall of 1967 scarcely a meeting of the president's advisers went by without a clash between the secretary of defense and Johnson's other counselors—particularly over the bombing of North Vietnam. Sometimes he argued directly with LBJ. The president had long worried about McNamara's "loyalty," but like the secretary of defense, he never let on in public he had any misgivings about the situation. Mrs. Johnson had warned him, LBJ once told Neil Sheehan of the *New York Times*, that it really was a wonder he hadn't destroyed Robert McNamara by making the other cabinet officers envious of his praise for the secretary of defense. McNamara was an expert in everything, Johnson added, economic matters, prices, strikes, taxes—all of them and more. "McNamara is the strongest Poverty and Head Start man except [Sargent] Shriver." He only wished that the man played more—had a little fun, made some friends. "He is like a jackhammer. He drills through granite rock till he's there."[2]

He had never heard a military man "badmouth McNamara," Johnson observed. No, sir, Robert McNamara got on with congressmen and the generals with only "minimal problems." That would all change in a few months, when McNamara's versatility and commitment to the ideals of the Great Society would come under attack by both—and from inside the White House itself. "No, don't go see Bob—," Johnson cautioned a senator who had asked some question about the war, "he's gone dovish on me."[3]

McNamara's high hopes for reimagining the Pentagon's role in society had led him to undertake such things as Project 100,000, an experiment that was supposed to offer opportunities to draftees normally turned down for service because of low scores on standardized tests. The army could train these men for jobs after they left the service, he believed, thereby contributing to the goals of the Great Society. Johnson liked the idea too. Accordingly, draft boards and recruiting centers were instructed to single out a certain number of men whose backgrounds identified them as "victims of poverty." McNamara was extremely proud of Project 100,000, but the inauguration of this social experiment coincided with a 1965 report that black fatalities in Vietnam composed 23.5 percent of all deaths in the war, a figure nearly double the percentage of the black population in the United States. Later those numbers came down, as more and more draftees were sent to Vietnam, but Project 100,000 remained controversial. Too few of the inductees actually received the kind of training that would improve their lot, and black leaders scored McNamara for luring poor blacks into the army "with promises of better jobs and then using them as cannon fodder."[4]

Another experimental project, the so-called "McNamara Line," appealed to the defense secretary because it held out the hope of an alternative to the bombing policy. The idea for an electronic barrier across the northern part of South Vietnam evolved out of a 1966 study on the ineffectiveness of trying to stop infiltration with B-52s. The authors of the study, scientists and engineers with long histories of working for the Defense Department, had suggested that infiltration might be hindered in another way—by erecting an electronic barrier just south of the "demilitarized zone" that separated North and South Vietnam. McNamara took over from there, quickly making the idea his own. He estimated the initial cost at $1 billion. But the dollars and the twenty thousand men it might take to monitor all the devices would be well worth it in the end. The barrier might not be effective at first, he advised Johnson, but in time it surely would, and it would "substantially change to our advantage the character of the war."[5]

Most important in this regard, it would "provide persuasive evidence both that our sole aim is to protect the South from the North and that we intend to see the job through." In other words, the barrier would solve McNamara's quest for a solid military alternative to the generals' proposals to escalate the bombing. Here was none too subtle evidence that McNamara had already begun to doubt the military chiefs' faith in victory through air power, and that he shared the war critics' concern about what the conflict was doing to America's position in the world. Work actually went forward on clearing a path through the jungle along a fifteen-mile stretch south of the DMZ, and McNamara announced to the public that the system would become operative by early 1968. The carefully chosen language in his announcement is of particular interest. The system's objectives, it read, were "consistent with those of our air campaign against the lines of communication." "We know, of course," the announcement concluded, "that no obstacle system can *stop* the infiltration of personnel or supplies."[6]

Sophisticated Pentagon-watchers could discern here the basic point McNamara had made in recent congressional testimony: nothing could completely *stop* the infiltrators. Not bombers, not high-tech electric fences. In the end, the McNamara Line was never implemented south of the DMZ, though electronic sensors were used to try to stop infiltration via the so-called Ho Chi Minh trail through Laos into South Vietnam. The defense secretary's remarks announcing the system stand out as part of the elaborate maneuvering going on inside the Pentagon to outflank the generals' offensive aimed at winning over the White House for an all-out campaign to blast North Vietnam.[7]

Thoroughly depressed as well about the war's impact on American society, Assistant Secretary John McNaughton had written almost in despair to McNamara:

> A feeling is widely and strongly held that 'the Establishment' is out of mind. The feeling is that we are trying to impose some US image on distant peoples we cannot understand (anymore than we can the younger generation here at home), and that we are carrying the thing to absurd lengths. Related to this feeling is the increased polarization that is taking place in the United States with seeds of the worst split in our people in more than a century.[8]

It may well be that McNaughton's death in a domestic plane crash deepened McNamara's own sense of gloom about the war and hastened his determination to take upon himself the burden of opposition to further escalations. When he did, in congressional testimony in late August 1967, it was clear for all to see that there was a major rift in the Defense Department, and not only there. Accounts vary, but they all agree that Johnson was furious that McNamara's performance had given critics a rallying point within the administration. What's more, the president was being challenged to choose between the generals and right-wing senators on one side, and Robert McNamara on the other. Either way he was sure to lose public support, and, he believed, internal control over straying subordinates.

Soon enough there was talk in the White House basement about the need to stop McNamara's "wickedness" before it did more damage to the war policy. It fed into many quarters. Disturbing news about General Eisenhower's attitude, for example, came from Johnson's liaison with the former president, General Andrew Goodpaster. Ike told Goodpaster that many of the people who came to see him, neither hawks nor doves, were discouraged about the apparent stalemate. "They say that nothing seems to be going well and that, perhaps, it would be better to get out than to continue." Goodpaster denied that was the case, of course, and explained the progress being made in terms of the percentage of South Vietnam's population under government control. "I showed him a chart on this matter given me by Mr. Rostow."[9]

Eisenhower's shakiness confirmed reports that Republican leaders were busy setting traps, insisting upon conditions that could not possibly be met, and, when they weren't, clobbering the administration from all sides. To counter such tactics, argued Johnson's political advisers, he must stick to centrist positions on both Vietnam and racial issues. In the last four elections, political analyst Richard Scammon reported to Johnson's advisers, the votes given Republicans and Democrats differed by a total of only 100,000! And those who voted in elections were neither radical nor black but were instead "the people who bowl regularly." Any talk of cutting out from Vietnam or condoning violence in the cities—and these people were lost to the Democrats. Harry McPherson reported bad news on yet another front. Many of the bright younger Democrats in the Senate were under intense pressure from supporters to attack the president to save their seats. "I won't do that," Maryland's Joe Tydings told McPherson, "but it's going to be tough."[10]

Things were tough everywhere. Under Secretary of State Nicholas Katzenbach had a hard time trying to defend the administration's Vietnam policies before the Senate Foreign Relations Committee, and wound up causing a furor. Senator Fulbright had scheduled hearings in mid-August 1967 on a proposed resolution expressing the sense of the Senate that foreign commitments required both executive and legislative "affirmative action" through a treaty, convention, or "other legislative instrumentality specifically intended to give effect to such a commitment."

It was a setup—designed to give Chairman Fulbright and his fellow "doves" the opportunity to challenge Johnson's frequent, and increasingly louder, assertions that the language of the Gulf of Tonkin Resolution gave him *carte blanche* to carry on the war as he saw fit. Johnson always carried a copy of the resolution around with him in his coat pocket, pulling it out dramatically whenever he felt challenged. Carefully unfolding the well-worn, deeply creased paper, he would read aloud, adding emphasis to the key words: "That language, just as a reminder to you, said, 'The Congress approves and supports the president as Commander in Chief to take all— all, ALL—necessary measures to repel any—any, ANY—armed attack against the forces of the United States.' "[11]

Fulbright hauled in constitutional experts to contest LBJ's claims to infallibility on matters of textual interpretation—and to find a way to get around his oft-expressed challenge to Congress: Repeal the Gulf of Tonkin Resolution if you don't like what it says, and take the consequences for leaving the nation without a foreign policy. The senator knew he couldn't go down that path—not yet anyway. So instead there was the resolution, which, even if passed, had no legislative standing. It was the best he could do. Katzenbach obliged the doves, however, by giving them something more potent than the resolution: a picture of an administration interpreting not only the Gulf of Tonkin Resolution to suit its fancy (and fantasies) but laying hands upon the Constitution itself.

Did the Department of State approve or disapprove of the proposed resolution? Fulbright began his questioning of Katzenbach, attorney general before moving to State. The former chief legal officer of the nation replied that he could not approve of it, because the resolution tried to redistribute the functions of government planned for by the Founding Fathers and inscribed in the Constitution. "Well, let's see if we can develop a few of the specific points," Fulbright responded. "How do you fit this in with the constitutional provision as to the declaration of war by the Congress?" Katzenbach had asserted in his prepared statement that cold war exigencies required speed and decisiveness: "His [the president's] is the responsibility of controlling and directing all the external aspects of the nation's power." Now, in answer to the chairman, Katzenbach added, "The expression of declaring a war is one that has become outmoded in the international arena. . . ." Hence the debate that preceded passage of the Gulf of Tonkin Resolution served as "the functional equivalent [for] the constitutional obligation expressed in the provision of the Constitution with respect to declaring war."

Katzenbach's "aggressive manner" in answering questions became "more and more vexatious to the senators," reported the New York Times. Afterward one member of the committee exclaimed, "This is the wildest testimony I ever heard. There is no limit to what he says the President could do. There is only one thing to do—take it to the country."[12]

Two weeks later Secretary McNamara appeared before a subcommittee of the Senate Armed Services Committee, the roosting place for Vietnam hawks, chaired by Mississippi's John Stennis. Like Senator Fulbright, albeit with a different purpose in mind, Stennis had prepared a trap for the administration's chief witness, the secretary of defense. When McNamara discussed with the president what he planned to say, a White House aide later recalled, "It was quite a scene. They were both pretty hot." Johnson told McNamara, in effect, that he was on his own. He wouldn't pull the rug out from under the defense secretary, but neither would he support him— or his arguments. "Believe me," Joe Califano said, "Johnson was mad."[13]

Particularly remarkable about the assault on McNamara was that he did not testify in favor of halting the bombing or deny its usefulness in causing the North Vietnamese considerable pain. His loyalty to the president overrode his own private convictions on both issues. But that was no longer enough. Exasperated by the senators' implication that Pentagon civilians lacked the nerve to let the generals win the war, McNamara put the question in starkest terms. Unless the obliteration of North Vietnam was America's objective, he said, no degree of bombing could prevent supplies from reaching the Viet Cong from the north in sufficient quantity to sustain the guerrilla war. No more than one hundred tons a day—and actually only a fraction of that amount—were needed to keep the VC going. It was illusory to believe that American bombers could ferret out and destroy all the tiny antlike lines that brought the enemy his weapons and supplies. Nor was there any prospect that Hanoi could be driven to negotiate on American terms by bombing cities and harbors. That was not only illusory, it was very dangerous. However tempting, pursuing that objective would not only be futile, it "would involve risks to our personnel and to our nation that I am unable to recommend."[14]

The report of the Stennis subcommittee claimed it was not pointing any fingers or second-guessing, "But the cold fact is that this policy has not done the job and it has been contrary to the best military judgment. What is needed now is the hard decision to do whatever is necessary, take the risks that have to be taken, and apply the force that is required to see the job through." At his press conference on September 1, 1967, the president leaned over backward to praise the Joint Chiefs and to minimize the differences among his advisers. Inevitably someone asked if McNamara had threatened to resign if a new bombing policy was initiated over his objections. "Absolutely not," shot back LBJ. "That is the most ridiculous, nonsensical report that I have seen, I think, since I have been President." Throughout the press conference, however, Johnson kept saying that the Joint Chiefs were able to communicate their views direct to him—a hint, at least, that McNamara's influence was waning. Back in March, during the Neil Sheehan interview, the president had stressed how many times a day he was in touch with McNamara and how the defense secretary always left word at the White House about where he was. Now the phone stopped ringing so often. Journalistic comments on the testimony (whose source,

McNamara's allies in the Pentagon suspected, was Walt Rostow) suggested that their boss was, of course, a brilliant "Defense Minister" but perhaps lacked the toughness of a "War Minister."[15]

At the first Tuesday Lunch after McNamara's testimony, the bombing debate began all over again when Secretary Rusk queried whether small storage sites on a target list proposed by the Joint Chiefs were worth the life of a single pilot. McNamara welcomed the comment. "That's why I don't recommend it," he snapped. But army General Harold Johnson would have none of this false sentimentality: "Men dying is a relative thing. The effect of the air campaign is a cumulative one and no one can predict which blow will be the crucial blow to them." The president seemed a bit hesitant to accept General Johnson's conclusion. "If we're not damaging targets why . . . ," he began. But again the JCS representative had the last word. "Every blow," he interrupted, "makes him stretch his resources and at some point his resources will not be able to be stretched anymore."[16]

Rusk intervened at this point to change the subject, and tempers cooled. The momentum behind the bombing policy ruled over all, and Lyndon Johnson's fate was in the generals' hands. A few minutes later Walt Rostow brought up the delicate question of VC participation in the political life of South Vietnam. Prospects for a stable government in Saigon had greatly improved: the struggle between Thieu and Ky had come to an end, with Ky having accepted second place on the military ticket; the elections were over, and the constitution was now in force. On the assumption that the Communist bid to take power had failed, Ambassador Ellsworth Bunker wanted to press Thieu to make some sort of gesture toward including the VC in South Vietnam's political life if they were willing to renounce their evil past. The constitution expressly forbade advocacy of communism, but President Thieu might find a way to say that as long as the Communists did not try to overthrow the government they could participate both as individuals and as a party. Rostow thought it would be a very helpful statement for Thieu to make. President Johnson liked the idea. He wanted to "be as liberal as possible." This time it was Rusk who dissented. Yes, he said, we should be very liberal—if South Vietnam's leaders were ready to buy the idea. Otherwise, he opposed putting any pressure on Saigon. McNamara urged the president to pursue a different course: "*acceptance* of the NLF is fundamental to any settlement. . . ."[17]

Johnson did not want to get that deeply involved. Send a cable to Bunker, he ordered.

> First tell them how to broaden the government and make it as much civilian as possible. Clean up the government. Give out their programs on reconciliation . . . ; land reform; peace initiatives. I'd have the New York Times believe that they will get what they want from this government.[18]

The meeting broke up a short while later. McNamara had lost on both questions. Not mentioned that day were the secret probings of Hanoi's attitude toward possible negotiations, code-named Pennsylvania. There were oblique references, to be sure, in the exchanges over the bombing and Rostow's query about a role for former VC.

McNamara's involvement in Pennsylvania had preceded his testimony before the Stennis subcommittee, and no doubt influenced what he said on that occasion. In that sense, the generals were right: McNamara slanted his testimony. On August 22 the defense secretary had "stopped by" Averell Harriman's office to give him a letter from Jackie Kennedy to Prince Sihanouk of Cambodia. Immediately they fell into conversation about Vietnam. The bombing policy, said McNamara, had to be tied to achieving the objective of negotiations. Hitting Hanoi at that moment—"with the Kissinger business going on"—Harriman complained, was not the way to suggest a serious interest in negotiations.[19]

The Kissinger business was the genesis of Pennsylvania. During a conference in Paris in June 1967, Harvard Professor Henry Kissinger had talked about Vietnam with a French microbiologist, Herbert Marcovich. Marcovich suggested that one of his friends, Raymond Aubrac, who had been on intimate terms with Ho Chi Minh going back to 1946, could be used as an intermediary to initiate secret negotiations. Kissinger then persuaded Rusk to use both Aubrac and Marcovich in that capacity. Off they went to Hanoi, where, on July 24, they met with Ho and Prime Minister Pham Van Dong.[20]

Kissinger had briefed A and M (as they were now known throughout the life of the Pennsylvania gambit) on American proposals to end the bombing in exchange for North Vietnamese restraint and assurances that negotiations would begin promptly. Prime Minister Pham questioned the two Frenchmen about hidden conditions, and, being told that the infiltration problem would have to be solved, replied that he had wondered when that issue would be raised. "This is our country," he exploded. "We cannot discuss the problem in this manner." Immediately, he added, however, "We want an unconditional end of bombing, and if that happens, there will be no further obstacle to negotiations."[21]

Something more was said by Pham at a second meeting with A and M. "We have been fighting for our independence for four thousand years. We have defeated the Mongols three times. The United States army, strong as it is, is not as terrifying as Genghis Khan." North Vietnam was ready for anything, he had said earlier, including a Washington decision to wreak havoc by bombing the irrigation dikes. Having made his point about North Vietnam's ability to sustain whatever pressure Washington imposed, the premier talked about "solutions." In this discussion, at least, the North Vietnamese leadership appeared to be flexible. Chester Cooper, who was working closely with Harriman, picked up on several crucial points in the record of the conversation. Pham Van Dong had said that "some U.S. forces would have to stay until the end of the process of political settlement"; second, he had said that the NLF envisaged a "broad coalition government," one which would include members of the present GVN; and, finally, he had said that Hanoi would not "push things toward unification" until after a political settlement.[22]

It took nearly a month, but Washington finally answered Pham Van Dong's "message" with a carefully crafted proposal to stop the bombing if that would lead to prompt and productive negotiations. During the period of negotiations, the United States would "assume" that North Vietnam would not take advantage of the situation to improve its position. McNamara claimed he had dictated the final wording of the proposal to Kissinger himself. Speaking with Harriman immediately thereafter, the defense secretary added, "We must make up our minds that the only way to settle this is by having a coalition government. We cannot avoid that." Harriman agreed. But that was not Secretary Rusk's view, he noted. After the Vietnamese elections "this issue must be brought to a head." If McNamara would make the issue, Harriman averred, he would support him. As had always happened at the conclusion of these "clandestine" meetings, McNamara pulled back from promising an open challenge. "Well, let's talk about it right after the election."[23]

The communication Kissinger handed to A and M for transmission to Hanoi, known as the August 25 proposal, included a covering oral message that the bombing around Hanoi would be curtailed for several days into early September. This effort at a conciliatory gesture backfired. When the North Vietnamese answer came on September 11, 1967, it denounced the proposal as yet another American ultimatum. Washington had no right to insist upon any conditions, or to advance its proposal in the wake of new bombing raids of August 21, or to threaten a resumption of the illegal bombing if its conditions were not met. Pham Van Dong's formal reply toughened North Vietnam's conditions as compared with what he had told the two Frenchmen earlier: the United States should cease its military actions against the north, withdraw its troops, recognize the National Liberation Front, and let the Vietnamese people themselves regulate their affairs. Yet it ended with a statement that after the bombing ceased, "it would be possible to engage in conversations."[24]

Pham Van Dong had told the Frenchmen in Hanoi that it was a very "complicated" business they had embarked upon, and this message certainly confirmed that statement. The North Vietnamese representative in Paris, Bo Van Mai, made it clear, however, that this was not a final turndown. As soon as there was a reply, Marcovich should get in touch with him "at any time of day or night." Kissinger was impressed with Bo's repeated references to a response, and he saw the statement about recognizing the NLF as an advance over earlier demands that the front be considered the only authentic representative of the people.[25]

After a confused discussion in Washington at the next Tuesday Lunch on September 12, 1967, Kissinger was told to reply to the North Vietnamese that the American proposal to halt the bombing did not stipulate conditions and was not an ultimatum. During the luncheon meeting Rusk had complained that the Communists were always trying to get the U.S. to say something new. Any message sent now should simply clarify the earlier communication. McNamara thought that reiterating the August 25 proposal would not suffice: "they charged us with conditions and I think it [a bombing halt] should be unconditional." A compromise of sorts was agreed upon, leaving out a reference to the wording of the August 25 message, but the new U.S. response contained an argumentative final paragraph about increased terrorist activities and Communist efforts to disrupt the South Vietnamese elections. Kissinger himself managed to get that deleted before he handed it over to A and M for delivery to Bo Van Mai in Paris, but the gist of the message was that the August 25 proposal "remained open." McNamara's plea, "I think it should be unconditional," left him isolated among the president's top advisers. Rusk recalled later that the A-then-B formula had not really been changed, that is, the U.S. would stop bombing in exchange for a North Vietnamese stand-down and prompt negotiations. "Stating it as an assumption was again an effort to find a way to let Hanoi proceed despite what they had been saying on the subject." There would be much discussion of whether the Pennsylvania proposals actually changed the American position, for if Hanoi had accepted the proposal both sides would have had to find some way of accommodating their interpretations to the reality of negotiations.[26]

However that may be, two weeks later Under Secretary Nicholas Katzenbach joined McNamara in arguing for continued restraint while waiting for a final answer. The Joint Chiefs wanted to intensify the bombing and restrike targets in Hanoi, said McNamara, but he believed that the "military progress" gained by such tactics would not be "great enough to change attitudes toward negotiations." Indeed, while the Paris channel remained open, the proposed strikes would have an adverse effect on the possibilities for peace. Katzenbach agreed: "I do not think we are going to get negotiations by bombing." But Johnson intervened in a way that indicated he was not convinced there was much to be gained from negotiations, even if Hanoi accepted the American proposal—"we are too quick to pick up what any professor may get going. I think we should get those targets now." Then maybe there could be a full pause.

Weary of the circular nature of the argument, McNamara suggested "the military" would always say we can't have a pause because there are still

targets to be hit. Increasingly, moreover, as in this instance, the defense secretary prefaced his comments with a phrase clearly dissociating himself
from the "military" view. LBJ could not have failed to notice what was happening. One hears in the president's comments all the bitterness, all the
frustration, mixed now into the plaintive note of a man unable to see any
reasonable way to end this torture:

> I think they are playing us for suckers. They have no more intention of
> talking than we have of surrendering. In my judgment everything you
> hit is important. It makes them hurt more. . . . I think we should get
> them down and keep them down. . . . [27]

Deeply worried, Katzenbach went back to the State Department to
write a long memorandum urging the president not to escalate the bombing while the Paris channel remained open. "Virtually every time we have
had a contact, direct or indirect, with Hanoi, they or their spokesman have
cautioned that an escalation of bombing would prejudice the condition of
discussions. . . . Whether or not there is any merit or substance to the
Hanoi statements the simple fact is that there have been actions widely
regarded as escalatory which coincide with our efforts to enter into negotiations." Cautious in broaching this subject, Katzenbach hastened to add
that these were no doubt excuses for Hanoi's predetermined attitude, yet "I
would like to eliminate all possible doubt with respect to the Kissinger
negotiations."

> I do not think we pay a heavy price in delaying hitting again a very small
> percentage of the targets in North Vietnam. We know that destruction
> of those targets this week or next week can have absolutely no signifi-
> cance in terms of the conduct of the war. There is an outside chance that
> it could have some impact on the search for peace. And I would play
> along with that chance—which I acknowledge to be very small indeed—
> because the consequences are so great.[28]

Outside the inner circle of the Tuesday Luncheons, the old Democratic pro and longtime Johnson supporter James Rowe had been present at
a dinner in the British embassy where Walt Rostow had held forth in tough
and unyielding language on the stakes of the war. Afterward, Rowe asked
Averell Harriman to drop by his house on N Street. Rostow had "scared the
Hell" out of him, Rowe explained, and he wanted to get a different view.
Chester Cooper accompanied Harriman and took down Rowe's comments:

> Rowe was very concerned about the impact of Vietnam on the domestic
> situation in the US. He felt that in the past six weeks the opposition to
> the Vietnam war in this country had very definitely intensified. He was
> worried that unless something was done well before next summer to

bring the war to a close, the Democrats would have great difficulty in winning the election against a Republican candidate.[29]

Harriman assured Rowe that he was working hard to get negotiations started, and it was agreed they would stay in close touch over the next several months. White House aides, meanwhile, were preparing speech drafts for Johnson's appearance in San Antonio, Texas, on September 29. The basic purpose of the speech was not to outline a negotiating position but to rally the nation to continue the struggle in Vietnam by restating in the most forceful terms why America was involved, and to detail yet again the "vicious campaign of Communist terror" that had reached new heights just before the South Vietnamese elections. As it went the rounds, the speech was actually toughened from Rostow's original draft to answer domestic critics so that it included a "Don't Tread on Me" assertion: "It has been said that they killed more civilians in 4 weeks trying to keep them from voting before the election than our American bombers have killed in the big cities of North Vietnam in bombing military targets."[30]

The San Antonio formula, as it became known, was sandwiched between such statements and a claim to victory. "Why," the president asked, "in the face of military and political progress in the South, and the burden of our bombing in the North, do they insist and persist with the war?" Because, Johnson answered himself, "They still hope that the people of the United States will not see this struggle through to the very end." The formula stated:

> As we have told Hanoi time and time and time again, the heart of the matter is really this: The United States is willing to stop all aerial and naval bombardment of North Vietnam when this will lead promptly to productive discussions. We, of course, assume that while discussions proceed, North Vietnam would not take advantage of the bombing cessation or limitation.[31]

It is difficult to say exactly what was on Johnson's mind when he repeated the most recent American proposals in this fashion. Context certainly cannot be ignored, either in terms of rhetoric or what was going on in the war. Both in the precise wording used, and where the formula was placed, the rhetorical context suggested a demand that North Vietnam surrender. Bo Van Mai told Marcovich that the speech had made a bad impression, it was "insulting." Marcovich warned Kissinger that it was necessary to be "very prudent in public statements." The least ambiguity was interpreted in its most unfavorable meaning. The fewer public declarations, the better at this stage.[32]

Bo also denounced the United States for playing the "usual American double game," talking peace while bombing. Johnson's speech was followed the next day by an attack on Haiphong that hit a school killing thirty children. The president's proposal, Bo said, had imposed conditions— "promptly" and "productive discussions" were conditions. Reviewing Pennsylvania, Ambassador Charles Bohlen, whose experience with Communist negotiators went back to World War II, agreed with Bo's interpretation. "To the communist mind, for us to insist that talks must be 'productive' means that we would already have determined how the talks should come out and would amount to the acceptance of an American solution . . . before they have even begun." [33]

The Paris channel remained "open" for several more weeks, and Kissinger tried his best to use the slight word changes Washington offered from day to day to get some sort of response. Rostow carefully explained that the changes were in the nature of "cosmetic" concessions to Hanoi, nothing more than that. "We have clearly turned the corner in this struggle for Vietnam and the future of Southeast Asia. We hope that through negotiations we are very nearly [at] the end. But, if negotiations do not succeed, we can be confident that we are already well on the road to success and to peace." [34]

Rostow's unstinting enthusiasm for what the bombing had accomplished brought another dissent from McNamara at the next Tuesday Luncheon. When the national security adviser went down the list to summarize the achievements of the bombing, McNamara replied simply, "I do not agree with that." Despite Rostow's optimism, Johnson seemed more depressed than usual. Referring to polls and debates, the president talked about the need to end the war quickly. Then he shocked everyone present by asking what effect a decision not to run again would have on the war? "You must not go down," exclaimed Dean Rusk. "You are the Commander-in-Chief, and we are in a war. This would have a very serious effect on the country. . . . Hanoi would think they have got it made." Then the president sounded another plaintive note:

> Our people will not hold out four more years. I want to get rid of every major target. Between now and election, I am going to work my guts out. I would be 61 when I came back in, and I just don't know if I want four more years of this. I would consider telling the American people that it is an awfully long period. But I am afraid it would be interpreted as walking out on our men. . . .
> . . . 95% of the people believe there has been a change of attitude on Vietnam. They all think that we will lose the election if we do not do something about Vietnam quick. They are all worried about expenses. [35]

Rusk picked up on Johnson's last comment. "In my opinion," he scoffed, "the tax bill made many doves." Rusk's contempt for the doves was of little comfort to LBJ, as he faced the prospect of another huge peace march on Washington as well as a balky Congress ready to pounce from all sides on proposed tax increases to finance the war. Yet in talking with a reporter from the *Cleveland Plain Dealer*, the president dramatically revised the comments he had made about Robert McNamara's limitless talents the previous spring. Asked to compare Rusk and McNamara, he said, "If you went in with a Cabinet of 13 men and you asked who is the ablest, wisest in the group to bet the lives of your wife and daughters, Rusk would get 12 of the 13 votes." The thirteenth would go to McNamara. He wanted to hold on to them both.[36]

That was not going to be possible much longer. McNamara was complaining to White House aides that both he and Rusk had lost credibility on the question of Vietnam, ostensibly in terms of making the case in public, but he was obviously also talking about having lost out in the Tuesday Luncheons. The *New York Times* editorial board sent one of its Washington bureau reporters to see Harry McPherson about rumors that McNamara's "disenchantment" had reached the critical stage. He couldn't build a story out of rumor, the reporter told McPherson. "But there is intense interest in this from New York."[37] As well there might be. A McNamara resignation would rattle windows in the White House with more intense vibrations than a bomb going off across the street in the Hay-Adams Hotel.

On Wednesday evening, October 18 at 7:30 p.m., a small group of presidential advisers met in the cabinet room to hear Professor Kissinger report on the Pennsylvania affair. Besides the usual guests at the Tuesday Luncheons, two of the president's closest political friends and counselors were present, Clark Clifford and Abe Fortas, the latter now sitting on the Supreme Court, as well as General Maxwell Taylor. Dean Rusk opened the discussion by congratulating the Harvard scholar for his skills in handling "a very delicate matter in a very professional manner."[38]

Kissinger then reviewed the whole series of exchanges going back to the original encounter with Marcovich at the Paris conference, followed by Rusk's presentation of the basic American formula and Hanoi's reply. "It seems to me that they're discussing a possible negotiate and fight strategy," concluded the secretary of state, conjuring up the vision of the frustrating and politically disastrous stalemate at the Panmunjom talks a decade and a half earlier. Johnson then asked Kissinger what he would recommend. Choosing his words carefully, Kissinger replied that he would "prefer" two options. If there was an intention to have a bombing pause, he thought it would be desirable to do it through the existing channel; if there was to be no pause, it was time to say that Hanoi's last message was deemed a refusal, and then to deal with the problem of how to wind up the channel diplomatically. Kissinger had weighted his remarks in favor of a pause, but not so heavily as to alienate anyone listening to him that evening. Katzenbach continued his effort to nudge the president toward a pause. To Rusk's assertion that Hanoi was simply stalling, the under secretary suggested he could see no motivation for Hanoi's stringing out the Paris contacts "unless it is considering some kind of talks."

But Johnson could. "I know if they were bombing Washington, hitting my bridges and railroads and highways, I would be delighted to trade off discussions through an intermediary for a restriction on the bombing. It hasn't cost him one bit. The net of it is that he has a sanctuary in Hanoi in return for having his Consul talk with two scientists who talked with an American citizen." "I disagree with that very much," Katzenbach rejoined. He would go for a pause starting in about a month. What about the argument that this would give the north the opportunity to resupply its forces in the south, asked Johnson? "Mr. President," Secretary McNamara said, "I believe I can show beyond a shadow of a doubt that bombing in Hanoi and Haiphong will not affect resupply in the South one bit." Both Katzenbach and McNamara urged on Johnson the argument that if the north did take military advantage of the pause, world opinion would support American retaliatory strikes.

"My reaction," began General Taylor, "is that this is one of the few times we have had an authentic link." But what had come back from Hanoi looked like a refusal. The goal could not be negotiations as an end in themselves. "Panmunjom wasn't pleasant." Then he trotted out the oldest cold war cliché. "Any indication of weakness is viewed with contempt. On the trip Clark Clifford and I made to our Asian allies, they could not understand our not using force. By showing weakness we could prejudice any possible negotiations."

Clark Clifford followed Taylor in the evening's speaking order. He too opposed a bombing pause. It would do no good, he believed, at this juncture, and only allow Hanoi precious time to build up its supplies. In his memoirs Clifford asserts that he was almost as full of doubts as McNamara about the ultimate end of it all. But he said nothing like that during the discussion. Nor did he argue with Taylor's assessment of the opinions of America's "allies" in Southeast Asia, although his view in his memoirs would be that they were "beginning to distance themselves—some slightly, some openly—from America's efforts in Vietnam, although they would not say so publicly."[39]

Instead Clifford reinforced Taylor's assertions. The attitude they had encountered in Asia, he said, was that without the bombing the war could go on "indefinitely."

> They are not concerned about the losses which are being sustained in their young men. They believe men are servants of the state, and the loss of men is not a serious matter. The fighting all takes place in South Vietnam. Without the bombing, Southeast Asians feel there is no inducement for the North Vietnamese to seek peace. This thing could go on

for twenty years. . . . *In my opinion a bombing pause makes the possibility of peace much more remote.* This is the unanimous opinion of the Asians out there.

The Clifford/Taylor mission that summer, to recruit more support from Asian nations in the way of combat troops, had been a dismal failure, as everyone in the room that evening knew, except perhaps Professor Kissinger. But Clifford was now seconded by Justice Fortas, who could see no "ray of hope" coming from the Paris channel. "We need to summon all our courage and strength from the Lord and maintain our position here."

Johnson then read from a memo he had received from McGeorge Bundy, without telling the group the source of the document. Bundy's view was that bombing in the Hanoi-Haiphong area did not affect supply in the south, despite what the top brass at the Pentagon claimed. Here was the opening McNamara had been waiting for, and he launched into a heartfelt exposition that challenged assumptions about the Pennsylvania channel and the imminence of victory.

On the matter of the Paris exchange, I consider this to be an important dramatic change in attitude.

Their behavior is consistent with the way they should act under pressure. They have not been forthcoming in these exchanges. *But my evaluation is that if bombing were to cease, talks will start quickly.*

There is some possibility this will lead to a settlement. . . . We need to move toward settlement in the next twelve months.

On September 12 we asked the Joint Chiefs of Staff to give us the ways to substantially shorten the war. Every action they recommended related to areas outside South Vietnam. I believe we need to probe this slight possibility to see if it can be productive. I do not believe we can maintain the support of our people in this country for twelve months.

I disagree with Abe (Fortas). I do not believe that the pauses have led to more dissension and division in this country. I believe a pause would increase rather than decrease support.

A pause need not have military disadvantages.

We should not cut off the Paris channel. I share the view of whoever wrote the memo the President just read. The bombing cessation isn't affecting how the war is carried on in the South.

But it was as if McNamara had not spoken at all, as if he were not even in the room. The conversation picked up where Taylor and Clifford and Fortas (with his summoning of the Lord's help to sustain them) had finished. "I recommend," Dean Rusk began, "that Professor Kissinger go on to Paris as planned tomorrow." Kissinger was to tell the French intermediaries that "we have had nothing back." The other side had been presented with a very serious, generous offer. "This doesn't smell like much yet." Rostow agreed. "When they are serious there is a way for them to say it." The enemy's military situation in the south was "weak," the national security adviser insisted. "The major field of battle is no longer in the South or even I Corps but in American politics. . . . A pause would be no more than an exercise of domestic politics and international politics." President Johnson ended the meeting with a statement that he too saw no desire to talk coming from the other side. As for a pause, he would wait to discuss the possibilities another time.

The Paris channel was thus allowed slowly to dry up. McNamara experienced the episode with keen regret that Washington never really made an offer to halt the bombing without conditions to see what would happen. The official American position was that Pennsylvania marked no change in the stiff DRV attitude that all *its* previous conditions had to be met first, including troop withdrawals and acceptance of the NLF as the government of South Vietnam, before a settlement could be reached. "I became convinced again," Johnson wrote in his memoirs, "that Hanoi had no interest in serious talk about peace except, as always, on its own stiff terms."[40]

At various points along the way, the two Frenchmen who had discussed the possibility of negotiations with Pham Van Dong back in July; Henry Kissinger, who carried on the tedious back-and-forth of message bearing; and Robert McNamara, all came to a different conclusion about Hanoi's diplomatic maneuverings. That these constituted nothing more than a clever artifice to disguise preparations for Tet, and to lull Americans into an unprepared state, became LBJ's final statement on the affair:

> We did not know then, but we soon learned, that Hanoi was already feverishly preparing its largest and most ambitious military campaign of the war. Reinforcements were crowding the infiltration trails and many had already arrived in South Vietnam.[41]

War-weariness, fear that the United States was preparing an invasion of North Vietnam, and, less well understood, arguments between NLF leaders and Hanoi, were all factors in the complicated maneuvers that Pham Van Dong had described to the Frenchmen at the outset of Pennsylvania. Clearly, as well, it was Hanoi's hope to drive a wedge between Saigon and Washington by posing the possibility of serious negotiations. Had the United States decided to implement a bombing pause, on the other hand, it might indeed have had a "corrosive" effect upon its enemy's cohesiveness. The impetus for the infiltration of supplies and men into South Vietnam leading to the Tet offensive was Hanoi's obvious desire to bring a halt to the bombing by military means. That meant forcing an end to the war as in the final stages of the struggle against the French. The United States did have it within its power to impose severe strains on the enemy—but perhaps, paradoxically, only by halting the bombing to see what would happen.[42]

Such speculations, in the end, do not tell us why Johnson refused to follow McNamara's proposed course, any more than do his postdictive explanations in his memoirs of enemy perfidiousness in preparing the Tet offensive while pretending to seek negotiations. On October 23, 1967, the president decided, instead of going for a pause, to resume air attacks in the Hanoi region. His explanation of this decision to Rusk and McNamara became a lengthy discourse on the travails of the presidency. LBJ borrowed from his defense secretary's analysis only to wind up with an argument for a near all-out bombing campaign.

> It doesn't seem we can win the war militarily. I asked the JCS [for] suggestions on how to shorten the war but all of their proposals related to suggestions outside South Vietnam.
>
> We can't win diplomatically either. We ought to make the proposals so clear and get such clear answers back that we can tell a farmer what has taken place and be able to have him understand it.
>
> Now we are back to where we started.
>
> . . . We've almost lost the war in the last two months in the court of public opinion. These demonstrators and others are trying to show that we need somebody else to take over this country. . . . The hawks are throwing in the towel. Everybody is hitting you. San Antonio did not get through. I cannot mount a better explanation.
>
> If we cannot get negotiations, why don't we hit all the military targets short of provoking Russia and China. It astounds me that our boys in Vietnam have such good morale with all of this going on.[43]

Over the next few days Johnson received two dissenting memoranda. The more famous was Robert McNamara's call for a bombing pause that reput all the arguments he had been making orally over the past several weeks into a formal paper. "This memo represents my personal views," he wrote in a covering note. "Because these may be incompatible with your own, I have not shown the paper to Dean Rusk, Walt Rostow or Bus Wheeler."[44] The other memorandum was from Harry McPherson. Professing no expertise on the specific military issues, what targets should or should not be hit, McPherson explained he wrote as a middle-road Democrat, one of those "who've supported American foreign policy decisions since 1948 and who believe we have to stay in Vietnam for one reason or another—[but who] have grown increasingly edgy about the bombing program."[45]

Continuing the present course in Vietnam, the defense secretary wrote, promised steady but slow progress in the war—but it would not be enough to sustain public support for the war. "As the months go by, there will be both increasing pressure for widening the war and continued loss of support for American participation in the struggle." Calls would be heard for hitting more and more sensitive targets in Hanoi and Haiphong, to prevent movement of goods into Vietnam by sea, to strike at the irrigation dikes. There would be increasing calls, as well, for American withdrawal. When the Joint Chiefs were asked for a "blueprint" of additional measures to bring the war to a speedy conclusion, their recommendations pertained only to actions outside South Vietnam. "I do not think adoption of any or all of these proposals would bring us significantly closer to victory in the next 15 months." [46]

What alternatives were there, then? "A decision to stop the bombing is a logical alternative to our present course in Vietnam." The remainder of McNamara's memorandum argued the case for an "indefinite" bombing halt. The North Vietnamese, it was to be hoped, might respond with a parallel reduction in military activity or moving toward talks, or both. Johnson scribbled on the memo words describing his serious doubts about such a conclusion. He wanted "chapter and verse" why anyone should believe Hanoi would respond in any other way than using the bombing halt for propaganda purposes, even if talks should begin. McNamara was blunt about the likely outcome of negotiations. The "internal dynamics" of the situation would create pressures "moving toward a settlement short of the total elimination of North Vietnam's intervention in the South but consistent with our objective of permitting the South Vietnamese to shape their own future." Along with that conclusion, McNamara suggested that the goal of American military policy should now be to train the South Vietnamese to do more of the fighting. Summing up, the defense secretary reiterated his belief that a bombing halt would lead to a reduction in North Vietnamese military activity and/or negotiations on at least some political issues. "No other course affords any hope of these results in the next 15 months"—or until the end of Johnson's term. [47]

McPherson's memo argued similar points. Like McNamara, he saw inevitable pressures building toward expansion of the bombing, from "less restraint" to "no restraint." "That means population bombing. It means LeMay's and Goldwater's policy." This kind of calculation created the greatest sense of moral unease. "If we are not (as McNamara says we are not) succeeding in disrupting the supply lines to the South, then the argument about shrapnel in Marines' backs doesn't hold up." It appeared to some people, McPherson made bold to say, that "you are escalating the air war, and running a kind of numbers game on remaining targets, solely in order to quiet or escape criticism from right-wing Senators and Congressmen and your own military leaders. But you are the Commander in Chief. . . . It appears to some people that the military are blackmailing you into following their policy toward North Vietnam."

Again like McNamara, the White house aide argued that if the bombing was designed to bring pressure on North Vietnam, it had become, paradoxically, the one kind of pressure Hanoi must resist. A bombing halt could create pressures for talks, on the other hand, by removing a unifying force in the North Vietnamese leadership. "It also appears to some that there is a vindictiveness in prosecution of the air war." Angry that this two-bit country would not come to terms, even if the bombing would not end the war, or if they would not be driven to the peace table, "we are going to pour it on and punish them for all the frustrations they are causing us."

Finally, the bombing created an endless circle which, McPherson argued, had spun out of control. Undertaken to boost morale in the south, now it had made Washington its prisoner. "Maybe you are wiping the slate of targets clean, so that you can pause later without attack from our own military and Congressional hawks. If so, I wonder if they can ever be quieted?"[48]

Whatever Johnson thought about McPherson's surprisingly dark reflections on the president's motivations, he believed McNamara's memo had to be answered. He gave it first to Walt Rostow, who, as expected, warned that it would push the president off the "middle ground you now hold at home." If the result in Vietnam was a Panmunjom situation, the Republicans would demand a "stronger" bombing policy. Conversely, "Bob's strategy . . . would, in my view, be judged in Hanoi a mark of weakness rather than evidence of increased U.S. capacity to sweat out the war."[49]

Rostow had something else to offer—a shadowy "contact" with the NLF, in the person of a captured Viet Cong agent, Sau Ha, who told his South Vietnamese interrogators that he had been instructed to open discussions about a prisoner exchange and "other matters." Rostow wrote Johnson that he had been looking for a long time for "a negotiation within South Vietnam." This looked like it might be it. It might yield nothing. "But the simple fact is this: it emerged while we were bombing the North full scale." The "contact" was elevated to full code status, Buttercup, a sign that someone in Washington took him seriously, even though the South Vietnamese themselves thought very little of Sau Ha's supposed credentials. To the national security adviser, however, the appearance of the "contact" gave him an option to throw back at McNamara. "Before changing our strategy in the direction suggested by Bob McNamara, I would certainly play this string out to the full." Buttercup indicated to the straw-grasping Rostow that "negotiations" were already under way, with the NLF bargaining for the highest position it could get in the postwar situation in South Vietnam. Were that the case, it was important to convince both the NLF and Hanoi that their leverage was decreasing as time went on—not increasing. "I believe Bob's strategy would ease their problem and permit them rationally to protract the negotiation. . . ."[50]

The other three people LBJ asked to comment on McNamara's memo were Max Taylor, Abe Fortas and Clark Clifford. Johnson sent them the "main elements" of the paper without McNamara's name attached. As he perhaps expected, the supposed anonymity of the author permitted the three commentators to make strong statements in response. In a Johnson/McNamara "showdown," it would be useful for the president to have such strong statements on the record. Taylor said the proposal would nullify all the American efforts to achieve its basic purpose, and would demonstrate weakness—always the worst thing one could say about a foreign policy idea. Fortas could not believe what he had read. "This is an invitation to slaughter. *It will, indeed, produce demands in this country to withdraw.* . . . In my opinion, it means *not* domestic appeasement, but domestic repudiation . . . ; a powerful tonic to Chinese Communist effectiveness in the world; and a profound retreat to the Asian dominoes." Clark Clifford, the once and future opponent of escalation, claimed that Hanoi continued to pursue a war it knew it could not win militarily, using its previous experience with the French as a guide, in the expectation of an American moral collapse. "If your pressure is unremitting and their losses continue to grow, and hope fades for any sign of weakening on our part, then some day they will conclude that the game is not worth the candle." The whole world was watching, he concluded, waiting to see if the United States meant what it said about defending South Vietnam. "Because of the unique position we occupy in the world of today, we cannot expect other countries and other peoples to love us. But with courage and determination, and the help of God, we can make them respect us." [51]

Johnson had also decided to summon a meeting of senior policy advisers, hoping to use them—after they were briefed by government officials—to counter the growing number of defectors to the peace movement. On October 21, 1967, protest marchers had surrounded the Pentagon, part of a huge crowd that streamed into Washington. A major event of this peace march was the effort made by its leaders to turn over to the Justice Department a briefcase containing the draft cards of hundreds of young men who refused to serve in the war. A lot of these characters, Johnson told a cabinet meeting on October 31, had turned up in FBI reports as "crazy people who had previous history in mental institutions." [52]

It was important to remobilize the American genro, the Wise Men of the cold war, to bring the country back together to see the Vietnam War through to a safe end. The natural leader of the Wise Men was Dean Acheson. He and LBJ had had serious differences over European policy, and Acheson had been known to compare Johnson unfavorably with his "boss" (insofar as Acheson ever called anyone boss), Harry S Truman. Joining Acheson at the Department of State on the evening of November 1, 1967, were the rock-solid veterans of many cold war battles: John McCloy, Arthur Dean, Douglas Dillon, Henry Cabot Lodge, Generals Omar Bradley and Matthew Ridgway, Cyrus Vance, Robert Murphy, and McGeorge Bundy, as well as Taylor, Fortas, and Clifford. The lone dissident was George Ball, who nevertheless agreed that the United States could not withdraw from Vietnam without severe repercussions.

During the first session Secretary McNamara appeared before the group, offering, it seemed, an odd apologia for his past advocacy. Perhaps, he said, his and Secretary Rusk's efforts since 1961 had been a failure. None of the Wise Men paid attention to what must have been, in their eyes, the result of too much attention to day-to-day reverses. Much more to their liking was the CIA briefing by Vietnam expert George Carver. Carver could not promise victory by the next fifteen months, but he was sure that Hanoi would make a strategic decision to end the war when convinced that the United States would not behave like the French in 1954, and when Saigon showed it had indeed established a viable state structure.[53]

Primed by the Carver briefing, the Wise Men picked up the argument precisely as Rostow and Clifford wished they might when they organized the meeting.[54] At the next day's session with Johnson, Acheson led off by praising "George Carver's restatement of what we are doing there. . . . I got the impression this is a matter we can and will win." We must understand, he continued, "that we are not going to have negotiations. The bombing has no effect on negotiations. When these fellows decide they can't defeat the South, then they will give up. This is the way it was in Korea. This is the way the Communists operate." As for the bombing, its importance was not military—Acheson spoke as if everyone knew that "fact"—but something else, psychological or political. But he did say that the targets should be "less dramatic."

Johnson interrupted at this point to say that *he* didn't play the bombing up or down. It had become front-page news as a result of McNamara's testimony in August before the Stennis subcommittee. "That generated both the hawks and the doves talking about bombing. . . . I am like the steering wheel of a car without any control. The Senate won't let us play down the bombing issue." All this rambling was akin, of course, to what Johnson said about draft card burners and his reactions to antiwar protests—"I'm not going to let the Communists take this government and they're doing it right now. . . . I've got my belly full. . . . I want someone to carefully look at who leaves this country, where they go, why they are going, and if they're going to Hanoi, how are we going to keep them from getting back into this country."[55]

In reply to Johnson's complaints, Acheson lectured the group on how he had behaved after "MacArthur took his licking at the Yalu . . . and there was a great outcry to get out." He had called in Dean Rusk, then assistant secretary, and George Kennan of the policy planning staff, he recalled with great relish, and had given them orders to go see Defense Secretary George Marshall. "We want less Goddamn analysis and more fighting spirit."

When Acheson finished, the others all responded like the Fighting Irish to a Rockne harangue at halftime. Mac Bundy wanted the president to emphasize how different Asia would be if the president had failed to act. "Getting out of Vietnam is as impossible [as] . . . it is undesirable." Douglas Dillon stressed that it was a communications problem. "I was surprised that last night, things were better than I expected." Henry Cabot Lodge affirmed the necessity of American endurance to the end. "In this war we are trying to divert a change in the balance of power." Robert Murphy said the problem was that "there is no hate complex like there was against Hitler. . . . Ho Chi Minh is not regarded as evil in many places in the United States and in Europe he is regarded as a kindly hero."

Only George Ball expressed doubts about the effort to bomb North Vietnam into submission, and even he rejected any notion of pulling up stakes and leaving the south to its fate. Later he would criticize the supercilious concentration on how to educate American opinion. He also remembered a private comment he made to Acheson and McCloy as they left the first briefing: "I've been watching across the table. You're like a flock of old buzzards sitting on a fence, sending the young men off to be killed. You ought to be ashamed of yourselves." Surprised at himself for this outburst, Ball voiced only the most circumspect of objections the rest of the way.[56]

Sitting in on the discussion was Averell Harriman. He claimed not to be cowed by Dean Acheson's condescending manner and *ex cathedra* pronouncements. "To you he's the great Secretary of State," Harriman growled to an aide. "But to me he's the freshman I taught to row at Yale."[57] Yet despite his disagreement with the man he once tutored, Harriman was even more quiescent than George Ball. Acheson's imposing presence at these meetings—he was clearly the dominant figure throughout—owed much to his reputation for having stared down the Communists during the Berlin Blockade in the early days of the cold war, and then, when challenged at home, coolly beating back the attacks of Senator Joseph McCarthy and the "neanderthals" during the Korean War. In the years since leaving the State Department, Acheson had not mellowed. Still contemptuous of unworthy foes, he was even more scornful of those who would give any quarter in the struggle with evil. Despite this apparent aloofness, a carefully cultivated image, Acheson's comments about the futility of negotiations suggest he was reliving the Korean trauma, and, in a sense, answering critics from a past era who had blamed him for being soft on communism.

Later Acheson would regret that he had accepted Johnson's invitation, and the testimony of "briefers," without having prepared himself to ask any of the tough questions—as he certainly would have while secretary of state. But the damage was done. Harriman tried to undo some of it in a memo to Rusk and Johnson written the following day. A number of the participants, he wrote, had expressed the opinion that proposals for negotiations only encouraged Hanoi to hold out. There was no evidence whatever to support that contention. Nor did he agree that there would never be negotiations, only a gradual fading away of the enemy, like the Cheshire cat in *Alice in Wonderland*. The Buttercup overtures, he reminded them, had been taken as a "bona fide attempt to begin talks." "I think it important that we not exclude the possibility that talks with either Hanoi or the NLF may be held before our elections and that our actions could increase the likelihood of talks." [58]

McGeorge Bundy took several days to respond to Johnson's request that he summarize the discussion along with his own comments. The delay, he said, was because he had found "my own mind stretched to some new thoughts. . . ." The results of his meditation proved to include some real stretches indeed, and some very curious twists, as the former national security adviser attempted to resolve both McNamara's defection from the November "consensus" and his own concerns about the "long haul." Bundy began by affirming that no one at the briefings wished to quit Vietnam without a satisfactory settlement, but there "may well be latent differences about the kind of settlement that would be acceptable." No one wanted to put any bets on the likelihood of early negotiations, he went on, except perhaps Averell Harriman, who was probably doing some wishful thinking about the road to peace through Communist capitals, and was too eager to demonstrate he knew the directions and should lead the way.

What about the bombing? Here Bundy came up against what had become the definitive issue—as McNamara understood full well—for if the bombing neither stopped the flow of supplies to the south nor was effective as a punitive weapon in forcing peace negotiations on American terms, the very basis of American strategy since the beginning of Rolling Thunder fell apart. In the event, Bundy flinched. The trouble, he wrote, centered in the squabbles between McNamara and the JCS. What was needed was a clear statement that no one intended to threaten China with a wider war. Then "Bob" should be persuaded to do his bit to help matters. Having stopped all the "foolish and false talk about a collision course with China," Johnson could lean on McNamara.

> Such an internal decision would . . . require—and permit—a gradual reframing of the position of the Secretary of Defense himself. Bob McNamara has tended to focus his attention very sharply upon the single issue of the relation between the bombing in the North and supply and reinforcement in the South. While I tend to agree with him on this emphasis, I do not think it was the emphasis of the majority of those who spoke on November 2, nor do I think it is the strongest position for you, all things considered, in the next fifteen months. I therefore believe that Bob should be asked to join in a rationale for the bombing which is a lit-

tle wider than what he has been using in his wholly understandable argumentation before the Stennis Committee. This is not a matter of a drastic change in his position, but simply a question of reframing it so as to give more emphasis to the element of increased military cost which is a legitimate purpose of bombing.[59]

This remarkable commentary treated McNamara's deepest concerns as "simply a question of reframing." It was all the more remarkable because Bundy was aware of and, at the president's instance, had commented upon the defense secretary's positions, later formalized in the November 1 memorandum, which went beyond McNamara's testimony to the Stennis subcommittee—a good distance beyond.[60] Now, swept up in the Achesonian dramaturgy, Bundy pretty much reversed his position from a letter he had written to the *Washington Post* in early September. There Bundy had argued that the Stennis subcommittee's report treated the generals' and admirals' opinions as virtually sacrosanct "simply because they are professionals," and denigrated the defense secretary's cogent rebuttal, even though it was fully supported by "extensive evidence." There, also, Bundy had cautioned against arguments without evidence from the dove side of the Vietnam debate, but the tone throughout was quite different from his November 10 memo to Johnson. Where earlier he had defended McNamara unconditionally, now the message was that the defense secretary needed to reframe his position to accommodate the views of the JCS, and, even more important, to support the conclusions of the Wise Men.

In a sudden shift, Bundy then raised, albeit in a somewhat oblique fashion, the whole question of how the war in the south was being conducted. He wondered, indeed, "what Westy's strategy really is?" Sending out soldiers to "search and destroy" the enemy in far-off areas had proved more and more costly in terms of money and men, and the results were not at all clear. But neither was Bundy's alternative, which seemed to hint at a modified enclave strategy, or, more directly, at what would later, in the Nixon years, be called "Vietnamization." Then came yet another remarkable commentary:

What I think I am recommending is simply that the Commander-in-Chief visibly take command of a contest that is more political in its character than any in our history except the Civil War (where Lincoln interfered *much* more than you have). I think the visible exercise of his authority is not only best for the war but also best for public opinion—and also best for the internal confidence of government.

Obviously, he said, he could not predict what policies would be adopted as the result of such a review, but they could be less expensive in lives by involving fewer exposures to ambush, and less expensive in money. And here Bundy's doubts about the ultimate outcome surfaced:

There just has to be an end of the cost of build-up at some point, and we ought not to let anyone believe that the dollar in Vietnam doesn't matter. It matters like Hell to our ability to stay the course. . . . If one thing is more clear than another, it is that we simply are not going to go on at the present rate for that length of time [five or ten years], and since I think the Communists have proved more stubborn than we expected at every stage, I think that sooner or later we are going to have to find a way of doing this job that is endurable in cost for a long pull.

The letter ended with Bundy's confession that "public discontent with the war is now wide and deep."

I still hold with all the things I said . . . and in earlier memoranda about not pausing, not negotiating, and not escalating. I now go on to say that I think some visible *de*-escalation, based on success and not failure, is the most promising path I can see. I can't prove this path exists, but I think we should search for it.

Thus Bundy's memorandum twisted and turned back upon itself, first demanding, in effect, that McNamara recant his recent advocacy of a bombing pause and negotiations, then calling for Johnson to assume a Lincoln-like personal control of the war to restore the internal faith of government in his leadership (another telling admission in itself), then sounding a loud warning about costs and the long haul, before finally settling nervously on a recommendation for "some visible *de*-escalation." Bundy was right to suggest that it would be difficult to prove such a tortuous path actually existed, or led anywhere.

In mid-November 1967 Johnson called General Westmoreland back to the United States to rally the home front. Speaking to a congressional briefing, the American commander asserted that out in Vietnam, "We feel that we are somewhat like the boxer in the ring, where we have got our opponent almost on the ropes. And we hear murmurs to our rear as we look over the shoulder that the second wants to throw in the towel." Westmoreland promised that "in two years or less . . . we will be able to reduce the level of our effort." How long victory would take, he did not know. "But I will say this," he repeated several times, "the best way I know of prolonging the war is to stop the bombing." [62]

That same day, November 17, according to a sketchy "chronology" put together by the White House press secretary, George Christian, Treasury Secretary Henry Fowler informed the president of the World Bank, George Woods, that "it was the decision of the government to recommend McNamara" to be his successor. [63] The defense secretary had not been informed of this meeting, nor that his name had actually been submitted as the American nominee. He learned about it from a London newspaper and rushed to the White House. After a conversation with Johnson, McNamara announced his "resignation" to take the position at a hastily convened press conference in the Pentagon on November 29. The assembled reporters "were shocked at his appearance . . . his haggard face, the loose hang of the dark medium-weight suit."[64]

"To this day," McNamara told a biographer more than twenty years later, "I don't know whether I resigned or was fired."[65] Reporters speculating on the events immediately afterward suggested that congressional sources believed that Westmoreland's influence would now rise, that there had been an ongoing struggle between the general and McNamara, between the JCS and the civilians, and that the military had won out at last. The White House's behavior added to the speculations. Almost as McNamara was making his announcement, Press Secretary Christian claimed to know nothing about an impending "transfer" of McNamara to the World Bank post. Told about rumors that the defense secretary was being ousted because of disagreements, Christian responded cryptically that there were always those in Washington who wanted nothing better than to divide people. "I'm not going to debate with phantoms," he said. "The facts on this thing, I'm sure, will come out." But he would not predict "whether they will come out today, or tomorrow or next week."[66]

McNamara had indeed expressed interest in the World Bank position back in mid-April 1967, when George Woods first approached him about the succession. And there had been conversations between McNamara and Johnson about the possibility during the summer and fall. An early McNamara biographer, Henry Trewhitt, commented that what few in Washington understood about the situation was the "depth of the differences, along with the paradoxically continuing respect, between the President and the Secretary of Defense." That, plus the better-understood problem of "separating gracefully from Lyndon Johnson," accounted for much of the confusion and speculation.[67]

Johnson biographer Doris Kearns records a similar paradoxical complication in the relationship between the two men—that LBJ always saw McNamara as a Kennedy man, yet alone among them a person who had developed a deep affection and loyalty for himself as well. But then the Kennedys began pushing harder and harder. "Every day Bobby would call up McNamara, telling him that the war was terrible and immoral and that he had to leave." Johnson also suggested to Kearns that McNamara had confided he felt like a murderer. "I never felt like a murderer, that's the difference. Someone had to call Hitler and someone had to call Ho. We can't let the Kennedys be peacemakers and us warmakers simply because they came from the Charles River."[68]

Accordingly, McNamara had to be relieved of this nutcracker pressure and moved to the presidency of the World Bank, a safe place out of reach of the Kennedys, who had been watching and waiting for him to crack ever since the August testimony. True, Bobby Kennedy had been closeted with McNamara soon after the defense secretary learned that he had in fact been nominated by Johnson for the World Bank position. It was the hope of those surrounding the New York senator that McNamara would not take this "humiliation" quietly but would resign from the government and join them in opposition. The timing would have been perfect, as Senator Eugene McCarthy, widely regarded then as a stalking horse for Robert Kennedy, announced on November 30 that he would oppose Johnson in Democratic primaries the next year.[69]

Had it been simply a case of Lyndon Johnson firing Robert McNamara, something like that might have happened, but the issues were far more complex. To begin with there was McNamara's loyalty to the presidency and his own sense of responsibility for what he called constitutional obligations upward, as well as his feeling of responsibility for what had become known in some quarters as "McNamara's War." In his Pentagon announcement, McNamara said he had told the president that as long as "Vietnam remains a serious problem and so long as he wishes me to remain in my present assignment, I shall do so." Here was a clear indication that McNamara would not join the doves but would instead work closely with the president's choice to succeed him, Clark Clifford, the most adamant of those who wrote critiques of the November 1 memorandum.

Nor could the story of McNamara's "resignation" be complete without considering the impact of the meeting of the Wise Men on November 1 and 2, 1967. Of those present, only George Ball gave approval—a somewhat qualified assent—to the idea of a bombing pause. None believed in the possibility or, more important, the desirability of negotiations—at least not as matters stood. In this regard, the Bundy memo to Johnson put the situation with McNamara precisely. Either he would have to "reframe" his position to bring it into line with the position adopted at that conference, or he would have to give way to someone who could make, or more likely had already made, that adjustment. Clark Clifford had established himself as the logical candidate.

Writing only a few days after the McNamara and White House announcements, *Washington Post* writer Chalmers Roberts entitled his story "McNamara: The Conflict Within." Describing McNamara as a man with a divided personality—the man with the steel-trap mind and computerized memory versus the intensely anguished individual struggling with moral and ethical questions—Roberts argued that Vietnam was only part of the reason for his action. There was also "McNamara's concern over the Nation's prodigal investment in new missiles and its comparatively modest expenditures in the ghettos."[70]

But the war, always the war, stood at the center. Months earlier, Roberts wrote, a friend had asked McNamara how he felt about the more than nine thousand Americans who had been killed in Vietnam. "There was a long silence, a sideward glance, a look at the floor. 'Some day,' he finally replied, 'I'll tell you how I feel about the war. But not now.'" The conflict within was not confined to Robert McNamara. Others present at the meeting of the Wise Men, the president perhaps most of all, suffered similar pain, if still unwilling to confront, as McNamara had, the reality of the Vietnam War on its own terms. And the consequences. For them and for the nation.

General Westmoreland had been summoned home to convince an increasingly skeptical public that the war would be won. "We have reached an important point," the general assured the National Press Club, "when the end begins to come into view." Comparing the Vietnam War to another experience, the general talked about the Indian Wars in the old West, where the army expanded into enemy territory like an ink spot soaking into cloth. And he defied the Communists to stage a massive attack. "I hope they try something," he told a magazine reporter, "because we are looking for a fight."[71]

There is an old saying: Be careful what you wish for, because you may get it. The Communists granted Westmoreland's wish.

Part Four

JOHNSON ALONE

EIGHTEEN

Tet

WHEN GENERAL WESTMORELAND RETURNED to Vietnam following his brief stay in Washington, he was more cautious about making predictions than he had been in public appearances back home. Away from Lyndon Johnson and Pentagon pressure to show real progress, "Westy" stopped talking about the light at the end of the tunnel and early troop withdrawals. His purpose in making those predictions, he explained to his second-in-command, General Creighton Abrams, had been to provide encouragement for those who supported the war. By picturing the Vietnamese as increasingly capable of carrying a heavier burden in the war, he further explained, he was actually providing arguments for a "protracted commitment."[1]

That was not all there was to it. The official history of the U.S. army in Vietnam suggests that Westmoreland's intentions during this period remain "difficult to fathom." The general and Ambassador Bunker had been advised in early November 1967, before they traveled home, that the "Saigon team" would be closely questioned about ways to end the war sooner. The "highest authority," the JCS cabled MACV headquarters, "is now thinking in terms of assigning top priority to those programs which would have a maximum impact on progress in South Vietnam in the next six months." Among the things he and Bunker were to consider, the message read, was the increased use of the ARVN in integrated operations.[2]

During these last months of 1967, enemy losses on the battlefield were heavy, encouraging false hopes that the "crossover" point between rising American combat forces and VC ability to absorb the pounding had finally been reached. Yet if the South Vietnamese were not ready to step in to assume the burden of preserving the "victory," all was for naught. At a commanders' conference with his generals on December 3, 1967, Westmoreland urged his lieutenants to concentrate on two coequal objectives:

grinding down the enemy and building up the confidence of the ARVN. If the Americans continued to distrust and avoid South Vietnamese combat commanders, added Creighton Abrams, "our cause here is hopeless."[3]

Westmoreland's rising confidence in the ultimate success of a war of attrition, given perseverance in Saigon and Washington, was not shared by all those present at such war councils. Lieutenant General Bruce Palmer, for example, could not see such a strategy producing a victory. "There was no way we could win that war," he argued later, "unless you could kill them all, and . . . I began to realize that this war of attrition wasn't going to work because first of all, they could control the tempo of the battle, and therefore the casualties. They were willing to take heavy casualties when they wanted to. They had the larger manpower base . . . about sixteen million people compared to twelve million that were available to the South. They had no materiel problem; anything they lost was replaced. . . . I just couldn't see any way of winning that war."[4]

The only possible way was to give up the war of attrition and go after the infiltration routes in Laos. "Our troops are in the wrong damned place," Palmer told Ambassador Ellsworth Bunker. "I agree with you," Bunker replied, "and Westy's been wanting to go into Laos . . . , but it doesn't look politically possible." If that was the case, it was better to negotiate. "We may in the end have to negotiate a compromise and accommodation," Palmer argued to the ambassador, "because I don't think we can kick them out of here."[5]

Westmoreland's visit to Washington had been aimed at countering such McNamara-type thinking, wherever it might arise. But LBJ wanted more; he needed to be able to point to visible progress in Vietnam by the summer of 1968. Not only was the presidential campaign looming, but Washington was beginning to have the jitters about an impending "gold crisis." Intermittent concern over the balance-of-payments problem went back to the last years of the Eisenhower administration, sometimes popping up as a major item to discuss at the National Security Council, but the situation had now reached an acute phase.

It was easy to blame French President Charles de Gaulle for instigating a gold crisis, and to label him a spoiler with an absurdly exaggerated notion of his self-appointed role as Europe's liberator from superpower hegemony. To which he would respond that it was not his doing the United States acted so irresponsibly around the world, dragging Europe along as an unwilling financier to help pay for its adventurist dreams. De Gaulle's annoying attacks on Washington's policies in Southeast Asia had always been tied to his alternative vision for Europe, but until recently they were bothersome primarily because his anti-Communist credentials legitimized his criticism of the Vietnam War.

Now it appeared that the French leader had found a way to exploit the war in striking a sharp blow at the United States as a prudent manager of the international economy. As the dominant reserve currency under the Bretton Woods system since World War II, the dollar had a fixed value in Europe. Every morning Europeans awoke to see that the price of gold had not changed overnight. It was still $35 an ounce. But something else was changing: there was a growing discrepancy between the value of the dollar in America and across the Atlantic. This produced a situation where de Gaulle could argue that Europe was, in effect, being "taxed" to pay for the American war in Vietnam.

While American inflation reduced the value of the dollar at home, this was not the case abroad. Because European treasuries held dollars as a reserve currency (like gold), American inflation meant that exports to the U.S. suffered while Americans who wished to invest in Europe enjoyed a premium—their cheaper dollars could buy European properties valued at the old rate. Vietnam was a factor in creating this situation, but it was not the only cause. American industry had towered over the postwar international economy, an unnatural state of affairs that was now coming to an end. And even without these factors, a shortage of new gold to back the currency demands of an expanding world economy was putting severe pressure on the official price of the precious metal. Speculators bet that the U.S. could not hold down the official price of gold much longer. Used to living in a world which paid daily obeisance to George Washington's engraved portraits, America had paid too little heed to warning signs that things were out of kilter. Determined not to abandon the Great Society programs, and loath to propose a tax increase that would play into the hands of conservatives, LBJ had chosen to pay for the war through inflation and deficits—in effect, by printing dollars. Only belatedly had he admitted the need for a surtax on incomes to cool the overheated American economy. As he feared it would, talk of raising taxes threatened the increasingly delicate equilibrium in Congress which had thus far allowed him to have it both ways: a war in Southeast Asia and the Great Society at home.

By the fall of 1967, with the budget deficit standing at $11.3 billion, Johnson was at loggerheads with Congress over ways to cut spending to head off an inflationary spiral. Wilbur Mills, the powerful chair of the House Ways and Means Committee, gave the president some blunt advice: Johnson should go on TV and explain that he had had to choose between guns and butter, and he had chosen guns. Once the president did that, Mills would back a tax increase "all the way."[6]

While the impasse between the Oval Office and Capitol Hill continued at home, the balance-of-payments deficit reached the then fearsome level of over $3 billion for 1967. In the last three months of the year it was running at a level of $7 billion per annum. The surplus dollars being returned for gold had a sobering effect on international perceptions of the strength of the American currency and the nation's ability to meet its various international and domestic responsibilities. De Gaulle had dramatized the issue by sending Air France planes to drop off dollars and pick up gold, instead of leaving it on deposit in the American Federal Reserve Bank. In 1965 alone he had "cashed in" more than $300 million and then issued a call for gold to be reestablished as the international standard at $70 an ounce, a level that would presumably stop American attempts to pay for the war with "greenbacks."[7]

De Gaulle also charged that the United States was using the two-level value of the dollar, sustained by the "unnatural" price of gold at $35 per ounce, to buy up European industry with overvalued dollars. It had long been de Gaulle's view that British membership in the European Economic Community was designed to further American domination of the Continent, part of a pattern that would aid American capitalists to use dollars to buy up European resources while denying French technology a chance to compete in the American market. This view was by no means an exclusively "Gaullist" resentment. The widespread popularity of Jean-Jacques Servan-Schreiber's book *The American Challenge* indicated the breadth of interest and concern about France's economic future in an "Americanized" Europe.[8]

France's second veto of British membership in the Common Market in 1967 gave Americans yet another opportunity, on the other hand, to focus on de Gaulle as their favorite nemesis. Treasury Secretary Henry Fowler summed up the impact of French policies at a National Security Council meeting on May 3, 1967:

> The French have been trying to use the Common Market structure for the past five years in an effort to diminish our economic, political and military influence. This French effort in Europe affects our ability to be effective in other parts of the world.[9]

President Johnson agreed that the economic situation was coming to dominate American-European affairs. "A showdown in this country is coming soon." If trade talks with Europe and financial discussions did not produce an agreement on sharing the costs of the American forces, he asked, "what do we do?" Besides the economic problem, noted UN Ambassador Arthur Goldberg, other countries were following the French example of complaining that the United States did not consult, only inform. "We no longer have a solid bloc of western allies behind us." National Security Adviser Walt Rostow responded. "Europe is neglecting the world. It is in an isolationist cycle. We should get one of our Senators to make this point in a major speech."[10]

The trouble with that abbreviated analysis and Rostow's proposed remedy was that de Gaulle had effectively turned the tables by using Vietnam as a pivot to discredit American policy morally, and his forays in "dollar-dumping" to raise questions about American solvency. American "Europe-firsters," who had supported the war because it supposedly demonstrated a willingness to take up the burdens the European empires had once shouldered, had become greatly worried about America isolating *itself* from world opinion because of Vietnam, thus permitting the French leader to exploit those feelings as well as to wreak havoc on the gold market. On the eve of Westmoreland's visit to Washington to rally public opinion behind the war, ominously enough, Rostow wrote Johnson that the British had been forced into devaluing sterling in order to save their gold reserves. The attack on the British pound was widely understood as an indirect assault on the dollar and presaged a full-gauged onslaught on reserves at Fort Knox.

Speculators were now convinced that the United States, its foreign expenditures for Vietnam adding to an already badly skewed balance-of-payments problem, could not hold the price of gold to $35 an ounce, the very basis of the postwar international economic system formulated at Bretton Woods.[11] Britain announced devaluation of sterling on a Saturday. The following Monday, France withdrew from the international gold pool. This group of European nations and the United States had pledged to contribute sufficient reserves to maintain the transactions of a smooth-running international economy and sustain the established price of gold. "This was one of several times when I was tempted to abandon my policy of polite restraint toward De Gaulle," Johnson wrote in his memoirs, "but I forced myself to be patient again."[12]

Johnson then declared on November 18, 1967, "I reaffirm unequivocally the commitment of the United States to buy and sell gold at the existing price of thirty-five dollars an ounce." The need for making such a statement chilled those who had attended the recent gathering of cold war Wise Men, those who had received the official briefings on the Vietnam situation with approving nods. It caused them to look with a different eye at the supposedly secure foundations of the Pax Americana, and to scrutinize Johnson's ameliorative steps for solving the crisis—unconvinced that merely asking American tourists to stay at home instead of going to Europe for a summer or two, or asking for voluntary curbs on foreign investments, demonstrated the will to do anything about the balance of payments. Johnson duly received a notice from the Council of Economic Advisers that commentators had sounded the tocsin in places like the *American Banker*, the *Journal of Commerce*, and London's *Financial Times*: only when substantial steps had been taken to correct the balance of payments would speculation in gold come to an end.[13] War strategy was now overlaid with graphs and charts showing trends in employment and inflation, export earnings and dollar-out flows. Concern about a wider war took on new dimensions, not simply fear of provoking China or Russia.

One of Westmoreland's first recommendations for shortening the war, submitted after returning to Saigon, was for B-52 strikes at supposed enemy enclaves in Cambodia. JCS chairman General Wheeler took the request to the White House and pushed hard for approval. "This recommendation is part of the four months' program for the conduct of the war and how to get it over quicker," he said. The president yearned to follow the generals' advice, but now he had many new worries, not least the increasingly shaky support of the "establishment." Both Rusk and McNamara disagreed with Wheeler—vehemently. Rusk feared "this action would make liars out of all of us who have been saying repeatedly that Bob McNamara's departure would have no effect on the conduct of the war." "If we undertook this action," he declared, "it would raise a credibility gap of proportions we could not stand."

Secretary McNamara's bombing pause had been "voted down" at the conference of Wise Men, but Rusk's comment confirmed that the defense secretary's announced resignation had been another jolt to the policy elite. McNamara expressed a hope at this meeting that LBJ would never refuse to take sound actions on such a basis. But bombing Cambodia was *not* a sound action, he went on. "I am scared to death. I am scared of a policy based on an assumption that by going somewhere else we can win the war. The war cannot be won by killing North Vietnamese. It can only be won by protecting the South Vietnamese so they can build and develop economically for a future political contest with North Vietnam." [14]

The strikes were ruled out—at least for the time being. As if awakening to what lay ahead, Johnson now compared himself not to Lincoln—as his aides had frequently done when the Vietnam War and the Great Society seemed to demonstrate the strength and wisdom of liberalism—but to Lincoln's successor, his namesake, Andrew Johnson of Tennessee, whose troubled years in the White House reflected the deep divisions of the Reconstruction Era. Receiving the first volume of Andrew Johnson's papers in a White House ceremony in mid-December, the president sounded almost diffident: "It is difficult to reach a clear judgment of the presidency of Andrew Johnson. Scholars are still fighting out some of the issues." Thrust into the whirlpool of post–Civil War politics, LBJ continued, Andrew Johnson was "sometimes blinded by his passion into taking an unwise and unnecessary course for the dominant political realities of that time."

"He had no chance for breeding," the president quoted a critic on Tennessee's Johnson, "and none for book education; none for that half-conscious betterment which comes from association with cultivated and morally excellent people." Like LBJ, in other words, Lincoln's successor had had to face the scorn of the Harvards of his day. After a series of anecdotes about Andrew Johnson's rise from poverty to the presidency, his courage in defying the secessionists, and his absolute loyalty to the Union, the president thanked his guests from the University of Tennessee for "making it possible for those who want the truth and who want to review the progress of this Nation in some of its most critical periods to see the works that you have prepared here."[15]

Leaving the White House under a cloud of impeachment and a Senate trial, after narrowly avoiding conviction, Andrew Johnson had to wait a century for a fair evaluation. Was that to be Lyndon Johnson's fate as well? But what could he do in the winter of 1967 to avoid such an outcome? A few days later Johnson appeared on national television for a year-end interview by representatives of the three networks. After a discussion of Vietnam, in which he defended the ARVN against the charge that it did not fight nearly as well as the NLF, and other topics, NBC's Ray Scherer bluntly asked about a comment from "one of the elder statesmen in our business" that President Johnson would not be able to govern effectively unless he regained the trust of the people. "I think there is some uncertainty in the country," came the president's reply. "I think there is some division in the country. I don't think that the opposition is in the majority and I don't think they will be on election day. But I don't discount it, and I don't ignore it."[16]

The same day this interview was taped, Johnson telephoned a former aide, Jack Valenti, who had left the White House to head the Motion Picture Association. "I am anxious to visit the pope," said Valenti's caller. Could Valenti get in touch with his Vatican contacts and make the necessary arrangements? He wanted to see if Rome could intercede with Hanoi to secure better treatment of American POWs. Johnson also had on his mind something he had mentioned in passing during the TV interview. Perhaps it would be possible to push President Thieu into opening serious talks with individual members of the NLF—though why he should do that, or what the results could possibly be, was never clear.

After a hectic hopscotching series of flights around the world, derided by White House reporters as a "flying circus," a helicopter with the president on board finally descended into an inner garden of the Vatican two nights before Christmas. Hanoi still expected to win the war in Washington, Johnson declared once he and Pope Paul VI sat down, just as they had defeated France in a test of wills.[17] If he hoped to discourage the pontiff from bringing up the subject of a bombing pause with this statement, he would be disappointed. Paul did press the idea, but the president said no, reciting the standard objections of past Communist behavior in using the pauses to rearm their forces. Johnson did reveal that after Glassboro he had asked Premier Kosygin what had happened to the American offer to stop bombing in exchange for a commitment to negotiate. Kosygin had replied, according to Johnson, "You are still bombing and nothing can be done." Shifting from what he did not want the pope to ask for, Johnson inquired if he would use his influence with President Thieu, a Catholic, to encourage meetings with former enemies. "It seems to me that if South Vietnam's government would more or less leave us and talk informally with the NLF— and thereby the NLF leave Hanoi—this could be a way for South Vietnam to settle its own fate and have Hanoi and the U.S. pull away."[18]

Did the pope really understand what Johnson was saying here? From the time Dean Rusk declared that the NLF would not be allowed to shoot its way into power there had been a series of retreats, first to the position that individual NLF members should be permitted to participate in the postwar politics of South Vietnam, then to the idea that the former guerrillas could reconstitute themselves as a party, now to this suggestion that the United States could leave Saigon alone to deal with its old enemies. As at the Guam conference, however, it was clear that American policymakers had thought of no safe way to put this half-formed idea into operation. The only thing that was clear was Johnson's increasingly desperate interest in finding some means of bringing matters to a conclusion, either by winning the war, or, never spoken aloud, by disengaging.

The series of tremors on the political Richter scale that reached major earthquake proportions in the Tet offensive began on the morning of January 23, 1968, when the North Koreans seized an American intelligence Ship, the USS Pueblo, and imprisoned its crew. Other reports of North Korean activities suggested to some officials the possibility that Pyongyang had chosen this moment to resume its attempt to conquer South Korea.[19] The Pueblo affair weakened the ground under Johnson because it appeared to demonstrate that a widening of the war in Vietnam might lead to crises elsewhere, in other cold war hot spots. Perhaps worse, even a continuation of the war at current levels might sharply limit U.S. ability to respond to a humiliating "provocation." It might be hard so neatly to connect the Pueblo affair to difficulties in Vietnam, but with 500,000 men in Southeast Asia, popular perceptions paid little heed to "details."

That some Communist master plan had been put into play was suggested by General Westmoreland's reports of increased military activity by enemy forces in several sectors. Westmoreland informed Washington that he saw two possibilities. "Either the enemy is making a major effort for a short period of time in order to gain exploitable victories for political purposes, or else the enemy has escalated the tempo and hopes to continue the protracted war at current tempo." The first had to be the correct explanation, he then argued, because the enemy simply could not sustain losses at 1967 levels. Hence his object was to conduct a short-term surge designed to force "negotiations leading to some form of a coalition government."[20]

Putting the alternatives that way always frightened—and was probably designed to frighten—timid civilians into backing chosen military strategies, out of fear that one day they would be blamed by the American public for "losing" China, or Cuba, or Vietnam, or even Tierra del Fuego.[21]

If, as Westmoreland assumed, the North Vietnamese were preparing a shift to conventional warfare to make a big splash, surely they would be able to sustain their attacks for only a relatively short period. In readiness to meet the anticipated attack(s), Westmoreland had moved American forces north toward the DMZ. Intelligence reported that the North Vietnamese had massed two divisions near a strategic area, Khe Sanh, in western Quang Tri Province, and Westmoreland was satisfied that was where the big attack would come. He sent in an additional six thousand marines and waited for the assault to begin.[22]

On January 21, 1968, North Vietnamese artillery began shelling American positions at Khe Sanh, just as the battle for Dien Bien Phu had opened a decade and a half earlier. French defeat at Dien Bien Phu, no one needed to be reminded, had set in train pressures for a political settlement—a *disastrous* political settlement, it was argued, that eventually caused the United States to involve itself in what had become a bloody and thankless task, and every day looked more daunting. In Washington, "Johnson had a scale model of Khe Sanh built in the White House situation room so he could follow the battle day-by-day and eventually hour-by-hour."[23]

On the day the *Pueblo* was captured, January 23, the president met with Democratic leaders in Congress. The incident could develop into a major international problem, he explained, but then passed quickly to the Vietnam situation. Hanoi had given indications it would talk, but only if "we cease all military activities." We must know what that means, he said. Meanwhile, the enemy was preparing a major effort. "Intelligence reports show a great similarity between what is happening at Khe Sanh and what happened at Dien Bien Phu." Having prepared the legislators for some kind of dramatic "happening" on the battlefield, Johnson passed on Westmoreland's analysis as his own conclusion.

> The President said that there is a rapid deterioration of the strength of the Viet Cong. They are having to replace their manpower with North Vietnamese. The current campaign is a short-term surge effort designed to gain political advantages.[24]

Going from that meeting to a Tuesday Lunch with his top advisers, Johnson brought up the question of possible Communist troublemaking in Berlin to divert attention, then pressed JCS Chairman Wheeler for assurances about Khe Sanh. As the shelling and the waiting went on, he appealed to Wheeler again and again for a definite promise that Americans would not lose the battle: "I don't want any damn Dinbinphoo."[25]

On January 25, meanwhile, Secretary of Defense–designate Clark

Clifford appeared before Congress to testify at his confirmation hearings. Clifford's reputation as a hard-liner led most of the reporters covering the hearings to stress his familiar positions. Only the *Washington Post* picked up on what appeared to be a change in the San Antonio formula. Clifford had stated that American conditions for a bombing pause did not require a prior cessation of military activity, including infiltration. "I assume," he said, "that they will continue to transport the normal amount of goods, munitions, and men to South Vietnam." The farthest any previous American statement on infiltration had gone had been to suggest that replacement and resupply might be allowed. Read one way, Clifford seemed to be saying that the North Vietnamese could *add* to their totals by maintaining their "normal" levels of infiltration. Even if one disregarded any deviance from the original San Antonio formula in Clifford's testimony, the emphasis on negotiating conditions just as the battle for Khe Sanh was getting under way seemed dangerous to Walt Rostow and Dean Rusk, both of whom complained to President Johnson that Clifford's testimony had weakened the American position. Interestingly, LBJ rejected their requests that the White House issue a clarifying statement retreating from the position Clifford had taken.[26]

Some Communist units jumped the gun and attacked too soon to make the Tet offensive a complete surprise, but when the assault began in full fury on January 29 and January 30, 1968, the siege of Khe Sanh was shown to be a ruse to draw Westmoreland's forces away from the cities, where the real attacks were to be staged. Both Saigon and the NLF had declared a truce for the Tet holidays, and the Communists made that stand-down a deception within the larger deception. First reports to reach the White House from CIA sources still talked about the attacks on eight principal cities and several key military installations as a "flurry" of activity "intended primarily for the psychological impact" it would have on the South Vietnamese on their most important holiday. General Westmoreland had declared that the situation was "well in hand" at all the locations, with heavy enemy casualties.[27]

Within a few hours new, more worrisome reports on the Tet offensive began piling into Washington—from the CIA, from MACV, and from American press and TV accounts. It now appeared that attacks within Saigon had taken place and that a Communist commando unit had penetrated the American embassy compound. More than any other, this story shaped the nation's perceptions of Tet. American briefing officers, from General Westmoreland on down, called the attack on the embassy a "piddling platoon action." But the feat stunned U.S. and world opinion.[28]

The contrast between General Westmoreland standing in a starched uniform inside the "recaptured" embassy, offering assurances that all was well, that the attack had failed, while film crews recorded dazed civilians and soldiers running around amidst the confusion and carnage outside, left an indelible impression on TV viewers. Also printed on the American consciousness was the picture of General Nguyen Ngoc Loan placing a pistol to the head of a VC captive and squeezing the trigger. The man crumpled to the ground, blood gushing as he hit the pavement. Loan's family had been killed in the attacks on Saigon, but the summary execution did not square with what remained of American illusions about the war.[29]

In many areas the Communists were able to hold the places they attacked for only a few hours. In other places, most notably the city of Hue, the fighting went on for weeks. The maximum aim of the offensive had been a general revolt in the south and an early peace. Below that came the hope that the shock would indeed, as in the battle for Dien Bien Phu, produce demands worldwide for a political settlement. And below that was a series of lesser goals designed to demonstrate that the Americans, no matter how long they stayed, could not secure any of their positions, either in the city or through strategic hamlets. The biggest losers, militarily, were the NLF cadres, who suffered the heaviest casualties. The offensive depleted ranks of the southern forces and cemented Hanoi's control over the war.

As additional reports came in from Saigon, it became clear that this was no "flurry" or "surge." Some eighty thousand North Vietnamese regulars and guerrillas had attacked more than a hundred cities. As one American officer attempted to track the assaults in the Saigon region, he thought it resembled a pinball machine, lighting up with each raid on a new post.[30] Asked to report on the situation, Westmoreland again stressed the psychological aspects, repeating that the offensive was an act of desperation to break South Vietnam's and America's will to resist. The ARVN was performing well, and President Thieu now had a chance to exercise "rare leadership." Someone in the White House carefully marked a sentence that read, "It will harden the government's position on negotiations with the Front."[31]

It can be argued, certainly, that Tet erased any possibility that Washington would pressure Thieu to negotiate with the NLF. The offensive swept away illusions on both sides. Hanoi soon realized it could not achieve its major objective without suffering heavy casualties and more long years of war. While the offensive perhaps hastened the opening of preliminary negotiations, it is questionable whether it shortened the war. President Thieu's leverage over Washington increased, enabling him to resist demands that he cooperate when Johnson did move toward formal peace talks later in the year. To the extent Lyndon Johnson was crippled politically by Tet and the aftermath, his role as a possible "connection" between Hanoi and Saigon diminished.

For the president and his advisers, such speculations were as yet a minor consideration. The news from Vietnam did not yet reveal whether

Tet was simply a psychological setback or a real military defeat. On February 4 Westmoreland finally reported to General Wheeler that from a "realistic point of view, we must accept the fact that the enemy has dealt the GVN a severe blow." The Communists had suffered tremendous casualties, at least fifteen thousand killed in action, but that did not rule out a second cycle of attacks on the cities. None of the enemy's military objectives had been achieved, and Westmoreland still doubted he had the capacity to win them in another round of assaults. But the tone of these later reports was far more somber about the future.[32]

At breakfast with Democratic leaders on February 6, Johnson reviewed the *Pueblo* affair, stressing that none of the military plans to recover the ship and its crew had much of a chance. Talks at the Panmunjom truce site were under way, without much progress. "We are going through some dangerous times," he said. "The best thing that has happened to us was not sending U.S. aircraft in to try to rescue the *Pueblo*." Senator Russell Long seemed displeased by the explanations, but Robert Byrd commended Johnson. "It was the only course open to us." Having said that, however, the Senate leader from West Virginia expressed deep misgivings about efforts to minimize the implications of Tet.

The *Pueblo*, he began, was only one chapter in the book on Vietnam. He was concerned:

1. That we had *poor intelligence.*

2. That we were not prepared for these attacks.

3. We underestimated the morale and vitality of the Viet Cong.

4. We over-estimated the support of the South Vietnamese government and its people.

"I don't agree with any of that," Johnson snapped. We knew there was going to be an offensive, he went on, but not the precise places where the attacks would occur. "There was no military victory for the Communists. Just look at the casualties and the killed in action." South Vietnam was mobilizing more troops. They had a constitution. They had held several elections.

Byrd did not step back from a confrontation with the president in the face of LBJ's blandishments, while the others present fell silent. "I have never caused you any trouble on this matter on the Hill. But I do have very serious questions about Vietnam. I think this is the place to raise these questions, here in the family." Johnson protested that he had never underestimated the Viet Cong morale. "They are not push-overs." The senator repeated, "Something is wrong over there." And Johnson likewise repeated, "The intelligence wasn't bad." Then the dialogue escalated:

Senator Byrd: That does not mean the Viet Cong did not succeed in their efforts. Their objective was to show that they could attack all over the country.

The President: That was not their objective at all.

Senator Byrd: You have been saying the situation with the Viet Cong was one of diminishing morale. When I say you, I mean the Administration.

The President: I personally never have said anything of the sort. I am not aware that anyone else has been saying that.

What do you think the American people would have done if we had sent in troops and lost 21,000 of them as the enemy has? . . .

I look at all these speeches that are in the [Congressional] Record. I look at all the people who are going around the country saying our policy is wrong. Where do they get us? Nowhere. . . .

I wish Mike (Senator Mansfield) would make a speech on Ho Chi Minh. Nothing is as dirty as to violate a truce during the holidays.

But nobody says anything bad about Ho. They call me a murderer. But Ho has a great image.

Senator Byrd: I don't want the President to think that I oppose you. I am just raising these matters.

The President: I don't agree with what you say.

Senator Byrd: I do not agree that the intelligence was good. . . .

The President: Everybody should say and do what they want to. But we have put our very best men that we have out there. I believe that our military and diplomatic men in the field know more than many of our Congressmen and Senators back here. Anybody can kick a barn down. It takes a good carpenter to build one. I just wish all of you would expose the Viet Cong and Ho. We have got some very crucial decisions coming up. . . .

Senator Byrd: I do not want to argue with the President. But I am going to stick by my convictions.[33]

Later that day Senator Byrd called the White House to apologize for his criticism, but Johnson recognized that he needed answers to each of the points that had been raised.[34] He was "alarmed," he told his top security advisers, at the attitude Byrd had expressed, as it reflected what he was hearing in many of the comments about Tet by politicians and in the press. "I told him he should be defending us rather than attacking us," Johnson said. "I disagreed with all the points that were made. I say this to let you know what is going on." General Wheeler suggested that Tet reminded one of the Battle of the Bulge, leaving the implication that while it had been a tactical setback, it could not change the outcome of the war. Less optimistic than the military for once, Walt Rostow hoped that was the case.

> If the war goes well, the American people are with us. If the war goes badly they are against us. The only way for us to answer this is for the military situation out there to come out alright. I think the men in uniform now have the burden in determining how much support or lack of support we get.[35]

General Wheeler had come to the White House that day to renew old requests for an end to restrictions on bombing targets inside the Hanoi and Haiphong areas. His outwardly calm assessment of Tet as another Battle of the Bulge could not hide a sense of outrage, nor conceal his concern about NLF reserves supposedly poised to launch a second wave:

> I am fed up to the teeth with the activities of the North Vietnamese and the Viet Cong. We apply rigid restrictions to ourselves and try to operate in a humanitarian manner with concern for civilians at all times. They apply a double standard. Look at what they did in South Vietnam last week. In addition, they place their munitions inside of populated areas because they think they are safe there.[36]

Once again both Rusk and McNamara objected to the proposal. It would cause extensive devastation and high civilian casualties, said McNamara. Civilian damage was nothing like it had been in World War II or Korea, Wheeler shot back, nor would be. "Frankly, this . . . does not bother me when I compare it with the organized death and butchery by the North Vietnamese and the Viet Cong during the last two weeks in South Vietnam." Johnson turned to Clark Clifford for a recommendation. Clifford showed some doubt, but came down on the other side from Rusk and McNamara: "I am inclined to move in the direction that their action over the past two weeks shows a dramatic answer to the San Antonio Formula and to the request for talks."[37]

Even had Clifford not recommended removing the restrictions, Johnson was effectively trapped. As Rostow put it, now was the time when the military would have to prove that things would come out all right if public support from the Senate majority leader on down was not to fall victim to the enemy's surprise attack. Indeed, Rostow called Wheeler's statements about NLF reserve forces in Vietnam "a firebell in the night . . . a most serious warning." "Since this is a battle which may determine the shape of Asia for a very long time—as well as the U.S. position on the world scene—it is a battle that must be won." Rostow thought it was time to extend enlistments in Vietnam and elsewhere, call up the reserves, and generally mobilize the nation both psychologically and militarily for war. Vietnam could no longer be treated as an adjunct to American responsibilities elsewhere, or something in tandem with the Great Society. What had to be done to win, had to be done.[38]

To start with, Rostow recommended that Johnson deliver a "war leader speech" to dispel the "growing feeling" that the administration was not leveling with the people. "The correspondents and the public know in their bones that we and our allies sustained a heavy blow last week. Yet there is a growing feeling that the Administration is attempting to pretend otherwise. It will do us no harm to tell them what they already know—and it will do us much good to do it in so unvarnished a way that the wonder will be at your candor and frankness."[39]

The proposed speech Rostow then submitted did contain some very candid admissions, calling Tet "more ambitious in concept, broader in scope, more savage in execution, and more secure in their development than we had thought possible." It listed 22,000 enemy dead, on the other hand, and labeled the offensive a "convulsive effort." The speech talked about the siege of Khe Sanh, still continuing, and still, in Westmoreland's mind, the prime objective of the offensive. Johnson should tell the people that there would be fierce fighting around Khe Sanh when the enemy tried to overrun the marines defending that outpost. "We expect that he will fail, and we expect that he will suffer appalling casualties before he discovers that there-is-not-going-to-be-any-Dien-Bien-Phu-in-this-war." There was nothing new to say about the reasons why America was in Vietnam. The only thing new was the enemy's effort to break the nation's will. He was waiting to see what the effect of Tet would be upon the American public.

> I believe that I can tell him what the effect will be. We have known savagery before. And we have known how to deal with it. We still do. Do not look to Iowa, or New York, or Oregon or Alabama for a reward for your deeds of last week. You will not find it.[40]

The speech draft rumbled on with a series of nearly melodramatic pledges. "We are going to give them the fight they want—and more than they want. We are going to mete out the measure they have asked for—and more than the measure. . . . As Winston Churchill put it to another enemy who specialized in savagery, 'you do your worst—and we will do our best.'" Questioning whether American forces should be in Vietnam, on the other hand, would give the enemy the victory he did not, nor would ever, deserve. If he saw he was succeeding with his psychological attempt, "he will redouble his efforts, with all that implies for the safety of the American men in Vietnam."[41]

As it turned out, Rostow's draft was the first in a series of papers that became a battleground in the struggle for Lyndon Johnson's mind over the next several weeks and months. On the other side was Harry McPherson. The same day Rostow sent his speech draft to the president, McPherson forwarded an Eric Sevareid commentary transcribed from the previous evening's TV news broadcast, noting that he agreed "in every particular." [42] Sevareid had begun by saying that the Tet casualty list included more than bodies. "It includes truth, the meaning of language and human reason." Then he quoted an American major, who, in a statement soon to be cited at war protest rallies across the nation, said of the city of Ben Tre, "It became necessary to destroy the town to save it." "The falling domino theory also applies in the realm of mind and spirit. Toppling truth, reason and language can, in the end, topple faith until the American people place no more credence in the summaries, analyses and predictions of their leaders than the Vietnamese people place in the statements of theirs." Sevareid ended his commentary with an appeal—as Rostow had—for the government to level with the people. "The American people have proved often enough, one would think, that they can stand up under bad news. Trust between people and leadership is a two-way street."

Sevareid had commented in closing that the American performance looked good only by comparison with enemy statements, and that was probably what McPherson wanted to emphasize. The president was not at all pleased with the direction of his aide's thinking, and wrote back a stinging rebuke. "I don't agree with any of it," Johnson scrawled. "Thanks for your judgment-L." [43]

The next day, February 9, the president called the Joint Chiefs of Staff to the White House to see what they now had to recommend. "Will we have to put in more men?" he asked at the outset. General Wheeler reviewed Westmoreland's cables on the fighting in various areas, and concluded with a stunner: Westmoreland needed reinforcements "to prevent the ARVN from falling apart." He also needed them for a strategic reserve to respond to any new initiative the enemy might spring, and to have troops ready in case a decision was made to launch an amphibious strike north of the DMZ. Later in the discussion Wheeler sprang his own initiative on Johnson. If he did make a decision to send reinforcements on the order of forty thousand to fifty thousand men, to fill out fifteen battalions, he would have no readily deployable strategic reserve left. "I know this will be a serious problem for you politically. In all prudence, I do not think we should deploy these troops without reconstituting our strategic reserve in the United States." [44]

Johnson was angry at Wheeler's attempt to force his hand. "All last week I asked two questions," he began. Did Westmoreland have what he needed, and could he take care of the situation with what he had in place? The answer to both had been yes. What had happened between then and now to change the situation? Wheeler produced a chart to show that North Vietnamese troops in South Vietnam had increased by fifteen thousand, changing the combat ratios dramatically. Johnson was incredulous. "Since last week we have information we did not know about earlier. . . . Because of that, do we need 15 U.S. battalions?" Wheeler flinched a bit. Westmoreland was going to put it all in a telegram. This was the first time the JCS chairman had addressed the matter of additional troops. Assistant Secretary of Defense Paul Nitze was also surprised: "I was not aware of this new intelligence."

Rostow shifted the topic to how well the ARVN was holding up. Wheeler's reply put a very different coloration on reported casualty figures. "They have been mauled. As of 11:00 p.m. our time last night, 1,698 ARVN were killed; 6,633 were wounded seriously. This totals about 10,000 ARVN lost." These new figures, not only of wounded and killed but of rapidly increasing enemy strength, continued to surprise the president's civilian advisers. Dean Rusk expressed his astonishment: "I have been asking for several days if there was a new order of battle. This is the first time that I have heard of this."

Army Chief of Staff General Harold Johnson dropped another bombshell. If the air strip at Khe Sanh fell to the enemy, the problem of resupply could become acute. "We think we have a 50-50 chance of sustaining our actions out there." Evacuating wounded under such conditions would mean nighttime helicopter flights. "This is one of the hazards you have to accept." As the recital of enemy capabilities went on, Johnson turned to Secretary Rusk. "Dean, should we have more than the Tonkin Gulf resolution in going into this? Should we ask for a declaration of war?" Rusk had no desire to get into that subject. Asking Congress for action on individual items would avoid problems inherent in a generalized declaration. "I do not recommend a declaration of war." What he did not say was that it was not at all a sure thing Congress would give the president a declaration of war. It might, he did say, provoke Moscow and Beijing "in a way we have never challenged them before. There would be very severe international effects."

Clark Clifford had been silent throughout the meeting. He found the discussion troubling. "There is a very strange contradiction in what we are saying and doing," he finally said. The American people had been told that the Tet offensive was not a victory for the enemy and had cost him between 20,000 and 25,000 troops. "Now our reaction to all of that is to say that the situation is more dangerous today than it was before all of this. . . . I think we should give some very serious thought to how we explain saying on the one hand the enemy did not take a victory and yet we are in need of many more troops and possibly an emergency call up."

Compared with his initial reactions to Wheeler's presentation, Johnson seemed almost fatalistic. "The only explanation I can see is that the enemy has changed its tactics. They are putting all of their stack in now. We have to be prepared for all that we might face." Intelligence showed the enemy had added fifteen thousand men. "We must do likewise. That is the only explanation I see." Dean Rusk was not satisfied, however. "I have a question. In the past, we have said the problem really was finding the enemy. Now the enemy has come to us. I am sure many will ask why aren't we doing better under these circumstances, now that we know where they are." But Johnson did not want to pursue that question at the moment. "Is there anything new on the *Pueblo*?" he changed the subject. Nothing, Wheeler replied, except North Korean threats of war.[45]

Johnson explained something of his reluctance to pursue Rusk's questions or his own skepticism about military intelligence at a meeting of civilian advisers. He had sensed a change from a position of sureness to uncertainty. "I don't want them to ask for something, not get it, and then have all of this placed on me." At the same time, he told his advisers, he was reluctant to send Westmoreland the 82nd Airborne Division, as the general had requested. "Frankly, I am afraid to move the 82nd because of the possibility of civil disturbances here in the U.S."[46]

That confession spoke volumes about the president's mood and recorded his growing pessimism that either Vietnam or the Great Society's War on Poverty could be won. McNamara promised he would try to come up with a plan to avoid the "disastrous consequences" of Wheeler's JCS recommendations and yet move additional troops to Vietnam. What was truly shocking about the Tet offensive was the realization that the United States could not protect its South Vietnamese clients so they could build and develop a viable society able to overcome their rivals for power. Throughout the cold war policymakers had often stated that ultimate questions of victory or defeat would be decided by the "people" themselves, that Americans were on hand only as a shield against outside intervention. After Tet, such an assumption lacked credibility in two ways. First, it was not at all clear the Americans could provide an effective shield. Second, in Vietnam the assumption of the "people's" innate opposition to Communist devilry had been challenged by the willingness of the NLF/NVN cadres to take incredibly heavy casualties for their cause. The issue was not whether the Vietnamese "people" wished to live under communism, but whether that cold war formulation any longer made sense as an explanation for Vietnam's struggle for self-determination.

Tet forced a painful reconsideration at another level as well. The enemy had not won a military victory over American forces, but he had never needed to drive the U.S. army back into the sea. To contemplate what another three years like the period since the decision to send the first 100,000 troops would cost, both spiritually and materially, compelled reconsidering each of the justifications put forward for the war. Hardest to abandon was the notion that world equilibrium depended upon defeating Ho Chi Minh, although some hard-liners were already beginning to develop the rationale that whatever happened next, the American presence in

Vietnam had bought time for Asia to right itself after the dizzying experience of World War II and decolonization in the menacing shadow of Communist China.

What demanded Johnson's attention was the dual question of disengagement, for now it was not the actual fighting in Vietnam but the need to get out from under the military's arguments that they had not been given a chance to win. The military case would begin with the contention that Tet resulted from the faulty strategy of gradual escalation, allowing the enemy time and space to mobilize his forces; it would culminate, as Johnson had already said he feared, in an accusation that he had denied reinforcements to destroy the enemy's capacity to launch more Tets in the future. The president proved unable to figure out a safe exit from Vietnam, and, in the end, neither did his successor.

Over the next week, February 11 to 18, 1968, LBJ's advisers began debating the question of sending Westmoreland immediate reinforcements. They took it for granted that the situation in Vietnam had reached a critical point. Later revisionist assessments of the Tet offensive as a great victory for American and South Vietnamese arms do not begin to convey the sense of crisis hanging over these "preliminary" debates. If, again, Tet was not a military victory for the enemy, it certainly raised military questions about American ability to prevail in the war, both in the short term and over the longer haul. Because later critics disparaged the NLF/North Vietnam offensive as nothing more than a "psychological" media triumph over an ill-informed public, it is well to look closely at what was being said and decided at the highest levels.

Those who wanted to send more men were especially concerned to portray a perilous situation but one that had to be, and could be, redeemed by responding to Westmoreland's appeals. Equally important, such a decision would, it was hoped—perhaps along with a presidential speech—mobilize the home front "for the duration," as in America's previous wars. General Wheeler's maneuvering, for example, was designed to force a commitment to call up the reserves. By having Westmoreland submit a request for a marine regiment and a brigade of the army's 82nd Airborne Division, and then promptly having the JCS turn him down on the grounds that no further forces should be deployed until the strategic reserve had been reconstituted, Wheeler hoped he would succeed in removing at least one of the constraints on the military effort. "With the crisis atmosphere in Washington surrounding the enemy offensive," writes military historian Andrew Krepinevich, "and the siege of Khe Sanh, Wheeler felt that he finally had the set of circumstances for which he had been looking in order to force Johnson's hand on the issue. Thus his encouragement of Westmoreland to request forces, which he then rejected in the hopes of forcing the president to call up the reserves."[47]

When Johnson met with his advisers to discuss Westmoreland's appeal, he had been given a CIA memorandum that confirmed the startling assertion Wheeler had made of a significant increase in the enemy's total combat capability. During the meeting, however, the JCS chairman took the position that he was not yet recommending that troops be sent. If he hoped to confuse the situation, he was eminently successful. The president tried his best to penetrate the maneuvering going on in the Pentagon, the games the brass and civilians were playing, and finally found a temporary position. "I think we should send anything available to get the number up to the 525,000 limit. We should live up to our commitment." Turning to Wheeler, he allowed himself a sarcastic quip: "'Just before the battle Mother' the JCS is now recommending against deploying emergency troop units." Wheeler replied, "At this time, yes sir."[48] Johnson's reference to an old Civil War tune had to do with his effort to get the military to commit itself. Was this the critical moment? he was asking. And were the generals saying no troops now? Wheeler wanted to sidestep a direct answer until his own strategy was in play.

Others present also insisted that Westmoreland had not made a firm request for additional forces. Asked to clarify his estimate of the situation, Westmoreland responded with a cable that achieved the balance General Wheeler was looking for—halfway between ultimate peril and marvelous opportunity. He did not fear defeat, Westmoreland said, but he could not fully seize the initiative from the "recently reinforced enemy" without the troops. If he tried with the reserves he had to reinforce his positions at the points of enemy infiltration, he would likely lose ground elsewhere. If Khe Sanh were abandoned, the enemy would have clear sailing all through the area and could threaten worse than Tet in the future. And so on.[49]

Walt Rostow worked this dichotomy into an argument that the enemy's "new" strategy, adopted out of desperation, had actually been foreseen in Saigon and Washington. "What was not understood and budgeted for was an attack on the cities and towns on the scale, with the concentration, and with the timing that it occurred." The enemy had failed in his maximum objective, but he had managed to shake confidence in America's ability to achieve its goals. Right now it looked as if the enemy hoped to pick up another victory in the I Corps area while preventing Westmoreland from being able to shift his forces to meet the attacks. So far as U.S. and world opinion were concerned, there could be only one answer: a clear defeat of the enemy. "Only such a demonstration is likely to permit us to end the war on honorable terms." Rostow therefore wanted the president to make a very strong response to Westy's cable. "Only you can make the political assessment of what it would cost to call up the reserves; but that would be the most impressive demonstration to Hanoi and its friends." As for the issue Clark Clifford had raised about the contradiction with past statements of progress, the proposed draft of a war leader's speech should take up the argument that Hanoi saw it was not winning and decided to go for broke. "Now they are rounding on I Corps; and we're not going to let them have it."[50]

Johnson barely had time to read Rostow's memo before the next meeting of his advisers, certainly not long enough to question the national security adviser's reasoning that Tet foretold final victory if Westmoreland got the reinforcements he wanted. Everyone present at the White House sessions on February 12 agreed there was no ambiguity about this message: Westmoreland believed he needed the troops. They all talked about the dramatic change of tone in this new message from Saigon. And everyone except Clark Clifford thought he ought to get the troops as soon as possible. McNamara wanted to send them to head off a call for a mobilization of the reserves, however, and that set him apart from some of the other troop advocates.

Clifford, on the other hand, put a series of questions to Wheeler in lawyerly fashion. This was the week that began the education of Clark Clifford as secretary of defense. When it was over, his doubts had hardened into firm convictions against accepting anything the military said—past, present, or future—about prospects for victory. Westmoreland had said, Clifford remarked, that it was national policy to keep the enemy from seizing and holding the two northern provinces. Hadn't that been the situation all along? Hadn't the enemy long controlled that area? Wheeler's answer was not really responsive to the question: "General Westmoreland believes that it would cost more to withdraw and go back later than to stand and fight now." Westmoreland talked about a new ball game, Clifford went on. Was that really so? Wheeler responded, "This thing has been building up for some time." Westmoreland's cable had a much greater sense of urgency in it than the previous one two days ago. Why was that? The General "realized that his earlier low-key approach was not properly based on a full assessment of the situation."[51]

Johnson seemed pleased with Clifford's approach. "I want to ask all the questions that I possibly can," he said, before a situation developed without having undertaken such an examination. "I hope all of you see what has happened during the last two weeks. Westy said he *could* use troops one day last week. Today he comes in with an urgent request for them." He wanted to look at all the issues now. He made it clear that this general observation applied to Khe Sanh as well. "Frankly, I am scared about Khesanh." There had been discussion about ammunition and fuel and medicine getting through to the besieged outpost. "I have a mighty big stake in this. I am more unsure every day."[52]

Do all of you feel that we should send troops? Johnson asked. They all said yes. McNamara, Rusk, CIA Director Richard Helms, General Wheeler, General Taylor, Walt Rostow—they all said yes. Then the president asked for objections. There were none. Clifford kept silent. He was not yet sworn in, he explained in his memoirs, and thought his "voting" was inappropriate. His personal views should be given to Johnson in private. In the past, Clifford had not hesitated to cast a "vote" in these meetings. Truth was, he was changing his vote on many issues.[53]

The announcement that 10,500 additional troops would be sent to General Westmoreland obscured the inner debates in the administration. Wheeler and the Joint Chiefs asked the very next day for the reserves to be mobilized, and Wheeler prepared for a visit to Vietnam during which he and Westmoreland would work out a plan for "victory." Clifford, meanwhile, had received a letter from one of the Pentagon doves who argued against troop reinforcements. The idea of a military victory in Vietnam, Assistant Secretary Townsend Hoopes wrote, is a "dangerous illusion." When he questioned the professional air staff about an assessment of the bombing's effectiveness, he went on, he found there was none. In some senses it was an unfair question, because it required the staff to question their raison d'être. "They come to the problem with a built-in predisposition to avoid the question whether air power can be efficacious in the circumstances where its application has been ordered; their tendency is to assume that it is or can be, and they prefer to concentrate their energies on developing the means and techniques that will prove them right." The studies commissioned by Secretary McNamara had demonstrated that the bombing had "diminishing relevance" to the struggle in the South. Its most useful service might well be, he concluded, as a counter to be traded away in serious bargaining.[54]

The ground strategy was no better, Hoopes continued. It often involved American troops in search-and-destroy battles in totally uninhabited areas, in the worst possible terrain for American soldiers, at a time of the enemy's choosing. As a result, American casualties were rising steadily, without any demonstrable progress in the war. The link between the two strategies, moreover, made it impossible for President Johnson to cut back on the bombing without also changing the ground strategy. It followed, therefore, that not only must the United States not send more troops to engage in Westmoreland's disastrous search-and-destroy missions, but the ground tactics must be changed if the basic necessary step toward negotiations, a bombing pause, was ever to be taken.

While Clifford was reading Townsend Hoopes's letter, President Johnson had devised a set of questions about calling up the reserves that he wanted answered before he accepted the JCS arguments. Why was it necessary to do this thing, he wanted to know: to be ready to provide further reinforcements to Vietnam? Or to be ready for contingencies outside Vietnam? Or to reassure NATO allies to whom the United States had commitments? Or, finally, to contribute to the nation's overall deterrent posture by adding to its visible strength in being?[55]

There is no indication where these and the rest of his questions came from, but the president reminded Walt Rostow two days later that he was determined to have answers before acting as the JCS wanted.[56] It seems unlikely from the purport of these questions that they emanated from Rostow's office. The national security adviser was occupied with supplying the Oval Office with new estimates of enemy dead in the Tet offensive. The figures, he said, were nearly 32,000, while U.S. and ARVN losses were a bit under 3,200. "The ratio over the whole period is, then, almost exactly 10 to 1."[57]

The ten-to-one ratio still cast its spell, but fewer and fewer were unaware that it was a spell, not reality. Besides setting questions about a reserve call-up, the president decided to prepare a draft message to Westmoreland informing him that he had "freedom of action to conduct his military operations as he thinks wise from a military point of view without being inhibited by political or psychological factors originating in the United States." This applied, in case Westy missed the point, specifically to Khe Sanh. The general on the spot should be the judge of where and under what circumstances "he wished to fight his battles." If he had italicized *his*, the president could not have made it plainer: Khe Sanh was on Westmoreland's shoulders.[58]

Johnson's vow that there would be no "American" Dien Bien Phu had thus given way to a larger concern about the consequences of sticking it out. The questionings and message to Westmoreland bespoke a skeptical attitude about any plan to send more troops to Vietnam beyond the 525,000 already pledged. The attention Johnson had paid to Clark Clifford's reevaluation suggested that the president sensed the need for another "certification" from the Wise Men. The political challenge from Senator Eugene McCarthy also troubled the White House, as predictions about the New Hampshire primary showed rising discontent among the rank and file of the Democratic party.

One other factor entered the equation. UN Secretary General U Thant sought meetings with top-level Washington officials to convey messages he had been receiving about a willingness of the North Vietnamese to begin negotiations almost immediately after a bombing halt. For the first time, Thant told Rusk and Clifford on February 21, 1968, Hanoi said it was also willing to talk about deescalating the war in the south.

Clifford welcomed Thant's overture, because he wanted to pursue these indications that Hanoi recognized the San Antonio formula did not demand the abandonment of its forces in the south. As he would do many times in future discussions, Secretary Rusk tried his best to put the genie Clifford had set free back in the bottle. The appearance of any new North

Vietnam division would be unacceptable, he said, implying that there could be endless debate over words like "reinforcement" or "replacement." Rusk also went back to the issue of "productive" negotiations. It was the U.S. view, he said, that peace "must bring about a North Vietnamese military disengagement from Laos and South Vietnam. We are concerned that we do not see much indication that Hanoi is ready to accept this result."[59]

Impatient, Thant admitted there was a basic difference between the two sides. "You want them to leave the South and they want you to get out." But now there must be first steps toward peace or there would be an intensification of the war. The secretary general's admonition thus set the stage for the last great debate of the Johnson administration. When General Wheeler returned from Vietnam to report his "findings," Clifford and Rusk mobilized their intellectual reserves for a fateful confrontation.

NINETEEN

"...From Which Americans Will Never Turn"

THERE WERE TESTS OF FREEDOM, Lyndon Johnson exhorted departing servicemen on board the *USS Constellation*, "from which Americans will never turn." "The past of nations, the past of powers, cannot guide or govern a nation whose power is greater than all the power of all nations past. Ours is such a power." Until freedom stood tall and strong in Asia, and until neighbors feared neighbors no more, he charged the sailors and marines, "Americans cannot sleep, and you Americans cannot be idle."[1]

Hurried into readiness, they left in late February 1968, either the last of a previous commitment or the first of thousands and tens of thousands yet to be called. While that fateful decision hung in the balance, Americans were dying in greater numbers than ever before. Ahead were the twelve bloodiest months of the war. Post-Tet U.S. combat deaths rose to more than five hundred a week. Estimates of enemy killed in the initial attacks kept climbing—thirty thousand, forty thousand, even fifty thousand. Despite these losses, the enemy's faith in ultimate victory remained largely unshaken. "I never think that the front could lose the war," said an enemy soldier captured during the offensive. "This is a war of the Vietnamese people fighting against American imperialists. As long as the Vietnamese people still exist and as long as the American people are still in Vietnam dominating the Vietnamese people, the war will go on."[2]

To American decision-makers, the estimate of enemy dead, in paradoxical fashion, focused attention on the treadmill nature of the war. The higher the numbers rose on updated casualty charts, the greater difficulty one had in explaining why things stayed the same. Entering the figures in computers to demonstrate the terrible losses the enemy had suffered during Tet, and distributing printouts confirming the inevitability that, sooner or later, enemy reserves would be exhausted, only increased amazement at the almost unbelievable determination of this foe to prevail against bombs and bullets or anything that could be put up against him. Quantitative change produces qualitative changes, but in this case not what the military quantifiers wanted—a change in attitude. How all this would play out was determined in the weeks between General Wheeler's mission to Saigon in late February and Lyndon Johnson's speech to the nation on the last day of March.

Wheeler arrived in Saigon prepared to coordinate with General Westmoreland on a proposal to send 200,000 more men to Vietnam. These were the men who would finally give MACV the strength to break the enemy's will. Of course, it was not just the troops that would do the job; Wheeler and his JCS confreres had seen the Tet offensive as one last chance to convince President Johnson to fight the war *their* way, using whatever it took to deliver a knockout blow to North Vietnam. It was assumed that if Johnson mobilized the armed forces of the nation in such a manner, he would have to allow the military to go into Laos and Cambodia. The nation would not tolerate a no-win strategy or a president who stayed his hand.

Previous messages from Washington had already coached Westmoreland on the proper way to make such requests, and how important it was to strike the right balance between alarm and reassurance. Yet Wheeler was apparently surprised at how grim the situation actually appeared. Exhausted from the trip and suffering from a heart condition, the JCS chairman had asked to rest before talks with the commander of MACV to determine how Washington's estimates tallied with Saigon's appraisal. He was awakened almost immediately by a cascade of mortar shells falling on the city. Believing he was the target, Wheeler told a surprised Westmoreland that American forces were "under siege."[3]

Westmoreland and his supporters argued later that the commander's reputation had been sacrificed by Wheeler in a failed attempt to coerce LBJ into fighting a different war in Vietnam. The argument depends, however, in part upon the idea that Westmoreland's optimistic assessments of Tet and the aftermath were more accurate than those of a purposely pessimistic Wheeler, whose goal was to scare the White House into action.[4] Vietnam historians who continue to minimize the importance of Tet militarily, and to stress the media's culpability for everything that went wrong, run into trouble here, not only because the argument requires a semi-conspiratorial interpretation of General Wheeler's behavior, adding someone to blame besides the media, but also because it requires denying that Tet brought home to Wheeler and the JCS the realization that the war could not be won without unacceptable leaps into military and political uncertainty.[5]

A variation on the argument is that Wheeler's efforts had nothing of conspiracy about them; he just never imagined there might be tests from which Lyndon Johnson might turn. Reporting to the Tuesday Luncheon on his trip to the *Constellation* and other military facilities, however, the president revealed, "I walked down rows of men. I told myself . . . that I sure regret having to send those men." A passing moment of uncertainty, perhaps, but also an augury.[6]

While reporters tried to force out of Press Secretary George Christian exactly what Wheeler's visit to MACV headquarters portended, the never idle Walt Rostow speculated on the enemy's next move. "I suspect Bus [Wheeler] will report considerable anxiety in Saigon," he advised Johnson, who had gone to the ranch for a few days. Rostow believed the "decisive battle of the war" was at hand. Obsessed with memories of 1954, the Communists would probably strike soon, hoping to dissipate Westy's reserves and achieve a maximum position in order to force a negotiation, perhaps via the San Antonio formula. "The Geneva Conference of 1954 opened on April 26. Dienbienphu fell on May 7/8."[7]

He had already explored the implications with Rusk and Clifford, Rostow continued, so as to "underline the diplomatic problem we might face if they tried, having expended their capital, to force us to negotiate before our power could be brought to bear." In reply, and not unexpectedly, Rusk had offered a familiar assertion that the way to handle this was to modify the San Antonio formula "and let them know that we wouldn't negotiate until North Vietnamese regulars are out of I Corps." Rostow recorded no comment from Clifford. All this speculating and jockeying took on greater focus when General Wheeler's preliminary report, cabled from CINCPAC headquarters in Hawaii, reached Washington. "Herewith Bus Wheeler's tentative conclusions," Rostow advised the ranch White House. Westmoreland needed three "troop packages," the first to be sent by May 1, the last by December 31—totaling 205,179 men.[8]

Wheeler's description of the enemy's Tet campaign was by far the somberest account of what had taken place—and was still going on—of all those that had emanated from "official" sources. Had Westmoreland not begun to move troops from border areas to the cities, Wheeler's first cable from Hawaii read, it could have been truly disastrous. "It was a very near thing. I will have on my return examples of how narrow the margin was between victory and defeat in certain key areas." While enemy losses were "very substantial," he still had "sizable uncommitted reserves." "It is my belief he has forces available for a second round of attacks against selected urban areas, including Saigon, and the disposition of his forces and his actions substantiate his intention to do so."[9]

First taken up at a luncheon meeting in the State Department before either the general or the president had returned to Washington, Wheeler's recommendations obviously threatened a sensation if they became public. Scheduled earlier as a speech-drafting session, the meeting at State was entirely given over to the more dramatic business at hand. Rusk appeared exhausted and worn down, recalled one of those present who had been summoned to work on the speech. McNamara's face was deeply lined and tense. Others at the table seemed "beyond pessimism."

In eerily calm tones, a dark parody of the crisply self-assured sentences with which he had disallowed doubt in past years, the secretary of defense began detailing what the proposals would cost: $10 billion in fiscal year 1969, $5 billion more in 1970, an overall Defense budget increase of $15 billion in 1970. "This will require a sizeable reserve call-up (minimum 150,000) as well as increased draft. In total, an increase in uniformed strength of 400,000." He had begun to outline alternatives for the president's speech, suggesting how he could use the announcement of a buildup to introduce a "new peace offensive," when Dean Rusk interjected yet another modification on the San Antonio formula. In exchange for an end to Communist assaults in Laos and Thailand, and if North Vietnam withdrew its forces from Quang Tri Province, he said, the president could offer either a partial bombing halt above the 20th parallel or a total bombing halt.[10]

Also present for speech-drafting duties was Harry McPherson. What he heard left him gaping in disbelief: "This is unbelievable and futile." For a moment the discussion went on as before, ignoring McPherson's protest. Clark Clifford suggested they consider another possibility. "I am not pushing it," he said, but what if the president were to announce that we intend to put in 500,000 to a million men? Clifford's words shattered the thin veneer of McNamara's self-control. "That," he snapped, "has the virtue of clarity." What was the point of putting in 200,000 more men. They would not be enough to win the war, only prolong it. This was "madness." "I've repeatedly honored requests from the Wheelers of the world, but we have no assurance that an additional 205,000 men will make a difference in the conduct of the war. . . . There is no [military] plan to win the war."[11]

Rusk and Rostow quickly protested that the enemy had taken a beating in Tet. Captured documents showed he had been disappointed, added the national security adviser, and might not be able to mount a new offensive in the cities, at least not yet. Reinforcing Westmoreland would allow time until good weather returned. "What then?" challenged McNamara. "Let's not delude ourselves into thinking [the enemy] cannot maintain pressure *after* good weather comes." He was thinking about air attacks, Rostow explained. "The goddamned Air Force," McNamara cried, "they're dropping more on North Vietnam than we dropped on Germany in the last year of World War II, and it's not doing anything!" A stunned Clark Clifford recorded McNamara's full agony: "His voice faltered, and for a moment he had difficulty speaking between suppressed sobs. He looked at me: 'We simply have to end this thing. I just hope you can get control of it. It is out of control.' "[12]

Clifford quickly intervened as they all sat silent in embarrassment. Let's look at the problem from another perspective, he said. How do we gain support for a major program if we have told the people things were going so well? "How do we avoid creating feeling that we are pouring troops down [a] rathole?" Before any decision was made, he concluded, there must be a full review of "our entire posture in SVN." Seemingly recovered, McNamara agreed. It would take a week at least, he said, to work out the defense and economic measures if we go big. McPherson was not deceived by the defense secretary's attempt to go on as if nothing had happened. "We are at a point of crisis," he wrote at the end of his notes on the meeting. "Q. is whether these profound doubts will be presented to President."[13]

Driving back to the White House, a shaken Califano turned to McPherson. "This is crazy," he said. McPherson nodded. "It really is all over, isn't it?" Califano said. "You bet it is," McPherson agreed. At this moment Califano knew that the president had somehow to wind down the war.[14] Early the next morning both Johnson and Wheeler returned to Washington in the middle of a rainstorm. They met at breakfast along with many of the same people who had attended the previous day's preliminary session. Wheeler began his oral report by saying, "I certainly learned things I did not know before." Then he repeated much of what had been in his cable. Among those things he had learned was that up to one-third of the South Vietnamese army had been rendered ineffective because of losses during Tet, pacification was at a halt, and the government believed it could not "afford" another such offensive in Saigon and the other towns. "The VC are prowling the countryside, and it is now a question of which side moves the fastest to gain control. The outcome is not at all clear." It was the consensus of responsible commanders, he concluded, that 1968 would be the pivotal year of the war.[15]

What was the alternative to sending Westmoreland the reinforcements? Johnson asked. We would have to be prepared to give up the two northern provinces of South Vietnam, came the reply, providing the North Vietnamese with a strong position for negotiations. "It would, I believe, cause the collapse of the ARVN." Turning to McNamara, the president asked what he thought. Adding 200,000 soldiers would not make much of a difference, McNamara repeated. The ultimate outcome depended on whether the ARVN could pull itself together and match the enemy's capabilities and will.[16]

All right, said Johnson, Clark Clifford would conduct a full review. He would not limit himself to considering only the troop question; he was also to consider other problems, including the balance of payments, whether or not to modify the San Antonio formula, and how to deal with congressional attitudes and public opinion. "We needed answers to many questions," Johnson wrote in his memoirs. "I thought that a new pair of eyes and a fresh outlook should guide this study."[17]

A still intriguing aspect of the Clifford appointment as secretary of defense centers on Johnson's expectations, or even his unconscious wishes. Did he expect Clifford to repeat his November 1967 performance when the Democratic counselor stood with the hawks to put down Robert McNamara's heretical notions? Or did he expect Clifford to reoffer the objections he had lodged in the summer of 1965 against sending the first 100,000 troops? After Clifford showed which way he would go, the word quickly spread that Johnson felt alienated from Truman's old mentor. That was undoubtedly the case. Relations cooled between them. But Johnson listened. He listened because it was not only Clark Clifford but now Dean Acheson; and not only Acheson but James Rowe, who went back with him to New Deal days; and not only James Rowe but a growing list of party notables all the way out to Governor William Guy in North Dakota and beyond.

"Now I make it a practice," Clifford commented on the way he approached the assignments Jonson had given him,

> to keep in touch with friends in business and law across the land. I ask them their views about various matters. Until a few months ago, they were generally supportive of the war. They were a little disturbed about the overheating of the economy and the flight of gold, but they assumed that these things would be brought under control; and in any event they thought it was important to stop the Communists in Vietnam.
>
> Now all that has changed. . . . The idea of going deeper into the bog strikes them as mad. They want to see us get out of it.
>
> These are leaders of opinion in their communities. . . . It would be very difficult—I believe it would be impossible—for the president to maintain public support for the war without the support of these men.[18]

Johnson had thus turned over Wheeler's report to the judgment of the establishment. Another report he set aside. On February 27, the day the Vietnam recommendations were first discussed, the first copy of the Kerner Commission's report was delivered to the White House. Formally titled the National Advisory Commission on Civil Disorders, it had been appointed by LBJ in the wake of the previous summer's riots in city ghettos. Chaired by Governor Otto Kerner of Illinois, the commission's findings were already being ballyhooed before publication as a challenge to the Great Society to commit huge sums several magnitudes above what Johnson had recommended for the War on Poverty. Its "nameplate sentence," wrote Joseph Califano, was sure to infuriate the president: "Our nation is moving toward two societies, one black, one white—separate and unequal." [19]

It did. Johnson refused to accept a bound copy of the report and remained silent for almost a month before even acknowledging its existence at a press conference. The president's attitude deeply worried Harry McPherson, who wrote that it was not the extreme liberals the White House had to answer, it was the moderates who, while they might not even be much interested in civil rights or the inner city's troubles, *were* concerned "about finding some way out of the tragic tailspin we are in." "One way to respond is by arming every white man in sight, but *I think* most people don't want that to be the country's answer. (If Vietnam has proved one thing, it is that heavy weapons cannot easily subdue an upheaval based even in part on social unrest.)" [20]

Few of the president's advisers focused, as McPherson did here, on the new ways the war in Vietnam was coming to resemble the War on Poverty. "I sometimes think that we are lonely voices speaking to the wind," Johnson told the cabinet. Critics were charging that liberalism had died with Kennedy. They had to get the message out about what the social budget meant to Americans, even as the war imposed limitations. [21]

Clifford's "task force" reported on March 4, 1968. Rostow had warned the president ahead of time that there had been "much debate" and a decision that Westmoreland should get not more than about twenty thousand additional troops. The reservations about anything beyond that number went "deep" in both the Defense and State departments. The common view was that additional forces would constitute "a gross over-commitment of U.S. military resources . . . without bringing us closer to a resolution of the problem." Behind that judgment, in turn, was a feeling "that we can only attain our objectives in Viet Nam by a negotiation which brings the Viet Cong into the political process, and this negotiation, in turn, may not be much advanced by putting additional U.S. forces into the country." [22]

The Clifford report, Rostow also cautioned, would contain a warning about congressional opposition to calling up the reserves or any package of measures that would extend tours of draftees. In preparing his report, Clifford had taken advantage of being the "new boy in town" to ask some very "simple" questions of the Joint Chiefs. No, he was told, there was no assurance that an additional 200,000 men would do the job. Yes, the enemy could, and probably would, add its own forces to match the American escalation. No, there was no way to tell if the ARVN could ever take over the job. And, finally, no, there was no plan for victory except continued attrition—unless the administration permitted broadening the war outside South Vietnam. [23]

Armed with the answers he had obtained from Wheeler and the other brass, Clifford presented his "brief" to the president. Even were we to meet this full request, he began, and the pattern continued as it had, it was likely that after a year or so there would be a call for another 200,000 to 300,000, "with no end in sight." The alternative was to send 20,000 and no more until a comprehensive survey of the current strategy had been completed. "Perhaps we should not be trying to protect all of the countryside, and instead concentrate on the cities and important areas in the country."[24]

Clifford tied this variation on the enclave strategy to a new argument: the demonstrated lack of effectiveness of the ARVN in the Tet crunch. When the fighting started, he said, President Thieu had not asked what more they could do, he requested more U.S. troops. McNamara had spoken critically of ARVN in recent months, but nothing like this slam at the basic assumptions of American policy. Next Clifford leveled an attack, albeit in a politer way, at the failure of imagination in the military's strategy for conducting the war:

> We can no longer rely just on the field commander. He can want troops and want troops and want troops. We must look at the overall impact on us, including the situation here in the United States. We must look at our economic stability, our other problems in the world, our other problems at home; we must consider whether or not this thing is tieing us down so that we cannot do some of the other things we should be doing; and finally, we must consider the effects of our actions on the rest of the world—are we setting an example in Vietnam through which other nations would rather not go if they are faced with a similar threat? . . .
> *Now the time has come to decide where do we go from here.*

In past meetings Dean Rusk had always taken up the cudgels to do battle with arguments that put a price limit on what America could or should do in Vietnam. But not today. Rusk had another plan in mind, but first the Wheeler-Westmoreland proposal had to be rejected because it risked forcing a decision on whether to stay or get out—the last thing the secretary of state wanted to see happen. "Mr. President," he began in a formal manner, as if addressing posterity, "without a doubt, this will be one of the most serious decisions you will have made since becoming President. This has implications for all of our society." Then he listed several. It was a very serious matter to take forces out of NATO to send to Vietnam. "We have also got to think of what this troop increase would mean in terms of increased taxes, the balance of payments picture, inflation, gold, and the general economic picture."[25]

But, he went on, the negotiation track was "quite bleak at the current time." After the discussion shifted to the economic consequences of a reserve call-up, and after Wheeler appeared to accept that no more than a tenth of the force he had proposed could be sent, Walt Rostow became alarmed at where the discussion was so clearly heading. "I think we should cast aside the generalities about military solution vs. diplomatic solution; or population strategy vs. real estate protection." Clifford's attack on basic premises and Rusk's ambiguous stance had put things in a stew. So he would attempt to clarify.

We need to look for a fresh summary of the reasons for mining Haiphong. There may be additional military steps to resolve the matter sooner.

The Russians really have not had difficult choices. We should look at a course of harder as well as softer policy.

Paul Nitze, one of the authors of NSC-68, the famous 1950 "blueprint" for waging the cold war, and now a Clifford aide, objected. Rostow was only too obviously trying to divert discussion into fantasies and to lead Johnson deeper into the morass with such speculation. It was up to the ARVN to pick themselves up. "We must get into negotiations some time soon. . . . We must make up our minds when we want to cease the bombings and see what happens." Rusk saw an opening to check the momentum toward a complete halt. "Well, we could try stopping the bombing during the rainy season in the north," he said. "It would not cost us much militarily, since our air sorties are way down at that time anyway." Clifford was surprised by Johnson's eagerness to try the idea. It was as if, he recalled, the president had seen a new life preserver in a stormy sea: "Dean, I want you to *really* get on your horse on that one—right away."[26]

Clifford had opposed bombing pauses in the past, because he felt that such ploys did not improve chances for negotiation. Instead they encouraged the enemy to believe Washington was desperate; and, on the other hand, they later became excuses for new escalations. Had he known about a memo Rusk sent the president that morning from an old booster, British economist Barbara Ward, he would have been even more suspicious. Ward had proposed that Johnson adopt his own fight-and-negotiate strategy, combining a bombing pause with sending more men to Vietnam. The idea was to put pressure on Hanoi by appointing negotiators while strengthening pacification programs in the south.[27]

While Clifford brooded about Rusk's motives, the president ended the meeting with an abrupt statement: "Tell him [Westmoreland] to forget the 100,000. Tell him 22,000 is all we can give at the moment." The next day at the Tuesday Lunch, LBJ asked what had happened to the suggestion about a bombing pause? Rusk produced a draft statement in which the president announced that he had ordered bombing "limited" to those areas integrally related to the battlefield. "Whether this step I have taken," it read, "can be a step toward peace is for Hanoi to determine." On its face this was something of a retreat from the San Antonio formula, which, it will be remembered, was an offer of a complete bombing halt in return for prompt and productive negotiations. Rusk explained, further, that the weather in the Hanoi area for the next month or so meant that the proposal would not make a major difference militarily. Should a new enemy offensive begin, the bombing could be resumed—or if Hanoi showed no corresponding military response, the bombing would be resumed. Areas integrally related to the battlefield would go as far north as the city of Vinh. "Bombing below that area should be intensive and without wraps."[28]

Rusk guessed that even this limited bombing halt would last "about three days." "By the time the bad weather has ended, if there is no response by Hanoi, we could resume it." As Clifford no doubt feared, by introducing this proposal the secretary of state would finally dislodge the problematic interpretation that the new defense secretary had attached to the San Antonio formula. When the partial pause was tried, and, as he imagined, failed, it would erase all previous diplomatic proposals from the books. Rusk finished laying out the scheme, but Clifford said nothing. He was already busy thinking about how this "public-relations move" could be turned around again in the direction he wanted to go—away from escalation.[29]

Amidst rumors that Johnson was demanding a loyalty oath on Vietnam from all Democratic candidates in the 1968 elections, and congressional speculation on Wheeler's report, outside pressure on the administration was building steadily. In a floor debate Senator Fulbright mentioned the figure 200,000—and then said the Gulf of Tonkin Resolution was now null and void. He was arguing that it simply could not cover all the things the president had done or proposed to do. But the senator had another reason for his protest: he was now taking the position that the original resolution had been obtained by deliberate deception. Fulbright had recently conducted new hearings into the events of August 1964 with Robert McNamara as the sole witness. The senator had received information that the second attack in the Gulf of Tonkin, which triggered the American response against North Vietnamese installations, had never taken place. McNamara stood his ground, but the intercept evidence he took with him to Capitol Hill really did not prove his case. And McNamara's insistence that American operations in the gulf were totally separate from South Vietnamese forays and could not have been the cause of the North Vietnamese attacks was now almost totally discredited. Fulbright still did not know at the time of the 1968 hearings how shaky McNamara's evidence really was, but he ended the hearings anyway with a statement of apology to the nation for having guided the Tonkin Gulf Resolution through the Senate. "I regret it more than anything I have ever done in my life."[30]

Pretty strong stuff even for the most "dovish" of the president's critics. Walt Rostow had drafted what he called a "Southeast Asia Resolution," reaffirming and going beyond the Tonkin Gulf Resolution, as "one option" for the president in dealing with congressional stubbornness. The national security adviser was not responding directly to Fulbright's denunciation of the 1964 resolution as null and void, but to his own concern that the initial "hawkish" reaction to Tet, found by pollsters, might be slipping away because Washington had suddenly seemed to lose its nerve. The idea that the "people" might know best about the situation in Vietnam contradicted, of course, the administration's favorite retort to critics that only those with access to all the secret cables really knew what Hanoi's position was or how things were going in the war. "You may wish to discuss it at lunch," Rostow said of his draft, "or drop it in the wastebasket." [31]

The Senate debate over Fulbright's accusations revealed that longtime hawks like Richard Russell, John Stennis, and Henry Jackson were unprepared to support a request for another 200,000 men for Westmoreland, unless the military strategy was changed. Inside the White House, meanwhile, Max Taylor tried to disperse some of the gloom with an encouraging memorandum, yet he had to confess that he too had left unanswered the primary concern that Vietnam "is a sponge with an inexhaustible capacity for absorbing U.S. resources and, hence, at some point we must call a halt. There is no positive answer to this fear which is a real one, other than to point to a few countervailing considerations." [32]

There was little here that Johnson could use as he faced questions about a sensational news story. The *New York Times* had reported both the request for 200,000 men and the rising tide of opposition it faced in administration policy debates. The *Times* quoted one official as saying, "Essentially we are fighting Vietnam's birth rate." The story left readers with a clear impression of a general breakdown of discipline in the ranks and the president's corresponding difficulty in controlling the policymaking process. Indeed, the article added that "some civilian officials" were now recommending that the United States change to a policy of buying time so as to allow the South Vietnamese to strengthen themselves to survive "after some sort of internal compromise" had been made. [33]

Added to the reports of an administration divided against itself came the results of the New Hampshire presidential primary. They suggested a party nearly riven in twain. Senator Eugene McCarthy's remarkably strong showing in that primary, which actually gave him more delegates than President Johnson, portended a run by Robert Kennedy, who had been nervously pacing the sidelines. A prescient letter from Governor William Guy of North Dakota arrived at the White House the day before the New Hampshire primary. "In the final analysis," said Guy,

> the public will vote for those candidates or that party in which they have the most confidence that a plan will be followed to get us out of this

costly Vietnam war and back coping with some gigantic domestic problems. Unless the Administration develops very soon a plan of disengagement so that the public knows what to expect in the years ahead, I would
have to rate Democratic chances in North Dakota, *and perhaps in the
nation*, as very poor.[34]

Such letters belied the notion that the polls demonstrated a post-Tet
surge in support for the war. Guy had written in another letter that he had
never publicly dissented, and when asked about Vietnam he would continue
to speak loyally. He knew the war had burdened Johnson with grief and
frustration. "I know that you yearn not only for peace, but for a truly great
society at home and abroad that is possible only under peaceful conditions."
Johnson's reply to the North Dakota governor, drafted by Rostow, promised
to consider his views, "but no matter how hard the choice, the President
can only do what, in the end, he concludes is best for the nation."[35]

Another major defector was Drew Pearson, who wrote that the president's domestic policies put even FDR's New Deal in the shade. "But they
are in serious danger of going down the drain if this war continues." Pearson blamed Rostow by name for leading the president astray. "In traveling
around the country I have found increasing resentment, even bitterness,
over the war, with much of it becoming personally directed against you. In
my opinion we cannot continue tearing the country asunder over an issue
so distant and so unrelated to the mainstream of our lives." Once again,
Rostow wrote the president's answer. This time he stressed the concern for
national security against an Asian threat from the time of Pearl Harbor, and
dwelt upon the responsibility of not excluding peoples of different color or
culture from American protection. "From all I know, the relations developed by our men fighting side by side with the Vietnamese . . . are as deep
and fraternal as any could be. You know the kind of ties we have developed
since June 1950 with the South Koreans."[36]

Dean Rusk tried to rouse the cabinet to withstand these outside
assaults on the once all-powerful ideological fortress of cold war assumptions. "If we don't keep our word in Southeast Asia, the inevitable result
would be isolationism in this country."

> The last few years demonstrate that the Communist world is no longer
> monolithic—they are in disarray. Unhappily, the West is also in disarray
> and General De Gaulle must bear a large share of the responsibility. We
> have no real alternatives but to stay on our course and encourage the
> South Vietnamese. We must avoid a withdrawal which would lead to a
> major war.[37]

Rusk had apparently finally mastered the non sequitur after many
hours of practice before the Senate Foreign Relations Committee. If the
Communist world was in disarray, how would an American withdrawal lead

to a major war? Indeed, how could the war even be called an effort to resist a worldwide Communist conspiracy? Rusk's predictions were outdone only by a private memorandum Abe Fortas sent to Johnson:

> Unless we "win" in Vietnam, our total national personality will, in my opinion, change—and for the worse. *If we do not "win" here, we will not participate elsewhere on a substantial scale.* If we do not "win" here, I think that a *long period of national self-doubt and timidity will be reflected in our economy, our social programs, etc.; and our nation will be sufficiently shaken so as to be in real danger from a demagogue* (who is not likely to have even the virtues of degaulle).[38]

De Gaulle comes in for almost as much blame here from Rusk and Fortas as Ho Chi Minh and his Communist allies. In a sense, certainly, their half-accusations have a real basis in the causes of the rising revolt within the establishment. French pressure on the American-led "dollar standard" was fast becoming a critical issue in elite debates over the war.

On March 14 Dean Acheson came to the White House to lunch with the president. Johnson wanted to hear from the former secretary of state what his recent examination of the Vietnam situation had revealed. Two weeks before, Acheson had confronted the president with the statement that the Joint Chiefs of Staff didn't know what they were talking about. This sudden about-face from his previous position left Johnson stunned. That was a shocking statement, LBJ had replied. "Then maybe you should be shocked," said Acheson. He would not say any more until he had studied the problem and had been fully briefed. No more dog-and-pony shows. Johnson agreed to those terms, and the reeducation of Dean Acheson began.[39]

Acheson was kept waiting for lunch because the president was discussing what was now frankly called the "gold crisis" with his top economic advisers. Indeed, the lunch meeting was held to one hour because Johnson had to return to that discussion to find a solution. The president began their dialogue by repeating in its essentials the Wheeler report on Tet. It had been a "serious knock" but not a disaster. After talking about the question of sending reinforcements, the president asked Acheson what he thought about the idea of a "committee" to review the situation and advise on ends and means in Vietnam. He was being pressed, he said, by "several quarters on the Hill and elsewhere" to set up such a committee. This casual reference, almost in passing, was something of an understatement, because Bobby Kennedy had just made the appointment of such a committee a "condition" of his willingness to stay out of the presidential race! Using intermediaries, RFK had even stipulated who the members of such a committee should be, and, beyond that humiliation, had asked for some sort of public confession of error.[40]

Acheson responded to the president's question not knowing about Bobby Kennedy's demands. It would be of no real use, he said, and would only cause confusion. To which Johnson added, again without mentioning the Kennedys, "it would give the impression that he had lost confidence in himself." Acheson then explained that what was needed was more information, not uninformed opinions. For instance, what about Westmoreland's claim to have killed or captured sixty thousand enemy troops? Acheson had grave doubts about such figures.

Reinforcements sent to Vietnam in the next six months, he went on, could not possibly affect the outcome. Hence the president should send only the minimum necessary to plug existing holes, and should make no major decisions until he had all the facts. Johnson agreed, adding that he thought both Dean Rusk and Clark Clifford felt the same way. Then came the Acheson recommendation, worded carefully to be sure, but clear enough:

> I took it that the purpose of . . . [American] efforts was to enable the GVN to survive, to acquire public support, and to be able to stand alone, *at least for a period of time*, with only a fraction of the foreign military support it had now. If this could not be accomplished at all or only after a very protracted period with the best that present numbers could do, it seemed to me that the operation was hopeless and that a method of disengagement should be considered.[41]

Acheson then suggested that he knew about a "younger group within the Government" who could prepare papers for "their cabinet superiors" to flesh out his suggestions. Before rushing off to another meeting on the gold crisis, Johnson assured the elder statesman that he would not make any precipitate decision, and turned him over to Walt Rostow. Summarize these points for Rostow, the president said as he left, and give him some names. But this encounter did not go well. "Walt listened to me," Acheson recorded, "with the bored patience of a visitor listening to a ten-year-old playing the piano."[42]

It would have been surprising, indeed, had Rostow displayed any other emotion. After all, Acheson had suggested that the "cabinet superiors" give way to the opinions of a "younger group within the government." Even more to the point, Acheson had introduced what would be called in the Nixon years by Rostow's successor, Henry Kissinger, the "decent interval" argument. To keep up the belief that America always met its commitments, disengagement had to be handled so as to produce a "decent interval," or, in Acheson's memorandum, *"at least for a period of time."*

But Rostow was not ready for such a minimalist approach to Vietnam outcomes. He coolly summarized Acheson's proposal for the presidential files as "progressive disengagement," and then sent Johnson a red-hot memo:

> We are at a most important moment in postwar history. Both the Communist world and the non-Communist world are in considerable disarray. The outcome—whether in Vietnam or in the gold crisis—depends on how free men behave in the days and weeks ahead.[43]

China was on the verge of civil war, he went on, and the Soviet Union was challenged by strong liberal forces throughout Eastern Europe. Heavy battles were ahead in Vietnam, but the situation could look much better by May. "If we lose our heads at this critical moment and listen to extremists, we might destroy the basis for the resistance to aggression in Southeast Asia; open the way to a new phase of Communist expansion; defeat the Communist moderates and liberals; and bring us all much closer to a third world war."

These arguments and prophecies were a strange concoction to offer a president needing, as Acheson thought, facts rather than more passion. Every critic of the war had become, in Rostow's line of sight, a dangerous extremist. Acheson, on the other hand, was highly sensitive to the "sound money" argument whenever it arose, going back to his shocked amazement at FDR's reckless disregard for the enshrined economic truths of his time. In any event, the gold question was sure to affect other "Atlanticists" among the policy elite. After the White House luncheon, Acheson wrote a friend, "The gold crisis has dampened expansionist ideas. The town is in an atmosphere of crisis." That very day the United States would lose $400 million in gold, forcing LBJ to order the gold markets closed.[44]

Yet the next day, as he delivered a speech to the National Alliance of Businessmen (created to give life to the administration's commitment to attacking the problem of minority underemployment), Johnson seemed fortified by Rostow's arguments. Three times in a short speech he vowed to win the war in Vietnam:

> We shall and we are going to win. . . .
>
> If that is what they choose, then we shall win a settlement on the battlefield. . . .
>
> But make no mistake about it—I don't want a man in here to go back home thinking otherwise—we are going to win.[45]

Elsewhere in the speech, the president reflected a bit too cleverly on his difficulties. "It seems everybody speculates these days. Some people speculate in gold—a primary metal. And some people just go around speculating in primaries." Earlier that day Bobby Kennedy had announced he was entering the campaign for the Democratic nomination for president. Johnson told the businessmen, "The press asked for my reaction to the recent activities of the Senator from New York. I don't want to tell you all of my reactions this morning."

The next day, March 17, Johnson delivered another fiery speech to a farmers' group in Minneapolis. America was going to win, he repeated, but it was not doing enough yet to win. Everyone must join in to help. "The time has come when we ought to stand up and be counted, when we ought to support our leaders, our government, our men, and our allies until aggression is stopped, wherever it has occurred."[46]

Whatever their impact on the nation, these speeches certainly polarized the men around the president. Clark Clifford felt shocked and dismayed. Harry McPherson wrote a ten-page letter urging the president to change his tactics in both foreign and domestic policy. "I think the course we seem to be taking now will lead either to Kennedy's nomination or Nixon's election, or both." But perhaps the most important reaction was a memo from James Rowe. Writing as an old friend as well as a Democratic party adviser, Rowe declared his surprise at the number of calls he had received in protest against the recent speeches. "The fact is, hardly anyone today is interested in winning the war. Everyone wants to get out and the only question is how."[47]

Rowe told the president he had asked Clark Clifford to "crank into the computer of decision" his views on the domestic political factor and Vietnam. Tet had changed everything. The middle group at home had disappeared. "The polls may show more hawks than doves but I insist, as does everyone of the 12 or 13 men at [Democratic] headquarters today who are talking around the country, that none of us ever find more than one or two isolated hawks. Everyone has turned into a dove."[48]

The immediate danger was the upcoming Wisconsin primary in early April, but unless changes were made the White House could be facing a series of defeats going right into the Chicago convention. At the next Tuesday Luncheon of senior advisers, the first topic was UN Ambassador Arthur Goldberg's proposal to revive the San Antonio formula and announce a halt to the bombings to see what Hanoi's reaction would be. Clifford objected. "I think it would be fruitless." Instead, he said, why not call the Wise Men together again? They had been nearly unanimous back in November, and perhaps it would be good to see if there had been any change.[49]

Clifford was anxious to blunt any attempt to play the bombing-pause game again—and particularly not within a framework of Dean Rusk's choosing. On his own, moreover, Clifford was now prepared to counter State Department "hawkishness" with some frank talking to the South Vietnamese. Calling Ambassador Bui Diem to his office, the new secretary of defense lectured him on the political realities of the situation. The American public, asserted Clifford, was not prepared "to go around the next corner." Washington and Saigon should be conferring immediately about how to bring the war to an end as soon as possible—"before the US public stops supporting the war." It was not going to be an ideal solution for any of the parties, but it would be much better than the solution that would result when the American public withdrew its support for the war. The public no longer believed in victory, and "when the President talks of winning, he means winning an honorable peace, not a military victory." Bui Diem said he understood fully what Secretary Clifford meant.[50]

Clifford's authority for saying things like this to the South Vietnamese ambassador, especially in the wake of Johnson's recent speeches, was doubtful. He was out on a very thin limb. Just how thin was made clear when the president's senior advisers, plus McGeorge Bundy, met later that day to go over McPherson's latest draft of the president's long-delayed address to the nation on further troop commitments. Clifford gave no hint of anything he had told Bui Diem as they discussed what was in every respect still a "war leader's" speech. Johnson began the discussion, however, with a concise statement of his dilemma: "I want war like I want polio. What you want and what your image is are two different things."[51]

Earlier in the day Johnson had phoned Clifford to tell him, "I've got to get me a peace proposal."[52] But now as the advisers inked in changes throughout the draft as they talked, almost all of them strengthened the picture of an implacable enemy operating from no other motive but conquest, as in the following instance:

> The enemy's attacks have demonstrated once again how difficult it is [—in an underdeveloped country, burdened with the legacy of colonialism and deprived of a sense of nationhood—] to preserve security against aggression directed and supported from without.[53]

The phrase enclosed in brackets was to be stricken from the final text. McPherson's draft had opened with a dramatic sentence: "I speak to you tonight in a time of grave challenge to our country." It then moved to an appeal to protect American soldiers on the battlefield and the American economy against the threat of inflation:

> In most countries such a challenge would be an unbearable strain upon the capacity of the nation and the confidence of the people.
>
> But this is America—the strongest nation and the greatest democracy on earth. This is the land that—four times in this century—has sent its men abroad to fight on foreign fields. . . .
>
> That is a proud history. It gives us cause to believe that now, as in the past, America has the capacity—the intelligence, the resources, and the will—to endure a distant struggle for freedom's sake.[54]

Clifford was terribly discouraged by the outcome of the discussion, at the end of which Johnson instructed McPherson to take out any references to peace initiatives. Yet it appeared that debate had not quite been shut off. Mac Bundy sent a memorandum the next day that argued the draft "will be profoundly discouraging to the American people." It did reflect what was decided in the session, but many Americans had begun to think that Vietnam really was a bottomless pit. "I think it is a miracle, in a way, that our people have stayed with the war as long as they have, but I do not see how we can carry them with us for very much longer if all we seem to offer is more of the same, with stalemate at a higher cost as the only prospect."[55]

In another memorandum the next day, Bundy added comments that he warned were just too private to go to anyone else, "even Walt and Harry." He told Johnson he agreed with critics of the Minneapolis speech to the farm organizations. "This damned war really is much tougher than—and very different from World War II and Korea, and I just don't think the country can be held together much longer by determination and patriotism alone." Only a bombing halt, as Ambassador Goldberg had argued, would impress the world as a serious peace gesture. He knew that was what McNamara had wanted earlier. "I've been against them all up to now—but no longer. . . . I think nothing less will do."[56]

Walt Rostow was equally unsatisfied with the draft of the speech, but for different reasons. He also believed that more of the same would not work after Tet. "I feel in my bones that after the Tet offensive, things can never be quite the same, and that a simple return to the 1966–67 strategy will not wash." There were two other options—a population-control strategy, and a policy of forcing a decision from Hanoi and its allies. This latter alternative would involve mining North Vietnamese harbors and attempting to interdict transportation routes from China; invading the southern part of North Vietnam and blocking the infiltration routes into South Vietnam; and moving into Laos to obstruct the Ho Chi Minh trail. He did not say exactly which one he favored, but the thrust of the memo was to carry the war to the enemy, particularly if a return to search and destroy was ruled out.[57]

Senator Kennedy's first speeches as a candidate for the Democratic nomination, meanwhile, had produced consternation in the White House. They were "the damnedest thing I'd ever heard of," complained Harry McPherson. The reason for this chagrin was Bobby's clever innuendo that LBJ was personally the reason for all the divisions in the country. Eugene McCarthy had stuck to specific issues, but Kennedy portrayed a nation slipping out of control. In Nashville, Tennessee, he reacted to screaming crowds reaching out to touch him by asking, "Who is it that is truly dividing the country?" Who was responsible for riots, drugs, and dropouts? It was not those who were calling for change, he answered himself. And then, his hand piercing the air to an ovation, "They are the ones—the President of this United States—President Johnson—They are the ones who divide us." And even more elaborately in Des Moines:

> Our gross national product now soars above $800 billion a year. But that counts air pollution and cigarette advertising, and ambulances to clear our streets of carnage. It counts the special locks for our doors and jails for the people who break them. It counts the destruction of our red-woods and the loss of natural wonder to chaotic sprawl. It counts napalm and nuclear warheads and armored cars for the police to fight riots in our cities. It counts Whitman's rifle and Speck's knife and television pro-grams which glorify violence to sell toys to our children.[58]

McPherson compared Kennedy's tactics to Richard Nixon's clever use of the Communist issue to assault Democrats as disloyal in past elections. He just implied it was the president's fault—whatever it might be. How could Johnson respond to such attacks? A fight for the nomination waged on Kennedy's terms was fast becoming a no-win situation. If the president had any hope of ending the war on "acceptable" terms, he would have to give himself a free hand by removing the reelection issue. Only in that way could he gain the space to maneuver toward whatever end the fates allowed.

At the moment the nation was divided by the war, his own party riven on a whole spectrum of issues. But there would not always be the war. Those whose resentments had arisen against the social dislocations of the 1960s would stay divided into the next generation. If it could be charged—and it certainly would—that the men who "lost the war" had also forced on the nation a socially engineered nightmare and called it a Great Society, then liberalism might be discredited for a time less than eternity but too long for living politicians. The need for Vietnam had become a need to limit its destructive capacity for the future, no longer to save the present. That was what weighed heavily on Lyndon Johnson.

There had been "a dramatic shift in public opinion on the war," the president agreed. "A lot of people are really ready to surrender without knowing they are following a party line." On March 23 Johnson secretly dispatched General Wheeler to the Philippines to meet Westmoreland and to give him two important pieces of news. There would be no more troops beyond a scheduled thirteen thousand, and he was being named army chief of staff. The president's personal message to Westmoreland hailed him as the protector of South Vietnam against "savage efforts to cut a nation in half," but the public reaction, of course, was that the general had been removed because of Tet and, some hoped, to enable Washington to change strategies.[59]

Prompted by Acheson and Clifford, the president had decided it was best to summon the Wise Men for a new look at how Vietnam fit in (or did not fit in) with the establishment's worldview. All day on March 25, 1968, the Wise Men began drifting into Washington for the opening dinner session at the State Department. During the meal Johnson stopped by to greet them but did not stay for the briefings. Afterward he would always believe that the briefers, CIA Vietnam specialist George Carver, a former army commander in Vietnam, General William DePuy, and the State Department's Philip Habib, had "poisoned the well." "What did those damned briefers say to you?" he demanded of George Ball.[60]

Actually the briefers could have said almost anything, because it really did not matter all that much what they had to say. Led by Acheson, the consensus "leader" of the Wise Men, the balance had swung almost to the opposite pole. Whereas in November 1967 all but George Ball and perhaps one or two other half-doubters had shunted aside any talk of a bombing halt or steps to disengage, now only one or two remained committed to seeing it through to the end. One of Acheson's former aides ran into his boss at a flower market in Georgetown a day or so before the Wise Men met. Greeting him with a flowerpot in his hand, Acheson declared, "I'm going to tell the President we have to get out of Vietnam."[61]

There was nothing particularly dreadful about the briefers' presentation of the immediate situation in Vietnam, but now the probings went deeper. Mac Bundy and his brother Bill, Acheson's son-in-law, had prompted the Wise Men to ask more questions than had been the case earlier. Clark Clifford had got Habib to admit that the war could not be won under present conditions. "What would you do?" he then asked. "Stop bombing and negotiate," came the answer. UN Ambassador Arthur Goldberg successfully challenged DePuy's new estimate of 80,000 enemy killed. What was the normal ratio of killed to wounded, he asked. Three to one. How many enemy were now estimated to be in the field? 230,000. If that was so, they were all in the hospital. "Then who the hell are we fighting?"[62]

Rostow was becoming more and more upset as he watched the discussion go on. At one point he passed a note to Richard Helms, the CIA director:

> Dick:
> About the only hope we've got, I conclude, is that:
> —the North Vietnamese *do* mount a big offensive (B-3, Hue, Quang Tri, Khe Sanh);
> —the 101, Airmobile, and the marines clobber them between now and May 15.
> Just like Lincoln in 1864.
>
> Walt[63]

"I smelled a rat," Rostow later recalled. "It was a put-up job." Clark Clifford had connived with Acheson and the Bundys to bring it off, he no doubt suspected. The only thing that could stop this steamroller to defeat, it appeared to him, would be a North Vietnamese offensive before mid-May! When the meeting broke up around 11 p.m., the national security adviser was gloomy. "I thought to myself," he told interviewers, "that what began in the spring of 1940 when Henry Stimson came to Washington ended tonight. The American Establishment is dead."[64]

Rostow had prepared a list of questions for Johnson to pose to the Wise Men when he met with them the next day. They seemed sadly out of date. "If you believe we should stay the course in Vietnam," read his last proposed question, "what measures would you suggest to rally and unite our own people behind the effort in Vietnam?"

Johnson learned what had taken place when he met the next morning with Wheeler and Creighton Abrams, Westmoreland's designated successor. Shorter, stouter than the handsome Westmoreland, General Abrams conveyed all the tenacity of a bulldog, and Johnson thought he had found the man to revive the sagging morale of the Wise Men. He wanted the new commander to stay and meet with the group when they arrived later at the White House. Abrams had brought with him some photos of Viet Cong "soldiers," teenagers practically dwarfed by their AK-47s. Johnson liked that. The ARVN was doing well, Wheeler offered. "Stress that, General Abrams," Johnson ordered.[66]

"Give them your plan, hope and belief," he added. "It is the civilians that are cutting our guts out." Rusk interjected another assignment for Abrams. "If we can't see some reasonable date, this country can't support a bottomless pit." While Clark Clifford watched with amazement, Johnson suddenly launched into a soliloquy lamenting in detail the wreckage the war had made of his presidency:

> Our fiscal situation is abominable. We have a deficit running over 20 [billion]. We are not getting the tax bill. The deficit could be over 30 [billion]. If it does, the interest rates will raise. The pound may fall. ... The dollar will be in danger. ...
>
> What happens when you cut poverty, housing and education?
>
> This is complicated by the fact it is an election year. I don't give a damn about the election. I will be happy just to keep doing what is right and lose the election.
>
> There has been a panic in the last three weeks. It was caused by Ted Kennedy's report on corruption and the ARVN and the GVN being no good. And now a release that Westmoreland wants 206,000 men, and a call-up of 400,000. That would cost $15 billion. That would hurt the dollar and gold.
>
> The leaks to the New York Times hurt us. The country is demoralized. ... A worker writes a paper for Clifford group and it's all over Georgetown. The people are trying to save us from ourselves. You must bear this in mind. ...

I will have overwhelming disapproval in the polls and elections. I will go down the drain. I don't want the whole alliance and military pulled in with it. . . .

I wouldn't be surprised if they repealed the Tonkin Gulf Resolution. Senator Russell wants us to go in and take out Haiphong. Senator McCarthy and Senator Kennedy and the left wing has informers in the departments. The Times and Post are all against us. Most of the press is against us.

How can we get this job done? We need more money in an election year, more taxes in an election year, more troops in an election year and more cuts in an election year.

As yet I cannot tell them what they expect to get in return. We have no support for the war. This is caused by the 206,000 troop request, leaks, Ted Kennedy and Bobby Kennedy.[67]

Wheeler and Abrams did their best at the meeting with the Wise Men. "I see no reason for all the gloom and doom we see in the United States press," said Wheeler. The biggest setback was here in the United States, which was one of the enemy's prime objectives. Abrams chimed in, "I feel good about the way the thing is going. The morale of the ARVN is high. Some have won battles, with the best of the NVA."[68]

Then Bundy summarized the views of the Wise Men. From the first sentence it was clear there was no support for more of the same. "There is a very significant shift in our position. When last we met we saw reasons for hope." There was no time left, Acheson interjected, to build up South Vietnam. "We cannot build an independent South Vietnam; therefore, we should do something by no later than late summer to establish something different." Challenged by Abe Fortas, still an unconverted hawk, Acheson said the issue was whether we could keep the North Vietnamese off the South Vietnamese by military means. "I do not think we can." Wheeler protested that we are not trying to win a military victory. Acheson exploded. "Then what in the name of God are five hundred thousand men out there doing—chasing girls? This is not a semantic game, General; if the deployment of all those men is not an effort to gain a military solution, then words have lost all meaning."[69]

Turning to Rostow, Johnson appealed for help. "What the hell do they want me to do? What *can* we do that we're not doing?" Rostow saw an opportunity. "Well, Mr. President, you know, as we've talked about before," he began—and launched into the case for invading North Vietnam and Laos. Harry McPherson was in the room and observed Johnson's reaction. "Johnson just *flinched*, just *jumped*." He did not want McPherson around to hear such things even being discussed. "No, no, no, I don't want to talk about that," he said. Johnson did not want somebody going out and saying, "Oh, my God, we're going to invade North Vietnam."[70]

The president demanded to hear for himself the briefings the Wise Men had been given, but, as he wrote in his memoirs, "the briefings had been much less important in shaping the views of these outside advisers than was the general mood of depression and frustration that had swept over so many people as a result of the Tet offensive." Walking back to his office after the final session with the Wise Men, the president mulled over what he had heard. "If they had been so deeply influenced by the reports of the Tet offensive, what must the average citizen in the country be thinking?" Still, he insisted, it was only a blow to morale, not a military defeat. "We were defeating ourselves."[71]

When the Wise Men departed, Johnson was left to ponder other advice, particularly the political advice of Lawrence O'Brien, the postmaster general. Larry O'Brien was a savvy Kennedy man, but his first loyalty was to the party and the presidency. LBJ appreciated (and desperately needed) such attributes. O'Brien had been watching developments after the New Hampshire primary and was deeply concerned about what would happen in Wisconsin on April 2. Just before he left for a look-see, he sent the president a memorandum about recent conversations with local Democratic leaders around the country. "Without exception, these people are your supporters and also without exception they express serious concerns about our current posture in Vietnam, both in political and in general terms."[72]

As a result of his review of the situation, O'Brien said, he felt it was necessary to suggest "some possibly dramatic moves" to allay fears in the party and buoy the spirit of the nation. First, he said, we should insist upon the government and people of South Vietnam taking greater responsibility for the war. At the same time Washington should publicly express disappointment and unhappiness with South Vietnamese failures, both in military terms and in terms of establishing a viable democracy. Saigon should grant a general amnesty to political prisoners and declare its willingness to negotiate with the enemy. To the latter end, furthermore, Thieu should announce a cease-fire, coordinated with a bombing pause to begin the same date. Vietnam policy should transcend political considerations, he ended, but "the widespread anxieties I have found among our political friends and associates convince me that their fears reflect an ever deepening disenchantment among many segments of the population who have heretofore supported our actions in Vietnam."[73]

In his memoirs O'Brien would write that it might have seemed presumptuous of him to set out a detailed plan of action for Vietnam, "but that had been the job of the experts for far too long." Apparently concerned that O'Brien would talk about his proposals elsewhere, Johnson sent Dean Rusk scurrying after him via telephone to tell the postmaster general about the proposal that *had* been decided upon: curtailment of the bombing above the 20th parallel in North Vietnam. Rusk had first broached the idea of such a partial bombing halt early in the month, explaining that with the weather overcast around Hanoi and Haiphong it would cost nothing militarily— and there was no expectation the North Vietnamese would respond, thus letting Washington off the hook with domestic and world opinion.[74]

Clark Clifford had feared exactly this ploy. He had pinned his hopes on countersubversion against Rusk's efforts to sabotage the groundwork he had laid with his interpretation of the San Antonio formula. Neither man was entirely happy with what the president planned to say to the nation. At long last the speech, which began in early drafts as a defiant response to the North Vietnamese for Tet, to the press for its supposed distortions, to de Gaulle for his gold policies, and to the whole world for its lack of faith, was ready. Only now it announced a partial bombing halt and put peace as its primary concern. Nor did Clifford or Rusk, apparently, have any real inkling of how Johnson intended to end his speech to the nation announcing the change in bombing policy.

The president had been thinking about not running for a second term for the past several months—if not years. He had asked various people what they thought the impact of such a decision would be on the war effort. But in recent days he had talked more like a candidate gearing up to take on any rival, Republican or Democrat. O'Brien's telephone report on the Wisconsin situation very likely decided the final paragraph of Johnson's speech. As O'Brien recorded the conversation, Johnson quizzed him closely about the primary:

> "Well, what do you think will happen?" he asked.
> "I don't think it looks good for you."
> "Can't you be more definite?"
> "Yes," I said, "I think you are going to be badly defeated."
> "How bad?" he inquired.
> "Sixty-forty," I told him. "Maybe two to one."
> His tone changed.
> "You were there only one day," he pointed out.
> "That's true," I said. "But that's my sense of the situation. Frankly, your supporters are very depressed."[75]

Lyndon Johnson knew very well that a decision not to stand for reelection would be interpreted in many (probably most) quarters as signaling a change in Vietnam policy—just as his "promotion" of General Westmoreland, no matter how fulsomely he might praise the former MACV commander, seemed a deliberate choice between competing military strategies. Perhaps, therefore, O'Brien's report on the likely outcome of the Wisconsin primary finally pushed Johnson through the door of decision. If so, he would fashion a virtue out of necessity.

Rusk and Clifford, meanwhile, were working on the final draft of the president's speech to the nation. They met once more on the morning of March 28, when the secretary of defense decided he had to take the plunge. The speech was all wrong, he said, it was still a war speech. It should not announce a pause of any sort but a cessation of bombing above the 20th parallel, and indicate that if the other side responded, further steps would be taken. Rusk's plan had been to announce a halt—and leave it at that. To Clifford's surprise, the secretary of state did not object, at least to the idea that the president be offered two drafts, the original and a softer speech.[76]

Johnson chose the latter. Scrawled on a piece of paper the president left behind after a meeting with his advisers were these words:

"Murderer—Hitler—"

"—Stop the War"

"—Escalate the Peace"[77]

As finally written and edited by the president, the speech balanced the peace gesture with a stern repetition of America's determination to see the war through to a successful end. It lectured Saigon on the need to take up more of the burdens of the war, but it asserted that progress in Southeast Asia would have been far less had Americans not made their stand in South Vietnam.

It repeated, quoting John Kennedy's exact words, nearly all the phrases that had led to involvement—"pay any price, bear any burden, meet any hardship, support any friend, oppose any foe to assure the survival and the success of liberty." But it talked about "division in the American house now." "There is divisiveness among us all tonight. And holding the trust that is mine, as President of all the people, I cannot disregard the peril to the progress of the American people and the hope and the prospect of peace for all peoples."

The passages on the bombing policy change followed Clifford's suggestions rather than Rusk's abbreviated proposal. Johnson announced that the United States was "taking the first step to deescalate . . . unilaterally, and at once." Even the "very limited bombing" of the north could come to an early end, he went on, if the restraint was met by Hanoi's restraint. "Whether a complete bombing halt becomes possible in the future will be determined by events."[78]

Johnson announced that he had named Averell Harriman as his personal representative to any peace conference that might be convened as a result of Hanoi's response to the offer to negotiate. And he called upon the United Kingdom and the Soviet Union, as cochairs of the Geneva conferences, to do all they could to move things to the peace table. Then came the famous peroration:

> With America's sons in the fields far away, with America's future under challenge right here at home, with our hopes and the world's hopes for

peace in the balance every day, I do not believe that I should devote an hour or a day of my time to any personal partisan causes or to any duties other than the awesome duties of this office—the Presidency of your country.

Accordingly, I shall not seek, and I will not accept, the nomination of my party for another term as your President.

The speech reflected the divisions among the president's advisers and was really the opening, not the climax, of an intense struggle to shape policy. Clifford's side in the ensuing debate started off with the advantage of the president's announcement that he would stand aside so as not to contaminate the peace process with politics. Johnson's withdrawal accentuated the idea that he had set in motion a process, not simply a bait-and-switch ploy. It also put pressure on Hanoi if it hoped to use world opinion to further its cause. In that sense Johnson's political self-immolation was more important than the change in bombing policy.

Secretary Rusk had remained calm at the witness table in the face of Senator Fulbright's sardonic questions, and was not one to flinch in this last endurance test. If he could keep the "process" from "getting out of control," the true situation after Tet could be allowed to reveal itself in the dying gasps of an exhausted enemy. State Department instructions to American diplomats in Asia advised them that Washington's priority now was to reequip ARVN forces for the tough battles to come.

You should make clear that Hanoi is most likely to denounce the project [the bombing halt] and thus free our hand after a short period. Nonetheless, we might wish to continue the limitation even after a formal denunciation, in order to reinforce its sincerity and put the monkey firmly on Hanoi's back for whatever follows.[79]

But it would be Lyndon Baines Johnson who chose what followed, not Clifford or Rusk or Rostow. Could it be that beyond the messages he got from the Wise Men and the predictions of what would happen in Wisconsin, this prideful man wished, at last, to save the nation from further tragedy in Vietnam? Talking late at night in the White House with his chief of staff, James R. Jones, and others, the president mused about the restrictions put upon an active candidate: "What if we're late in the campaign and I have to make a decision that might result in a peace settlement but will be politically risky. I want my hands free to do what's necessary to end this thing."[80]

Houses Divided

THE FINAL PARAGRAPHS of Johnson's March 31 speech surprised everyone. The announcement he would not seek a second full term put a quite different face on what was really a very modest peace gesture. Secretary of Defense Clark Clifford deeply regretted that Johnson had kept his intentions secret. Had he known what the president planned, Clifford argued later, he would have pushed for a total cessation of the bombing. The speech, as drafted, was deliberately "ambiguous," intended for an embattled candidate needing a respite from criticism. Clifford wished that Johnson had had a chance to redraft it in more suitable terms for a peace searcher. The temporary unity among the president's advisers over a partial bombing halt actually masked a "continuing and profound disagreement" over the nation's goals for the remainder of Johnson's term of office.[1]

If White House insiders were uninformed, the Vietnamese, enemies and clients alike, were left dumbfounded. For once, Hanoi lacked a ready response. Apparently planning their own dramatic offer to begin peace discussions to take advantage of the supposed post-Tet shift in American opinion, North Vietnamese leaders did not wish to make it appear they were accepting LBJ's terms—a partial bombing halt—as anything like a reasonable basis for opening talks. His statement said nothing about troop withdrawals, DRV spokesmen in Beijing told a Japanese news agency, and was therefore "out of the question for the Vietnamese people." Yet Johnson's "abdication" was too big an event to dismiss in that fashion. "We are very happy about President Johnson's decision," said the North Vietnamese ambassador to Czechoslovakia. "I am of the opinion that this will bring this war to an end. Negotiations can now start and they can start soon."[2]

In Saigon, Ambassador Ellsworth Bunker, concealing his own surprise, rushed to see President Thieu—"for obvious reasons"—to reassure him about American steadfastness. Thieu's first question was whether Johnson's decision not to run was really final. "Was there no possibility of a draft at the convention?" Bunker sidestepped the real import of Thieu's inquiry and replied that he could only offer his "personal opinion" that the president had decided upon this drastic step to cut the ground from under his critics and thus give himself a free hand. "He has lifted Vietnam out of domestic politics and is asking the country and his opposition to face up squarely to what must be done."[3]

Thieu quipped that Johnson's maneuver was "very Asian." But Bunker knew his explanation had done little to relieve the South Vietnamese leader's deepest suspicions. Thieu had been hearing disturbing things from Ambassador Bui Diem, whose reflections on the changing atmosphere in Washington were filled with forebodings. On one recent occasion, Diem had arrived at the White House eager to talk about the new spirit of unity that permeated his country. He found President Johnson preoccupied with his own thoughts, looking drawn and exhausted, and little interested in discussing Saigon's successes in mobilizing its people for the ultimate struggle against the common enemy. When Diem finished his recital, the president sat silent for a long moment. Then, slowly, he delivered what Diem took to be a warning that he could not sustain the American commitment. "If we don't win," the president said, "we are in deep trouble. I've tried my best, but I can't hold alone."[4]

And the gloom was not confined to the Oval Office. Just before flying home to report on Washington developments, Diem met with Dean Rusk. Only eighteen months earlier, he remembered, the secretary of state had told him, "When Americans decide to do something, they do it." Now Rusk was saying, "We have no choice. Now we have to win not a military victory but an honorable peace." It was the first time, Diem noted, that he had heard an American leader suggest anything like that particular combination of words: "an honorable peace." They stayed with him, he would write, all during the flight back to Saigon, and he was to remember them again in October 1972 when Henry Kissinger announced that the United States had gained a "peace with honor."[5]

As events unfolded over the next several months, Dean Rusk reconvinced himself that North Vietnam was trying to conceal its own desperation, and he did everything he could to prevent the White House from surrendering to the blandishments of the peace contingent within the administration. Back in Saigon, meanwhile, Thieu predicted to Bunker that the North Vietnamese would react to the president's offer in two days. Publicly they would denounce it and repeat their demand for a complete cessation of the bombing; but privately they would circulate rumors that the speech showed how even Johnson had lost faith in his hawkish policy, and that he had abandoned it.[6]

Those were Thieu's predictions to Bunker, so they were carefully worded. What he meant was that Hanoi would not only circulate rumors, it would *conclude* that Johnson had acknowledged failure, and act accordingly. He was right on target. Hanoi's official response, broadcast on April 3, denounced American duplicity but ended with a statement that it was willing to appoint a representative to "contact" a U.S. representative "with a view to determining with the American side the unconditional cessation of the U.S. bombing raids and all other acts of war against the Democratic Republic of Vietnam so that talks may start."

In Washington anonymous officials professed to be "flabbergasted" that Hanoi had accepted. "We had all thought Hanoi was not going to pick this offer up."[7] So perhaps they had. Certainly embattled administration hawks had hoped the speech would, as Ambassador Bunker told Thieu, cut the ground from under critics without yielding anything of substance. But that was before Johnson added his surprise ending to the speech. Clifford might be chagrined that he had not had an opportunity to argue the case for total cessation, but the hawks had even greater problems in dealing with the implications of Johnson's astonishing peroration. If Hanoi had concealed its eagerness to get to the peace table by the strident language of its reply, Washington "officials" now had to conceal their alarm at the possibility of negotiations under the cloud of Johnson's "abdication" by asserting that Hanoi had made a huge concession in agreeing to talks while the bombing continued.

However that may be—and there were many other possible ways of calculating the elements involved—Johnson already had good reason not to shut off the possibility of serious peace discussions. The Wise Men had delivered their verdict—a powerful one. But there was more. Late in the afternoon of April 4 the president was on the phone with Ambassador Llewellyn Thompson in Moscow, talking about prospects for peace negotiations, when a wire service bulletin was passed across his desk. Martin Luther King had been shot on the balcony of his motel room in Memphis, Tennessee. King had gone to the city to rally support for striking sanitation workers, whose plight reflected the persistence of both economic and social malaise in the cities, which indeed now approached crisis stage. A few minutes later Johnson's secretary, Juanita Roberts, typed a second message. "Mr. President," it read, "Martin Luther King is dead." Everything Johnson had attempted with the Great Society and the War on Poverty suddenly seemed to have come to an end with a single assassin's bullet, just as three years of promises about Vietnam had ended with a single raid on the embassy compound during Tet.[8]

King's martyrdom firmly established the new fault lines in American politics. The Democratic coalition which had lasted from 1932 to 1968 had come apart. Did Vietnam only accelerate the process? On one side the war demonstrated a whole series of national shortcomings and raised political consciousness leading to disillusionment with the "tepid liberalism" of the cold war years. Conservatives likewise saw the war as a product of liberal "theorizing." When questions were first raised about Vietnam's corrupting influence on domestic policy, it will be recalled, Johnson had seized upon the notion of race prejudice to denounce Northern liberals who supported civil rights but supposedly turned their backs on the plight of the brown men in Asia—and to hammer away at Arkansas senator William Fulbright, his nemesis as chairman of the Senate Foreign Relations Committee, whose record on civil rights had disqualified him as a possible secretary of state nominee. And again, Johnson had recently talked about the struggles on the frontiers of Southeast Asia and in the inner cities as part of the same overall quest for the Great Society.

King had repudiated all such notions. In his last sermon the Southern Baptist leader had turned the connection between Vietnam and America inside out. "Something is happening in our world," he had said. "The masses of people are rising up. And . . . if something isn't done, and in a hurry, to bring the colored peoples of the world out of their long years of poverty, their long years of hurt and neglect, the world is doomed." By the time he said those words, King was a moderate. Black panther leader Eldridge Cleaver had written that the uprisings in the cities had brought out the true nature of American society and its "police" forces. "Blacks," he wrote in *Soul on Ice* (1968), "all over America could now see the Viet Cong's point: both were on the receiving end of what the armed forces were dishing out."[9]

A majority of Americans, while disgusted with the war, had no patience with such arguments, but that was not the point. Within hours of King's assassination, the nation's major cities were in a state of siege. In Chicago, Mayor Daley gave instructions to shoot to maim looters, and to kill suspected arsonists. Such orders did little good. Americans were puzzled and angered, one aide wrote the president, by television scenes showing policemen standing around as looters had a field day. It was the same confusion they felt about Tet. "The tactics raise the same deeply frustrating questions as the Vietnam War. How can this great country allow itself to be pushed around and humiliated by a violent minority?"[10]

Well aware that television pictures from Vietnam and American cities showed only surface reality, Johnson also knew he could no longer deal with the deeper realities by sending more troops to Southeast Asia or providing emollients at home. Like all political leaders, he sometimes hid these understandings, even from himself. The original premise of the Great Society was that federal funds for Head Start and other programs would provide inner-city children with something like the opportunity the middle class had always enjoyed. Near the end of his presidency, LBJ would establish a secret Interagency Task Force on Rural-Urban Migration to look into the question of keeping Southern blacks from moving to the cities. Richard Nixon openly adopted the idea. "We must create a new rural environment," Nixon said in his 1970 State of the Union message, "which will not only stem the migration to urban centers but reverse it."[11]

Vietnam too had been based upon a theory about city and country, from the time of the strategic hamlets through the development programs of later years. Harvard's Samuel Huntington had even proclaimed that the United States had stumbled upon the answer to wars of national liberation: forced-draft urbanization and modernization. "The depopulation of the countryside struck directly at the strength and appeal of the Viet Cong. . . . The Maoist-inspired rural revolution is undercut by the American-sponsored urban revolution."[12] Tet destroyed such assumptions, while at home the Great Society's hopes for resolving the tensions created by the internal black migration to the cities went aglimmering as the war starved federal programs of funds and created an increasingly polarized atmosphere—which may have been more important than the actual cutbacks. The impression that the Democratic party was under the influence of silk-stocking liberals and a trendy intelligentsia, neither of whom suffered any social or economic cost from the war or Great Society programs, alienated many traditional supporters.[13]

Johnson had no time left after King's assassination. His death probably made few, if any, new converts to the antiwar cause, but the stakes had been raised. Only blocks from the White House, whole areas of the city were aflame. "By the dawn of April 6," a British observer wrote, "a pall of black smoke hung over the national monuments. The capital of the United States was under military occupation." An American witness in Vietnam asserted that the assassination "intruded on the war in a way that no other outside event had ever done." King's death, recalled a black infantryman, first gave black soldiers in his unit "a feeling of unity and got them thinking about black issues." Over the next several months, writes the historian Ronald Spector, "increasing racial antagonisms in the United States, growing black consciousness and a growing sense of injustice among African-American soldiers in Vietnam, and frustration with a war that appeared increasingly costly and pointless had all begun to converge to move the armed forces toward racial crisis."[14]

It is important to note in this regard that LBJ had told the cabinet he feared the racial crisis, and understood its connection with Vietnam, on the day *before* King was assassinated. In the midst of an emotional recounting of his meeting that morning with Robert Kennedy, and all his efforts to carry on after JFK's death, Johnson suddenly launched into a rambling soliloquy about why he had given the "abdication" speech:

I did it out of my beliefs of 30 years, my beliefs and hopes for this country. . . . *Country is in damn serious danger. Danger in Vietnam—danger in Middle East. . . . Negroes are marching in cities.* . . . we have difficulties in Europe and troubles that could be very deadly here at home, right here in this Nation's Capital. . . . So I think that I did the right thing in the interest of unity, in our Nation's best interest.[15]

One of President Johnson's closest aides, Joseph Califano, has recently written, "Once Johnson had withdrawn from the race, he was determined to end the war before he left office." The first test of that conviction came almost immediately. Johnson had announced that if peace talks were held, his representative would be Averell Harriman. Long associated with the view that a primary requirement of successful negotiations was the involvement of the Soviet Union—and, of course, that he was the single most qualified American to undertake that assignment—Harriman's lack of sympathy for the South Vietnamese added to the concerns of National Security Adviser Walt Rostow and the other Vietnamese "hands" that things were starting off in the wrong direction. Rostow complained to Johnson that Harriman should not stay on beyond the early stages of any negotiations because of his age, and because "he lacks—and has always lacked—an understanding of the South Vietnamese." This failed to dissuade the president, but the struggle would be continued over the terms of the negotiating "instructions."[16]

Harriman had already initiated preliminary contacts with Ambassador Anatoly Dobrynin over drinks in his Georgetown home in his new role as special negotiator. "I . . . went after him pretty hard on the necessity of the Soviet Union taking real responsibility" for a successful outcome of Vietnamese peace negotiations, he noted of their conversation. That sort of approach was exactly what concerned Rostow and the others. They wanted Russia involved, to be sure, but not to arrange a big-power deal at the expense of Saigon. If Harriman succeeded in convincing President Johnson at some point down the road to sacrifice Vietnam on the altar of superpower hegemony, LBJ and the Democrats could be blamed (and with reason) for a Far Eastern "Yalta." It made matters no less troubling that Averell Harriman's name was already associated with the supposed defeats of World War II diplomacy, even though he was actually a hard-liner by the time of FDR's death and well before.[17]

Joining Rostow and Rusk on the hard-line side of deliberations on the final draft of Harriman's instructions were General Westmoreland and Ambassador Bunker. The general made himself perfectly clear. "In the negotiations," he told Secretary Clifford, stressing every word, "Governor Harriman will have a hand with four aces and the enemy will have two deuces." What conditions did he imagine would be acceptable for a cease-fire? asked the defense secretary. None, came the reply. "I do not see any acceptable cease-fire. We would just like the North Vietnamese to go home and turn in their weapons." Clifford was dismayed, in turn, by Westmoreland's self-righteousness and entrenched delusion. But Johnson understood. "Westy is bitter," he said. "He feels he has been made the goat of Tet and is being recalled because he got no support in Washington."[18]

Johnson asked Westmoreland to fly with him in his helicopter to Camp David, probably with a specific purpose in mind beyond giving the general a lift. As he looked down on Washington, Westmoreland saw the fires still burning over widespread areas of the city. "It looked considerably more distressing," the general wrote in his memoirs, "than Saigon during the Tet offensive." Westmoreland apparently failed to draw any conclusion, however, military or political, from what he saw below as they flew on to the president's retreat.[19]

At Camp David, Ambassador Ellsworth Bunker took a somewhat different tack. He delivered glowing reports of South Vietnam's recovery from Tet, and heaped praise on President Thieu's personal initiatives on the political front. But when Rostow asked if the South Vietnamese were prepared for negotiations, Bunker shot back, "Not at all. They think those who want to live under Marxism should go north." Rostow pressed a favorite idea. Had they given any thought to the VC coming in as a political party, but not in government? Bunker liked that idea not at all. The NLF was a highly organized bunch of Communists that would take over a coalition as they had in Czechoslovakia twenty years earlier. "From the standpoint of the GVN this is not a good time for negotiations. In three or four months they'll be stronger." Clifford pounced on the contradiction. If the Saigon government was getting stronger, why did it feel such concern for the NLF? "They are not afraid of them militarily, but politically," Bunker replied. "They are fearful if they take [them] to their bosom, they'll end up running the show." Later he added, "The most important thing is to keep Thieu going—don't let him think we're selling him out."[20]

Bunker had prepared a formal paper detailing the reasons why Hanoi felt itself to be in such a strong bargaining position. Almost all of these reasons had to do with conditions inside the U.S. rather than on the battlefields of Vietnam. "In short," he wrote, "they see us now as especially vulnerable at the negotiating table because of the divisions in the U.S., racial violence, and the widespread depression, defeatism or despair about South Vietnam as a result of Tet." If Washington could tough it through this period, "we stand a good chance not merely of saving something from what appears to be the wreckage of our policy, but turning Tet into a new and more hopeful stage for the future. . . ."[21]

Rostow continued to brood about Bunker's statements long after the meeting at Camp David. Eventually he tried to come to terms with his own view that Harriman was too soft, and the ambassador's hints that political

negotiations were not to be countenanced—ever. Bunker's continued opposition to any talk of a postwar NLF-VC political party brought out a fascinating attempt to reconcile Rostow's notion of what would happen in
postwar Vietnam with Washington's longtime opposition to imposing a
coalition government. After the war, read a draft telegram to Bunker that
Rostow submitted for Rusk's approval, it was unrealistic to assume that the
Communists would all go north or be converted. That being so, Saigon
should give consideration to the right of the NLF to compete as a political
party "after a period of delay." "The President's formulation is a one-man-
one-vote solution. It leaves, as it was meant to leave, many problems unre-
solved, but *it leans clearly away* from a coalition solution." The only
alternative was a military dictatorship in South Vietnam and an Indonesian-
type massacre. "We can take U.S. casualties to oppose aggression, but not
to buy time for non-Communist political unity." This came pretty close, in
fact, to Henry Kissinger's later talk about the need for a "decent interval"
before the collapse of the Saigon government in order to save America's
reputation."[22]

Harriman had watched Bunker's performance at Camp David with a
sense of amazement at his capacity to undo prospects for peace negotiations. "Bunker seems to lack an understanding that President Johnson has
the balance of this year to carry out his policies, and that there is little
chance that American opinion will support a 30-billion dollar war in Vietnam, with the present rate of losses, for much longer." During the discussion of Harriman's instructions, Bunker kept trying to insert new
conditions, particularly a demand that the North Vietnamese reduce the
flow of men and supplies going south. Rusk had wanted to demand that the
North Vietnamese withdraw entirely from the northern provinces of South
Vietnam before any settlement, but in this discussion he kept silent. Clifford turned back Bunker's challenge by suggesting that these were matters
that could be treated instead as "guidelines." Johnson agreed, and the
instructions stayed as drafted.[23]

The essence of Harriman's instructions became the terms under which
the North Vietnamese finally agreed—after nearly seven months—to full-
scale negotiations. The U.S. would cease all bombing and artillery attacks
on North Vietnam, read the draft, when, according to North Vietnamese
statements, such a decision would, first, lead to prompt (within a week) and
"serious" (instead of productive) talks; second, "not exclude" the government of South Vietnam on issues affecting its interests; third, not permit
North Vietnam to improve its military position while discussions continued.[24]

Harriman appreciated Clifford's efforts to ward off Bunker's assault on
the draft instructions, but he complained nevertheless that they were too
rigid. "When I went to Moscow in 1942 [1941?]," he told the defense sec-

retary, "Roosevelt simply instructed me to accompany Churchill and explain our position to Stalin. I had no further guidance, I didn't need any then—*and I don't need any now!*" Thus far it seemed that Johnson had followed the Harriman-Clifford leads, but when a snag immediately developed over the site for the first Vietnamese-American meeting, Harriman's impatience once more aroused all of LBJ's suspicions about Eastern-liberal-Kennedy treachery. On April 11 Harriman called Johnson to support Warsaw as a possible location. "I wanted you to know," he began, "I feel very strongly that Warsaw has a number of advantages over any other place." Johnson exploded—more at Harriman's tone, perhaps, than at the issue under discussion. As long as he was president, he declared, "we are not going to Warsaw." Others agreed with him, including Ellsworth Bunker. Harriman persisted, saying that he hoped to be consulted. "Yes, you have told me your opinion," said Johnson. "I would also like to be consulted and decide before the State Department decides." Harriman realized he had overstepped. "I will obey orders." Johnson did not let him off the hook. "I hope so." Harriman could not resist taking a shot at Bunker. "I am a fellow who takes orders. I have dealt with these countries for a long time, and I think my judgment is better than Bunker's." "It may be," replied the president. "It may be better than mine." The conversation closed on an acrimonious note with Harriman suggesting that he wanted to be able to tell Johnson how he felt about these matters, and with the president's studied reply, "You did, you see." [25]

It took very little for the president to see Harriman as no more loyal than any of the other Harvards he had always despised. Harriman was a Yale man, as was Bunker, but in this context he had become an honorary Harvard. How important this early contretemps was in the subsequent history of what happened, and what did not happen, during the Paris peace negotiations may be debated. Certainly insignificant in itself, it reflected the wariness and weariness of a highly sensitive man, now a lame-duck president, who had long feared being pushed around by his advisers. And that had serious implications for the peace negotiations and the presidential campaign.

It took almost a month to get agreement on Paris as the location for the talks, further convincing Johnson that he would be viewed as a weakling. The peaceniks inside the administration had little more to lose than those who had stood outside the gates to the White House shouting, "Hey, hey, LBJ, how many kids did you kill today?" Intelligence reports, meanwhile, showed that the North Vietnamese were readying another offensive. Even Clifford complained that the evidence did not indicate a country moving toward peace. "I do not want Ho to get the impression he can take this country away from us," Johnson told his advisers. "We are not reeling under the Dove's attack." The next day, May 1, Clifford unburdened himself to a guest in the Pentagon, David Lilienthal, who had been enlisted in the early optimistic years of the war to plan for the Mekong River Valley scheme and other "postwar" economic developments. Yes, the North Vietnamese were building for some new adventure, Clifford admitted, and the JCS were after him all the time. Despite these pressures, he insisted, Vietnam policy could go only one way now. It was simple arithmetic: the U.S. could not stand the drain much longer. The balance-of-payments crisis was real. If the war went on, it would have to become "their war." "They've been put on notice that all of them, all the Asians that have been depending on Uncle Sam to fight for them, have got to get off their big fat Asian ass and defend themselves."[26]

Like Johnson, Lilienthal was loath to give up the dream of building a Tennessee Valley Authority in Southeast Asia. The two discussed how the "grass roots story" could be portrayed, "as we did the story of the Tennessee Valley," if the networks could be persuaded to divert some of their energies from the "horrors of war to the exciting story of how peace can be built through building the underpinnings of people's lives." "Such a picture of the future rests on the foundation of your statement at Johns Hopkins," Lilienthal told the president, "in what should be known even more widely than the Marshall Plan, as the Johnson Plan."[27]

Illusions die hard. When Johnson and Lilienthal talked about such New Deal dreams, it momentarily stripped away all the layers of disappointment and war-weariness. "Tell Thieu," Johnson exclaimed as they finished one discussion, "Tell Thieu that until January 20th at least they will not be let down." Johnson felt vindicated at the moment, too, by his "victory" in holding out against those like Harriman and Nicholas Katzenbach who had been willing to go to Warsaw—a Communist capital—to negotiate peace. In confused fashion, the president reeled off how Jews could not go to Warsaw, and how that related somehow to "our friends of South Vietnam." Lilienthal recorded an amazing scene: " 'How would it be if I were told—no Negroes can be present—no brown people.' And as he roared out this he flung his hand to the right and left—Hanoi brushing off Negroes over here, brown people over there."[28]

Johnson's victory in holding out for Paris changed little, either at home or on the international scene. At a discussion of what the U.S. delegation should say at the opening session, the president still had Lilienthal's heroic references in mind, not hard realities. "We should talk about the new Marshall Plan for that area," he told a meeting called to consider the speech. "The statement doesn't give [an] 'effective pitch.' We need something a truck driver can understand." But in opening the talks Harriman had planned to say some other things that disturbed the White House, particularly references to Ho Chi Minh as an Asian Tito, and an overall theme of "peace this year." The hawks tried to rein Harriman in by sending a former high Defense Department official, Cyrus Vance, along as a watchdog and cohead of the American delegation. The JCS also had its representative, General Andrew Goodpaster, to report any deviations from the agreed-upon negotiating instructions.[29]

No sooner had the plane taken off for Paris than Harriman and Goodpaster fell into an argument. "Now it's our job to end this war," Harriman told his colleagues. "To get the best terms we can, but to end the war." General Goodpaster shook his head. "That's not my understanding." The delegation was to negotiate with the North Vietnamese but was not in any way to compromise the maximum pressure on the battlefield. "That's not right, General," Harriman rejoined. "I think it's clear what our position is—what the president ordered." "No sir," Goodpaster said. "The president would not want us to endanger American lives. We have not been instructed to end the war on the 'best terms we can.' " Harriman was furious. "We're going to end this war. That's what the president said we should do." Goodpaster would not back down. "Sir," he said, "that is not what the president said. Those are *not* our instructions."[30]

The Joint Chiefs had their own negotiating "terms" which they presented to Clifford, and which, it may be assumed, President Johnson knew fully as well. The Harriman-Goodpaster dispute reflected the president's unwillingness to challenge the military directly by allowing the delegation leeway to go beyond the questions involved in a bombing cessation. Hanoi had agreed to send a delegation to talk about that issue, and the JCS wanted to be sure that nothing more than that was discussed. Unlike the State Department or the national security adviser, the military chiefs had clearly in mind the outlines of a political settlement they wanted. Their terms were a victor's terms. The basic objective of the American negotiating team should be, General Harold Johnson wrote Clifford, to secure the sovereignty of the government of Vietnam. Included in that objective should be a North Vietnamese withdrawal of all military and subversive forces from South Vietnam, Cambodia, and Laos; guarantees of Saigon's control throughout South Vietnam; and a settlement on the basis of the "general philosophy" of the 1954 Geneva accords. Anything that departed from that objective, such as the imposition of a coalition government on Saigon; agreement on a cease-fire in place; a premature withdrawal of Free World forces before the South Vietnamese government was strong enough to cope with the politico-military threat; or a cessation of reconnaissance to insure compliance with peace terms, would prevent accomplishment of the American national purpose. The JCS, concluded General Johnson in an admonitory tone, "are of the view that the United States is bargaining from a position of strength."[31]

The sessions at Paris quickly turned into speechmaking occasions while, all too plainly, both sides waited for their stepped-up military actions to force the other into the next concession. The American fear of another Panmunjom endurance trial had already become Johnson's newest burden. The president's party seemed hopelessly split. Vice-President Hubert Humphrey, now the unhappy warrior weighted down with the administration's standard as he sought the presidential nomination, appeared to be almost an onlooker as Eugene McCarthy and Robert Kennedy fought over the right to redeem the liberal heritage. They and their supporters blamed the president for the impasse. Johnson himself suggested that his support now came from the Republican opposition, that he was their "candidate." In remarks to the annual dinner of the White House Correspondents Association, he treated the situation in a humorously sardonic fashion that hid nothing of the bitterness underneath that gnawed at his very being:

> You know somehow, people just never do seem to quite understand me. On March 31st, I clearly said in very measured words, 'I will not seek and I shall not accept the nomination of *my* party.' I repeat—*my* party! And ever since that night, I have been waiting for Everett Dirksen to drop by.[32]

Neither party would give Johnson the tax bill he believed he had to have to prevent speculation against the dollar and, it was, feared, an international financial crisis like the debacle that produced the Great Depression. Treasury Secretary Henry Fowler told a special cabinet meeting, "We can't be responsible for another 1932 . . . none of us . . . not the President, not any of you, any of us, this Cabinet." The issue was still budget-cutting. Liberals would support no cuts; conservatives would vote no tax increases without the cuts.[33]

Rusk and the Vietnam hawks had insisted almost from the beginning that Tet was only a psychological victory for the enemy; but Clifford and his coterie of doves had taken the position that while that was probably true, Tet meant the war was nowhere near close to being ended. Issues like the tax-increase debate demonstrated how Vietnam had completely undermined the administration's plans and programs. It was idle, and worse than idle, therefore, to go on dreaming about the Mekong Valley project or imposing terms on the enemy.

While the talks remained stalled in Paris, Johnson vented his frustration over and over again, threatening continually to accept proposals to show the enemy "they can't push us back by this kind of pressure." But he never did so. When American ground forces turned back North Vietnamese attacks over the summer months, the argument for bombing in the vaguely restricted area between the 19th and 20th parallels lessened. Harriman did deliver a personal warning to Soviet Ambassador Valerian Zorin in Paris that if Johnson were forced to resume the bombing, there would be enormous pressure on him to remove all previous restraints. "This could be a dangerous situation."[34]

Zorin maintained he was unable to help resolve the impasse. Despite Harriman's pleas that the United States could not cease the bombing until it had a positive indication what the response would be, the Russian diplomat repeated there was no other way to move matters to the next stage. Unconditional cessation. That was Hanoi's public position, and it was its private position as well. The only glimmer was Zorin's agreement—at Harriman's urging—to continue these private contacts.

Averell Harriman had banked heavily on his ability to encourage Moscow's intervention in the negotiations to bring Hanoi around. He viewed the previous instances when Soviet diplomats had displayed interest in a settlement as missed opportunities, signals that went right by Dean Rusk's supposedly sensitive antennae. Believing himself more experienced than any of the Kennedy or Johnson men when it came to fathoming the Soviet mind, Harriman held out a powerful temptation: equal prestige with the United States. He described to Zorin the USSR's weighty role on the world scene and the special influence it had in Vietnam. Moscow had the capacity to help Hanoi and all of us out of this impasse, he said. The ambassador listened, and repeated again what he had said at the outset. The Soviets had never suggested they could bring North Vietnam anywhere except on Hanoi's terms.

When Harriman's private conversation with Zorin was discussed in Washington, Secretary Rusk expressed pleasure that the warning of resumed bombing would get around to the North Vietnamese. "I believed the time would come," the secretary recalled later, "when the North Vietnamese would find the job ahead of them too tough, come to the table, negotiate at least a cease-fire, and call off their aggression." Harriman's ploy—designed for a very different purpose—fit into Rusk's plans for the ultimate outcome of the Paris talks. Clifford was aghast at this reaction. It was no time to be issuing threats or contemplating new bombing scenarios. "Something will come out of Paris," he asserted. "I hope so." He hoped so, he went on, because there was no plan to win the war otherwise. The president had long ago put limitations on the war: no invasion of the north, no mining of harbors, no invasion of sanctuaries. With those limitations the war could not be won. "Our hopes must go with Paris." Since the North Vietnamese had also come to Paris, he concluded, they may have at last grasped what Tet revealed: neither side could win militarily.[35]

Johnson was not ready for such a bold admission. "I disagree," he said. The JCS Chair, General Wheeler, did not quite know what to say. "I disagree to some extent," he finally offered. Wheeler's predicament was an interesting one. The military had long argued that the limitations placed on its freedom of action made winning problematic, but if Wheeler now agreed with Clifford, he would also have to concede that diplomacy was the only road out of Vietnam. And that he most certainly did not wish to do. Rusk stayed with his faith in Communist understanding of Western resolve. "We sought to keep North Vietnam from overtaking South Vietnam with force. We have succeeded. We win when they know they can't win." Exasperated, Clifford challenged everyone in the room: "Can anybody here tell me what our plan is if the Paris talks fail? If Paris fails, we have no alternative but to turn back to the military—and they have no plan to bring it to an end."[36]

Clifford's challenge went unanswered. Johnson put off, yet again, a decision on resuming bombing in the area between the 19th and 20th parallels. How long the defense secretary could have held the fort against all the others had nothing happened to suggest the logjam in Paris might be breaking up is impossible to say. At one point in their several seemingly fruitless conversations, Ambassador Zorin commented to Harriman that he wondered if the Americans had ever said directly to the North Vietnamese what they had told him, that the required sign from Hanoi did not have to be in the form of a public statement about its intentions. Harriman said it had been conveyed in these terms, and more than once. But he did so again in a conversation with the leftist Australian journalist Wilfred Burchett on June 1, 1968. Burchett had long enjoyed a special status with the North Vietnamese, and Harriman took some encouragement from his attitude in this conversation: he was reasonable, and he freely admitted what Hanoi's delegates had absurdly continued to deny, that there were North Vietnamese troops in South Vietnam and Laos.[37]

Three days later Soviet Premier Alexei Kosygin dispatched a long letter to President Johnson. It began with a statement that a real possibility now existed of finding a way out of the bloody war that so disturbed the region and made a relaxation of international tensions impossible. Kosygin then raised a hitherto unexamined issue. Suppose North Vietnam agreed to substantive talks *before* a bombing cessation? The first item on the agenda would then become a cessation. Ending the bombing was the only way to get to the next stage, otherwise the official discussions would never get started. "I and my colleagues believe—and we have grounds for this—that a full cessation by the United States of bombardments and other acts of war in relation to the DRV could promote a breakthrough in the situation that would open perspectives for peaceful settlement. Such a step cannot bring about any adverse consequences whatever for the United States neither in the sense of a loss for the interests of their safety nor even in the sense of a loss for their prestige." To show good faith, Kosygin added that Harriman had expressed the wish that the Soviets help in bringing about unofficial contacts with the Hanoi delegation. "I take this opportunity to advise you that we brought this to the cognizance of our Vietnamese friends since we for our part consider that all forms of contact between the sides must be used."[38]

Rostow advised Johnson that the letter might be a "breakthrough." "Obviously, we must come to grips with Moscow bilaterally to clarify these matters." It took no special diplomatic skill to see that Kosygin's letter addressed at least two of the three conditions set forth in Harriman's instructions for a bombing halt—that substantive negotiations begin promptly, and that Hanoi refrain from taking military advantage of the situation. The third was a very sticky point for both sides—Saigon's participation. Obviously, Hanoi would insist upon the NLF being present as well. Harriman understood the difficulty and had floated the notion of meetings between Saigon and NLF representatives in South Vietnam itself.[39]

It had not been anticipated that the Soviets would involve themselves in quite this fashion. To accept Kosygin's letter as a basis for halting the bombing might mean having to abandon the third point. Averell Harriman was happy to do so, but not the majority of the president's advisers. It would have been better had Kosygin worked quietly behind the scenes to make the North Vietnamese more amenable. Now there was this awkwardness to deal with. Neither Saigon nor the NLF recognized the other's legitimacy, a problem Washington wanted to finesse with an "our side, your side" solution, allowing anyone to sit at the table with the delegations. Naturally, Saigon, as an actual government in being, stood to lose the most that way. It would be much worse if the U.S. delegation abandoned its third condition for a bombing halt.

Fate also worked against Johnson's acceptance of the Kosygin letter to order a bombing halt. The day it arrived in Washington was also the day of Robert Kennedy's assassination by Sirhan Sirhan in Los Angeles. Kennedy had just won the California primary, establishing him as a truly powerful contender for the nomination. If King's martyrdom made it impossible for Johnson to turn back from a peace direction, RFK's death put diplomacy on hold. Johnson did not wish to appear to be merely following another Kennedy lead, but it was more than that. The assassination revealed another aspect of the president's growing uncertainty about what was real and what was illusion. "How could the Kennedys do this to me?" he exclaimed. "Can you imagine, one getting killed at the beginning and another at the end of my term?"[40]

Addressing the nation on television, the president struck an uncertain note about what the assassination meant. Of course there were connections between hatred and acts of violence. It would be wrong to conclude otherwise. "It would be just as wrong, and just as self-deceptive, to conclude from this act that our country itself is sick, that it has lost its balance, that it has lost its sense of direction, even its common decency." There was an eerie ring to these words, as if intended as a defense of his bombing policy. Neither did he leave the matter there, for he then suggested a need to examine all those possibilities. He was appointing a commission, he said, to answer, "What in the nature of our people and the environment of our society makes possible such murder and such violence?"[41]

Harriman and Cyrus Vance had returned to Washington, meanwhile, for consultations when the Kosygin letter arrived, and were thus included in the top-level discussions. Also present were Charles Bohlen and Llewellyn Thompson, both Soviet experts and the latter currently serving as ambassador to Moscow. Rusk opened the discussion by summarizing the letter and giving a running commentary on its importance, which he readily granted. But the gist of his remarks was that Kosygin needed to supply the specifics of what Hanoi would do if the United States agreed to stop the bombing. Harriman was shocked at Rusk's performance. At a prior meeting at the State Department, Clifford had suggested, without serious dissent, that they advise the president to take Kosygin at his word and see what followed. But when they got to the White House, the secretary of state led off the formal discussion with this new insistence upon "clarification." "I have never participated in any discussion in the White House," Harriman noted, "where there was such a clear attempt made on the part of one member of the President's Cabinet to destroy the position of another before the second man had a chance to present it."[42]

How much difference Rusk's disingenuous behavior made can be questioned. Johnson also called on an old crony, Abe Fortas, for his negative comments. But the real clincher came from General Wheeler, who, sensing the president's state of mind in this week of Kennedy's death, pressed the issue of infiltration rates. May was the highest month so far, he said. The enemy had shown absolutely no restraint since the partial bombing halt. How long can we stand it, Johnson asked, without jeopardizing our position? "We could hold for about a month," Wheeler replied. "Morale may go to hell in a handbag." He would take the chance, the president mused out loud, if there was a reasonable chance of results, and he could start it up again if nothing happened. The JCS chair disagreed with Rusk's comment that the Kosygin letter was important. "I don't see anything new and startling in the Kosygin letter."

After all this, Clifford had a tough time arguing that the letter was a "great opportunity." Johnson reminded his secretary of defense that he had taken up Russian hints of serious peace talks at the time of the thirty-seven-day pause. Circumstances were different, Clifford argued. "Let's give it a test. The aid [from the Russians] to North Vietnam was not great until we started bombing their sister Socialist state." At best, the bombing was stopping only 25 percent of the flow of men and supplies down infiltration routes. "We should accept his letter as assurances. He honestly wants war to end. If we stop bombing, the Soviets will turn pressure on North Vietnam to stop the fighting. The Soviets are sending 80% of supplies. They have the means to make them stop the war."[43]

Johnson responded to Clifford's arguments with a sour comment that ignored his reasoning and displayed all the president's frustration with domestic critics. It was if the ghost of Robert Kennedy sat across the table, not Clark Clifford. "I don't think being soft will get us peace." What about the bombing, General, he turned to Wheeler, how important is it? Johnson got more than he expected in the general's answer. It sounded like an accusation—and it struck home. "Nobody wins a war by being on the defensive. The only offensive pressure we have had . . . [is] the bombing, which has been unduly restricted."[44]

After a lengthy debate about the precise wording of a reply to the Soviet leader, what emerged was something pretty much along the lines of Walt Rostow's comment. "We need to force Kosygin to be explicit about his assumptions." Johnson's response duly asked Kosygin to be "precise" about what Hanoi was prepared to do, putting the Soviets in an untenable position. It is interesting that not once, either in the Washington discussion or in the letter of reply, did the subject of the Sino-Soviet rivalry come up, even obliquely. Clifford and the old Russian hands present could have pointed out to good effect that to demand of the Soviets that they attempt to pressure Hanoi on specifics posed an impossible requirement for both Moscow and the North Vietnamese. Russia could not afford to appear to be "selling out" the interests of a socialist country; neither could Hanoi afford to offend the Chinese in such a direct fashion.[45]

During the ride back to the State Department, Rusk said to Harriman, "The trouble with Clark is that he has lost his nerve since he has been over at the Pentagon." Harriman was again outraged. It was a contemptible attack, he believed, and he thought Rusk used it privately to destroy Clifford's credibility in the White House. But Clark Clifford was perfectly capable of taking care of himself. He had once outmaneuvered Secretary of State George C. Marshall over recognition of Israel, and he was not about to let Dean Rusk best him over this crucial matter. A few days later the secretary of defense told reporters at the Pentagon that there were certain "straws in the wind" at the Paris talks, little indications of progress that gave him hope. "What I think we must do if there is ever any occasion," Clifford told Harriman privately, was "in the most guarded manner to indicate that something is happening." Otherwise the attitude of those who were at the president every day—"some very militarist gentlemen"—would prevail, producing an ultimatum to Hanoi that could bring everything down.[46]

Rusk retaliated with his own press conference the very next day, June 22, his first in nearly six months. He wouldn't quarrel, he said, with the characterization of "bits and straws in the wind," but there was no real reason to believe that a breakthrough was near. Reporters gained the clear impression that the secretary of state wished that his colleagues had not spoken so optimistically. "We are a long way from substance when we have to point to the fact that coffee breaks are becoming longer." Harriman had used this example to suggest to reporters in Paris that the North Vietnamese were increasingly willing to leave off propaganda for a few minutes at least during these planned interruptions for coffee and tea.[47]

Informal contacts, both with Ambassador Zorin and the North Vietnamese, did in fact increase over the next several weeks. Cyrus Vance even had the opportunity to present yet another variation on the standard American proposal for ending the bombing during one of these private sessions, this time suggesting that the United States would make no public statements about any "conditions" for a cessation, pretending, in effect, that it had not stipulated any. It was turned down immediately, but the contacts continued. Clifford, meanwhile, went to Saigon to prepare for a Vietnamese-American summit meeting in Hawaii. He found there exactly what he expected to find: the Saigon government really wanted no settlement with Hanoi, and the American embassy encouraged this attitude.[48]

The time had long passed, Clifford decided, for playing by Dean Rusk's rules. While Ellsworth Bunker stood by shocked at what he was hearing, Clifford informed Thieu and Vice-President Ky that absent visible signs of progress, the American public would not support the war much longer. If no settlement was reached at Paris, the administration expected the South Vietnamese gradually to take over the war. Later, in an emotional confrontation with Bunker and his aides, the secretary of defense declared that they would all be derelict in their duty if they failed to make use of the final six months of the Johnson presidency to seek an honorable end to the war.[49]

It was an uncomfortable flight to Hawaii. Deeply depressed by what he had seen in Vietnam, and his veritable isolation among the president's top advisers, Clifford sent ahead a message asking for a private meeting with the president. Bunker rushed from the airplane to alert Rusk to what was coming. Clifford did not get to see Johnson alone. Rostow and Rusk were also present, along with Press Secretary George Christian. But this time he did get the first word. Playing off "Bus" Wheeler's statement that wars can't be won defensively, Clifford began by stating the South Vietnamese had no idea how they could win the war. They were fighting well enough on the defense, but with the enemy fading away every time into Laos and Cambodia, one had to conclude they could not be defeated. But Saigon did not want the war to end, Clifford said. Protected by half a million American soldiers and a "golden flow of money," the South Vietnamese leaders had no reason to want anything to change. Of that he was "absolutely certain." Johnson was taken aback, recalled Clifford, and Rusk visibly offended by these statements. Where are we then? Johnson asked. Where do we go? Bunker had told him, Clifford answered, that Thieu believed the talks had started six months too soon; Saigon needed time to build up. The situation was actually quite the reverse, Clifford said. Thieu should understand this was the best time for a settlement. He would have Lyndon Johnson for six months and after that uncertainty. All the presidential candidates except George Wallace were moving away from support of the war, and they would all have a mandate to end it. He did agree with Bunker on one point. The ambassador said the Vietnamese did not do much until they were jarred off their duffs. Well, now was the time to do some jarring.[50]

Rusk denied everything Clifford had said. Korea had demonstrated, he shot back, that defense can win wars. He simply did not believe the charge that Saigon wanted to continue the fighting to secure American aid. Clifford could see that Johnson was uncomfortable with the sight of his two chief advisers constantly at odds. The meeting ended there, another defeat, the secretary of defense feared, for rational consideration of the problem. Then Ambassador Bunker came into the room. Johnson questioned him and revealed his fears. How much sentiment was there, he asked, that Washington was "selling them out"? Thieu understood the situation, Bunker replied, but there was a great deal of public concern, particularly among the northern Catholics who had come south a decade earlier. No one could accept a coalition.[51]

Johnson had played with the idea of writing a second letter to Kosygin to take him up on his "offer," but he seemed distracted by the Hawaii meeting with Thieu. *New York Times* columnist Tom Wicker commented on the contrasting images between the search for peace in Paris and the incongruous assembly near Honolulu, "held with the usual military trappings of marines at attention, starry-collared admirals and generals, and in the spit-and-polish surroundings of Camp Smith, the Pacific command headquarters. . . ."[52]

Returning from Hawaii, Johnson expressed a desire to sit down with the putative Republican candidate, Richard Nixon, "to see what kind of world he really wants." Nixon had said, the president went on, that he was "for our position in Vietnam." If the Democrats "go the other way," the GOP might be of more help in the final months of his administration. This oblique reference to a likely fight in the platform committee over the "peace plank" at the Chicago convention suggests another related reason why the summer months were proving so difficult, why the search for peace seemed so weighted down. Johnson was like a man in a nightmare, trying to run from danger with leaden legs. He feared that Edward Kennedy might pick up the banner and take the nomination from Hubert Humphrey. That gave him a supposed reason to intervene in the nominating process as well as in the writing of the platform, to prevent it from happening. In the midst of all evidence to the contrary, he had not quite given up hope there might be a spontaneous upsurge for LBJ at that convention—that the party might turn to him to restore unity as a way of avoiding a suicidal intraparty struggle. And he could not answer the call to run on the peace planks being submitted by antiwar activists![53]

The meeting with Nixon took place on July 26, scheduled for later in the same day as a briefing session for George Wallace, a piece of minor deception to distract attention from the far more serious nature of the Nixon-Johnson encounter. Secretary Rusk opened the session with a statement that the administration was trying to find out what would happen if it stopped the bombing. The Soviets had been discussing these things with Hanoi, he went on, but they did not want to push the North Vietnamese into the arms of China. Here was, of course, the argument Clifford had failed to make a month earlier for responding to Kosygin's letter affirmatively. Nixon said his own advisers wanted to stop the bombing, but it was the only leverage left to American negotiators. "That's right," agreed Rusk. And it was militarily important, too. Was there any indication they were hurting? asked Nixon. They were willing to listen, Rusk replied. What would make them talk seriously? Nixon continued. This time Rusk's answer began as a sardonic, half-facetious, comment on the war. "100,000 casualties since Jan.[uary]," he said. "Only women in [the] field." But then he caught himself and returned quickly to favorite cold war theses about Communist behavior. "There was no reason why guerrillas had stopped sending men into Greece. There is no obj.[ective] reason why Berlin blockade was lifted."[54]

Rostow came into the room to repeat once again the story of how well the South Vietnamese had fought during Tet, how much stronger they were now than then. At Honolulu, interjected the president, the American side had put forward the one-man, one-vote solution to South Vietnam's future. "We will not put [a] coalition gov't over them unless they choose it." But Thieu had told him, he said, that he was willing to take the risk of allowing former VC to participate as individuals, not as a political party. Rostow continued the explanation and took it down a dangerous path: "It could be cosmetic or means to a Communist takeover." No one wanted to follow him onto that treacherous ground.[55]

Nixon then launched into his problem as a candidate. What he needed was a reassurance on the commitment that Johnson would not abandon Saigon. Given that, he implied, he would leave Vietnam alone during the campaign, or at least not attack President Johnson. The discussion ended with a series of brave words decrying defeatism:

"I have admired [the] way all of you have stood up through great fire. *This is a hard time*," Nixon averred. Public opinion had taken a strange turn. Congress was a bunch of jelly. "Where has the war been lost?"

"In the editorial rooms of this country," Rusk answered bitterly.

"I do not intend to advocate a bombing pause," Nixon vowed, as if making a pact with Johnson that reached beyond party loyalty to a higher patriotism.[56]

The encounter appeared to deepen LBJ's antagonism toward critics, especially antiwar Democrats; indeed, he had sought the meeting as if to confirm that his own party was in the grip of a temporary aberration. Nixon thus filled a crucial role in Johnson's attempt to make sense of what was causing the national malaise. The next day he told advisers, "I believe the International Communists have a movement under way to get me to stop the bombing." The idea that Communists had successfully infiltrated the antiwar movement and now directed the campaign to end the bombing was of a piece with the president's long-held fears of personal disgrace at the hands of an Eastern elite. Filled with resentment at his Vietnam legacy, Johnson had shunted aside all of Clifford's entreaties.[57]

He was listening to other voices beyond those who assembled for the Tuesday Lunches. A few weeks after their meeting, Nixon sent the president a message via the Reverend Billy Graham. Asked if he would take a personal message to the White House, Graham took out a scratch pad and made notes. He would never embarrass Johnson, Nixon dictated. He was the hardest-working president in 140 years. After the election he wanted a working relationship with Johnson and would like him to undertake special assignments. Once Vietnam was settled, Nixon would give his predecessor a major share of the credit and do everything possible to secure his place in history. It was certainly a better deal, Johnson probably reflected, than his own party was offering. After Graham transmitted the message, Nixon was eager to hear how it had gone? "I told him over the telephone," Graham recorded, "that the President was deeply appreciative of the gesture."[58]

Unlike Robert McNamara, whose troubled conscience finally could no longer rationalize the war, Clifford could not quit—or be relieved by the president from his burdens. Theirs was a political pact of a different sort than McNamara's loyalty to both Kennedy and Johnson. The longtime Democratic counselor's mandate was to extricate Lyndon Johnson and the party from the morass of Vietnam, however far apart the two men stood at the end of the day. Clifford described it, nevertheless, as a maddening experience. Meeting with Dean Rusk privately on one occasion, he hoped they could reach an agreed position on requirements for ending the bombing. But Rusk had nothing to say. "All you are suggesting is that we keep fighting and having our men killed indefinitely," Clifford charged. But the secretary of state replied with bland calmness, "You never can tell when Hanoi will break and give in."[59]

As Johnson's gropings for some face-saving alternative to his own statements of American obligations became more and more desperate, Clifford ceased for a time to argue openly against the position of his adversaries. What effect would a complete bombing halt have, the president wondered aloud with his advisers, knowing full well the answer he would get. "It would permit 30% more troops and supplies to reach South Vietnam," rehearsed General Wheeler. No, insisted Secretary Rusk, "It would add 50% to what is getting through now." What about this offensive the enemy was planning, came the next question? Clifford assured him American forces were ready for anything. "I would like to see us knock hell out of them," said Johnson. Wheeler felt the moment was right to pose again the idea of bombing right up to the 20th parallel. The president demurred while trying to appear not to. "I want to get back up to the 20th parallel. Let's get ready for that if they hit us. Dean, you go out to Vance and Harriman and tell them to hold on to their hats if attacks against our forces occur."[60]

After meetings like these, Clifford would retire to the Pentagon and continue to plead his case with written communications. The entire experience of the war, he wrote, had demonstrated that the bombing had produced neither a sufficient physical or psychological burden on the enemy to compel him to cease his military activity in the south. "As a practical matter, moreover, I believe that the suggested linkage of our bombing of the north to deaths caused by the enemy in the south is unworkable. The amount of fighting in the south, and hence the number of our casualties, is dependent upon our own actions as well as those of the enemy." Obviously, Johnson did not like to receive letters like this one. Vance and Harriman had just recommended that Johnson halt the bombing, on the assumption that a current lull on the battlefield was in fact the demonstration of restraint the president had asked for in his March 31 speech. And the diplomatic correspondent of the *Washington Post* reported, meanwhile, that a high-ranking member of the Vietnamese delegation in Paris, later identified as Ha Van Lau, had confirmed that the lull had "political significance." The Americans must be aware of that fact, he told the reporter. "If the president wished to make use of the situation," Lau said, "he could do so and stop the bombing."[61]

This seeming "collaboration" between the American delegation and Lau further infuriated the president, who ordered Rusk to hold another press conference and rule out any possibility of a bombing halt unless the North Vietnamese had said beforehand what would happen. Reporters were also told privately that the administration had stiffened its attitude because of the "ambiguous" nature of the lull and intelligence reports that an enemy offensive was being prepared. But the *New York Times* dismissed the argument:

What Mr. Rusk is asking for, in effect, is a unilateral commitment by Hanoi to de-escalate the war on its side without a comparable commitment from the United States and in the face of a continuing allied buildup and continuing aggressive action by allied troops throughout the South. This is an impossible demand that can only lead to the new enemy activity the President has predicted.[62]

The offensive did come, beginning August 17, with numerous rocket and mortar attacks on American installations and South Vietnamese towns. It had been planned, according to captured enemy documents, as a general offensive to last longer than Tet. Saigon was still the ultimate target, but not until the attacks in the countryside had been successful. This time, however, there was no question of any sort of victory for the enemy, military or psychological. Met by effective resistance, the offensive quickly sputtered to a halt. Many of the planned attacks never materialized.[63]

In a sense, what happened on the battlefield in Vietnam was now irrelevant to decision-making. It could not change the ultimate reality of stalemate. Political battle lines had been drawn in the United States. A fight to the death at the Democratic National Convention was now a certainty. Governor Richard Hughes of New Jersey, a strong supporter of the Vietnam War, had tried to persuade Johnson that the military issues of the debate over a bombing halt were no longer sufficient reason to deny Hubert Humphrey a chance to "emerge clearly and decisively as his own man, as a fresh and creative candidate for the Presidency." The best way, indeed the only way, to secure that opportunity would be for Johnson to permit Humphrey to recommend the bombing halt to the president. But then what? For Johnson to adopt this scheme would produce charges of total cynicism and favoritism of the worst sort.[64]

Humphrey had tried on his own to edge out from under LBJ's shadow as the convention approached. Unfortunately his timing was bad. On the day before the August offensive began, the vice-president spoke about the lull, confirming that some administration officials felt that Hanoi had sent a signal of deescalation—one sufficient to justify a bombing halt. The primary need was to protect American troops, Humphrey said. "We are also engaged in peace negotiations," he continued, "and if the stopping of the bombing can aid the peace negotiations, then that helps protect the men."[65]

The 1968 Democratic National Convention was the most uproarious affair in the party's history. While Mayor Richard J. Daley's police tried their best to scourge "Yippies" and other protesters from Chicago's streets, inside the convention hall nominee Hubert Humphrey summoned followers of Eugene McCarthy and the Kennedy stand-in, George McGovern, to put aside recrimination and dissension and follow him to victory. "I say to this great convention tonight, and to this great nation of ours, I am ready to lead our country!"

In private, Johnson mocked Humphrey's capabilities, even as he kept the vice-president bound and gagged on anything that touched Vietnam. Under such circumstances Nixon could present himself as an alternative without breaking his promise not to attack Johnson. McGeorge Bundy tried to present the case for a bombing halt on different terms that might appeal to the president's obvious need to claim success for his policy. Bundy, now head of the Ford Foundation (and himself enmeshed in a deeply divisive effort to improve education in the inner city), made the case that the military significance of the bombing had always been exaggerated from the outset of Rolling Thunder, and it had now become a symbolic issue that might cause the loss of all that had been gained in three years of resistance to Communist aggression.

> What I hope for is a decision of imaginative courage, not *because* of soft-headed pressure from doves, but really in *in spite of* them. I think stopping the bombing is now the right course for those who want to defend the gains we have made in Southeast Asia since 1964.[66]

He had come to this position, Bundy admitted, somewhat to his own surprise, after years of thinking the opposite. Arguing that a military case for bombing had to be made on the grounds that the policy would be decisive, the former national security adviser contended that one could no longer make such a case. Signals from the other side that a bombing halt would produce substantive talks amply justified a change in American posture. As long as the bombing continued, furthermore, it was impossible to make the issue of Hanoi's troops in the south stand out.

Then Bundy ventured boldly into a difficult area, as unpromising as a barefoot walk across hot coals: a bombing halt would send the proper signal to Saigon. Evidence in the press indicated that the American authorities in South Vietnam were wary of a bombing halt for its possible disquieting effect on a government neither as stable or strong as we would like. That was a natural but a limited view of the matter. A bombing halt would convey the increased need for self-reliance. "Conversely, a continuation of the bombing would strengthen the continuing illusion of some in Saigon that the Americans can be forced to carry the main burden indefinitely."

Having suggested what a change in policy would accomplish in Vietnam, Bundy turned to what the absence of change would do at home. "There is no force on earth that can hold the American people to more years of the same." The president, by sheer force of will, could hold to the present course for the remainder of his term. But no new administration of either party could carry it on. "This is not what the American people now want, and what they want will be decisive." A more modest level of effort would preserve the gains made, allow Saigon gradually to take over the war, and sustain support at home. A bombing halt was the best available first step in that direction. By moving to lower the level of the fighting, the United States would have a much better chance of ultimate success. "In this respect a halt in the bombing now would have even greater value than the President's first limitation of March 31. It is the right next step."[67]

Johnson's reply to Mac Bundy went through several drafts by Walt Rostow. They all began with the sentence, "I was pleased to get your letter and memorandum of August 15 and to enjoy again the sharpness and clarity of your mind." Clearly, the successor national security adviser was going to enjoy matching wits with his old boss. The arguments Bundy made, Rostow wrote for Johnson, were all consistent with arguments for previous pauses—and equally invalid, therefore, as a guide to what might happen. Meanwhile, the buildup of enemy forces showed no disposition to talk about peace.

> When they are ready to move towards peace they will know how to indicate to us—in one way or another—what will follow if we stop the bombing. I have no doubt that—one day—they will do so.[68]

Where Bundy had sought to bring into the open the hardest question of all, the political future of South Vietnam, Johnson cut out of Rostow's draft a discussion of Thieu's willingness to contemplate the "sort of settlement that we have in mind and regard as honorable."

> And he is trying to build a new big non-Communist coalition to run against the Communist popular front he someday expects to confront at the polls. Thieu's coalition will probably prove to be as contentious as the Democratic Party; but it might agree on running one non-Communist candidate rather than eleven.[69]

The letter closed with a clever reference to their changed positions, and a twist on Bundy's own argument against critics in his time who lacked access to the "in-boxes." "I know it's hard to believe *on the outside*, but the simple fact is the other side is not yet ready for a settlement. I do not despair that they might be ready sometime in the weeks and months ahead—although I am not counting on this."[70]

Sooner than Rostow and Johnson expected, the Vietnamese accepted terms for an end to the bombing. Actually, only Hanoi accepted, not Saigon—and there, lamented Harry McPherson, Johnson ended his term, "the American Gulliver . . . tied down by South Vietnamese Lilliputians."[71]

TWENTY-ONE

October Surprises

SEPTEMBER PROVED TO BE the cruelest month. In Paris, Harriman and Vance despaired of any sign from the other side, sifting each day's words in search of some new word or phrase. Nothing turned up. Across the Atlantic both candidates also waited for news of a possible breakthrough. They heard nothing. Without any propelling discussion of Vietnam, the presidential campaign drifted into the farther shoals of irrelevance. There it lodged in the stagnant backwash of sullen resentment. That did not alarm Richard Nixon. Far ahead in public opinion polls, the Republican ticked off each remaining day until the election with but one fear troubling his sleep during the small hours of the night: what if President Johnson should break their "pact"? If at the last minute Johnson decided to halt the bombing, Nixon could lose the election.

For the time being at least, LBJ had no such intention. Instead he was busy shoring up rationalizations and dreaming of a final triumph over his critics, the denizens of Georgetown and summer places off the coast of Massachusetts.

The president had ordered CIA director Richard Helms to produce a report on Communist infiltration and leadership of peace movements, particularly those on college campuses. Helms appeared in the cabinet room to make his report on September 18, armed with charts and graphs, but they illustrated a disappointing conclusion. "There is no convincing evidence," he said, "of Communist control, manipulation, or support of student dissidents."

"No support?" marveled Dean Rusk, who obviously could not believe what he was hearing. "That's right," said Helms. "But there is support," Johnson protested, almost pleading: "There is, isn't there?"

Treasury Secretary Henry Fowler thought he knew what Helms had meant to say, or should have said. "Aren't they giving the same kind of support that the Communists gave to the labor movement in this country." "Let's leave it at that"—Helms was ready to settle for that ambiguous conclusion.

But Secretary of Agriculture Orville Freeman did not want the discussion to end, nor did the others. "I find that very hard to believe," said Freeman. "I'm travelling around this country and all kinds of people tell me about Communist involvement in this thing." Dean Rusk cited numbers. "Let me say one thing," he began. "I was told by a trustee of an Ivy League University that he had 30 Communists on his faculty. He said that to me." No matter what his CIA director said, Johnson just did not "believe this business that there is no support." All these student groups, the Students for a Democratic Society and the DuBois Clubs, were infiltrated. "Maybe they are not Communist led, but they are Communist agitated and aggravated."[1]

Helms gave up. He offered his colleagues a way to go away with their minds at rest that the opposition had been duped by Communist agents. Without changing his conclusion, Helms said he was talking about the world situation and trying to stay away from U.S. problems. That statement brought a sardonic quip from Vice-President Hubert Humphrey. "Well, just come out and travel with me." The remark brought laughter around the table. It was deeply upsetting to Humphrey that at almost every campaign stop he was heckled and jeered by leftist protesters while Richard Nixon was largely ignored by the placard-waving demonstrators.

A Communist taint in the peace movement offered some relief from the ennui surrounding the president's men, offered also some desultory hope for a revitalization of cold war ranks, and provided a measure of justification for refusing to listen to demands that the bombing be halted. Cabinet reactions to the CIA report filled certain ritual needs, but counting Communists on an Ivy League faculty was in the end only a way of getting riled up. No one present that day really believed that eliminating Communists from the peace movement would solve the administration's problems with the Vietnam negotiations.

Once the Communist "question" was dealt with, Secretary Rusk very formally asked permission to speak "on a subject about which I feel very strongly." The subject was the effort by the press and "some politicians" to paint a "false picture of differences between the President and the Vice President. This gets in the way of the peace talks in Paris. It doesn't do anyone any good. I know that the Vice President has the same views." Either by coincidence or by design, Johnson had brought with him copies of statements he had made supporting Humphrey's candidacy. "If any of you need reference sources they are now available to you in these documents." Perhaps the vice-president had left the meeting. The minutes do not record anything he said in response.[2]

It was a bit odd: reference sources handed out to prove that Lyndon Johnson supported his "handpicked" candidate to succeed him? Around the table were those who had heard LBJ say cruel things about Hubert Humphrey only a day or so before. At the time of the Democratic Convention, Johnson had been "negotiating" for a summit meeting with Soviet Premier Alexei Kosygin. It would steal attention from the convention, and, if it came off, provide LBJ with a final, dramatic triumph over his critics. See what the Democrats had done, it would say, they had taken the presidency away from the man the Soviets trusted, one with whom they had agreed to meet in order to resolve the great issues before the world: not just Vietnam but the arms race and the Middle East.

But the Soviets had spoiled Johnson's dream in late August with a brutal military intervention to suppress a liberalizing government in Czechoslovakia. Then they announced a new "Brezhnev Doctrine," under which the USSR "unselfishly" obligated itself to protect all sister socialist states from Western subversion. The Czech intervention did not put a stop to contacts between Ambassador Anatoly Dobrynin and National Security Adviser Walt Rostow, looking toward some way to salvage a summit meeting. But LBJ found himself in a more awkward position than President Eisenhower in 1960, when the Russians shot down the U-2 spy plane on the eve of a planned Soviet-American summit conference. Eisenhower had refused to apologize to save the summit then, and Johnson could not now agree in the wake of Czechoslovakia to a summit that appeared to condone even the slightest appearance of a Russian-American deal at South Vietnam's expense.

The president's quest for a triumphal exit from the White House, then, had put him in the position of having to seek tougher terms because of the Soviet intervention, whether or not a summit took place. It was an intensely frustrating predicament and may help to explain Johnson's overheated reactions to the Communist "issue" in domestic politics (in part pique at Moscow's "betrayal") and his continuing jaundiced eye on the Humphrey campaign.

By mid-September the impetus for a summit conference had shifted somewhat from the White House to the Kremlin. Dobrynin's conversations with Walt Rostow made it clear that the Russians were at least as anxious, if not more so, for such a meeting. The trap for Johnson was that if a summit did not bring "positive" results on almost all the issues the United States wished to discuss, the outcome would be an American ratification of sorts of the Brezhnev Doctrine. The ambassador had given Rostow a message from Moscow which discussed the usual points in regard to the need for America to negotiate directly with Hanoi on all questions at issue, but he more than hinted that if the United States had reservations, Washington should come back with a proposition that the Russians could press on Hanoi.[3]

Rostow put his mind to work on that "invitation" and came up with a longer set of conditions for a bombing halt. Some of these elaborated the basic three points the United States had already demanded (productive peace negotiations, an end to mortar and artillery attacks on South Vietnamese cities, and participation of the Saigon government in the negotiations) in stronger terms, and some were new (the release of all U.S. pilots in the hands of the North Vietnamese). When Dobrynin read over the American memorandum based on Rostow's drafts, the only sticking point seemed to be the issue of the GVN's representation. That question, he said, was between Hanoi and the United States. Russia could not commit itself to get a positive answer. From the tenor of these conversations, however, Rostow got the impression that Russia was ready to reinvolve itself in the peace negotiations. If it would not guarantee Hanoi's acceptance of the GVN at the table, the ambassador had found no difficulty with the other conditions, and that suggested the Soviets would give good advice on the third point as well.[4]

The memorandum Rostow handed to Dobrynin recalled Johnson's response to Premier Kosygin's June 5 letter in an attempt to pin the Russians down. "If, after appropriate exploration and consideration," it read, "the leaders of the Soviet Union . . . are prepared to advise the President to proceed on the basis of what is now being said, the President would take their advice with the utmost seriousness." Moscow's formal response to the memo merely repeated Kosygin's claim that an end to the bombing would produce positive results, yet it also suggested an exchange of views between Foreign Minister Andrei Gromyko and Secretary Rusk could "prove useful." When they met, Gromyko put two questions to the secretary: Was the issue of the South Vietnamese at the peace table the sole obstacle to ending the bombing, and, second, was it possible to eliminate the present leaders, Thieu and Ky, as parties to the situation? Rusk replied that South Vietnamese presence was a most important issue, perhaps the most difficult for Hanoi. As for Thieu and Ky, their participation was essential. Whatever "strong views" Hanoi might have about Thieu and Ky were matched by the latter's feelings about the authorities in the DRV, but they were willing to let them have the NLF at the negotiating table. Here were hints, certainly, that Russia was, despite continuing disclaimers, seeking to act as a facilitator (if not something more), or that North Vietnam was considering on its own a change in its negotiating position.[5]

Averell Harriman, meanwhile, had come to a somewhat similar conclusion about Russian attitudes after Czechoslovakia. He also believed that

Moscow could be coerced into playing a more active role in settling the Vietnam War in order to redeem itself in the eyes of American and world opinion. The present leaders of the Soviet Union were weak, he wrote in a memorandum to himself, and even feared their ability to control their own people with the example of a liberalized Czechoslovakia so nearby. Besides domestic concerns, the Soviets foresaw the rise of German influence in Eastern Europe. That being so, they badly needed a boost from some major gain in Russian-American relations.[6]

Harriman and Vance seldom talked about using this supposed leverage in such specific fashion, but they pushed Soviet diplomats in Paris "to weigh in heavily" in moving the talks to the next stage, repeating over and over again that now was the time for Moscow to act. And instead of the usual bland responses that such questions were really none of Moscow's business, they were told that their views were being transmitted to the Kremlin.[7] Harriman came back to the United States in mid-September and once again pushed the case for a bombing halt so as to allow Soviet diplomacy a chance to work, basing his argument on private conversations he had been having with a new man from Hanoi, Le Duc Tho. Measuring his words carefully, the special ambassador said he felt the North Vietnamese delegation was now serious about making progress. Without telling him about the exchanges with Dobrynin, Johnson repeated the list of conditions he had had Rostow communicate to the Soviet representative. And if the North Vietnamese should violate these understandings after a bombing halt began, Johnson said, "I shall count on you, Averell, to lead the Party and the Government in demanding a resumption of bombing. . . ."[8]

Harriman took his meaning. Press stories out of Paris describing the American delegation's supposed concern about Washington's unbending insistence on its conditions had kept Johnson's fires of suspicion smoldering. Before he met with the president, moreover, Harriman had talked with Clark Clifford to get a feel for where matters stood. Did the president really wish to see Humphrey defeated? Harriman asked. Clifford waited a moment before answering, "If you agree it is just between you and me, I believe you're right: the President wants to see him defeated." Their interview certainly did nothing to dissuade Harriman that Johnson cared little about what happened to the vice-president, if he did not actually want to see him defeated. When George Ball, now the U.S. ambassador to the United Nations, came to Paris a few days later, they talked about what could be done, not only to save the vice-president but—especially in Ball's case—the president from himself. Ball told Harriman he was considering resigning to become a Humphrey adviser, a step that would cause immediate speculation about a rift between the White House and the Democratic nominee. Harriman thought it was exactly the right thing to do. He would do it himself, except he might still somehow be able to move things off dead center in the negotiations. Passing through Paris, *New York Times* columnist C. L. Sulzberger had dinner with the Harrimans. Afterward he wrote in his diary, "Harriman now obviously detests President Johnson. . . ."[9]

For George Ball the moment of decision came on September 25 at a National Security Council meeting. What happened there did not convince him to resign; he had already decided that. It convinced him that Hubert Humphrey must give a speech as soon as possible establishing his independence from the administration's policy. Johnson was in an especially truculent mood that day. When Ball launched into a Harriman-like argument that the Soviets could not help in resolving the war until a bombing halt gave them the chance to use their leverage, the president said he wanted a reason for risking such a halt. He doubted that even acceptance of all three conditions was enough of a reason now.[10]

General Wheeler thought a bombing halt was a terrible idea. "We are in a strong position in Vietnam," he began. To stop applying pressure made no sense militarily or politically. "The morale of our forces would suffer. Friends and enemies would interpret this as victory for Hanoi." After he finished, Leonard Marks, head of the United States Information Agency, posed a direct question. What would be the actual military costs if Ball's suggestion were adopted? Wheeler reluctantly admitted that it would take the North Vietnamese two or three weeks to mount an offensive—though he insisted there might be a large increase in casualties. These were academic points, Secretary Clifford rejoined, and this was a practical test. If the buildup continued, the bombing could be restarted, "and you can go as far as you want to." "No," said Johnson, "we will debate it as we did before." Debate for that day on a bombing halt was over.[11]

After the NSC meeting adjourned, Rusk, Clifford, and Rostow went on to the Tuesday Luncheon with the president. The main topic was not military strategy but Ball's decision to resign "as an act of conscience." Clifford said Ball had told him that morning he could no longer permit himself to remain quiet about Nixon, that he needed to be free to help Humphrey say the things he should be saying. Well, said an obviously displeased Dean Rusk, Ball had told him the same thing, but he was misestimating the political situation. The announcement was bound to be interpreted as a "break" with the administration. Clifford denied that was Ball's intention. Rusk was more than skeptical: "Ball quits two months after he takes office." He should have decided this, Johnson grumbled, when he agreed to serve. "Ball's going to Humphrey is part of [a] moyement to the 'dove' side— special sale number one."[12]

Johnson was closer to the mark than Clifford, who was obviously trying to mollify the president so as not to intensify his determination to resist any and all pleas to halt the bombing. If Ball's leaving did not signal a break, his purpose was to enable Vice-President Humphrey to make a break. It could also be argued, however, that in some deep area of his unconscious mind, President Johnson's purpose was the same: to force Humphrey to make a break. Johnson had bullied Humphrey throughout his term as vice-president, exiling him for long periods from meetings of his top advisers as punishment for suggesting doubts about the war. Eventually Humphrey clambered onto the bandwagon—and took a front seat to lead the cheering. Apparently the president watched this performance without noting any qualities necessary for someone aspiring to the White House.

As the presidential campaign developed along predictable lines, LBJ was clearly angered by Humphrey's little "infidelities," such as a speech suggesting that troops would start coming home soon. Clark Clifford really didn't care if Johnson was upset with Hubert Humphrey, only if that anger made him less willing to think about peace steps. The night before Ball's resignation, Clifford had pressed especially hard on the Nixon "issue." He should have the honor of ending the war, Clifford urged, not leave it to Richard Nixon. He had not mentioned Humphrey, but the president brought him into the conversation. He doubted, he said, that "Humphrey had the ability to be President." He would have respected him more, he said, if he "showed he had some balls."[13]

Clifford mused later that Johnson refused to recognize that the only way for Humphrey to show the strength the president wanted to see in his successor would be to break with the administration. Probably that was so, yet Johnson must certainly have recognized that his rigidity would eventually drive someone to "desperate" action, whether it was Averell Harriman or McGeorge Bundy or, as it happened, George Ball. For most traditional liberals, Hubert Humphrey's campaign was already a lost cause. It was going nowhere. He was seventeen points behind in the polls and seemingly out of touch with everyone. But that was not all. In many places where liberals gathered, Humphrey had become an anathema.

George Ball could not allow the degradation to go on without trying to do something about it. Humphrey was his good friend, Ball told an interviewer later, but he was not sure "he would have been the man among all men I would have picked as the candidate...." The point was, the way things were going Humphrey was going to lose, and lose very badly indeed. "I had a feeling that too shattering a defeat would have hurt the party and would install Mr. Nixon with too great a mandate." With his mind thus made up, Ball called Johnson at the ranch and explained that for the first time he was not asking or giving advice but "telling you what I'm going to do, because this is a matter of conscience with me."[14]

Then he telephoned Humphrey. His resignation would command newspaper and television attention for maybe three days, he said, and before that time was up he intended to create a real stir by being "very outrageous." He had a Vietnam speech already outlined in his mind for the vice-president to give in Salt Lake City on September 30. He flew to the West Coast to join Humphrey and to complete the drafting. Ball was also planning a "deep background" press conference immediately after the speech, during which he would decode what had been said and clue reporters so that their stories would say the things the vice-president had not dared to utter.[15]

Ball called the president before the speech was delivered, to read him the Vietnam passages. When the president finally got on the line—he had been talking with Richard Nixon—he listened, then said, "George, I know you'll be able to persuade them [the press] that this doesn't mark any change from the line we've all been following." "I'm sorry, Mr. President," came the reply, "but that's not quite the name of the game."[16]

Carefully crafted, Humphrey's actual statement, according to one White House aide's assessment, fell just within positions the Johnson administration had taken in the San Antonio speech a year earlier. "But Humphrey staffers," wrote Joe Califano, "let reporters know that the Vice President was in fact committing himself to a bombing halt without any qualifications."[17]

Not anonymous Humphrey "staffers"—George Ball guided the reporters. Humphrey's speech read:

> As President, I would stop the bombing of the North as an acceptable risk for peace because I believe it could lead to success in the negotiations and thereby shorten the war. . . . In weighing that risk—and before taking action—I would place key importance on evidence—direct or indirect—by deed or word—of Communist willingness to restore the demilitarized zone between North and South Vietnam.
>
> If the Government of [North] Vietnam were to show bad faith, I would reserve the right to resume the bombing.[18]

Ball began his "speech" to the reporters with a sly disclaimer. The Vietnam debate had become a theological study, he said, "and every formulation of a position of minor reference to Viet Nam is interpreted as though by a group of medieval monks sitting around analyzing a manuscript." Then Ball proceeded to lead them through just such an exercise. Reporters needed the guidance, he knew very well, because the vice-president's words in themselves marked no significant difference from White House positions. Calling Humphrey's statement by far the strongest and most useful that had ever been made, Ball said that it went right to the limit "without passing over the line toward irresponsibility." The reporters appeared puzzled. As one said, "It seems to me to be exactly the same as the Administration position. . . ." If anything, it asked for specifics on the demilitarized zone. The general tenor of the questions continued to express doubt that anything significantly new had been said. Finally, Ball spelled it out, revealing as he did so the president's actual negotiating position.

Well, I am not going to tell you what has been secretly made by the Administration, obviously. But you have seen what is on the public record and as far as the Administration is concerned, you know what the Administration is saying now, that they must know precisely what the other side is going to do. . . . All that this [Humphrey's speech] says is that he is going to look for some token of good faith, and on the basis of that, he is going to stop the bombing.

At last they got it!

Ambassador, it sounds to me as though you are saying that if Vice President Humphrey is elected, he is going to stop the bombing and this business about a token of good faith is in effect a mechanism to protect what is going on in Paris now.

Ball replied,

Well, you can interpret that any way you like. That is not what I am saying. But you can put any interpretation on it which you like.[19]

Accounts of the Humphrey speech highlighted his promise to end the bombing, blurring (as Ball had hoped) what he required of North Vietnam in return. Yet Rostow and Rusk professed to see little different in the speech from White House statements on negotiating conditions. "We should not go looking for marginal differences," said Rusk, perhaps to play down an issue that threatened a Johnson blowup. Soon the press was linking Humphrey's speech with supposed pleas from Harriman and Vance for greater flexibility in conducting the negotiations. According to Joseph Califano, LBJ never forgave Humphrey; but it is also possible that the vice-president's forcing the issue had a strangely liberating effect on Johnson. Angered as he might be at Humphrey's apostasy, now "it" had been said (never mind what "it" precisely was—"it" could be many things), and the taboo against talking about a bombing halt had been broken.[20]

What impact the Humphrey speech, and Ball's exegesis, had on Hanoi's leaders, on the other hand, cannot be determined. Still, it would seem that it took no great insight to figure out that an important change had taken place on the American political scene. Suddenly it made a difference who was elected. After Rusk's conversation with Andrei Gromyko, the American negotiators in Paris were instructed to "hammer first" on the issue of Saigon's representation—not exactly a switch in priorities, but more like an effort to follow up on the Russian foreign minister's hints imparted by the questions he had asked. On October 9, during the tea break conversation, which by now had become the occasion for any serious discussion, Le Duc Tho listened to Harriman and Vance expound on the need for GVN representation, and then replied, "If you want to discuss this matter further we are prepared to do so." He even wished immediately to set a time and place, gesturing toward the walls and ceiling of the Majestic Hotel, where the formal sessions took place, to indicate that they were not then in a secure location for such a talk. What was needed, Tho concluded, was goodwill and serious intent, an attitude the DRV was ready to display.[21]

Two days later, on Friday, October 11, 1968, Le Duc Tho and Xuan Thuy met the Americans at a prearranged site in a Paris suburb. The Vietnamese wanted to know, Tho said, whether the U.S. would stop the bombing if it had a clear answer on the question of Saigon's representation as a party in the peace negotiations. For the next hour or so the two sides took turns trying to get some wording that would commit the other. The Vietnamese insisted they could not go first with such a commitment because they had reason to fear that if they did, the United States would raise other "conditions." Harriman and Vance countered that it was not a condition, rather a statement about what would permit serious negotiations. Eventually Tho was more forthcoming. The American negotiators should report to Washington as follows: If North Vietnam accepted the participation of the Saigon government, would the president immediately stop the bombing? The Americans agreed to communicate the question that way and to report if they had an answer in three days' time, on Monday. Over a parting cup of tea, the two Vietnamese said they believed "rapid progress could be made if we were really determined to move toward peace."[22]

Rostow took the Vietnamese statements to mean they had concluded that the Tet offensive and subsequent attempts to stimulate an uprising against President Thieu had failed, and that they had also decided to accept an unsatisfactory political settlement in the south—at least for the time being. To save face they would claim they had driven the aggressive U.S. troops out of the south. "If this is so, we have a monumental job of fast negotiation ahead, in which the most critical job will be to help Thieu keep his country stable as the new situation unfolds."[23]

The break in the impasse signaled by the North Vietnamese query thus forced Washington to consider how actual peace talks could be sold to Saigon. Rusk had already told Gromyko that the United States had accepted (thus far without serious consultation with the South Vietnamese) the idea of the NLF being present under the loose formulation of "your side, our side." This circumlocution avoided the charge that Washington was ready to do something it said it would never do—deal directly with the Viet Cong about the political future of South Vietnam.

A formidable task now faced Johnson. The process of bringing President Thieu into the picture began with a telegram to Ambassador Bunker containing the proposed instructions to Paris and asking for his reaction. These instructions, read the Washington commentary sent to Saigon, constituted a "hard proposition," which, exactly as Le Duc Tho and Xuan

Thuy feared would happen, set forth further "conditions" for a bombing halt, including a demand that serious talks begin "within 24 hours," and that *all* military activity in the area of the demilitarized zone, not just actual attacks, cease. The important thing about these instructions, advised the cable, was that they were consonant with "Thieu's public statements" as well as those of President Johnson. In other words, with this telegram negotiations with Saigon to secure approval for peace talks had commenced. As matters unfolded, these proved to be the most difficult negotiations.[24]

Ambassador Bunker and General Abrams both gave a favorable response to the proposed instructions to Paris, and said they were themselves "comfortable" about facing negotiations in view of the improved military situation in the south. They even got President Thieu's approval—or thought they had. A third "party" to these preliminary rounds was the Joint Chiefs of Staff, whose adamant opposition to a bombing halt had given Johnson both a rationale for his own rigid refusal to hear of anything less than total capitulation by the North Vietnamese on the "conditions" for a cessation, and a fear they would go public and add to his woes. Meeting with the Joint Chiefs on October 14, Johnson had Rostow and Clifford review the recent developments and Saigon's assessment of the military situation. Perhaps to everyone's surprise, JCS Chairman General Wheeler bought on at once. Abrams's assessment, he explained, along with Thieu's ready acceptance to a bombing halt, indicated to the JCS that "the military war has been won." "I am in full accord with the approach and recommend it."[25]

Throughout the meeting, however, Rusk kept adding to the list of items to be resolved, almost as if he expected North Vietnam to provide solutions for America's foreign policy problems all across Southeast Asia. The Communists must shut down their guerrilla activities in Laos and Thailand, he said, and there could be no cease-fire unless "South Vietnamese authority runs to every part of South Vietnam." In short, surrender. Everyone present thought that Le Duc Tho's "concession" had been, in part, a result of Soviet impairment after the Czech intervention. Perhaps it was useful to think such things to convince oneself that the other side was hurting, but that was not what the secretary of state believed. Rusk apparently still had Greece on his mind. The NLF, like the Communist rebels in the late 1940s, were ready to fold their tents and fade away after some tough words at the peace table. For him the tricky part was not to be chivied into substantive negotiations by the fainthearted. The tough negotiations for Rusk were here, and his opponents were the Cliffords and Harrimans.[26]

Johnson had asked his old friend and mentor, Richard Russell, to attend this meeting. After each of the military chiefs had spoken, the president asked Russell for his assessment. It turned out to be a less than welcome contribution. The Georgia senator had serious doubts about trusting the North Vietnamese to carry out any of the conditions. And if they violated the terms agreed upon, he said, the president would have a deuce of a time resuming the bombing. Russell's objections went on for quite a while, producing responses from both Clifford and Rusk before Johnson revealed more of his mind than he had thus far in any of the discussions. It would be on his conscience, he said, if the negotiators had to say the president had kept them from reaching a settlement. "One can figure out what the condition of this country would be if the critics were to say we didn't try, that therefore additional casualties were our fault. *If this isn't the way to stop it, I don't have any way to end it.*" [27]

Back on the "frontlines" in Paris, the North Vietnamese negotiators had received the latest version of the American proposal and were not happy with the preemptory demand that they produce an NLF delegation within twenty-four hours of a bombing halt. Instead of a simple answer to the question of whether the U.S. would stop the raids if they agreed to allow Saigon a seat at the table, here were a new set of niggling requirements. The North Vietnamese were trying everything they could, concluded American policymakers, to bolster the status of the NLF, in this instance by suggesting that its leaders could not make the trip from South Vietnam to Paris in such a short time. Truth was, however, that Hanoi did not need such ploys. The Americans had accepted the presence of the NLF at the peace table, and, by their own formula, "your side, our side," had given it equal status with the supposedly "legitimate" and "independent" government of South Vietnam; or, conversely, still by the same formula, had reduced Saigon to the identical puppet status as the NLF. Either way, the South Vietnamese regime suffered the most loss of face. No doubt Rusk had grasped this point, and that accounted for his stalling tactics. One could not imagine a negotiation that somehow ignored the status of the NLF as a political factor in South Vietnam's future. Else why were they there?

To this point Washington had finessed these questions. But no longer. Late in the afternoon of Friday, October 18, Ambassador Bui Diem came into Walt Rostow's office with new messages from Saigon. Thieu had instructed him that if the NLF participated in the peace talks it would have "very dangerous repercussions" for South Vietnam's political stability. Thus he opposed the presence of the NLF at the Paris conference and warned it would be very difficult for the GVN to participate otherwise. Rostow said he understood the problem but was depressed by President Thieu's attitude. He should be approaching the peace conference in a spirit of confidence, not filled with anxiety. "It was a time to roll up our sleeves and get to work to see how we handle the conference to our advantage." [28]

Rostow continued this pep talk for some time, declaring it a "great stroke of good fortune" that having triumphed in the foxholes of Vietnam, they would now be able to work together in the foxholes of Paris in the same spirit. Bui Diem assured Rostow that he agreed with this great and good friend of his country, but President Thieu faced heavy pressures from the Assembly. This was a particularly effective little jab at the results of American-imposed "democracy" in South Vietnam. The United States had said it couldn't live with a dictatorship in Saigon; fine, now it would have to put up with democracy's unruliness![29]

Thieu did not confine his objections to private messages sent through Ambassador Diem. He had learned the game well. Press reports of his speeches opposing a bombing halt and negotiations with the NLF infuriated the Johnson administration. "Obviously," Dean Rusk cabled Ambassador Bunker, "we have as much of a problem with Saigon on theology as we have with Hanoi." Perhaps Saigon had earlier consented to the American proposals because it did not really believe in the eventuality. However that might be, the United States could not let such questions "determine our ability to grapple with the serious issues of substance. . . ." Bunker was instructed to do what he could before more damage was done to the prospects for negotiations. Rusk must have felt considerable unease at having to send such instructions to Bunker because, as we have seen, his own position was close to Thieu's. But the worst thing, worse even than having to sit down at the peace table, would be an open split between Washington and Saigon—that would wreck any chance of thwarting the peaceniks in the administration.

Bunker thought his best approach would be along the lines Rostow suggested. If the GVN decided to go into a sulk and refused to attend, he would tell Thieu, it would indicate a lack of confidence in their own position, which would be very unfortunate. Thieu's speeches had already had a very bad effect, the ambassador planned to say, particularly in revealing to Hanoi the potential for a split between Washington and Saigon.[30]

Still impressed with what they thought had been a major North Vietnamese concession, and irritated by this insubordination, Rusk and his aides had tried to dismiss as "theology" what was in fact an issue of major substance. What one agreed to about the level of representation at the peace table had quite definite implications for any postwar political settlement. In Paris, meanwhile, the North Vietnamese had begun pressing the Americans to accept the idea of a "joint communiqué" to spell out the agreement on a bombing cessation, and a concurrent announcement of a "four-party" conference "to seek a political settlement to the Viet-Nam problem on the basis of respect for the Vietnamese peoples' national rights." Greatly alarmed at this ploy, Harriman and Vance shook their heads. Washington would hear of no such thing. There could be no "written communiqué," especially not one saying anything about a four-party conference. It had been understood from the start, the Americans said, that "we had described the meetings as our side—your side, and for their part they could call it whatever they wish."[31]

There were other issues to iron out, including the timing of the first meeting after agreement was reached, but the joint communiqué and the description of the conference (our side—your side, or four-party) now became the central points of contention. Xuan Thuy made good use of Thieu's public declarations opposing a bombing halt or discussions with the NLF to put pressure on the U.S. negotiators. Harriman could not deny Thieu's remarks or that they had created difficulties. Finally he offered the possibility of an "agreed minute" as one alternative to the North Vietnamese demand for a joint communiqué.[32]

That evening a Soviet official from the Paris embassy phoned Cyrus Vance to ask for a meeting the next day, October 22. When they met the Russian diplomat explained he had been in contact with the North Vietnamese, who were very "emotional" and "suspicious." It became apparent, he went on, that the real problem was with the translations back and forth. On instructions from his government, he had suggested possible compromises. The gist of these was that the North Vietnamese would give up the demand for a joint communiqué and the announcement of a four-party conference, and settle instead for a secret minute about the terms of the bombing halt and the makeup of the conference. As to the timing question, the North Vietnamese had agreed that the first meeting could take place no later than a week after the bombing stopped. "The Russians are obviously trying very hard to pull this off," Rostow advised the president, "—and in a hurry."[33]

A week was too long, insisted General Wheeler at the next meeting of Johnson's advisers. It would ruin South Vietnamese morale. If the ARVN had to sit around on their hands, the momentum that had been generated since the summer counteroffensives would be lost. Thieu's behavior added weight to such a concern. He had to worry about Nixon's reactions as well, said President Johnson. Thieu had protested the NLF presence, and the Republican candidate would no doubt pick up on that point.

> *The President*: Nixon will ask me if this isn't like putting a fox in the chicken coop. (Laughter)

> *Secretary Clifford*: It seems Thieu gains enormously to have the GVN at the Table.

> *The President*: We do, in effect, recognize them [the National Liberation Front] by letting them sit down with us.

> *Secretary Rusk*: It's about like letting Stokely Carmichael sit at Cabinet Meeting.

> *Secretary Clifford*: It still seems like [a] greater benefit than detriment.

The President: Factually, that's correct.

Secretary Rusk: Emotionally, that's not correct.

Walt Rostow: The South Vietnamese are afraid of how we play them in Conference—push them toward accepting a slippery slope—jam into coalition government.[34]

After the meeting Rostow and William Bundy drafted new instructions for Paris. These stipulated that the first meeting should take place on November 2, three days after a bombing halt, and that if the North Vietnamese still insisted upon it, a secret minute describing the conference could be offered by Harriman and Vance, supposedly on their own initiative. The minute would say: "The US has indicated that representatives of the RVN will be present, and the DRV has indicated that representatives of the NLF will be present. The foregoing in no way implies recognition of those represented at the meeting."[35]

From Thieu's perspective, of course, such a secret arrangement between Hanoi and Washington only worsened matters. The wording not only classified the NLF and Saigon as equivalent but seemed to suggest there was no requirement for Hanoi to recognize President Thieu's government as an independent entity. If this was mere "theology," the Americans were getting better at it than many of the church's most notorious casuists.

As it turned out, the North Vietnamese objected to the sentence about nonrecognition in the proposed secret minute. When President Johnson talked individually with members of the Joint Chiefs and other subordinate commanders to make sure, as Rostow put it, they all stayed on the reservation, the whole thing seemed really to fall apart over timing of the initial negotiating session and North Vietnamese insistence upon naming the participants in order in the secret minute. Rusk even asked Ambassador Bunker at one point if he thought it was worth it, from Saigon's perspective—but without telling Thieu about the secret minute—to press for the nonrecognition sentence?[36]

Bunker did not need to inform Thieu about a secret minute or discuss wording to explain the intricacies of the diplomatic dance going on in Paris. Vice President Ky told the ambassador in plain language, "If we sit down with the NLF as equals, the whole *raison d'être* of this regime is finished." The only way Saigon could agree to attend such a conference, Foreign Minister Thanh explained in equally clear language, was if it was agreed that questions of internal politics of either North Vietnam or South Vietnam were not to be raised, and if the NLF was prohibited from signing any international agreement that resulted from the conference.[37]

Thanh was told those were impossible conditions to put upon the negotiations. And there matters rested. None of these encounters convinced Washington officials that, when it came right down to it, they would not be able to persuade or cajole the South Vietnamese into showing up in Paris if the conference actually took place. Negotiations with the North Vietnamese, meanwhile, had hit another roadblock. While the Americans complained about new "conditions" on the North Vietnamese side, delegate Xuan Thuy declared that if the South Vietnamese failed to appear, such a boycott—absent the secret minute saying the bombing halt was unconditional—would provide an excuse for Johnson or his successor to resume the attacks.

Rostow asked Ambassador Dobrynin to come to his house late in the afternoon of October 25 in order to present a memorandum from Johnson urging Soviet intervention to move the negotiations along. "There could be no outcome worse for all our efforts," it read, "than to have a resumption of the bombing and the break-up of what we have tried to achieve since March 31." The ambassador responded to this appeal by suggesting that the Americans were holding up an agreement over "third level" questions. No such thing, Rostow insisted, these were matters of the first importance. After more sparring in this fashion, Dobrynin interjected a query about stalled Soviet-American arms talks, implying a quid pro quo. Rostow brushed this aside. Johnson couldn't think about anything but Vietnam at this crucial moment, he said. When Dobrynin got up to leave, the national security adviser looked at his watch. "Anatoly," he intoned, "it is now midnight in Paris. You'd better get to work to clear up these issues of third importance."[38]

At noon on October 27 an excited Cyrus Vance called the White House from Paris. "We have now got *everything* we have asked for," he said. The North Vietnamese had backed off on demanding the words "without condition" and had agreed to a first meeting on November 2, three days after the proposed bombing halt. *"We should accept,"* he concluded. What had happened? "I smell vodka and caviar in it," Rusk asserted when Johnson's advisers assembled that evening at dinner to consider this startling development. "We have substantial compliance with this. The Soviets have moved in." Another hard-liner, Maxwell Taylor, agreed, "I have been a hard-nosed man, Mr. President, but I am for this. They are hurting." But Johnson refused to share in the euphoria Vance's phone call had created. "I think we are being herded into this under pressure." He would not consider a final decision to halt the bombing until he had one last assurance from General Abrams and one last shot at explaining the "facts of life" to the North Vietnamese so they understood that the American action really depended upon their good behavior.[39]

Both Clark Clifford and Walt Rostow were puzzled by Johnson's adamant refusal to go ahead promptly now that the North Vietnamese had moved so far. The secretary of defense argued that they had taken eight steps out of ten toward the U.S. position. Dean Rusk made it nine. "We may be motivated by evils we know not of," insisted the president. "I would rather be stubborn and adamant rather than [a] t[r?]icky, slick politician. They think everybody is working toward electing Humphrey by doing this." Johnson suspected everybody. He suspected that the North Vietnamese were playing politics, doling out concessions at selected intervals to force Johnson's hand at the last moment. Probably they planned to declare the halt was "unconditional." "I won't stand for that. Let's not leave them under the impression that it is unconditional. We can't sell Nixon's and Russell's on that. . . . I have my own credibility problems already." Johnson couldn't afford, in other words, to be accused of breaking his "pact" with Nixon not to back off American demands. A key to preventing any slash-back, the president believed, was getting General Abrams back in Washington, where he could be photographed with Johnson mulling over the situation. He wanted to look Abrams in the eye and have him say there was no danger involved in a bombing halt.

Clifford thought it was unnecessary to bring Abrams back. "I am not sure Wheeler can't do everything Abrams can do and do it better." "I disagree," snorted Johnson. "He has the color of [a] military commander who is in [the] field. He can say here are the conditions—he can assure that this won't risk lives. I want him to talk straight and direct. . . . All of you are playing with this like you have been living in another world—with a bunch of doves." Referring to his own party as a separate entity, Johnson ended, "The Democrats and George Ball have been putting out that we were about to do this."[40]

The president may have believed, as certain of his advisers did, that the North Vietnamese had sued for peace and were seeking a way to save face through negotiations. When he spoke of being tricked by Hanoi and Moscow, however, as he did that evening, what really concerned him were not violations of the understanding about a bombing halt, but a more profound fear that the new Communist strategy was aimed at destroying South Vietnamese morale—just as Thieu and Ky had been saying. Panmunjom was not the real danger, then, but a Far Eastern Yalta. Would it be said of Johnson that he was on the verge of military victory, like FDR at the end of World War II, only to throw it away, as conservatives charged Roosevelt had done at Yalta—in the agreements on Poland and China—under the influence of advisers like Averell Harriman?

Yalta had remained a powerful symbol of American diplomatic failures when an ill president lacked the fortitude to face down the Russians at the very moment the American Century began—with trouble ever since. Whether or not the analogy was fair, Johnson could be sure the Republicans would raise the cry, "Who lost Indochina?" Why had the North Vietnamese suddenly turned tail on these questions, if not to trick him into negotiations? And from the first reactions of the South Vietnamese, he knew they would not buy Rostow's line about comrades in arms and comrades forever. Finally, if "liberals" wanted to herd him into a "quick" decision on a bombing halt and beginning peace talks with the NLF as well as Hanoi (under a Russian aegis!), that only made him more suspicious. "We may be motivated by evils we know not of," he said. It was a paradoxical situation. For years Washington had tried to get the Russians involved, for example, to exercise a moderating influence on the ambitions of their client "state." Now that it had happened, LBJ regarded it as a subtle Communist trick abetted by the naiveté of the doves.

Rostow wrote the president a late-night letter trying to ease his mind by letting him know that the men at dinner, except for Clifford, had lived through Vietnam with all its pain for seven years. Yes, he would be accused of playing politics with the war, the national security adviser said. But he would anyway if he now delayed, "—and politics against the party you lead. Harriman and the Russians will see to that." With all its supposed uncertainties, the deal now being offered was the best that could be had, "—vastly better than any we thought we could get since 1961."[41]

But Johnson's antipathy toward the doves had depths that Rostow's memo could not touch. Speculation was rife, moreover, that he was about to cave in all the way—even to forcing a coalition government on South Vietnam to achieve victory in the presidential election. Johnson was ambiguous at best about Humphrey, and he feared the Republicans would seize upon a bombing halt to accuse him of playing politics with soldiers' lives. A week earlier columnist Joseph Kraft, in the *Washington Post*, had written that "Lyndon Johnson is more than ever the total master of his regime." His tough stand now gave him room to maneuver for a "deal" to bring about a full-dress peace conference to enhance his reputation. It could be made to look like a very big thing, indeed, wrote Kraft, but "It could almost certainly not yield an early resolution of the Vietnamese conflict."[42]

Whether Kraft's story was inspired by Republican sources, that was indeed the line the Nixon camp decided upon—and pursued vigorously not only with U.S. media but with South Vietnam as well. The details would emerge later, but Johnson had learned that the Nixon staff was in touch with the South Vietnamese through various intermediaries. Thieu was being promised a better deal if the Republicans won the election. That meant, it took no great political savvy to understand, a showdown with Saigon over a decision to go it alone, especially if Johnson acted before the election.

The day that Johnson demanded Creighton Abrams be brought back to Washington for a face-to-face meeting, FBI reports were on his desk concerning the activities of Anna Chennault, widow of famed World War II

"Flying Tiger" hero General Claire Chennault. Madame Chennault, another daughter of the prominent Soong family along with Madame Chiang Kai-shek, was a key figure in the "China Lobby," the powerful anti-Communist pressure group. A fund-raiser who helped to secure $250,000 for Nixon's candidacy, she had also offered her services as a go-between for the Republicans and President Thieu. Her primary contact points were John Mitchell in campaign headquarters and South Vietnamese Ambassador Bui Diem. The message Mitchell gave her to transmit to Saigon via Ambassador Diem was that if Johnson declared a bombing halt, President Thieu should resist going to the peace table. The bombing halt would then backfire on the Democrats, insuring Nixon's election—and a better deal for South Vietnam.[43]

Nixon had inside sources about the impending decision, including future national security adviser Henry Kissinger, who transmitted information he had gleaned about the Paris negotiations, as well as a "mole" inside the White House who reported to Bryce Harlow, an old Eisenhower aide who was now one of Nixon's closest advisers. Harlow's informant had supplied very good information about LBJ's concern with the American military. "They're having a hell of a time with the Joint Chiefs," Harlow told the candidate. "Lyndon is bringing them around. He's twisting and turning it so that they'll go with it. He's forcing them to go with it."[44]

Harlow's counter to LBJ's arm-twisting was to alert press reporters to the president's plan in an effort to expose the double-dealing going on— holding Nixon to a no-first-criticism pledge while selling out for a Humphrey victory. Johnson apparently had no knowledge that he was being spied upon, nor was it really necessary for Harlow to supply information to Joseph Kraft or anybody else for there to be speculation about the impact of a bombing halt. Whatever accounts for the president's forebodings as the American election approached, Hanoi's concessions spurred the momentum toward confronting Saigon in spite of all doubts. Johnson would be damned either way he decided to go.

Rostow proposed sending Thieu a letter to soften this confrontation with new assurances of continuing American support. It praised Thieu and his government for surviving the "shock of the Tet attacks" to rebuild South Vietnam's military strength, asked him to be ready to exert every bit of military pressure in the near future, and, in a strangely contradictory paragraph, called upon him to "mount a major political and psychological effort in the days ahead to bring the VC over to your side." Then this:

> I know the question of the NLF in the Paris talks is awkward for you. But you can feel sure that we shall make clear that no question of recognition by the U.S. is involved. . . . Your people can also be sure that we have no intention of imposing a coalition government upon them. On

the other hand, I count on you to move towards reconciliation and peace in South Vietnam in the spirit of our talks at Honolulu in July and of our communiqué.

"You can count on Ambassador Bunker, General Abrams, and me," it closed, "to be at your side in the days ahead as we have been in the years that are behind us."[45] Even this phrasing suggested a yearning to be done with the war, and to put the onus on Thieu for any and all failures in its final chapter. Meanwhile, Washington sent Ambassador Bunker a proposed joint announcement of a bombing halt, along with similar private assurances for President Thieu that the United States had no intention of trying to impose a coalition government on Saigon. "The two presidents wish to make it clear," read the proposed declaration, "that neither the government of the Republic of Viet-Nam nor the United States Government recognizes the so-called National Liberation Front as an entity independent of North Viet-Nam."[46]

Thieu seemed to agree. "I do not see how we can ask for anything more," he told Bunker, who then cabled Washington, "I think we are in the clear here. . . ." When this welcome message arrived, Rostow was busy composing yet another letter from Johnson, this one to Ho Chi Minh to be given to the North Vietnamese at the first session of the peace conference. Rostow's prose reached for Lincolnesque themes. It depicted a generous victor seeking to bind up the wounds of war. After stern reminders that the American people were not likely to put up with another Panmunjom experience—still a bitter memory—and expected the conclusion of a "stable peace . . . at the earliest possible date," the tone softened to recall Johnson's offer at Johns Hopkins University. It was still open—albeit now without the specific promise of a billion dollars for the Mekong River project:

> I should also wish you to know that I have never deviated from a vision of the future in which the remarkable capacities of the people of North Vietnam would be turned to the works of peace in collaboration with their neighbors in Southeast Asia. In the months and years ahead, it would give me great satisfaction to know that the people of South Vietnam were living in the dignity of independence, forging their own peaceful destiny, in an environment of rapid economic and social progress.[47]

Very late the night of the day Rostow wrote his "Lincoln" letter, General Creighton Abrams arrived from Saigon and was taken to the White House where the president and his advisers had gathered at 2:30 a.m. for a final time before sending the signal to Paris that the bombing halt was "on." Johnson opened the meeting with a review of events since early summer when Kosygin sent his letter suggesting that a bombing halt would produce negotiations. From mid-October to this evening, the president continued, there had been two weeks of very hard negotiations, and on each issue the North Vietnamese had backed down, until finally they had "fully met our position." Then he outlined the proposed agreement. "As we have always said," Johnson quickly slipped around the one awkward corner, "there is no obstacle to the NLF having an opportunity to express its view on a settlement. But no recognition of the NLF is involved."[48]

It was the "universal judgment of our diplomatic and military authorities," he concluded, that these concessions had set the stage for an honorable settlement of the war. Then he turned to Abrams. Leaked newspaper accounts of this meeting highlighted, as Johnson intended they should (complete with pictures of the two men), Abrams's answers to the president's searching questions.[49] In August the military had said ending the bombing would increase enemy capabilities severalfold, Johnson began his inquiry. Why could we do it now? Because, explained Abrams, the enemy had left the staging areas where it had been preparing attacks. "There isn't enough enemy left in I Corps to keep 1st Cavalry Division up there. . . . The enemy moved out." What about casualties? Johnson demanded. "I am going to put more weight on your judgment than anybody else. Can we do this without additional casualties?" Abrams assured him that was so. On and on this recital went, questions and answers, Johnson probing for some doubt that would come back later to set off an avalanche of criticism. He could discover not one. Enemy forces were weaker and less capable, American morale was great, the ARVN was improving, and so on.

"This is a critical period here," Johnson asked one last question. "In light of what you know, do you have any reluctance or hesitance to stop the bombing?" Abrams did not. "If you were President, would you do it?" "I have no reservations about doing it. I know it is stepping into a cesspool of comment. I do think it is the right thing to do. It is the proper thing to do." Satisfied with the results of his interrogation, Johnson sat back while the others continued. Would South Vietnam survive politically if we decided to halt the bombing? asked Secretary Rusk.

Secretary Rusk: We have lost 28,000 men. We can't stand another coup. Do they understand this can't happen?

General Abrams: Yes, they understand that.

Secretary Rusk: Will this action precipitate a coup?

General Abrams: No, Sir. They know it's the end of the U.S. Government in Vietnam if they have a coup.[50]

Clifford nudged the general in a different direction. Did he have any expectation that Hanoi or the NLF was ready to abandon the field? No, admitted Abrams, they would continue with terrorist activities, biding their time. "I do not expect this to be wound up in a month," Rusk interrupted.

"This may go on while you men wrap it up in South Vietnam." Abrams nodded vigorously, "I subscribe to that 100%." "The loudest voice in Paris," the general said, "is what we accomplish in South Vietnam." Rostow beamed at that: "We agree." "That's right," added Rusk. That left it to General Wheeler to pronounce a military benediction: "I think this is as much a symbol of defeat as erection of [the] Berlin Wall. They have been clobbered. If they don't act in good faith, I would urge resumption and really let them have it. I would use [a] fire hose rather than [an] eyedropper."[51]

The meeting had now gone on for two and a half hours. It was 5 a.m., and it would be another hour before Bunker called from Saigon to report on President Thieu's readiness to issue the joint declaration. Rusk had returned to the State Department. The president grew impatient, asking why a cable had not arrived, Bunker had been meeting with Thieu for over an hour. A few minutes past six, Rusk finally relayed the message to Johnson: Thieu was stalling. The president looked up from the phone, "That's the old Nixon." The Republican candidate must have gotten jittery, said Johnson, and was sending word to Saigon to hold off until after the election.

What could be done? If we said that Thieu was conniving with the Republicans, the president pondered, it would "rock the world" and destroy what we had hoped to get out of stopping the bombing. Indeed, Nixon's behavior threatened the defeat of South Vietnam. His proxies might have persuaded the Saigon leaders that they would get a better deal if he were elected, and that they should hold out against a bombing halt to defeat Humphrey, but it was the "old Nixon" double-dealing again. Proof was in a letter Walt Rostow produced from his brother, Eugene, who had heard from an informant about a luncheon where a prominent member of the New York banking community—someone "very close to Nixon"—explained the supposed strategy.

It was a bizarre piece of skulduggery, if true, but not entirely implausible with the stakes so high, ranging from winning an election to providing Nixon with an exit from a war that the establishment wanted to be rid of fully as much as any radical protester. The conversation reported to Eugene Rostow took place in the context of a "professional" discussion about the future of the financial markets in the next term. Prospects for a bombing halt were dim, the Nixon confidant had explained, because the candidate intended to play a blocking role, thereby inciting Saigon to be difficult and Hanoi to wait. Part of this strategy involved the expectation that with peace talks stalled, the North Vietnamese would launch a new offensive—forcing the outgoing administration to suffer more casualties and spend a great deal more. The adverse impact of these Vietnam developments on the stock market would serve Nixon's real purposes:

These difficulties would make it easier for Nixon to settle after January. Like Ike in 1953, he would be able to settle on terms which the President could not accept, blaming the deterioration of the situation between now and January or February on his predecessor.[52]

"It all adds up," Johnson said when he had finished reading the letter. "I have no doubt there is some substance in this." Abrams had assured him that stopping the bombing would reduce casualties; now it appeared that, in this deepening mystery play where everything had a paradoxical double life, his only chance to come out of the situation was to increase the tempo of the ground war, a policy sure to swell casualties. If he stopped the bombing and South Vietnam went its own way, prospects for a safe exit from the war and an "honorable peace" would rapidly diminish; but equally so if he failed to carry through on this decision, and Nixon's supposed strategy for tricking the South Vietnamese into betraying their own best interests played out as envisioned in this strange report he had been given by Eugene Rostow. He hinted something of his dilemma to the historian who had previously chronicled decisions of the Tuesday Luncheons. "All the evil forces around town," he told Henry Graff about the decision to end the bombing, "started rearing their ugly heads."[53]

Since mid-October Johnson had been holding a "gung-ho" message that Walt Rostow had drafted to Abrams in the event of a decision to halt the bombing. It had become even more pertinent in light of the revelations about secret manipulations. A hundred years ago, it began, Lincoln found a general. Johnson had been lucky enough to find two, Westmoreland and Abrams. What General Abrams must now do, what he must also inspire the ARVN to do, was to pursue the enemy relentlessly. "Don't give them a minute's rest. Keep pouring it on. "With luck and with Abe, we shall conquer ourselves a peace in the next three months—without the loss of a single battle or skirmish—as General Winfield Scott did 120-some years ago."[54]

As happened before when Walt Rostow resorted to American history to defend or rationalize the war, he got tangled up. Abraham Lincoln found himself a general in U.S. Grant, but he had opposed the Mexican War—where Winfield Scott promised a victory in three months—as an immoral undertaking. Mixed-up history was the least of Johnson's problems, of course. Angered and frustrated with Thieu, the president ordered Rusk to have Bunker tell the South Vietnamese leader that if it got out that he had blocked American efforts at peace talks, South Vietnam wouldn't have much support in the United States. Clark Clifford wanted to go further. The situation "could become so grave" that it could be untenable even in the weeks remaining in President Johnson's term. Only Rusk pulled back, fearing, as his questions to Abrams had hinted, that Hanoi's concessions at

Paris actually could have a destablizing impact on Saigon—enough so to cause either a breakdown or an American decision to pull out in disgust, either of which perfectly suited the enemy's purpose.[55]

To protests that Thieu had to be shown at once that he could not hijack a peace effort, Rusk pleaded for patience:

We've invested 29,000 killed and $70 billion.
The whole thing could blow up.
The allies could come apart.
If we had [a] public blowup it would be a disaster.[56]

The secretary of state had argued from the beginning that America was in Vietnam to assure the world of its reliability. Despite all criticism that it was instead demonstrating an irrational fixation on thwarting a minor-league player in the great game of nations, or some other piece of monstrous foolhardiness, Rusk had clung to that position. Now he could see everything unraveling all the way back to the Truman Doctrine.

Rostow left the meeting to write a memo to the president urging him to treat information about Richard Nixon's involvement with the South Vietnamese with some care. These materials were so explosive that they could "gravely damage the country," he said, whether or not the Republican was elected. "If they get out in their present form, they could be the subject of one of the most acrimonious debates we have ever witnessed." He should consider having a private talk with him instead, to say that he believed Nixon was not personally involved, but to warn him to be "exceedingly circumspect in dealing with inexperienced and impressionable South Vietnamese."[57]

Like Dean Rusk, Walt Rostow could forsee a terrible dilemma emerging from this confusion. To allow Saigon to stand in the way of an honorable peace, or to allow President Thieu to determine the outcome of the American election on November 5, was intolerable. But to bring down the South Vietnamese government after all the sacrifice by applying methods not unlike those—hawkish critics would charge—that had toppled Diem in 1963, would undo all those things supposedly accomplished in Southeast Asia and undermine public support for cold war policies elsewhere.

Such were the thoughts that swirled in and about the cabinet room as the president's advisers reassembled only a few hours later to hear the results of Thieu's meeting with *his* national security council. "If I were Thieu," Johnson mused, "I wouldn't feel very kindly about it." Johnson had some understanding, however, of why Nixon had decided to play it this way and intervene with Thieu. Humphrey's speech in Salt Lake City, Mac Bundy's speech dissociating himself from the administration's position in October—all this publicity "all had an effect on Nixon." When the Republicans thought the president had gone back on his word, "they went to work

on the [South Vietnamese] Embassy. They made Bui Diem think he could
get a better deal from Nixon than us." As for other statements out of South
Vietnam, "I think Ky is getting just as independent as Hubert." When
another message came through from Saigon, it was clear American appeals
had been turned down. "This may mean that everything we have done is in
vain," Johnson reported to the group. But Johnson still had General
Abrams's cross-examination to fall back on. "Based on Abrams' views, the
JCS views, and all of you, I was ready to go. I was 80% ready before General Abrams came here. *Now I am ready to go.*"

Thieu's NSC had decided they could not meet as soon as three days
(which the United States had demanded for so long from the North Vietnamese!), and Thieu was now alleging that Averell Harriman had insulted
his representative in Paris by telling him that Saigon could not veto NLF
presence at the conference. Official American reports of what Harriman
said seemed scarcely to warrant such a reaction, but a newspaper account
had the American negotiator telling Pham Dang Lam that South Vietnamese "pretensions" were "out of this world. . . . Your Government does
not represent all of South Vietnam, Mr. Ambassador, and you would do well
to remember that."[58]

Ambassador Lam's mission had apparently been designed to produce
some such remark Thieu could treat as a major insult to the dignity of his
government, perhaps to see if Washington would repudiate what had been
done in its name in Paris. If so, the ploy did not work. Johnson agonized
over what to do, but he knew very well that if he failed to go ahead with a
bombing halt, leaks of how close "peace" had been would absolutely ruin
the nation's support for any policy in Vietnam—no matter who was elected.
"If he keeps us from moving," Johnson declared, "God help South Vietnam—because I can't help him anymore, neither can anyone else who has
my job."[59]

That message, in almost precisely those words, was sent to Bunker for
his use in persuading Thieu to change his mind.

> The President is deeply concerned that President Thieu does not suffi-
> ciently understand the American people and their government. If Presi-
> dent Thieu makes himself responsible for preventing the very peace
> talks which have cost so much to obtain, the people of this country
> would never forget the man responsible. No American leader could res-
> cue the position of such a person with the American people. If President
> Thieu keeps us from moving at this moment of opportunity, God help
> South Vietnam, because no President could maintain the support of the
> American people.[60]

Here was the first instance for Johnson to use the Abrams leverage as
well. Johnson wanted Thieu to understand that the attitude of the Ameri-

can military was of crucial importance to the security of his [Thieu's] own country. "Our top military men are unanimous that the understandings reached in Paris provide a substantial military benefit to U.S. and allied forces in the field. These men, who have been responsible for the conduct of the battle, will respond with disgust to a rejection of this present opportunity for petty and trivial reasons." Bunker was also to allude to the Chennault connection. There might be individuals in the Saigon government, he was to say, who were speculating about the internal politics of the United States. Decisions based upon such speculation "carry the gravest danger because the American people would react in fury if they should discover that lives were being lost because people of other countries were trying to intrude their own judgments into the judgments of the American people about our future leadership."

Thieu's reaction was emotional and disjointed, reported Ambassador Bunker. "You are powerful," he reproached Bunker. "You can say to small nations what you want. We understand America's sacrifice for Vietnam. All Vietnamese know our life depends on US support. But you cannot force us to do anything against our interest. This negotiation is not a life or death matter for the US but it is for Vietnam."[61]

Bunker thought Thieu's objections were not totally without merit. He was particularly concerned that if the "secret minute" became public—and it was almost unavoidable that, one way or another, it should—it would severely damage the American position in Vietnam, and be regarded as evidence of Washington's perfidy. What would happen, Bunker asked, if at the first meeting of the peace conference either the U.S. or the GVN challenged the credentials of the NLF delegate? The other side would produce the secret minute as proof that an agreement had been reached on the NLF as a separate entity. The upshot would be that Saigon could claim, with good reason, that the United States had agreed with Hanoi on the very thing Washington had said it would never accept, a four-power conference.[62]

Clark Clifford was furious. "We have known before how Thieu would react," he charged. "Now they have been asked [by Republican provocateurs] would you rather have three months of Johnson or four years of Nixon. Their whole approach is delay. This message is 'horseshit.' This message is thoroughly insulting." Rusk suggested it was not so surprising. After all, both sides are pushing for key concessions.[63] In a last appeal to Thieu, Secretary Rusk informed him that the North Vietnamese had withdrawn their demand for a "secret minute," that they had agreed to a six-day delay before the first meeting, and that the United States was prepared to state publicly that its view of the NLF was the same as Saigon's. "If he breaks with us," Rusk told Bunker to say, "we are finished. The American people will not take this."[64]

Accompanied by deputy ambassador Samuel D. Berger, Bunker took this message to Thieu. They argued for seven hours in an effort to produce Thieu's agreement to the cessation, and his willingness to announce the sending of a delegate to the peace conference convened after the bombing halt. The Vietnamese leader was adamant. "At the very moment you are assuring me of Hanoi's good faith," read an account of the exchange, "they are shelling Saigon." "Yes," Bunker responded, "and we are still bombing North Vietnam." Berger then warned Thieu that if Saigon continued to play the game this way, "we will not support you." Picking up a pen, Thieu said, "Let me write that down. You say you will not support us. I thought you were the Ambassador to the Republic of Vietnam, not Hanoi." The meeting broke up a short while later—just three hours before Johnson went on television to announce the halt.[65]

In yet another letter, meanwhile, Thieu had sent a frank statement to Washington that touched the heart of the whole situation. Without the war there was no basis at all for his government. He did not say it that way, but it was the only conclusion to draw.

> Any prospect of recognition of the "NLF," explicit or implicit, is considered as a sure sign of surrender to the Communists. This will promptly and inevitably create the demoralization of the whole nation, and the collapse of our entire defense efforts. The regular armed forces, the regional and popular forces, the rural development cadres, the civil servants and others, will consider it to be utterly futile to make further efforts and sacrifices for a goal doomed in advance. Conversely, the morale of enemy troops and cadres will immediately raise. . . . Street demonstrations will immediately resume in Saigon and other cities, more violent than ever, leading to the most chaotic political instability.[66]

A few hours before Johnson was to announce on television the bombing decision, LBJ's feet again began to grow cold. He demanded still more assurances from the Joint Chiefs that they backed him all the way. A letter was solicited from General Wheeler that stated that after a "thorough discussion," the JCS agreed the bombing halt would constitute "a perfectly acceptable military risk." In a second paragraph, however, they implied doubts about the political outcome. The Joint Chiefs hope, it read, that "the current problem of reaching agreement with the GVN can be handled in such a way that the effectiveness and prestige of the current government in Vietnam would not be jeopardized."[67]

"They are weasling out," Johnson complained to Clark Clifford. Forget about the chiefs, his old counselor implored him. The letter was sufficient. "In any case," Clifford wrote in his memoirs, "it was the most I could get in writing from them."[68] Walt Rostow urged the president to call Nixon. Tell him about the evidence the White House had concerning

Republican meddling in the Vietnamese peace negotiations, and then explain that if it became known Thieu was holding up a deal that could bring peace nearer, the basis of public support for the "enterprise would dissipate." "We simply cannot let these inexperienced men snatch defeat from the jaws of victory."[69]

As the day went by in almost surreal fashion, Johnson seemed to wonder about that statement—not about Nixon's supposed inexperience costing a victory, but whether this announcement was to be a victory celebration. Over and over again he asked for reassurances. Early in the afternoon he turned again to Clark Clifford. Are we really winning the war? he asked. Is the enemy washed up? Clifford said he did not think so. In his opinion the enemy "was definitely not washed up. Hence we ought to go ahead and seek progress in peace talks."[70]

Whether LBJ fully grasped what Clifford was saying, he well understood that the step he was about to take had much more political than military significance. The ultimate battle for Vietnam was about to begin. Hoarse from a cold brought on by the all-night meetings, Johnson met for one last time with his advisers before his speech announcing the bombing halt. Thieu had refused to go along, so the speech had to be amended. He had originally planned to say that representatives of the government of South Vietnam would be present; now he could only explain that representatives of the government of South Vietnam were "free to participate." As for the NLF presence in Paris, he had planned to say that "Their participation in no way involves recognition. Yet it conforms to our consistent position that their views could be heard in the course of making peace in Vietnam." What he actually said was, "I emphasize that their attendance in no way involves recognition of the National Liberation Front in any form." There was no mention in the speech that NLF voices "could be heard."[71]

All he could do, Johnson felt, was try to hold things together to thwart whatever schemes were afoot to undo all that had been sacrificed to save Vietnam—now completely transfigured and reified into an abstraction. Nixon's "conspiracy" was liberating in a way. It allowed Johnson to support a bombing halt with new enthusiasm, and without feeling he was betraying the legacy of three presidents—a predicament he had, of course, defined himself into with repeated invocations over the past half-decade.

As he prepared to speak to the nation announcing the bombing halt, LBJ sent a self-revealing appeal to General Abrams:

> It is now clear, Abe, that our course is set. We must go forward fearlessly, without division if possible, but we must go forward.
>
> I hope you will use all your imagination and all the persuasiveness you can summon on Thieu, Ky and your military counterparts to the end that South Vietnam hangs together.

If you and Bunker are unable to do this—there will be, as Franklin said, a lot of separate hangings.

In the meantime summon the strength of every American and everyone else you can—quartermasters included—to put on an effort in South Vietnam and Laos as it has never been put on before.

We have only 80 days left.[72]

TWENTY-TWO

The Last Chapter?

DEAN RUSK'S NEWS CONFERENCE on November 1, 1968, was filled with clues to the internal debates that had preceded the bombing-halt decision. In his opening remarks, for example, the secretary of state reiterated that Hanoi had to be held accountable for peace throughout Southeast Asia. "The decision of last evening was not the end of a struggle," he went on in a Freudian double entendre. Others were now expected to help with managing Hanoi. "Now, I am also saying to all of those who have said, oh, things will be wonderful if you stop the bombing, we are saying to them, all right, get busy, get busy. See what you can do. We have made our move, now you make yours."[1]

When reporters asked about Saigon's refusal to issue a joint announcement and its obstructionist attitude about the convening of the peace conference, Rusk did his best balancing act. The South Vietnamese objected, he said, not to the bombing halt; "their problem has been with questions that we normally call modalities . . . questions of procedure, questions of status and things of that sort." Washington's attitude was to try to set aside "unnecessary complications" about procedure and get to substance. "It may be the pragmatic Anglo-Saxon approach at work, if you wish. . . . If the talks evolve as we now expect they will, perhaps everyone at the table will have a different view as to the situation of the other people at the table."

At least part of Dean Rusk wanted nothing to do with pragmatism of any sort, Anglo-Saxon or otherwise. Instructions personally drafted by Rusk himself were going out to Paris to guide the American negotiators even as he spoke to reporters. The highest priority, began his cable, must now be given to close and friendly working relationships with the South Vietnamese. "With the cessation of the bombing we are now in a position to insist upon the most simple and fundamental demands we have to make upon the North Vietnamese. They must stop their aggression. We can no longer accept any sensitivities on their side about such words as 'reciprocity,' 'conditions,' and other such nonsense. They must liquidate their aggression in South Vietnam and Laos." The fact that Hanoi had sent men with guns into South Vietnam gave them no right to issue demands about the internal political structure of that country, any more than Saigon's leaders had a claim on Washington to demand changes in the political structure of North Vietnam.[2]

The schoolmaster's tone evident throughout the cable was directed at his errant pupils—not the North Vietnamese, but Harriman and Vance. What else could "other such nonsense" refer to, except the rumors out of Paris about the delegation's dismay about Washington "hard-liners"? A few days later, moreover, Rusk told *Washington Post* diplomatic correspondent Murrey Marder not to waste his time by going to France to cover the peace talks. Nothing would happen in Paris. Both sides held views that could not be compromised. As long as Lyndon Johnson was president and he was secretary of state, there would be no "progress" in the negotiations. If Marder wanted the real story on what was happening, he should pay attention to the military reports from Vietnam, not focus on what floated out of Paris.[3]

In his quiet, calm way, Dean Rusk played many roles. He would serve longer as secretary of state than any other man except FDR's Cordell Hull, whose greatest boast was that he had outlasted all the radical New Dealers to preserve the Wilsonian version of true American liberalism. To many, Rusk had become the cold war's Samuel Johnson, holding back the forces of untamed romanticism by the strength of his personality. In the diplomatic game Rusk was a cautious player, whose favorite line was uncomplicated adherence to a few central beliefs. The concessions Hanoi had yielded in order to get the bombing halt, he believed, constituted the real truth about this end game. Black's moves signaled defeat, if only white could get past a preoccupation with quick results. North Vietnam had, in effect, sued for peace.

The bombing halt was indeed the right piece to play, but not in the way the doves imagined. Rusk had favored the stand-down because it would ease public criticism in the United States and allow the North Vietnamese to save face while at last surrendering to the inevitable. If the American delegates were so foolish as to overlook their basic advantages in a rushed attempt to make peace, the North Vietnamese would, of course, accommodate them. In any event, the enemy could be expected to play its side well at the expanded talks. Patience and discipline for only a few months more, he pleaded, that was all, for time was on the American side.

National Security Adviser Walt Rostow held similar views. In forwarding a report on the fighting from one of his aides on the NSC staff, Rostow advised the president that the odds were becoming more favorable to a bid by Hanoi for a quick settlement "if we hold steady." The report itself had suggested that no conclusions could be drawn about North Vietnamese strategy at Paris, but Rostow thought the determining factor would be the accelerating pacification rate. "The enemy simply cannot afford to sit still." Control over the population was proving to be a wasting resource for the NLF and North Vietnam. According to Rostow's calculations, the Communists were losing the battle for hearts and minds at a rate that had now reached 3 percent of the population a month. Hence the need to be ready when Hanoi asked for terms.[4]

But the secretary of state's strategy and Rostow's arithmetic rested on a shaky premise. How could American diplomats get closer to the South Vietnamese who had thus far refused to come to Paris and were vowing never to attend under the terms Washington had negotiated? President Thieu's embarrassing denunciations of American actions not only irritated Washington, they actually bolstered Hanoi's claims that the bombing halt was a great victory for their side. The South Vietnamese simply had to trust Johnson, and they did not. From Saigon a reporter wrote for the *New York Times*, "The policy may be to let Thieu kick shins for a while in order to keep him in power. Now, however, there are indications that the kicks are beginning to hurt badly."[5]

That was not the only problem. Rusk's memory of the Korean experience conjured up a related peril. He argued at the Tuesday Luncheons that it was quite likely that, if elected, Richard Nixon would pull an "Eisenhower" and try to fashion a cobbled peace that would mock Johnson's efforts to preserve a "free" Vietnam. All the more reason, then, to use the interim to establish a solid barrier against a bugout. As it turned out, of course, this was a misreading of Nixon's intentions, but Rusk could just as easily have argued the other side—that the Democrats owed the new administration an obligation not to present it with a surrender document.

Radio Hanoi, meanwhile, added to the secretary's woes in a not unexpected way, declaring that Washington had been forced by world opinion to halt the bombing and was now facing "great defeats" in Vietnam. It boasted, "This is a great victory for the entire Vietnamese people."[6] The Nixon camp also moved to discredit American diplomacy. Although he himself did not mistrust the president for having made the decision just before the election, Nixon said, his advisers had their own opinions—and were entitled to express them. In a sanctimonious comment, the Republican candidate promised he would not do anything to undercut peace hopes. "Peace is too important for politics, and that's the way we're going to play it." Even if John Mitchell's efforts to persuade Thieu not to send a delegate to Paris were superfluous, given Saigon's all too clear understanding of the meaning of admitting the NLF to the peace talks, Nixon picked up at once on

Johnson's statement in his speech to the nation that the South Vietnamese were "free" to attend, not that they would. All Nixon had to do was wait.[7]

Over the next few days the polls showed a dramatic shift toward Humphrey. The Harris poll of November 2 actually showed that the vice president had moved ahead, 43 to 40 percent. But with Thieu's announcement that "the government of South Vietnam deeply regrets not being able to participate in the [peace] talks," the pro-Democratic impetus came to a dead halt. Now Nixon could simply feign surprise and point out what Thieu's refusal to play meant: "In view of the early reports that we've had this morning [from Saigon], the prospects for peace are not as bright as we would have hoped a few days ago."[8]

For one of the few times during this confused period, Rostow, Rusk, and Clifford (each for his own reason) were agreed on what should be done: not only must Nixon's hand be called, but evidence of the Anna Chennault intrigue must be presented to Senate Republican leader Everett Dirksen, with a threat to go public, unless the candidate reversed his efforts and actually pushed Thieu to go to Paris. If Nixon continued to suggest that the president had misled the nation, Rostow recommended, Dirksen should be told, "We will reveal the evidence which will destroy him and any effectiveness he would have if he's elected."[9]

The president did summons Dirksen, and, in a dramatic flourish, told him he knew all about the Chennault affair. The senator hastened to warn Nixon that LBJ was threatening to go public with the evidence. Nixon turned that threat to his advantage, however, by claiming on television that he was ready to go to Vietnam if that would help. "I believe they ought to go to the conference table. . . . If my influence could be helpful, I will be helpful." It was a brilliantly bold and brazen maneuver, writes Nixon biographer Stephen Ambrose, in a career built on such boldness and brazen effrontery. Having schemed to keep Thieu from signing on to Johnson's policy, here he was imitating Ike's "I shall go to Korea" pledge.[10]

Johnson's threat to go public was effectively skewered by Nixon's ploy, though he probably never intended to go through with it anyway. To reveal that American intelligence operations had been directed not only against an ally's diplomats but against its own citizens would only add to Johnson's troubles—as Nixon found out during the Watergate investigations. Saigon was releasing details, meanwhile, of Washington's pressure on Thieu before the bombing halt, in a successful campaign to suggest that LBJ's credibility gap yawned wider than ever. And Nixon continued to have it both ways. In his final appeal for election, he declared that the "diplomatic disaster" of the Paris talks could be laid to a failure of the president's men to provide the groundwork for the bombing halt. His election was necessary, he declared, to give new men with "fresh ideas" the opportunity to find solutions that had eluded "the tired men around the president."[11]

On November 5, 1968, Richard Nixon finally achieved his lifelong ambition. He was elected president by the narrowest of margins. It was a late-night thriller, fully satisfying to those who loved staying up until dawn for the final returns from the famous playgrounds of political bosses—like, for example, Illinois. Nixon won 43.4 percent of the popular vote to Humphrey's 42.7 percent. In the electoral college the margin was much wider, 302 votes to 191. Pundits claimed that one vote, President Thieu's, swung the election. Maybe so, maybe not. Had Johnson held off on a bombing halt announcement for two or three days, and not given Thieu an opportunity to cast his vote before the American election, many people, including Republican insiders, believed the outcome would have been different. Yet if one added to Nixon's popular vote the 13.5 percent received by Alabama Governor George Wallace, the swing to the political right was clear, and that was a more complicated phenomenon than the war itself.

Just how complicated all this had become was evident in the message traffic between Saigon and Washington. Ambassador Bunker reported that, as expected, Hanoi was claiming the bombing halt as a clear victory, insisting it was unconditional and declaring that the NLF had been admitted to the talks as a separate entity. "I recommend that we pull out all stops in making clear that we never have and do not now recognize the NLF as a separate entity." American policymakers could repeat until they were blue in the face that the only thing they had agreed to was that the North Vietnamese could bring whomever they wished—their French chauffeur if it pleased them—to sit on their side of the table. President Thieu's vehement insistence that Washington had conceded the point made such disclaimers seem ridiculous. As matters stood, therefore, both Hanoi and Saigon agreed that the prehalt understanding called for a four-power conference.[12]

On one level, of course, Saigon's behavior suited the purposes of those who imagined a "fight and talk" strategy until the other side got tired and gave up. But that was not the way Lyndon Johnson saw it. He had pronounced the understandings a justification for all the suffering Vietnam had caused the American people. He had explained how others had urged him to end the bombing, but he had held out against such demands until American conditions had been met. Thieu's repudiation of the arrangements thus struck a serious blow to what was left of the president's rationale for the war. It was harmful on both the left and the right. For the right, Thieu's outrage confirmed criticism of the war as a half-hearted endeavor begun without a clear military purpose, and now ending inevitably in confusion and capitulation. For the left, Thieu's obstinacy demonstrated that the war had begun in confusion and capitulation to cold war fixations, and was now prisoner, inevitably, to the desperate struggle of a reactionary warlord to maintain his clique in power. The short respite from criticism achieved by the bombing halt was already over.

Certainly those who held the views from either of these perspectives had had little incentive to vote for Hubert Humphrey. Conservatives believed the only chance to break with a policy of defeat would be a Nixon victory; liberals despaired at this new evidence of Vietnam's death grip on American politics. One day Nixon would find out how much this election cost when he tried to make peace. In Paris, meanwhile, Harriman and Vance were left with Rusk's instructions to get closer to a delegation that was not there. The only alternative was an embarrassing announcement that the opening of the wider conference would have to be delayed. North Vietnam's claim that the NLF could not be produced on short notice had been judged by the Americans as little more than a gimmicky way of boosting the guerrillas' stature; now it was Washington's representatives who had to ask for a delay. The DRV delegates were able to whipsaw the Americans on American terms. To Cyrus Vance's suggestion that the meeting continue on a two-party basis, discussing procedural arrangements and agenda items until Saigon's representatives appeared, the North Vietnamese replied that was out of the question. The NLF was present and ready, and besides, the American formula was "our side—your side." What difference did it make that the GVN had failed to show up?[13]

The North Vietnamese reminded the Americans that each side would arrange its delegations as it pleased. Here was another embarrassment. If the conference went ahead as a three-party affair, that would only emphasize the Communist argument that the GVN was a puppet government— precisely the reverse of American denigrations of the NLF's status. A paradox more tangled, and certainly more deadly, than any in Gilbert and Sullivan had arisen to bewilder American policymakers. Assistant Secretary of State William Bundy instructed the Paris delegation to keep stalling, at the same time ordering Ambassador Bunker to warn the Saigon government that the American public would not tolerate a delay to satisfy every one of its reservations. Bundy wanted comments from both Paris and Saigon about a proposal to make the GVN the "chairman" of our side. Would it help, he asked, or would this only invite Hanoi to make the NLF chairman on its side? He had answered his own question.[14]

Furious with all this back and forth over what had been considered a done deal, President Johnson instructed his national security adviser to draft a back-channel message to Bunker for transmission to Thieu and Ky. They should know, it read, that the president's confidence in them was deeply shaken, "very deeply shaken." He was in no mood to make any more reassurances. "If a viable relation is to be re-established, it is their task—and they should set about it promptly—very promptly."[15]

Johnson tried to bring pressure on Saigon by invoking President-elect Nixon's aid to get Thieu to Paris. No one contemplated imposing a coalition government on South Vietnam, the intermediary, Senator Everett

Dirksen, told Ambassador Bui Diem, but President Thieu must be aware of the negative public reaction building against him that could "create difficulties" for the new administration. Dirksen had literally appeared, unannounced, on Diem's doorstep on November 9, four days after the election. The ambassador had been working alone on a Saturday morning in the chancery when the doorbell rang. To his amazement it was the Republican Senate leader, alone and huddled against the wind. "I am here," Dirksen intoned in his low, husky voice, "on behalf of two presidents, President Johnson and President-elect Nixon." The message was simple. "South Vietnam has got to send a delegation to Paris before it is too late." Dirksen had no sooner left than Joe Alsop appeared, also unannounced. "You know, my friend," he began, "your president, Mr. Thieu, is playing a deadly game. I saw the old man yesterday, and he is really furious." It took Diem a moment to realize Alsop was talking about Lyndon Johnson. These "messengers" brought bad news. Dirksen and Alsop were trusted friends, and critics of any dovish tendencies in the administration's Vietnam policy. It began to dawn on Bui Diem that Richard Nixon had no "secret plan" to end the war, and that while he would perhaps not be susceptible to criticism from the left, "the Republicans' long-range eyesight was just as good as the Democrats'." [16]

Nixon met with Johnson and his advisers on November 11 and promised, somewhat opaquely, that he would do nothing to undermine the president. "I don't want anybody messing it up." They would present a united front, he assured Johnson—against both Vietnams. Defense Secretary Clark Clifford watched the president-elect's performance at this session, noting the contrasts as they talked on: LBJ expansive as always, filling the room with a stream of Texas stories and rhetoric; Nixon just the opposite, drawn into himself, almost painfully self-controlled, every word weighed twice before it was spoken aloud. "You can be very helpful in the next 65 days *[especially with Saigon]*," Clifford interjected. "I know you want to wind this up as soon *[as much]* as we *[do]*." "The quicker the better," Nixon rejoined. [17]

Clifford's attempt to nail down the president-elect, and his press conference the next day, focused attention on the crucial issue that had been shoved into the background in all the uproar over Saigon's refusal to send a delegation to Paris. There was no agenda for the expanded conference. That was the way Dean Rusk and Walt Rostow wanted things, because they had imagined or had talked themselves into seeing the conference as a face-saving cover for a Communist surrender under an arrangement whereby the NLF would be allowed to reenter Vietnamese politics.

When Saigon's information minister, Ton That Thien, stated publicly that Washington had halted the bombing and agreed to the Paris talks without his government's approval, LBJ was enraged and asked Clifford to rebut the charge. It was a golden opportunity for the secretary of defense to take the initiative once again, as he had done at the outset of his tenure when he recast the San Antonio formula. "I was the only one who could do it," Clifford asserted. He felt immensely sorry, he would write, as he watched Lyndon Johnson's thirty-two-year political career coming to an end in such disarray. "Gradually, though, as he [Johnson] began to perceive Saigon's intransigence and Nixon's treachery more clearly, his impatience with Rusk and Rostow became manifest."[18]

Whether or not Johnson was growing impatient with the remaining hawks, the truest picture of the administration's final days was indeed one of disarray. On that point Clifford was dead right. At his news conference on November 12, the secretary of defense reviewed the history of the talks from their opening in May. Far from being kept in the dark, he declared, Saigon had been informed about each point at every step of the way. It had been known that the NLF would "accompany" the Hanoi delegation from the outset, and that the "Saigon Government would accompany the United States." Clifford may not have chosen these particular phrases for their symbolic meaning. He was a political "counsel," not a diplomat. But even if he had said only what came to mind, he had effectively equated the NLF and the "Saigon Government," thereby negating all the efforts to insist that the "our side—your side" formula offered the Liberation Front no new status.

Clifford went on to reveal that President Thieu's only objection, originally, concerned the timing of the first session of the wider conference. He couldn't get a delegation there in three days. "That was the only reason he gave." Then came the other reasons, piled on top of this one in a stack of excuses. With his next three paragraphs Clifford set off a series of bombshells:

> I think the President owed it, under his constitutional duty, I think he owed it to the American people to proceed with the talks.
>
> Now, I say that I believe we should make every reasonable effort to demonstrate to Saigon why it should come in and join the talks. At the same time, if they choose not to, I believe the President has the constitutional responsibility of proceeding with the talks.
>
> There are a great many subjects that can be covered between the United States and Hanoi of a military nature and that's our real function. We have been there as a military shield for South Vietnam. I have not anticipated that we would get into the political settlement of South Vietnam. That is up to South Vietnam and Hanoi.[19]

What constitutional obligation did Lyndon Johnson have to enter into peace talks—except his general obligations to conduct the affairs of office? Clifford made it sound like it was somewhere written that LBJ must go to Paris. But the real piece of clever wizardry came in the discussion of Amer-

ica's "real function" in the war. President Thieu had been insisting that
Hanoi talk with Saigon—but about military questions, not the "political
settlement of South Vietnam." Clifford's attempt here was to set an agenda
for the Paris talks that would allow the United States to extricate itself militarily, leaving the South Vietnamese government to fend for itself. The
State Department had to continue to get along with Saigon, Clifford jotted
down about the press conference, but "my motive was the ending of the
war...."[20]

Johnson knew what was going on. "Take the principal things," he
ordered Walt Rostow, "particularly where he quotes me—and analyze
them." Clifford had said the U.S. might go ahead without the GVN, and
Johnson wanted Rostow to note that he had not authorized such a statement. He did not, however, publicly criticize anything Clifford had said,
and so the defense secretary's comments stood as the only American public
statement on a proposed agenda. At a press conference in Saigon, the minister of information denied that President Thieu had ever gone back on his
word. Asked what would happen if the United States negotiated a withdrawal and left, the minister replied with a neat thrust that of course the
United States was an independent country and could do as it pleased.
"Some say we can't win the war without the US, but it is also true that the
US cannot win the war without us." The same thing applied to a negotiated peace—that is, neither Washington nor Saigon could make peace alone.
Predictably, the South Vietnamese also responded to Clifford's ploy with a
suggestion they were willing to meet in secret with an NLF representative
someplace outside the formal conference. Thus on one level the drama was
playing out as Rusk hoped it would. His recent instructions had ordered the
American delegates to stand firm with the GVN in refusing to discuss the
internal politics of South Vietnam, and Harriman had responded that in
that case there would be nothing to negotiate. He was right, admitted Walt
Rostow. "The central issue—and test of will—should come ... over how
and when Saigon talks to the NLF." And that would depend, he argued, on
how steady the American side was in Paris and the pace of pacification on
the ground.[21]

Meanwhile, a slight change was ordered in the instructions to the
American delegates. When the other side brought up the question of South
Vietnam's internal structure, the answer should be that this was better discussed between the South Vietnamese parties themselves in separate, private talks. This was and wasn't a significant alteration. It was if one thought
it fit Clifford's notion that the U.S. would pull out without a final agreement being reached on military action in the south; it wasn't if one interpreted the instructions to mean that after an agreement had been reached
on an NLF decision to lay down its arms, bilateral political talks could take
place. Avoided, of course, was any notion of how a cease-fire could be nego-

tiated without political conditions. The South Vietnamese minister of information seemed to understand this crucial point perhaps better than either Clifford or the State Department.[22]

The disarray in the American government revealed itself again when Averell Harriman tried to define a mutual step-by-step withdrawal policy. He called such a proposal "our strongest card," but Rostow's assistant, air force Colonel Robert Ginsburgh, immediately saw what was afoot. Harriman had pointed out that there was complete disagreement between the Americans and the South Vietnamese about what the 1966 Manila Communiqué meant. At that time Johnson had declared American troops would be withdrawn by six months after the end of fighting. It had been a deliberately ambiguous statement, designed to satisfy Russian Foreign Minister Andrei Gromyko's argument in a private conversation with the president that what was needed for negotiations to take place was a promise to set a firm evacuation timetable. Nowhere did the Manila Communiqué define exactly what was meant by linking the withdrawals to a subsidence of the level of violence. Now Harriman wanted to put forward such a definition. "We are not now in agreement with the GVN on what the Manila Communiqué means," he cabled.

> The GVN position is that all people, either of Northern or Southern region, who are fighting with the Communists must either withdraw to the North or else rally under the Chieu Hoi [amnesty] program. The US position is that NVA and any other personnel infiltrated since 1964 must be withdrawn.[23]

Ginsburgh picked up at once on what Harriman was attempting to do. It was of a piece with Clark Clifford's maneuvers. "I believe we must get off this kick immediately," the colonel wrote Rostow. "Paris must be made to understand that we seek an honest-to-God settlement, not simply a step-by-step de-escalation leading to (1) a bugout or (2) a reduction of the commitment of U.S. resources to a war to be continued for a longer period of time at a lower level of intensity. . . . Before we start fighting with the GVN on this issue, we need to get agreement within the U.S. government."[24]

Here the situation stood near the end of November 1968, and here, in essence, were exactly the choices as Richard Nixon would put them to the American people: a bugout, or a reduction of the commitment—which he would label Vietnamization. As for the South Vietnamese, they understood only too well that once they went to Paris, the military and political talks could not be disentangled. Little wonder, then, that Bui Diem's efforts to explain the American political system to President Thieu, and why Saigon was wrong to expect that a new president could find support for a "winning strategy," proved unavailing.

Nixon's biographer, Stephen Ambrose, speculates on the might-have-been had Johnson simply taken Thieu's unwillingness to go to Paris as a reason to carry through with an offer along the lines Averell Harriman had contemplated, redefining the Manila Communiqué and testing Hanoi's savvy about a real decision to withdraw American forces promptly in exchange for a similar demonstration of North Vietnamese restraint to allow at least a "decent interval." "Of course it borders on madness to even suggest that either Johnson or Nixon could have done such a thing." Each man had sworn not to be the first president to lose a war.[25]

Ironically, Nixon's willingness to join Lyndon Johnson in pressing Thieu to go to Paris drew him into the framework of his predecessor's policy, and imposed limits of a sort on his possible alternatives. Ngo Dinh Diem's death in 1963 had put Johnson under obligation to Kennedy's policy, even though JFK might have made a decision later to change that policy; in a different manner, LBJ's determination to force Thieu to his will may have had the effect of lengthening the war, even though Johnson had no clear idea of the peace talks agenda. The safest place for the Vietnamese government, at least temporarily, was Paris, as a negotiating partner.

It took some time for Saigon to come to this conclusion. Clifford urged Johnson to begin withdrawing American forces ostensibly to give Thieu a shove: "It would be a great day to pull out 5000." Rusk agreed that Thieu needed a shove, but to prevent a further erosion of support in the United States. Congress will murder us with Thieu acting like he's acting now, the secretary admitted. Two weeks later Clifford renewed his appeal. The South Vietnamese still had not agreed to go to Paris. They're stalling, the secretary of defense complained, all we can see ahead is "delay and delay and delay." Rusk had a better answer this time. The North Vietnamese had withdrawn troops from the DMZ, but there were still some around the area. Hanoi's claims that the activities in the DMZ were Liberation Front movements was no excuse. "I would work toward clearing out the DMZ," he said. As for Clifford's and Harriman's approach of a mutual withdrawal of five thousand men, "that is the wrong way to get peace in South Vietnam."

We must be careful about a token withdrawal of forces. We agreed to pour it on in South Vietnam after the bombing was halted.

Johnson's head was spinning. He had stood just about all the delay from South Vietnam he could, he said. Then he immediately added, "I think we are justified in *resuming the bombing.*"

I would like to leave office de-escalating—not escalating—but I do not want to make a phony gesture. I do not want to run. We have listened to dovish advisers. We have tested them. We don't want a sellout.

At the end of November, Rusk felt the moment had come to push for a new military effort in the DMZ—the way Johnson was swinging back and forth, he might all of a sudden tell Clifford to take out five thousand or maybe ten thousand. We should go all out unless we get some quick answers from North Vietnam, urged Rusk, we should go all out in the DMZ. Rostow agreed. They won't talk sense unless we do, he said. Rusk pressed hard. "Today is Tuesday. Tomorrow we should look at this. Let's meet at 5:00 tomorrow. Do it at 1:30 p.m. Lunch tomorrow."[26]

Everyone knew that the talk about the DMZ was really a series of ploys. Hanoi wanted to force the pace of the conference by asserting the NLF was not bound by any agreements previously reached until the meetings began; Washington raised the DMZ question to divert attention from its inability to get Saigon to fall in line with American diplomacy. And every time the president and his advisers met they reviewed with satisfaction the stepped-up air war over Laos, where the bombing of the Ho Chi Minh trail had been increased threefold.[27]

Clifford tried at these meetings to stress the vagueness of the status of the DMZ in relation to the peace talks. Abuses in the DMZ, he said, were not to be tolerated—after the talks started. "Talks haven't started. They have not violated any agreement. It has been thirty-five days." Rusk protested vigorously that specific commitments had been made at the time of the bombing halt. "We asked do they understand three facts of life— DMZ, cities, GVN. If the enemy gets away with the DMZ, what else do we let them get away with?"[28]

The initial request for sending patrols into the DMZ had come from the American delegates in Paris. They had wanted to capture one or two North Vietnamese regulars to disprove Hanoi's argument that only NLF operated in the area. This gave Rusk his opportunity to press the case for cleaning out the DMZ, an argument seconded by JCS chairman General Wheeler. Wheeler suggested sending a battalion to "drive the enemy forces back north. . . ." Back from Paris for a short visit, Harriman tried to cut off the momentum building for a general offensive. Aerial reconnaissance had done the job, he now contended, and the delegation had withdrawn the request. Perhaps that was so, Wheeler said, but there was the danger of an enemy buildup—the old argument against a bombing halt. "If this goes on for three weeks to a month," he concluded in ominous tones, "I don't know what will happen." Rusk rushed through the opening with an "impassioned statement that he wanted it as a matter of record that he was in support of any measures to protect American lives."[29]

"Far-fetched," Harriman grumbled under his breath. "A farce." Only the day before in a private discussion, Harriman recorded in a private memorandum, Dean Rusk had lectured him about how it was still necessary to ask Americans to die in an all-out effort to preserve South Vietnam from communism. Harriman did not directly challenge Rusk by saying that the best way to preserve lives was to begin bringing the troops home, but he did reintroduce Clifford's proposal for negotiating mutual troop withdrawals. Johnson was indecisive, refusing to allow a battalion-size incursion but authorizing Wheeler to send company-size "posses" into the DMZ. As for the idea of negotiated troop withdrawals, at first he reacted sharply. "I don't want any more talk in the press about withdrawal of American troops." In private, away from Rusk and Wheeler, Harriman insisted to Johnson that he had reason to believe North Vietnam wanted to go on talking on a bilateral basis about current issues—and postwar relations. These talks could be kept completely secret, he said. "Go ahead," the president responded at last. "Talk to them about anything you want."[30]

During this visit to Washington, Harriman had found the president in a "philosophic" mood, while Clark Clifford was deeply worried about the possibility that Rusk and Rostow would align themselves with the Joint Chiefs to persuade Johnson to resume bombing North Vietnam. After the DMZ discussion, the defense secretary pulled Harriman aside. Warn the North Vietnamese about the risks of intransigence, he told him, about the "strong element" in Washington pushing resumption. They should be made aware of the need to make "real progress as rapidly as possible in mutual steps to deescalate the war. . . ."[31]

Harriman had long since come to the conclusion that Dean Rusk was an obsessed man, that almost alone he stood between Lyndon Johnson and serious peace negotiations.

> The only thing I can gather about Rusk is that he wants to end his career as the strong Cold War warrior, with all the guns firing, with Nixon giving in and being the appeaser. Of course I believe in loyalty to President Johnson that we should start the negotiations for mutual reduction of violence, for reduction in American casualties and begin movement of troops home. His historic position will then be justified as the man who was primarily responsible for bringing this unhappy conflict to a close.[32]

Harriman's notations raise important, if ultimately unanswerable, questions about the transition from Johnson to Nixon, the continuation of the war under the guise of "Vietnamization," and might-have-beens. Leaving aside Harriman's bitterness about Dean Rusk's role, and his overdrawn belief that the secretary of state alone stood in the way of peace, what would have been the consequences of a Johnson decision to begin a troop withdrawal? If Harriman was right that he had had indications of Hanoi's interest in such a planned phasedown, it is certainly possible that the United States could have obtained better terms than it did when President Nixon began unilaterally withdrawing American forces. The realities of the "final" settlement were clouded, and remain so, by Nixon's attacks on the antiwar movement and claims that his "Vietnamization" scheme salvaged the best that could be salvaged of the war as the result of bold strikes against the enemy that the Democrats had feared to risk.

Nevertheless, the transition period from Johnson to Nixon continues to raise questions about missed opportunities. If Saigon hoped for a new, more vigorous military policy from a Nixon administration, so too, obviously, did Hanoi have to concern itself with such a possibility. Harriman and Vance may have read too much into North Vietnamese "hints" about a phased mutual withdrawal, but they were certainly aware that Hanoi had no intention of abandoning the NLF or their determination to reunify the country by military or political means. Johnson's negotiators understood that their very presence in Paris—whatever Dean Rusk believed or feared—presupposed either a willingness to talk about South Vietnamese's future in terms of a political settlement that would include the NLF, or a desire to find some sort of escape hatch to get the Americans out in an orderly fashion. Nevertheless, had negotiations begun during this transition, before formal positions were entrenched and before new reputations were at stake, momentum and contingency might have combined to produce a different mix of political and military means, and possibly an earlier and less bloody end to the war. A *New York Times* editorial noted that Averell Harriman had given an interview on New Year's Day 1969 in which he had expressed the hope that substantial American and North Vietnamese troop withdrawals could begin "early in the year." Harriman had suggested that "the Vietnamese . . . get together and work out a solution in their own way" to the political problems of South Vietnam. The *Times* applauded this effort to put pressure on Saigon "to come to grips with the political realities of South Vietnam. . . ."[33]

Thieu needed no prompting to understand where the Americans were going. He knew, he told Ambassador Bunker, that American public opinion would demand a troop withdrawal in 1969. What he did not know was how America would handle this "Vietnamization" policy. How many troops, he wondered, would be withdrawn over the next year? As many as 100,000? He could not accept an imposed coalition, but there was room to think about NLF participation in a special general election or in local elections on a one-man, one-vote basis. The GVN, he said, was approaching the position when "The system could absorb some bacteria."[34]

For all his talk about the substance of what was to be decided at the peace conference, President Thieu still had not agreed to participate. A GVN delegation had arrived in the French capital, but there had yet to be a formal opening session. Saigon was now arguing about the shape of the table, and whether or not identifying flags on the table suggested an independent status for the NLF. Patience exhausted, Johnson sent Thieu a blunt letter about the "dangerous implications" of his position. It began with a dismissive comment on the table controversy, pointing out Hanoi's willingness to forgo identifying flags or nameplates. Then it moved past symbols to the central issue:

> At the present moment, the situation in Congress and in the American public is as dangerous and volatile as I have seen it at any time in the last four years, or indeed in my 40 years of public service.[35]

He had no regrets, the president ended, about the course they had followed thus far, and he hoped he had supported South Vietnam's cause, "so that we may emerge with an honorable settlement that preserves your country's right to determine its future without external interference. You and I have a long history of close and constructive collaboration." If that collaboration was to continue, however, Thieu must now do the "right thing" and put aside further complaints about such petty things as the shape of the table and the ornaments in front of the negotiators. "Please do not force the United States to reconsider its basic position on Vietnam."[36]

As usual, Ambassador Bunker tried to cushion Washington's criticism, but this time he had been instructed to give Thieu the letter, not deliver an oral message. Thieu had to understand, Bunker explained, that the issue was not one leader showing empathy for the other's problems with public opinion. Both of us, he said, have the same urgent problem—"to avoid a situation where American opinion will make it impossible to continue our commitment here." Saigon must not think it would be any less urgent when Richard Nixon moved into the White House. Interestingly, Dean Rusk had sent an oral message of his own for Thieu, which Bunker then read to the Vietnamese leader. "I hope the Vietnamese Government is not taking undue comfort from the fact that the time being saved in Paris may be well used on the battlefield, because the damage to their cause by adverse reactions here could become irreparable."[37]

Rusk, of course, had to walk a tightrope. He wanted to use the time on the battlefield, but with a new Congress about to assemble, what Johnson called in his letter to Thieu an "avalanche of criticism" could bury them all. The South Vietnamese president responded to all this with a comment that Bunker understood he was no "super-hawk." He had known for a long time, at least two years, that the war would not end in a clear military victory, he said, and that his government would have to be prepared for a "decisive" political competition with the Communists. They just needed time to prepare for the contest on the principle of one-man, one-vote. "This showed how far we had come in those two years," he said. "The Vietnamese people now understand that there will be peace without victory, that they must expect a difficult contest with the Communists, *and that the US also wants and expects this.*"[38]

Thieu then explained why he thought the table shape and nameplates mattered. If South Vietnam was to prepare itself for the political war-after-the-war, such matters were not trivial but significant for face and prestige. Holding out against the enemy's propaganda claims directly affected troop morale, and the strength of government depended in part upon the morale of the people and the troops. The shape of the table came into play because it signified the position of the NLF. To give in on this first issue suggested a willingness to give in on others, including the question of a coalition government. Perhaps Thieu remembered John Kennedy's comments on the outcome of the Cuban missile crisis. It did not matter whether Russian missiles in Cuba altered the actual balance of military power, Kennedy had explained to television commentators afterward; they "would have politically changed the balance of power . . . would have appeared to, and appearances contribute to reality."[39]

It would seem, indeed, that the problem of appearances imperiled small countries much more than they would a superpower. But Bunker interrupted Thieu's recitation to point out that so far all the concessions had come from the other side, from the question of where the talks should take place to "virtual conditions" for ending the bombing, to a willingness to give in on nameplates and flags. Thieu finally said it came down to the problem of how to reconcile the need to satisfy American public opinion with the requirements of Vietnamese morale. He would try to come up with a solution.[40]

In his formal reply to Johnson, Thieu asserted his willingness to "alleviate gradually the burdens nobly assumed by the United States" on the battlefield. But then he cited Rusk's recent statement at a press conference to justify his position. "Procedural matters," the secretary of state had said, "do conceal important questions of substance." In Paris, meanwhile, Harriman and Vance were rejoicing over Johnson's letter to the Vietnamese leader. It reflected, Vance felt, the president's new philosophical attitude— "much less interested in military action, and more interested in peaceful progress."[41]

With this interpretation of the president's mind providing additional stimulus, the two Americans met with their North Vietnamese counterparts, Xuan Thuy and Le Duc Tho, on January 14, 1969, for what turned out to be a *tour d'horizon* of where matters stood at the end of the Johnson administration. All four agreed that what was said would remain entirely private. Harriman began by talking about the Nixon "team" to be headed by Henry Cabot Lodge, suggesting there would be continuity between the Democrats and the Republicans. It was clear, however, that in this penultimate discussion with the "other side," the old diplomat hoped to set in motion a process that would prompt both sides to move toward a peace settlement. He wanted their ideas, Harriman told the Vietnamese, on postwar relations between the United States and the Democratic Republic of Vietnam, indicating that he was in a position to discuss these with President Nixon. The new president, he felt confident, was committed to finding not only peace in Vietnam but a general settlement for Southeast Asia.[42]

Trying to divide the issues, Harriman argued that the United States and North Vietnam should talk about mutual deescalation, with the hope that the Vietnamese would settle amongst themselves the political issues connected with South Vietnam's future. Le Duc Tho began his response by questioning Harriman's premise. He was not so sanguine about the new American "team," citing comments in the press about Nixon and Lodge, and about Thieu's choice to head the GVN delegation, Vice-President Ky. Reports in the press suggested a "special relationship" between Nixon and Ky. "This situation makes the DRV wonder."

Then there was the impression, which American military action since the bombing halt had certainly done nothing to dispel, that Washington's aim was still to try to settle from a "position of strength." If the U.S. wished to "drag on the discussions, and wants to oblige the DRV to accept its position on the basis of strength," Le Duc Tho warned, "then the talks will be prolonged and there will be no results." He continued in this vein for some time, ruminating about Nixon's choices, then shifted somewhat obliquely to Harriman's effort to divide the tasks of the peace conference into military and political questions. In reality, he said, the belligerents in South Vietnam were all four parties, and all four together must resolve both the military and political issues. "We must sit together." He then introduced what would become the most difficult issue of all: the present regime in Saigon had given no indication that it desired peace. The DRV had indicated such a desire, and the U.S. also apparently wanted peace. But how could a settlement be reached with such warlike leaders as Thieu and Ky? "It is very difficult."

They had done all they could, he went on, to prevent the talks from getting started, and what would happen even if they did begin? It was likely, he implied, that the GVN delegates would try to sabotage the negotiations at every stage. Progress in resolving these doubts, he concluded, would have to await what Nixon and Lodge actually did. About future relations, Tho was especially reticent, saying only that the example of good Franco-Vietnamese postwar relations indicated what could develop.

Harriman tried to argue that newspaper speculations about Nixon's or Lodge's relationship to Ky should be "disregarded." He then cut to the heart of Tho's presentation. He had heard him mention the NLF program for South Vietnam, Harriman said, and how it contemplated a neutral, independent, and prosperous South Vietnam. How did Le Duc Tho envision future relations between the north and south? South Vietnam must move toward a coalition government, came the reply, "through elections." Pending reunification, there would be two different regimes. "Every political force which is sensible and reasonable and which approves of the points of the NLF program can join the coalition government."

Le Duc Tho made things even less clear with a statement that for the "immediate future" the war cabinet in Saigon would have to give way to a "peace cabinet." Presumably this would include members of the NLF. In any event, Tho said, South Vietnam would eventually have, through elections, "a coalition Government, and that Government will include all tendencies provided their members want South Vietnam to be independent and peaceful." Harriman quickly realized that he had reached too far and was now hearing things he really did not care to hear. "We said we did not want to comment on how South Vietnam would solve its problems," he reported to Washington. "We do not want to impose a coalition Government and we hope that the Vietnamese will get together and find a solution. Tho's assumption that the present Government of South Vietnam does not want peace was one which we could not accept. We did not want Tho to feel that we accepted everything he said."

The key to translating Harriman's demurrer is in the first sentence, *"We do not want to impose a coalition Government . . ."* Thieu had grasped the point, as he told Bunker, "The Vietnamese people now understand that there will be peace without victory, that they must expect a difficult contest with the Communists, *and that the US also wants and expects this.*" The dialogue between Harriman and Le Duc Tho ended, however, with the latter's insistence that the DRV never "imposed" anything, "but the reality of the situation will require a coalition government." What he was arguing, in other words, was that a coalition government was the only government that would have the will to make peace.

Harriman was not unduly discouraged by the seeming impasse over a coalition government. He recalled in an interview that on several occasions the North Vietnamese had been more forthcoming about their desire to be independent of both Moscow and Beijing, and their interest in American technology. In his talks with President Nixon and his chief policymakers, he tried to convey this leverage. He envisioned an interim period of two separate states of possibly up to fifteen years, more than enough for a "decent interval" between the withdrawal of American forces and the unification of Vietnam. Such a time period would also diminish Hanoi's domination of the whole situation. The sticking point always, however, was Harriman's insistence that this could best come about by a military stand-down by American and North Vietnamese forces, which would, he hoped, propel the NLF and Saigon into serious talks. Le Duc Tho made it plain, on the other hand, that the United States could not extricate itself that easily and hope that peace talks in South Vietnam would follow. Without American participation in the political questions, the validity of any agreements would be suspect.[43]

Harriman also held a last conversation with the Soviet ambassador in Paris, Valerian Zorin. The gist of his remarks combined gratitude for what the Russians had done to facilitate the peace negotiations with expectations that they could provide further "encouragement" to Hanoi at the right moment in the future. The old Russian hand encouraged Zorin to believe that President Nixon would be anxious to end "military activities as quickly as possible" if a peace with honor could be concluded. "Of course," he went on, " 'honor' was a flexible word, and included both saving of face *and* substance." He then rambled on about what the *Soviets* could get out of the situation in terms of a settlement of all Southeast Asia, and economic programs for regional development. He concluded by saying that Nixon had told him, Harriman, specifically, that he wanted the USSR to continue to play a role in the affair.[44]

Like the two Hanoi representatives, Zorin pressed the point that the Americans could not bypass the political situation in South Vietnam. He thanked Harriman for the kind words about Moscow's previous help in getting talks under way, but he did not think that his American friends quite understood the situation. The National Liberation Front was a "real thing," and if the U.S. underestimated its importance, the USSR would be in no position to help in the next stage of the peace conference. Harriman's response was a study in the uses of ambiguity. "We did not recognize the FLN," he said, "and considered them as Hanoi's agents, but the fact that their representatives were here in Paris showed our interest in them and in their role." He went on to argue for a mutual deescalation of the fighting, suggesting that if the United States and Russia were to clamp down on their respective clients, the Vietnamese would have little choice but to negotiate the political settlement themselves. Zorin repeated that the United States could not disengage prematurely and expect the peace to work. To which Harriman hinted as broadly as he could what the Russians could tell Hanoi about American attitudes:

> *The Governor* [Harriman] said this was something like the table situation, where one said one thing publicly and another privately. He had already admitted we sometimes underestimated the FLN; the truth was somewhere between our underestimation and Soviet overestimation. They were southerners; they would have a great influence on the settlement; he agreed they must be dealt with—which is why last spring we said we had no objection to their coming to Paris.[45]

The next day Harriman gave a final interview to the press as head of the American delegation, at Orly Airport near Paris. What he said was sure to infuriate the anonymous "hard-liners" he implied were responsible for the current impasse in getting the expanding talks started. "In a limited war there is no such thing as victory . . . and I think it is very well for people to stop talking about winning a war, but are we achieving our objectives, that is the question." The way out of Vietnam, he repeated, was to separate the military and political questions. "I say the military settlement should come first." The *Washington Post* writer observed, "This was a diplomatically oblique way of expressing strong disagreement with the hardline American and South Vietnam strategists, many of whom would be just as happy to see a 'no exit' sign posted over the new talks."[46]

Upon his return to Washington, Harriman had talks with Secretary of State William Rogers, Under Secretary Eliot Richardson, and National Security Adviser Henry Kissinger. They were all cordial, especially Kissinger, who expressed a keen desire to keep "in touch." But when he came away form his "blunt" talk with Richardson about the realities and the personalities involved, Harriman was less than satisfied. "The advantage of a new administration," he said, "is to get out of dead ends and personal commitments." America's objective, he continued in the vein of his press conference, was not the survival of any particular government in Saigon but South Vietnam's ability to decide its own future without outside interference. Hence his hope to produce political talks by depriving the contenders of their military backers. Richardson took it all right, Harriman wrote of the interview, but didn't commit himself. "He didn't seem to fully grasp what I was trying to get across."[47]

In his Orly press conference, Harriman had said that serious peace talks could begin at once if there was a will to do so. Combined pressure by Johnson and Nixon did produce a breakthrough with South Vietnam. The shape of the table, arranged at Saigon's demand by a concession from the other side, now delineated two sides. By this point, however, symbols could be read to mean the opposite of intentions. The negotiations had taken on the attributes of the croquet game in *Alice in Wonderland*, where mallets suddenly bent into long-necked birds, and balls unrolled into hedgehogs. If the table shape reduced the NLF role to that of a subordinate, how did it affect Saigon except in the same fashion? Moreover, as Le Duc Tho and Valerian Zorin had predicted, the United States found itself continually distracted by such "local" questions.

Walt Rostow still held out to Johnson the idea that, in the end, American military force would prevail, and the world come to know that the war had not been a lost cause. "You will enjoy this copy of General Abrams' order to his subordinate commanders," the national security adviser wrote late in the afternoon on January 17. Abrams's order read:

> 1. The Paris peace talks are scheduled for resumption at 1730 hours, Saigon time, 18 January 1969.
>
> 2. There have been constant indications from the enemy that he plans to stage attacks at such times as he can best influence the Paris talks.

3. Request that each addressee take such action as is necessary to pre-empt the enemy and destroy him completely.[48]

Appearing at the National Press Club for his own final press conference, President Johnson told reporters what he intended to do when he left office. "I am going down to the ranch Monday afternoon, and I am going to sit on that front porch in a rocking chair for about 10 minutes. And then I am going to read a little and write a little. Then I am going to put on my hat and go out and find Walter Lippmann."[49]

What things went through Lyndon Johnson's mind down on the front porch of the ranch? Did he think about that day when George Brown argued with him in the kitchen at Christmastime 1963, telling him to get out of Vietnam? John Kennedy's assassination had burdened Johnson with obligations. None was more fateful, when all's said and done, than the onus of Ngo Dinh Diem's death, a terrible burden made all the worse by LBJ's knowledge that Americans had abetted the coup that brought about his downfall.

Johnson tried to overcome that burden by picturing himself as the trustee of the legacy of the three presidents before him. At times, indeed, he felt himself simply the prisoner of the Kennedy legend, already grown to daunting size. Believing he was denied access to the establishment, Johnson had kept on all of JFK's key advisers. To those who argued he should select his own team, he had explained his need to have them by his side if he were to achieve acceptance for the Great Society program. He probably over-estimated their importance to his success with Congress.

At first he intended that the Big Three, Mac Bundy, Bob McNamara, and Dean Rusk, keep him free from criticism on foreign policy while plans for the Great Society went forward—the culmination of LBJ's career-long efforts to build a coalition of Southern and Western interests to reimagine the New Deal. As Vietnam began to intrude upon his presidency, these advisers were to provide him with the same counsel that had guided John Kennedy through the Cuban missile crisis. Bundy, especially, argued for a "crisis management" approach to Vietnam. "It seems to me at least possible that a couple of brigade-size units put in to do specific jobs about six weeks from now might be good medicine everywhere," he had written the president in midsummer 1964 in an expression of confidence that Vietnam could be kept under control.[50]

Kennedy's spirit thus expressed itself over and over again through the counsel of McGeorge Bundy and Robert McNamara, both of whom carried forward the lost leader's passionate faith in the myths of America's special mission to the world, repeated in ringing phrases in his inaugural speech. "Let every nation know," he had said, "whether it wishes us well or ill, that we shall pay any price, bear any burden, meet any hardship, support any friend, oppose any foe, in order to assure the success of liberty." McNamara began to have doubts first. In many ways he lived a double life from mid-1965 until late 1967. McNamara's private tragedy may have been his feeling that he must stay on to protect Johnson and the country from the forces set in motion by such rhetoric. Toward the end of his ordeal, McNamara took up the notion of an electronic barrier to slow infiltration from the north, primarily, it would seem, to provide a barrier against demands that the bombing be carried even to the obliteration of Hanoi and other cities.[51]

Dean Rusk's private feelings about Vietnam may have been as troubled as those experienced by McNamara. But they rarely showed in public as anything more than a slight blush on the back of his neck, as when he testified in front of Senator Fulbright's committee in 1966. "I do believe there is a fundamental difference between the kind of revolution which the Communists call their wars of national liberation, and the kind of revolution which is congenial to our own experience, and fits into the aspirations of ordinary men and women right around the world."[52]

Rusk's unswerving loyalty to that conviction, and a related belief that to show weakness in Vietnam meant the ultimate collapse of the postwar world order, kept him at his post after others departed in despair. LBJ often referred to McNamara as his military fist and Rusk as his extended hand for peace. It was just the reverse, even after McNamara left. Clark Clifford, who had opposed escalation in 1965 but then opposed all subsequent bombing pauses, had a reputation in Washington as a Vietnam "hawk." This old-time Democratic counselor became the leading voice for finding a political exit from the war. Johnson may have appointed Clifford because McNamara "had gone soft" on him, but in the debates that raged all through the last year of the administration, from the Joint Chiefs' effort to send 200,000 men to Vietnam to follow up the Tet "victory," to the bombing-halt decision, his was the skeptic's demand for proof.

Rusk's chief ally was Walt Rostow. Johnson took comfort from having Rostow's unstinting conviction in ultimate victory to answer the antiwar intellectuals. Mac Bundy's successor drafted Lincolnesque memos for Johnson, as for example, after the 1966 Manila Conference when he suggested that the main obstacle to peace had become North Vietnam's inability to figure out how to surrender gracefully without putting NLF cadres in danger of reprisals. An offer to participate in South Vietnamese politics might not be worth much, he confessed, but Hanoi "could be concerned to save some face for their proteges and protect them from the reprisals that could come if they persist in violence once the game from the North is called off."[53]

Rostow was also a bridge between day-to-day advice and Johnson's longtime interest in modernization and government's role in promoting economic development. It is difficult to say how heavily Johnson's faith in

New Deal accomplishments during the Great Depression influenced his vision of Ho Chi Minh realizing that a better path for North Vietnam could be found in the offer Johnson had made at Johns Hopkins in April 1965. The Mekong River project never got off the ground, yet LBJ's fascination with the "other war" in Vietnam remained to the end. Perhaps, as with his advisers, his faith needed nothing immediately concrete, only the conviction that ultimately it would happen. "On the fifth floor of this building [the new American Embassy in Saigon]," Ambassador Henry Cabot Lodge reported at a discouraging moment in the war, "I can see the port of Saigon, thick with shipping and in the green flat fields through which the Saigon River winds, I see more ships constantly making the sixty-mile trip to and from the open sea. . . . This is American mass, which none can produce as we can."[54]

Early warnings from George Ball and the later efforts of Averell Harriman made no serious dent in such convictions. From the time of Diem's overthrow to the bombing-halt decision exactly five years later, policymakers insisted that their goal was Vietnamese self-determination, and their enemy the implacable forces of something John Foster Dulles had once called "International Communism" and Ronald Reagan would label the "Evil Empire." Yet whenever any government in Saigon showed signs of wishing to negotiate for itself, Washington moved to halt the process before it could get started. As for the enemy, the United States invoked Moscow's aid from 1965 onward as almost a partner in persuading Hanoi to abandon its efforts to seize South Vietnam. The trouble with the basic cold war formulation, as France's Charles de Gaulle pointed out often enough, was that it gave no credence to powerful cultural and nationalist impulses outside the bands of this narrow thinking.

It was still possible in 1966 for Vice-President Hubert Humphrey to reassert government pledges to "defeat aggression, to defeat social misery, to build viable, free political institutions, and to achieve peace," and to insist that the nation stood on the verge of realizing "the dream of the Great Society in the great area of Asia, not just here at home."[55] But by 1967 this same vision had darkened considerably. "As we stand at the outer frontier of disorder in Southeast Asia," declared an embattled Lyndon Johnson on November 9, 1967, "we stand also at the inner frontier of disorder in our cities."[56]

Vietnam revisionists now argue that Tet was a defeat for North Vietnam and the National Liberation Front, turned into a victory by the American media. In short, the United States psyched itself out of victory. All through the Johnson years the president's advisers scoffed at the French analogy, except for cautionary words about allowing it to shape American policy. The United States could be defeated, it was admitted, as the French had been, by allowing domestic antiwar arguments to go unanswered.

Otherwise it was impossible. Tet revisionism is an offshoot of that assertion. There can be little doubt that the initial panic, influenced heavily by the pictures sent back to the United States by the media, unduly portrayed South Vietnam as near total defeat. The Tet offensive did not achieve its major objective, a widespread uprising against the government in Saigon. But the change in American attitudes reflected more than the events in Vietnam itself; from any perspective the war had long since ceased to be simply a "limited" struggle.

Tet demonstrated that the war could not be won with 500,000 Americans in Vietnam, that the bombing campaign could not interdict supplies to the enemy, and that the costs of continuing at current levels, let alone new escalations, were prohibitive. Unless there was an argument to be made that American physical security was actually endangered—hardly a rational position given Soviet-American engagement in seeking peace—Johnson had run out of appeals for support. Over and over again the president's advisers had urged him to "level" with the American people. The trouble was, he had. He had used all the arguments they gave him. The unbridgeable credibility gap was not Johnson's attempt to deceive the nation about how well the war was going, it was between arguments for the war and a reality that did not correspond to the famous Munich analogy. The one last, great effort to make the war understandable in abstract terms became instead LBJ's "abdication" speech. After it was over, he told the cabinet what had been on his mind as he delivered the speech, a heartfelt summation of the collapse of his hopes for the Great Society.

> I did it out of my beliefs of 30 years, my beliefs and hopes for this country. . . . *Country is in damn serious danger. Danger in Vietnam—danger in Middle East. . . . Negroes are marching in cities.* . . . We have difficulties in Europe and troubles that could be very deadly here at home, right here in this Nation's Capital. . . . So I think that I did the right thing in the interest of unity, in our Nation's best interest.[57]

It is difficult to argue that Johnson would have acted differently however he came to the presidency. As he suggested in this apologia to the cabinet, Johnson had *lived* the modernization policies his advisers prescribed for Vietnam during the New Deal and Fair Deal years. When Johnson criticized war critics for harboring racial prejudices, it was part of an increasingly desperate (and increasingly ironic) search for a new rationale for conducting a war that had already eaten into the vitals of the nation's self-image—the basic foundation for any political program, let alone one as ambitious and fraught with challenge as the Great Society. Johnson's congressional "alliances," with Western and Southern Democrats grouped at the center, elaborated a series of delicate balances. He felt a personal obligation to do all he could to guarantee to blacks the civil rights every American was supposed to enjoy, and he updated New Deal programs to wage a War on Poverty. He hoped that "not losing" in Vietnam would keep the alliances intact; instead, "not winning" split off the hawks, and "Mr. Johnson's War" alienated those who would now be called doves.

On May 1, 1970, former President Lyndon Johnson left his ranch in Texas to deliver a speech in Chicago. It was a week after his successor had sent American forces into Cambodia to seek out the central headquarters of the NLF and the North Vietnamese army, where, it was supposed, strategy was coordinated for the war in South Vietnam. Protests swept college campuses, culminating in the tragic shootings at Kent State University in Ohio. Johnson's speech was an appeal for unity in the Democratic party. If the party forgot its historic mission to bring together the small businessman, the corn farmer, the taxi driver along with the Mexican-American migrant worker and the black man, it would fail the nation. "Unless we remember and balance all these interests, the Democratic Party *could become a minority party* . . . or *even worse*, several minority parties. . . . This nation is strong enough to stand a reasonable degree of contention. But when contention turns to violence; when argument hardens into hatred; when polarization destroys . . . *beware*. In this atmosphere, a political party and its people *can lose the way*." [58]

There could hardly be a better commentary on the costs of the Vietnam War. Conservatives would blame Johnson and his advisers for leaving the country with the "Vietnam syndrome," a malaise that nearly destroyed American influence in the world and undermined confidence in national institutions. Liberals tried to recreate the world of the 1960s without Lyndon Johnson. Writing in the introduction to a new edition of his *The Death of a President*, prepared for the twenty-fifth anniversary of John Kennedy's assassination, William Manchester asserts that the martyred president had personally assured him American involvement in Vietnam would come to an end by 1965, even down to "the last helicopter pilot." "After his funeral," Manchester informs readers, "Johnson countermanded these orders." [59]

That is not the way the war—or liberal difficulties with Johnson's heritage—began. Still, it is easier to think that the trajectory of a single bullet draws an indelible line across our history, and to believe we have been separated from a different, presumably better, world by that shot. There is no passage back. The history of the world we have been forced to leave behind will never be written. That sense of loss of an imagined past explains, in large part, the continuing fascination with conspiracy theories. Claims to inside knowledge about the dead president's intentions, moreover, give such theories a strange sort of authority, tempting nonbelievers as well as proponents of the various scenarios to forsake the quest for understanding the 1960s in any other way.

For liberals, especially, the celebration of presidential leadership ever since Franklin Delano Roosevelt and the New Deal has been crucial to their self-understanding, providing a supposed offsetting force against the inertia of provincialism and the power of corporate capitalism. From this perspective, Kennedy's death cut short a promising beginning in overcoming the cultural drag of the 1950s—until Lyndon Johnson took the nation down a perilous path. By expelling Johnson from the honor roll of Wilson, FDR, Truman, and Kennedy, the war also becomes a terrible aberration. Calling Vietnam a noble cause betrayed by the liberals, as Ronald Reagan did to overcome the "syndrome," hardly makes the struggle more understandable. We are still apparently willing to pay any price for Vietnam—for military theories that posit victory, for all the other illusions that sustain belief in the demanding dream.

Coda

IMMEDIATELY UPON TAKING OFFICE, Richard Nixon vowed not to get trapped in the Vietnam quagmire. "I call it the madman theory, Bob," he told aide H. R. Haldeman. "I want the North Vietnamese to believe I've reached the point where I might do anything to stop the war. We'll just slip the word to them that, 'for God's sake, you know Nixon is obsessed about Communists. We can't restrain him when he's angry—and he has his hand on the nuclear button,'—and Ho Chi Minh himself will be in Paris in two days begging for peace."[1]

One trouble with this calculation was that Nixon's other actions— opening doors to China, negotiating with the Soviets over fundamental political and military questions—belied the notion that a slathering madman with an itchy nuclear trigger finger sat in the White House. His carefully planned troop reductions, moreover, demonstrated considerable skill in defusing the peace protests. Ending the draft put the finishing touches on a successful campaign to neutralize large segments of the antiwar movement, depriving it, for example, of a broad base on college campuses.

The announcement of the so-called Nixon Doctrine, at Guam in the summer of 1969, came very close, finally, to admitting that the war had been a mistake (at least the way it had been fought), and that it would not be repeated. "Except for the threat of a major power involving nuclear weapons," he declared, the United States had a right to expect Asian nations to handle the problems of internal conflict by themselves. Since there had never been an atomic threat in Vietnam, this statement went as far as Nixon ever went in criticizing the original decision to send troops. His policy, instead, was to support regional stabilizers, for example Iran in the Middle East, and send aid but not troops to help third-world countries defeat Communist forces.

These nonmadman steps helped Nixon gain considerable freedom of action diplomatically, though the war was prolonged until the end of his first term and until 1975 for the Vietnamese. More than 15,000 of the

58,000 American deaths in the war came in those last four years. Nixon ordered the heaviest bombing raids of the war, clandestine attacks on suspected bases in Cambodia, strikes around Hanoi during the spring 1972 North Vietnamese offensive, and the so-called Christmas bombings carried out by waves of B-52s after the failure of a peace accord that fall. But neither the bombings nor the land incursions into Cambodia (1970) and Laos (1971) demonstrated that Vietnamization could succeed where half a million American troops had failed.

Nixon's chief negotiator in Paris, National Security Adviser Henry Kissinger, always insisted in bitter terms that the war had been won by 1972—a victory thrown away by Congress when it cut off funding in a spasm of anti-Nixon rage during Watergate. When his Vietnamese counterpart, Le Duc Tho, pointed out the chief weakness of the theory behind Vietnamization, Kissinger admitted in his memoirs that he was hard-pressed for an answer. "All too acutely," Kissinger wrote, "he pointed out that our strategy was to withdraw enough forces to make the war bearable for the American people while simultaneously strengthening the Saigon forces so that they could stand on their own. He then asked me the question that was also tormenting me: 'Before, there were over a million U.S. and puppet troops, and you failed. How can you succeed when you let the puppet troops do the fighting?' "[2]

Nixon imagined himself an American Disraeli—a conservative open to radical solutions to preserve the whole. But first the whole had to be restored in a viable political compact. The New Deal alliance had dominated American politics from 1932 to 1968 before finally bursting into flames at a whole series of locations that consumed its intellectual and political resources. Nixon invented and then proclaimed the "Silent Majority" as a replacement for the New Deal alliance. An inherently unstable amalgam that gave him only a little time to reformulate a more viable political combination, it could not withstand a powerful shock such as would occur if the new administration moved swiftly to liquidate the war.

The war had fallen heavily on American cities, where protest movements helped to spark angry outbursts of black outrage and white discontent, as well as on areas of small-town and rural America, where anger at the antiwar movement was exacerbated by frustration with draft calls. There was another French analogy that Nixon dare not risk: de Gaulle's rapid exit from the Algerian war. He could not repudiate the war in Vietnam without implying the bankruptcy of cold war theories about its origins; nor could he disengage without securing a "decent interval" to avoid the impression of military defeat. For the sake of his presumed constituency, the "silent majority" which had few common bonds, he must act as if he believed the war required (and honored) the sacrifices young men unable to escape the draft had endured. If he was to retain their support, he must emphasize, and empathize with, injuries (real and perceived) done to them by the liberal-dominated federal government. His would-be successor, George McGovern, and his actual successors, Jimmy Carter and Ronald Reagan, all ran anti-Washington campaigns in an effort to throw a net around the fragments of the old political alliance.

So, even though Nixon and his advisers *had* listened to Averell Harriman's descriptions of Soviet interest in a post–cold war relationship once the Vietnam War ended, and they *had* grasped what he was trying to say about the opportunities, Vietnam (memory) stood in the way of action. Indeed, Nixon's vision of what would be called détente had already taken shape before the presidential campaign. "It is a time when a man who knows the world will be able to forge a whole new set of alliances," he told an interviewer during the campaign. "We are now in a position to give the world all the good things that Britain offered in her Empire without the disadvantages of nineteenth-century colonialism."

It was simply not possible, politically, to brush aside the deep injuries the war had caused to the national conscience and consciousness by calling upon Americans to understand that it had been a dreadful mistake. One could not construct détente on a foundation of needless graves. Neither could Richard Nixon accept, personally, a defeat in Vietnam as the major event of his first term. Whatever happened in the end must appear to be a victory; like LBJ, Nixon was a captive of what Garry Wills has called the "Kennedy Imprisonment." Kennedy's enshrinement in American memory, the continuing fascination he exerted, burdened not only LBJ but Richard Nixon as well. Vietnam played a multidimensional role in that predicament. On the one hand Kennedy had faced down the Russians in the Cuban missile crisis, imposing the burden of "victory" on his successors; on the other, it was already the stuff of legend that Kennedy intended to withdraw from Vietnam, imposing on his successors the burden of a tragically unnecessary war.

For their part, the North Vietnamese had no inclination to settle quickly if it meant forsaking goals fought for for so long. They had been down that path before at Geneva in 1954, when even their backers, Russia and China, urged the compromises that produced the second Indochina war. By insisting upon a simultaneous military and political settlement, including the immediate replacement of the Thieu regime with a coalition government, the North Vietnamese posed impossible conditions for Nixon when the enlarged Paris talks finally got under way. They held to that position for nearly three years. Nixon walked on the Great Wall, meanwhile, and traveled to Moscow to sign an arms-control agreement. New statements recalled the World War II summit conferences promising an era of cooperation among the superpowers. But there was still Vietnam. None of Nixon's journeys revealed a path out of the jungles of Southeast Asia.

In October 1972 Kissinger dropped the mutual withdrawal demand, and Le Duc Tho stopped insisting that the political settlement be made coincident with the military agreement. That compromise confirmed all that South Vietnam had feared about the peace talks when they opened. The putative agreement negotiated in 1972, and eventually signed with minor modifications in early 1973, allowed North Vietnamese troops to remain in the south while something called a "council of national reconciliation," composed of representatives of the Saigon government, the NLF, and "neutrals," was set the task of supervising elections for a new government. It foreshadowed a coalition government, and it never functioned.

Thieu had objected to nearly all the terms of the proposed agreement, causing Kissinger and Le Duc Tho to break off negotiations just as they were about to sign the formal documents. Although Nixon ordered the Christmas bombings to demonstrate to the world that America had forced the North Vietnamese to accept his terms, the changes Hanoi agreed to did not alter the reality of the deal: America was leaving Vietnam. One of Kissinger's assistants, John Negroponte, argued that the bombing had indeed produced a condition where the North Vietnamese would finally accept American demands to withdraw their forces from the south. The national security adviser responded that President Nixon had set a deadline of January 20, 1973. The war must be over when his second term began. Bitter, Negroponte told friends, "We bombed the North Vietnamese into accepting our concession."[3]

American involvement in Vietnam had been sealed by a decision in 1963 to intervene—against Ngo Dinh Diem, whose government had proved incapable of waging America's war in Vietnam. A decade later, Richard Nixon warned Nguyen Van Thieu to sign a peace agreement he admitted was not "an ideal one," or face a total cutoff in American aid. "If you refuse to join us," he wrote, "the responsibility for the consequences rests with the Government of Vietnam. . . ."[4]

With that threat, Thieu caved in. "We have finally achieved peace with honor," President Nixon told the American people. American prisoners of war came home, along with the remainder of the half-million troops Lyndon Johnson had sent to Vietnam to prevent a Communist victory. Promises were made that the Americans would come back in force if the terms of the truce were violated; and assurances were offered that Washington would help in the economic recovery of North Vietnam. But thirty years after World War II, and one hundred years after the French came, the Vietnamese had reasserted control of their own history and the right to make their own mistakes.

When Saigon "fell" in 1975, Walt Rostow declared in a television interview that it was the darkest day in Western history since the Japanese invasion of Manchuria more than forty years earlier. The allusion may not have been entirely clear to most Americans, with its suggestion that the destruction of the twenty-year-old Republic of South Vietnam presaged an all-out assault on what remained of American influence in Asia on a level with the Japanese challenge leading to Pearl Harbor. By 1975 this reassertion of the original premise of the war could command only limited attention compared with other national issues. Bitter arguments continued to rage over the conduct of the war, but these were largely directed at the notion that once "committed," the war should have been fought all out, not that the "commitment" itself was a wise or unwise thing.

President George Bush promised to deliver the nation from the Vietnam syndrome at the time of the Gulf War in 1991: "When this war is over, the United States, its credibility and its reliability restored, will have a key leadership role in helping to bring peace to the rest of the Middle East." [5] The sentence could mean that Vietnam had indeed been a dreadful aberration, not simply that Lyndon Johnson had misled the nation or that his successors had left the Vietnamese to their fate. However one read Bush's affirmation of the just cause at issue in opposing Iraq's invasion of Kuwait, the stakes were higher for America than protecting access to Middle Eastern oil reserves or orderly processes in resolving international disputes. Reducing the history of the Vietnam War to the abstractions "credibility" and "reliability" made it possible to deal with that history on terms established by the outcome of the Gulf War. But the end of the cold war raised more profound questions about how to interpret the Vietnam experience and the meaning of the "syndrome," questions others besides historians must ponder.

What does this sudden uneasiness mean,
and this confusion? (How grave the faces have become!)
Why are the streets and squares rapidly emptying,
and why is everyone going back home so lost in thought?

    Because it is night and the barbarians have not come.
    And some men have arrived from the frontiers
    and they say that barbarians don't exist any longer.

And now, what will become of us without barbarians?
They were a kind of solution.
                —C. P. Cavafy, "Waiting for the Barbarians"

Notes

Acheson Papers	The Papers of Dean G. Acheson, Harry S Truman Library, Independence, Missouri
Armstrong Papers	The Papers of Hamilton Fish Armstrong, Seely Mudd Library, Princeton University, Princeton, New Jersey
Ball Papers	The Papers of George Ball, Lyndon B. Johnson Library, Austin, Texas
Bundy Papers	The Papers of McGeorge Bundy, Lyndon B. Johnson Library, Austin, Texas
Clifford Papers	The Papers of Clark Clifford, Lyndon B. Johnson Library, Austin, Texas
Fowler Papers	The Papers of Henry Fowler, Lyndon B. Johnson Library, Austin, Texas
FR	U.S. Department of State, *Foreign Relations of the United States* (Washington: GPO, v.d.)
Harriman Papers	The Papers of W. Averell Harriman, Library of Congress, Washington, D.C.
JFK/OH	Oral History at the John F. Kennedy Library, Boston, Massachusetts
Johnson Papers	The Papers of Lyndon Baines Johnson, Lyndon B. Johnson Library, Austin, Texas. (Certain files are also abbreviated in the notes as follows: NSF, National Security Files; CF, Confidential Files; DSDUF, Documents Sanitized and Declassified from Unprocessed Files.)
Krock Papers	The Papers of Arthur Krock, Seely Mudd Library, Princeton University, Princeton, New Jersey
LBJ/OH	Oral History at the Lyndon B. Johnson Library, Austin, Texas

545

Lilienthal Papers	The Papers of David E. Lilienthal, Seely Mudd Library, Princeton University, Princeton, New Jersey
McGovern Papers	The Papers of George S. McGovern, Seely Mudd Library, Princeton University, Princeton, New Jersey
Pentagon Papers: GE	The Senator Gravel Edition, *The Pentagon Papers: The Defense Department History of United States Decision-making on Vietnam* (4 vols., Boston: Beacon Press, 1971).
PP	Office of the Federal Registrar, *Public Papers of the Presidents of the United States* (Washington: GPO, v.d.)
Rowe Papers	The Papers of James Rowe, Franklin D. Roosevelt Library, Hyde Park, New York

PREFACE

1. Quoted in Lloyd C. Gardner, *A Covenant with Power: America and World Order from Wilson to Reagan* (New York: Oxford University Press, 1984), pp. 45, 123.
2. Maxwell D. Taylor, *Swords and Plowshares* (New York: W. W. Norton, 1972), p. 165.

1. DECODING LYNDON JOHNSON

1. Doris Kearns, *Lyndon Johnson and the American Dream* (New York: Harper & Row, 1976), p. 91.
2. *Ibid.*, pp. 41–42.
3. The Johns Hopkins speech is reprinted in a useful collection of documents that provide the context in U.S. Senate, Foreign Relations Committee, *Background Information Relating to Southeast Asia and Vietnam*, Committee Print, 90th cong., 1st sess. (Washington: GPO, 1967), pp. 148–153.
4. Eric Goldman, *The Tragedy of Lyndon Johnson* (New York: Alfred A. Knopf, 1969), p. 46; George Reedy, *Lyndon B. Johnson: A Memoir* (New York: Andrews and McMeel, 1982), p. 39.
5. Tyrell Webb Interview, pp. 3, 8, LBJ/OH.
6. James Rowe Interview, I, p. 14, LBJ/OH.
7. Philip Reed Rulon, *The Compassionate Samaritan: The Life of Lyndon Baines Johnson* (Chicago: Nelson-Hall, 1981), p. 61. When he was deciding what approach to take about problems of poverty in the Great Society years, Johnson naturally turned back to the NYA, modeling the Jobs Corps after that New Deal agency. George Reedy adds the important point that Johnson always valued education and educators for one thing: what it and they could accomplish for "the cotton fields and the slums." Reedy, *Lyndon B. Johnson*, pp. 22–23.
8. Robert Caro, *The Years of Lyndon Johnson: The Path to Power* (New York: Random House, 1981), pp. 392–395. Discussion of the polls, and Wirtz's conclusions therefrom, are in the interview with Ray E. Lee, a newspaper reporter who aided in the first campaign. Lee, LBJ/OH, Interview II, pp. 23–24.
9. Caro, *Path to Power*, p. 449.
10. Robert Dallek, *Lone Star Rising: Lyndon Johnson and His Times, 1908–1960* (New York: Oxford University Press, 1991), pp. 174–176.
11. Caro, *Path to Power*, p. 469.
12. George Brown, Interview III, July 11, 1977, LBJ/OH, p. 8.
13. Caro, *Path to Power*, p. 471–472.
14. For a brief summary, see Paul Conkin, *Big Daddy from the Pedernales: Lyndon Baines Johnson* (Boston: Twayne, 1986), pp. 88–90.
15. Claudia T. Johnson, *A White House Diary* (New York: Holt, Rinehart & Winston, 1970), p. 156.
16. Dallek, *Lone Star Rising*, p. 178.

17. Undated partial transcript, 1939, Johnson Papers, Handwriting File, Box 1.

18. Walter Prescott Webb, *Divided We Stand: The Crisis of a Frontierless Democracy* (New York: Farrar & Rinehart, 1937), pp. 86–87.

19. *Ibid.*, p. 220.

20. *Ibid.*, pp. 238–239.

21. Quoted by Alan Brinkley in his article "The Idea of the State," in Steve Fraser and Gary Gerstle, eds., *The Rise and Fall of the New Deal Order* (Princeton, N.J.: Princeton University Press, 1989), p. 97.

22. James Rowe, Interview, LBJ/OH, p. 9.

23. Undated partial transcript, 1939, Johnson Papers, Handwriting File, Box 1.

24. George Brown, Interview II, August 6, 1969, pp. 10–11, LBJ/OH.

25. Interview I, April 6, 1968, pp. 23–24, 7–8, LBJ/OH.

26. Chandler Davidson, *Race and Class in Texas Politics* (Princeton, N.J.: Princeton University Press, 1990), p. 68.

27. Dallek, *Lone Star Rising*, p. 228.

28. George Brown, Interview I, pp. 12–13, LBJ/OH. Friendly and unfriendly biographers alike are fascinated by Johnson's agglomeration of personal wealth. Clearly, Johnson felt uneasy about revealing very much about how he acquired his money. Ronnie Dugger finds the roots of Johnson's later problems with the "credibility gap" in his largely successful efforts to hide from public view the manipulations of these years. Dugger's conclusion is one of a Faustian bargain unmatched in the nation's history: "By about 1958 his mature employment of these forms had evolved into a compound system for producing power and wealth from politics that in its range, professionalism, caution, and cynicism was unlike anything known before in the American democracy." Ronnie Dugger, *The Politician: The Life and Times of Lyndon Johnson* (New York: W. W. Norton, 1982), pp. 382–385.

29. Dallek, *Lone Star Rising*, p. 293.

30. Davidson, *Race and Class in Texas Politics*, p. 25.

31. Davidson, *Race and Class in Texas Politics*, pp. 64, 105; Robert Caro, *The Years of Lyndon Johnson: Means of Ascent* (New York: Alfred A. Knopf, 1990), pp. 285–286.

32. Caro, *Means of Ascent*, p. 298.

33. Dallek, *Lone Star Rising*, p. 341–342.

34. Donald Worcester, *Rivers of Empire* (New York: Pantheon, 1985), pp. 14–15.

35. Monroney, Interview, LBJ/OH, p. 30.

36. James Rowe, Interview I, LBJ/OH, pp. 24–26.

37. Dallek, *Lone Star Rising*, pp. 418–422.

38. Dugger, *Politician*, pp. 372–377; James Rowe, Interview I, pp. 30–36, LBJ/OH.

39. Dallek, *Lone Star Rising*, p. 430; and see George Reedy to Arthur Krock, November, 14, 1956, with enclosures of Johnson memoranda, Krock Papers, Box 30. Johnson had announced that he wanted no "Democratic" bills, only amendments to Eisenhower's proposals, so that they could say they were "saving" Ike from conservatives in his own party. Reedy, *Lyndon B. Johnson*, pp. 85–86.

40. Interview I, p. 31, LBJ/OH.

41. While secondary sources, including Dallek, *Lone Star Rising*, pp. 521–522, discuss the "deal" in detail, Senator Frank Church of Idaho, in an interview for the Johnson Library, denied that was the way it happened, although he agreed it was Johnson's intervention with Southern senators that secured passage of the Hell's Canyon bill. It failed, nevertheless, in the House. Church, LBJ/OH, pp. 3–4.

42. Reedy to Johnson, October 17, 1957, Senate Papers, Johnson Papers, Box 420.

43. *Ibid.*

44. *Ibid.*

45. Interview, LBJ/OH, p. 17.

46. Interviews with Bryce Harlow, LBJ/OH, I, p. 43, and II, pp. 3, 13–14.

47. U.S. Senate, Preparedness Investigating Subcommittee of the Armed Services Committee, *Hearings: Inquiry into Satellite and Missile Programs*, 85th cong., 1st and 2nd sess. (2 parts, Washington: GPO, 1958), I, 3.

48. Teller's fame, and controversial views, had won him more praise from generals, financiers, industrialists, and politicians than among his scientific colleagues, who ostracized him after the 1954 Oppenheimer security hearings. Teller had testified against Oppenheimer on the basis of the latter's opposition to the H-bomb. He had become fixed on the notion of using "clean" bomb blasts to dig harbors, etc. ". . . Possessed by his muse, he could behave as if he were ordained by some supernatural power, promoting ideas and dismissing foes with self-righteous

ire. Increasingly, he seemed to be driven from the inside out, not the outside in, just the opposite of how a scientist should operate." So concludes William J. Broad in *Teller's War: The Top-Secret Story Behind the Star Wars Deception* (New York: Simon & Schuster, 1992), p. 26.

49. *Ibid.*, p. 28.

50. *Ibid.*, p. 39.

51. Senate Preparedness Subcommittee, *Hearings*, pp. 280, 161.

52. *Ibid.*, II, 1971–1972.

53. *Ibid.*, p. 1976.

54. Rowe to Johnson, November 15, 1957, Rowe Papers, Box 99.

55. Statement of the Democratic Leader . . . , January 7, 1958, Johnson Papers, Statements File, Box 23.

56. *Ibid.*

57. Quoted in Dallek, *Lone Star Rising*, p. 532.

58. Walter McDougall, . . . *The Heavens and the Earth: A Political History of the Space Age* (New York: Basic Books, 1985), pp. 406–407.

59. McDougall, *Heavens and Earth*, p. 388. McDougall also elaborates on the role that Webb's namesake, James Webb, played in the development of American space policy as head of NASA, *ibid.*, chapter 18. James Webb was fascinated with the frontier historian's work, citing it in his own speeches. He was an absolute believer in the government-science-industry team pioneered by NASA, as a model for combating communism in places like the Congo and Vietnam.

60. Terrell Maverick Webb Interview, LBJ/OH, pp. 13–14. Mrs. Webb had been married to Maverick, and this interview traces LBJ's relations with Maverick as well as the developing friendship with Webb.

61. William E. Leuchtenburg, *In the Shadow of FDR: From Harry Truman to Ronald Reagan* (Ithaca: Cornell University Press, 1985), pp. 132–133. "Somewhere along the line, the realization must be driven home to the 'liberals' that spending has no more relationship to liberalism than the salt content of sea water," he told Arthur Krock. If liberalism came equipped with a price tag, it wouldn't have much of a future in America. The Republicans enjoyed themselves immensely at this game, always bidding low to create an impression that liberals wanted to reach into the public's hip pocket to extract as much money from the wallet as possible. LBJ to Krock, early 1960, Krock Papers, Box 30.

62. Douglas G. Brinkley, *Dean Acheson: The Cold War Years, 1953–71.* (New Haven: Yale University Press, 1992), pp. 71, 99.

63. Dallek, *Lone Star Rising*, p. 541.

64. McPherson Interview, LBJ/OH, pp. 14–15.

65. Kearns, *Lyndon Johnson*, p. 154. On foreign policy specifically, LBJ also told her that while the American people were usually apathetic, once they were aroused there was always the possibility of "a mass stampede, a violent overreaction to fear, an explosion of panic," as in the heyday of Senator Joseph McCarthy. *Ibid.*, p. 142.

66. Harry Truman's exaggeration of American atomic capabilities at the time of Hiroshima and Nagasaki, not LBJ's deviousness in the 1960s, should probably be looked at as the beginning of the "credibility gap" in American foreign policy. See Lloyd C. Gardner, "The Atomic Temptation," in Lloyd C. Gardner, ed., *Redefining the Past: Essays in Diplomatic History in Honor of William Appleman Williams* (Corvallis, Ore.: Oregon State University Press, 1986), pp. 169–194.

2. LIBERAL ANXIETY IN THE EISENHOWER YEARS

1. William L. O'Neill, *Coming Apart: An Informal History of America in the 1960s* (Chicago: Quadrangle Books, 1971), p. 5.

2. Daniel P. Moynihan, *Maximum Feasible Misunderstanding: Community Action in the War on Poverty* (New York: Free Press, 1969), pp. 7, 9.

3. Barbara Ehrenreich, *Fear of Falling: The Inner Life of the Middle Class* (New York: Pantheon, 1989), p. 33.

4. O'Neill, *Coming Apart*, p. 8.

5. *Ibid.*, p. 10.

6. Quoted in Lloyd C. Gardner, *Imperial America: American Foreign Policy Since 1898* (New York: Harcourt, Brace, Jovanovich, 1976), p. 237.

7. Henry Kissinger, *Nuclear Weapons and Foreign Policy* (New York: Harper & Row, 1957), p. 428.

8. For discussions, see Robert D. Schulzinger, *Henry Kissinger: Doctor of Diplomacy* (New York: Columbia University Press, 1989), pp. 11–13, and Walter Isaacson, *Kissinger: A Biography* (New York: Simon & Schuster, 1992), pp. 86–90.

9. Max F. Millikan and W. W. Rostow, *A Proposal: Key to an Effective Foreign Policy* (New York: Harper, 1957), pp. 8, 149–150.

10. U.S. Senate, Foreign Relations Committee, *Executive Sessions of the Senate Foreign Relations Committee* (Historical Series), XIV, 1962, 99th cong., 1st sess. (Washington: GPO, 1986), 585.

11. Millikan and Rostow, *Proposal*, p. 132.

12. For accounts of the DAC, and Acheson's determination that the Democrats follow a hard-line foreign policy and head off heresies such as that espoused by George F. Kennan, who had called for "disengagement" in Germany and Central Europe, see Brinkley, *Dean Acheson*, pp. 63–65, and David Callahan, *Dangerous Capabilities: Paul Nitze and the Cold War* (New York: HarperCollins, 1990), pp. 162–165.

13. John Kenneth Galbraith, *A Life in Our Times: Memoirs* (Boston: Houghton-Mifflin, 1981), p. 359.

14. *Ibid.*

15. Typewritten memo included in Ward to Valenti, March 8, 1965, Johnson Papers.

16. David Halberstam, *The Best and the Brightest* (New York: Random House, 1972), pp. 438–439.

17. Quoted in Hans J. Morgenthau, "The International Aspects of the Great Society," in Bertram M. Gross, ed., *A Great Society?* (New York: Basic Books, 1968), p. 120.

18. Bruce J. Schulman, *Lyndon Johnson and American Liberalism: A Brief Biography with Documents* (New York: St. Martin's, 1994), p. 54.

19. Thomas Paterson, ed., *Kennedy's Quest for Victory* (New York: Oxford University Press, 1989), p. 11.

20. Victor Lasky, *J.F.K.: The Man and the Myth* (New Rochelle, N.Y.: Arlington House, 1968), pp. 362–363.

21. Paterson, *Kennedy's Quest*, p. 11.

22. Merle Miller, *Lyndon* (New York: Putnam, 1980), p. 242.

23. For an account of the maneuvers at the convention, see Dallek, *Lone Star Rising*, pp. 575–580, and for more details, "Notes on the Democratic Convention" by Phil Graham, July 19, 1960, copy in Rowe Papers, Box 100.

24. Untitled, unsigned memorandum, headed "July 13, 1960," and marked, "Rec'd for filing, 11/18/64," Johnson Papers, Office of the President Files, Bill Moyers, Box 8.

25. John Singleton, LBJ/OH, II, p. 48.

26. Henry Fairlie, *The Kennedy Promise: The Politics of Expectation* (New York: Doubleday, 1973), p. 58.

27. *New York Times*, August 27, 1960.

28. The quotes are reproduced in William Appleman Williams, *The United States, Cuba, and Castro* (New York: Monthly Review Press, 1962), pp. 149–150.

29. Paterson, *Kennedy's Quest*, p. 37.

30. Herbert Parmet, *The Democrats: The Years After FDR* (New York: Macmillan, 1976), p. 197.

31. Arthur M. Schlesinger, Jr., *A Thousand Days: John F. Kennedy in the White House* (Boston: Houghton-Mifflin, 1965), p. 109.

32. Michael Beschloss, *The Crisis Years: Kennedy and Khrushchev, 1960–1963* (New York: HarperCollins, 1991) p. 48.

33. Quoted in Moynihan, *Maximum Feasible Misunderstanding*, p. 62.

34. Letter to the Editor, *New York Times*, November 1, 1960.

35. Interview with Walt Rostow, JFK/OH, pp. 100–101.

36. Frank Costigliola, *France and the United States* (New York: Twayne, 1992), p. 109.

37. William Borden, "Foreign Economic Policy," in Paterson, *Kennedy's Quest*, pp. 57–86.

38. U.S. Congress, Joint Economic Committee, *Hearings: Foreign Economic Policy, 1961*, 87th cong., 1st sess. (Washington: GPO, 1961), p. 18. Italics added.

39. *Ibid.*, p. 14.

40. Frank Costigliola, "Nuclear Arms, Dollars, and Berlin," in Paterson, *Kennedy's Quest*, pp. 24–56. Quotation is from p. 30.

41. News Conference, September 16, 1965, quoted in U.S. Congress, Senate Committee on Foreign Relations, Staff Study, *Arms Sales and Foreign Policy*, 90th cong., 1st sess. (Washington: GPO, 1967), p. 2. All of the material in this section is based on this Staff Study.

42. *Ibid.*, p. 4.
43. Borden, "Foreign Economic Policy," p. 72.
44. General Services Administration, National Archives, *Public Papers of the Presidents, John F. Kennedy, 1962* (Washington: GPO, 1963), pp. 360–361.
45. William Clayton and Christian Herter, "A New Look at Foreign Economic Policy in Light of the Cold War and the Extension of the Common Market in Europe," U.S. Congress, Joint Economic Committee, Committee Print, 87th cong., 1st sess. (Washington: GPO, 1961), p. 2.
46. *Ibid.*, p. 8.
47. *Ibid.*, p. 4.
48. Schlesinger, *A Thousand Days*, pp. 927–930.
49. Walter Heller, *New Dimensions of Political Economy* (Cambridge, Mass.: Harvard University Press, 1966), pp. 12–14.
50. Kevin Phillips, *The Emerging Republican Majority* (New Rochelle, N.Y.: Arlington House, 1969), pp. 37, 166.

3. AFTER THE BAY OF PIGS

1. Quoted in Theodore Sorensen, *Kennedy* (New York: Harper & Row, 1965), p. 302.
2. Beschloss, *Crisis Years*, pp. 116–128.
3. Walter LaFeber, *Inevitable Revolutions: The United States in Central America* (New York: W. W. Norton, 1983), pp. 149–150.
4. See, for example, the article by Richard E. Welch, Jr., "Lippmann, Berle, and the U.S. Response to the Cuban Revolution," *Diplomatic History*, 6 (Spring 1982), 125–143.
5. Wayne S. Smith, *The Closest of Enemies: A Personal and Diplomatic History of the Castro Years* (New York: W. W. Norton, 1987), pp. 68–70.
6. For a recent brief summary of Allen Dulles's attempts to manipulate Kennedy, see Peter Grose, *Gentleman Spy: The Life of Allen Dulles* (Boston: Houghton-Mifflin, 1994), pp. 519–525.
7. Schlesinger, *A Thousand Days*, pp. 242, 257–258.
8. Fairlie, *Kennedy Promise*, pp. 180–181.
9. Howard B. Schaffer, *Chester Bowles: New Dealer in the Cold War* (Cambridge, Mass.: Harvard University Press, 1993), pp. 206–210.
10. Walter LaFeber, *America, Russia and the Cold War, 1945–1990* (New York: McGraw Hill, 1991), p. 216.
11. *Ibid.*
12. See the discussion in Paterson, *Kennedy's Quest*, pp. 135–138.
13. David Di Leo, *George Ball, Vietnam, and the Rethinking of Containment* (Chapel Hill: University of North Carolina Press, 1991), pp. 46–47; George Ball, *The Past Has Another Pattern: Memoirs* (New York: W. W. Norton, 1982), p. 365.
14. W. W. Rostow, "Beware of Historians Bearing False Analogies," *Foreign Affairs*, 66 (Spring 1988), 863–868.
15. De Lesseps Morrison, *Latin American Mission: An Adventure in Hemisphere Diplomacy* (New York: Simon & Schuster, 1965) pp. 113–114.
16. William C. Westmoreland, *A Soldier Reports* (Garden City, N.Y.: Doubleday, 1976), pp. 410–411.
17. Two very different readings of *Why England Slept* are offered by Schlesinger, *A Thousand Days*, pp. 84–85, and Fairlie, *Kennedy Promise*, pp. 69–71.
18. Office of the Federal Register, *Public Papers of the Presidents of the United States: John F. Kennedy, 1961* (Washington: GPO, 1962), pp. 305–306. Italics added.
19. *Ibid.*
20. Beschloss, *Crisis Years*, p. 129.
21. Rostow to Secretary of State, Secretary of Defense, and Director of Central Intelligence, April 24, 1961, Kennedy Papers, President's Official File, John F. Kennedy Library, Box 115.
22. *Ibid.*
23. Rostow, Oral History Interview, JFK/OH, p. 48.
24. Sorensen, *Kennedy*, p. 640. The Eisenhower-Kennedy exchanges on Laos became important later in the decade, when Lyndon Johnson attempted to build a consistent historical record to support his July 1965 decision to send 100,000 men to Vietnam. What emerged from a

new examination of existing records of the conversation, and from still later evaluations, provided a significantly different picture of what transpired that day. Johnson's people found that Kennedy memoir writers had built their own record to show that JFK had been pushed into Southeast Asia by his predecessor. What Kennedy had actually sought to learn that day was whether Eisenhower would support *his* initiatives, not simply what Ike recommended he do. According to notes taken by Robert McNamara and Kennedy himself, Eisenhower had serious reservations about any unilateral intervention. See Fred I. Greenstein and Richard H. Immerman, "What Did Eisenhower Tell Kennedy About Indochina? The Politics of Misperception," *Journal of American History*, 79:2 (September 1992), 568–587.

25. Sorensen, *Kennedy*, pp. 641–642.

26. Chester L. Cooper, *The Lost Crusade: America in Vietnam* (New York: Dodd, Mead, 1970), p. 171.

27. *Ibid.*, p. 172.

28. Paterson, *Kennedy's Quest*, p. 136.

29. Mansfield to Kennedy, May 1, 1961, Johnson Papers, Vice-President's Security Files, Box 1.

30. Beschloss, *Crisis Years*, p. 203–204.

31. *Ibid.*, p. 212.

32. LaFeber, *America, Russia and the Cold War*, p. 231.

33. Halberstam, *Best and the Brightest*, p. 76.

34. Lloyd C. Gardner, *Approaching Vietnam: From World War II Through Dienbienphu* (New York: W. W. Norton, 1988), p. 341.

35. *Ibid.*, pp. 340–341.

36. For a succinct discussion of these developments, see Marilyn Young, *The Vietnam Wars, 1945–1990* (New York: HarperCollins, 1991), pp. 60–65.

37. Gabriel Kolko, *Anatomy of a War: Vietnam, the United States, and the Modern Historical Experience* (New York: Pantheon, 1985), pp. 66–68.

38. Stanley Karnow, *Vietnam: A History* (New York: Viking, 1983), pp. 238–239.

39. John Mecklin, *Mission in Torment: An Intimate Account of the U.S. Role in Vietnam* (Garden City, N.Y.: Doubleday, 1965), pp. 82–83.

40. *Ibid.*, p. 123; George McT. Kahin, *Intervention: How America Became Involved in Vietnam* (New York: Alfred A. Knopf, 1986), pp. 122–123.

41. Senator Gravel Edition, *The Pentagon Papers* (4 vols., Boston: Beacon Press, 1971), II, 53.

42. Memorandum of a Conversation, March 27, 1961, *FR, 1961–1963*, I, 52–57.

43. Memorandum by Robert Komer, April 28, 1961, *ibid.*, 85–86.

44. Nancy Dickerson, *Among Those Present* (New York: Random House, 1976), p. 79.

45. Evelyn Lincoln, *Kennedy and Johnson* (New York: Holt, Rinehart & Winston, 1968), pp. 166–167. Johnson's adviser on national security affairs, Colonel Howard Burris, had given the vice-president a memorandum on the implications of the Laos crisis that emphasized how difficult it would be to persuade the South Vietnamese government that the United States had any policy to "stem Communist advances in the area." Burris to Johnson, April 28, 1961, Johnson Papers, Vice-President's Security Files, Box 5.

46. Goldschmidt to LBJ, May 4, 1961, Johnson Papers, Confidential Files, "Mekong River," Box 167.

47. Miller, *Lyndon*, p. 466.

48. Frederick Nolting, *From Trust to Tragedy* (New York: Praeger, 1988), p. 21.

49. Kennedy to Diem, May 8, 1961, Johnson Papers, National Security File, International Meetings, Box 1–2.

50. An important controversy has developed around this conversation. Most recently, John M. Newman, *JFK and Vietnam: Deception, Intrigue, and the Struggle for Power* (New York: Warner Books, 1992), pp. 72–96, has argued that Johnson was operating either as a lone wolf or in collaboration with Pentagon figures to encourage Diem to ask for American troops, as a way of forcing Kennedy's hand. The authors of the famous "Pentagon Papers," the study ordered by Secretary Robert McNamara of the decision-making process that led to America's involvement in the Vietnam War, had concluded several years ago, on the other hand, that "no strong inference" can be drawn from the fact that it was Johnson who first raised the issue. He had been sent to find out, after all, what it was Diem really wanted. Even if Kennedy had already decided not to provide troops at that time, given the nature of Johnson's mission of reassurance, there was "nothing outrageous" about his posing the question. *Pentagon Papers: GE*, II, 55–56. George Kahin went further, however, writing that Johnson had been "charged" with asking Diem if he

wanted combat troops and a bilateral treaty. *Intervention*, p. 132. Newman's case is filled with suppositions at critical points in the argument, but neither is there any firm evidence that Kennedy actually "charged" Johnson to raise the question of providing American combat troops. In his report to the president, Johnson stressed that "Asian leaders," sensitive to the colonial issue, did not want combat troops except in the case of "open attack." And, he added, the administration should seek to allay that concern for another reason, to gain support from Congress. "We might gain much needed flexibility in our policies if the specter of combat troop commitment could be lessened domestically." *Pentagon Papers: GE*, II, 57–59.

51. Nolting to Department of State, May 15, 1961, *FR, 1961–1963*, I, 139.

52. Nolting to Secretary of State, May 15, 1961, Johnson Papers, Vice-President's Security Files, Box 1.

53. Carl T. Rowan, *Breaking Barriers: A Memoir* (Boston: Little, Brown, 1991), p. 188. Newman, *JFK and Vietnam*, p. 76, uses an edited version of this quotation to suggest that Johnson was concerned that Diem did not understand he was supposed to ask for combat troops in the letter to Kennedy. As the full quote indicates, the conversation with Rowan had quite the opposite implication.

54. Lyndon B. Johnson, *The Vantage Point: Perspectives of the Presidency, 1963–1969* (New York: Popular Library, 1971), p. 57.

55. United Nations Press Services, "UN-Aided Projects in Asia Discussed in Visit of United States Vice-President to ECAFE Headquarters," Press Release ECAFE/88, May 17, 1961, and Cesar Ortiz-Tinoco, "Mr. Johnson's Visit to ECAFE," undated, both in Johnson Papers, Confidential Files, "Mekong River," Box 167.

56. Karnow, *Vietnam*, p. 214.

57. *Pentagon Papers: GE*, II, 58–59.

58. "Report by the Vice President," undated [May 1961], *FR, 1961–1963*, I, 152–157. The editors of this volume of the *Foreign Relations* series could not discover anything about the drafting of this document. The language and viewpoint are both different from the parts of Johnson's report most frequently cited.

59. *Ibid.*

60. "Address by Vice President Lyndon B. Johnson," Howard University, June 9, 1961, copy in Rowe Papers, Box 100.

61. Harris Wofford, *Of Kennedys and Kings: Making Sense of the Sixties* (New York: Farrar, Straus, Giroux, 1980), p. 156.

62. Taylor Branch, *Parting the Waters: America in the King Years, 1954–1963* (New York: Simon & Schuster, 1988), p. 838.

63. *Ibid.*, pp. 843–844.

64. Johnson to J. J. Neville, August 14, 1961, Johnson Papers, Confidential Files, "Mekong River," Box 167.

65. Draft Instructions, October 11, 1961, *FR, 1961–1963*, I, 345–346; undated, untitled memorandum, Krock Papers, Box 1; Nolting to Department of State, October 18, 1961, *FR, 1961–1963*, I, 391–392.

66. Kahin, *Intervention*, p. 135; Taylor, *Swords and Plowshares*, pp. 226, 238–239.

67. Schlesinger, *A Thousand Days*, pp. 546–547.

68. Nolting, *Trust to Tragedy*, p. 36.

69. Ball, *Past Has Another Pattern*, p. 300.

70. Draft Memorandum for the President, November 8, 1961, *FR, 1961–1963*, I, 561–566; Bundy to Kennedy, November 15, 1961, *ibid.*, pp. 605–607.

71. Notes on the National Security Council Meeting, November 15, 1961, *ibid.*, pp. 607–610.

72. *Ibid.*

73. Kennedy to Khrushchev, November 16, 1961, *ibid.*, pp. 636–638.

74. *Pentagon Papers: GE*, II, 120.

75. Nolting to Department of State, November 18 and 25, 1961, *FR, 1961–1963*, I, 642–644, 666–668.

76. *Ibid.*, pp. 683–689.

77. "Memorandum of Understanding," December 4, 1961, *ibid.*, pp. 714–716.

78. Rusk to Nolting, December 5, 1961, *ibid.*, p. 716.

79. William J. Rust, *Kennedy in Vietnam: American Vietnam Policy, 1960–63* (New York: Scribner, 1985), p. 59.

80. Kahin, *Intervention*, p. 140.

81. Burris to Johnson, August 17, 1962, *FR, 1961–1963*, II, 601–603.

82. Halberstam, *Best and the Brightest*, p. 208.
83. James S. Olson and Randy Roberts, *Where the Domino Fell: America and Vietnam,* *1945–1990* (New York: St. Martin's, 1991), p. 95.
84. Press Conference, December 12, 1962, Office of the Federal Register, *Public Papers of the Presidents of the United States: John F. Kennedy, 1962* (Washington: GPO, 1963), pp. 866–874.
85. Mecklin, *Mission in Torment*, p. 20.
86. Kahin, *Intervention*, p. 169.

4. THE AMERICAN COUP

1. Ellen Hammer, *A Death in November: America in Vietnam, 1963* (New York: Oxford University Press, 1987), p. 211.
2. "Memorandum for the Record . . . , January 3, 1962, *FR, 1961–1963,* II, 3–4.
3. Robert Johnson, Memorandum to Rostow, January 11, 1962, *ibid.,* 21–23.
4. Lawrence J. Bassett and Stephen E. Pelz, "The Failed Search for Victory," in Paterson, *Kennedy's Quest,* p. 244.
5. Johnson, *Vantage Point,* p. 62.
6. Kahin, *Intervention,* p. 140.
7. U.S. Senate, Foreign Relations Committee, *Executive Sessions of the Senate Foreign Relations Committee* (Historical Series), XVII, 89th cong., 1st sess., 1965 (Washington: GPO, 1990), 38.
8. Olson and Roberts, *Where the Domino Fell,* pp. 94–97; Cooper, *Lost Crusade,* pp. 195–197.
9. Cooper, *Lost Crusade* pp. 195–196.
10. Memorandum to U. Alexis Johnson, February 15, 1962, *FR, 1961–1963,* II, 129–132.
11. Halberstam, *Best and the Brightest,* pp. 205–206.
12. Nolting to State Department, March 11, 1962, *FR, 1961–1963,* II, 215–216.
13. Nolting, *Trust to Tragedy,* p. 102.
14. "Memorandum of a Conversation . . . ," April 6, 1962, *FR, 1961–1963,* II, 309–310, and Galbraith to Kennedy, April 4, 1962, *ibid.,* pp. 297–298.
15. "Memorandum from the Acting Assistant Secretary of Defense . . . ," April 14, 1962, *ibid.,* pp. 324–327.
16. Galbraith to Harriman, May 5, 1962; Galbraith to Harriman, May 10, 1962; Rusk to Galbraith, May 16, 1962, *ibid.,* pp. 375, 379, 399.
17. "Memorandum of a Conversation . . . ," July 22, 1962, *ibid.,* pp. 543–546; Rust, *Kennedy in Vietnam,* p. 76.
18. Hammer, *Death in November,* pp. 101–102.
19. Harriman to Nolting, October 18, 1962; Nolting to Harriman, October 20, 1962; Harriman to Nolting, October 22, 1962; Nolting to Harriman, October 25, 1962, *FR, 1961–1963,* II, 707, 716, 717–718, 719–720.
20. Hammer, *Death in November,* pp. 31–32.
21. "Memorandum for the Files . . . ," December 27, 1962; Report by the Senate Majority Leader, December 18, 1962, *ibid.,* pp. 797–798, 779–787.
22. Kahin, *Intervention,* p. 142.
23. *Ibid.,* p. 143.
24. "Report by an Investigative Team . . . ," dated only January 1963, *FR, 1961–1963,* III, 73–94.
25. *Ibid.*
26. *Ibid.,* note 2, p. 73.
27. Andrew F. Krepinevich, *The Army and Vietnam* (Baltimore: Johns Hopkins University Press, 1988), p. 81.
28. Memorandum to Harriman, January 29, 1963, *FR, 1961–1963,* III, 65.
29. Nolting to Harriman, February 27, 1963, *ibid.,* pp. 126–128.
30. Kahin, *Intervention,* p. 147.
31. Memoranda of Conversations, April 1 and 3, 1963, *FR, 1961–1963,* III, 193–195, 198–200.
32. Young, *Vietnam Wars,* p. 95; Kahin, *Intervention,* p. 144.
33. Nolting to State Department, April 5, 1963, *FR, 1961–1963,* III, 207–213.
34. Karnow, *Vietnam,* pp. 279–280.
35. Rusk to Nolting, June 3, 1963, *FR, 1961–1963,* III, 348.
36. Department of State to Embassy, June 11, 1963, *ibid.,* pp. 381–383.

37. Hammer, *Death in November*, p. 144.
38. Karnow, *Vietnam*, p. 281.
39. Hammer, *Death in November*, p. 145.
40. Truehart to Department of State, June 25, 1963, *FR, 1961–1963*, III, 413–414.
41. Karnow, *Vietnam*, p. 284.
42. Memorandum to the Acting Secretary of State, August 6, 1963, *FR, 1961–1963*, III, 554–555.
43. Kahin, *Intervention*, p. 151.
44. Karnow, *Vietnam*, p. 285.
45. Department of State to Embassy in Vietnam, August 24, 1963, *FR, 1961–1963*, III, 628–629.
46. Karnow, *Vietnam*, p. 288.
47. Hammer, *Death in November*, p. 186.
48. "Memorandum for the Record . . . ," August 26, 1963, *FR, 1961–1963*, III, 638–641.
49. *Ibid.*
50. "Memorandum of a Conference . . . ," August 28, 1963, *FR, 1961–1963*, IV, 3–6.
51. *Ibid.*, and Editorial Note in *ibid.*, pp. 6–9.
52. "Memorandum of a Conversation . . . ," 6 p.m., August 28, 1963, *ibid.*, pp. 12–14.
53. Rusk to Lodge, August 28, 1963, *ibid.*, pp. 15–16.
54. Lodge to State Department, August 29, 1963, *ibid.*, pp. 20–22.
55. Kennedy to Lodge, August 29, 1963, *ibid.*, pp. 35–36.
56. Kahin, *Intervention*, pp. 160–161.
57. Memorandum of Conversation, August 31, 1963, *FR, 1961–1963*, IV, 69–74.
58. *Ibid.*
59. Kahin *Intervention*, p. 166.
60. Hammer, *Death in November*, p. 198.
61. Lodge to Rusk, September 2, 1963, *FR, 1961–1963*, IV, 84–85.
62. *Ibid.*, pp. 96–97, 100–103, 104–106.
63. Lodge to Rusk, September 5, 1963, *ibid.*, pp. 109–110.
64. Lodge to Rusk, September 7, 1963, *ibid.*, pp. 131–132.
65. Lodge to Rusk, September 9, 1963, *ibid.*, pp. 140–142.
66. Gardner, *Approaching Vietnam*, p. 270.
67. Kahin, *Intervention*, p. 169.
68. Memorandum of a Conversation, September 10, 1963, *FR, 1961–1963*, IV, 161–167.
69. See, for example, McNamara's report of an interview with a Vietnam specialist, identified only as "Professor Smith," a pseudonym. *Ibid.*, pp. 293–294.
70. Deborah Shapley, *Promise and Power: The Life and Times of Robert McNamara* (Boston: Little, Brown, 1993), pp. 260–265.
71. Memorandum, October 2, 1963, *FR, 1961–1963*, IV, 336–346; William J. Duiker, *U.S. Containment Policy and the Conflict in Indochina* (Stanford: Stanford University Press, 1994), pp. 300–301.
72. Memorandum, October 2, 1963, *FR, 1961–1963*, IV, 336–346.
73. Kahin, *Intervention*, p. 171. Indeed, even before Kennedy accepted the recommendations of the report, the generals sent word through one of their number, Tran Van Don, that they were anxious to have "private conversations." Telegram from Central Agency Station to CIA, Washington, October 3, 1963, *FR, 1961–1963*, IV, 354–355.
74. Hammer, *Death in November*, p. 243.
75. Central Intelligence Agency to Lodge, October 9, 1963, *FR, 1961–1963*, IV, 393.
76. U.S. Senate, Foreign Relations Committee, Staff Study, "U.S. Involvement in the Overthrow of Diem, 1963," 92nd cong., 2d sess. (Washington: GPO, 1972), pp. 13–15.
77. Bundy to Lodge, October 25, 1963, *FR, 1961–1963*, IV, 437.
78. Lodge to Rusk, October 28, 1963, *ibid.*, p. 449.
79. Memorandum of a Conference, October 29, 1963, *ibid.*, pp. 468–471.
80. *Ibid.*
81. Memorandum of a Conference, 6 p.m., October 29, 1963, *ibid.*, p. 472.
82. Harkins to Taylor, October 30, 1963, *ibid.*, pp. 479–482.
83. Lodge to Rusk, October 30, 1963, *ibid.*, pp. 484–488.
84. *Ibid.*
85. Bundy to Lodge, October 30, 1963, *ibid.*, pp. 500–502.
86. Lodge to Rusk, November 1, 1963, *ibid.*, p. 513.
87. Hammer, *Death in November*, p. 300.

88. *Ibid.*, p. 290.
89. Lodge to Kennedy, November 6, 1963, *FR, 1961–1963*, IV, 575–578.
90. Kennedy to Lodge, November 6, 1963, *ibid.*, pp. 579–580.
91. Memorandum for the Record, November 24, 1963, *ibid.*, pp. 635–637; the quotation about not losing Indochina appeared in Tom Wicker, *JFK and LBJ* (Baltimore: Penguin Books, 1972), p. 205. Wicker later confirmed that Moyers had been his source. Wicker, LBJ/OH.
92. McNamara to Lodge, *FR, 1961–1963*, IV, 702–703; Krepinovich, *Army and Vietnam*, p. 90; Louis Heren, *No Hail, No Farewell* (New York: Harper & Row, 1970), p. 42.

5. TRANSITIONS

1. Quoted in Kathleen Turner, *Lyndon Johnson's Dual War: Vietnam and the Press* (Chicago: University of Chicago Press, 1985), p. 251.
2. George Reedy, LBJ/OH, p. 25.
3. The standard account of friction between Kennedy and Johnson men in the immediate aftermath of the events in Dallas is William Manchester, *The Death of a President: November 25, 1963* (New York: Harper & Row, 1967), esp. pp. 310–329; but see also Lawrence F. O'Brien, *No Final Victories: A Life in Politics from John F. Kennedy to Watergate* (Garden City, N.Y.: Doubleday, 1974), p. 164.
4. Richard N. Goodwin, *Remembering America: A Voice from the Sixties* (Boston: Little, Brown, 1988), p. 243.
5. Miller, *Lyndon*, p. 336.
6. These reached their height with the publication of Kennedy's private secretary's memoir. See Lincoln, *Kennedy and Johnson*, pp. 204–205. For a refutation of Lincoln's assertions, see Arthur M. Schlesinger, Jr., *Robert Kennedy and His Times* (Boston: Houghton-Mifflin, 1978), pp. 604–605. Schlesinger notes in this same place, however, that LBJ had always worried about that possibility. "Johnson was chronically nervous about his prospects."
7. Quoted in Schlesinger, *Robert Kennedy*, pp. 622–623.
8. Harry McPherson, *A Political Education: A Washington Memoir* (Boston: Houghton-Mifflin, 1988), p. 200.
9. McPherson, *Political Education*, p. 248.
10. Kearns, *Lyndon Johnson*, pp. 177–178.
11. Ball, *Past Has Another Pattern*, p. 313.
12. Paul R. Henggeler, *In His Steps: Lyndon Johnson and the Kennedy Mystique* (Chicago: Ivan R. Dee, 1991), p. 141.
13. "Remarks in Boston . . . ," October 27, 1964, *Public Papers, 1963–1964*, II, 1466–1470; and see "Remarks in Madison Square Garden . . . ," October 15, 1964, *ibid.*, pp. 1348–1354; "Remarks in New York City . . . ," October 16, 1968, *ibid., 1968*, II, 1041–1043.
14. Bill D. Moyers, "Second Thoughts," in Bernard J. Firestone and Robert Vogt, eds., *Lyndon Baines Johnson and the Uses of Power* (New York: Greenwood Press, 1980), pp. 352–353.
15. Hugh Sidey, *A Very Personal Presidency* (New York: Atheneum, 1968), pp. 30–31.
16. Dickerson, *Among Those Present*, p. 96.
17. "Remarks to State Governors After President Kennedy's Funeral," November 25, 1963, Office of the Federal Register, *Public Papers of the Presidents: Lyndon B. Johnson, 1963–1964* (Washington: GPO, 1965), pp. 4–5.
18. Address to Joint Session of Congress, November 27, 1963, *Public Papers, 1963–1964*, pp. 63–64.
19. Reedy to Johnson, November 27, 1963, and Memo of Yarborough's statement by Les Carpenter, November 27, 1963, Johnson Papers, Handwriting File, Box 2; James Rowe to Johnson, November 30, 1963, Rowe Papers, Box 100.
20. Johnson, *Vantage Point*, pp. 30–34.
21. Ken Thompson, *The Johnson Presidency: Twenty Intimate Perspectives on Lyndon B. Johnson* (Lanham, Md.: University Press of America, 1986), p. 228.
22. Roberts, LBJ/OH, II, p. 36.
23. Reedy, *Lyndon B. Johnson*, pp. 146–147. Tom Wicker reached much the same conclusion about Johnson and his advisers during the transition: "He would look around him and see in Bob McNamara that it was technologically feasible, in McGeorge Bundy that it was intellectually respectable, and in Dean Rusk that it was historically necessary." Halberstam, *Best and the Brightest*, p. 530.
24. Armstrong to Bundy, December 11, 1963, Armstrong Papers, Box 11.

25. Halberstam, *Best and the Brightest*, p. 305.

26. Bundy to Rusk and McNamara, February 18, 1964, Johnson Papers, NSF, Files of McGeorge Bundy, Box 1.

27. McGeorge Bundy, "The Presidency and the Peace," *Foreign Affairs*, 42 (April 1964), 353–365.

28. *Ibid.*

29. George Ball, LBJ/OH, I, 14–15.

30. *Ibid.*

31. Congressional Research Service, *The U.S. Government and the Vietnam War: Executive and Legislative Roles and Relationships*, Pt. 3, 100th cong., 2d sess. (Washington: GPO, 1988), pp. 2–3.

32. Theodore White, *The Making of the President 1964* (New York: Atheneum, 1965), pp. 170–172.

33. Kearns, *Lyndon Johnson*, p. 154.

34. Branch, *Parting the Waters*, p. 762.

35. *Ibid.*

36. Richard Neustadt, *Presidential Power: The Politics of Leadership from FDR to Carter* (New York: John Wiley, 1980), pp. 150–151.

37. Branch, *Parting the Waters*, p. 808; White, *Making of the President 1964*, p. 173.

38. Nicholas Lemann, *The Promised Land: The Great Black Migration and How it Changed America* (New York: Alfred A. Knopf, 1991), p. 116.

39. U.S. Senate, Committee on Commerce, *Hearings: Civil Rights—Public Accommodations*, 88th cong., 1st sess. (Washington: GPO, 1963), Part 1, pp. 287–288.

40. Moyers, "Second Thoughts," in Firestone and Vogt, *Lyndon Baines Johnson*, pp. 352–353.

41. Wicker, *JFK and LBJ*, p. 170.

42. *Ibid.*, pp. 204–205; Wicker had taken this down from what Bill Moyers told him about that first discussion. It is one of several recollections Moyers had of his conversation with Johnson. Wicker, LBJ/OH, I, 33.

43. See, for example, Beschloss, *Crisis Years*. p. 24.

44. Gardner Ackley, "Troika Meeting with President Johnson," November 25, 1963, Johnson Papers, Diary Backup, Box 1.

45. Walter Heller, *New Dimensions of Political Economy* (New York: W. W. Norton, 1967), p. 12.

46. Lemann, *Promised Land*, p. 141.

47. Nicholas Lemann, "The Unfinished War," *Atlantic Monthly*, December 1988, pp. 37–56.

48. *Ibid.*, pp. 142–143.

49. *Ibid.*

50. *Ibid.*, p. 149.

51. Lloyd C. Gardner, *Economic Aspects of New Deal Diplomacy* (Madison: University of Wisconsin Press, 1964), p. 174.

52. Lemann, *Promised Land*, p. 150.

53. Goodwin, *Remembering America*, p. 257.

54. *Ibid.*, and see Moynihan, *Maximum Feasible Misunderstanding*, pp. 79–80.

55. James T. Patterson, *America's Struggle Against Poverty, 1900–1985* (Cambridge, Mass.: Harvard University Press, 1986 ed.), p. 137.

56. Michael B. Katz, *The Undeserving Poor: From the War on Poverty to the War on Welfare* (New York: Pantheon, 1989), p. 23.

57. James C. Thomson, Jr., "How Could Vietnam Happen? An Autopsy," *Atlantic Monthly*, April 1968, pp. 47–53.

58. Halberstam, *Best and the Brightest*, p. 314.

59. George R. Brown, LBJ/OH, III, 19–20.

60. Sidey, *Very Personal Presidency*, p. 135.

61. Goodwin, *Remembering America*, p. 270.

6. THE TWO WARS

1. Charles Morris, *A Time of Passion: America, 1960–1980* (New York: Penguin Books, 1986), pp. 98–99; for a leftist critique that makes much the same point, see Michael Lewis, *The Culture of Inequality* (Amherst: University of Massachusetts Press, 1978), p. 52.

2. Rowan, *Breaking Barriers*, pp. 238–239.

3. *Ibid.*

4. Johnson, *Vantage Point*, pp. 69–71.

5. *Ibid.*, pp. 70–75.

6. U.S. Senate, Committee on Foreign Relations, *Background Information Relating to Southeast Asia and Vietnam* (Washington: GPO, 1967), pp. 118–119.

7. *Ibid.*, pp. xv–xvi, 3–4, 99–100; Patterson, *America's Struggle Against Poverty*, p. 113; Lemann. *Promised Land*, pp. 149, 154, 156–158.

8. Heller, LBJ/OH, Interview I, p. 27.

9. Claudia T. Johnson, *White House Diary*, pp. 112–113.

10. "Why Should Conservatives Support the War on Poverty," undated, 1964, Johnson Papers, Office Files of Bill Moyers, Box 39.

11. Richard Lichtman, "Introduction," in Marvin E. Gettleman and David Mermelstein, eds., *The Failure of American Liberalism: After the Great Society* (New York: Vintage Books, 1971), pp. 46–47.

12. Walter Heller, LBJ/OH, Interview I, p. 23.

13. Heller to JFK, June 16, 1962, appended to *ibid.*

14. *Ibid.*, p. 25.

15. "Remarks to Members of the Communications Satellite Corporation Board," August 17, 1964, *LBJ/PP*, 1963–1964, II, 971–972.

16. Kearns, *Lyndon Johnson*, p. 190.

17. Watson to LBJ, September 29, 1964, Johnson Papers, Handwriting File, Box 4.

18. Joseph A. Califano, Jr., *The Triumph and Tragedy of Lyndon Johnson: The White House Years* (New York: Simon & Schuster, 1991), p. 62.

19. Goodwin, *Remembering America*, pp. 273–274.

20. Louis Harris, *The Anguish of Change* (New York: W. W. Norton, 1973), pp. 15–16.

21. Barbara Jordan and Elspeth Rostow, eds., *The Great Society: A Twenty Year Critique* (Austin: Lyndon B. Johnson Library, 1985), p. 79.

22. U.S. House of Representatives, Committee on Rules, *Hearings: Civil Rights*, H.R. 7152, 88th cong., 2d sess. (Washington: GPO, 1964), pp. 203–204.

23. *Ibid.*, p. 90.

24. *Ibid.*, pp. 156, 90.

25. *Ibid.*, p. 156.

26. Joseph A. Califano, Jr., "Tough Talk for Democrats," *New York Times Magazine*, January 8, 1989, pp. 28–29ff.

27. David J. Garrow, *Bearing the Cross: Martin Luther King, Jr., and the Southern Leadership Conference* (New York: Vintage Books, 1988), p. 338.

28. Richard A. Cloward and Frances Fox Pliven, *The Politics of Turmoil: Essays on Poverty, Race and the Urban Crisis* (New York: Pantheon, 1974), pp. 320–321.

29. Moynihan, *Maximum Feasible Misunderstanding*, pp. 91, 94–95.

30. Wickenden to Myer Feldman, January 4, 1964, Johnson Papers, White House Central File, Gen. WE9 Poverty Program, Box 32.

31. Lemann, *Promised Land*, p. 158.

32. Patterson, *Struggle Against Poverty*, p. 147.

33. White, *Making of the President 1964*, p. 224.

34. Garry Wills, *The Second Civil War: Arming for Armageddon* (New York: New American Library, 1968), p. 22.

35. Patterson, *Struggle Against Poverty*, p. 147.

36. Lemann, *Promised Land*, p. 158.

37. For an elaboration on this theme, see Ira Katznelson, "Was the Great Society a Lost Opportunity?" in Fraser and Gerstle, *Rise and Fall of the New Deal Order*, pp. 185–211. "This policy perspective that constituted the kit bag of ideas available to the Democratic presidents of the 1960s was principally that of economists who were concerned with human capital and incentives to opportunity, and of sociologists and social work professionals who had developed theories of blocked opportunity. Joined together, this package of orientations to policy had a coherent analysis and prescriptive perspective: its central intent was the integration of the poor into the growth

economy and social insurance state from which they had been excluded both for reasons of economic structure and individual behavior." Pp. 200–201.

38. Quoted in Michael Charlton and Anthony Moncrieff, *Many Reasons Why: American Involvement in Vietnam* (New York: Hill and Wang, 1989), pp. 105–106.

39. Quoted in William Appleman Williams, et al., eds., *America in Vietnam: A Documentary History* (New York: W. W. Norton, 1989), p. 258.

40. U.S. Senate, Foreign Relations Committee, *Executive Sessions of the Senate Foreign Relations Committee* (Historical Series), XVI, 1964, 88th cong., 2d sess. (Washington: GPO, 1988), 195.

41. Wallace Thies, *When Governments Collide: Coercion and Diplomacy in the Vietnam Conflict, 1964–1968* (Berkeley: University of California Press, 1980), pp. 250–253; "Resolution of the Ninth Conference of the Lao Dong Party Central Committee," December 1963, printed in Gareth Porter, *Vietnam: A History in Documents* (New York: New American Library, 1981), pp. 255–257; Karnow, *Vietnam*, pp. 329–331.

42. Porter, *Vietnam: Documents*, p. 255.

43. William P. Bundy, unpublished manuscript on Vietnam, Lyndon B. Johnson Library, Austin, Tex., chapter 12, p. 7.

44. Mansfield to Johnson, January 6, 1964, *FR, 1964–1968*, I, 2–3.

45. Bundy to Johnson, January 9, 1964, *ibid.*, pp. 8–9.

46. *Ibid.*, pp. 9–13.

47. Congressional Research Service, Library of Congress, *The U.S. Government and the Vietnam War: Executive Roles and Relationships*, prepared for the Committee on Foreign Relations, U.S. Senate, Part 2, 1961–1964, 98th cong., 2d sess. (Washington: GPO, 1985), pp. 213–214.

48. McGeorge Bundy to Johnson, January 7, 1964, *FR, 1964–1968*, I, 4–5.

49. Lodge to Department of State, January 21, 1964, *ibid.*, pp. 28–31.

50. Kahin, *Intervention*, chapter VII, "The Pentagon's Coup," pp. 182–202.

51. *Ibid.*, and for a contrary view, see William Bundy, unpublished manuscript, chapter 12, p. 15.

52. Lodge to Department of State, January 31, 1964, *FR, 1964–1968*, I, 45–48.

53. Kahin, *Intervention*, p. 202.

54. Halberstam, *Best and the Brightest*, p. 352.

55. Bundy, unpublished manuscript, chapter 12, p. 15.

56. Mansfield to Johnson, February 1, 1964, Johnson Papers, NSF, Bundy Memos to the President, Box 1.

57. "The President's News Conference of February 1, 1964," *PP, 1963–1964*, p. 254.

58. *Ibid.*, pp. 259, 289.

59. Lodge to Johnson, February 22, 1964, *FR, 1964–1968*, I, 102,–103.

60. Johnson to Lodge, February 22, 1964, *ibid.*, p. 104.

61. Bundy, unpublished manuscript, chapter 12, p. 18.

62. See, for example, Thomson to Bundy, July 24, 1964, Johnson Papers, NSF, Country Files, France, Box 170.

63. Johnson to Lodge, March 20, 1964, *FR, 1964–1968*, I, 184–185.

64. "Memorandum of a Conversation . . . ," March 4, 1964, *ibid.*, pp. 129–30. Taylor wrote in his memoirs that he and McNamara went around to various towns, and on a platform in each of the town squares carried out the president's instructions down to the last detail, "in a posture befitting the victorious finale of a prize fight or of a party convention. When it was all over, there was no doubt that he was the 'American Boy,' at least for the time being." Taylor, *Swords and Plowshares*, p. 310.

65. *FR, 1964–1968*, I, 129–130.

66. For Johnson's intervention, see Goodwin, *Remembering America*, p. 351; the report, dated March 16, 1964, is in *FR, 1964–1968*, I, 153–167.

67. McNamara Report, March 16, 1964, *FR, 1964–1968*, I, 153–167.

68. *Ibid.*

69. Krepinevich, *Army and Vietnam*, pp. 92–93.

70. Goodwin, *Remembering America*, p. 271.

71. Thomas Powers, *The War at Home: Vietnam and the American People, 1964–1968* (New York: Grossman, 1973), p. 3.

72. Sidey, *Very Personal Presidency*, p. 218–219.

73. Summary Record of the 528th NSC Meeting, April 22, 1964, *FR, 1964–1968*, I, 258–262; Rowe to Bill Connell, May 5, 1964, Rowe Papers, Box 98.

74. Bohlen to LBJ, April 2, 1964, *FR, 1964–1968*, I, 216–219.

75. Memorandum of a Conversation, April 18, 1964, *ibid.*, p. 244.
76. Summary Record of the NSC Meeting, May 15, 1964, *ibid.*, pp. 328–332.
77. Summary Record of the NSC Meeting, May 24, 1964; *ibid.*, pp. 369–374; Rusk to Lodge, May 21, 1964, *ibid.*, pp. 344–346; Lodge to Rusk, May 22, 1964, *ibid.*, pp. 346–348.
78. Draft Memorandum, May 25, 1964, *ibid.*, pp. 374–377.
79. For an early draft of such a resolution by Walt Rostow, dated February 13, 1964, see *ibid.*, pp. 72–74.
80. William Bundy, unpublished manuscript, pp. 13–24.
81. See, for example, Bundy to Johnson, June 3, 1964, *FR, 1964–1968*, I, 440–441.
82. Bowles to Moyers, with enclosed letter for Johnson, May 19, 1964, and Moyers to Bowles, June 2, 1964, Johnson Papers, White House Central File, CF 12.
83. Journal Entry, June 16, 1964, Lilienthal Papers, Box 208.
84. Cater to Moyers, June 9, 1964, Johnson Papers, Reference File, Vietnam, Box 1.
85. Cater to Johnson, June 23, 1964, Johnson Papers, Office Files of Douglass Cater, Memos to the President, Box 13 (emphasis added).
86. Jack Valenti, *A Very Human President* (New York: W. W. Norton, 1975), pp. 133–134.
87. Cater to Johnson, with Johnson's handwritten note, June 29, 1964, Johnson Papers, Handwriting File, Box 3.
88. John McCone, director of the Central Intelligence Agency, drafted the memo of this conference, on November 24, 1963. The quotation is his conclusion about the new "President Johnson tone" as it differed from the Kennedy "tone." As such, it may have reflected his approval of what he believed had dramatically changed, more than any real change. See *FR, 1961–1963*, IV, 635–637.
89. McCloy, Oral History, LBJ/OH, p. 10.
90. Bundy to Johnson, June 25, 1964, *FR, 1964–1968*, I, 530–531.
91. Cater to Johnson, May 4, 1964, Johnson Papers, Office Files of Douglass Cater, Memos to the President, Box 13.

7. THE PEACE CANDIDATE

1. *PP, 1963–1964*, II, 1109–1112.
2. Remarks at Akron University, October 21, 1964, *ibid.*, pp. 1387–1392.
3. *Ibid.*, pp. 1368–1373.
4. Bayard Rustin, "From Protest to Coalition Politics," reprinted in Gettleman and Mermelstein, *Failure of American Liberalism*, pp. 275–276.
5. Johnson, *Vantage Point*, p. 95.
6. Rowan, *Breaking Barriers*, p. 246. For other accounts of Johnson's obsession with removing Bobby from the scene, see Kearns, *Lyndon Johnson*, p. 200, and Miller, *Lyndon*, p. 389.
7. Goldman, *Tragedy*, p. 199.
8. Goodwin, *Remembering America*, p. 348.
9. *PP 1963–1964*, II, 1160–1169.
10. Sidey, *Very Personal Presidency*, p. 89.
11. Johnson, *Vantage Point*, p. 95.
12. *New York Times*, July 24, 1964, p. 1.
13. Transcript of July 23, 1964, press conference, in Johnson Papers, NSF, Country File, France, Box 170.
14. *Ibid.*
15. *Ibid.*
16. McCone, "Comments on De Gaulle's Speech," July 24, 1964, *ibid.*
17. Johnson quote from Kahin, *Intervention*, p. 216. Kahin, relying on the Gravel edition of the *Pentagon Papers*, suggests here (p. 217) that the United States had said that attacks on the north "might begin" if "the pressure from dissident South Vietnamese factions became too great." See, *Pentagon Papers: GE*, II, 329. Publication of the relevant documents in *FR, 1964–1968*, I, indicates somewhat less emphasis ought to be placed upon the conclusions of the authors of the *Pentagon Papers*, although it is certainly possible they had access to other sources. See Department of State to Taylor, July 25, 1964, and Taylor to Department of State, July 27, 1964, *FR, 1964–1968*, I, 569–571, 576–579.
18. Taylor to Department of State, July 27, 1964, *FR, 1964–1968*, I, 576–579.

19. Quoted in William Conrad Gibbons, *The U.S. Government and the Vietnam War: Executive and Legislative Roles and Relationships* (3 parts, Princeton, N.J.: Princeton University Press, 1986), part 2, p. 297.

20. *Ibid.*, p. 302.

21. "Notes Taken at Leadership Meeting on August 4, 1964," Johnson Papers, Meeting Notes File, Box 2; Herrick and Rusk quotes from Anthony Austin, *The President's War* (New York: Lippincott, 1971), pp. 292, 75.

22. George Ball, LBJ/OH, I, 22.

23. *Ibid.*

24. Gibbons, *U.S. Government and Vietnam War,* Part 2, p. 287.

25. See U.S. Senate, Committees on Foreign Relations and Armed Services, Joint Hearing, *Southeast Asia Resolution,* 88th cong., 2d sess. (Washington: GPO, 1966); for the McNamara quote, U.S. Senate, Foreign Relations Committee, *Executive Sessions* (Historical Series), XVI, 1964, 88th cong., 2d sess. (Washington: GPO, 1988), 293.

26. Rusk to Taylor, August 3, 1964, *FR, 1964–1968,* I, 603–604; see also lunch notes, August 4, 1964, Bundy Papers, Box 1, where the following anonymous exchange took place at the White House: "What is 34-A role in all this?" "Must be cause; no other is rational." "But not a sufficient cause?"

27. Gibbons, *U.S. Government and Vietnam War,* part 2, p. 288.

28. *Ibid.*, pp. 290–292.

29. *Ibid.*, p. 291.

30. Ulysses S. Grant Sharp, *Strategy for Defeat: Vietnam in Retrospect* (San Rafael, Calif.: Presidio Press, 1978), p. 44.

31. Whether McNamara ever had serious doubts about the intercepts cannot be finally determined. His biographer suggests, without offering proof, that information disputing their reliability was never given to him. On the other hand, she concludes that in both 1964 and again in 1968, when he offered the intercepts as proof to a skeptical Senate Foreign Relations Committee, McNamara performed acts of loyalty to Lyndon Johnson by keeping the debate over the Gulf of Tonkin out of the presidential campaigns. Shapley, *Promise and Power,* pp. 453–459.

32. Ray Cline, LBJ/OH, II, 27–29; see also the accounts in Gibbons, *U.S. Government and Vietnam War,* part 2, pp. 298–301, and the article "The 'Phantom Battle' That Led to War," *U.S. News & World Report,* July 23, 1984, pp. 56–67.

33. "Notes Taken at Leadership Meeting . . . ," August 4, 1964, Johnson Papers, Meeting Notes File, Box 2.

34. *Ibid.*

35. *Ibid.*

36. LBJ to de Gaulle, August 4, 1964, Johnson Papers, Handwriting File, Box 3.

37. De Gaulle to Johnson, August 8, 1964, and Johnson note on text, August 8, 1964, *ibid.*

38. Kolko, *Anatomy of a War,* p. 157.

39. Halberstam, *Best and the Brightest,* p. 414.

40. Ball, *Past Has Another Pattern,* p. 379; Rowan, *Breaking Barriers,* p. 266. Johnson said the same thing to a number of people—see Halberstam, *Best and the Brightest,* p. 414; Frank Cormier, *LBJ, The Way He Was* (Garden City, N.Y.: Doubleday, 1977), p. 102. The only thing that changed in these accounts was what the sailors were shooting at—whales, flying fish, or waves.

41. See Jim Sleeper, *The Closest of Strangers: Liberalism and the Politics of Race in New York* (New York: W. W. Norton, 1990), pp. 60–61.

42. Sidey, *Very Personal Presidency,* p. 122.

43. Powers, *War at Home,* pp. 26–28; Valenti to Johnson, August 4, 1964, Johnson Papers, Handwriting File, Box 3.

44. Ward to Johnson, August 30, 1964, Johnson Papers, Handwriting File, Box 3.

45. Taylor to Department of State, August 15, 1964, *FR, 1964–1968,* I, 682–684.

46. Taylor to Department of State, August 31, 1964, *ibid.*, pp. 719–721.

47. Bundy to Johnson, August 31, 1964, *ibid.*, pp. 723–724.

48. Bundy to Johnson, September 8, 1964, *ibid.*, pp. 746–749; Memorandum of a Meeting, September 9, 1964, *ibid.*, pp. 749–755.

49. *Ibid.*

50. See Newman, *JFK and Vietnam.*

51. Goodwin to Johnson, September 1, 1964, Johnson Papers, Handwriting File, Box 4; unsigned (Bill Moyers?) to Johnson, September 7, 1964, *ibid.*, White House Aides Files, Moyers, Box 53.

52. Rostow to Bundy, September 9, 1964, *ibid.*

53. Patrick Lloyd Hatcher, *The Suicide of an Elite: American Intellectuals and Vietnam* (Stanford: Stanford University Press, 1990), p. 97.

54. Memorandum for the Record, September 20, 1964, *FR, 1964–1968*, I, 778–781.

55. *Ibid.*

56. Gibbons, *U.S. Government and Vietnam War*, part 2, p. 356.

57. Memorandum for the Record, September 20, 1964, *FR, 1964–1968*, I, 778–781.

58. "Remarks in Oklahoma at the Dedication of the Eufaula Dam," September 25, 1964, *PP, 1963–1964*, II, 1122–1128.

59. "Remarks in Manchester . . . ," September 28, 1964, *ibid.*, pp. 1160–1168.

60. Memorandum of a Conversation, August 6, 1964, *FR, 1964–1968*, I, 643–645.

61. Memorandum for Record, September 15, 1964, Johnson Papers, NSF, Bundy Memos for the President, Box 2.

62. There are several accounts of U Thant's August 6 visit to Washington, each of which uses different language to describe Thant's impressions, but none completely confirms the secretary general's apparent belief that he had been given a specific go-ahead to arrange talks. In addition to Memorandum of Conversation, August 6, 1964, *FR, 1964–1968*, I, 643–645, see Kahin, *Intervention*, pp. 243–244; Thies, *When Governments Collide*, pp. 48–49; Walter Johnson, Editorial Note, in Walter Johnson, ed., *The Papers of Adlai E. Stevenson* (8 vols., Chicago: University of Chicago Press, 1972–1979), VIII, 661–665; Philip L. Geyelin, *Lyndon B. Johnson and the World* (New York: Praeger, 1966), pp. 202–213.

63. In addition to sources cited in note 62, see Harlan Cleveland, LBJ/OH, I, 19–23.

64. Cleveland, LBJ/OH, I, 23; Geyelin, *Johnson and the World*, p. 207.

65. Rusk, LBJ/OH, II, 7; Thies, *When Governments Collide*, pp. 50–51.

66. George Ball, LBJ/OH, I, 1–15; C. L. Sulzberger, *An Age of Mediocrity: Memoirs and Diaries, 1963–1972* (New York: Macmillan, 1973), p. 137.

67. For a good summary of Ball's various arguments in this memo and elsewhere, see Di Leo, *George Ball*, pp. 71–81. Quotation is from p. 75.

68. Young, *Vietnam Wars*, p. 127.

69. Ball, LBJ/OH, I, 16–17.

70. Bundy, unpublished manuscript, chapter 16, pp. 22, 11. (I have reversed the order of the sentences quoted.)

71. Memorandum of Conversation, October 16, 1964, Johnson Papers, NSF, Files of McGeorge Bundy, Boxes 18–19.

72. See note 65.

73. Rusk to Taylor, November 1, 1964, *FR, 1964–1968*, I, 878–879.

74. Cormier, *LBJ*, pp. 133–134.

75. "Remarks . . . ," November 2, 1964, *PP, 1963–1964*, II, 1578–1581; Young, *Vietnam Wars*, p. 130.

8. GROPING TOWARD A DECISION

1. Press Conference, November 28, 1964, *PP, 1963–1964*, pp. 1611–1620. I have reversed the order of the quotations in this instance.

2. Bundy, unpublished manuscript, chapter 18, p. 12.

3. Taylor to Rusk, November 10, 1964, *FR, 1964–1968*, I, 899–900; for other statements about the "pulmotor treatment," see Bui Diem with David Chanoff, *In the Jaws of History* (Boston: Houghton-Mifflin, 1987), pp. 128–129, and Bundy, unpublished manuscript, chapter 19, pp. 4–6.

4. Halberstam, *Best and the Brightest*, p. 507.

5. For a full account of the Working Group's sometimes tortuous efforts to develop these options, see Bundy, unpublished manuscript, chapter 18.

6. "Memorandum . . . ," November 27, 1964, *FR, 1964–1968*, I, 958–960; W. P. Bundy, Draft Position Paper, November 29, 1964, *Pentagon Papers: GE*, III, 678–683.

7. Memorandum for the Secretary, January 6, 1965, *Pentagon Papers: GE*, III, 684–686.

8. This paragraph is taken from two sets of notes of the December 1 meeting. John McNaughton's notes are reproduced in *FR, 1964–1968*, I, 965–969, while McGeorge Bundy's more cryptic notes are in Bundy Papers, Box 1.

9. *Ibid.*

10. Instructions to Ambassador Taylor, December 3, 1964, *ibid.*, pp. 974–978; Kahin, *Intervention*, pp. 253–255.

11. U.S. Senate, Foreign Relations Committee, *Executive Sessions of the Senate Foreign Relations Committee (Historical Series)*, XVI, 88th cong., 2d sess., 1964 (Washington: GPO, 1988), 368.

12. *Ibid.*, pp. 368–369.

13. Kahin, *Intervention*, p. 255.

14. *Ibid.*, and Rusk to State Department, December 16, 1964, Johnson Papers, NSF, Subject Files, Box 24.

15. Memorandum of Conversation, December 13, 1964, *ibid.*, NSF, International Travel, Boxes 33–34.

16. Busby to Johnson, December 4, 1964, marked "Never Sent," Johnson Papers, Office Files of Horace Busby, Box 52.

17. Busby to Johnson, December 18, 1964, *ibid.*

18. Cater to Johnson, December 30, 1964, Johnson Papers, Office Files of Douglass Cater, Box 13.

19. Cater to Johnson, December 8, 1964, *ibid.*

20. "Confidential Memo on Turner Catledge's Conversation with President Johnson," December 15, 1964, Krock Papers, Box 1.

21. Gibbons, *U.S. Government and Vietnam War*, part 2, p. 384.

22. Halberstam, *Best and the Brightest*, p. 507.

23. Nguyen Cao Ky, *Twenty Years and Twenty Days* (New York: Stein & Day, 1976), p. 50.

24. *Ibid.*, p. 52.

25. *Ibid.*, p. 53.

26. *Pentagon Papers: GE*, II, 346–347.

27. *Ibid.*

28. Westmoreland, *Soldier Reports*, p. 94.

29. *Ibid.*, pp. 94–95.

30. Kahin, *Intervention*, pp. 258–259.

31. Johnson to Taylor, December 30, 1964, *FR, 1964–1968*, I, 1057–1059.

32. See, for example, Sharp, *Strategy for Defeat.*

33. Taylor to Johnson, January 6, 1965, Cable #2052, Johnson Papers, NSF, NSC Histories, Box 40.

34. For the elaboration of this argument, see Krepinevich, *Army and Vietnam.*

35. Taylor to Johnson, January 6, 1965, Cable #2055, Johnson Papers, NSF, NSC Histories, Box 40. Italics added.

36. Taylor to Johnson, January 6, 1965, Cable #2058, Johnson Papers, NSF, NSC Histories, Box 40.

37. Quoted in Halberstam, *Best and the Brightest*, p. 500.

38. Westmoreland, *Soldier Reports*, pp. 96–98.

39. *PP, 1965*, I, 40–42; II, 634–635.

40. Johnson to Taylor, January 7, 1965, Johnson Papers, NSF, NSC Histories, Box 40.

41. Taylor to Johnson, January 7, 1965, and Rusk to Taylor, January 14, 1965, *ibid.*

42. Gibbons, *U.S. Government and Vietnam War*, part 2, pp. 400–401.

43. Kahin, *Intervention*, p 272.

44. *Ibid.*

45. "Memorandum for the President," January 27, 1965, Johnson Papers, NSF, NSC Histories, Box 40.

46. *Ibid.*

47. *Ibid.*, italics added.

48. Johnson to Taylor, January 27, 1965, *ibid.*

49. Bundy to Taylor, January 28, 1965, *ibid.* It is significant that the first "signal" that the Phase I, Phase II sequence had begun was resumption of the De Soto patrols. At the time of the Gulf of Tonkin crisis, the administration argued that these were basically routine intelligence-gathering missions. Quite clearly they were intended, both in the summer of 1964 and in early 1965, as evidence of a willingness to carry the war to the Democratic Republic of Vietnam.

50. Westmoreland, *Soldier Reports*, p. 115.

51. Bromley Smith to Johnson, quoting Bundy, February 4, 1965, Johnson Papers, NSF, International Travel, Boxes 28–29.

52. Kahin, *Intervention*, pp. 276–277.

53. Summary Record of National Security Council Meeting, February 10, 1965, Johnson Papers, NSF, NSC Meetings, Box 1.

54. Johnson, *Vantage Point*, p. 122.

55. Summary Notes of NSC Meeting, February 6, 1965, *ibid.* Another account of this meeting has the president asking Mansfield directly what he should do—and being totally surprised at the response. "I think you should negotiate, Mr. President." Johnson recoiled at this and instead of attempting to draw out the majority leader, launched into an emotional reply about our men dying while we sat still with our hands behind our backs. Mansfield had felt compelled to speak his mind, but he had not wanted to stir up LBJ before the NSC, where, he certainly understood, the president felt least confident of his opinions. His letter to Johnson a day or so later tried very hard to move their relationship back to a calmer level. Mansfield was no doubt correct in feeling that the least effective way of persuading Lyndon Johnson was by open confrontation, but his well-reasoned memos to Kennedy and LBJ were no more successful. For the confrontation, see William Bundy, unpublished manuscript, chapter 22B, p. 6.

56. Johnson, *Vantage Point,* p. 125.

57. Summary Notes of NSC Meeting, February 8, 1965, 10:30 a.m., Johnson Papers, NSC Minutes, Box 1.

58. Rowan, *Breaking Barriers,* pp. 268, 271. For a similar comment about LeMay, and Johnson's claim he was protecting everyone against the general as much as the Viet Cong, see Galbraith, *A Life in Our Times,* p. 479.

59. Bundy, "Memorandum for the President," February 7, 1965, Johnson Papers, NSF, NSC Histories, Box 41. Bundy's use of the royal "we" in this memorandum is certainly one of the more interesting developments in the evolution of American policy in Vietnam. He speaks as a viceroy might in reporting back to the seat of power.

60. Halberstam, *Best and the Brightest,* p. 533.

61. Public opinion polls eventually showed broad support for the bombing, but the way in which pollsters ask their questions often determines the answer. In the immediate aftermath of the first raid on North Vietnam, McGeorge Bundy reported that telegrams to the White House were running at more than twelve to one against government policy. The national security adviser offered several explanations, but concluded, "We have an education problem that bears close watching and more work." McGeorge Bundy to Johnson, February 9, 1965, Johnson Papers, NSF, NSC Histories, Box 40; Bundy, unpublished manuscript, chapter 22, p. 11.

62. Mansfield to Johnson, February 8, 1965, Johnson Papers, NSF, Name Files, Box 6.

63. *Ibid.*

64. Bundy, unpublished manuscript, chapter 21, pp. 7–20.

65. Sullivan to Rusk, January 29, 1965, Johnson Papers, NSF, International Travel, Boxes 28–29.

66. Typical was Dean Rusk's statement to a congressional briefing session about the origins of the war. "President Eisenhower decided that it was necessary for us to give substantial economic and material and military support to South Vietnam to prevent its being overrun from the North, because the North had left behind cadres of Communist cells and were trying even in 1954 and 1955 to make it impossible for South Vietnam to survive as a sovereign state." Nothing in the 1954 agreement envisioned two permanent sovereign states in Vietnam. Congressional Briefing, February 16, 1965, Johnson Papers, Congressional Briefings, Box 1.

67. Bundy, unpublished manuscript, chapter 23, pp. 13–14.

68. See Central Intelligence Agency, "The Kosygin Delegation to North Vietnam," February 1, 1965, Johnson Papers, NSF, NSC Histories, Box 40.

69. Gibbons, *U.S. Government and Vietnam War,* part 3, pp. 100–101.

70. Kahin, *Intervention,* p. 279. An intriguing side effect of the Vietnam War was its role in furthering the Franco-Russian entente that de Gaulle desired. As one observer wrote, "The blossoming *rapprochement* with Moscow gave de Gaulle still greater freedom of movement; the role of an endlessly moving figure in the eternal ballet was now his." See John Newhouse, *De Gaulle and the Anglo-Saxons* (New York: Viking, 1970), p. 278.

71. Harold M. Wilson, *The Labour Government, 1964–1970* (London: Weidenfeld and Nicolson, 1971), pp. 79–80.

72. *Ibid.*

73. Congressional Briefing, February 23, 1965, Johnson Papers, Congressional Briefings, Box 1.

74. Memorandum of Conversation, February 19, 1965, Johnson Papers, NSF, Country Files, France, Box 171.

75. Congressional Reception, February 11, 1965, Johnson Papers, Congressional Briefings, Box 1.

76. Bundy to Johnson, February 19, 1965, Johnson Papers, NSF, NSC Histories, Box 40.

77. Memorandum of Meeting, February 17, 1965, Johnson Papers, Meeting Notes File, Box 2.
78. *PP, 1965*, I, 131–139.
79. Young, *Vietnam Wars*, p. 137.
80. Minutes of NSC Meeting, February 18, 1965, Johnson Papers, NSF, NSC Meetings, Box 1.
81. Kahin, *Intervention*, p. 295.
82. Memorandum of Conversation, February 19, 1965, Johnson Papers, NSF, Country Files, France, Box 171.
83. Bundy to Johnson, February 16, 1965, Johnson Papers, Bundy Memos for the President, Box 2.
84. Kahin, *Intervention*, pp. 294–303.
85. *Ibid.*, p 305.
86. Johnson, *Vantage Point*, p. 132.
87. Claudia T. Johnson, *White House Diary*, pp. 248–249.

9. THE JOHNSON DOCTRINE

1. Goodwin, *Remembering America*, p. 378.
2. Admiral U.S. Grant Sharp, for example, would always believe that the way the bombing campaign was conducted displayed to the enemy a "fatal lack of will . . . at the highest level of our government. . . ." Instead of using America's vast technological superiority to make our wishes prevail, Washington adopted a go-slow approach that allowed the North Vietnamese to cease worrying about the extent of U.S. power and to prepare their defenses. *Strategy for Defeat*, p. 70.
3. Handwritten Draft, February 12, 1965, Johnson Papers, NSF, Bundy Files, Box 17.
4. *Ibid.*
5. Paterson, *Kennedy's Quest*, p. 11.
6. Cooper, *Lost Crusade*, pp. 264–266.
7. *Ibid.*
8. Wilson, *Labour Government*, pp. 85–86.
9. "Commencement Address at Catholic University," June 6, 1965, *PP, 1965*, II, 640–644.
10. Brian Van DeMark, *Into the Quagmire: Lyndon Johnson and the Escalation of the Vietnam War* (New York: Oxford University Press, 1991), pp. 94–95.
11. Transcript of Congressional Reception, March 2, 1965, Johnson Papers, Congressional Briefings, Box 1.
12. *Ibid.*
13. *Ibid.*
14. "Johnson Report Outline," March 14, 1965, Johnson Papers, NSF, NSC Histories, Box 40.
15. The fullest account of General Johnson's report is in Gibbons, *U.S. Government and Vietnam War*, part 3, pp. 166–168.
16. *Ibid.*
17. Krepinevich, *Army and Vietnam*, pp. 140–143.
18. Taylor to Rusk, cables 2888 and 2889, March 8, 1965, Johnson Papers, NSF, NSC Histories, Box 40.
19. Taylor, *Swords and Plowshares*, pp. 341–343; Halberstam, *Best and the Brightest*, pp. 566–567.
20. Bundy to Johnson, March 6, 1965, Johnson Papers, NSF, NSC Histories, Box 40.
21. *Ibid.*
22. March 7, 1965.
23. "Memorandum for Discussion," March 16, 1965, Johnson Papers, NSF, NSC Histories, Box 40.
24. *Ibid.*
25. Copy of Taylor cable 3003, March 16, 1965, *ibid.*
26. Diem, *In the Jaws*, pp. 130–135.
27. Memorandum for the President, March 20, 1965, Johnson Papers, Files of McGeorge Bundy, Memos to the President, Box 3.

28. "Vietnam—what is our interest there and our object," March 22, 1965, Johnson Papers, NSF, Files of McGeorge Bundy, Box 17. During this same period, Assistant Secretary of Defense John McNaughton sent Robert McNamara several memoranda that reflected the same concerns as those expressed by Bundy. In one, the most famous, McNaughton argued that American objectives could be listed as 70 percent to avoid a humiliating U.S. defeat and thus to our reputation as a guarantor, 20 percent to keep South Vietnam out of Chinese hands, and 10 percent to permit the people of South Vietnam to enjoy a better, freer way of life. "It is essential—however badly SEA may go over the next 1–3 years—that U.S. emerge as a 'good doctor.' We must have kept promises, been tough, taken risks, gotten bloodied and hurt the enemy very badly." For a discussion, see Kahin, *Intervention*, pp. 310–313.

29. Handwritten Notes on the Agenda, March 23, 1965, *ibid.*, Boxes 18–19.

30. Statement, March 25, 1965, *PP, 1965*, I, 319; for a very similar statement to Mexican newspaper editors in 1918, promising them economic development after the issues of the revolution had been settled according to American ideas, see Lloyd C. Gardner, *Wilson and Revolutions* (Philadelphia: Lippincott, 1975).

31. Moyers to Johnson, March 25, 1965, *ibid.*, Reference File, Vietnam, Box 1.

32. For the response the night Johnson delivered this speech, see Califano, *Triumph and Tragedy*, pp. 55–57; Reuther to Johnson, March 16, 1965, Johnson Papers, Handwriting File, Box 6; E. Frederic Morrow to Johnson, March 17, 1965, *ibid.*

33. *PP, 1965*, I, 332–333.

34. Summary Notes of NSC Meeting, March 26, 1965, Johnson Papers, NSF, NSC Histories, Box 1.

35. "Points for Vietnam Discussion," March 26, 1965, and "Statement of Senator George McGovern to President Johnson: Private Conversation at the White House," March 26, 1965, both in McGovern Papers, Box 11.

36. *Ibid.*

37. Memorandum for the President, March 29, 1965, Johnson Papers, NSF, Subjects, Box 42.

38. Bundy to Rusk, March 26, 1965, Johnson Papers, NSF, Country File, Vietnam, Box 15.

39. Cooper to Bundy, n.d. [March 1965], *ibid.*

40. Unsigned Memorandum, February [?] 1965, *ibid.*, NSF, International Travel, Boxes 28–29. The memo has notes in McGeorge Bundy's handwriting, but the basic themes were common enough in Bundy's day and in that of his successor, Walt Rostow.

41. Rostow to Bundy, March 30, 1965, *ibid.*, NSF, Country File, Vietnam, Box 200.

42. *Ibid.*

43. Rostow to Rusk, March 29, 1965, *ibid.*, White House Central File, Confidential File, Box 44.

44. Memorandum for the President, April 1, 1965, *ibid.*, Bundy Memos, Box 3.

45. *Ibid.* For the background to this memo, see Averell Harriman to Bundy, April 1, 1965, with enclosure, Harriman Papers, Box 439. Harriman stressed that the idea could have appeal not only to "liberals" but to the interested Communist nations as well, suggesting to the North Vietnamese that they could have a chance at economic development free from Chinese domination, and to the Chinese that they could have a buffer state. Russia would profit from assurances that China would not expand southward. As usual, such cold war "realism" ill-suited the actual situation in Vietnam. It was just not going to be possible to submerge the crisis there into a regional economic scheme. See also Chester Cooper to Bundy, April, 1, 1965, Johnson Papers, NSF, Country File, Vietnam, Box 200.

46. Jack Valenti's Notes re Johns Hopkins Speech, *ibid.*, Statements File, Box 143.

47. Bundy to LBJ, March 28, 1965, Johnson Papers, NSF, Country File, Vietnam, Box 15.

48. Jack Valenti Notes, "The Johns Hopkins Speech," n.d., *ibid.*, Statements File, Box 143; Rutherford Poats to Valenti, March 26, 1965, *ibid.*, NSF, Country File, Vietnam, Box 15; Karnow, *Vietnam*, p. 418; Goodwin, *Remembering America*, pp. 272–278.

49. Valenti to LBJ, March 29, 1965, Johnson Papers, Handwriting File, Box 6.

50. Goodwin, *Remembering America*, pp. 365–366.

51. "The War in Vietnam," Draft #1, Johnson Papers, Statements File, Box 143.

52. The Johns Hopkins speech is reprinted in a useful collection of documents that provide the context in U.S. Senate, Foreign Relations Committee, *Background Information Relating to Southeast Asia and Vietnam*, Committee Print, 90th cong., 1st sess. (Washington: GPO, 1967), pp. 148–153.

53. Valenti Notes, "Johns Hopkins Speech," n.d., Johnson Papers, Statements File, Box 143.

54. *Ibid.*

55. Cooper to Bundy, April 6, 1965, *ibid.*, NSF, Country File, Vietnam, Box 200.

56. *PP, 1965*, I, 394–399.

57. *Ibid.*

58. *Ibid.*

59. *Ibid.*

60. This and subsequent quotations are from Goldschmidt, "The Development of the U.S. South," attached to LBJ to Goldschmidt, September 24, 1963, Johnson Papers, Confidential Files, "Mekong River," Box 167.

61. LBJ to Goldschmidt, September 24, 1963, *ibid.*

62. Valenti Notes, "Johns Hopkins Speech," n.d., Johnson Papers, Statements File, Box 143.

63. Valenti Notes, *ibid.*, Statements File, Box 143; Bundy to LBJ, April, 6, 1965, *ibid.*, Diary Backup, Box 15.

64. Bundy to LBJ, *ibid.*, April 6, 1965, *ibid.*, Diary Backup, Box 15.

65. Bundy to Johnson, April 6, 1965, *ibid.*, Diary Backup, Box 15.

66. Ronald Steel, *Walter Lippmann and the American Century* (Boston: Atlantic–Little, Brown, 1980), pp. 562–563.

67. *Ibid.*

68. *Ibid.*, p. 564.

69. Chester L. Cooper, "Memorandum for the Record," April 13, 1965, Johnson Papers, NSF, NSC Histories, Box 41.

70. Karnow, *Vietnam*, p. 419.

71. Miller, *Lyndon*, p. 466.

72. Kearns, *Lyndon Johnson*, p. 267.

73. Cater to Johnson, April 8, 1965, *ibid.*, Office of the President Files, Cater Memos, Box 13.

74. *New York Times*, April 8, 1965.

75. *Washington Post*, April 14, 1965.

76. "The Works of Peace," Remarks, April 8, 1965, McGovern Papers, Box 11.

77. Memorandum to the President, April 10, 1965, Johnson Papers, Bundy Files, Memos to the President, Box 3.

78. *Ibid.*

79. *Washington Post*, April 13, 1965.

80. Memorandum of Conversation, April 8, 1965, Johnson Papers, NSF, Name File, The Vice-President, Box 4. Humphrey forwarded a copy of this memorandum to Dean Rusk.

81. *Ibid.*

82. Halberstam, *Best and the Brightest*, p. 572.

10. THE DEMANDING DREAM

1. "Memorandum," April 22, 1965, Krock Papers, Box 1. Succeeding quotations are from this source as well.

2. Unsigned Memo, "Key Elements for Discussion," April 1, 1965, Johnson Papers, NSF, NSC Histories, Box 41; Van DeMark, *Into the Quagmire*, pp. 107–111.

3. McCone to Secretary of State, et al., April 2, 1965, Johnson Papers, NSF, NSC Histories, Box 41.

4. U.S. Senate, Foreign Relations Committee, *Executive Sessions* (Historical Series), XVII, 1965, 89th cong., 1st sess. (Washington: GPO, 1990), 394.

5. Taylor to Rusk, April 14, 1965, Johnson Papers, NSF, NSC Histories, Box 41.

6. Memorandum for the President, April 14, 1965, *ibid.*

7. Joint State-Defense Message, April 15, 1965, *ibid.*

8. Bundy to Taylor, April 15, 1965, *ibid.*

9. Bundy to Donald Graham, April 20, 1965, Johnson Papers, Files of McGeorge Bundy, Boxes 18–19.

10. Van DeMark, *Into the Quagmire*, pp. 126–127.

11. Sullivan to Rusk, April 21, 1965, Johnson Papers, NSF, NSC Histories, Box 41.

12. Van DeMark, *Into the Quagmire*, p. 127; Ball to Johnson, April 21, 1965, Johnson Papers, NSF, NSC Histories, Box 41; Gibbons, *U.S. Government and Vietnam War*, part 3, pp. 235–237, 240; Jack Valenti [?] to Johnson, April 23, 1965, Johnson Papers, Reference File, Vietnam, Box 1.

13. Ball, *Past Has Another Pattern*, p. 393.

14. Memorandum of Telephone Conversation, April 23, 1965, Harriman Papers, Box 583.

15. Memorandum of Conversation, April 26, 1965, *ibid.*; Harriman to Johnson, *ibid.*

16. Press Conference, April 27, 1965, *PP, 1965*, I, 448–449.

17. Bundy to Johnson, April 26, 1965, Johnson Papers, Bundy Memos to the President, Box 3.

18. Bruce to Secretary of State, April 29, 1965, *ibid.*, NSF, Country File, Box 207.

19. Rusk to American Embassy, London, May 1, 1965, *ibid.*, NSF, Country File, United Kingdom, Box 207.

20. David Klein to McGeorge Bundy, April 29, 1965, *ibid.*, NSF, Country File, France, Box 171.

21. Gibbons, *U.S. Government and Vietnam War*, part 3, p. 240.

22. *Ibid.*

23. *Ibid.*, 238.

24. For a brief review of the crisis in the cold war context, see LaFeber, *America, Russia and the Cold War*, pp. 244–247.

25. *Ibid.*, and see B. A. Adams to Gordon Chase, May 12, 1965, with enclosure, "The Communist Role in the Dominican Revolt," Johnson Papers, NSF, Country File, Dominican Republic, Boxes 49–51, 52–54.

26. LaFeber, *America, Russia and the Cold War*, p. 246; see also Young, *Vietnam Wars*, pp. 150–151.

27. Ball, LBJ/OH, II, 33–34; Kahin, *Intervention*, p. 321.

28. Ball, LBJ/OH, II, 33–34.

29. Mohr, "Memo on Chat with Johnson," April 29, 1965, Krock Papers, Box 1.

30. *Ibid.*

31. *Ibid.*

32. LaFeber, *America, Russia and the Cold War*, p. 246.

33. "Radio and Television Report to the American People on the Situation in the Dominican Republic," May 2, 1965, *PP, 1965*, I, 469–474.

34. Gibbons, *U.S. Government and Vietnam War*, part 3, p. 242; "Remarks to the Committee Members . . . ," May 4, 1965, *PP, 1965*, I, 484–492.

35. Gibbons, *U.S. Government and Vietnam War*, part 3, p. 242.

36. *Ibid.*, p. 248.

37. Bundy to the President, May 5, 1965, Johnson Papers, Files of McGeorge Bundy, Memos to the President, Box 3.

38. On Krock's efforts to win favor with Johnson, see Horace Busby to Johnson, May 7, 1965, Johnson Papers, Office Files of the President, Busby Memos, Box 51.

39. *New York Times*, May 9, 1965.

40. Bohlen to Secretary of State, May 4, 1965, Johnson Papers, NSF, Country File, France, Box 171.

41. *Ibid.*

42. Johnson to Taylor, May 10, 1965, *ibid.*, NSF, NSC Histories, Box 41.

43. Kahin, *Intervention*, pp. 330–331.

44. Quoted in John Prados, *The Keepers of the Keys* (New York: William Morrow, 1991), p. 227.

45. "Memorandum for Record," May 13, 1965, Johnson Papers, NSF, Name File, Box 3.

46. Rostow to Rusk, May 17, 1965, *ibid.*, NSF, Files of McGeorge Bundy, Boxes 18–19.

47. Jack Valenti's Notes, May 16, 1965, *ibid.*, Meeting Notes File, Box 2.

48. *Washington Post*, May 23, 1965.

49. Kearns, *Lyndon Johnson*, p. 313.

50. Dugger, *Politician*, p. 42.

51. *Washington Post*, May 23, 1965.

52. Diary Entry, May 26, 1965, Lilienthal Papers, Box 209.

53. Bundy to Johnson, May 28, 1965, Johnson Papers, NSF, Vietnam, Southeast Asian Development.

54. Message to Congress, June 1, 1965, *PP, 1965*, II, 609–617.

11. THE FIRST 100,000

1. Westmoreland to Admiral Sharp and General Wheeler, June 7, 1965, Johnson Papers, NSF, NSC Histories, Box 41.

2. "Summary Notes of 552nd NSC Meeting," June 11, 1965, Johnson Papers, NSF, NSC Meetings, Box 1.

3. Sharp, *Strategy for Defeat*, pp. 92–93.

4. Bundy, Memorandum for the President, June 3, 1965, Johnson Papers, Files of McGeorge Bundy, Memos for the President, Box 3. I have reversed the order of these sentences. Nearly thirty years later, Bundy admitted that "We did misread the potential of the antiwar movement." But he insisted that it failed intellectually because it did not address the "real questions," which presumably had to do with what could be done when the other side was convinced of victory. Bundy then conflated his objections to intellectuals with his disdain for the *New York Times* editorial policy which asked the administration to negotiate, when there was nothing to negotiate. See Ted Gittinger, ed., *The Johnson Years: A Vietnam Roundtable* (Austin: Lyndon B. Johnson Library, 1993), p. 98.

5. See, for example, Larry Berman, *Planning a Tragedy: The Americanization of the War in Vietnam* (New York: W. W. Norton, 1982), and, on the other side, David M. Barrett, *Uncertain Warriors: Lyndon Johnson and His Vietnam Advisers* (Lawrence: University of Kansas Press, 1993).

6. Hobart Rowen, *Self-Inflicted Wounds: From LBJ's Guns and Butter to Reagan's Voodoo Economics* (New York: Times Books, 1994), p. 4; Goodwin, *Remembering America*, pp. 403–404.

7. News Conference of July 28, 1965, *PP, 1965*, II, 794–803.

8. *Ibid.*

9. Taylor to Rusk, June 5, 1965, Johnson Papers, NSF, NSC Histories, Box 41.

10. Most of what follows about this meeting is taken from Bundy's handwritten notes, June 5, 1965, Bundy Papers, Box 1; see also Van DeMark, *Into the Quagmire*, p. 152.

11. Van DeMark, *Into the Quagmire*, pp. 155–157; Reedy ran into major difficulties trying to contain the speculation. He met with reporters twice on June 9 to try to answer all the questions. See News Conferences, 12:10 and 4:35 p.m., June 9, 1965, Johnson Papers, NSF, NSC Histories, Box 41.

12. Charles Mohr, "Memo on Dean Rusk Luncheon with Reporters," June 10, 1965, Krock Papers, Box 1.

13. *Ibid.*

14. Mansfield to Johnson, June 9, 1965, Johnson Papers, Famous Name File, Box 6.

15. Ky, *Twenty Years and Twenty Days*, p. 65.

16. Van DeMark, *Into the Quagmire*, p. 154.

17. Ball, LBJ/OH, I, 33.

18. Gibbons, *U.S. Government and Vietnam War*, part 3, p. 288.

19. *Ibid.*

20. McGeorge Bundy's notes for this meeting are the principal source for what happened. They are rough jottings, never rethought into a typed memorandum. Bundy Papers, Box 1.

21. "Summary Notes of 552nd NSC Meeting," June 11, 1965, Johnson Papers, NSF, NSC Meetings, Box 1.

22. For background, see Henry F. Graff, *The Tuesday Cabinet: Deliberation and Decision on Peace and War Under Lyndon Johnson* (Englewood Cliffs, N.J.: Prentice-Hall, 1970). The original article that resulted from these interviews was "Decision in Vietnam: How Johnson Makes Foreign Policy," *New York Times Magazine*, July 4, 1965, pp. 4–5ff. What follows is taken, as cited, from either the article or the book. There are some very significant differences in places.

23. Graff, *Tuesday Cabinet.*, pp. 51–52.

24. *Ibid.*, p. 37.

25. *Ibid.*, pp. 42–43.

26. *Ibid.*, p. 48.

27. Graff, "Decision in Vietnam," p. 17. Bundy was troubled by the appearance of this colloquy, and wrote a letter to the *New York Times* which appeared on July 5, 1965, the day after Graff's article in the Sunday Magazine, protesting that he opposed such a view. "But . . . since coming to Washington, I have learned to understand better the emphasis which Mr. Acheson and others correctly place on the importance of responsible energy in the conduct of American foreign policy." *Tuesday Cabinet*, pp. 48–49. Graff later changed the wording of their exchange when the book was published in an apparent effort to ease Bundy's concern. His effort, like Bundy's emendation, only demonstrated how difficult it was to come up with a less controversial statement: "Bundy said he had come to accept also what he had learned from Dean Acheson—that, in

the final analysis, the United States was the locomotive at the head of mankind, and the rest of the world the caboose—*meaning, I thought,* that he was not expressing chauvinism but simply passing judgment on the usefulness to the world of American energies." Phrased this way, Graff appears to be answering Bundy's caveat with one of his own that could be read different ways: (1) Graff did not know what Bundy meant, or (2) Yes, I agree with Bundy's demurrer.

28. *Ibid.,* p. 55.

29. *Ibid.,* p. 56.

30. "Decision in Vietnam," p. 20; *Tuesday Cabinet,* p. 57.

31. *Tuesday Cabinet,* p. 58. Johnson had hitched a ride on a B-26 when it was attacked by eight Zeros. The tail gunner believed he might have shot one of the attackers down. It was the one combat mission he flew during his abbreviated tour of duty in the navy. He did receive a silver star for this "mission." See Dugger, *Politician,* p. 246.

32. Goodpaster, "Meeting with General Eisenhower 16 June 1965," Johnson Papers, NSF, Name File, Box 2.

33. Press Conference, June 17, 1965, *PP, 1965,* I, 669–685.

34. "Telcon: The President," June 14, 1965, Ball Papers, Box 7.

35. *Ibid.*

36. Di Leo, *George Ball,* p. 114.

37. "Memorandum for the President," June 18, 1965, Johnson Papers, NSF, NSC Histories, Box 42.

38. *Ibid.*

39. Johnson to Reston, June 19, 1965, with column of June 14 attached, Johnson Papers, Handwriting File, Box 8.

40. Telcon, June 21, 1965, Ball Papers, Box 7.

41. Telcon, June 24, 1965, Ball Papers, Box 7; Bruce to Rusk, June 22, 1965, Johnson Papers, NSF, Country File, United Kingdom, Box 207.

42. Unsigned Memo, "Meeting with the President," June 23, 1965, Johnson Papers, NSF, NSC Histories, Box 42.

43. Memorandum, "Pomfret with LBJ," June 24, 1965, Krock Papers, Box 1.

44. Undated draft statement. Johnson Papers, NSF, NSC Histories, Box 43. The draft was not used.

45. Berman, *Planning a Tragedy,* p. 108.

46. Kearns, *Lyndon Johnson, p. 253.*

47. McPherson to Johnson, "Thoughts on Bobby Kennedy and Loyalty," June 24, 1965, Johnson Papers, Office of the President Files, McPherson Memos, Box 7.

48. *Ibid.*

49. *Ibid.*

50. See the discussion in Shapley, *Promise and Power,* pp. 340–343.

51. McNamara, Memorandum for the President, June 26, 1965, Johnson Papers, NSF, NSC Histories, Box 43; Press Conference, June 17, 1965, *PP,* 1965, I, 669–685.

52. McNamara, Memorandum to the President, June 26, 1965, Johnson Papers, NSF, NSC Histories, Box 43.

53. Bundy to McNamara, June 30, 1965, Johnson Papers, NSF, NSC Histories, Box 43.

54. *Ibid.*

55. *Washington Post,* July 6, 1965.

56. Ball to Rusk, et al., June 28 and June 29, 1965, Johnson Papers, NSF, NSC Histories, Box 43.

57. Bundy to Johnson, June 27, 1965, Johnson Papers, NSF, Bundy Memos, Box 3.

58. Bundy to Johnson, June 30, 1965, Johnson Papers, NSF, Bundy Memos, Box 3.

59. Cooper to Bundy, June 30, 1965, Johnson Papers, NSF, NSC Histories, Box 43.

60. Bundy, unpublished manuscript, chapter 27, pp. 5–6.

61. Bundy, Memorandum, July 1, 1965, Johnson Papers, NSF, NSC Histories, Box 43.

62. Rusk to Johnson, July 1, 1965, Johnson Papers, NSF, NSC Histories, Box 43.

63. Graham to Johnson, July 11, 1965, Johnson Papers, Handwriting File, Box 8.

64. Wofford, *Of Kennedys and Kings,* pp. 317–318.

65. Bundy to Johnson, July 1, 1965, Johnson Papers, NSF, Bundy Memos, Box 4.

66. Gibbons, *U.S. Government and Vietnam War,* part 3, pp. 344–345.

67. *Ibid.*

68. *Ibid.*

69. Gilpatric to Bundy, July 9, 1965, Johnson Papers, NSF, NSC Histories, Box 43.

70. Walter Isaacson and Evan Thomas, *The Wise Men: Six Friends and the World They Made* (New York: Simon & Schuster, 1986), pp. 651–652; Brinkley, *Dean Acheson*, pp. 247–248.
71. Brinkley, *Dean Acheson*, p. 246. See also Di Leo, *George Ball*, p. 89.
72. Thus Brinkley in *Dean Acheson* writes: "Throughout the war, Acheson sounded one theme. Vietnam was like Korea, with only one glaring difference: unlike Johnson, Harry Truman had had the self-confidence and stamina to see his commitment through" (p. 252). Actually, Acheson did not urge Johnson to see it through when the Wise Men were summoned to Washington after the Tet debacle, but Brinkley's point illustrates a key aspect of the mind-set of the American cold war genro at the time of Johnson's decision.
73. McNaughton to Bundy, July 13, 1965, Johnson Papers, NSF, NSC Histories, Box 43.
74. Harry McPherson to Johnson, July 16, 1965, Johnson Papers, White House Aides, McPherson, Box 52.
75. Memorandum for the President, July 20, 1965, Johnson Papers, NSF, NSC Histories, Box 43.
76. *Ibid.*
77. *Ibid.*
78. "Cabinet Room, Wednesday, July 21, 1965," Johnson Papers, Meeting Notes File, Box 2.
79. Rudy Abramson, *Spanning the Century: The Life of Averell Harriman, 1891–1986* (New York: William Morrow, 1992), pp. 638–639. See also *New York Times*, July 17, 1965.
80. Bundy to Johnson, July 21, 1965, Johnson Papers, NSF, NSC Histories, Box 43.
81. Busby to Johnson, July 21, 1965, Johnson Papers, Office Files of Horace Busby, Box 3.
82. *Washington Post*, July 25, 1965.
83. Cabinet Room, July 22, 1965, Johnson Papers, Meeting Notes File, Box 2.
84. Cabinet Room, July 22, 1965, 3:00 p.m., Johnson Papers, Meeting Notes File, Box 2.
85. Handwritten Notes, July 22, 1965, Bundy Papers, Box 1.
86. Valenti to Johnson, July 22, 1965, 7:45 p.m., Johnson Papers, Office of the President Files, Box 12.
87. Shapley, *Promise and Power*, pp. 345–346; Sidey, *Very Personal Presidency*, pp. 230–234.
88. Telcon, Clark Clifford, July 23, 1965, Ball Papers, Box 7.
89. Camp David, July 25, 1965, Johnson Papers, Meeting Notes File, Box 2.
90. Clark Clifford, with Richard Holbrooke, *Counsel to the President: A Memoir* (New York: Random House, 1991), pp. 418–419; Shapley, *Promise and Power*, p. 347.
91. Shapley, *Promise and Power*, p. 345.
92. Summary Notes of 553rd Meeting of the National Security Council, July 27, 1965, Johnson Papers, NSC Meetings, Box 1.
93. Unsigned memorandum prepared in December 1968, Johnson Papers, Meeting Notes File, Box 2.
94. Congressional Leadership Meeting, July 28, 1965, Johnson Papers, Meeting Notes File, Box 2.
95. Rowland Evans and Robert Novak, "Johnson's Home Front," *Washington Post*, July 30, 1965.
96. Memorandum, prepared in December 1968, Johnson Papers, Meeting Notes File, Box 2.
97. *Washington Post*, July 31, 1965, and *New York Times*, July 29, 1965.
98. Alsop and Lippmann columns, *Washington Post*, July 30, 1965.
99. Telcon, July 30, 1965, Ball Papers, Box 7.
100. Telcon, July 29, 1965, Ball Papers, Box 7.
101. Reuther to Johnson, June 15, 1965, *ibid.*
102. Johnson to Reuther, July 7, 1965, Johnson Papers, Handwriting File, Box 8.

12. A FEARFUL SYMMETRY

1. Cater, "Memorandum for Mr. Bundy," July 28, 1965, Johnson Papers, Reference File, Vietnam, Box 1.
2. *Ibid.*
3. The following paragraphs on the August 3, 1965, meeting are taken from handwritten notes on Cater's memorandum to Bundy, cited above, and from Gordon Chase, "Memorandum

for Record: August 3, Dinner Meeting on the Information Problem," August 4, 1965, Johnson Papers, Confidential File, PR 18, Box 83.

4. Lodge, Memorandum for the President, August 11, 1965, Johnson Papers, NSF, Name File, Box 2.

5. Rowan, *Breaking Barriers*, pp. 272–273.

6. Johnson to Mrs. Clifford Long (drafted by Harry McPherson), September 8, 1965, Johnson Papers, Files of White House Aides, McPherson, Box 28. Emphasis added.

7. Califano, *Triumph and Tragedy*, p. 58.

8. *Ibid.*, and Allen J. Matusow, *The Unraveling of America: A History of Liberalism in the 1960s* (New York: Harper & Row, 1984), pp. 183–184.

9. Matusow, *Unraveling of America*, pp. 184–185.

10. Goldman, *Tragedy*, p. 315.

11. Hugh Davis Graham, *The Civil Rights Era: Origins and Development of National Policy* (New York: Oxford University Press, 1990), pp. 24–25.

12. Goodwin, *Remembering America*, p. 417.

13. Ackley to Johnson, July 30, 1965, quoted in Matusow, *Unraveling of America*, pp. 156–157.

14. Califano quoted in Matusow, *Unraveling of America*, p. 196.

15. Califano, *Triumph and Tragedy*, p. 62.

16. *Ibid.*, p. 361.

17. *Ibid.*, pp. 64–65.

18. Rowan, *Breaking Barriers*, p. 258; Garrow, *Bearing the Cross*, p. 440; Irwin Unger and Debra Unger, *Turning Point: 1968* (New York: Scribner, 1988), p. 176.

19. Lemann, *Promised Land*, pp. 236–237; Garrow, *Bearing the Cross*, pp. 452–455, 465–466.

20. Garrow, *Bearing the Cross*, pp. 453.

21. Lemann, *Promised Land*, p. 236.

22. Kearns, *Lyndon Johnson*, p. 305.

23. Unger, *Turning Point*, p. 39.

24. Moynihan, *Maximum Feasible Misunderstanding*, pp. 144–146; David Zarefsky, *President Johnson's War on Poverty: Rhetoric and Reality* (University, Ala.: University of Alabama Press, 1986), p. 120.

25. Graham, *Civil Rights Era*, p. 209; Katz, *Undeserving Poor*, pp. 24–25

26. Lemann, *Promised Land*, p. 177.

27. Sleeper, *Closest of Strangers*, p. 90.

28. *Ibid.*, p. 92.

29. Hayes Redmon to Bill Moyers, November 27, 1965, Johnson Papers, Files of White House Aides, Moyers, Box 11.

30. Hayes Redmon to Bill Moyers, November 30, 1965, *ibid.*

31. Dean Rusk, with Richard Rusk and Daniel S. Papp, *As I Saw It* (New York: W. W. Norton, 1990), p. 422.

32. Moynihan, *Maximum Feasible Misunderstanding*, p. 148.

33. Robert Lampman, Interview, LBJ/OH, I, 37; Lemann, *Promised Land*, p. 170.

34. Ackley, LBJ/OH, II, 1–5.

35. Notes of a Telephone Conversation, November 18, 1965, Fowler Papers, Box 8B.

36. McPherson to Moyers, December 13, 1965, Johnson Papers, White House Aides Files, McPherson, Box 41.

37. Califano, *Triumph and Tragedy*, pp. 106–111.

38. *Ibid.*, pp. 112–117.

39. Matusow, *Unraveling of America*, pp. 160–161.

40. Annual Message on the State of the Union, January 12, 1966, *PP, 1966*, I, 3–12.

41. "Talking Points for the President," February 7, 1966, Johnson Papers, NSF, International Meetings, Boxes 1 and 2.

42. Ky, *Twenty Years and Twenty Days*, pp. 83–84.

13. THE PAUSE THAT FAILED

1. Diem, *In the Jaws*, p. 153.

2. *Ibid.*, p. 154.

3. Telcon, October 7, 1965, Ball Papers, Box 7.

4. Krepinevich, *Army and Vietnam*, pp. 169–170.

5. Shapley, *Promise and Power*, pp. 356–361.

6. Wilson, *Labour Government*, p. 187.

7. Bundy to Johnson, November 5, 1965, Johnson Papers, NSF, Country File, Vietnam, Boxes 92–95; Johnson, *Vantage Point*, p. 234.

8. Townsend Hoopes, *The Limits of Intervention* (New York: David McKay, 1969), p. 125.

9. Kahin, *Intervention*, pp. 244–245.

10. Telcons with Johnson, November 16, 1965, and Rusk, November 17, 1965, Ball Papers, Box 7.

11. Telcon with Bundy, November 19, 1965, Ball Papers, Box 7; Hayes Redmon to Moyers, November 26 and November 27, 1965, Johnson Papers, White House Aides, Moyers, Box 11.

12. See Charles DeBenedetti (Charles Chatfield, Assisting Author), *An American Ordeal: The Antiwar Movement of the Vietnam Era* (Syracuse: Syracuse University Press, 1990), pp. 124–128.

13. *Ibid.*, p. 129, and Shapley, *Promise and Power*, pp. 353–355.

14. DeBenedetti, *American Ordeal*, p. 130.

15. *Ibid.*, p. 132.

16. *New York Times*, December 1, 1965.

17. *Ibid.*, December 3, 1965.

18. *Ibid.*

19. Bundy, unpublished manuscript, chapter 33, p. 18.

20. Armstrong to Bundy, November 17, 1965, Armstrong Papers, Box 109.

21. Bundy, unpublished manuscript, chapter 33, p. 18.

22. Bundy to Johnson, November 27, 1965, Johnson Papers, NSF, Country Files, Vietnam, Boxes 92–95.

23. Bundy to Johnson, December 4, 1965, *ibid.*

24. This and following paragraphs on the December 17 meeting are taken from an edited version of Jack Valenti's notes in Johnson Papers, Meeting Notes File, Box 2; and Valenti, *Very Human President*, pp. 223–228. There are important differences in what has been omitted from each account.

25. These paragraphs on the December 18 meeting, except where noted, are based on a typed transcript, Johnson Papers, Meeting Notes File, Box 2; and Valenti, *Very Human President*, pp. 228–240.

26. Typed Transcript, December 18, 1965, Johnson Papers, Meeting Notes File, Box 2. The account of McNamara's important statement varies in Valenti, *Very Human President*, p. 233, and in Clifford, *Counsel to the President*, p. 434. Valenti records that McNamara said they must find "alternative solutions," while Clifford has the defense secretary saying they must "search" for a diplomatic solution.

27. McNamara's testimony at the libel trial *Westmoreland v. CBS*, cited in Bob Brewin and Sydney Shaw, *Vietnam on Trial: Westmoreland vs. CBS* (New York: Atheneum, 1987), p. 102.

28. *Very Human President*, p. 240. There remains some question when the pause was decided upon, however. Clark Clifford talks about another meeting on December 19, 1965, when the matter was finally decided. *Counsel to the President*, p. 436. And it is clear from the minutes of yet another meeting on December 21 that Johnson was still wavering. Minutes of Meeting in the Cabinet Room, Johnson Papers, Office of the President Files, Box 13.

29. Bundy to Johnson, December 27 and December 28, 1965, Johnson Papers, NSF, Country Files, Vietnam, Boxes 92–95; Telcon, December 28, 1965, Ball Papers, Box 7.

30. "Notes on Telcon with the President," December 28, 1965, Harriman Papers, Box 583.

31. "Memorandum for Personal Files," December 28, 1965, *ibid.*, Box 499.

32. Telcon, December 28, 1965, Ball Papers, Box 7.

33. Johnson, *Vantage Point*, p. 239.

34. Lodge to Rusk, January 4, 1966, enclosed in Bundy to Johnson, January 4, 1966, Johnson Papers, NSF, Country Files, Vietnam, Boxes 92–95.

35. Bundy to Johnson, January 3, 1966, with enclosed draft, January 3, 1966, *ibid.*

36. "Notes on Talk with McGeorge Bundy," January 22, 1966, Harriman Papers, Box 437.

37. Telcon, January 8, 1966, Ball Papers, Box 7.

38. See Telcon, January 11, 1966, Ball Papers, Box 7; and McNamara's private remarks at a dinner given by Arthur Schlesinger, Jr. His objective, he said, was "withdrawal with honor." "He seemed deeply oppressed and concerned at the prospect of indefinite escalation. Our

impression was that he feared the resumption of bombing might well put us on the slippery slide." Schlesinger, *Robert Kennedy*, pp. 734–735.

39. Notes by Valenti, "Meeting in the Cabinet Room," January 22 and January 24, 1966, Johnson Papers, Office of the President File, Box 13.

40. There are at least two sets of notes of this meeting, neither obviously complete. My quotation here is from an unsigned transcript headed "Meeting in Cabinet Room—January 25, 1966," Johnson Papers, Diary Back-Up, Box 28. A copy of the paper Mansfield brought with him is in the same location. Another set of minutes, transcribed from Valenti's notes, also headed "Meeting in Cabinet Room," January 25, 1966, is in *ibid.*, Office of the President Files, Box 13.

41. In the paper, dated January 24, 1966, and located in Johnson Papers, Diary Back-Up, Box 28, this sentence is scratched out, whether by Mansfield or by one of Johnson's aides cannot be determined. Perhaps, however, the "scratching" was done by one of the note takers present, who observed that Mansfield had self-censored this key point.

42. Valenti Notes, January 25, 1966, Johnson Papers, Office Files of the President, Box 13. The word "enough" in parentheses is taken from the other set of notes, in *ibid.*, Diary Back-Up, Box 28. There are other important differences in these notes, e.g., "We killed many, many civilians in World War II and nobody really got exercised about that. I would rather see civilians killed than have American boys die."

43. Valenti Notes, January 25, 1966, Johnson Papers, Office of the President Files, Box 13.

44. Kai Bird, *The Chairman: John J. McCloy, The Making of the American Establishment* (New York: Simon & Schuster, 1992) p. 584.

45. Valenti Notes, "Meeting in Cabinet Room," January 28, 1966, *ibid.*

46. Valenti Notes, "Meeting in Cabinet Room," January 27, 1966, *ibid.* Emphasis added.

47. January 31, 1966.

48. Valenti Notes, "Meeting in President's Office," January 29, 1966, Johnson Papers, Office of the President Files, Box 13.

49. The text was reprinted in *New York Times*, January 29, 1966.

50. Cooper, *Lost Crusade*, p. 296.

51. "Talking Points for the President," February 7, 1966, Johnson Papers, NSF, International Meetings, Boxes 1–2.

52. Minutes, February 7, 1966. *ibid.*

53. Westmoreland, *Soldier Reports*, pp. 159–160.

54. Graff, *Tuesday Cabinet*, p. 102.

55. U.S. Senate, Foreign Relations Committee, *Hearings: Supplemental Foreign Assistance Fiscal Year 1966–Vietnam*, 89th cong. 2d sess. (Washington: GPO, 1966), p. 6.

56. *Ibid.*, p. 15.

57. *Ibid.*, pp. 74–75.

58. *Ibid.*, p. 77.

59. *Ibid.*, p. 302.

60. Kennan to Armstrong, February 3, 1966, Armstrong Papers, Box 13.

61. Hearings, *Supplemental Foreign Assistance–Vietnam*, pp. 350–354.

62. Untitled Notes, February 15, 1966, Bundy Papers, Box 2.

63. Graff, *Tuesday Cabinet*, p. 73.

64. R. W. Komer to Bundy, February 23, 1966, Johnson Papers, Reference File, Miscellaneous Documents.

65. Claudia T. Johnson, *White House Diary*, pp. 359–360.

66. Johnson, *Vantage Point*, p. 235.

67. Valenti to Johnson, January 22, 1966, in Valenti, *Very Human President*, pp. 240–242.

68. *Ibid.*, p. 243.

14. ROSTOW TAKES OVER

1. Carl Solberg, *Hubert Humphrey: A Biography* (New York: W. W. Norton, 1984), pp. 285–289. It is interesting, in this regard, that when Humphrey's conversion on the road to Saigon took place, he recalled his fight with the Communists in the Minnesota Democratic Farmer Labor party. "I fought those bastards then and I'm going to fight them now" (p. 288).

2. "Notes on Meeting of the Vice President with Members of his Staff," February 18, 1966, Johnson Papers, Confidential File, Box 166.

3. *Ibid.*

4. *New York Times*, April 26, 1966.

5. Theodore Draper, *Abuse of Power* (New York: Viking, 1967), p. 112.

6. Moyers to Johnson, June 9, 1966, Johnson Papers, White House Aides File, Moyers, Box 12. See also Hayes Redmon to Moyers, May 26 and June 9, 1966, *ibid.*

7. McNamara to Johnson, March 2, 1966, Johnson Papers, White House Central File, ND 9-4, Box 147.

8. Sidey, *Very Personal Presidency*, p. 269.

9. William J. Connell, Interview, LBJ/OH, p. 32.

10. Solberg, *Humphrey*, p. 290.

11. Humphrey to Johnson, March 3, 1966, Johnson Papers, NSF, Name File, Box 4.

12. Quoted in full in Miller, *Lyndon*, pp. 419–420.

13. *Ibid.* Arthur Schlesinger writes in his biography of Robert Kennedy that Bobby wrote the letter at a time when his old friend Bob McNamara had confided his concern about the generals and their demand for a resumption of the bombing. It was intended to encourage the president to resist their blandishments. Schlesinger leaves out those parts of the senator's letter, however, that Johnson seized upon as justification of the rightness of his course in following Lincoln's example. See Schlesinger, *Robert Kennedy*, pp. 734–735.

14. Johnson to Robert Kennedy, January 27, 1966, Johnson Papers, Diary Back-Up, Box 28.

15. Chronology of statements, undated, Johnson Papers, Reference File, Vietnam, Box 1.

16. Solberg, *Humphrey*, p. 290; William J. Connell, Interview, LBJ/OH, p. 33. Connell also recalls that Humphrey talked about experiences in Minnesota to back up his conclusions.

17. Notes of Meeting in Cabinet Room, February 26, 1966, Johnson Papers, Office Files of the President, Box 13.

18. Brewin and Shaw, *Vietnam on Trial*, p. 234. Komer's formal appointment came on March 28, 1966. He was to coordinate all programs for "peaceful construction relating to Vietnam." National Security Action Memorandum No. 343, NSF, Komer Files, Box 6.

19. Notes of Meeting in Cabinet Room, February 24, 1966, Johnson Papers, Office Files of the President, Box 13.

20. Notes of Meeting in Cabinet Room, February 26, 1966, *ibid.*

21. Young, *Vietnam Wars*, pp. 167–168.

22. Notes of a Meeting in the Cabinet Room, March 11, 1966, Johnson Papers, Office Files of the President, Box 13.

23. Young, *Vietnam Wars*, p. 168.

24. Eyes Only: Notes on Vietnam, March 24, 1966, Johnson Papers, Confidential File, Vietnam, Box 168.

25. Notes of Meeting in the Mansion, April 2, 1966, Johnson Papers, Office Files of the President, Box 13.

26. Valenti Handwritten Memo entitled "A Final Note, Mr. President," April 3, 1966, Johnson Papers, Office of the President Files, Box 12. It is not entirely clear that this one in the series was actually sent to Johnson. Valenti to Johnson, April 4, 1966, *ibid.*, Reference File, Vietnam, Box 1. For this memo, and others in the series, see Valenti, *Very Human President*, pp. 244–249. George Ball thought everything was "really unraveling," yet he correctly predicted that the final decision would be to go forward. Telcon, Ball with James Reston, Ball Papers, Box 7.

27. Rostow to Johnson, April 5, 1966, Johnson Papers, Rostow Memos for the President, Box 7. Joining Rostow in urging against a "take over or get out" attitude toward Vietnam was Maxwell Taylor, now an addition to the list of White House advisers. He also urged, with a somewhat different slant, stepped-up military action on the ground and in the air. "If we are suffering a reverse on the political front, we need to seek compensation on the military front." Taylor to Johnson, April 12, 1966, Johnson Papers, NSF, Country File, Vietnam, Boxes 259–260.

28. Kahin, *Intervention*, pp. 422–430.

29. Ky, *Twenty Years and Twenty Days*, pp. 96–99.

30. William M. Hammond, *United States Army in Vietnam: Public Affairs: The Military and the Media, 1962–1968* (Washington: Center of Military History, GPO, 1988), p. 260.

31. Rostow to Johnson, April 5, 1966, Johnson Papers, Rostow Memos for the President, Box 7.

32. Rostow to Johnson, April 5, 1966, Johnson Papers, Rostow Memos for the President, Box 7.

33. *Ibid.*

34. Rostow to Johnson, June 3, 1966, Johnson Papers, Files of Walt Rostow, Memos to the President, Box 8.

35. Halberstam, *Best and the Brightest*, p. 628.; Miller, *Lyndon*, p. 413.

36. Bromley Smith, "Summary Notes of 557th NSC Meeting," May 10, 1966, Johnson Papers, NSF, NSC Meetings, Box 2; see also Komer to Johnson, May 9, 1966, *ibid.*, Komer Files, Boxes 1–3.

37. Komer to William Porter, May 11, 1966, Johnson Papers, Komer Files, Boxes 1–3.

38. Diem, *In the Jaws*, p. 153.

39. Karnow, *Vietnam*, p. 442.

40. See Jonathan Schell, *The Real War: The Classic Reporting on the Vietnam War* (New York: Pantheon, 1987), pp. 7, 10, 165, 173–174.

41. Karnow, *Vietnam*, p. 442.

42. Krepinevich, *Army and Vietnam*, p. 196.

43. Komer Interview III, LBJ/OH, pp. 60–61; Schell, *Real War*, p. 10.

44. Taylor, *Swords and Plowshares*, p. 340.

45. McPherson to Johnson, May 18, 1966, Johnson Papers, Office Files of the President, McPherson Memos, Box 7. A few days earlier, however, McPherson had chided the president for attacking Senator William Fulbright at a Democratic banquet in Washington, for, in effect driving a wedge in the party. "It seemed you were trying to beat Fulbright's ears down before an audience of Democrats who, I am told, had earlier applauded him strongly." McPherson to Johnson, May 13, 1966, *ibid.*

46. *New York Times*, May 19, 1966.

47. Henry L. Trewhitt, *McNamara: His Ordeal in the Pentagon* (New York: Harper & Row, 1971), pp. 234–235; Shapley, *Promise and Power*, pp. 383–384.

48. Harriman to Rusk, May 10, 1966, Harriman Papers, Box 520; Memoranda of Conversations, May 14 and 30, 1966, *ibid.*, Box 486.

49. Bromley Smith, "Summary Notes of 559th NSC Meeting," June 17, 1966, Johnson Papers, NSF, NSC Meetings, Box 2. For Wilson's warning, see Bruce to Acting Secretary, June 2, 1966, and Johnson to Wilson, June 14, 1966, *ibid.*, Rostow Files, Memos to the President, Box 8. For concern about Goldberg, see Rostow to Johnson, June 16, 1966, *ibid.* "I shall try to stay close to him," Rostow promised.

50. George Christian, "Notes of the President's Meeting with the National Security Council," June 22, 1966, Johnson Papers, NSF, NSC Meetings, Box 2.

51. *Ibid.*

52. Olson and Roberts, *Where the Domino Fell*, p. 154.

53. *Los Angeles Times* clipping in Johnson Papers, White House Aides File, Moyers, Box 12.

54. *PP, 1966*, I, 694–695.

55. *Ibid.*

56. Hayes Redmon to Moyers, July 26, 1966, Johnson Papers, White House Aides Files, Moyers, Box 12.

57. McPherson to Moyers, August 4, 1966, Johnson Papers, White House Aides File, McPherson, Box 28.

58. *PP, 1966*, II, 855–856.

59. Press Conference, August 24, 1966, *ibid.*, pp. 876–884.

60. Lodge Cable, August 10, 1966, Johnson Papers, NSF, Rostow Memos to the President, Box 9.

61. State Department Translation, "General de Gaulle's Speech of September 1, 1966," Johnson Papers, NSF, Country File, France, Box 172.

62. *Ibid.*

63. Lodge Cable, September 2, 1966, Johnson Papers, NSF, Country File, Vietnam, Boxes 35–36.

64. Rostow to Johnson, October 1, 1966, Johnson Papers, NSF, Country File, United Kingdom, Boxes 210–212.

65. Cooper, *Lost Crusade*, pp. 310–316.

66. Memorandum of Conversation, October 10, 1966, Johnson Papers, NSF, Country File, USSR, Box 228.

67. *Ibid.* It is difficult to be sure, except in general terms, what Gromyko said, since the State Department has yet to declassify portions of the memorandum, relying on a very broad interpretation of its rules on "foreign-originated" information. Johnson told British Foreign Secretary George Brown what his understanding of Gromyko's position was, particularly the claim that Russia now had "some influence in North Vietnam and that, if the bombing were to cease, there was reason to hope" for a "positive action on the part of the North." Memorandum of a

Conversation, October 14, 1966, Johnson Papers, NSF, Country File, United Kingdom, Boxes 210–212.

68. Memorandum of Conversation with Secretary McNamara, October 10, 1966, Harriman Papers, Box 520.

69. McNamara to Johnson, October 14, 1966, Johnson Papers, NSF, NSC Meetings, Box 2.

70. *Ibid.*

71. *Ibid.*

72. *Ibid.*

73. *Ibid.*

74. Wheeler to McNamara, October 14, 1966, *ibid.*

75. Bernard Fall, "Viet Nam in the Balance," *Foreign Affairs*, 45 (October 1966), 1-18.

76. Remarks, October 20 and 21, *PP, 1966*, II, 1236–1237, 1246–1247.

77. "Parliament House Discussions . . . ," October 21, 1966, Johnson Papers, Diary Back-Up, Box 48.

78. "Notes re the President's meeting w/Arthur Calwell," October 22, 1966, Johnson Papers, Diary Backup, Box 48.

79. Cooper, *Lost Crusade*, p. 312; McPherson, *Political Education*, p. 315.

80. Miller, *Lyndon*, p. 456.

81. Rostow, "Meeting of the President with Thieu and Ky," October 23, 1966, Johnson Papers, Diary Back-Up, Box 48.

82. *Ibid.*

83. The "inside" story of the Manila Conference is best told in Cooper, *Lost Crusade*, pp. 314–319.

84. *Ibid.*, p. 319.

85. Jorden, "Notes on the President's Trip to Viet-Nam," undated [October 26, 1966], Johnson Papers, Diary Back-Up, Box 48.

86. Sidey, *Very Personal Presidency*, p. 151.

87. *PP, 1966*, II, 1316–1325. See also Sidey, *Very Personal Presidency*, p. 147.

88. Califano, *Triumph and Tragedy*, p. 150.

15. WINTER OF DISCONTENTS

1. Leo Janos, "The Last Days of the President: LBJ in Retirement," *Atlantic Monthly*, July 1973, pp. 35–41.

2. Dugger, *Politician*, p. 397.

3. Transcript, November 12, 1966, Johnson Papers, Office of the President Files, Box 12.

4. Johnson, *Vantage Point*, p. 356.

5. Todd Gitlin, *The Sixties: Years of Hope, Days of Rage* (New York: Bantam Books, 1987), p. 294.

6. David E. Lilienthal, *The Journals of David E. Lilienthal*, vol. VI, *Creativity and Conflict* (New York: Harper & Row, 1976) 351–352.

7. John Taft, *American Power: The Rise and Decline of U.S. Globalism* (New York: Harper & Row, 1989), p. 305.

8. Lilienthal, *Journals*, VI, 328.

9. Taft, *American Power*, p. 305.

10. Rostow, "Memorandum for the President," December 9, 1966, Johnson Papers, NSF, Country File, Vietnam, Box 200.

11. Press Conference, November 5, 1966, *PP, 1966*, II, 1325–1327.

12. Rostow to Johnson, November 17, 1966, Johnson Papers, NSF, Rostow Memos to the President, Boxes 11–12.

13. *Ibid.*

14. Trewhitt, *McNamara*, p. 235; Halberstam, *Best and the Brightest*, p. 633.

15. Abramson, *Spanning the Century*, pp. 644–645; Harriman, "Report on Post-Manila Trip," November 22, 1966, Johnson Papers, NSF, Rostow Memos to the President, Box 11.

16. *Ibid.*

17. "Addition to McNamara Conversation," November 26, 1966, Harriman Papers, Box 486.

18. Rostow to Johnson, November 28, 1966, Johnson Papers, NSF, Rostow Memos to the President, Boxes 11–12.

19. Raphael Littauer and Norman Uphoff, eds., *The Air War in Indochina* (Boston: Beacon Press, 1972), pp. 11, 40; John Schlight, *The War in South Vietnam: The Years of the Offensive*,

1965–1968, The United States Air Force in Southeast Asia (Washington: Office of Air Force History, 1988), p. 214.

20. Donald J. Mrozek, *Air Power and the Ground War in Vietnam: Ideas and Actions* (Maxwell Air Force Base: Air University Press, 1988), pp. 92–93.

21. For a good, brief account of how the Vietnam War upset cold war air power and nuclear theorists, see Fred Kaplan, *The Wizards of Armageddon* (New York: Simon & Schuster, 1983), chapter 23.

22. Robert Sherrill, *The Accidental President* (New York: Grossman, 1967).

23. Barbara Garson, *The Complete Text of MacBird* (New York: Grove Press, 1967), p. 97.

24. Gitlin, *Sixties*, p. 313.

25. Heren, *No Hail, No Farewell*, p. 129.

26. Roche wrote Johnson that he had held President Kennedy in high regard and worked with him from 1956 to 1962, "when he cut me dead because I refused to support Teddy" for the Senate. The episode did not "alter my admiration for him," Roche also wrote, but the bitter tone in his memos whenever a member of the Kennedy "clan" is under discussion suggests otherwise. Roche to Johnson, December 23, 1966, Johnson Papers, Special File on the Assassination of John F. Kennedy, Box 1.

27. Roche to Johnson, November 16, 1966, Johnson Papers, Office of the President Files, Roche Memos, Box 11. For another example, see Roche to Johnson, February 1, 1967, Johnson Papers, Office of the President Files, Marvin Watson, Box 29.

28. A special file on the assassination and the Manchester book in the Johnson Papers under that heading includes a page-by-page rebuttal of several of the charges made in *The Death of a President*. It contains a wealth of material on several subjects, including correspondence and newspaper clippings.

29. Manchester, *Death of a President*, pp. 4, 228.

30. Theodore Sorensen's *Kennedy* and Arthur M. Schlesinger's *A Thousand Days* both appeared in the year of the first major escalation. Sorensen wrote that Kennedy had told him in the aftermath of the coup that ended Diem's government and life that it would be a mistake to abandon the commitment to a shaky ally. "I think we should stay" (p. 661). Schlesinger notes that choices had been "fatally narrowed" as early as 1961 when Kennedy started adding to the two thousand American troops already there, though the president worried about the point when intervention might turn Vietnamese nationalism against the U.S. (p. 998).

31. Moyers to Goodwin, December 10, 1966, Johnson Papers, Office of the President File, Moyers Memos, Box 8.

32. Vietnam does not warrant an index entry in *The Death of a President*, but in the 1988 introduction to a new edition, Manchester claimed that Johnson reversed JFK's Vietnam decision, quoting a private statement Kennedy had made to him. "His withdrawal operation, which had already begun at the time of his death, would have ended this country's Vietnam commitment in 1965 with the evacuation, as he had put it to me, of 'the last helicopter pilot.' After his funeral Johnson countermanded these orders."

Manchester's claim to inside knowledge about what Kennedy intended was largely irrelevant, except as it might have influenced what he wrote in *The Death of a President* about relations between the two men—which, in turn, increased LBJ's defensiveness about Vietnam. Manchester, *Death of a President*, p. xx. Manchester was in a very different frame of mind, however, when he wanted an interview with Johnson during the writing of the book. He wrote to both McGeorge Bundy and Jack Valenti to advise them that he was scheduled to give a commencement address at the University of Massachusetts, where he would insert some sharp comments about the antiwar Teach-in movement. "I intend to make the point," he informed Bundy, "as strongly as possible, that foreign policy ought not to be the occasion for a panty raid." Apparently he had not yet grasped what JFK allegedly told him. Manchester to Bundy, May 18, 1965, and Manchester to Valenti, June 26, 1965, Johnson Papers, Special File on the Assassination of John F. Kennedy, Box 1.

33. Henggeler, *In His Steps*, p. 251; Janos, "The President in Retirement," p. 39.

34. Henggeler, *In His Steps*, pp. 202–203; Lilienthal, *Journals*, VI, 328–329.

35. Henggeler, *In His Steps*, pp. 202–203.

36. For reprints of the articles, and other commentary, see Harrison Salisbury, *Behind the Lines–Hanoi* (New York: Harper & Row, 1967); Powers, *War at Home*, pp. 172–173.

37. Salisbury, LBJ/OH, p. 13.

38. *Ibid.*, p. 17, and see Dean Rusk's memorandum, "Highlights of Harrison Salisbury Private Report to Me," January 14, 1967, and its enclosure, the minutes of the interview with Pham Van Dong, January 2, 1967, in Johnson Papers, DSDUF, Box 3.

39. Salisbury Interview with Pham Van Dong, January 2, 1967, Johnson Papers, DSDUF, Box 3.

40. "Memorandum of Meeting," December 1, 1966, Harriman Papers, Box 520.

41. Salisbury, LBJ/OH, p. 21.

42. Rusk to Johnson, January 14, 1967, Johnson Papers, DSDUF, Box 3.

43. Diary Entry, January 14, 1967, Lilienthal Papers, Box 212.

44. Harry S. Ashmore and William C. Baggs, *Mission to Hanoi: A Chronicle of Double Dealing in High Places* (New York: Putnam, 1968), pp. 24, 28.

45. Quoted in *ibid.* p. 39.

46. *Ibid.*, p. 46.

47. *Ibid.*, p. 50. The detailed report Ashmore and Baggs provided the State Department also suggested that Ho had implied he had serious problems of "face" in dealing with the NLF, and, more problematically, that NLF representatives would not have to be present at an "exploratory conference." The report also suggested that without the DRV's guiding hand, there could be an increase in Chinese influence in the NLF. Ashmore and Baggs also predicted a conflict between the NLF and the DRV sometime in the future when things began to be sorted out. There is no indication State Department recipients of this report picked up on such nuances. Ashmore and Baggs, "Report on Visit to Hanoi . . . ," January 18, 1967, Johnson Papers, NSF, Rostow Memos to the President, Box 12.

48. Ashmore and Baggs, *Mission to Hanoi*, p. 60.

49. *Ibid.*, p. 65.

50. *Ibid.*, p. 67.

51. *Ibid.*, p. 71.

52. *Ibid.*, p. 73.

53. For a full account of what was called Marigold, see George Herring, ed., *The Secret Diplomacy of the Vietnam War: The Negotiating Volumes of the Pentagon Papers* (Austin: University of Texas Press, 1983), pp. 211–370. Quotation here is from p. 272.

54. *Ibid.*, pp. 239, 284.

55. Rusk to London, November 16, 1966, *ibid.*, 271.

56. Rusk to London, November 20, 1966, *ibid.*, 271.

57. Johnson, *Vantage Point*, pp. 251–252.

58. Rusk to Warsaw, December 10, 1966, in Herring, *Secret Diplomacy*, p. 296.

59. Memorandum of a Conversation, December 22, 1966, *ibid.*, pp. 314–315.

60. Rostow to Johnson, February 4, 1967, Johnson Papers, NSF, Rostow Memos to the President, Box 13.

61. Rostow to Johnson, January 3, 1967, Johnson Papers, NSF, Office Files of Rostow, Box 6.

62. He could easily draw such conclusions, for example, from the conversation Assistant Secretary of Defense John McNaughton had with Soviet Chargé Alexander Zinchuk, the Russian diplomat who had talked with William Bundy along similar lines. But there were many other contacts as well, certainly more than enough to convince a man who wanted to be convinced, as Rostow did, of his own assumptions. McNaughton, "Memorandum of Conversation," January 3, 1967, Johnson Papers, NSF, Rostow Memos to the President, Box 12. See also Dean Rusk's appeal to the Russian ambassador on the responsibility of the United States and the Soviet Union to keep their client states from ruining prospects for progress on other issues. "If Moscow cannot tell us with assurance what Hanoi would do if we stopped the bombing, Moscow could at least tell us privately what Moscow could do." Rusk, "Memorandum of Conversation," January 5, 1967, *ibid.*

63. Rostow to Rusk, January 5, 1967, Johnson Papers, NSF, Rostow Memos to the President, Box 12. As it happened, Senate Majority Leader Mike Mansfield sent Johnson a memorandum on the meaning of Hanoi's "signals" that reached a much sounder conclusion, pointing out that the difficulty was not persuading the North Vietnamese to come to the peace table, or to provide "help" to enable them to save face, but what the negotiations were to be about—the composition of the South Vietnamese government. Mansfield to Johnson, January 6, 1967, Johnson Papers, DSDUF, Box 3. Rostow drafted the reply, which, in the normally circuitous language used on these occasions, insisted that the U.S. could only offer "self-determination by the South Vietnamese people," and ended, "I'm sure you have derived encouragement over the past year, as I have, in the real progress towards constitutional government made in South Vietnam." Johnson to Mansfield, January 9, 1965, *ibid.*

64. Rostow to Johnson, January 10, 1967, Johnson Papers, Rostow Memos to the President, Box 12; Rostow to Lodge, January 18, 1967, *ibid.*, Box 13.

65. "Letter from President Johnson to Ho Chi Minh," January 5, 1967, Johnson Papers, NSF, Rostow Memos to the President, Box 12.

66. Much of the documentation concerning Sunflower is printed in Herring, *Secret Diplomacy*, pp. 373–517. Even so, many important documents remain classified, or partially classified, and one must rely upon memoirs for crucial points. Where no specific citation is given, the narrative here is largely taken from documents from Herring's edited version.

67. Marvin Watson, "Meeting with the President . . . ," January 17, 1967, Johnson Papers, Diary Back-Up, Reference File, Miscellaneous Vietnam Documents, Box 1.

68. Cooper to Rusk and Harriman, February 5, 1967, Herring, *Secret Diplomacy*, p. 430.

69. *Ibid.*

70. Quoted in Heren, *No Hail, No Farewell*, p. 140.

71. Herring, *Secret Diplomacy*, p. 415.

72. *Ibid.*, pp. 416–422.

73. Clipping from *Washington Daily News*, November 30, 1966, in Johnson Papers, Special File on the Assassination of John F. Kennedy, Box 1.

74. Robert Kintner to Johnson, with enclosures, January 18, 1967, Johnson Papers, Special File on the Assassination of John F. Kennedy, Box 1.

75. Claudia T. Johnson, *White House Diary*, pp. 472–473.

76. Jake Jacobsen to Johnson, with enclosure, January 11, 1967, Johnson Papers, Special File on the Assassination of John F. Kennedy, Box 1. See also Edwin Weisel to Johnson, December 23, 1966, enclosing an article by Theodore White from *Life* magazine, with a featured quotation from Jackie Kennedy: "She wanted to make sure that the point came clear and went on: 'There'll be great Presidents again—and the Johnsons are wonderful, they've been wonderful to me—but there'll never be another Camelot again." *Ibid.*

77. Roche to Johnson, December 23, 1966, Johnson Papers, Special File on the Assassination of John F. Kennedy, Box 1. A writer for the North American Newspaper Alliance, Vera Glaser, under the headline "Uneasy Rests the Crown of JFK's Jackie," wrote, "When Franklin D. Roosevelt died in 1945, his widow Eleanor observed a decent period of mourning, then returned to public life, working tirelessly for the less fortunate. Perhaps no First Lady in history endured as much ridicule and vilification. She bore it with sweetness and dignity. . . . Mrs. Kennedy opted for La Dolce Vita—the world of high fashion, society and the arts. While pointedly snubbing Ms. Johnson's invitations to the White House, Jackie has accepted every official prerogative available to her." Clipping from *Cincinnati Enquirer*, December 22, 1966, in *ibid.*

78. "Memorandum of Meeting," February 2, 1967, Harriman Papers, Box 520.

79. Harriman, "Memorandum for the President," February 2, 1967, Johnson Papers, NSF, Rostow Memos to the President, Box 13; Harriman to Rusk and Johnson, February 2, 1967, *ibid.*; Lodge to State Department (Saigon 17053), February 1, 1967, *ibid.*; and Lodge to Johnson (Saigon 17054), February 1, 1967, *ibid.* Somewhat later, Harriman told Kennedy on the telephone in a frustrated tone that "some time ago" he had explained to him that Russia was swinging into position. "We are moving into a place where maybe we are going to get something done." For the senator to support Hanoi's positions was not going to help. Telecon, February 27, 1967, Harriman Papers, Box 520.

80. Lodge cables, 17053 and 17054, February 1, 1967, Johnson Papers, NSF, Rostow Memos to the President, Box 13.

81. Bohlen to Rusk, February 1, 1967, Johnson Papers, NSF, Country File, France, Box 173.

82. Rostow to Johnson, undated [February 4 or 5], 1967, with draft enclosed, dated February 4, 1967, Johnson Papers, NSF, Rostow Memos to the President, Box 13.

83. Much of the narrative below is taken from Cooper, *Lost Crusade*, pp. 342–368, and from his Oral History Interview at the Johnson Library.

84. Rostow to Johnson, February 6, 1967, Johnson Papers, NSF, Rostow Memos to the President, Box 13.

85. *Ibid.*

86. Johnson, *Vantage Point*, p. 253.

87. Rostow to Johnson, February 6, 1967, Johnson Papers, NSF, Rostow Memos to the President, Box 13.

88. The account that follows is from Schlesinger, *Robert Kennedy*, pp. 767–769. See also Johnson's comment on the meeting in Drew Pearson, Notes of a Meeting with LBJ, March 13, 1967, Drew Pearson Papers, Johnson Library, Box G 246.

89. Roche to Johnson, February 9, 1967, Johnson Papers, Office Files of Marvin Watson, Box 29.

90. Cooper to Rusk, February 7 and 8, Johnson Papers, NSF, Rostow Memos to the President, Box 13.
91. Cooper, *Lost Crusade* p. 357.
92. Wilson, *Labour Government*, p. 348.
93. Johnson, *Vantage Point*, p. 252.
94. Undated text, February 7, 1967, in Johnson Papers, NSF, Files of Walt Rostow, Box 5.
95. Johnson watched closely what the military leaked about any change in the bombing. After the criticism of the mid-December raids that destroyed civilian dwellings and public buildings in Hanoi, for example, an anonymous air force source told reporters that targets had been taken off the list in response to the "protests." AP clipping, Johnson Papers, Special File on the Assassination of John F. Kennedy, Box 1.
96. Johnson, *Vantage Point*, p. 254; and Wheeler's presentation on February 8, 1967, to the National Security Council, Johnson Papers, NSF, NSC Meetings, Box 2.
97. Rostow to Johnson, February 7, 1967, 8 p.m., Johnson Papers, NSF, Rostow Memos to the President, Box 13.
98. Rostow to Bruce and Cooper, February 10, 1967, Johnson Papers, NSF, Rostow Memos to the President, Box 13.
99. Wilson, *Labour Government*, pp. 358–359.
100. *Ibid.*, p. 364.
101. Interview with Averell Harriman, LBJ/OH, p. 26.
102. Wilson, *Labour Government*, p. 365.
103. "Meeting of the President with Hugh Sidey . . . ," February 8, 1967, Johnson Papers, Meeting Notes File, Box 3.
104. "Congressional Briefing," February 15, 1967, Johnson Papers, Congressional Briefings, Box 1.
105. Cooper, *Lost Crusade* p. 368.
106. Roche to Johnson, February 20, 1967, Johnson Papers, Office Files of Marvin Watson, Box 29.
107. Diary Back-Up, November 27, 1963, Johnson Papers, copy in Special File on the Assassination of John F. Kennedy, Box 1.

16. WARS OF ATTRITION

1. Diary Entry, May 12, 1967, Johnson Papers, Daily Diary, Box 11.
2. *Ibid.*
3. Congressional Briefing, February 23, 1967, Johnson Papers, Congressional Briefings, Box 1.
4. Diary Entry, May 12, 1967, Johnson Papers, Daily Diary, Box 11.
5. Congressional Briefing, February 23, 1967, Johnson Papers, Congressional Briefings, Box 1.
6. Rostow to Johnson, March 8, 1967, enclosing text of CIA Report, "North Vietnamese Civilian Reaction to U.S. Air Strikes," Johnson Papers, NSF, Rostow Memos to the President, Box 14; Johnson to Jackson, March 2, 1967, *PP, 1967*, I, 267–269.
7. McPherson to Johnson, March 7, 1967, Johnson Papers, Office of the President Files, Box 7.
8. McNamara to Johnson, June 12, 1967, quoted in Larry Berman, *Lyndon Johnson's War: The Road to Stalemate in Vietnam* (New York: W. W. Norton, 1989), pp. 52–53.
9. Hoopes, *Limits of Intervention*, p. 51.
10. For a brief discussion, see Shapley, *Promise and Power*, p. 413.
11. Henry Owen, "Memorandum: 1964–1967," undated, enclosed in Rostow to Johnson, March 17, 1967, Johnson Papers, DSDUF, Box 3.
12. Rostow to Johnson, March 17, 1967, Johnson Papers, DSDUF, Box 3.
13. Rostow to Johnson, March 12, 1967, enclosing CIA report, March 10, 1967, Johnson Papers, NSF, Rostow Memos to the President, Box 14.
14. See "Background Paper: National Reconciliation," undated [March 1967], Harriman Papers, Box 532; Lodge to Rusk, March 17, 1967, *ibid.*; Rusk to Lodge, March 17, 1967, *ibid.* Rostow to Johnson, March 23, 1967, Johnson Papers, Rostow Memos to the President, Box 14; Harriman, Memorandum for Record, March 24, 1967, Harriman Papers, Box 420.
15. Notes by Drew Pearson, March 13, 1967, Pearson Papers, Box G 246.

16. Rostow to Johnson, March 20, 1967, Johnson Papers, Files of George Christian, Box 2.

17. Lilienthal, *Journals*, VI, 413.

18. *Ibid.*, p. 417.

19. *Ibid.*, p. 418.

20. *Ibid.*, pp. 418–419.

21. Barrett, *Uncertain Warriors*, pp. 75–78.

22. Martin to Harry McPherson, April 4, 1967, Johnson Papers, Office Files of Harry McPherson, Box 28.

23. Martin McPherson, May 1, 1967, Johnson Papers, Office Files of Harry McPherson, Box 28

24. DeBenedetti, *American Ordeal*, p. 172.

25. McPherson to Johnson, April 4, 1967, Johnson Papers, White House Aides, McPherson Memos to the President, Box 53.

26. Roche to Johnson, April 18, 1967, Johnson Papers, Office Files of Marvin Watson, Box 29.

27. Schlesinger, *Robert Kennedy*, pp. 774–775.

28. DeBenedetti, *American Ordeal*, pp. 178–179.

29. *Ibid.*, p. 177.

30. Melvin Small, *Johnson, Nixon and the Doves* (New Brunswick, N.J.: Rutgers University Press, 1988), p. 103.

31. On the difficulties associated with trying to explain the significance of the protest marches, see Powers, *War at Home*, pp. 184–186.

32. Small, *Johnson, Nixon and the Doves*, p. 101.

33. Roche to Johnson, May 19 and June 15, 1967, Johnson Papers, Office Files of Marvin Watson, Box 29; Small, *Johnson, Nixon and the Doves*, p. 102.

34. McPherson to Johnson, May 4, 1967, with enclosure, Johnson Papers, Office of the President Files, McPherson, Box 7.

35. *Ibid.*

36. Small, *Johnson, Nixon and the Doves*, p. 107.

37. James C. Thomson, Jr., "Minutes of a White House Meeting, Summer 1967," *Atlantic Monthly*, May 1967, pp. 67–68, enclosed in Rostow to Johnson, May 1, 1967, Johnson Papers, DSDUF, Box 1.

38. *Ibid.*

39. Rostow to Johnson, April 27, 1967, Johnson Papers, NSF, Rostow Memos to the President, Box 15.

40. *Ibid.*

41. Address, April 24, 1967, copy in Johnson Papers, NSF, Country File, Vietnam, Box 43.

42. See, for example, Rostow's account of a conversation with Joseph Alsop, May 1, 1967, Johnson Papers, NSF, Country File, Vietnam, Box 43.

43. Barrett, *Uncertain Warriors*, p. 82; see also Rostow to Johnson, May 6, 1967, recounting a discussion afterward during which the national security adviser himself backed off. Johnson Papers, NSF, Country File, Vietnam, Boxes 74–75.

44. Rostow to Bunker, May 5, 1967, Johnson Papers, NSF, Country File, Vietnam, Box 43.

45. Rostow to Johnson, May 9, 1967, 11:00 a.m., and 7:30 p.m., both in Johnson Papers, NSF, Rostow Memos to the President, Box 16.

46. Rostow to Johnson, May 15, 1967, Johnson Papers, NSF, Rostow Memos to the President, Box 16. Evans had been hearing things from people outside the Pentagon as well. Richard Russell had told him that for the first time in thirty-five years he did not know what to suggest; moderate Democrats were complaining that LBJ was going toward the LeMay-type resolution of the crisis by bombing population centers; even some of the president's real friends in the Senate were beginning to think that Johnson had gotten himself into Truman's predicament in 1952, and that only a Republican could begin negotiations. Harry McPherson reported all that Evans had said to him to Press Secretary George Christian, May 12, 1967, Johnson Papers, White House Aides, McPherson, Box 32.

47. Barrett, *Uncertain Warriors*, p. 86; for the Bunker reports see Douglas Pike, ed., *The Bunker Papers: Reports to the President from Vietnam, 1967–1973* (2 vol., Berkeley: Institute of East Asian Studies, University of California, 1990), I, 1–37.

48. The fullest account of the relationship of the Vietnam War to events in the Middle East is Judith A. Klinghoffer, "The Johnson Administration, Israel and American Jewry: Linkages to the Vietnam War," Ph.D. dissertation, Rutgers University, 1994. This fine study suggests how the Vietnam War served as an essential background to decisions in many capitals as the Middle East went to war for a second time in little more than a decade.

49. Rostow to Johnson, May 19, 1967, Johnson Papers, NSF, Country File, Vietnam, Boxes 74–75.

50. McPherson to Johnson, June 13, 1967, Johnson Papers, Files of White House Aides, McPherson, Box 29.

51. *Ibid.* (Italics added.)

52. See the discussion in Tom Wells, *The War Within: America's Battle over Vietnam* (Berkeley: University of California Press, 1994), pp. 154–159.

53. "Summary of Notes . . . ," June 15, 1967, Johnson Papers, Files of George Christian, Box 1.

54. *Ibid.*

55. *Washington Post* clipping, June 13, 1967, in Johnson Papers, Office Files of Marvin Watson, Box 32. In Watson's clipping, the lines quoted are heavily underlined and also marked in the margin.

56. Wills, *Second Civil War.*

57. "Remarks in Baltimore . . . ," June 27, 1967, *PP, 1967,* I, 654–659.

58. Califano, *Triumph and Tragedy,* pp. 209–222.

59. Patterson, *America's Struggle Against Poverty,* pp. 151–153.

60. Schlesinger, *Robert Kennedy,* p. 797.

61. Humphrey to Johnson, July 27, 1967, Johnson Papers, Office Files of Joseph Califano, Box 20.

62. Wills, *Second Civil War,* pp. 109, 60, 93, 39.

63. "Notes of Meeting . . . ," July 28, 1967, Johnson Papers, Files of George Christian, Box 1. In this meeting with reporters from news magazines, Johnson predicted "considerably more trouble." "When someone is kept as a slave, he said, there is a minimum of trouble. As suppressed people begin to rise from prejudice and discrimination there is [sic] naturally going to be more problems."

64. Califano, *Triumph and Tragedy,* pp. 220–221.

65. *Ibid.,* p. 221.

66. Rostow to Johnson, July 28, 1967, Office Files of White House Aides, McPherson, Box 53.

67. Associated Press Article, New Brunswick (N.J.) *Home News,* July 31, 1967.

68. *Ibid.*

69. *Ibid.,* p. 226.

70. Rostow to Johnson, June 14, 1967, Johnson Papers, NSF, Rostow Memos to the President, Box 17; Harriman, Memorandum of Conversation, April 18, 1967, Harriman Papers, Box 520; Rostow, Memorandum of Conversation, April 18, 1967, Johnson Papers, NSF, Rostow Memos to the President, Box 15.

71. Johnson, *Vantage Point,* p. 257.

72. Harriman, "Memorandum for the President," June 17, 1967, Johnson Papers, NSF, Rostow Memos to the President, Box 17.

73. William Krimer, State Department Interpreter, Memorandum of Conversation, June 23, 1967, Johnson Papers, NSF, Country File, USSR, Special Addendum on Glassboro, Box 295.

74. *Ibid.*

75. *Ibid.*

76. *Ibid.*

77. Rostow to Johnson, June 21, 1967, Johnson Papers, NSF, Rostow Memos to the President, Box 18.

78. Rusk to Johnson, with enclosure, June 24, 1967, Johnson Papers, NSF, Country File, USSR, Special Addendum on Glassboro, Box 295.

79. A. Akolovksy, Memorandum of Conversation, June 25, 1967, Johnson Papers, NSF, Country File, USSR, Special Addendum on Glassboro, Box 295.

80. Johnson, *Vantage Point,* p. 257.

81. Jeffrey J. Clarke, *Advice and Support: The Final Years, 1965–1973* in *United States Army in Vietnam* (Washington: Center of Military History, 1988), p. 275.

82. Tom Johnson, Memorandum to the President, July 12, 1967, Johnson Papers, Tom Johnson's Notes, Box 1.

83. Shapley, *Promise and Power*, pp. 425–428; Moyers to Johnson, July 18, 1967, Johnson Papers, Office of the President Files, Box 8.

84. "Notes of the President's Meeting . . . ," July 13, 1967, Johnson Papers, Tom Johnson's Notes, Box 1.

85. Quoted in Barrett, *Uncertain Warriors*, p. 104.

86. News Conference, July 13, 1967, *PP, 1967*, II, 693–694.

87. Berman, *Lyndon Johnson's War*, p. 57.

88. Tom Johnson to Johnson, August 5, 1967, Johnson Papers, Tom Johnson's Notes, Box 1.

89. "Notes of the President's Meeting . . . ," August 8, 1967, Johnson Papers, Tom Johnson's Notes, Box 1.

90. "Notes of the President's Meeting with Labor Leaders," August 9, 1967, Johnson Papers, Tom Johnson's Notes, Box 1.

91. Berman, *Lyndon Johnson's War*, p. 59.

17. THE LAST DAYS OF ROBERT McNAMARA

1. Halberstam, *Best and the Brightest*, pp. 615–616.

2. "Meeting Between the President and Neil Sheehan . . . ," March 24, 1967, Johnson Papers, George Christian Files, Box 1.

3. Halberstam, *Best and the Brightest*, p. 645.

4. Shapley, *Promise and Power*, pp. 344–348.

5. James William Gibbons, *The Perfect War: Technowar in Vietnam* (Boston: Atlantic Monthly Press, 1986), p. 396; *Pentagon Papers: GE*, IV, 349.

6. Press Release, September 7, 1967, Johnson Papers, NSF, Country File, Vietnam, Boxes 74–75.

7. Karnow, *Vietnam*, p. 41.

8. McNaughton to McNamara, May 6, 1967, *Pentagon Papers: GE*, IV, 478–479; for a discussion of the memorandum, see Young, *Vietnam Wars*, pp. 206–210.

9. Halberstam bluntly puts responsibility for the reference to McNamara's "wickedness" in Walt Rostow's office—*Best and the Brightest*, p. 638; Goodpaster, Memorandum for Record: Meeting with General Eisenhower, October 18, 1967, Johnson Papers, NSF, Name File, Box 2.

10. Douglass Cater to Johnson, August 12 and 19, 1967, Johnson Papers, Files of Douglass Cater, Box 17; McPherson to Johnson, August 25, 1967, *ibid.*, Files of Harry McPherson, Box 29.

11. James Reston, *Deadline: A Memoir* (New York: Random House, 1991), p. 309.

12. *New York Times*, August 18, 1967.

13. Trewhitt, *McNamara*, p. 272; Shapley, *Promise and Power*, p. 432.

14. Hoopes, *Limits of Intervention*, p. 87.

15. Berman, *Lyndon Johnson's War*, p. 73; *PP, 1967*, II, 818; Hoopes, *Limits of Intervention*, p. 84.

16. Jim Jones, Notes of Weekly Meeting, September 5, 1967, Johnson Papers, Meeting Notes File, Box 2.

17. *Ibid.*, emphasis added.

18. *Ibid.*

19. "Memorandum of Conversation with Secretary McNamara," August 22, 1967, Harriman Papers, Box 486.

20. For a short discussion of Pennsylvania, see Isaacson, *Kissinger*, pp. 121–124.

21. A full record of the negotiations can be found in Herring, *Secret Diplomacy*, pp. 717–751.

22. Memorandum, August 2, 1967, *ibid.*, pp. 717–719. For a somewhat different assessment, see Herring's own comments on Pennsylvania, *ibid.*, pp. 521–523.

23. *Ibid.*, p. 729; Memorandum of Conversation, August 22, 1967, Harriman Papers, Box 486. It is hard to determine exactly what McNamara meant in his conversation with Harriman about dictating the final message to Kissinger. Drafts of the "August 25" proposal appear in Johnson Papers, NSF, Files of Walt Rostow, Box 9.

24. Herring, *Secret Diplomacy*, pp. 737–738.

25. *Ibid.*, p. 738; Paris Cable 3143, September 11, 1967, Johnson Papers, NSF, Files of Walt Rostow, Box 9.

26. Jim Jones to Johnson, enclosing Minutes of Weekly Luncheon, September 12, 1967, Johnson Papers, Meeting Notes File, Box 2; Rusk to Kissinger, September 12, 1967, *ibid.*, NSF,

Files of Walt Rostow, Box 9; Kissinger to Rusk, September 13, 1967, *ibid.;* Rostow to Johnson, September 13, 1967, *ibid.;* Rusk, LBJ/OH, II, 3.

27. "Notes of the President's Meeting . . . ," September 26, 1967, Johnson Papers, Tom Johnson's Notes, Box 1.

28. Katzenbach to Johnson, September 26, 1967, Johnson Papers, NSF, Rostow Memos to the President, Box 23.

29. Cooper, Memorandum for Record, September 28, 1967, Harriman Papers, Box 499.

30. For partial drafts and communications, see Rostow to Johnson, September 26 and 29, 1967, Johnson Papers, NSF, Rostow Memos to the President, Box 23; the speech as delivered is in Johnson, *PP, 1967,* II, 876–881.

31. *PP, 1967,* II, 876–881.

32. Marcovich to Kissinger, translated by Kissinger, October 2, 1967, enclosed in Rostow to Johnson, October 7, 1967, Johnson Papers, NSF, Files of Walt Rostow, Box 9.

33. Kissinger/Read Telecon, October 8, 1967, Johnson Papers, NSF, Files of Walt Rostow, Box 9; Herring, *Secret Diplomacy,* p. 772.

34. Rostow to Johnson, October 6, 1967, Johnson Papers, NSF, Files of Walt Rostow, Box 9.

35. "Notes of the President's Meeting . . . ," October 3, 1967, Johnson Papers, Tom Johnson's Notes, Box 1.

36. "Notes of the President's Meeting with Jack Leacacos . . . ," October 14, 1967, Johnson Papers, Files of George Christian, Box 1.

37. McPherson to Johnson, October 10, 1967, and McPherson to George Christian, October 17, 1967, both in Johnson Papers, Office Files of Harry McPherson, Boxes 32 and 53.

38. All quotations from the October 18, 1967, meeting are from Johnson Papers, Tom Johnson's Notes, Box 1.

39. Clifford, *Counsel to the President,* p. 452.

40. Johnson, *Vantage Point,* p. 268.

41. *Ibid.*

42. This conclusion is an extrapolation based in part upon Olson and Roberts, *Where the Domino Fell,* pp. 181–183, and Larry Cable, *Unholy Grail: The United States and the Wars in Vietnam, 1965–1968* (New York: Routledge, 1991), pp. 206–213.

43. "Notes of the President's Meeting . . . ," October 23, 1967, Johnson Papers, Tom Johnson's Notes, Box 1.

44. McNamara to Johnson, November 1, 1967, Johnson Papers, Meeting Notes File, Box 2.

45. McPherson to Johnson, October 27, 1967, Johnson Papers, NSF, Country File, Vietnam, Boxes 81–84.

46. McNamara to Johnson, November 1, 1967, Johnson Papers, NSF, Country File, Vietnam, Box 127.

47. *Ibid.*

48. McPherson to Johnson, October 27, 1967, Johnson Papers, NSF, Country File, Vietnam, Boxes 81–84.

49. Rostow to Johnson, November 2, 1967, Johnson Papers, NSF, Country File, Vietnam, Box 127.

50. *Ibid.* References to Buttercup are scarce. It is not even certain that Rostow was referring to the specific agent, Sau Ha, in this memo to the president. The dates are not precise, for example. On the other hand, the contention that there was now in operation a "contact" in South Vietnam is the crucial matter. Johnson referred, moreover, to Buttercup in his memorandum for record on the McNamara proposals, using it as a reason for rejecting the defense secretary's arguments. See "Memorandum of the President for the File," December 18, 1967, *ibid.* In this memorandum, LBJ writes as if Buttercup remained a live possibility, even though other evidence suggests interest had wilted long since. It is important to remember that in the aftermath of McNamara's resignation, the president was anxious to keep the record straight in terms of reasons why the defense secretary's final recommendation had been rejected. About the only account extant of Buttercup, sketchy as it is, is in Don Oberdorfer, *Tet!* (Garden City, N.Y.: Doubleday, 1971), pp. 62–65.

51. Taylor to Johnson, November 3, 1967; Fortas to Johnson, November 5, 1967; Clifford to Johnson, November 7, 1967, Johnson Papers, NSF, Country File, Vietnam, Box 127.

52. Tom Wells, *The War Within,* p. 211.

53. Rostow to Johnson, November 2, 1967, Johnson Papers, Meeting Notes File, Box 2.

54. Jim Jones to Johnson, November 2, 1967, enclosing summary minutes, Johnson Papers, Meeting Notes File, Box 2. All quotations below from this meeting are from this source.

55. Jim Jones to Johnson, November 4, 1967, *ibid.*

56. Ball, *Past Has Another Pattern*, p. 407.

57. Isaacson and Thomas, *Wise Men*, p. 681.

58. Harriman Memorandum, November 3, 1967, Johnson Papers, DSDUF, Box 4.

59. Bundy to Johnson, November 10, 1967, Johnson Papers, Reference File, Miscellaneous Vietnam Documents.

60. See Bundy to Johnson, October 17, 1967, Johnson Papers, NSF, Country File, Vietnam, Boxes 95–96; Rostow to Johnson, November 4, 1967, Johnson Papers, DSDUF, Box 4.

61. *Washington Post*, September 11, 1967.

62. Congressional Briefing, November 16, 1967, Johnson Papers, Congressional Briefings, Box 1.

63. Christian to Johnson, November 30, 1967, Johnson Papers, Office of the President Files, Box 7.

64. Trewhitt, *McNamara*, p. 275.

65. Shapley, *Promise and Power*, p. 439.

66. From press tape copy, November 29, 1967, Johnson Papers, Office of the President Files, Box 7.

67. Trewhitt, *McNamara*, p. 276.

68. Kearns, *Lyndon Johnson*, pp. 320–321.

69. Shapley, *Promise and Power*, pp. 438–440; Karnow, *Vietnam*, pp. 510–513.

70. *Washington Post*, December 3, 1967.

71. Karnow, *Vietnam*, p. 514.

18. TET

1. Jeffrey J. Clarke, *Advice and Support: The Final Years, 1965–1973* in *United States Army in Vietnam* (Washington: Center of Military History, 1988), p. 280.

2. Wheeler to Westmoreland, November 8, 1967, Johnson Papers, DSDUF, Box 4.

3. Clarke, *Advice and Support*, pp. 280–282.

4. Palmer, LBJ/OH, I, 30–31.

5. *Ibid.*, p. 33.

6. For international aspects of the "gold crisis," see David P. Calleo, *The Imperious Economy* (Cambridge, Mass.: Harvard University Press, 1982), pp. 9–79; on the American budget deficit, see Matusow, *Unraveling of America*, pp. 169–173.

7. Richard Barnet, *The Alliance: America-Europe-Japan, Makers of the Postwar World* (New York: Simon & Schuster, 1983), p. 250.

8. Alfred Grosser, *The Western Alliance: European American Relations Since 1945*, trans. by Michael Shaw (New York: Vintage Books, 1982), pp. 220–223.

9. "Summary Notes of the 569th NSC Meeting," May 3, 1967, Johnson Papers, NSF, NSC Meetings, Box 2.

10. *Ibid.*

11. Rostow to Johnson, November 22, 1967, Johnson Papers, NSC Histories, Box 53; "The Balance of Payments Program of New Year's Day, 1968, *ibid.*, Box 54.

12. Johnson, *Vantage Point*, pp. 316–317.

13. Gardner Ackley to Johnson, December 23, 1967, Johnson Papers, Handwriting File, Box 27.

14. "Notes of the President's Meeting . . . ," December 5, 1967, Johnson Papers, Tom Johnson's Notes, Box 1.

15. Remarks, December 14, 1967, *PP, 1967*, II, 1133–1135.

16. "A Conversation with the President," December 19, 1967, *ibid.*, pp. 1159–1173.

17. For a discussion of the background of the trip and an account of the conversation in Rome, see Valenti, *Very Human President*, pp. 278–317; informal notes of the meeting are also in Johnson Papers, Meeting Notes File, Box 2.

18. "Meeting of the Pope and President," December 23, 1967, Johnson Papers, Meeting Notes File, Box 2.

19. Johnson, *Vantage Point*, p. 385.

20. Rostow to Johnson, January 22, 1968, enclosing Westmoreland message of same date, Johnson Papers, NSF, Country File, Vietnam, Box 127.

21. *Ibid.*
22. Olson and Roberts, *Where the Domino Fell*, pp. 178–180.
23. *Ibid.*
24. "Notes of the President's Meeting with the Democratic Leadership," January 23, 1968, Johnson Papers, Tom Johnson's Notes, Box 2.
25. "Notes of the President's Tuesday Security Lunch," January 23, 1968, *ibid.*; Olson and Roberts, *Where the Domino Fell*, p. 181.
26. Clifford, *Counsel to the President*, p. 471.
27. CIA Memorandum for Walt Rostow, January 30, 1968, Johnson Papers, NSF, NSC Histories, Box 48.
28. CIA Memorandum, "The Situation in South Vietnam No. 3, " January 30, 1968, *ibid.*; Oberdorfer, *Tet!*, pp. 3–30; Karnow, *Vietnam*, p. 525.
29. Karnow, *Vietnam*, p. 529.
30. Berman, *Lyndon Johnson's War*, pp. 147–148; Karnow, *Vietnam*, p. 527.
31. Ginsburgh to Rostow, January 31, 1968, Johnson Papers, NSF, NSC Histories, Box 47.
32. Wheeler to Rostow, February 4, 1968, Johnson Papers, NSF, NSC Histories, Box 47.
33. "Notes of the President's Meeting with the Democratic Congressional Leadership," February 6, 1968, Johnson Papers, Tom Johnson's Notes, Box 2.
34. "Notes of the President's Tuesday Luncheon Meeting," February 6, 1968, Johnson Papers, Tom Johnson's Notes, Box 2.
35. "Notes of the President's Meeting with Senior Foreign Policy Advisers," February 6, 1968, Johnson Papers, Reference File, Miscellaneous Vietnam Documents.
36. "Notes of the President's Tuesday Luncheon Meeting," February 6, 1968, Johnson Papers, Tom Johnson's Notes, Box 2.
37. *Ibid.*
38. Rostow to Johnson, February 7, 1968, Johnson Papers, NSF, NSC Histories, Box 47.
39. Rostow to Johnson, February 8, 1968, Johnson Papers, NSF, Country File, Vietnam, Box 100.
40. *Ibid.*
41. *Ibid.*
42. McPherson to Johnson, February 8, 1968, Johnson Papers, Handwriting File, Box 28.
43. *Ibid.*
44. "Notes of the President's Meeting with the Joint Chiefs of Staff," February 9, 1968, Johnson Papers, Tom Johnson's Notes, Box 2.
45. *Ibid.*
46. "Notes of the President's Meeting with the Senior Foreign Affairs Advisory Council," February 10, 1968, Johnson Papers, Tom Johnson's Notes, Box 2.
47. Krepinevich, *Army and Vietnam*, p. 240.
48. "Increase in Enemy Forces in Vietnam Since December," February 11, 1968, Johnson Papers, NSF, NSC Histories, Box 47; "Notes of the President's Meeting with Senior Foreign Policy Advisers," February 11, 1968, Johnson Papers, Tom Johnson's Notes, Box 2.
49. Wheeler to Westmoreland, February 11, 1968, and Westmoreland to Wheeler, February 12, 1968, Johnson Papers, NSF, NSC Histories, Box 47.
50. Rostow to Johnson, February 12, 1968, 11:45 a.m., Johnson Papers, NSF, Files of Walt Rostow, Box 6.
51. "Notes of the President's Meeting with Senior Foreign Policy Advisors," February 12, 1968, Johnson Papers, Tom Johnson's Notes, Box 2.
52. *Ibid.*
53. Clifford, *Counsel to the President*, p. 478.
54. *Ibid.*, Hoopes to Clifford, February 13, 1968, Clifford Papers, Box 1.
55. "Notes of the President's Luncheon Meeting . . . ," February 13, 1968, Johnson Papers, Tom Johnson's Notes, Box 2.
56. Johnson to Rostow, February 15, 1968, Johnson Papers, NSF, NSC Histories, Box 47.
57. Rostow to Johnson, February 12, 1968, *ibid.*
58. Draft, February 15, 1968, Clifford Papers, Box 1. In this instance, General Taylor had prompted the president to take a second look at the Khe Sanh position, and may, by his questioning, have allowed LBJ to make a "military" recommendation. Rostow to Johnson, February 13, 1968, Johnson Papers, NSF, NSC Histories, Box 47.
59. Memorandum of Conversation, February 21, 1968, Johnson Papers, Meeting Notes File, Box 2.

19. ". . . FROM WHICH AMERICANS WILL NEVER TURN"

1. "Excerpts from the President's Remarks," February 18, 1968, Johnson Papers, NSF, NSC Histories, Box 47.

2. Ronald H. Spector, *After Tet: The Bloodiest Year in Vietnam* (New York: Free Press, 1993), p. 87.

3. Mark Perry, *Four Stars: The Inside Story of the Forty-Year Battle Between the Joint Chiefs of Staff and America's Civilian Leaders* (Boston: Houghton-Mifflin, 1989), p. 187.

4. See the discussion in Samuel Zaffiri, *Westmoreland: A Biography of General William C. Westmoreland* (New York: William Morrow, 1994), pp. 306–311.

5. An extreme example of the argument is Phillip B. Davidson, *Vietnam at War: The History 1946–1975* (Novato, Calif.: Presidio Press, 1988), esp. pp. 485–525. In these pages every disputed issue is presented as a media conspiracy of the left, or, novel to most observers, of a "liberal" CIA. Davidson was Westmoreland's intelligence chief during the war.

6. "Notes of the President's Luncheon Meeting," February 20, 1968, Johnson Papers, Tom Johnson's Notes, Box 2.

7. News Conference with George Christian, February 23, 1968; Rostow to Johnson, February 23, 1968, both in Johnson Papers, NSF, NSC Histories, Box 47.

8. Rostow to Johnson, February 25, 1968, Johnson Papers, NSF, NSC Histories, Box 47.

9. *Ibid.*

10. Accounts of the meeting are in notes made by Harry McPherson, "Notes of Meeting, February 27," Johnson Papers, Meeting Notes File, Box 2; Clifford, *Counsel to the President*, pp. 484–485, which appears to be based primarily on McPherson's notes, but with important additions (and omissions); and Califano, *Triumph and Tragedy*, pp. 262–264, which is based on the author's own notes and has several additional comments by Robert McNamara.

11. This description of McNamara's comments is put together from McPherson's notes cited above, and Califano's account also cited above.

12. McPherson's notes and Clifford's account, cited in note 10.

13. McPherson's notes, cited above.

14. Califano, *Triumph and Tragedy*, p. 264.

15. "Notes of the President's Meeting . . . ," February 28, 1968, Johnson Papers, Tom Johnson's Notes, Box 2; Wheeler to Johnson, February 27, 1968, Johnson Papers, NSF, Country File, Vietnam, Box 127.

16. "Notes of the President's Meeting . . . ," February 28, 1968, Johnson Papers, Tom Johnson's Notes, Box 2. These notes are incomplete, however, and must be supplemented at present with the account in Johnson, *Vantage Point*, pp. 391–392.

17. Johnson, *Vantage Point*, pp. 392–393.

18. Quoted in Young, *Vietnam Wars*, p. 229.

19. Califano, *Triumph and Tragedy*, p. 260.

20. McPherson to Califano, March 1, 1968, Johnson Papers, Office Files of Harry McPherson, Box 32.

21. "Cabinet Meeting of February 18, 1968," Johnson Papers, Cabinet Papers, Box 12.

22. Rostow to Johnson, March 4, 1968, Johnson Papers, DSDUF, Box 4.

23. Clifford, *Counsel to the President*, pp. 492–493; Perry, *Four Stars*, p. 190.

24. "Notes of the President's Meeting with Senior Foreign Policy Advisers," March 4, 1968, Johnson Papers, Tom Johnson's Notes, Box 2.

25. *Ibid.*

26. *Ibid.*, and Clifford, *Counsel to the President*, p. 496, which contains fuller notes on this exchange.

27. Johnson, *Vantage Point*, p. 399.

28. Draft and Comments, dated March 5, 1968, Clifford Papers, Box 2.

29. Notes of the President's Meeting with Senior Foreign Policy Advisers, March 5, 1968, Johnson Papers, Tom Johnson's Notes, Box 2; Clifford, *Counsel to the President*, p. 497.

30. News Conferences with George Christian, March 7 and 8, 1968, Johnson Papers, NSF, NSC Histories, Box 47; Shapley, *Promise and Power*, pp. 454–456.

31. Rostow to Johnson, March 8, 1968, Johnson Papers, NSF, NSC Histories, Box 47.

32. Taylor to Johnson, March 9, 1968, Johnson Papers, NSF, Country File, Vietnam, Box 127.

33. *New York Times*, March 10, 1968.

34. Guy to Marvin Watson, March 9, 1968, Johnson Papers, Office Files of Marvin Watson, Box 32. Italics added.

35. Guy to Johnson, March 7, 1968, and Johnson to Guy, March 12, 1968, Johnson Papers, NSF, Country File, Vietnam, Box 127.

36. Pearson to Johnson, March 11, 1968, and Johnson to Pearson, March 12, 1968, Johnson Papers, NSF, Country File, Vietnam, Box 127.

37. Minutes of Cabinet Meeting, March 13, 1968, Johnson Papers, Cabinet Papers, Box 13.

38. Juanita Roberts, Johnson's private secretary, to Clark Clifford, forwarding the Fortas memo, March 13, 1968, Clifford Papers, Box 1.

39. Isaacson and Thomas, *Wise Men*, pp. 686–687.

40. Acheson, "Meeting with the President," March 14, 1968, Acheson Papers, Box 88; Clifford, *Counsel to the President*, pp. 503–505.

41. "Meeting with the President," March 14, 1968, Acheson Papers, Box 88. Emphasis added.

42. *Ibid.*

43. Rostow to Johnson, March 14, 1968, Johnson Papers, NSF, Country File, Vietnam, Box 127, and Rostow to Johnson, March 15, 1968, *ibid.*, NSF, Subject File, Box 42.

44. Lloyd C. Gardner, "Lyndon Johnson and Vietnam: The Final Months," in Robert A. Divine, ed., *The Johnson Years*, III, *LBJ at Home and Abroad* (Lawrence: University Press of Kansas, 1994), p. 207.

45. Speech, March 16, 1968 *PP, 1968*, I, 402–405.

46. Clifford, *Counsel to the President*, p. 507; Isaacson and Thomas, *Wise Men*, p. 695.

47. Clifford, *Counsel to the President*, p. 507; McPherson to Johnson, March 18, 1968, Johnson Papers, Papers of White House Aides, McPherson, Box 53; Rowe, Memorandum to the President, March 19, 1968, *ibid.*, Office Files of Marvin Watson, Box 32.

48. Rowe, "Memorandum to the President," March 19, 1968, Johnson Papers, Office Files of Marvin Watson, Box 32.

49. "Notes of the President's Meeting . . . ," March 19, 1968, Johnson Papers, Tom Johnson's Notes, Box 2.

50. "Meeting with Ambassador Bui Diem," Clifford Papers, Box 7.

51. "Notes of Meeting of March 20, 1968," Johnson Papers, Tom Johnson's Notes, Box 2.

52. Karnow, *Vietnam*, p. 559.

53. Second Draft, March 20, 1968, Johnson Papers, NSC Histories, Box 128.

54. *Ibid.*

55. Bundy to Johnson, March 21, 1968, Johnson Papers, Office Files of the President, Box 1.

56. Bundy to Johnson, March 22, 1968, Johnson Papers, Reference File, Miscellaneous Vietnam Documents.

57. Rostow to Johnson, March 21, 1968, NSF, Office Files of Walt Rostow, Box 6.

58. McPherson to George Christian, with enclosure, March 22, 1968, Johnson Papers, White House Aides File, Box 30; Power, *War at Home*, pp. 292–293.

59. Luncheon Meeting, March 22, 1968, Johnson Papers, Meeting Notes File, Box 2; Johnson to Westmoreland, March 24, 1968, *ibid.*, NSF, NSC Histories, Box 48.

60. Isaacson and Thomas, *Wise Men*, p. 703.

61. *Ibid.*, p. 698.

62. *Ibid.*, p. 700.

63. Note dated "3/25/68," Johnson Papers, Files of Walt Rostow, Box 6.

64. *Ibid.*

65. Rostow to Johnson, March 25, 1968, Johnson Papers, NSF, Country File, Vietnam, Box 127.

66. "Notes of the President's Meeting . . . ," March 26, 10 a.m., Johnson Papers, Tom Johnson's Notes, Box 2.

67. *Ibid.*

68. "Notes of the President's Meeting . . . ," March 26, 1968, 1:15 p.m., Johnson Papers, Tom Johnson's Notes, Box 2.

69. "Summary of Notes," March 26, 1968, Johnson Papers, Tom Johnson's Notes, Box 2; Clifford, *Counsel to the President*, p. 517.

70. Wells, *War Within*, pp. 251–252.

71. Johnson, *Vantage Point*, p. 418.

72. O'Brien to Johnson, March 27, 1968, Johnson Papers, Reference File, Vietnam, Box 1.

73. *Ibid.*

74. O'Brien, *No Final Victories*, pp. 228–229.

75. *Ibid.*, p. 229.
76. Clifford, *Counsel to the President*, p. 520.
77. Ca. March 30, 1968, Johnson Papers, Handwriting File, Box 28.
78. *PP, 1968*, I, 469–476.
79. Rusk to various American embassies, March 30, 1968, Johnson Papers, NSF, NSC Histories, Box 48.
80. James R. Jones, "Behind L.B.J.'s Decision Not to Run in '68," *New York Times*, April 16, 1988.

20. HOUSES DIVIDED

1. Clifford, *Counsel to the President*, pp. 524–526.
2. Several sources record the efforts of Hanoi to convey their new approach by inviting Walter Cronkite of CBS to come to the North Vietnamese capital. Cronkite declined, but Charles Collingwood later came in his place. See Karnow, *Vietnam*, p. 566. Teletype transcript of the Reuters dispatch carrying the story about North Vietnamese reactions, April 1, 1968, Johnson Papers, NSF, Country File, Vietnam, Boxes 95–96.
3. Bunker to Rusk, April 1, 1968, Johnson Papers, NSF, Country File, Vietnam, Boxes 95–96.
4. Diem, *In the Jaws*, p. 224.
5. *Ibid.*, p. 225.
6. Bunker to Rusk, April 1, 1968, Johnson Papers, NSF, Country File, Vietnam, Boxes 95–96.
7. *New York Times*, April 4, 1968.
8. Lewis Chester, Godfrey Hodgson, and Bruce Page, *An American Melodrama: The Presidential Campaign of 1968* (New York: Viking, 1969), p. 16.
9. Wofford, *Of Kennedys and Kings*, p. 237; John Morton Blum, *Years of Discord: American Politics and Society, 1961–1974* (New York: W. W. Norton, 1991), p. 266.
10. Fred Panzer to Johnson, Suggestions for a Riot Speech, April 6, 1968, Johnson Papers, Office Files of Harry McPherson, Box 44.
11. Lemann, *Promised Land*, p. 211.
12. Young, *Vietnam Wars*, p. 221.
13. Phillips, *Emerging Republican Majority*, pp. 108–111.
14. Young, *The Vietnam Wars*, pp. 230–231; Spector, *After Tet*, pp. 242–259.
15. This quotation is taken from two sets of minutes of the cabinet meeting of April 3, 1968. The italicized portion is from Johnson Papers, Tom Johnson's, Notes, Box 2. The remainder is from *ibid.*, Cabinet Papers, Box 13.
16. Califano, *Triumph and Tragedy*, p. 326; Rostow to Johnson, April 3 and 4, 1968, Johnson Papers, NSF, Country File, Vietnam, Box 96.
17. Memorandum of Conversation, April 8, 1968, Harriman Papers, Box 571.
18. Clifford, *Counsel to the President*, pp. 532–533.
19. Westmoreland, *Soldier Reports*, p. 362.
20. "Notes of the President's Meeting at Camp David," April 9, 1968, Johnson Papers, Meeting Notes File, Box 2.
21. Bunker, "Viet-Nam Negotiations: Dangers and Opportunities," April 8, 1968, Johnson Papers, NSF, Country File, Vietnam, Boxes 95–96.
22. Rostow to Rusk, enclosing draft of April 19, 1968, *ibid.*, NSF, Country File, Vietnam, Box 96. Italics added.
23. Harriman, "Meeting and Lunch at Camp David," April 9, 1968, Harriman Papers, Box 571; Rostow to Johnson, April 4, 1968, Johnson Papers, NSF, Country File, Vietnam, Box 96.
24. Draft, "Instructions for Governor Harriman," April 6, 1968, Johnson Papers, NSF, Country File, Vietnam, Box 96.
25. Memo of Telecon, April 11, 1968, Harriman Papers, Box 583.
26. "Notes of the Tuesday Luncheon," April 30, 1968, Johnson Papers, Tom Johnson's Notes, Box 3; Diary Entry, May 1, 1968, Lilienthal Papers, Box 213.
27. Lilienthal to Johnson, May 2, 1968, Johnson Papers, NSF, Komer-Leonhart Files, Box 14.
28. Diary Entry, May 4, 1968, Lilienthal Papers, Box 213.

29. "Notes of the President's Meeting with Negotiating Team," May 8, 1968, Johnson Papers, Tom Johnson's Notes, Box 3; William Jorden to Rostow, May 4, 1968, Johnson Papers, NSF, Country File, Vietnam, Boxes 95–96.

30. Perry, *Four Stars*, p. 196.

31. Johnson to Clifford, May 8, 1968, Clifford Papers, Box 26.

32. Remarks, May 11, 1968, *PP, 1968*, I, 599.

33. "Minutes of Special Cabinet Meeting," May 14, 1968, Johnson Papers, Cabinet Papers, Box 13.

34. "Notes on the Meeting in the Cabinet Room," May 18, 1968, Johnson Papers, Tom Johnson's Notes, Box 3; Memorandum of Conversation, May 19, 1968, Harriman Papers, Box 553.

35. Rusk, *As I Saw It*, pp. 472–473; "Notes of the Tuesday Lunch Meeting . . . ," May 21, 1968, Johnson Papers, Tom Johnson's Notes, Box 3; Clifford, *Counsel to the President*, pp. 540–542. The minutes cited in Clifford's memoirs differ in many respects from Tom Johnson's notes.

36. Clifford, *Counsel to the President*, p. 541, gives the best account of this part of the debate.

37. Memorandum of Conversation, June 1, 1968, Harriman Papers, Box 556.

38. Kosygin to Johnson, June 4, 1968, Johnson Papers, NSF, Files of Walt Rostow, Box 10.

39. Rostow to Johnson, June 5, 1968, *ibid*.

40. Harris, *Anguish of Change*, p. 16.

41. "Address to the Nation . . . ," June 5, 1968, *PP, 1968*, I, 691–692.

42. "Notes of the President's Meeting with Foreign Policy Advisers," June 9, 1968, Johnson Papers, Tom Johnson's Notes, Box 3; Harriman, "General Review of Last Six Months," December 14, 1968, Harriman Papers, Box 555.

43. "Notes of the President's Meeting With Foreign Policy Advisers," June 9, 1968, Johnson Papers, Tom Johnson's Notes, Box 3.

44. *Ibid.*

45. Johnson to Kosygin, June 11, 1968, Johnson Papers, Files of Walt Rostow, Box 10.

46. Harriman, "General Review of Last Six Months," December 14, 1968, Harriman Papers, Box 555; Notes on Telephone Call, June 21, 1968, *ibid.*, Box 447.

47. *New York Times*, June 22, 1968.

48. Gardner, "Lyndon Johnson and Vietnam: The Final Months," in Divine, *Johnson Years*, III, *LBJ at Home and Abroad*, 220–221; Clifford, *Counsel to the President*, p. 550.

49. Clifford, *Counsel to the President*, p. 551.

50. *Ibid.*, p. 551–552; George Christian Notes, July 19, 1968, Johnson Papers, Files of George Christian, Box 12.

51. George Christian Notes, July 19, 1968, Johnson Papers, Files of George Christian, Box 12.

52. Rostow to Johnson, with enclosure, July 14, 1968, Johnson Papers, Files of Walt Rostow, Box 10; *New York Times*, July 20, 1968.

53. "Notes of the Meeting . . . at Lunch," July 24, 1968, Johnson Papers, Tom Johnson's Notes, Box 3; Califano, *Triumph and Tragedy*, pp. 318–320.

54. "Nixon," June 26, 1968, Johnson Papers, Tom Johnson's Notes, Box 3.

55. *Ibid.*

56. *Ibid.*

57. "Notes of the President's Meeting with Foreign Policy Advisers," July 30, 1968, Johnson Papers, Tom Johnson's Notes, Box 3.

58. Graham, "Notes for President Johnson," undated, September 1968, Johnson Papers, Ranch Files, Box 8.

59. Clifford, *Counsel to the President*, pp. 568–569.

60. *Ibid.*

61. Clifford to Johnson, August 1, 1968, Johnson Papers, DSDUF, Box 4; Harriman, "General Review of Last Six Months," December 14, 1968, Harriman Papers, Box 555; *Washington Post*, August 3 and 6, 1968.

62. "Once Upon a Time—," *New York Times*, August 2, 1968.

63. Spector, *After Tet*, chapter 10, esp. pp. 235–236.

64. Hughes to Johnson, July 30, 1968, Johnson Papers, Confidential File, Box 73.

65. "Humphrey on Bombing," *New York Times*, August 16, 1968.

66. Bundy to Johnson, August 15, 1968, Johnson Papers, NSF, Country File, Vietnam, Boxes 91–95.

67. *Ibid.*
68. Johnson to Bundy, August 23, 1968, *ibid.*
69. Draft, August 22, 1968, *ibid.*
70. *Ibid.*, emphasis added.
71. McPherson to Clark Clifford, August 13, 1968, Johnson Papers, Office Files of Harry McPherson, Box 53.

21. OCTOBER SURPRISES

1. All quotations here and below are from Minutes of Cabinet Meeting, September 18, 1968, Johnson Papers, Cabinet Papers, Box 15.
2. *Ibid.*
3. Rostow to Johnson, September 13, 1968, with enclosure, 1:45 p.m., and 3:00 p.m., Johnson Papers, Files of Walt Rostow, Box 12.
4. Rostow to Johnson, September 14 and 16, 1968, *ibid.*
5. Memorandum, September 16, 1968, *ibid.*; Rostow to Johnson, October 2, 1968, *ibid.*
6. "Memorandum for the Files: Re Soviet Intervention in Czechoslovakia," October 2, 1968, Harriman Papers, Box 556.
7. See, for example, Vance to Rusk, September 21 and 25, 1968, Harriman Papers, Box 554.
8. Rostow, "Memorandum for the Record," September 17, 1968, Johnson Papers, NSF, Country File, Vietnam, Box 137.
9. Harriman, "General Review of Last Six Months," December 14, 1968, Harriman Papers, Box 555; Sulzberger, *Age of Mediocrity,* p. 464.
10. Notes on the National Security Council Meeting, September 25, 1968, Johnson Papers, Tom Johnson's Notes, Box 3.
11. *Ibid.*
12. Di Leo, *George Ball,* p. 174; "Notes of the President's Weekly Luncheon Meeting," September 25, 1968, Johnson Papers, Tom Johnson's Notes, Box 3.
13. Clifford, *Counsel to the President,* p. 571.
14. Ball, LBJ/OH, II, 42.
15. *Ibid.*, pp. 44–46.
16. Di Leo, *George Ball,* p. 174.
17. Califano, *Triumph and Tragedy,* p. 325.
18. Quoted in *ibid.*
19. Transcript of Deep Background Press Conference, September 30, 1968, Rowe Papers, Box 152.
20. Rostow to Johnson, September 30, 1968, Johnson Papers, NSF, Country File, Vietnam, Boxes 137–138; Califano, *Triumph and Tragedy,* p. 325; Editorial, "Precious Momentum for Peace," *New York Times,* October 8, 1968.
21. Harriman and Vance to Rusk, October 9, 1968, Johnson Papers, NSF, Country File, Vietnam, Box 137.
22. Harriman and Vance to Rusk, October 11, 1968, Johnson Papers, NSF, Country File, Vietnam, Box 137.
23. Rostow to Johnson, October 11, 1968, *ibid.*
24. Untitled cable, October 11, 1968, *ibid.*
25. "Notes of the President's Meeting . . . ," October 14, 1968, Johnson Papers, Tom Johnson's Notes, Box 3.
26. *Ibid.*
27. *Ibid.*, emphasis added.
28. Rostow, "Memorandum of Conversation," October 18, 1968, Johnson Papers, NSF, Country File, Vietnam, Box 137.
29. *Ibid.*
30. Rusk to Bunker, October 19, 1968; Bunker to Rusk, October 19, 1968, *ibid.*
31. Harriman and Vance to Rusk, October 21, 1968, *ibid.*
32. *Ibid.*
33. Rostow to Johnson, October 22, 1968, 11:25 a.m., with enclosure, *ibid.*
34. "Notes on the President's Tuesday Luncheon," October 22, 1968, Johnson Papers, Tom Johnson's Notes, Box 4.

35. Cable to Paris, October 23, 1968, Johnson Papers, NSF, Country File, Vietnam, Box 137.

36. Harriman and Vance to Rusk, October 24, rec'd 9:19 p.m., Clifford Papers, Box 6; Rostow, "Memorandum for the Record," October 23, 1968, Johnson Papers, NSF, Country File, Vietnam, Box 137; Rusk to Bunker, October 24, 1968, Clifford Papers, Box 6.

37. Bunker to Rusk, October 25, 1968, Clifford Papers, Box 6; Bunker to Rusk, October 24, 1968, rec'd 8:27 a.m., Johnson Papers, NSF, Country File, Vietnam, Box 137.

38. Untitled memorandum handed to Dobrynin, October 25, 1968, and Rostow to Johnson, October 25, 1969, 9 p.m., Johnson Papers, Files of Walt Rostow, Box 10.

39. Memorandum of Vance Phone Call, October 27, 1968, Clifford Papers, Box 6; "Notes of the President's Meeting . . . ," October 27, 1968, Johnson Papers, Tom Johnson's Notes, Box 4.

40. "Notes of the President's Meeting . . . ," October 27, 1968, Johnson Papers, Tom Johnson's Notes, Box 4.

41. *Ibid.*; Rostow to Johnson, October 28, 1968, 12:40 a.m., Johnson Papers, NSF, Files of Walt Rostow, Box 6.

42. Draft, "Vietnam Guidelines," October 20, 1968.

43. For details, see Stephen Ambrose, *Nixon: The Triumph of a Politician, 1962–1972* (New York: Simon & Schuster, 1989) pp. 207–213, and Diem, *In the Jaws*, pp. 244–245.

44. Isaacson, Kissinger, pp. 130–133, and Harlow, LBJ/OH, II, 58.

45. Draft, October 27, 1968, Johnson Papers, NSF, Country File, Vietnam, Box 137.

46. Draft letter to Thieu, and Rusk to Bunker, October 27, 1968, Johnson Papers, NSF, Country File, Vietnam, Box 137.

47. Bunker to Rusk, October 28, 1968, Johnson Papers, NSF, Country File, Vietnam, Box 137; Rostow to Johnson, October 28, 1968, with enclosure, *ibid.*, Files of Walt Rostow, Box 5.

48. "Notes of the President's Meeting," October 29, 1968, Johnson Papers, Tom Johnson's Notes, Box 4.

49. Bernard Gwertzman, "Halt Militarily Acceptable, Abrams Advised Johnson," *New York Times*, October 31, 1968, p. 1.

50. *Ibid.*

51. *Ibid.*

52. Eugene Rostow's letter, read by Johnson in *ibid.*

53. Graff, *Tuesday Cabinet*, p. 162.

54. Rostow to Johnson, October 15, 1968, with enclosed letter to Abrams, and Johnson to Abrams, October 29, 1968, Johnson Papers, NSF, Country File, Vietnam, Box 137.

55. "Notes of the President's Meeting," October 29, 1968, Johnson Papers, Tom Johnson's Notes, Box 4.

56.. *Ibid.*

57. Rostow to Johnson, October 29, 1968, Johnson Papers, NSF, Files of Walt Rostow, Box 5.

58. "Notes on Tuesday Luncheon," October 29, 1968, Johnson Papers, Tom Johnson's Notes, Box 4; Harriman to Rusk, October 29, 1968, Clifford Papers, Box 6; Drew Pearson and Jack Anderson, "Washington-Saigon Feud," *Washington Post*, November 17, 1968.

59. "Notes on Foreign Policy Meeting," October 29, 1968, Johnson Papers, Tom Johnson's Notes, Box 4.

60. Rusk to Bunker, October 30, 1968, Harriman Papers, Box 554.

61. Bunker to Rusk, October 30, 1968, Clifford Papers, Box 6.

62. Bunker to Rusk, October 30, 1968, tels. 41539 and 41542, Clifford Papers, Box 6.

63. "Notes on Foreign Policy Meeting," October 30, 1968, Johnson Papers, Tom Johnson's Notes, Box 4.

64. Rusk to Bunker, October 30, 1968, tel. 263813, Harriman Papers, Box 554.

65. Murrey Marder, "LBJ Version of Bomb-Halt Negotiations Is Challenged," *Washington Post*, November 6, 1968, p. A3.

66. Bunker to Rusk, October 30, 1968, Clifford Papers, Box 6.

67. Wheeler to Johnson, October 31, 1968, *ibid.*

68. Clifford, *Counsel to the President*, p. 592.

69. Rostow to Johnson, October 31, 1968, Johnson Papers, NSF, Country File, Vietnam, Box 137.

70. Notes on Diary Back-Up for October 31, 1968, Johnson Papers, Diary Back-Up, Box 114.

71. Harry Middleton, "Meeting in the Cabinet Room," October 31, 1968, *ibid.*; speech draft, October 31, 1968, Johnson Papers, White House Aides, Harry McPherson Files, Box 67; Clifford, *Counsel to the President*, p. 593.

72. Johnson to Abrams, October 31, 1968, Johnson Papers, NSF, Country File, Vietnam, Box 137.

22. THE LAST CHAPTER?

1. Transcript of Rusk's News Conference, November 1, 1968, Johnson Papers, DSDUF, Box 2.

2. Rusk to Harriman and Vance, November 1, 1968, Johnson Papers, NSF, Country File, Vietnam, Box 137.

3. Averell Harriman, "Memorandum of Conversation," December 5, 1968, Harriman Papers, Box 571.

4. Rostow to Johnson, with enclosure, November 16, 1968, Johnson Papers, DSDUF, Box 4.

5. Douglas Robinson, "In Saigon, Trouble with an Ally," *New York Times*, November 3, 1968, part iv, p. 1.

6. *New York Times*, November 3, 1968.

7. Ambrose, *Nixon*, p. 212.

8. *Ibid.*

9. Jim Jones, untitled memo, November 2, 1968, Johnson Papers, NSF, Country File, Vietnam, Boxes 137–138; Jim Jones to Johnson, November 2, 1968, *ibid.*, Diary Back-Up, Box 114.

10. Clifford, *Counsel to the President*, p. 594; Ambrose, *Nixon*, p. 213.

11. *New York Times*, November 5, 1968.

12. Bunker to Rusk, November 2, 1968, Johnson Papers, NSF, Country File, Vietnam, Box 137.

13. Benjamin Read, Memorandum of Vance telephone call, November 5, 1968, *ibid.*

14. Bundy to Paris and Saigon, November 4, 1968, *ibid.* Harriman and Vance replied anyway, pointing out that not only would Hanoi seize upon such a ploy for its own ends, but that naming Saigon's representative as chairman would "greatly complicate" working relationships with its delegates, "which promise to be difficult enough as it is." Harriman and Vance to Rusk, November 4, 1968, *ibid.*

15. Rostow to Johnson, via Jim Jones, November 5, 1968, *ibid.* Johnson's amendments to this message, leaving out everything after the dashes, made it somewhat less peremptory.

16. Bundy to Harriman and Vance, November 10, 1968, Johnson Papers, NSF, Country File, Vietnam, Box 138; "Notes of the President's Meeting with the President-Elect, Richard Nixon," *ibid.*, Tom Johnson's Notes, Box 4; Diem, *In the Jaws*, pp. 245–246, 248.

17. "Notes of the President's Meeting with the President-Elect, Richard Nixon," November 11, 1968, Johnson Papers, Tom Johnson's Notes, Box 4. The phrases in italics do not appear in Tom Johnson's record of the meeting; they are from Clifford's own account. See Clifford, *Counsel to the President*, p. 600.

18. Clifford, *Counsel to the President*, p. 600; untitled, undated notes, Clifford Papers, Box 6.

19. Rostow to Johnson, November 12, 1968, enclosing transcript of press conference, Johnson Papers, DSDUF, Box 2.

20. Untitled, undated outline, Clifford Papers, Box 6.

21. Johnson to Rostow, November 12, 1968, Johnson Papers, DSDUF, Box 2; Rostow, "Memorandum for Record," November 23, 1968, *ibid.*, NSF Country File, Vietnam, Box 138; Bunker to State Department, November 13, 1968, Clifford Papers, Box 6; Rostow to Johnson, November 18, 1968, 8:55 a.m. and 4:25 p.m., with enclosure, Johnson Papers, NSF, Country File, Vietnam, Box 138.

22. State Department to Harriman and Vance, with Rostow amendments, November 18, 1968, Johnson Papers, NSF, Country File, Vietnam, Box 138.

23. Harriman to Rusk, November 21, 1968, Johnson Papers, NSF, Country File, Vietnam, Box 138.

24. Ginsburgh to Rostow, November 21, 1968, *ibid.*

25. Ambrose, *Nixon*, pp. 230–231.

26. Notes on President's Meetings with Tuesday Luncheon Group, November 20 and December 3, 1968, Johnson Papers, Tom Johnson's Notes, Box 4.

27. "Notes on the President's Foreign Policy Meeting," December 5, 1968, *ibid.*

28. *Ibid.*

29. *Ibid.*, and Averell Harriman, "Notes on Trip to Washington, December 6–10, 1968," December 10, 1968, Harriman Papers, Box 551. The notes taken at this meeting by Tom Johnson are particularly sketchy. Harriman's account fills in substance as well as details.

30. Averell Harriman, "Notes on Trip to Washington, December 6–10, 1968," December 10, 1968, Harriman Papers, Box 551.

31. *Ibid.*

32. Harriman, "Notes on Conversation with Dean Rusk," December 14, 1968, Harriman Papers, Box 551.

33. "Running Around in Circles," *New York Times,* January 2, 1969.

34. Bunker to Rusk, December 28, 1968, Johnson Papers, NSF, Country File, Vietnam, Box 138.

35. Rusk to Bunker, January 7, 1969, enclosing Johnson's letter to Thieu, Johnson Papers, NSF, Country File, Vietnam, Box 122.

36. *Ibid.*

37. Bunker to Rusk, January 10, 1969, Johnson Papers, NSF, Country File, Vietnam, Boxes 259–260.

38. *Ibid.* Emphasis added.

39. Kennedy, *PP, 1962,* pp. 897–898.

40. Bunker to Rusk, January 10, 1969, Johnson Papers, NSF, Country File, Vietnam, Boxes 259–260.

41. Bunker to Rusk, January 13 1969, *ibid.*, Box 138; undated addendum to Harriman, "Notes on Trip to Washington, December 6–10, 1968," Harriman Papers, Box 551.

42. The subsequent discussion of this meeting and all quotes are from Harriman and Vance to Rusk, January 17, 1969, Johnson Papers, NSF, Country File, Vietnam, Boxes 259–260.

43. Harriman, LBJ/OH, p. 30.

44. Memorandum of Conversation, January 18, 1969, Harriman Papers, Box 554.

45. *Ibid.*

46. January 20, 1969.

47. Memoranda of Conversations, January 21 (with Rogers), January 22 (with Richardson), and January 29, 1969 (with Kissinger), Harriman Papers, Box 556.

48. Rostow to Johnson, January 17, 1969, Johnson Papers, DSDUF, Box 2.

49. News Conference, January 17, 1969, *PP, 1968,* II, 1351.

50. Bundy to Johnson, August 31, 1964, *FR, 1964–1968,* I, 723–724.

51. Robert McNamara's *In Retrospect: The Tragedy and Lessons of Vietnam* (New York: Times Books, 1995), appeared as this book was in proofs. Despite its heartfelt confession of error and misjudgment, McNamara's book has been greeted with a surprising measure of disappointment and even antagonism. Although McNamara had access to materials that other historians have yet to be permitted to see, his book adds remarkably little to what we already know about many key issues, provides a tenuous defense of earlier positions on others (such as the Gulf of Tonkin incident), and stops short with his formal resignation as secretary of defense. This last is particularly disappointing, because McNamara's post-Tet opposition to the Westmoreland troop request probably played a significant part in finally determining Clark Clifford's position.

52. U.S. Senate, Foreign Relations Committee, *Hearings: Supplemental Foreign Assistance Fiscal Year 1966–Vietnam,* 89th cong., 2d sess. (Washington: GPO, 1966), pp. 74–75.

53. Rostow to Johnson, November 17, 1966, Johnson Papers, NSF, Rostow Memos to the President, Boxes 11–12.

54. Lodge Cable, August 10, 1966, Johnson Papers, NSF, Rostow Memos to the President, Box 9.

55. Quoted in Draper, *Abuse of Power,* p. 112.

56. "Remarks in New York City . . . ," November 9, 1967, in *PP, 1967,* II, 1010.

57. This quotation is from two sets of minutes of the cabinet meeting of April 3, 1968. The italicized portion is from Johnson Papers, Tom Johnson's Notes, Box 2. The remainder is from *ibid.*, Cabinet Papers, Box 13.

58. "Remarks by President Johnson," May 1, 1970, copy in Rowe Papers, Box 100. Emphasis in original.

59. New York: Harper & Row, 1988, p. xx.

CODA

1. Quoted in Young, *Vietnam Wars*, p. 237.
2. Gardner, *Covenant with Power*, p. 188.
3. Nguyen Tien Hung and Jerrold L. Schecter, *The Palace File* (New York: Harper & Row, 1986), p. 146.
4. *Ibid.*, p. 150.
5. *New York Times*, January 29, 1991, p. A13.

Index

A NOTE ON THE AUTHOR

Lloyd C. Gardner is the Charles and Mary Beard Professor of History at Rutgers University. Born in Delaware, Ohio, he studied at Ohio Wesleyan University and the University of Wisconsin, Madison, where he received a Ph.D. in history. He has been a Woodrow Wilson Fellow, a Guggenheim Fellow, and a Fulbright Exchange Professor, and in addition to a great many articles has written and edited more than a dozen books dealing with American diplomatic history.